HENRY JAMES, 1866-1916

a reference guide

A Reference Guide to Literature

Jack Salzman
Editor

HENRY JAMES, 1866-1916

a reference guide

LINDA J. TAYLOR

G.K.HALL & CO.

70 LINCOLN STREET, BOSTON, MASS.

Library of Congress Cataloging in Publication Data

Taylor, Linda J.
Henry James, 1866-1916, a reference guide.

Includes bibliographical references and indexes.
1. James, Henry, 1843-1916—Bibliography. I. Title.
Z8447.T39 [PS2123] 016.813'4 82-979
ISBN 0-8161-7874-7 AACR2

This publication is printed on permanent/durable acid-free paper
MANUFACTURED IN THE UNITED STATES OF AMERICA

For Mark and Phoebe Taylor

Contents

The Author

Linda J. Taylor received the A.B. from Cornell University in 1969, and the Ph.D. in English and American Literature from Brown University in 1975. From 1972 to 1975 she was Rhetoric Analyst for the Rhode Island Supreme Court. She is now associate professor of English at Oglethorpe University in Atlanta, Georgia, where she teaches American literature, composition, modern poetry, and creative writing. She has published articles on Henry James and Emily Dickinson.

Preface

In the introduction to his 1968 Critical Heritage volume on Henry James, Roger Gard asserted "the need for fairly exhaustive documentation" of the nineteenth-century response to James's novels.[1] This need continues, especially given the very important and problematical question of James's relation to American culture, as well as the contradictory opinions about his fluctuations in popularity. A further very interesting yet really unexplored and undocumented issue is that of his relation to the provincial press. This volume attempts to provide Gard's "fairly exhaustive documentation" of the American response to James, as well as address the particular question of what southerners and westerners wrote about him. In addition to including the items listed in other compilations of published American criticism of James during his lifetime, I have searched forty-three major and geographically representative newspapers and some additional periodicals for reviews of sixty-four James titles (this number does not include titles of stories published in volumes of short stories). Over three-fifths of the 2,600 items cited in this volume were previously undiscovered.[2] This great bulk of new reviews shows not only how widely, consistently, and substantively James was noticed by the American press, but also how much more there is to nineteenth-century American literary criticism than we had documented.

Within a restricted field, this bibliography attempts comprehensive coverage of published American criticism of James from 1866, when the _Nation_ was beginning to review his short stories, through the year of his death, 1916. I limit myself to American items because of the aforementioned large amount of material. I have covered the forty-three newspapers, and have included all American periodical reviews cited in major bibliographical works by Richard N. Foley,[3] Beatrice Ricks,[4] and others. I have checked the Library of Congress's collection of books about American Literature written between 1866 and 1916 for references to James. In addition to items listed in major bibliographic sources, I have incorporated those from Clayton L. Eichelberger's _William Dean Howells: A Research Bibliography_[5] which make mention of James. I also included E. R. Hagemann's list of 240 comments on James from the humor magazine _Life_ (New York, 1883-1937),[6] and unpublished reviews given to me by George Monteiro, Philip Eppard, and Gary Scharnhorst.

From this field, I have included items that make some critical or biographical comment on James, generally omitting summaries of contents, announcements of publication, and advertisements. I have excluded portraits of James other than those that accompany some printed commentary. The items have been arranged chronologically by year, and within each year alphabetically by author. Items with the same author (usually anonymous) are ordered chronologically, and those with the same author and the same date are arranged alphabetically by title of periodical.

The annotations are summaries rather than evaluations. I have condensed virtually all the major critical points from the given review and speak in the voice of the reviewer, commenting directly on James and expressing rather than describing the contents of the review. The exceptions are the remarks in parentheses, which are in my own voice commenting on the reviews themselves. The annotations are sometimes rather long because I wanted to provide a real summary, without the distorting effect of extracting a point or two from an article and leaving out ten others. Also, because much of the material is very hard to get, in many cases only on microfilm in one or two libraries, I wanted to make the contents of the reviews so accessible that most users of the bibliography would not need to consult the originals.

The index has five parts: Subjects, Authors, Newspapers and Periodicals, Titles, and James Titles. The Subject Index includes proper names but not names of characters. I have not indexed the titles of anonymous articles or, generally, of reviews. These titles tend to be headlines like "Some Recent Fiction" or "Books of the Week," which, repeated weekly with regular review columns, are of very little use to the index user seeking a particular article by its title. I have separated references to James's longer works into two categories: reviews, and mentions other than reviews. This distinction gets fuzzy when applied to long discussions of individual novels in general articles on James or to reviews of installments of novels, but I have tried to include among reviews any critical commentary made about a given work within a few months of its serialization and publication. The references other than reviews tend to be mentions of the work, usually in a discussion of another of James's books.

NOTES

1. Henry James: The Critical Heritage (London: Routledge & Kegan Paul, 1968), p. 1.

2. See Linda J. Taylor, "The Portrait of a Lady and the Anglo-American Press: An Annotated Checklist, 1880-1886," Resources for American Literary Study, 5 (1975), 166-198; and "Contemporary Critical

Response to Henry James's The Bostonians: An Annotated Checklist," RALS, 7 (1977), 134-151.

3. Criticism in American Periodicals of the Works of Henry James from 1866 to 1916 (Washington, D.C.: Catholic University, 1944).

4. Henry James: A Bibliography of Secondary Works (Metuchen, N.J.: Scarecrow Press, 1975). See also William T. Stafford, "The American Critics of Henry James: 1864-1943," Diss. University of Kentucky, 1956; Maurice Beebe and William T. Stafford, "Criticism of Henry James: A Selected Checklist," Modern Fiction Studies, 12 (Spring 1966), 117-177; and Clayton L. Eichelberger, A Guide to Critical Reviews of United States Fiction, 1870-1910 (Metuchen, N.J.: Scarecrow Press, 1971).

5. (Boston: G. K. Hall, 1976).

6. "Life Buffets (and Comforts) Henry James, 1883-1916: An Introduction and Annotated Checklist," PBSA, 62 (April-June 1968), 207-225.

Acknowledgments

I want to acknowledge the help of many people in this seven-year process of searching, annotating, and compiling. Indispensable to me were my researchers at the Library of Congress, Linda Rehling, Dorothy Holton, and Jeneane Johanningmeier. I thank George Stewart of the Oglethorpe University library, the Interlibrary Loan librarians at Brown University, and Sue Rames, formerly of the Brown University library, for their help with obtaining microfilmed newspapers through interlibrary loan. George Monteiro, of the Brown University English Department, provided me with my start on this project. He gave much advice and moral support along the way, as well as review references from standard bibliographies and a large number of previously undiscovered reviews from nineteenth-century religious periodicals.

I thank Sandi Riggs, who typed the manuscript, for her extreme patience and competence, and Terri Guth, Sue McDonald, and Prudy Hughes for incidental typing. Thomas A. Tenney gave advice and leads. Dean G. Malcolm Amerson and President Manning M. Pattillo, Jr., of Oglethorpe University, provided released time from teaching and financial support to complete the work. I received a Shell Assist to help pay for the typing. The editors of Resources for American Literary Study gave me permission to use annotations from my checklists of reviews of The Portrait of a Lady and The Bostonians published in 1975 and 1977.

Special thanks go to Betsy Dzuro, who did the index, checked finding lists, and helped order and number the items. I appreciate the assistance of the librarians in the Newspaper and Current Periodicals Room at the Library of Congress, and librarians at the American Antiquarian Society, California State Library, Colorado State Historical Society, Denver Public Library, University of Illinois-Urbana library, Milwaukee Library, Oregon State Library, Samford University library, and San Diego Public Library for searching newspaper indexes. I appreciate also the use of collections at the Providence Public, Boston Public, Cleveland Public, Brown University, Yale University, Emory University, and Georgia State University libraries. Finally, I want to thank Mark Taylor and his mother, Phoebe Taylor, to both of whom this book is dedicated.

Introduction

Without the help of a computer and the authority of a systematic survey of this material, I hesitate to interpret it for very specific trends. Throughout James's career, though, certain kinds of comments followed him everywhere. From 1876 to 1916, reviewers say, for example, both that his characters were astonishingly real and that they were puppets, not real at all. From start to finish commentators complain of inconclusive endings and a lack of incident. James is considered too cold and keenly analytical, not emotionally invested enough in the fates of his often rather dull and disagreeable people. His painstaking, fine workmanship and literary skill usually win praise, even when the obscurity of his later style evokes automatic comment and his elaboration and refinement are considered extreme. He was always thought a subtle analyst of character and motive, but nineteenth century reviewers were disturbed by his moral relativism and alleged condescension toward America. Perceptive early reviewers saw his works of the 1870s and 1880s as gently satirical social histories with accurate portrayal of types; even more perceptive late reviewers saw deep and difficult-to-express meaning behind his difficult style. They eventually replaced distress at his "amorality" with respect for his long-standing artistic integrity, his capacity to tell the truth. The early hope for great things and sense of a James vogue changes eventually to the image of James as almost Olympian himself, even if his writing was often thought unpleasant, inaccessible, or trivial.

Certain landmarks in the history of James criticism during these years are useful for the student seeking direction amid so much volume. As literary historians from William Dean Howells to the present maintain, James was the subject of controversy after the 1878 publication of his early novelette *Daisy Miller*, although the actual number of reviews is not so large as we might expect. In 1881-82 the appearance of *The Portrait of a Lady*, coinciding with James's return to the United States at the deaths of his parents, made him famous all across the continent, from the Louisville *Courier-Journal* to the *San Francisco Chronicle*. It was James's most widely reviewed work and created a peak in his reputation.

Borne on the momentum of this publicity was Howells's November 1882 Century essay on James (1882.39), in which he made the controversial remark that James's art was finer than that of Dickens and Thackeray. This assertion helped ignite what Edwin Cady has called the "Realism War," in which critics and journalists of the 1880s and less so the 1890s debated in print the relative merits of realism and idealism in fiction.[1] It was fueled by other essays such as Walter Besant's and James's own on the art of fiction,[2] and Louis John Jennings's vitriolic 1883 criticism of James and Howells.[3] The war also provoked extensive editorial comment by provincial newspapers like the Atlanta Constitution, where Joel Chandler Harris was an editorial writer in the 1880s.

In 1885 the early installments of The Bostonians compounded the controversy, as indignant northeastern journals huffed about James's alleged distortions of Boston culture, while some southern and western papers (the New Orleans Daily Picayune, for example) expressed tolerant amusement. A year or two after the 1886 publication of this and James's other big "social" novel The Princess Casamassima, he informed Howells in a letter that he had "entered upon evil days" because of reduced demand for his work.[4] Modern critics tend to conclude that both novels were failures with the public,[5] but the evidence I have found (including about four times the number of American items cited elsewhere) suggests that The Princess did enjoy some acclaim.

The Reverberator in 1888, like "The Point of View" in 1882, reflected James's ambivalent attitude toward American journalism. These stories suggest some relation between his treatment by the press and the development of his art in the 1880s, the years when he first attained international fame and seemed, more than later, to court a large audience. The Tragic Muse in 1890 was the last of his big novels before his forays into the English theater during the next five years. These unsuccessful stage ventures culminated in the hooting and hissing he received at the 1895 London opening of Guy Domville. From then until the end of the century he suffered what his biographer Leon Edel has called a "spiritual illness" and "failure of confidence," as he wrote a series of works about children and ghosts in a kind of artistic healing of "the lingering wounds within his psyche."[6] During these years, as James experimented with ways of showing what the mind can come to know and how it comes to know it, he grew more fully into the elaborate style of his "later manner." Yet, many reviewers after 1900 would refer nostalgically to one or more of these novels as among his most memorable.

Resurgences of public interest came in 1903 following the publication of William Wetmore Story and The Ambassadors, and in 1904-1905 during James's American visit and lecture tour. After 1905 he was often called great, and even the most prominent American novelist, but he was also alleged to have been read and celebrated since the 1890s by only a small group of devoted enthusiasts. The appearance of the New York Edition of his works in 1908-1909 provoked much commentary, including comprehensive assessments of his literary career, though he was depressed the following year over its low sales. James continued to be interesting to the American public for himself as well as for his writing, getting considerable coverage at the time of his change to British citizenship in 1915 and his death in 1916. The only three full-length critical studies of him published in America during his lifetime were done in the new century (see 1905.86, 1915.37, 1916.97).

Literary historians tend to agree that after 1890 James's involuted style and the subtlety of his subjects helped alienate further an already waning audience that remembered him primarily for *Daisy Miller* and *The Portrait of a Lady*. Yet, though he may have been, in the words of one reviewer, "more celebrated than read," he was very much discussed, and at his death considered by many to be the greatest contemporary American novelist (see 1916.70). Some of the newspapers and periodicals, such as the *Atlanta Constitution* and the *Indianapolis Journal*, reviewed James much less after 1890 than they had before, but a greater number, including the *Nation*, *Independent*, Louisville *Courier-Journal*, *Chicago Tribune*, *Detroit Free Press*, *San Francisco Chronicle*, *Boston Evening Transcript*, and *New York Times*, remained steadily attentive to the production of new James volumes, thus keeping his name before the public. Interestingly, I found more reviews of *What Maisie Knew* (1897) than of *Daisy Miller* (1878), more reviews of *The Ambassadors* (1903) or *The Wings of the Dove* (1902) than of *The American* (1877). In fact, the average number of reviews per book (26) is the same before 1890 as it is after.

NOTES

1. *The Realist at War* (Syracuse, N.Y.: Syracuse University Press, 1958), pp. 28-29.

2. See Besant's lecture "Fiction as One of the Fine Arts," delivered in April 1884 at the Royal Institution; and James's "The Art of Fiction," *Longman's*, 4 (September 1884), 502-521.

3. "American Novels," (London) *Quarterly Review*, 155 (January 1883), 111-113.

4. Percy Lubbock, ed., *The Letters of Henry James* (New York: Scribner's, 1920), p. 135.

5. See, for example, F. W. Dupee, *Henry James* (1951; rpt. New York: Dell, 1965), pp. 139-140; Werner Berthoff, *The Ferment of Realism: American Literature, 1884-1919* (New York: Macmillan, 1965), p. 105; Lyall Powers, *Henry James and the Naturalistic Movement* (East Lansing: Michigan State University Press, 1971), p. 124.

6. Leon Edel, *Henry James: The Treacherous Years, 1865-1901* (Philadelphia: J. B. Lippincott, 1969), pp. 14-16.

Reference Works Consulted

BEEBE, MAURICE, and STAFFORD, WILLIAM T. "Criticism of Henry James: A Selected Checklist." Modern Fiction Studies 12 (Spring 1966): 117-77.

Book Review Digest. Vols. 1-12. Minneapolis and New York: H. W. Wilson Co., 1905-1916.

EICHELBERGER, CLAYTON L. A Guide to Critical Reviews of United States Fiction, 1870-1910. Metuchen, N.J.: Scarecrow Press, 1971.

_____. William Dean Howells: A Research Bibliography. Boston: G. K. Hall, 1976.

FOLEY, RICHARD N. Criticism in American Periodicals of the Works of Henry James from 1866 to 1916. Washington, D.C.: Catholic University, 1944.

HAGEMANN, E. R. "Life Buffets (and Comforts) Henry James, 1883-1916: An Introduction and Annotated Checklist." PBSA 62 (April-June 1968):207-25.

RICKS, BEATRICE. Henry James: A Bibliography of Secondary Works. Metuchen, N.J.: Scarecrow Press, 1975.

Newspapers Searched

The following list includes only those newspapers that have been searched for reviews of all of James's titles included in the annotated bibliography. Variant titles are given with the dates applicable to each title.

Albany Evening Journal
Atlanta Constitution
Boston Daily Advertiser
Boston Evening Journal
Boston Evening Transcript
Chicago Evening Post
Chicago Inter-Ocean
Chicago Times (1875-1894); Chicago Times-Herald (1895-1901); Chicago Record-Herald (1901-)
Chicago Tribune
Cincinnati Commercial (1875-1882); Cincinnati Commercial Gazette (1883-June 15, 1896); Cincinnati Commercial Tribune (June 16, 1896-)
Cleveland Daily Plain Dealer (1875-1886); Cleveland Plain Dealer (1887-)
Colorado Springs Weekly Gazette
Detroit Evening News (1875-August 22, 1905); Detroit News (August 23, 1905-)
Detroit Free Press
Hartford Daily Courant (1875-July 8, 1887); Hartford Courant (July 9, 1887-)
Indianapolis Journal
Indianapolis News
Iowa State Register
Louisville Courier-Journal
Minneapolis Tribune
New Orleans Daily Picayune (1875-April 5, 1914); New Orleans Times-Picayune (April 6, 1914-)
New York Commercial Advertiser (1875-January 30, 1904); New York Globe and Commercial Advertiser (January 30, 1904-)

Newspapers Searched

New York *Daily Graphic*
New York *Evening Post*
New York Herald
New York *Sun*
New York Times
New York Tribune
New York *World*
Omaha Republican
Philadelphia *North American*
Philadelphia *Public Ledger and Daily Transcript* (1875-August 11, 1902); Philadelphia *Public Ledger and Philadelphia Times* (August 12, 1902-January 13, 1913)
Portland *Morning Oregonian*
St. Louis Post-Dispatch
St. Louis Republican (1875-1876); St. Louis *Missouri Republican* (1876-1888); *St. Louis Republic* (1888-)
St. Paul *Daily Pioneer Press* (1875-1909); *St. Paul Pioneer-Press* (1909-)
Salt Lake Tribune
San Francisco Chronicle
San Francisco Examiner
Springfield (Mass.) *Republican*
Washington Post

The following newspapers have been searched for reviews appearing in the years indicated.

Brooklyn Daily Eagle 1894-1902
Providence Sunday Journal 1893-1903

Writings by Henry James

Parenthetical dates for short stories indicate the year of initial publication in periodicals.

"After the Play"	1893 (1889)
"The Album"	1894
"The Altar of the Dead"	1895
The Ambassadors	1903
"The American" (play)	1891
The American	1877
The American Scene	1907
"An Animated Conversation"	1893 (1889)
"The Art of Fiction"	1884
"The Aspern Papers"	1888
The Aspern Papers	1888
"The Author of Beltraffio"	1885
The Author of Beltraffio	1885
The Awkward Age	1899
"The Beast in the Jungle"	1903
"The Beldonald Holbein"	1903 (1901)
"The Bench of Desolation"	1910
The Better Sort	1903
"The Birthplace"	1903
"Black and White"	1893 (1889)
The Bostonians	1886
"Broken Wings"	1903 (1900)
"Brooksmith"	1892 (1891)
"A Bundle of Letters"	1880
"The Chaperon"	1893 (1891)
"Collaboration"	1893 (1892)
Confidence	1880
"Covering End"	1898
"The Coxon Fund"	1895 (1894)
"Crapy Cornelia"	1910 (1909)
Daisy Miller	1878
Daisy Miller: A Comedy	1883
"The Death of the Lion"	1895

Writings by Henry James

A Diary of a Man of Fifty	1880 (1879)
"Disengaged"	1894
Embarrassments	1896
English Hours	1905
Essays in London and Elsewhere	1893
"Eugene Pickering"	1875 (1874)
"Europe"	1900 (1899)
The Europeans	1878
"The Figure in the Carpet"	1896
The Finer Grain	1910
"Flickerbridge"	1903 (1902)
"The Four Meetings"	1885 (1877)
French Poets and Novelists	1878
"Georgina's Reasons"	1885 (1884)
"The Given Case"	1900 (1898-99)
"Glasses"	1896
The Golden Bowl	1904
"The Great Condition"	1900 (1899)
"The Great Good Place"	1900
"Greville Fane"	1893 (1892)
"Guest's Confession"	1919 (1872)
Guy Domville	1894
Hawthorne	1880
"The High Bid"	1949
"Impressions of a Cousin"	1884 (1883)
"Impressions of New England"	1905
In the Cage	1898
An International Episode	1879
Italian Hours	1909
"John Delavoy"	1900 (1898)
Julia Bride	1909
"Lady Barberina"	1884
"A Landscape Painter"	1920 (1866)
"The Lesson of Balzac"	1905
"The Lesson of The Master"	1892 (1888)
The Lesson of the Master	1892
"The Liar"	1889 (1888)
"A Light Man"	1885 (1869)
A Little Tour in France	1884 (1883-84)
"A London Life"	1889 (1888)
A London Life	1889
"Longstaff's Marriage"	1879 (1878)
"Lord Beaupre"	1893 (1892)
"Louisa Pallant"	1888
"Madame de Mauves"	1875 (1874)
"The Madonna of the Future"	1875 (1873)
"The Marriages"	1892 (1891)
"Maud-Evelyn"	1900
"The Middle Years"	1895 (1893)
"Miss Gunton of Poughkeepsie"	1900

"The Modern Warning"	1888
"Mora Montravers"	1910 (1909)
"Mrs. Medwin"	1903 (1901)
"Mrs. Temperly"	1889 (1887)
"My Friend Bingham"	1950 (1867)
"A New England Winter"	1884
New York Edition	1907-1909
"The Next Time"	1896 (1895)
"Nona Vincent"	1893 (1882)
Notes of a Son and Brother	1914
Notes on Novelists	1914
"Occasional Paris"	1884 (1878)
"The Old Things"	1897 (1896)
The Other House	1896
The Outcry	1911
"Owen Wingrave"	1893 (1892)
"Pandora"	1885 (1884)
"The Papers"	1903
Partial Portraits	1888
"A Passionate Pilgrim"	1875
A Passionate Pilgrim	1875
"Paste"	1900 (1899)
"The Patagonia"	1889 (1888)
"The Path of Duty"	1885 (1884)
"The Pension Beaurepas"	1883 (1879)
Picture and Text	1893
"The Point of View"	1882
The Portrait of a Lady	1881
Portraits of Places	1884
The Princess Casamassima	1886
"The Private Life"	1893 (1892)
The Private Life	1893
"A Problem"	1950 (1868)
"The Pupil"	1892 (1891)
"The Question of Our Speech"	1905
"The Real Right Thing"	1900 (1899)
"The Real Thing"	1893 (1892)
The Real Thing	1893
"The Reprobate"	1894
The Reverberator	1888
Roderick Hudson	1875
"The Romance of Certain Old Clothes"	1875 (1868)
"A Round of Visits"	1910
The Sacred Fount	1901
"The Siege of London"	1883
"Sir Dominick Ferrand"	1893 (1892)
"Sir Edmund Orme"	1892 (1891)
A Small Boy and Others	1913
The Soft Side	1900
"The Solution"	1892 (1889-90)

The Spoils of Poynton	1897	
"The Story in It"	1903	(1902)
"The Story of a Masterpiece"	1950	(1868)
Tales of Three Cities	1884	
"Tenants"	1894	
Terminations	1895	
Theatricals: Second Series	1894	
Theatricals: Two Comedies	1894	
"The Third Person"	1900	
"Tommaso Salvini"	1948	(1883)
"The Tone of Time"	1900	(1903)
The Tragic Muse	1890	
Transatlantic Sketches	1875	
"The Tree of Knowledge"	1900	
"The Turn of the Screw"	1898	
"Two Countries"	1888	
The Two Magics	1898	
"The Velvet Glove"	1910	(1909)
Views and Reviews	1908	
"The Visits"	1893	(1892)
Washington Square	1880	
Watch and Ward	1878	
"The Way It Came"	1896	
What Maisie Knew	1897	
"The Wheel of Time"	1893	
The Wheel of Time	1893	
The Whole Family	1908	
William Wetmore Story and his Friends	1903	
The Wings of the Dove	1902	

Writings about Henry James, 1866-1916

1866

1 ANON. "The Magazines for February." Nation, 2 (February 1), 151.
(Review of Atlantic Monthly.) "A Landscape Painter" is "a very charming love-story," written with "grace and spirit."

1867

1 ANON. Review of Atlantic Monthly. Nation, 4 (February 28), 168.
Like other James stories, "My Friend Bingham" shows "marked skill in analysis of character" and a liking for "fine shades of feeling," especially the complexities of love. His stories are finished, and the result of meditation.

2 ANON. "Magazines for March." Nation, 4 (February 28), 168.
(Review of Atlantic Monthly.) In "My Friend Bingham," as well as his other stories, James does finished work, shows "marked skill in analysis of character," and likes to dwell on "fine shades of feeling."

1868

1 ANON. "The Magazines for February." Nation, 6 (January 30), 94.
(Review of Galaxy.) "The Story of a Masterpiece" is "very well thought out" and James's best so far. Within his somewhat narrow limits, James is "the best writer of short stories in America." He is never commonplace or slipshod. "The Romance of Some Old Clothes" is tantalizing but trivial.

1868

2 ANON. "Magazines for June." Nation, 6 (May 28), 434.
(Review of Galaxy.) James's "A Problem" is "the good thing" of this issue. It is the carefully finished work of "a thoughtful and clever writer." It shows James's "subtlety in the dissection of motive," and his ability to create a real character without too much of an atmosphere of "voluptuousness."

1871

1 ANON. "The Magazines for August." Nation, 13 (August 3), 78.
(Review of Atlantic Monthly.) Watch and Ward is interesting, the word perhaps most often applied to James's work. Yet, this story also "merits words of praise more valuable" to a writer.

2 ANON. "The Magazines for September." Nation, 13 (August 31), 148.
(Review of Atlantic Monthly.) Watch and Ward has all James's excellences and "promises to be one of his best."

3 ANON. "The Magazines for October." Nation, 13 (September 28), 212.
(Review of Atlantic Monthly.) The October installment of Watch and Ward is not as "perfectly characteristic of its author" as the other parts have been.

4 ANON. "Notes." Nation, 13 (October 5), 228.
(Apology for possible misunderstanding of the meaning of comment on James and Howells in the September 28 review of the Atlantic.) The October Atlantic installment of Watch and Ward has less of James's "elaborateness of analysis" than other parts of this "excellent story," and an undesirably and uncharacteristically large number of "'fallings in love.'"

5 ANON. "The Magazines for November." Nation, 13 (November 2), 295.
(Review of Atlantic Monthly mentions installment of Watch and Ward.)

6 ANON. "The Magazines for December." Nation, 13 (November 30), 358.
(Review of Atlantic Monthly.) These last chapters of Watch and Ward have an unreality, and the characters compel the reader's attention less than they did. As a rule, despite the nice observation and fine sensibilities in their composition, James's characters are not "very recollectable."

James is not yet perfectly successful in the novelist's business of painting society.

1872

1 ANON. "Magazines for November." Nation, 15 (October 31), 284.
(Review of Atlantic Monthly.) In "Guest's Confession," a study of character, James is so intent on dissecting the human nature of his characters that he does not make them live. The story is acute and clever, but not very pleasing.

1875

1 ANON. "Literary Items." Boston Evening Transcript, January 23, p. 4.
(Notice of publication of A Passionate Pilgrim.) These stories are among the finest ever printed in the Atlantic Monthly, and constitute "one of the most noteworthy collections of short stories in American literature."

2 ANON. "Literary Notices." Philadelphia North American, January 23, p. 1.
(Review of Atlantic Monthly.) This installment of Roderick Hudson contains "fine lines and delicate shades," but does not disclose "the nature of the whole."

3 ANON. "A Passionate Pilgrim." New York Herald, January 31, p. 6.
(Review in dialogue.) James is cosmopolitan, has studied French models, and in "The Last of the Valerii" resembles Hawthorne. "A Passionate Pilgrim" is wonderful, with unique characters and excellent descriptions of scenery, but "Eugene Pickering" is unpleasant. James is more picturesque than Howells, "more of a romancer than a novelist," but although his plots are good, his women are often such "cold-blooded, selfish creatures" that he seems "a little of a cynic."

4 ANON. "New Publications." Boston Evening Journal, February 12, p. 1.
(Review of A Passionate Pilgrim.) These stories are clever, "fresh, original and entertaining."

5 ANON. "Literary." Appleton's, 14 (February 13), 214-215.
(Review of A Passionate Pilgrim.) James is "the most unsatisfactory of our story-writers" because he shows great promise and potential he never realizes. His work is

always unsatisfying, fragmentary, incomplete. He seems "too indolent to use his powers for stronger work," but enjoys details and episodes and so remains a dilettante. Yet, judged by ordinary standards rather than by his own promise, his "episodes and characters are admirable studies," with bright, memorable touches of description.

6 ANON. Review of A Passionate Pilgrim. Detroit Free Press, February 21, Supp. p. 1.
These readable stories are in James's "best vein," and the first one is particularly interesting.

7 ANON. Review of Atlantic Monthly. Philadelphia North American, February 25, p. 1.
The new chapter of Roderick Hudson describes Rome "with delicate touches" and works in "a little action."

8 ANON. "Minor Book Notices." Literary World, 5 (March 1), 157.
(Review of A Passionate Pilgrim.) James is "one of the most artistic writers" of current fiction. He is "a keen observer" with "good knowledge of human nature within a limited range," but his work "lacks geniality and realism." It is "too artistic and too unsympathetic ever to be popular."

9 ANON. "Recent Fiction." Independent, 27 (March 25), 10.
(Review of A Passionate Pilgrim.) The hero of the title story is an unmanly, unheroic, "feeble fool," but James has "great and peculiar powers as a storyteller." This collection is one of the best by an American in many years. "The Madonna of the Future" and the exquisite "Madame de Mauves" have genuine sadness. Though James's genius is different from that of William Morris, one finds similar pleasure in their works.

10 ANON. "Culture and Progress . . . 'A Passionate Pilgrim.'" Scribner's, 9 (April), 766-767.
(Review.) Going abroad seems neither to have hurt nor to have helped James. These stories show the influence of the French, but James's "sturdy imagination and compact realistic drawing" are his own. His style is fastidiously polished, with boldness of outline as well as delicacy of touch. James narrowly limits his range, has "resolute integrity of literary purpose," adheres to an aesthetic ideal rather than writing for a wide popularity, and, despite his perfection of skill, fails "to move us strongly." The exception is "Madame de Mauves," a masterpiece with "a harvest of most living passion" and a main character much stronger than those of the other stories. This book is unusual in

that all the tales are good, and all are "nearly equally well written."

11 ANON. Review of Transatlantic Sketches. Boston Daily Advertiser, May 1, p. 2.

These essays are "intelligent, spirited, and graceful," showing James's "power to charm," his "rare facility in description," his "fascinating grace of thoughtful, sympathetic comment," and his clear sight, worthwhile thought, and "accomplished skill."

12 ANON. "Transatlantic Sketches." Literary World, 5 (May 1), 182-183.

(Review.) This book shows "the effect of foreign residence," and has a "cold cynicism." Distinctive character, "broad and tender humanity," and vigorous creative force are lacking, but the art is skillful, the style strong and elegant, and the diction felicitous, despite "many inexcusable errors."

13 ANON. "Literary Notices." St. Louis (Mo.) Republican, May 2, p. 11.

(Review of Transatlantic Sketches.) These poetic sketches express the feeling of travel rather than describe the sights. This "keenly sympathetic and nobly enthusiastic" observer writes "solely for the thoughtful and studious." A Passionate Pilgrim had "marked originality" and "great power in character drawing."

14 ANON. Review of Transatlantic Sketches. Independent, 27 (May 6), 9.

James is "an improved Irving," without Geoffrey Crayon's sentiment, humor, and storytelling ability, but with more learning, better sketching ability, "a keener eye for the picturesque," a more fluent style, and more accuracy with facts.

15 ANON. "Literary Notices." Philadelphia North American, May 14, p. 1.

(Review of Transatlantic Sketches.) James can see and sympathize, dwells on the subjective, and includes little humor. The book educates and charms and imbues the familiar with "much novelty and life."

16 ANON. "Essays." Chicago Tribune, May 15, p. 3.

(Review of Transatlantic Sketches.) These "clear and complete impressions," containing "really substantial information," are conveyed "with cool, still nerves, and a sense of abundant leisure." The descriptions are "carefully drawn," and entirely filled in, with "a satisfactory air of finish."

17 ANON. "Briefer Notices." Advance, 8 (May 27), 672.
(Review of Transatlantic Sketches.) This book is "very fresh and piquant." James makes his readers see with him, in fine descriptive writing.

18 ANON. Review of Transatlantic Sketches. Minneapolis Tribune, May 30, p. 4.
Unlike some travel books, this volume is neither stale, flat, nor unprofitable. The style is "forcible and flexible," and can describe with either "bold strokes" or "an artistic diffuseness and delicate suggestiveness." James shows balance, good sense, and an "American acuteness and humor."

19 ANON. "Some New Books./Notable Contributions to American Literature." New York Sun, June 11, p. 2.
(Review of A Passionate Pilgrim and Transatlantic Sketches.) In A Passionate Pilgrim, the title story is perhaps the best, and "The Romance of Certain Old Clothes" lacks the "genial inspiration" and good taste of the rest. Except for a number of conspicuous lapses into extravagance and affectation, the diction is "fit, forcible, and elegant," "uncommonly fine." James has "a genial imagination," a "pleasant, but not overflowing fancy." In the sketches, his landscapes tend to be populated, and the most valuable sections are perhaps the reviews of paintings. The spirit of these books is "candid, fine and catholic," and if their author goes on as he has begun, "his position in American literature should be a proud one."

20 ANON. "James's Tales and Sketches." Nation, 20 (June 24), 425-427.
(Review of A Passionate Pilgrim and Transatlantic Sketches.) James's writings show "the marks of intelligent purpose and of the graceful ease that comes only of conscientious training" of a generous native talent. He is an artist and not careless, and his literature may be light and yet thoughtful. James's culture is modern, and, like the modern traveler, he records the scenery of his own mind as affected by external sights. His knowledge of the world has kindled rather than dampened the ardor of his fancy. The only fault of his conspicuously elegant style is the use of French words where English would do, and if James needs any caution, it is against handling his characters too delicately. In Roderick Hudson they are being drawn more boldly than in these stories.

1875

21 ANON. "Recent Literature." Atlantic Monthly, 36 (July), 113-115.
(Review of Transatlantic Sketches.) James's travel writing is "saturated with the essence of a penetrating individuality," and he conveys more fully than anyone else "the peculiar feelings of an American in Europe." His style is the "chief charm" of the work, despite his tendency toward over-refining his expressions. Although James's writing on other countries is exquisite, charming, playful, and true, only Italy "calls forth his full poetic power."

22 ANON. "'Transatlantic Sketches.'" Scribner's, 10 (July), 389-390.
(Review.) James has a genius for letter writing, and has "rich verbiage and [a] splendidly colored style." No travel book since Hawthorne has had such "high literary finish," and sometimes James sounds like him, with delicate fancy and happy phrasing. He is here seldom analytical but gives a sense of the charm of places and the leisured mood of the cultured traveler.

23 ANON. Review of A Passionate Pilgrim. Unitarian Review, 4 (July), 108-109.
These stories have been "greatly praised," but they are not "to our taste." They are written with power and an easily flowing style, but are improbable and have "uncanny, immoral" characters, no worthy purpose or end, and "little to make one better or happier." The European sketches are "more attractive," with keen, though not sympathetic, observation.

24 ANON. "Editor's Literary Record." Harper's, 51 (August), 452.
(Review of Transatlantic Sketches.) The poetic life in these sketches gives them charm.

25 ANON. "The Atlantic Monthly." Boston Daily Advertiser, September 20, p. 2.
(Review of tenth chapter of Roderick Hudson), which is "dramatic and intense." The characters act "at the height of their power," and the chapter ends with "an exciting and mysterious situation."

26 ANON. "The Atlantic Monthly." Boston Daily Advertiser, October 20, p. 2.
(Review of November installment of Roderick Hudson), whose characters slowly work through the crisis of their fates, "peculiarly unhappy."

27 ANON. "Other New Books." Christian Union, 12 (October 27), 344.

1875

(Review of Transatlantic Sketches.) These sketches do not contain practical information and are different from other travel letters. Readers of taste and culture who have been to Europe will enjoy them, but others will find that despite the "excellent English and graceful (frequently fastidious) fancies," the book is so indefinite that it is tiring.

28 ANON. "Literary Matters. New Publications." Boston Evening Transcript, November 23, p. 6.
(Review of Roderick Hudson.) James has an analytical turn of mind, and although he sometimes dwells on disagreeable human traits, he invariably excites his readers' interest. This book will be "widely read and generally liked."

29 ANON. "Literary and Journalistic." Indianapolis News, November 24, p. 2.
(Review of Galaxy.) James's study of Balzac "will be relished by people of literary taste."

30 ANON. "Magazines." Advance, 8 (November 25), 219.
(Review of Galaxy.) James's sketch of Balzac is delightful.

31 ANON. "New Publications." Boston Daily Advertiser, November 27, p. 2.
(Review of Roderick Hudson.) Roderick Hudson is "an unusually good story," a "strong, picturesque and interesting romance," with its interest centered in the fate of individuals. It has received a favorable reception.

32 ANON. "Literature." Chicago Inter-Ocean, November 27, p. 5.
(Review of Roderick Hudson. Much sentimental plot summary.) The book is more a study of character than a novel, and "the entire romance [can be] expressed by the formula, one plus two equal to x." Rowland Mallet is "the beau ideal of an American gentleman of leisure," but Roderick is an egotist and "a good deal of a knave," his actions strange for a genius. There is much to admire in this treatment of "a very difficult subject," and the story will be warmly welcomed among "lovers of artistic work and admirers of magnificent descriptive writing."

33 ANON. "New Books. Henry James's New Novel." New York World, November 29, p. 2.
Review of Roderick Hudson finds it surprisingly powerful for James, who has made an excellent reputation as "a graceful and cultivated essayist and charming" short story writer rather than as a great author. Probably no living American

writer has a style more facile, pure, and warm, and this is the best American romance since The Marble Faun. Despite Roderick's moral offenses, he is a natural character and illustrates James's power not of drama but of subtlety. James's characters constantly recall Thackeray's, and Rowland Mallet is as good in his way as Major Dobbin. The lesser characters lack roundness and fullness because James is too much the artist to be interested in the superficially uninteresting, and because his beautiful style reduces his book's dramatic force. One does not expect the equals of the three main characters to appear in American literature for a long time.

34 ANON. Review of Roderick Hudson. St. Louis Globe Democrat, December 5, p. 6.
James is "one of the most entertaining and instructive of recent writers," and Roderick Hudson is as good as any of his other work.

35 ANON. "Literariana." New York Daily Graphic, December 9, p. 299.
(Review of Roderick Hudson. Abstracts New York World review, November 29, 1875, unattributed.) This book shows more power of conception and delineation than any, if not all, of James's previous works. The story is not pleasant, although it has beautiful incidents and places where "sunlight plays . . . in a most delightsome fashion." James's worst fault is his bias toward the morbid, melancholy, gloomy, and morose. This work lacks the joy, cheer, and electric qualities, the "tonic and invigorating properties" most people seek in literature.

36 ANON. "New Publications." New York Times, December 10, p. 2.
(Review of Roderick Hudson.) This book of "marked merit" and "unusual interest" is "remarkably successful" for a first novel, and "one of the best" American novels in recent years. James shows constructive and narrative faculty, dramatic power, skill with details, and that he is what many popular writers are not--a literary artist. Some of the characters are very vital, but they all talk like James, and they tend to lack "strong unity." The style is "remarkably neat, clear, and . . . picturesque," but consciously prim. The story is "cleverly although not vigorously constructed" and holds one's interest.

37 ANON. "Literature. A Novel." Chicago Tribune, December 11, p. 1.
(Review of Roderick Hudson.) James's talent lies in "a broad, rich style, in brilliant colloquy, and in a rare

faculty for making impossibly-sumptuous characters, electric in their intense vitality," but he lacks "the firm, sure, even power of a finished artist." He should have had Rowland marry Christina to save her, and thus have achieved by harmonizing these counterparts a "far more artistic creation." The book is distinguished from others by its power to provide "very agreeable recreation."

38 ANON. "Recent Literature." Hartford (Conn.) Daily Courant, December 11, p. 2.
Roderick Hudson is James's "excellent story."

39 ANON. "Literary." Appleton's, 16 (December 18), 793.
(Review of Roderick Hudson.) As "ingenious and sustained psychological analysis," Roderick Hudson is "wonderful." Its story is "finely conceived" and it has "an indescribable charm," especially in the atmosphere of Rome. Yet, as a novel it fails the "crucial test" of creating real characters. James has great knowledge of human nature, can trace with "marvelous skill" the influence of various factors on characters, and can dissect them with perhaps too much "precision and minuteness," but he explains rather than dramatizes them.

40 ANON. "Laurel Leaves." Independent, 27 (December 23), 8.
(Review of Roderick Hudson.) This novel has the admirable artistic finish and polished style of James's short stories, but the bloodless, "cold and heartless tone becomes very tiresome."

41 ANON. "Literature." New York Herald, December 26, p. 3.
(Review of Roderick Hudson.) None of the characters in James's romances is real, and they seem more like marble than flesh and blood. They evoke no human sympathy, but only an irresistible fascination. Mrs. Hudson is the only real character, and consequently the least interesting. James is one of the best romanticists living, and his stories, with their unconventional endings, are charming more for their beautiful language and wonderful description than for their plots.

42 ANON. "Literary Notices." Philadelphia North American, December 27, p. 1.
(Review of Roderick Hudson.) The substance of this tale is not great. The story is an incomplete drama, with an imperfect plot. In its psychological emphasis it centers more on the erratic and impetuous than on the regulated, principled, and consistent. The portraiture is clear and the incidents well built together.

43 [HOWELLS, WILLIAM DEAN.] "Recent Literature." Atlantic Monthly, 35 (April), 490-495.

(Review of A Passionate Pilgrim.) Readers have not been indifferent to James, and he has given this reviewer "the highest pleasure that a new, decided, and earnest talent can give." These stories are "a marvel of delightful workmanship," and in "richness of expression and splendor of literary performance" James is unexcelled by the greatest. His style is distinctive, even stately, with a good vocabulary; the tales are "freshly and vigorously conceived." All are striking, but "A Passionate Pilgrim" is the best, while "The Madonna of the Future" is almost as perfect. Yet, although the stories have great force and novelty, the characters may be "often a little narrow in their sympathies and poverty-stricken in the simple emotions."

1876

*1 ANON. Review of Roderick Hudson. Library Table, 1 (January), 16-17.

(Cited in Ricks.)

2 ANON. "Recent Literature." Atlantic Monthly, 37 (February), 237-238.

(Review of Roderick Hudson.) Because this book continues to give pleasure, and will likely attract the better readers' attention for many years, James has "a high place among the keenest" American and English literary artists. The texture has "a clear sparkle," the organization is crystalline, and the execution even. The book's main triumph is Christina Light, and Roderick is James's "most abundantly vigorous creature," but there is a coldness, a lack of appropriate pathos about some of the scenes, however fitly handled. James is "a unique and versatile writer of acute power and great brilliancy in performance."

3 ANON. "Culture and Progress . . . James's 'Roderick Hudson.'" Scribner's, 11 (February), 588-589.

(Review.) This book disappoints James's admirers to some extent and seems less a novel than a "curious" biological and psychological study of types. The story has "a vigorous reality," but its details are overelaborated, its subject is abstract and removed from most readers' concerns, and it is too little generated from "some strong, untamable artistic impulse." Its subject "'is too cold and hard, and the treatment, brilliant as it is, is saturated with a sophistication that at times becomes almost repellent.'" Except for Mary Garland, the characters are flawed or "treated with a barren sneer." Some of James's verbal habits "seriously blemish his rich style," but few novels of the season are better than this one, and James is an artist who can give us "admirable compositions."

4 [WISTER, S. B.] "James's Roderick Hudson." North American Review, 122 (April), 420-425.
(Review.) This book is less fresh and crude than most first novels, and if not an original work of genius, it is an unimitative, "entirely peculiar" character study with little plot. The characters are realistic and all have "the finest finish," Roderick's mother being the best. The conversations are too long and analytical, and the style is "sometimes slipshod," with too much repetition of certain striking words. The minute pieces of the whole present a picture that is real, but until the last chapters lacking in richness, high relief, and vividness as the result of a mistaken purpose rather than a failure of method. The ending is "beautiful, powerful, tragical," yet not overstrained, but should have been told with more feeling.

1877

1 ANON. Review of Atlantic Monthly. Springfield (Mass.) Republican, January 24, p. 3.
(General praise of James and other contributors.)

2 ANON. "Our Boston Literary Letter." Springfield (Mass.) Republican, February 21, p. 4.
(Review of Atlantic Monthly.) Though highly improbable, the plot of The American is the best James has ever written, and if he can manage his "catastrophe" well he will have a great success. This novel is far better than Daudet's Sidonie. Mrs. Bread is perhaps the best character and drawn with photographic exactness.
Howells's current novel is second only to James's in "lively interest."

3 ANON. "April Magazines." Springfield (Mass.) Republican, March 17, p. 4.
(Review of Atlantic Monthly.) James leaves us in suspense about the denouement of The American.
James has a good critical article in the Galaxy on the Theatre Français

4 ANON. Review of Atlantic Monthly. St. Paul (and Minneapolis) Daily Pioneer Press, April 24, p. 4.
The close of The American will be read eagerly by those who have been following the story.

1877

5 ANON. Review of Atlantic Monthly. Springfield (Mass.) Republican, April 25, p. 4.
The ending of The American shows James unable to keep the novel up to the too high mark that was set for it. In other respects the last chapter is "good and effective."

6 ANON. "New Publications. Three Novels." New York Tribune, May 8, p. 6.
(Review of The American.) James's successful use of his great gifts and fine education will depend on an informing power of temperament not yet evident in his works. His characters are cut like intaglios, more clearly outlined than in his other books (the Bellegardes are equal to anything like them in Balzac), but they are presented too coldly and objectively, without the "profound and universal human sympathy" needed to temper James's "scientific apprehension" of human nature. The great charm of the book is in the brilliant dialogue and by-play between the main characters. The descriptive passages are faultless.

7 ANON. "Literary Notes." Cincinnati Commercial, May 9, p. 3.
(Notice of publication of The American, "one of the most noteworthy of all recent novels by American authors.")

8 ANON. "New Publications." Boston Evening Journal, May 12, Supp., p. 2.
(Review of The American.) This book "will earn a deserved appreciation from the many admirers of this talented author" and is the best of his longer works. It has carefully studied character delineations and clear-cut, vivid description, and in these respects can easily be called the best American novel of the present time. The mental portraits of the characters are imperfect, unfinished, and the ending is disappointing.

9 ANON. "Literary Notices." St. Louis Missouri Republican, May 12, p. 4.
(Review of The American.) A new novel by James will be hailed with pleasure by his already large circle of readers. James has much originality of thought and strong inventive faculties, and is one of the rising novelists of the day. Portraying the American "from an objective point of view" and bringing him "into bold relief" in foreign surroundings is a good idea, and the book is "thoroughly entertaining."

10 ANON. "Literary Items." Louisville Courier-Journal, May 13, p. 3.
(Review of The American.) The American is James's best work and has been admired by all who read it in the magazine.

1877

It is "a capital story, well conceived and finely executed, and full of original situations and delicate humor."

11 ANON. "Henry James's Latest Novel." New York World, May 14, p. 2.
(Review of The American.) The main characters are not so individual, alive, and real as those in Roderick Hudson, but the minor characters are more lifelike, and the whole is broader and more finished. In portraying the very large social question of patrician versus plebeian James has overstated the difference. Yet, given the difficulty of the task James has taken on (more difficult than in Roderick Hudson), his success in presenting not only a social problem but also things less tangible and more elusive is surprising. Nothing in recent fiction is "so artistic--so almost scientific in its art" as the endings of this novel and Roderick Hudson. One wishes that James, "our best American novelist," would write an American novel.

12 ANON. "Literary Notes." New York World, May 14, p. 2.
(Review of Galaxy.) James's article on De Musset is "very keen and sympathetic," one of the nicest pieces of criticism likely to appear this month.

13 ANON. "Literature." Independent, 29 (May 17), 9.
(Review of The American.) What keeps James from being a writer "of the first rank" is a ruinous flaw of spirit rather than of art. His English is faultless, his observation is wise and keen, and his works are readable. Yet, they are also cold-blooded, with supercilious culture and glimmer rather than soul.

14 ANON. "Scribbler's Produce." Chicago Times, May 20, p. 11.
(Review of The American.) The book "is not what it is cracked up to be." Some people call it good simply because James wrote it, but it is "utterly devoid of one striking point," it is heavy and monotonous, and although the conception is good, the presentation is "vague, unsatisfactory, and occasionally . . . stupid," lacking vigor and subtlety. The story is vapid, the plot scarcely worth mentioning, and Newman is too languid and soft, a "stupid Englishman."

15 ANON. Review of The American. New York Times, May 21, p. 3.
Opinions differ widely about James. He writes clever things, with "extraordinarily painstaking variety," but here the characters do not inspire much sympathy and the ending is disappointing. Newman lacks vitality and is not quite credible.

1877

16 ANON. "Literature." Chicago Tribune, May 26, p. 12.
(Review of The American.) Pale, passionless, and unduly protracted, this book will earn few admirers. It ends in a "miserable failure of the hopes of the hero" which he could have averted with ordinary wit and energy, so the failure is unforgivable.

17 ANON. "Literariana." New York Daily Graphic, May 26, p. 610.
(Review of The American.) As a piece of literary work, this is far above the average novel, James is "one of our cleverest writers," and his sketches and articles are excellent. His "Passionate Pilgrim" showed "brilliant promise," with its obvious defects, and Roderick Hudson showed more power, but was not much improvement. The American has "fine and striking passages" but is "inferior to many poorer tales in plot and characterization" and continuity of interest. James cannot project himself into "widely dissimilar characters," his people "speak pieces" instead of talking, and at the end the moral is disappointing. The book is "richly worth reading," but this is not James's best field of literary art.

18 ANON. "James's 'American.'" Nation, 24 (May 31), 325-326.
(Review.) Newman's capitulation to the Bellegardes is "the great disappointment of the story," and shows a want of passion. Yet, there is much to admire in this novel, whose threads are "managed with rare skill," and whose chapters have "great completeness and symmetry." The delicacy with which Mme de Cintré is drawn is the best thing in the book, and places it "among the best modern studies of society."

19 ANON. "Our Boston Literary Letter." Springfield (Mass.) Republican, May 31, p. 3.
(Review of The American.) By far the best of the recent novels on the reviewer's desk is The American. It is not a great novel like Daniel Deronda, and has an air of frustration, but the characters are real and contradict themselves naturally. The book has "immense merits of detail and some fine strokes" in the arrangement and general effect. James has made a very near approach to a thoroughly successful novel, the nearest approach by any American for a long time.

20 ANON. "The Contributors' Club." Atlantic Monthly, 39 (June), 741-742.
James's works have "a certain indescribable flavor of refinement," but few other indispensable qualities of a novel. He uses minute rather than broad strokes, his women are unrealistic, and he has struck an original track where he stands without a rival.

1877

21 ANON. "Current Literature." Indianapolis Journal, June 1, p. 5.
(Review of The American.) James is to be praised highly for originality of diction, and given a high place among American story writers. His style is original, and his stories have culture, refinement, and "a charm of elegance." He is "a close student of human nature" and his books are valuable to students of human character.

22 ANON. "New Publications." New Orleans Daily Picayune, June 3, p. 12.
(Review of The American.) James is "the most original of novelists" in sending a hero not conventionally charming to women, and with unlimited money and no knowledge of the world, on a European tour to find adventure.

23 ANON. "Literary Matters. New Publications." Boston Evening Transcript, June 6, p. 6.
(Review of The American.) Not even those who dislike James's work can deny the fascination of this novel, which compels the reader to read all of it. Yet, it is one of the most unsatisfactory American novels ever written, has no emotion, and is cold, keen, and polished. James dissects his characters, and inspires wonder at his knowledge and admiration for his skill, but no sympathy for him or his characters. The ending is abrupt and disappointing.

24 ANON. Review of Galaxy. Albany Evening Journal, June 25, p. 1.
The most readable paper in this issue is James's on George Sand.

25 ANON. "Recent Literature." Atlantic Monthly, 40 (July), 108-109.
(Review of The American.) This book is an advance over Roderick Hudson. The characters are more intrinsically interesting. James's treatment of them has "more of that symbolic quality essential to the best artistic successes" and comes nearer to "an air of simple human fellowship." The early portrait of Newman is as acute and vigorous as virtually any other in recent fiction, though James can be verbose. His plot and situation are original and carried out with "a brilliancy and a nice application of details" that make the book "delightful to a refined taste." The fates of some of the characters are not credible and the ending is not entirely satisfactory, but it may have been the necessary conclusion to this forceful, "impressive composition."

1877

26 ANON. "Current Literature." Galaxy, 24 (July), 135-138.
(Review of The American.) This book is so good that one regrets it is not better. James's "purely literary work is always good," with an "air of elegance" too rare among American writers. In this respect The American is better than Roderick Hudson, though the latter has passages of "greater vivacity and stronger imaginative power." The American's plot is original and well constructed, but the ending is "lame and impotent." The hero is not a representative enough American, is inadequate to the part he plays, and sometimes speaks uncharacteristically. Mme de Cintré is too vague, but the other Bellegardes and the Nioches, especially Noemie, are vividly, strongly imagined.

27 ANON. "Recent Fiction." Literary World, 9 (July), 29-30.
(Review of The American.) This is a "very modern novel," with thorough, clear, and accurate characterization. Yet, the characters are either "utterly detestable" or not attractive, and presented for inspection rather than for sympathy. The story is very slight, but no book was ever less dull. The literary execution is brilliant, like good painting. James's "admirable talent demands a better field" and nobler characters to illustrate a "higher purpose." The book comes "perilously near being a French novel."

28 ANON. "Culture and Progress./'The American.'" Scribner's, 14 (July), 406-407.
(Review). This book showed promise of becoming the great American novel, but is a "conspicuous failure." With his "genuine and hearty manliness," the "big, rich, frank, simple-hearted, straightforward, and triumphantly successful" hero seemed the best American type and ideal and inspired "a living interest." James, however, did not understand him, and replaced his "masculine vigor" with weakness so that the ending is miserable, shocking, and disappointing. Reviewers have praised James's style, which is very good. He has been perhaps too influenced by Turgenev.

29 ANON. "Books of the Day." Appleton's, n.s. 3 (August), 189-190.
(Review of The American.) James's works have "a certain sameness" relieved by "his fertility of invention." This story has "many admirable and delightful qualities," including "exceptionally well defined" and vivid minor characters, a sense of power well applied, and a charming atmosphere of culture, refinement, and high thought. The social perspective is "admirably harmonious and sustained," the characters pique curiosity if not genuine interest, James's mind is "rich and full," and Mme de Cintré is the

best thing he has done. The first two-thirds of the book approaches greatness, but the story "breaks down sadly toward its close."

30 ANON. "Literary Notices." Eclectic, n.s. 26 (August), 249-250.
(Review of The American.) With its opulent power, "consistent and well-constructed" plot, interesting characters portrayed with delicacy and precision, "brilliant and picturesque" descriptions, effective situation, and elegantly cultured atmosphere, this novel should be "of the first rank." Yet, it fails to be because James subordinates his characters' individuality and force to the development of his interesting and suggestive situation. The ending is unsatisfactory, but the book as a whole is "a stimulus and an enjoyment."

31 ANON. "New Novels." Library Table, 3 (August 30), 154-155.
(Review of The American.) James has "rare abilities as a novelist," but his "nicety of expression," "cultivated taste," and "keen analytic ability" make him "preeminently the critic," a "severe but just and impartial judge." Newman retains both his individuality and his representative Americanness. The book is "excellent in conception," but in places lacks "sufficient warmth, a greater depth of coloring."

32 BURLINGAME, EDWARD L. "New American Novels." North American Review, 125 (September), 309-315.
(Review of The American and Julian Hawthorne's Garth.) This book has deserved and had "a somewhat exceptional reception," and the perfection of James's literary skill is almost beyond dispute. This novel appeals to the intellect more than to the imagination, and James is a critic and analyst rather than a sharer of strong feelings. He has thoroughly mastered all he has attempted and stands near the head of his school, but the school has limitations. Mme de Cintré is the least successful character, and the ending is blurred, ineffective, and disappointing, but the minor characters are vivid. James is a more careful, detailed painter than Julian Hawthorne is.

*33 HAYWOOD, J. C. How They Strike Me, These Authors. Philadelphia, 1877.
(Unlocated. Cited in Ricks.)

34 TEMPLETON [pseud.]. "Boston Correspondence. Literary." Hartford Daily Courant, May 17, p. 1.
(Review of The American.) The book is selling better and is more popular with the general reading public than

James's other works. The only serious drawback is the ending, but the disappointment is lessened because the reader does not feel sympathy with the characters. James is the most brilliant and in some respects the best American novelist. His work should put him in the first rank.

1878

1 ANON. Review of French Poets and Novelists. Cincinnati Commercial, March 22, p. 2.
James is an enthusiastic and careful student of these writers. The book "will attract the attention of all lovers of French literature, and is an agreeable addition to our own."

2 ANON. "Literature." Chicago Tribune, April 20, p. 9.
(Review of French Poets and Novelists.) This book has "an uncommon degree of merit," "an intimate and intelligent understanding" of its subjects, and "a singularly felicitous and opulent style." James's "admirably keen, candid, and generous" criticism reflects "a broad and kindly catholicity of appreciation and judgment."

3 ANON. "Editor's Literary Record." Harper's, 56 (May), 939-940.
(Review of French Poets and Novelists.) These studies of French literature are not comprehensive or "profoundly true." They lack the right moral tone and assume too much reader knowledge. Yet, James has "a notable power of intellectual analysis," real insight into character, and artistic skill.

4 ANON. "New Books." Penn Monthly, 9 (May), 402-403.
(Review of French Poets and Novelists.) James is very fit to write on the French authors, but these thoughtful and enjoyable essays' treatment of them may not always be right. The best are on De Musset, Gautier, and George Sand, and the worst is on Balzac.

5 ANON. "New Publications." New York Times, May 13, p. 3.
(Review of French Poets and Novelists.) America is "singularly wanting" in this kind of book, and in good critics. The "coldness" which sensitive people dislike in James's fiction is useful in criticism. James "does honor to American letters by his thoroughness, sobriety, and intellectual force," and will win a respectful, even enthusiastic reception in England. No one writes criticism "of finer flavor and sounder quality."

1878

6 ANON. "Reviews./Cultivated Criticism." New York World, May 20, p. 2.

(Review of French Poets and Novelists.) These "graceful and discriminating" essays are "some of the best literary criticism that has been written in America." Yet, James's novels are better than his essays. His conscientious, thorough, consistent account of Balzac is the best extant. The essays' main fault is that James's cultivation sometimes hampers his "natural force" and spontaneity of feeling.

7 ANON. Review of Watch and Ward. Boston Evening Transcript, May 27, p. 6.

In volume form, Watch and Ward "will find a multitude of readers," some of whom remember its charm. It is less artistic and strong than The American, but "infinitely more pleasant reading."

8 ANON. Review of Watch and Ward. Philadelphia North American, May 31, p. 4.

This story has not much material, and no tragedy, but is "pleasing, well-proportioned, and well-colored."

9 ANON. Review of Watch and Ward. New York World, June 10, p. 2.

In contrast to Roderick Hudson and The American, this story is "of slight interest" and "not too well managed," with almost all its interest in its "verbal elegance."

10 ANON. Review of Atlantic Monthly. New York World, June 17, p. 2.

The Europeans opens admirably and promises to be one of the year's "few notable works of fiction," but James focuses too much on its American characters.

11 ANON. Review of Atlantic Monthly. Springfield (Mass.) Republican, June 20, p. 2.

The contrasts between the "minutely touched" portraits in The Europeans are interesting. James has come into his estate as a novelist and may be establishing "a school of his own." His novels resemble those of Howells.

12 ANON. Review of Watch and Ward. Chicago Tribune, June 22, p. 9.

Though not equal to James's later efforts, this story shows "much of his felicity of thought and expression," and will repay reading.

*13 ANON. Review of Watch and Ward. Library Table, 4 (June 22),

313.
(Foley refers to this review's negative comments, p. 16.)

14 ANON. "Recent Literature." Atlantic Monthly, 42 (July), 118-119.
(Review of French Poets and Novelists.) James is more like Sainte-Beuve "than any other English writer," and the chapter on Balzac is "splendid," of its kind the most "abundant and interesting" treatment yet of that author. It is "a mixture of the frankest admiration and . . . of brutal snubbing." In these essays "the want of some positive or negative result clearly enunciated" distinguishes the "highly suggestive, charming" James from the "systematic" critics like Matthew Arnold and Sainte-Beuve. He should take more of a stand, but "the ease and brilliancy of his style," and his felicitous praise, are "irresistible." The piece on Turgenev is perhaps "a masterpiece of criticism," and the notably ardent paper on De Musset is also very enjoyable.

15 ANON. "New Books." Churchman, 38 (July 6), 14.
(Review of French Poets and Novelists.) These essays are "in the best style of critical writing," and the ones on De Musset, Gautier, Balzac, George Sand, and the Ampères are remarkably thorough and finished, "among the highest examples of modern literary criticism." James is a better critic than Taine.

16 ANON. Review of Watch and Ward. Springfield (Mass.) Republican, July 9, p. 8.
Although most people disagree that James's art has improved since the 1871 publication of this book, his style in more recent works is more finished and his excessively beloved details are subordinated to the "important elements of the story." James still describes with a minuteness both effective and tiresome, but now he includes no details without a purpose. He has "real power," and sees so much so clearly, with such clever expression, that even his most disagreeable books give "a certain pleasure."

17 ANON. Review of Watch and Ward. New York Times, July 12, p. 3.
The many admirers of "the most distinguished" of American novelists will enjoy this interesting early book which shows the progress James has made since writing it. The "troublesome topic" is very "cleverly handled," Nora Lambert is "wonderfully natural," and the "keen analysis" of character, the "very perfect study" of Hubert Lawrence, show James's skill. His "sharp crystalline method" discards anything

1878

tawdry, flashy, or sensational, and though the book is not always impassioned, it has "warm color." James "should be classed with the very few leading romance writers of England and America." In A Passionate Pilgrim he reached an excellence that none have equaled in many years.

18 ANON. "August Magazines." New York Daily Graphic, July 17, p. 107.
(Review of Atlantic Monthly.) The Europeans is a pleasant story.

19 ANON. "The Magazines." Hartford Daily Courant, July 18, p. 2.
(Review of Atlantic Monthly.) The Europeans "will be read with enjoyment by all who take up the magazine."

*20 ANON. "Our Book Column." St. Louis Post-Dispatch, July 20, p. 2.
(Review of Watch and Ward.)

21 ANON. Review of Atlantic Monthly. Louisville Courier-Journal, July 21, p. 2.
In The Europeans James is saying that we Americans are too grave a people and take life too arduously.

22 ANON. "Our Boston Literary Letter." Springfield (Mass.) Republican, July 23, p. 8.
(Review of Atlantic Monthly.) Nearly all our successful authors, including James, have been successful critics. The Europeans is "as subtle and original a study from life" as was The American, but it is less picturesque, and much less picturesque than Hardy's Return of the Native. The Europeans may become as exciting as James's last novel, but is now devoted to minute drawing and penetrating of rather commonplace characters who may not be worth it.

*23 ANON. Review of French Poets and Novelists. Independent, 30 (July 25), 13.
(Cited in Foley as laudatory, p. 14n.)

24 ANON. "The Magazines." Detroit Free Press, July 27, p. 8.
(Review of Scribner's.) James is both careful and industrious. "Longstaff's Marriage," in the August Scribner's, is a "rather analytical" sketch.

25 ANON. "Books of the Day." Appleton's, n.s. 5 (August), 189.
(Review of Watch and Ward.) This book is readable and interesting as one of James's early works, and it will not hurt his established reputation. It has the same "insight

into character," "firmness of delineation," skill in projecting characters onto a setting, and sense of proportion as his later more famous and ambitious novels, and almost as much "vigor and grace of style." The ending is conventional, and James's "opulence of intellectual resource" is missing. James may turn out to be the long-awaited great American novelist.

26 ANON. Review of Watch and Ward. Cottage Hearth, 5 (August), 286.
This is perhaps one of the best stories from this "writer of rare excellence--indeed a real genius."

27 ANON. "Recent Fiction." Literary World, 9 (August), 47.
(Review of Watch and Ward.) This story just misses being perfect, failing a bit toward the end, and it has "the unmistakable Atlantic stamp." No current book is written with more "careful grace." James's "studiously critical temper" helps him be "very full and delicate" in his analyses and descriptions.

28 ANON. "The September Atlantic [Monthly]." New York Daily Graphic, August 15, p. 306.
(Editorial review.) The Europeans is "highly interesting."

29 ANON. "The September Magazines." Atlanta Constitution, August 18, p. 2.
(Review of Atlantic Monthly.) This installment of The Europeans gives "fresh proof" of James's "rare felicity of style" and his deftness in character portrayal.

30 ANON. Review of Atlantic Monthly. Springfield (Mass.) Republican, August 20, p. 4.
James makes the conversations in his novels so lively he might try a play.
The characters in The Europeans move forward circuitously and hesitatingly, and the plot's intricacies are too complex to be pleasurable, but the principal characters are clearly drawn, and the whole has "an unmistakable, though not quite natural flavor of Boston." The story is witty and piques curiosity, but "leaves the moral sense a little in the lurch" as James's novels tend to do.

31 ANON. "Recent Novels." Nation, 27 (August 22), 117-118.
(Review of Watch and Ward.) James has well-known good gifts and holds too high a place for anything he deliberately acknowledges to be slightly regarded. Yet, this story will not rank high among his works.

1878

32 ANON. "Literary Notes." St. Louis Post-Dispatch, August 24, p. 2.
A Tauchnitz edition of The American has been published, and the publisher describes James as "'a rising writer.'" (Also printed in the Virginia City [Nevada] Territorial Enterprise, September 1, p. 2.)

33 ANON. "Our Book Column." St. Louis Post-Dispatch, August 24, p. 2.
(Review of Atlantic Monthly.) The Europeans "marches bravely on" in the September issue.

34 ANON. Review of Atlantic Monthly. Louisville Courier-Journal, August 25, p. 3.
The Europeans pleases not from "ingenuity of plot and effectiveness of incident, but by the power of a fine style and keen analyses of character and a delicate humor" with "occasional touches of inimitable satire."

*35 ANON. Reviews of The Europeans. Library Table, 4 (August 31), 383; (December 7), 511-512.
(Foley notes these reviews' claim that the characters are not real, p. 16.)

36 ANON. Brief reference. Springfield (Mass.) Republican, September 4, p. 3.
James's and Thomas Bailey Aldrich's novels stand "with one foot in one country and the other in a foreign land."

37 ANON. "Literariana. The October Magazines." New York Daily Graphic, September 18, p. 545.
(Review of Atlantic Monthly.) The Europeans continues to increase in interest.

38 ANON. "Our Boston Literary Letter." Springfield (Mass.) Republican, September 25, p. 3.
(Review of Atlantic Monthly.) This critic thinks better of The Europeans than the Republican does. James needs to have or show more patriotism, and though The Europeans shows he still has his firm, delicate grasp of individual character, it does not show much advance toward "that perception of universal character" that distinguishes genius from talent. Yet, what he does is good, "a very high kind" of work.

39 ANON. "The Contributors' Club." Atlantic Monthly, 42 (October), 508-509.
(Comments on French Poets and Novelists.) This "is the most perversely uncertain book of criticism I have ever read." James is too "anxiously impartial," and he "sees

so widely" that he loses "the entirety, the plain effect of the whole." Therefore, despite his "delightful style," the book, "as a whole, is unsatisfactory."

40 ANON. Review of Watch and Ward. Sunday Afternoon, 2 (October), 384.
(Negative review.) The word choices in descriptions are very good, but the characters are like mounted dead beetles or photographs, and are presented with no moral purpose.

41 ANON. Note. New York Tribune, October 12, p. 8.
(Notice of publication of The Europeans. Favorable quotations from the Christian Union and the New York Evening Post.)

42 ANON. "Literary Notes." New York Times, October 14, p. 3.
James "has outstripped his father as a popular author," but his father has written many fine volumes.

43 ANON. Review of The Europeans. New York Commercial Advertiser, October 15, p. 1.
This work is intensely interesting and the story is well sustained and has a delightful style. The Europeans is one of the best American novels ever written, and certainly adds to James's reputation.

44 ANON. "Books and Authors." Christian Union, 18 (October 16), 313.
(Review of Watch and Ward.) Despite its "good points characteristic" of James's style, this book is disappointing after his recent works. It is surprising, given his "well merited reputation," that he decided to republish it.

45 ANON. "Literary Notes." New York Daily Graphic, October 17, p. 744.
(Review of The Europeans.) James is a charming writer familiar to cultivated readers. His book was an admirable serial story whose merits were so often praised that further comment is unnecessary.

46 ANON. "Literature. . . . Literary Notes." Chicago Inter-Ocean, October 19, p. 10.
(Note on The Europeans.) The (New York?) Evening Post thinks The Europeans will strengthen James's reputation as a novelist more than anything he has done before.

47 ANON. "Politics and Literature: A View of the Field from London." New York Times, October 20, p. 4.
(Note on The Europeans.) James has no reason to complain

of the reception of The Europeans, an "entertaining and graceful view of American life." Even the Athenaeum praises it, but the "Americanisms" its critic mentions are really Anglicanisms.

48 ANON. "Literary Matters." Boston Evening Transcript, October 21, p. 6.
(Note.) The Europeans is "in great favor with English critics." (Quotes favorable comments from the London and the London World.)

49 ANON. "Literary Notes." New York Times, October 25, p. 3.
(Quotation from the Athenaeum review of The Europeans about that novel's happy dearth of "Americanisms.")

50 ANON. "Literary Notes." Louisville Courier-Journal, October 27, p. 5.
James "is said to be highly valued in England, both as a reviewer and a novelist."

51 ANON. "Literary Notes." New York Tribune, October 28, p. 6.
Daisy Miller and The Europeans have received "warm praise" from the London Academy. (Quotes favorable comments from the Academy and the Examiner.)

52 ANON. Review of The Europeans. Christian Union, 18 (October 30), 361.
In this entertaining story James shows the objectivity and acute, penetrating analytical powers of an anatomist. His types are not familiar to most people, but they do exist and do present a "very effective" contrast. Except possibly for Daisy Miller, no stronger character drawing than Gertrude's has been done "for a long while."

53 ANON. "Literary Notices." Philadelphia North American, October 31, p. 4.
(Review of The Europeans.) This story is a disappointment because the Baroness figures less prominently than the early minute description of her suggests, and the ending fails to satisfy the reader's expectations. James does contrast American and European thought, manners, and conduct, but the loss midway of the master motive diminishes the story's connection and force.

54 ANON. "The Europeans." Chicago Tribune, November 2, p. 9.
This book will do much to place James among the first of American fiction writers, and he is in some respects superior to any who might dispute his claim to preeminence. He has much of Hawthorne's power of analysis and an even more

complete synthetic faculty, with Howells's charm of style and more than his energy, but he has not yet shown the dramatic skill of Mrs. Stowe in her one great work. The Europeans is appropriately a sketch because it lacks the great motive and robust tone of a full-blown book. Yet, it has the even more necessary admirable studies of character, loving appreciation of Boston local color, and "cosmopolitan sympathy with strange ideas and tastes."

55 ANON. "Literary." Chicago Inter-Ocean, November 2, p. 10.
(Review of The Europeans.) The Europeans is a well-defined novel with many attractions. There is no ingenuity of plot. The Baroness is not lovable, her career ends rather tamely, and the other characters are managed much better. The denouement is rather pleasing and the book "decidedly readable."

56 ANON. "Literary Notices." St. Louis Missouri Republican, November 2, p. 3.
(Review of The Europeans.) The story is interesting and fresh, original, and healthy in tone. James's descriptions are "wonderfully vivid," he describes "the spirit of things" and not their dull outside, and his work is "always mentally invigorating." The Europeans is one of his best books and will largely increase his circle of readers.

57 ANON. "Literature . . ./Literary Notes." Indianapolis Journal, November 3, p. 3.
(Note.) The Athenaeum says The Europeans is defaced by very few Americanisms.

58 ANON. "Literary Notes." New York Times, November 4, p. 3.
The publication of Daisy Miller in volume form "will be welcome to a very large class of readers."

59 ANON. "New Publications." New York Times, November 4, p. 3.
(Review of The Europeans.) In some respects this work is superior to James's others, but it is not satisfactory as a whole. Its excellence is not in its insignificant plot, with its unlikely, even feeble, crisis. James can interest with details, elaborate with "fine art," and charm with "delicate and generally truthful touches," but his mind is undramatic and he does not do enough with the Baroness.

60 ANON. "Book Reviews." New York World, November 4, p. 2.
(Review of The Europeans.) One wishes that this book's nearly perfect workmanship had been concerned with a subject more vital and lofty, and that it amounted to as much as The American. The unexpected conclusion is disappointing because

1878

many of the characters, if not heroic, had the potential to develop into "something large and intrinsically important."

61 ANON. "New Publications." Boston Daily Advertiser, November 7, p. 2.
(Review of Daisy Miller.) This study of a very independent but at heart a good girl should have a place in some American families.

62 ANON. "Literary Notices." Philadelphia North American, November 8, p. 4.
(Review of Daisy Miller.) This work is so purely a study of character as "to sink the narrative in its philosophy." Its slight disagreeableness is because of its presumably educational and monitory purpose; it may teach other Daisies a lesson about the difference between American and European social laws. The art of the story is in conveying "an absolute conviction" of the innocence and independence of such young women.

63 ANON. "Literary Notes." New York Tribune, November 9, p. 6.
In its review of The Europeans, the London Spectator says James promises to be a new figure in Anglo-American literature.

64 ANON. "Our Book Column . . . Literary Notes." St. Louis Post-Dispatch, November 9, p. 2.
Daisy Miller "has attracted great attention."

65 ANON. Review of Daisy Miller. New York Times, November 10, p. 10.
This work surpasses all James's others for clearness of conception and accuracy of observation. Despite its satire it is gentle, true, and patriotic. James's other books have been "elaborate and well finished," and this story's method is excellent. No other English or American story is "so well balanced and clever."

66 ANON. "Literary Notices." Hartford Daily Courant, November 11, p. 2.
(Review of Daisy Miller.) This book is a "delightful study of the American girl," which also sketches the American boy with "an amused and most respectful admiration."

67 ANON. "Our Boston Literary Letter." Springfield (Mass.) Republican, November 11, p. 4.
(Review of story by Cherbuliez.) James's stories, including The Europeans which is in many ways "an exquisite novel of the Franco-American school," never have a good ending.

68 ANON. "New Books." Detroit Free Press, November 15, p. 8.
(Review of The Europeans.) The American was meritorious, but this book is even better, and will command the highest praise. It has James's "finished elegance" of style. The story is abundantly attractive, with truly artistic character sketches, and suggestive "hints and touches." It establishes James, if he had not been before, "in the front rank of modern novelists."

69 ANON. "The Blight of Our Literature./Waiting for the Foreign Verdict." New York Tribune, November 18, p. 6.
(Reprinted from the New York Evening Post.) If James had been French, The American and The Europeans would almost certainly "have been crowned by the Academy" and made American readers rave over the translations. As it is, only a few are bold enough to declare James the equal of Cherbuliez and Daudet. American critics tend to underestimate their own authors' books and to wait for the verdict of foreign critics.

*70 ANON. Review of The Europeans. Independent, 30 (November 21), 9.
(Cited in Foley as saying the characters are puppets, p. 16.)

71 ANON. Review of Daisy Miller. New Orleans Daily Picayune, November 24, p. 5.
Daisy Miller is certainly a study. A more "imperturbable, cool and placid young woman cannot readily be imagined." The little story is a very pleasant half-hour's entertainment.

72 ANON. "The American Novel--With Samples." Catholic World, 28 (December), 331-334.
(Comments on The American.) The American has been "much-admired and generously-lauded" as natural and probable, but it lacks the "vitalization of interest" essential to popular success. James has talent, and more friends than critics. The book is somewhat accurate, but also vague and sketchy, with no apparent purpose or moral. The plot is sometimes feeble, the style is not impressive, the characters are not ladies and gentlemen, Newman caricatures Americans, and the conception lacks "breadth, clearness, vigor, life."

73 ANON. Review of The Europeans. Boston Evening Transcript, December 4, p. 6.
This delightful book is "as original in plan and vigorous in execution" as any of James's previous works.

1878

74 ANON. "Our Book Column." St. Louis Post-Dispatch, December 7, p. 2.

(Review of The Europeans.) This story interests but does not much excite the reader. How it all would end was less important than the ongoing "fine and minute study" of contrasting ways of life, which is amusing and interesting. Felix is delightful, and it is healthy that writers are beginning to draw "healthy, wholesome, happy characters." The book is in many respects one of the most charming in years, its flavor is new and fresh with a "surprising touch of nature or truthful character painting" on nearly every page. It produces unique sensations in the reader, captivates us in spite of ourselves, and makes a lasting impression.

75 ANON. "Books for Christmas." New York Tribune, December 14, p. 6.

The Europeans is among the "new and important works suitable for holiday gifts."

76 ANON. Review of Daisy Miller. Nation, 27 (December 19), 386-389.

It seems superfluous to comment on this "true, clever, painful little story" since no American book of its size in this critic's memory has been "so much read and so much discussed." It is the best James has ever done, the completest and least touched by his mannerisms or limitations. Although a perfect study of a not uncommon type, it is not offensively anatomical and the characters live and move. James shows his inability to get his dramatis personae off the stage except by killing them. Americans going to Europe should read this book to see themselves truthfully portrayed, and take heed. Thus, James is a kind of moral reformer.

*77 ANON. Review of An International Episode. Library Table, 4 (December 21), 527.

(Foley refers to this reviewer's comments on the story's subtle social satire, p. 19.)

78 ANON. "Literary Notes." New York Tribune, December 21, p. 6.

(First of two notes. In the context of a Boston "carnival of authors," James is mentioned with other well-known writers.) The (London?) Examiner has called "An International Episode" in Macmillan's perhaps the best thing in the magazines this month. (Quotes favorable comments from the Examiner.)

79 ANON. "Literary Notes." Detroit Free Press, December 22, p. 11.

(Quotation from Richard Grant White's January 1879 North

American Review notice of The Europeans and Daisy Miller, about James's belonging to the French school.)

80 ANON. "Items." Boston Evening Transcript, December 23, p. 6.
(Note.) The (London) Examiner says that "An International Episode" in Macmillan's Magazine is "'the best thing in the shilling magazines, and perhaps in all the magazines for this month.'" (Noted also in Chicago Inter-Ocean, December 28, 1878, p. 12.)

81 ANON. "Books of the Day . . . Sundry Fact and Fiction." Springfield (Mass.) Republican, December 31, p. 2.
(Review of Daisy Miller.) Daisy Miller is the traditional Yankee girl abroad and would be considered exceedingly ill-bred in any civilized society, yet the reader believes her "not bad at heart but pure and maidenly."

*82 MATTHEWS, BRANDER. Review of French Poets and Novelists. Library Table, 4 (March 30), 197.
(Cited in Foley, who quotes Matthews that this is the best American or English purely literary criticism since Lowell, and that except for Lowell and Matthew Arnold, James is "the foremost literary critic" in English, pp. 13-14.)

83 S[MALLEY], G[EORGE] W. "London Literary Topics./Mr. James, Jr., and His Reviewers." New York Tribune, November 2, p. 8.
(London letter.) The London Athenaeum's estimate of The Europeans is inadequate, too critical, but the London Daily News and London World reviews are good. In England James has a large and expanding audience responsive to "that refinement and restraint of style" rare in current English fiction. Though The Europeans shows "a want of proportion," British readers have discovered in James the power of drawing "in a few masterly strokes" characters who are different from "the conventional and hackneyed types in vogue."

84 SMALLEY, G. W. Note. Chicago Tribune, November 9, p. 9.
(Quoted item from New York Tribune.) James now has an admiring public in England. Even the Athenaeum and Matthew Arnold liked French Poets and Novelists.

85 SMALLEY, G. W. Chicago Tribune, November 30, p. 9.
(Item from New York Tribune London letter.) When Turgenev was in London, he inquired eagerly for Henry James.

86 TEMPLETON [pseud.]. "Boston Correspondence. Literary." Hartford Daily Courant, October 21, p. 1.
(Review of The Europeans.) The Europeans contains an

excellent sketch of a well-known Boston hotel and the view from its windows, as well as "some subtle sketches of New England character."

1879

1 ANON. "Books of the Day." Appleton's Journal, n.s. 6 (January), 94-95.

(Review of The Europeans.) The Europeans is quite different from the elaborate American, and it contains some of James's best and most artistic work. The picture of the "typical American family" is "an unmistakable achievement of genius," done with delicate and unobtrusive art, yet with power and imaginative truth. It would be hard to conceive "a finer and truthfuler picture" of the virtues of American life. The art is almost too subtly delicate for its purpose, and its model is not English or American, but French.

2 ANON. "Literary Notices." Eclectic, n.s. 29 (January), 123.

(Review of The Europeans.) This book is James's "most artistic, most satisfactory, and most characteristic work," even better than The American. It is much more vivid and brilliant, done in "bold, distinct, rapid, and luminous outlines," with both definiteness and an almost too obvious finish and refinement.

3 ANON. "Editor's Literary Record." Harper's, 58 (January), 309-310.

(Review of The Europeans.) The Europeans is "a series of brilliant sketches" without "the intimate fusion of parts essential to narrative or dramatic unity." James describes scenes better than people because his characters are not copied from reality but are "fictions of the intellect" portrayed by description and assertion rather than by natural unfolding. Although they are cleverly conceived and presented entertainingly, they are not real enough to rouse the reader's sympathies or make the story seem probable.

4 ANON. "The Literary Movement in America." International Review, 6 (January), 95-96.

(Review of The Europeans and Daisy Miller.) These works are "better worth reading than many far more pretentious" ones, and they show James's increased powers and confidence. In The Europeans the dialogue is brilliant and the characters real, but there is "too much talk for the action." Daisy Miller is even better, "the best short story we have read for many a day." Daisy is a triumph, the ending is inevitable, and if James follows his genius he may do great things.

5 ANON. "James's 'The Europeans.'" Scribner's, 17 (January), 447.

(Review.) James is noted for "the neatness and finish of his work, for the delicateness of his satire," and the carefulness of his character study. Cultured audiences will delight in this book's "gentlemanliness, excellent diction," and fastidious thought, without missing "the want of life and incident." Although he fails to strike "a ringing note," James is an "earnest and observant" artist who steadily improves and who in many ways leads American writers.

6 ANON. Review of The Europeans. Literary World, 10 (January 18), 28.

James is "quite abreast of any living American novelist" in his "keen, analytic delineation of character and motive" and his "carefully studied and exquisitely finished style." His is purely artistic fiction that is "subjectively rather than objectively true" and "faithfully idealistic rather than faithfully natural." The Baroness is not edifying, but James's book is "fastidiously correct" in all particulars and shows great talent.

7 ANON. "The Woman Who Talks. A Sketch After Henry James." St. Louis Post-Dispatch, January 18, p. 2.

(A short parody of James's fiction.)

8 ANON. "Recent Periodical Literature." Atlanta Constitution, January 25, p. 2.

(Review of Atlantic Monthly.) The critical paper in the February Atlantic on James's The Europeans and other novels is "admirable of its kind" and has "daintiness of discrimination."

9 ANON. "Periodicals." Indianapolis Journal, January 25, p. 9.

(Review of Atlantic Monthly.) An "anonymous but skillful hand" in the February Atlantic criticizes The Europeans.

10 ANON. "The Europeans, and Other Novels." Atlantic Monthly, 43 (February), 167-173.

James intellectually tickles one with his incessant wit, and he studies his human specimens "with the methodical minuteness . . . of a microscopist." With his analytical habit of mind, he focuses on each separate detail and his "romance is a series of situations imperfectly vivified by action." The conversations are "exquisitely real and just." We can hear his characters better than we can see them perhaps because James is so spirituel and his conceptions so subtle that he cannot give them form or flesh and thus is

1879

not an artist. American authors should stop comparing their countrymen and women with Europeans, and evolve some "new forms adapted to our new environment."

11 ANON. "The Contributors' Club." Atlantic Monthly, 43 (February), 258-259.
(Authorship attributed to both C. F. Woolson and W. D. Howells.) It is shocking that some experts regard Daisy Miller's "exquisitely loyal service to American girlhood abroad" as snobbish and unpatriotic. The Europeans is perfect of its kind. James provides an intellectual treat, but lacks the storytelling gift. He has instead "keen observation and fine discrimination of character," portrayed subtly and delicately. People should not expect him to be what he is not.

12 ANON. "Henry James's 'Daisy Miller.'" Scribner's, 17 (February), 609-10.
This story has been much criticized in America for the "uncomplimentary character of its heroine," but it is told with more than James's usual skill and good style. He satirizes Americans who act as if the prejudices of foreigners were not worth the slightest thought, and he also brings out in powerful relief "the filial impiety of many American girls," their disobedience to parents.

13 ANON. "Recent Fiction." New York Times, February 2, p. 8.
(Review of An International Episode.) The style is charming and the characters are "all realistic sketches," efforts to portray types. The English are done better than the Americans, but the story is "distinctly favorable to Americans" despite its indirect satire. It is not thrilling, but is "of uniform high excellence" and will add to the "high repute" of James's work.

14 ANON. "Literature." Chicago Tribune, February 8, p. 16.
(Review of An International Episode.) This story raises some of the social problems considered in "Irene Magillicuddy," but with a far more delicate touch. The satire is "decently clothed" and justice dealt out impartially between Americans and British; the snubbing the Americans get is made amusing, and patriotic pride is soothed in an unexpected and gratifying way by the story's upshot.

15 ANON. "Current Literature/Literary Notes." Indianapolis Journal, February 15, p. 5.
In a review of English literature for 1878, the London Daily News cites The Europeans as the only American work

of that year "worthy of attention." The News writer finds it European in subject and style.

16 ANON. "Literature." Chicago Tribune, February 22, p. 9.
(Review of W. D. Howells's The Lady of the Aroostook.) Howells stands supreme among American writers in "careful study of character" and "easy handling of subtle social conditions." He and James have some traits in common, but James's works lack the "breath of life" that Howells puts into his.

17 ANON. Review of An International Episode. San Francisco Chronicle, March 2, p. 6.
This book is pleasant reading and deserves to meet with general favor. It is one of James's best efforts, "a brilliant little narrative" of life in Newport. James is fast earning fame on both sides of the Atlantic as "a master in the delineation" of features of American, English, and French society.

18 ANON. "Howells' New Novel." New York Times, March 15, p. 3.
(Review of W. D. Howells's The Lady of the Aroostook.) In the realism and cleverness of his dialogue, Howells is very much like James, but Howells's story has more movement.

19 ANON. "World Biographies." Literary World, 10 (March 29), 105-106.
(Biographical sketch of James with long quote from Spectator review of Daisy Miller, "An International Episode," and "Four Meetings.") James is moving to "a foremost place in the younger school of American writers," and has published twelve critical papers of "exceptional value" as well as the "three brilliant novelettes" reviewed by the Spectator. In the future we may look to James for "some of the strongest and choicest contributions to American fiction."

20 ANON. "Literature . . . The April Magazines." San Francisco Chronicle, March 30, p. 6.
(Review of Atlantic Monthly.) "The Pension Beaurepas" is "worth the price of the number," which "is filled with unusual articles of more than usual excellence."

21 ANON. "Literature . . . Literary Lines." San Francisco Chronicle, April 13, p. 6.
Bret Harte and James have been elected members of the London Rabelais Club, "formed to promote earnestness, erudition and manly strength in literature."

22 ANON. "James's 'International Episode.'" Scribner's, 18

(May), 148.
(Review.) James is one of the most thorough and artistic reporters of the day, and among the most unobtrusive but effectual American critics of the English. Here he makes Americans seem cleverer, but the ending is weak because a type like Bessie Alden would not reject Lord Lambeth.

23 ANON. Editorial. New York Times, June 4, p. 4.
Many New York ladies indignantly declare Daisy Miller a shamefully untrue portrait of American girlhood, but many fashionable Americans would see Daisy as representative of a real class outside "good society."

24 ANON. Note. Literary World, 10 (August 30), 287.
(A long quoted remark from the London Saturday Review notice of Daisy Miller, "An International Episode," and "Four Meetings," to the effect that readers see James's characters physically but not from within, "seems to us a very just and intelligent criticism" on James.)

25 H[AZELTINE], M[AYO] W[ILLIAMSON]. "American Women in Europe." New York Sun, February 2, p. 2.
(Review of Daisy Miller and An International Episode. Long discussion of Americans and the European upper classes in the context of James's stories.) Daisy Miller is "charming and touching." James does not intrude the felicitous moral of An International Episode. He is a "patient and scrupulous" photographer whose affirmations we trust.

26 HIGGINSON, THOMAS WENTWORTH. "Short Studies of American Authors. . . . VI.--Henry James, Jr." Literary World, 10 (November 22), 383-384.
James has had too little contact with the mass of mankind, his early works are too unfinished, his later critical essays are too prolix and hasty, and he is indifferent to local coloring. Yet, his short stories, with their originality and "fine delineations of character," are the best in recent American literature. He has avoided the disagreeable qualities of French fiction, and his most successful social stories, Daisy Miller and "An International Episode," convey lessons. He holds our sympathy and affection for Daisy's essential innocence. James has not yet produced a satisfactory novel. He "habitually deals with profounder emotions" than does Howells, and is therefore more likely to be overpowered by his characters and produce an inadequate ending. The "very disappointment which the world felt at the close of 'The American' was in some sense a tribute to its power," and the final irresolution of the hero was "simply perfect" for his character, but art should be more than "a true

transcript from nature" and must have a beginning, middle, and end.

27 [HOWELLS, WILLIAM DEAN.] "The Contributors' Club." Atlantic Monthly, 43 (March), 399-401.

Many silly criticisms of Daisy Miller have been printed and uttered, but the book is startlingly simple and authentic. Daisy commits no great sins, and the story's usefulness and literary excellence are beyond doubt.

28 [PRESTON, HARRIET WATERS.] "The Contributors' Club." Atlantic Monthly, 43 (January), 106-108.

(Comments on The Europeans.) Except for two or three of his short stories, The Europeans is James's best work so far. The style is "even more delightful than usual, despite the large number of "stage directions" that accompany the conversation. Like Charles Reade, James "seldom tells us what his characters mean, intend, or think," but Reade's characters do such tremendous things that their "mere bodily activity sufficiently defines their mental processes," whereas James's characters "do nothing at all." In this book there is only "contrast of character, and conversation." Mr. Wentworth is "excellent," distinct, and "carefully finished," showing some of "James's finest art," but Mr. Brand is made too "ludicrous."

29 PRESTON, HARRIET W. "Recent American Novels." Atlantic Monthly, 43 (June), 758-759.

(Review of An International Episode.) This "elegant trifle" has James's "daintiest workmanship," and "brilliant" but aimless mockery by an objective intelligence. Americans will like this portrayal of "the very best kind of American girl." The British critics were complimentary after the first act, but rather entertainingly annoyed after the second.

30 WHITE, RICHARD GRANT. "Recent Fiction." North American Review, 128 (January), 101-106.

(Review of The Europeans and Daisy Miller.) Among living writers only Matthew Arnold gives a greater impression of self-knowledge, self-restraint, or perpetual self-consciousness, and writes with greater "fastidious taste, cautious proceeding, and careful elaboration." James belongs to the French school. The great defect of all his novels is his characters' "lack of individuality and vital force." They talk very well, but are shadowy and bloodless and have no existence for James beyond the range of his own consciousness. The best thing James has yet produced is "Madame de Mauves," which is worthy of Balzac, who seems to be James's model.

With her vulgar talk and lack of mental tone, Daisy Miller is a kind of American young woman "unfortunately too common." James's portrait is "very faithful" and is admirable especially in the difficult portrayal of the Millers' "characterless . . . inane and low-bred" conversation. This study may have some corrective effect and show Europeans what Americans think of the likes of Daisy Miller, but instead she will probably become in European journals the accepted type of the young American woman.

1880

1 ALDEN, H. M. "Editor's Literary Record." Harper's, 60 (May), 945-946.

(Review of Confidence.) This novel is brilliant but cold, clever but deficient in storytelling power, with characters who are interchangeable intellectual abstractions rather than individuals and who fail to excite our interest. The narrative is without body.

2 ANON. Note. Boston Evening Transcript, January 8, p. 6.

The "brilliant novelette" "A Bundle of Letters" is published in the Parisian.

3 ANON. Note. Boston Evening Transcript, January 10, p. 6.

(Notice of publication of Hawthorne.) James is "one of the most brilliant of living writers."

4 ANON. "Literary Matters." Boston Evening Transcript, January 15, p. 6.

(Review of Hawthorne.) Although readers may be annoyed by James's unfavorable comparison of American with European life, and by his "occasional flippancy of tone and carelessness of style," this work will interest them. The merit of its "close scrutiny and careful analysis" is unquestionable. The book shows James's "zealous study and thorough knowledge" of his subject, as well as the capacity for fine "shades of thought" and "delicate flights of fancy" necessary to an appreciation of Hawthorne.

5 ANON. "New Publications." New York Times, January 18, p. 10.

(Review of Hawthorne.) This book will awaken much dissent, but will be "eagerly read." James has criticized Hawthorne "much more freely" than has anyone else, and his "allusions to American life" have an irritating, even unwarrantable, "tone of depreciation." Yet, he admires and defends Hawthorne "with skill and ingenuity," writes in "a spirit of intelligent appreciation," and will provoke interest in Hawthorne. The style is "plain, familiar," and easily comprehensible.

6 ANON. "Current Literature." New York Evening Post, January 19, p. 1.
(Review of Hawthorne.) Although it contains some "very excellent" interpretive criticism, of which James is a master, this book is "in some respects disappointing and depressing." Its tone is intensely and narrowly English. James has failed to learn the facts about his subject, and adopts the prevalent English opinion of American literature.

7 ANON. "Literature." New York Herald, January 19, p. 5.
(Review of Hawthorne.) James is an exquisite author in another sense from Hawthorne, and his novels are largely criticisms, like this volume which is more critical than biographical. James portrays Hawthorne with an indefinable, vague, elusive quality, and one feels "a natural resentment" of James's "shadowy, bloodless portraiture of an American author" who was more solid than that. The criticism is keen and earnest, but with a suggestion of "dainty sneering" and condescension.

8 ANON. "Book Reviews. . . . Literary Notes." New York World, January 19, p. 2.
(Review of Hawthorne.) James too much depreciates G. P. Lathrop's study of Hawthorne, and seems to be trying to describe Hawthorne's early surroundings for European readers. He takes up important issues; the whole book is interesting and very pleasant reading, but it is far from definitive. James is very good with particulars, and keenly sensitive to Hawthorne's style, but does not arrive at "a character of Hawthorne" as a man or a writer.

9 ANON. "New Books." St. Louis Globe-Democrat, January 19, p. 3.
(Review of Hawthorne.) This work "deals with every important occurrence in Hawthorne's life, is beautifully written and doubly endears the subject to memory."

10 ANON. "Henry James, Jr., on Hawthorne." Boston Daily Advertiser, January 20, p. 2.
Coming unexpectedly from James's "light and mocking pen" is a very amusing biography of Hawthorne. The description of "the utter forlornness" of New England life fifty years ago is "very funny," as James lavishes on it "satire, contempt, and a kind of amused pity." The indictment of New England is "accurately true," and the chapter on Brook Farm

and Concord is "one of the most entertaining ever written on those fruitful subjects of enthusiasm and irony." For James provincialism is the one unpardonable sin. His purely literary criticism is "always delightful," and is keen, clear, and delicate. He makes his censure frank, his praise cordial, and fully appreciates Hawthorne's literary gift.

11 ANON. Review of Hawthorne. New York Commercial Advertiser, January 21, p. 1.
(Comments mainly on Hawthorne himself.) Like other American writers, Hawthorne is more appreciated today in England than in the United States.

12 ANON. "Letters and Science." Chicago Tribune, January 24, p. 9.
(Review of Hawthorne. Summarizes Hawthorne's life, with quotations from James's book.)

13 ANON. "New Publications." Cincinnati Commercial, January 24, p. 4.
(Review of Hawthorne.) This book is difficult to evaluate. James writes "a very popular kind of fiction" whose scope and style are not unlike those of this biography, but here his self-conscious manner ill fits the subject. It is painfully incongruous when one with James's "somewhat mechanical fancies" tries to measure the "immeasurable" depth, nobility, and simplicity of Hawthorne's soul. James is not large-souled and broadly comprehensive enough to be a competent critic, as indicated by his narrow view of Hawthorne the man and writer, and by his "half cynical, half contemptuous flings" at G. P. Lathrop's psychological and delicately divining study of Hawthorne. The latter writer's works will be prized as masterpieces after James is forgotten. Yet, James is a bright, keen writer, this book has merit, and readers will approach it with "curiosity, admiration and strong disapprobation."

14 ANON. "Literary Notices." St. Louis Missouri Republican, January 24, p. 12.
(Review of Hawthorne.) This book is a critical review rather than a biography.

15 ANON. "Provinciality in Literature--A Defense of Boston." Atlanta Constitution, January 25, p. 2.
(Editorial.) Comments in those primary representatives of literary Boston, the Atlantic Monthly and the Boston Daily Advertiser, suggest that Boston has been "stung to the quick" and "quite overwhelmed" by James's "casual remarks" on New England's defect of provinciality in Hawthorne.

Hawthorne is more a study of New England social life fifty years ago than a study of the author, and James, with his "exquisite culture" and "initiated" rather than "provincial" intellect, is "the most delightful literary snob of the period." His piece on Hawthorne is "exceedingly clever," "delightfully written," with keen satire and delicate humor. Nonetheless, Boston should realize that provinciality is no defect but rather "the very essence and marrow of American literature" and all literature.

16 ANON. "Books of the Week." New York Daily Graphic, January 29, p. 648.

(Review of Hawthorne.) In this "remarkable study" James should have given more of a biographical account of Hawthorne, but his critical analysis is fine and will rank high. He is sometimes too cool and discriminating, and, contrary to James's assertion, Hawthorne's genius and growth were independent of his environment. James says much that is interesting and valuable in the chapter on "Three American Novels," and although repetitious, he has "delicacy and beauty of expression," pleases the reader, and wins his attention if not his sympathy.

17 ANON. "James's Hawthorne." Nation, 30 (January 29), 80-81.

(Review.) James has the advantages of a fresh subject and appropriate distance from it, and he leaves the reader with a single, consistent impression kept always in view.

18 ANON. "Literature. . . . Hawthorne, by Henry James, Jr." Chicago Times, January 31, p. 8.

(Review.) The book is in many respects well done, but not on the whole satisfactory, and its prevailing characteristics are egotism, intellectual straining, verbosity, and rhetorical gaudiness. It has an air of precocity and reads like "the work of an alert, immature, vigorous, and ambitious mind" seeking "definite conceptions." In this "experimental search" James does not wholly miss Hawthorne's character, but, guided by flashes, shows us glimpses. James's worst fault of style is his "strenuous effort to be always striking." He tries to conceal his "radical want of thorough comprehension by gaudy and bizarre devices."

19 ANON. "James's Hawthorne." Atlantic Monthly, 45 (February), 282-285.

(Review.) James puts "too slight a value" on some of Hawthorne's work, notably The Scarlet Letter, and criticizes as material for fiction the American social structure which presents "the only fresh and novel opportunities left to fiction." Yet, James's characterization of Hawthorne is most satisfactory despite small errors, and overall the book is skillful and manly, "a miracle of tact and of self-respect," with nothing to regret in its attitude. It is "delightful and excellent," "refined and delicate in perception, generous in feeling." Its closing words present Hawthorne with subtle justice and rich expression.

20 ANON. "Bits of Critical Opinion. . . . Henry James's Worldly Idylls." New York Tribune, February 8, p. 8.

(Item from Pall Mall Gazette to the effect that James's books are narrow because they omit the everyday aspects of life and focus on the graces and adornments.)

21 ANON. "New Publications." St. Paul (and Minneapolis) Pioneer Press, February 9, p. 4.

(Review of Julian Hawthorne's Sebastian Strome.) An "acute critic complains" that in Hawthorne James "confuses his admirable estimate of the genius of the great writer of romances" by using the terms novel and romance interchangeably. (A "Literary Notes" item says James thinks Hawthorne "the most valuable example of the American genius" in the field of letters.)

22 ANON. "James's Hawthorne." Christian Union, 21 (February 11), 133-134.

(Review.) This book has charming qualities: "grace, cleverness, artistic proportions," modulated tints. Its tone, art, and style are French, suggestive of Sainte-Beuve. Its "radical fault" is its foreign attitude and failure to see what is "vital and creative" in American life. Hawthorne would have "repudiated vigorously" James's "pitiful plea" of the poverty of American materials for fiction. In details, the book is satisfactory, and it finely delineates Hawthorne's art. It fails, however, to present him clearly and comprehensibly, and misses his "masculine genius."

23 ANON. "Literature/The Magazines." Chicago Times, February 14, p. 8.

(Review of Appleton's Journal.) James is "capable, but by no means remarkable," belittles American literature, and has contempt for American culture, yet American reviewers habitually give him "a chorus of adulation." However, the Appleton's Journal review of Hawthorne defends Hawthorne "with perfect justice" against James's patronizing attitude, the "objectionable tone" that appears throughout his work. (Long quotation from Appleton's.)

24 ANON. "Literature . . ./Other Books./Mr. James' 'Confidence.'" Chicago Times, February 21, p. 8.

(Review.) Confidence has not much depth or substance, and its characters are fools, but though it will not add to James's reputation, it will add to his income. He has enjoyed "so much puffery" recently from authors of similar "literary syllabub" that he is "making money, if not fame."

25 ANON. "Literature." San Francisco Chronicle, February 22, p. 6.

(Review of Hawthorne.) This book in the English Men of Letters Series does not pretend to biographical value, and was written from "a purely English standpoint for English readers." Except Matthew Arnold's essays, no recent addition to English critical writing compares with it for delicacy of thought or finish of expression. It is exquisite in form and has an unusually large amount of careful criticism for its size, but James has been in Europe too long to really know New England. The American reader will rebel instinctively at many of his conclusions and object to the "half-patronizing pity" with which he looks at Hawthorne's Salem. James errs profoundly when he calls Hawthorne a novelist rather than a romancer.

26 ANON. "Literature." New York Herald, February 23, p. 8.

(Review of Confidence.) The characters are very similar to those in James's other books. In courtship the heroes do not love the ladies but, rather, scientifically analyze their character. Confidence is a "clever bit of workmanship," and will mollify those who have thought James's works unpatriotic. James draws mothers well, and a book like Confidence "contrasted with the novels of the day stands alone."

27 ANON. "March Magazines." New York Tribune, February 25, p. 6.

(Review of Lippincott's. Quotations from the review of Hawthorne, which review is "discriminating and just, showing a wise appreciation of that admirable piece of critical art.")

28 ANON. Review of Hawthorne. Independent, 32 (February 26), 12.

This work deserves study, but James's ideas about the dearth of artistic material in America are "cockneyish" rather than cosmopolitan.

29 ANON. Review of Hawthorne. Detroit News, February 26, p. 2.

This book, and its inclusion in a series on English authors, has provoked some "hostile criticism." Yet, except for "an uncalled for and ill-natured fling" at Poe, it contains nothing offensive.

1880

30 ANON. "Bits of Criticism./Another English Critic on Mr. Henry James." New York Tribune, February 29, p. 7.
(Comments quoted from the Westminster Review to the effect that James's novels are excellent because they are detailed and painstaking, they get on good terms with the reader, and they have much art as well as humor.)

31 ANON. "Books of the Day." Appleton's Journal, n.s. 8 (March), 282-284.
(Review of Hawthorne.) Major faults of this otherwise admirable work are James's detachment, his "hypercritical method," and his subtle, exhaustive analysis's failure to make Hawthorne concrete and real. James's estimates of Hawthorne are always fresh, individual, and interesting. They are often "delicately discriminating and appreciative," even exceptionally good.

32 ANON. "Literary Notices." Eclectic, 31 (March), 378-379.
(Review of Hawthorne.) This book is "wonderfully subtle, acute, penetrating, and discriminating," the "finest piece of purely literary criticism" in American literature, but its overelaboration and overqualification bury our general conceptions of Hawthorne in "minute distinctions." In his dread of provincialism, James is too guarded and tentative about Hawthorne, and his attitude toward "everything American" is too condescending. Although "unsatisfactory as a whole, and somewhat provoking in manner," the essay contains "much excellent criticism very beautifully expressed."

33 ANON. "Editor's Literary Record," Harper's, 60 (March), 633.
(Review of Hawthorne.) James's "deft and artistic" use of materials makes "exquisitely graceful" biography. His criticisms are "sparkling and subtle," but often hypercritical, and he sometimes sneers at American literature.

34 ANON. "Literature of the Day." Lippincott's, 25 (March), 388-391.
(Review of Hawthorne.) No American writer has so much natural affinity to Hawthorne as James has. James analyzes and dissects his characters as Miles Coverdale did his friends, and he sees a deep significance in the ordinary. With a sense of fitness, James outlines Hawthorne's life simply, and in tracing it shows "wonderful skill," keenness of insight, and "subtlety of divination." When he denies Hawthorne is a pessimist, though, he is very wrong and shows his own "determination to take nothing seriously." James writes of America with "sympathy and comprehension," and an "almost faultless" style. This study deserves itself to be the subject of a study. (See 1880.27.)

1880

35 ANON. "Literary Notes." New York Tribune, March 1, p. 6.
When the first edition of 1,500 copies of Confidence was published, there were already 2,100 orders for it.

36 ANON. "New Publications." Cincinnati Commercial, March 3, Extra Sheet, p. 1.
(Review of Confidence.) Except for Roderick Hudson, James's least known and best story, this book is the most sustained he has ever made. It has James's elegance and refinement of finish, rather than any largeness of views or positive convictions. He gives us microscopic studies of life, and one regrets that he does not apply his "Meissonier-like" touch to objects of greater mental interest or intellectual worth. The most enjoyable of James's often insubstantial "artistic delineations" is in "A Bundle of Letters." In Confidence Blanche Evers, though silly, is a slight improvement over Daisy Miller, and the denouement is unexpected and very skillfully done. The characters are very good material for James's "artistic romancing," and his elegance and brightness are always refreshing.

37 ANON. "New Publications." New York Tribune, March 5, p. 6.
(Review of Confidence.) This novel has little material or incident, and few actors. James's genius produces an art not epic, tragic, gorgeous, or sensational, but "more remarkable for acute observation, deep insight, and refined analysis." The story has faithful and exquisite pictures of European scenery, "subtle artifice," fine invention, "a natural and credible denouement," and "admirable, amusing" minor characters. The book provides piquant mental enjoyment and James's style has been "justly commended" as a model of terse, vigorous, elegant expression, but he overworks certain words such as "clever."

38 ANON. "Late Publications." Philadelphia North American, March 5, p. 4.
(Review of Hawthorne.) James's analysis of Hawthorne's character and genius is undoubtedly the best yet published, and James, with his French subtlety and nicety of expression, was well fitted to produce this "brilliant piece of work." Hawthorne's admirers may be disappointed in it because that writer's subtle genius "eludes the keenest criticism."

39 ANON. Review of A Bundle of Letters. Detroit Free Press, March 6, p. 3.
This "clear little satire" contains some "very interesting letters" from a German and a Frenchman.

1880

40 ANON. "New Publications." Boston Evening Journal, March 9, p. 1.
(Review of Confidence.) The plot has some delightful surprises, the dialogue is sparkling and clever, and the analysis, or dissection, is as "keen, cold and pitiless" as usual in James's books. The final impression is not entirely agreeable, perhaps because none of the characters enlists the reader's sympathy. James's book suggests that life and love are merely jest and mocking banter.

41 ANON. Review of Confidence and A Bundle of Letters. Independent, 32 (March 18), 11-12.
Confidence has James's "sparkle and brightness," a good plot except the farcical ending, and clever character study. "A Bundle of Letters" is also bright and interesting, but its characters are "fragmentary and exaggerated."

42 ANON. "New Publications." Detroit Free Press, March 20, p. 3.
(Review of Confidence.) Because James is so much more a critic than a novelist, American readers have not given him a fair hearing and have been even further alienated by Daisy Miller. His more recent novels, though, have made him more popular, and so will Confidence. Without pretense to brilliancy or sensational emotional appeals, this "thoughtful study" has also "singular force and interest" as a story. The style is "a model of terseness, vigor and elegance."

43 ANON. "Some April Magazines." Atlanta Constitution, March 24, p. 2.
(Editorial review of International Review.) James, the "highly cultured story-writer," "formerly of America, but now of the entire continent of Europe," writes daintily of the letters of Eugene Delacroix. This article seems one of James's hastiest efforts, since he has in it "little opportunity to advertise his well-known merits as a snob" of culture and parts.

44 ANON. "Recent Novels." Nation, 30 (March 25), 289-290.
(Review of Confidence.) The book is a study rather than a story, and the improbability of the situation is a flaw in the work of a writer who has been a realist since Roderick Hudson. Everything else flows naturally, is captivating reading, and is remarkably good. In recent years all James's best people have been "everyday characters whose respect for convention amounts to a code of morals." Confidence has very alive, individual, and interesting characters of whom the best is Blanche. Her "exquisite" monologues and subtle, intricately motivated "chess-playing" are both entertaining and realistic.

1880

45 ANON. "New Publications." St. Paul (and Minneapolis) Daily Pioneer Press, March 29, p. 4.

(Review of Confidence.) James has taught his readers to expect so much "rare entertainment" that they are perhaps inevitably disappointed with this book. He is best in short stories, "gems of searching analysis and delicate conscientious portraiture." It is because of limitations of form rather than of his genius that this work may charm less than Daisy Miller and An International Episode. It has less excellent dialogue than usual, but its style and construction are "painstaking perfection."

46 ANON. "Mr. Henry James's Latest Novel." New York Evening Post, March 29, p. 1.

(Review of Confidence.) James's facility of expression and his ability to pursue a subtlety to its innermost hiding place are combined with much triviality. Despite the graceful lines, "too heavy a superstructure rises from slim foundations." This flimsy narrative is not an advance for James, and is inferior to Daisy Miller. It has scanty material and colorless characters. James knows little of his own country, but if he observed it better, he would gain in "breadth, freshness, and power."

47 ANON. "Culture and Progress." Scribner's, 19 (April), 943-944.

(Review of Hawthorne.) James sounds superior and condescending rather than properly reverent toward his subject, and he utterly lacks sympathy for the United States, New England, and Hawthorne. The book has some redeeming passages, but James's traveling has been wider than his thoughts have been deep, and he is as self-conscious as he accuses some New Englanders of being. His belief that literary growth requires "ivied ruins" is "astonishingly crude" from a man "so discriminating and observant," and he lacks "the true artistic sense."

48 ANON. Note. Boston Evening Transcript, April 9, p. 6.

"A Diary of a Man of Fifty" and "A Bundle of Letters" are written "in the usual sparkling style of this brilliant author, and are keen but good-natured satires."

49 ANON. Review of A Diary of a Man of Fifty and A Bundle of Letters. New York Commercial Advertiser, April 12, p. 1.

These sketches are "characteristic and entertaining." Despite some "carelessness and inelegancies" absent from James's earlier and more carefully polished work, this book shows no "marked deterioration." James is "one of the best" young American men of letters.

1880

50 ANON. Note. Springfield (Mass.) Republican, April 15, p. 3.
"A Diary of a Man of Fifty" and "A Bundle of Letters" are "lively sketches."

51 ANON. "The May Magazines." Chicago Times, April 24, p. 8.
(Review of Harper's.) Harper's makes the very fair criticism that the much-puffed Confidence fails to tell a story and interest the reader.

*52 ANON. Review of Hawthorne. Churchman, 41 (April 24), 462.
(Foley cites this as a favorable review.)

53 ANON. "The Rabelais Club." New York Tribune, April 25, p. 8.
James has been selected as a member of this group devoted to earnestness, erudition, and manly strength in literature.

54 ANON. "Several Recent Novels." Christian Union, 21 (April 28), 398.
(Review of Confidence.) Such characters have appeared before in James, but instead of allowing us to understand them they disappear when we try to define them, as James analyzes them to the vanishing point. He is less inflexibly neutral than usual about these characters, but neither his keen, unemotional men and cool, calculating women, who form one set of his automata, nor his insipid volatile women and dull stolid men "are in any sense representatives of average American society." Their fragmentary and mysterious dialogues are not typical either.

55 ANON. "Literary Notices." Eclectic, n.s. 31 (May), 634-635.
(Review of Confidence.) James's style and manner are "delightful" and the book is charming, but the people and situations, though amusing, are too "flimsy and artificial" to hold the reader's sympathy or to justify serious treatment by "a really great" artist. This novel shows increased command over materials and "an exquisite gracefulness and delicacy of art" that almost implies genius, but it reveals no "growth of imaginative vigor" or widening of creative vision and faculty. Thus, James fails to fulfill any "large expectations" based on his earlier stories, and he seems to avoid the "broad currents of human life" to explore "little side eddies."

*56 ANON. Review of Confidence. Churchman, 41 (May 1), 490-491.
(Cited in Foley, who quotes this reviewer's praise of James, p. 23.)

57 ANON. "New Books." New York Times, May 3, p. 3.
(Review of A Diary of a Man of Fifty and A Bundle of

Letters.) These stories have James's "usual clever stamp." "A Bundle of Letters" deals with "typical Americans" in France.

58 ANON. Notice of A Diary of a Man of Fifty and A Bundle of Letters. Independent, 32 (May 6), 10.
The first of these is "charmingly told," fresh, and interesting. The second has some good points, but has a "distasteful picture of the vulgar American woman abroad."

59 ANON. "Literary Lines." San Francisco Chronicle, May 16, p. 6.
(Quotation from a James essay on Gautier refers to Gautier's "Le Capitaine Fracasse.")

60 ANON. "Literature." San Francisco Chronicle, May 16, p. 6.
(Review of Hawthorne. Summary of Hawthorne's life.)

61 ANON. "Topics of the Day." New Orleans Daily Picayune, May 23, p. 2.
(Note.) James, "the anti-provincialist, is a favorite in the cultured society of London and Paris."

62 ANON. "Literature." San Francisco Chronicle, May 23, p. 6.
(Review of A Diary of a Man of Fifty and a Bundle of Letters.) These stories have James's usual "finish of style and felicity of phrase," his Gallic "delicate suggestiveness of thought and fancy." The letters in the "bundle" are "marvelously well done" and true to life.

63 ANON. Review of Confidence. Boston Book Bulletin, 3 (June), 40-41.
James is popular and has attracted more attention recently than any other American writer, though mainly for methods scarcely literary. This novel's plot is improbable and complicated, and though it is worked out with skill, style, and interest, it remains unsatisfying, with no strong characters. James is at his best in the description of Baden-Baden.

64 ANON. "Culture and Progress. . . . James's 'Confidence.'" Scribner's, 20 (June), 311.
It is surprising that with all the "artistic perfection of his style, the keenness of his observation and the strength and brilliancy of his thought," James has "so little real depth of insight." Although James shows us love as too tame and devoid of passion, his book is entertaining and skillfully constructed. We see the whole inner life and character of James's people, but more the influence of

their emotion on their conduct than their real emotion itself. Each character is a skillful study, and many are so originally and piquantly portrayed that they almost seem new creations despite their affinities with other fictional characters. The plot is simple, yet contains "a series of delightful surprises dexterously managed."

65 ANON. "'Washington Square.'" New York Tribune, June 13, p. 8.
(Comments on the first installment of Washington Square.) James has done some good work, but here and in Confidence he draws characters "intensely unimportant if true." He and the school which he heads write "little nothings" about dull, dreary, stupid people, but with "an air of languid profundity," a "deep intensity of expression" suggesting "mountainous labor."

66 ANON. Review of Harper's. Nation, 30 (June 24), 474.
In the first installment of Washington Square the heroine is already interesting, if only by contrast with previous subjects of James's analysis.

67 ANON. "The July Harper's." New York Herald, June 28, p. 10.
(Review of Harper's.) Washington Square begins well, and will probably be one of James's "telling stories."

68 ANON. "The Contributors' Club." Atlantic Monthly, 46 (July), 140-41.
(Comments on Confidence.) James's work is like the painter's, and one describes it using terms belonging to art. In Confidence "a scheme of color" relates all the parts. We do not follow the characters with a lively interest in their fortunes, but rather, like James, take an analytic attitude toward them. Most of the novel is told from the point of view of Bernard Longueville, "a clever device for holding the story together without the . . . disadvantages of an autobiographic form." But, it even further reduces the characters' individuality and separateness. The story's workmanship is as finished as in James's other books, and the story is pleasanter though not more interesting; it has a happy ending. It refutes the "dreadful accusation" brought against this "delightful" writer of being a cold-blooded, "indifferent dissector of human nature." James should, though, attempt more difficult tasks than this kind of book.

69 ANON. "Books Received." Californian, 1 (July), 92.
(Review of Confidence.) In this "somewhat plotless novel" the aimless people have nothing to do or say and all sound like James. Their ingenious remarks grow wearisome.

1880

70 ANON. "New Publications/Recent Fiction." New York Times, July 1, p. 3.
(Review of W. D. Howells's The Undiscovered Country.) The leading American authors, Howells, James, and Thomas Bailey Aldrich, stand far above the others. Though their delicate subtlety requires reflective readers, their books are read all over America and are being devoured by the English readers of the higher class, who are amazed, if not always delighted by this peculiar school of romance. Like Howells, James has accurate perceptions about women and about good society.

71 ANON. "Literary Items." Louisville Courier-Journal, August 4, p. 3.
James's earliest stories from a dozen years ago did not satisfy him and "are now buried in the magazines where they appeared."

72 ANON. "Literary Notes." Chicago Tribune, September 4, p. 9.
The London Examiner thinks that Washington Square will be one of James's most popular works.

73 ANON. "Literary Notes." Chicago Tribune, September 18, p. 16.
The cosmopolitan view of Concord culture expressed in Hawthorne has led a young woman devotee of that culture to hate James and wish him in love with and married to "'a perfect Daisy Miller.'"

74 ANON. "Literary." Louisville Courier-Journal, September 18, Supp., p. 1.
(Review of Atlantic Monthly. Reference to William James as "a brother of Henry.")

75 ANON. "Literary Items." Louisville Courier-Journal, September 22, p. 3.
(Same note as 1880.73.)

76 ANON. Reviews of Atlantic Monthly. Atlanta Constitution, September 26, p. 2; November 4, p. 2; November 24, p. 2; December 31, p. 2.
James is connected with Boston and its "provincialism." (Early notices of The Portrait of a Lady in serial praise the characters.)

77 ANON. Reviews of Macmillan's Magazine. Boston Daily Advertiser, October 15, p. 2; December 13, p. 2.
In The Portrait of a Lady Mr. Touchett's son and wife are "queer" and Isabel is well-drawn and agreeable despite her saying some "silly things, of which American girls are quite

1880

innocent." The story, "like all good things, begins rather indifferently," and "the Americans of the novel" are so far not of the finest type. Henrietta is impertinent and offensive, the workmanship is delicate, and "the novel itself . . . neither strong nor great."

78 ANON. Review of Atlantic Monthly. Boston Evening Journal, October 16, Supp., p. 2.
The November installment of The Portrait of a Lady suggests a scope pretty sure to permit the "keen analyses and contrasts of character" which so delight James.

79 ANON. Review of Atlantic Monthly. Boston Evening Transcript, October 18, p. 6.
The November Atlantic contains the opening chapters of The Portrait of a Lady, which are "bright and full of point." Despite what the critics have said about James, few writers of fiction have "a wider circle of readers."

80 ANON. "Literary." Louisville Courier-Journal, October 19, p. 3.
(Review of Atlantic Monthly.) In The Portrait of a Lady and elsewhere, James "is adept" at painting a certain type of lady, in a usually "unflattering style."

81 ANON. "Literary Items." Louisville Courier-Journal, October 21, p. 3.
James replied to the Boston Journal's request for a story that he has already promised enough literary work to keep him busy for many months.

82 ANON. "New Publications." Philadelphia Public Ledger and Daily Transcript, October 23, Supp., p. 1.
(Review of Atlantic Monthly.) The best of the Atlantic this month "is decidedly its fiction," and The Portrait of a Lady is in James's "best style," is "far superior to the languid interest of his last stories," and will be enjoyed.

83 ANON. Review of Atlantic Monthly. Boston Daily Advertiser, November 13, p. 2.
The English characters in The Portrait of a Lady are "less spontaneous than the Americans, and none of them particularly discreet or reverent."

84 ANON. "Book Reviews. . . . The Magazines." New York World, November 22, p. 2.
(Review of Atlantic Monthly.) The Portrait of a Lady promises much more of a story than Washington Square, and "is certainly very good reading."

1880

85 ANON. "Book Reviews. . . . The Magazines." New York World, November 22, p. 2.

(Review of Harper's.) Washington Square, now concluded, has been lengthened not by padding, but by detail that "sharpens and deepens the outlines" of the characters. Only the aunt and lover repay the pains taken with them, while the father remains vague and the daughter wooden.

86 ANON. "New Publications." New York Times, November 28, p. 10.

(Review of Washington Square.) James depicts character "faithfully and accurately," showing that with insight and descriptive power one can find "various and distinctive types of American character" that are good subjects for fiction. He should, however, combine his successful, "intensely realistic" characterizations with "a good striking plot."

87 ANON. "Boston Books. Henry James, Jr., in Miss Fletcher's New Novel." New York Herald, November 29, p. 9.

A satirical description of James appears in Miss Fletcher's (George Fleming's) novel of Americans in Rome, The Head of Medusa, in which a selfish, unscrupulous Italian nobleman marries an American girl of "noble nature" and then, becoming indifferent to her, stands between her and a better love. (Quotation from description of James.)

88 ANON. "Washington Square." Boston Evening Transcript, December 2, p. 6.

(Review.) This latest of James's "curious studies of human nature" shows that he sees that our society does have "types." It is valuable as a picture of society past and present, and it is an example of the current trend toward anatomical rather than imaginative fiction of ideality.

89 ANON. "New Publications." Philadelphia Public Ledger and Daily Transcript, December 4, Supp., p. 2.

(Review of Washington Square.) The portrait of Catherine is "very well done," Morris Townsend is not consistent, Mrs. Penniman is "perfect," and Dr. Sloper is "capital, as any of his brother physicians will recognize."

90 ANON. "Literature. . . . 'Washington Square.'" New York Herald, December 6, p. 5.

James leisurely tells his stories in the manner of "a cynical dandy lying back in his easy chair" talking to friends. His "little dainty turns" of narration have "a certain piquancy." The story, though thin, is refreshing, and will be avidly read and relished by a great many people.

1880

91 ANON. "New Publications. . . . Notes." Boston Evening Traveller, December 8, p. 1.
(Review of Washington Square.) Du Maurier's illustrations compare unfavorably with the best work of American artists. Washington Square is "a society study" rather than a novel, and "a delightful piece of analysis," to be ranked with James's best work.

92 ANON. "New Books and New Editions. . . . Washington Square." New York Daily Graphic, December 10, p. 297.
Interest is well sustained from beginning to end. The story has the particular attraction of the father's "more than common keenness and acumen," and the novelty of the heiress's not marrying the adventurer but becoming an almost contented old maid.

93 ANON. "Literary Notices." Cleveland Daily Plain Dealer, December 15, p. 2.
(Review of Washington Square.) Knowing that James, the author of Daisy Miller, has produced another "society story" will make the public inquire heartily for the book. Du Maurier's illustrations lack the "pen and ink spirit" of his work in Punch.

94 ANON. Review of Atlantic Monthly. Boston Evening Traveller, December 16, p. 1.
The Portrait of a Lady is "of great promise" and "of much interest." Without losing his "inimitable faculty" for character analysis, James "infuses" it with "a little more blood and sinew" than his other works and "thus comes nearer to his ideal" than in any previous effort.

95 ANON. "Literary Notices." Hartford Daily Courant, December 16, p. 1.
(Review of Washington Square.) The story, like everything James writes, is entertaining for its "analysis of motives and of feeling, and for his exquisite style, but it has less 'go' in it than any others by him," and revolves around characters who do not interest us. The wooden Catherine has constancy and power of will, but not interest.

96 ANON. "Literary." Louisville Courier-Journal, December 17, p. 4.
(Review of Washington Square.) James's heroines anger young women, but many people admire him and his exquisite powers, though they may wish he were less cynical. Here, he analyzes and etches four characters with "his peculiarly delicate and unfaltering strokes," and it is in the characterization that the book's merit lies. Those who

appreciate "the art of a writer" will be charmed, but others will not be interested. This work is not as good as some of James's others.

97 ANON. Review of Atlantic Monthly. Hartford Daily Courant, December 17, p. 2.
The Portrait of a Lady is a "vastly entertaining story."

98 ANON. "Late Publications." Philadelphia North American, December 17, p. 4.
(Review of Washington Square.) Like James's other works, this is a study of character rather than a novel. When through, James "shuts the puppet-box" without regard for the feelings of his spectators. This book is very clever, as James always is, but disappointing in its artificiality and lack of characters with whom the reader sympathizes. The characters also behave unrealistically.

99 ANON. "Recent Novels." Chicago Tribune, December 18, p. 10.
(Reviews of Washington Square and George Fleming's The Head of Medusa.) James is "supercilious, too dilettante, talks too much and says too little." He finishes neither character nor plot, yet draws characters well and "has depicted certain types with remarkable accuracy." This book lacks "absorbing interest," has a weak substructure, an uninviting superstructure, and a failed heroine. In her novel Miss Fletcher (George Fleming) gives a "not unflattering likeness" of James (quoted).

100 ANON. "Literary. . . . New Publications." Chicago Inter-Ocean, December 18, p. 14.
(Review of Washington Square.) This story has had "a multitude of readers" as a serial, "will doubtless, as it deserves, find many more," and the general reader will think it "capital." James provokingly works up his characters until the reader is fully interested, and then leaves him on his own.

101 ANON. "Literary Items." Louisville Courier-Journal, December 19, p. 2.
(Note.) George Fleming's novel The Head of Medusa has a passage describing a character apparently modeled on and satirizing James. (Passage is quoted.)

102 ANON. "Miscellaneous Literature." Springfield (Mass.) Republican, December 23, p. 3.
(Review of Macmillan's Magazine.) Nothing in Macmillan's for December leads The Portrait of a Lady "in ability or interest," and no serial in any English magazine of the past quarter has "equaled it."

1880

103 ANON. "New Publications." Portland Morning Oregonian, December 29, p. 1.

(Review of Washington Square.) This writer's powers assure that any story by him will be worth reading, and a story like this, in James's style, "will win the attention of the multitude of readers of lighter fiction."

104 ANON. "Our Boston Literary Letter. Women in America and in Europe." Springfield (Mass.) Republican, December 29, p. 4.

The Portrait of a Lady calls attention to the difference between American and European women, a "good theme for fiction." The adorable Isabel and the audacious Henrietta "excite the most eager curiosity" about their fates. They "are wrapped in the folds of the American flag," and their destiny is an international concern.

105 B. "A Bookworm's Waymarks." Literary World, 11 (September 25), 325.

The trouble with Daisy Miller is not James's lack of patriotism, but rather his tendency to look too determinedly at the seamy side of things. Because he refuses to look at beauty rather than deformity, he is "all wrong" as an artist, whatever may be his merits as a possibly "great teacher of manners and morals."

106 BIANCIARDI, MRS. E. D. R. "Letters From Italy.--XXXVIII./James, Jr., and Americans Abroad." Springfield (Mass.) Republican, June 15, pp. 2-3.

Hawthorne is one of "two grievous inflictions" on the American colony in Italy. The consensus from "the endless discussions" of it is that it says very little about Hawthorne. It has some "keen, fine strokes of criticism," but fails to make a "comprehensive judgment." James reveals some limitations in point of view, showing again his lack of affection for and "persistent disparagement of anything American." He has "greatly retarded" English appreciation of America and the establishment of cordial relations between the two countries.

107 COOLIDGE, SUSAN. "Mr. James's Confidence." Literary World, 11 (April 10), 119-120.

In real life this kind of imbroglio would have ended in murder or the madhouse, and by closing with the wedding gifts and hand-shaking James shows he can make his characters do the impossible. It is regrettable that one capable of such refined and delicate work should have "indulged in a plot so objectionable and preposterous" just to show how cleverly he can untangle his own snarl of circumstances. (Much plot summary.)

108 FOXCROFT, FRANK. "Mr. Henry James, Jr., On Hawthorne." Literary World, 11 (February 14), 51-53.
(Review.) Americans have awaited this volume with interest. It is valuable only as criticism, having little biographical content. James's estimate of Hawthorne is appreciative, but "almost coldly calm," with a perpetual consciousness of an English audience. His list of negatives in the American environment is "appalling" and inaccurate, but his analysis of Hawthorne's novels is for the most part admirable.

109 HAZELTINE, MAYO WILLIAMSON. "Some New Books." New York Sun, January 25, p. 2.
(Review of Hawthorne.) This book is not satisfactory as either a biography or a critical estimate. James writes too much on the model of Sainte-Beuve, when Americans need critics who are not equivocal and evasive but who tell the truth directly. James fails to probe and boldly avow Hawthorne's intellectual gaps and deficiencies, to expound his philosophy that would be the key to his works. James merely intimates, and his repetition of certain adjectives is annoying.

110 H[AZELTINE], M[AYO] W[ILLIAMSON]. "Some New Books." New York Sun, May 23, p. 2.
(Review of Confidence, A Diary of a Man of Fifty and A Bundle of Letters.) Though a work of talent rather than of genius, A Diary is one of James's best. With no humor and little pathos, which faculties James generally lacks, this story is charming, amiable, nearly perfect, showing impressive literary skill. It and A Bundle are "happily conceived and carefully finished." James feels an habitual "critical superiority" toward American society, and Americans are ambivalent toward him. The heroine of Confidence is one of James's "strongest and most engaging figures," but the characters too consistently repudiate Americanisms in speech.

111 H[AZELTINE], M[AYO] W[ILLIAMSON]. "Some New Books. . . . Some New Novels." New York Sun, June 27, p. 2.
We have had "more chaff than wheat from the crop of society literature" inspired by "the marked commercial success" of "An International Episode" and "Daisy Miller."

112 HIGGINSON, THOMAS WENTWORTH. "Henry James, Jr.," Short Studies of American Authors. Boston: Lee & Shepherd, pp. 51-60. Enl. ed. 1888; New York: Longmans, Green, 1906.
James's books lack the hearty, robust men found in Howells, but James deals with stronger emotions. His literary workmanship is so hasty that his essays are prolix and repetitious. He misses points of excellence in well-known books.

He is indifferent to local coloring and is only a limited cosmopolitan, being not at home in his own country. His short stories are the best in recent American literature, but, despite strong characters and skillful plots, his novels are unsatisfactory because of their endings.

113 LATHROP, G. P. "Cockney Americanism." New York Tribune, February 9, p. 6.
(Letter to the Editor. Long, satirical objection to James's criticisms of America in Hawthorne.)

114 P[ERRY?], T. S. "Contemporary Literature." International Review, 8 (April), 447-450.
(Review of Hawthorne.) This is "a readable and interesting book," with a charming style and manner. Contrary to the charges of his condescension and lack of patriotism, James is very skillful in portraying both Hawthorne and the intellectual life of his time with occasional irony of only "the gentlest kind." James shows "the essential quality" of Hawthorne's genius as well as his shortcomings.

115 PERRY, T. S. "Some Recent Novels." Atlantic Monthly, 46 (July), 125-126.
(Review of Confidence.) Confidence is not a novel but a study of an ingeniously devised situation "analyzed and described with the utmost skill." It is not morally profound, and its "life-like figures" move as in a well-played game of chess. The story is breathlessly interesting and as a bit of social imagination deserves high praise, but James should try to be more than merely entertaining and, with his "generous equipment," give us "novels of a higher flight."

116 [SANBORN, F. B.] "Our Boston Literary Letter." Springfield (Mass.) Republican, February 10, pp. 2-3.
(Review of Hawthorne.) James must be careful when he tries to include among his puppets a real literary man. This book is egotistical, with "laughable condescension" and "airy impertinences" toward Hawthorne's New England, and a French disrespect for serious-minded women. Hawthorne's personality was far more profound and capacious than that of James, who lives among the "little creatures" of his imagination and is the victim of his own illusions. Despite his large experience, his nature has remained narrow, and the provincialism of which he accuses others is his own. He has many qualifications to be the American Sainte-Beuve, but he reduces the objects of his criticism to "microscopic dimensions." Yet, despite some inaccuracies, this book has much value, especially the analysis of the romances. James

is now "at the head of American fiction," as Hawthorne was in his day.

117 SHARP, LUKE [pseud.]. "The Portrait of a Lady." Detroit Free Press, December 26, p. 9.
(Possible parody on The Portrait of a Lady.)

118 TEMPLETON [pseud.]. "Boston Correspondence. . . . Joseph Cook and Henry James." Hartford Daily Courant, February 21, p. 1.
(Reviews of Hawthorne and Confidence.) Confidence is one of James's best books, and one of his most characteristic in its minute study of character and analysis of motive. The plot is simple and the narration more satisfactory and interesting than "the perversities" of The American and "the over-subtleties" of The Europeans. Despite his faults, James is the "first of living American novelists." Within its limits his mind is rich and fertile. His treatment of Hawthorne and the literary prophets and apostles of Concord, for which he is "'catching it' on all hands," results from his lack of mental affinity with them. They would think James "a dainty product of conventionalism and artificiality." James was not good on Hawthorne and his surroundings, and he might have shown in general "a more robust taste and more catholic appreciation," but all must admire "his exquisite analysis" of Hawthorne's works. G. P. Lathrop wrote a loud attack on the book for the New York Tribune, and F. B. Sanborn reviewed it more effectively in the Springfield (Mass.) Republican.

1881

1 ALLEN, GRANT. Review of The Portrait of a Lady. American, 3 (December 31), 186-187.
James's influence is "morbid and unwholesome" and his novel, although "a masterpiece in a literary sense," is "one of the most disheartening books ever written." Its moral emptiness and decadence make it an "abnormal, unreal, unhealthy" affair for which "[t]he working, suffering . . . world has no use."

2 ANON. Review of Washington Square. Dial, 1 (January), 195-196.
Washington Square shows James's characteristic moderation and modesty in undertaking these "simple 'studies.'" His people are agreeable and restrained, his stories never strain the nerves, and he "attempts no statement or solution of great social or moral problems, no dissemination of

1881

pessimistic theories." The reader appreciates these traits. Morris Townsend's motive in deserting Catherine is difficult to understand.

3 ANON. Review of Washington Square. Literary World, 12 (January 1), 10.

This book is "a clever bit of psychological anatomy" which we admire as we might admire a brilliant experiment or skillful operation, but mainly it is "a piece of literary dilettanteism." It shows cunning workmanship, but does not give James credit for being "even an earnest trifler."

4 ANON. Review of Atlantic Monthly. Springfield (Mass.) Republican, January 3, p. 3.

The Portrait of a Lady is one of the stories in the January Atlantic whose authors' subjects "are all within their composes and are well treated."

5 ANON. Review of Atlantic Monthly. Portland Morning Oregonian, January 8, p. 2.

The Portrait of a Lady is "an effort at portraiture, and hardly a narrative at all," with "little action," incidents "few and commonplace," and an emphasis on the study of character. The characters all have "a marked individuality outside of all the conventional types."

6 ANON. "The Literary Succession." Boston Evening Journal, January 20, p. 2.

The (Boston) Literary World suggests that when Longfellow, Emerson, Whittier, Holmes, and Lowell are gone, the likes of Howells, Aldrich, Stedman, James, Scudder, and Fawcett may rise to fill the void of greatness. Or, there may be "an interregnum of mediocrity" until young writers mature.

7 ANON. "Our Book Column." St. Louis Post-Dispatch, January 22, p. 3.

(Review or bookseller's notice of Washington Square.) Washington Square is "the latest and probably the best" work by "this very brilliant author." It is "well-told and well worth telling," and the delineation of character is, as always with James, "wonderfully artistic."

8 ANON. Reviews of Atlantic Monthly. Atlanta Constitution, January 26, p. 2; February 22, p. 2; April 1, p. 2; May 1, p. 2; May 26, p. 2; June 21, p. 2; August 25, p. 2; September 25, p. 4; November 27, p. 4.

(Reviews of The Portrait of a Lady in serial use vocabulary of science and mechanism to call the characters unreal, not human, mere puppets which the "majolican" "Junior James" dissects or directs "in the character of a showman.") James is "interested in society groups" rather than in individual manifestations of human nature. He is too obviously manipulative and lacks human sympathy, but "one or two" of the characters are likely to endure.

9 ANON. "Literature of the Day." Lippincott's, 27 (February), 215.

(Review of George Fleming's The Head of Medusa.) George Fleming (Miss Fletcher) is not as deeply indebted to or influenced by James as the (London) Saturday Review suggests. Her "wicked little sketch" of an international novelist is "one of the brightest things" in The Head of Medusa.

10 ANON. "Literature of the Day." Lippincott's, 27 (February), 214-215.

(Review of Washington Square.) The conscious subtlety of James's works makes demands on the reader's subtlety of perception. Long experience and "nicety of perception" have given James "an immunity from failure," but his characters still lack roundness and he is not a robust writer. He has followed the "established English" pattern of the novel to the extent of having a solid, practical situation, unexceptional characters, and a natural ending, but even with these features this book is no more realistic or substantial than his others. Although the book has his fine touch, James's "compromise with the commonplace" may have "cramped his opportunity for being brilliant and spirituel." The social texture is not thick, and no minor characters appear.

11 ANON. "New Publications." New York Tribune, February 6, p. 8.

(Review of Washington Square.) This book is worthwhile and worth reading, but it is neither a very good story nor very lively. Despite the "vivid description," dramatic dialogue, and "ingenious situations" which gave promise in his earlier works, James "lacks the constructive art of the novelist," even in The American with its bold, remarkably powerful incidents. Washington Square lacks incident, and Aunt Penniman is its best character. It contains nothing to anger Americans, and James is equally critical of all societies. His popularity is dubious and his works somewhat cynical and mocking because neither he nor his readers care much about his characters. His analyses are cold-blooded, and he should devote himself to "wholesome satire" like Daisy Miller instead of to these amusing but unsympathetic and unprofitable character pictures.

12 ANON. Reviews of Atlantic Monthly. Detroit Free Press, February 19, p. 5; November 13, p. 3.

This installment of The Portrait of a Lady is "sure to have wide reading without any special urgency on the part of critics," and the novel progresses "slowly, but pleasantly."

13 ANON. "The Canadian." Wasp, 6 (February 19), 116.
(Parody on James emphasizing his cultural prejudice in favor of Boston.)

14 ANON. "Some Recent Novels." Appleton's Journal, n.s. 10 (March), 274-275.
(Review of Washington Square.) The book is lively and maintains interest, but includes a disappointingly small amount of the local color of the period and place it portrays. No other living novelist "makes less use of those externals and surroundings" that help furnish the atmosphere of a story, and James's characters evolve from their own impulses and the influence of other personalities, "isolated as far as possible from the 'environment.'" Though his heroine is quite ordinary and does not very much grip the reader, James has "consummate literary skill" and is "beyond doubt the cleverest writer who now entertains the public with fiction."

15 ANON. "Culture and Progress. . . . James's 'Washington Square.'" Scribner's Monthly, 21 (March), 795-796.
Except for Thomas Hardy, no one writing current fiction in English has "so complete a training and so fine a hand" as James. Hardy has "an imaginative side" that James lacks, but the latter is remarkable for the care he gives his style and for "the elaboration of his notes on modern society." Industriously, like a scientist, he records minute observations of the daily conduct of ordinary people. Though most people think Washington Square dull, it seems one of James's "best and cleverest" tales. Its being set in America may be a weakness, since, for all its realism, the book shows a limited understanding of the complicated courtship code of American society. As with Daisy Miller, James portrays in Catherine "the bad minority" of American women. We do not care about the characters, who are not truly real, and, like James's other works, the novel is worked up with great care, skill, and cleverness, but comes to nothing.

16 ANON. Review of Washington Square. Californian, 3 (April), 376-377.
Washington Square's execution is nearly perfect, but its design is a blunder in that James handles tragedy with a "dispassionate, realistic method" and a spiritualized Zola's assumption about suffering. He does a fine portrait of

Catherine, without his usual overload of detail, but his matter-of-fact, scientific manner does not lift us to the fervent or sympathetic response we associate with tragedy.

17 ANON. Editorials. Cincinnati Commercial, April 17, p. 4; April 19, p. 4.
(Reference to and quotation from James's "rich collection of personal recollections" of Carlyle in the May 1881 Atlantic Monthly, including one "amusing" incident.)

18 ANON. Editorial review of Scribner's Monthly. "Some June Magazines." Atlanta Constitution, May 26, p. 2.
In A Fearful Responsibility Howells seems to be imitating James, whose work, aside from "the exquisitely finished literary embroidery," is "of the flabbiest description." We depend on Howells to give us something different from James's "whimsy-flimsy stuff."

19 ANON. Review of Atlantic Monthly. Cincinnati Commercial, May 28, extra sheet, p. 1.
James "continues to drag along his fine-spun, colorless, metaphysical romance," The Portrait of a Lady.

20 ANON. "Typical Americans." New York Times, June 22, p. 4.
(Editorial.) The "typical American" of James and Howells has replaced the "vanished 'Yankee'" and is generally accepted as "a truthful portrait." James's Newman is rich, honest, sincere, and energetic, but his characteristically American traits are his vulgarity and ignorance of the rules of polite society. Americans should not be libeled by their "best story-writers," and someone should protest this inaccurate portrayal.

21 ANON. "July Magazines." Atlanta Constitution, July 2, p. 2.
(Editorial review of Scribner's Monthly. In discussion of the conclusion of Howells's A Fearful Responsibility, refers to "Mr. Junior James" as "the great chief of the majolicans.")

22 ANON. "New Publications." New York Tribune, July 3, p. 8.
(Review of Edgar Fawcett's A Gentleman of Leisure.) James has inspired great hope but should have done more work like Daisy Miller, "an admirable portraiture of a typical American girl," instead of studying "the manners of the tourist." The "tragic sketch" of Daisy was his only "notable attempt" at satire. Fawcett pursues a larger object, his satire cuts deeper, and he has "a more tender feeling for his countrywomen."

1881

23 ANON. Review of W. D. Howells's A Fearful Responsibility. Atlanta Constitution, July 30, p. 2.

James is a "literary Majolican" making "curious efforts to dissect the refined ruffianism which Americans call culture." (The writer implies that James is an influence with which writers and critics must come to terms, and other Atlanta Constitution reviewers of 1880-81 mention him in a similar light, e.g., in reviews of S. B. Russ, October 1, 1880, p. 2, and Mrs. Burnett, January 1, 1881, p. 2.)

24 ANON. Review of Atlantic Monthly. Chicago Tribune, September 17, p. 9.

The Portrait of a Lady "increases in interest."

25 ANON. "Literary Matters./The October Magazines." Boston Evening Transcript, September 19, p. 6.

(Review of Atlantic Monthly.) This issue, which includes an installment of The Portrait of a Lady, is "exceptionally entertaining."

26 ANON. "The American Novel." New Orleans Daily Picayune, October 16, p. 2.

(Editorial. General comments on James.) James is "the most finished, observant and subtle of all contemporary American novelists." He has a "quiet strength" and understated way of exciting the reader's emotional response to his characters, and his deemphasis of plot makes his novels more rather than less true to life. However, the novels, with their European settings, do not answer the need for the use of contemporary America as setting and material for fiction.

27 ANON. "Literary Buddhism." Louisville Courier-Journal, October 23, p. 8.

(Editorial.) James and Howells have "established a new school of romance from which romance has been entirely eliminated" and in which the "phantom," "porcelain," "wil-o'-the-wisp" characters have "the habit . . . of cold and ruthless self-analysis" and "are controlled, not by emotion or passion or intellectual force, but by theory." James's women are "all Daisy Millers" and the men also inexplicable, not of "this age or country." (Vocabularies of science and of art are combined to emphasize the unreality of the characters and of the atmosphere, the dearth of emotion and positive values in favor of triviality and indifference.)

28 ANON. Review of Atlantic Monthly. Philadelphia Public Ledger and Daily Transcript, November 5, p. 2.

The characters in The Portrait of a Lady are not only

unrealistic but also "disagreeable." A "wearisome" straining after "epigrammatic effects" is noted, but the novel is to be credited with a "singular intellectual interest."

29 ANON. "New Books." Charleston (S.C.) News and Courier, November 8, p. 2.
(Review of J. Brander Matthews's French Dramatists of the 19th Century.) Matthews's essays "lack the literary finish and grace of style which lend such a charm" to James's studies of nineteenth-century French poets and novelists.

30 ANON. Note. New York Tribune, November 14, p. 6.
The ending of The Portrait of a Lady leaves the "chief characters in a forlorn and unsatisfactory state."

31 ANON. Review of The Portrait of a Lady. New York Commercial Advertiser, November 18, p. 3.
James's style, his "graces of mind and execution," have "done so much to embellish American letters," and the story is one of great interest.

32 ANON. Reviews of Atlantic Monthly and The Portrait of a Lady. New York World, November 18, p. 4.
The Portrait of a Lady and Howells's Dr. Breen's Practice are "two of the best novels that have ever appeared in . . . [the Atlantic] or . . . in any magazine." The Portrait of a Lady is "a remarkable novel," "without doubt" James's most "'important'" work so far, and "one of the most important of American works of fiction." All who are likely to read it already know about it.

33 ANON. Review. Boston Evening Journal, November 19, Supp., p. 1.
The Portrait of a Lady is "unquestionably among the most noteworthy books of the year in . . . fiction." The dialogue, the delineation of character, the natural behavior of most of the characters, and the studies of life and society in European cities are admirable. However, the story is too slow moving, the ending too abrupt, and the "real motive" behind what goes on, especially Isabel's actions, is often hard to determine.

34 ANON. "Late Literature." Akron Daily Beacon, November 19, Supp., p. 5.
(Review of Atlantic Monthly.) The Portrait of a Lady and Howells's Dr. Breen's Practice "have been such notable features."

1881

35 ANON. Review of Atlantic Monthly. Detroit Evening News, November 21, p. 2.

The Portrait of a Lady is "brought to a triumphant conclusion."

36 ANON. "Periodicals." Boston Evening Transcript, November 22, p. 6.

(Review of Atlantic Monthly.) The closing installment of The Portrait of a Lady is one of the principal "good things" in the December Atlantic.

37 ANON. Review of Atlantic Monthly. Philadelphia North American, November 22, p. 4.

The Portrait of a Lady "is finished in a dramatically powerful, but unsatisfying, even tantalizing, fashion."

38 ANON. Note. Indianapolis Journal, November 23, p. 7.

The Portrait of a Lady is an "interesting romance."

39 ANON. Review of The Portrait of a Lady. Philadelphia North American, November 25, p. 4.

The ending, if made more "definitive and comfortable," would render the novel faultless, with "nothing to be desired." The work, as it is, is "brilliant," "very powerful and impressive," and "the masterpiece of its author." Its heroine is James's "most elaborate and most successful essay at psychological analysis."

40 ANON. Review of The Portrait of a Lady. Albany Evening Journal, November 26, p. 1.

Some writers are possibly more popular than James, but "none more readable," and The Portrait of a Lady is "characteristic of his style and manner." It is a "society novel" "as fascinating as it is refined," and James strikes a balance between social realism and conventional standards of morality, taste, and decorum.

41 ANON. Humorous item. Boston Evening Journal, November 26, p. 2.

A mock interview with Madame Merle of The Portrait of a Lady "reveals" an epilogue to James's novel emphasizing incident more than analysis.

42 ANON. Review of The Portrait of a Lady. New York Daily Graphic, November 26, p. 181.

Isabel is "clever, intelligent, conceited," and stubborn, the novel "a psychological puzzle," and both, apparently, dominated by intellect. The characters, with the exception of Ralph, are immoral, unpleasant, or simply odd, and, though they "are close studies from life, doubtless," there is "no earthly reason," certainly no moral or aesthetic purpose, "for trotting them out except the morbid one of seeing what sort of a combination show they will make." The ending is inconclusive.

43 ANON. Review of Atlantic Monthly. San Francisco Chronicle, November 27, p. 6.
The ending of The Portrait of a Lady may be as unsatisfactory as those of The American and Washington Square.

44 ANON. Review of The Portrait of a Lady. New York Times, November 27, p. 5.
This is "a deeply interesting study of men and women, of motives and moods," but "unsatisfactory in its beginning and in its end," "spun out too much," and sometimes dull. A quality of "thinness and unnaturalness" is found in the characters, who do not "often elicit sympathy from their charm or nobility," and in whose "accessories" (the minuteness of description, the adroitness with which an apparent commonplace is given a point) rather than in whose "central spirit" James is "a modern follower of naturalism." There is melodrama in the story, and the novel is too long and analytical, but much of the thought that went into it is excellent, and the tone, if not bracing, is elevated.

45 ANON. Review of Atlantic Monthly. San Francisco Examiner, November 27, p. 6.
(Reprints November 18, 1881, New York World review of installment of The Portrait of a Lady, 1881.32.)

46 ANON. "New Publications . . . Literary Notes." St. Paul Daily Pioneer Press, November 28, p. 4.
"The whole of the first edition of The Portrait of a Lady was sold on the day of publication."

47 ANON. Review of The Portrait of a Lady. Boston Evening Traveller, November 29, Supp., p. 1.
The lack of plot, the lack of local color, and the failure to end a novel by neatly rewarding virtue and punishing vice are not grounds for condemning James as an artist. James's self-imposed limitations of scope and lack of emphasis on incident and action manifest rather than detract from his realism, yet he is "not a creative artist." James is criticized for ill-chosen subjects, superficial management of them, and "superb indifference" to any ulterior "considerations beyond the limited area of a given personality." (The writer notes this novel's "distinct human interest," and employs language of science and art to praise James's

"natural method" of "minute analysis" of character development, which does not violate or ignore nature, but rather makes faithfulness to its complexity a possibility.) Chapter 42 and the portrayal of the characters are praiseworthy, especially the portrayal of Osmond, and the novel is itself James's "best work so far," standing "distinctively without a peer" in its field among the productions of contemporary novelists.

48 ANON. Review of The Portrait of a Lady. Cincinnati Commercial, December 1, p. 7.

James is "in the front rank of living novelists," and has "an honest naturalness and a power of dramatic effect." The female characters are less sharply defined than the males but "far from being like Dickens' heroines, mere pegs to hang the story upon," and Henrietta is "representative of dozens of American young women known to us all." (Reviewer recognizes her, Ralph's, and Osmond's androgyny, admires Isabel, emphasizes the melodramatic in her situation, and finds the ending unfinished and ambiguous, yet makes no moral judgments about it.)

49 ANON. Review of The Portrait of a Lady. Indianapolis Journal, December 2, p. 2.

(An unfavorable review, which disapproves of James's European point of view, the characters, and "the moral tone.")

50 ANON. Review of The Portrait of a Lady. Chicago Inter-Ocean, December 3, p. 10.

The characters are "soulless" and materialistic, the ending is unfinished, and James's use of expatriates rather than rural yeomen as heroes and heroines to "serve as representatives of American people" is regrettable.

51 ANON. Review of The Portrait of a Lady. San Francisco Chronicle, December 4, p. 6.

This is the "best work" so far by James, and "the best novel of the year" by any author. There is a lack of action, and the chief merits are the character drawing, the dialogue, and the style.

52 ANON. Humorous item. Springfield (Mass.) Republican, December 4, p. 4.

(Reprint of the spoof interview with Madame Merle in the Boston Evening Journal, 1881.41.)

53 ANON. "Personal." Baltimore American and Commercial Advertiser, December 6, p. 2.

(Note.) James, "who is about to write a novel of life at Cambridge," is described as resembling the Prince of Wales and looking like an Englishman. (Noted also in Indianapolis Journal, December 8, 1881, p. 4.)

54 ANON. Review of The Portrait of a Lady. Chicago Tribune, December 10, p. 10.
James's attitude toward and fictional treatment of America and Americans are negative and fault-finding. The book is clever, probably entertaining to the general reader, and the best of James's works, except for the inconclusive ending and James's tendency to overexplain.

55 ANON. Review of The Portrait of a Lady. Minneapolis Tribune, December 11, p. 4.
The main characters are vaguely outlined, the conversation is meaningless, commonplace, and inane, and the novel itself is "a shadowy, unfinished picture."

56 ANON. "The Portrait of a Lady, The English Critics on Mr. James's New Novel." New York Tribune, December 11, p. 8.
(Quoted excerpts from reviews in the Spectator [at some length], the Athenaeum, and the Academy.)

57 ANON. Review of The Portrait of a Lady. New York Herald, December 12, p. 5.
(The Portrait of a Lady and Thomas Hardy's A Laodicean are compared, emphasizing James's distinctive artistic "method" and the idea that both writers portray modern society as "genteel comedy," as self-repressed, and as lacking "real seriousness.")

58 ANON. Note. Iowa State Register, December 13, p. 4.
(Reprints the item from the New York Tribune, 1881.30.)

59 ANON. Review of The Portrait of a Lady. Detroit Free Press, December 17, p. 3.
The novel is an interesting study, mainly "of American character both in its natural and Europeanized forms," but too prolonged. Isabel is a sort of atonement for "Daisy Miller."

60 ANON. Review of The Portrait of a Lady. Literary World, 12 (December 17), 473-474.
This novel is representative of its age, of nineteenth-century society in its decline of morality and morale. A "few [of the characters] are hardly fit to live."

1881

61 ANON. Review of The Portrait of a Lady. Portland Morning Oregonian, December 18, p. 4.
(Paraphrases very closely parts of the New York Times review, 1881.44.)

62 ANON. Brief quoted reference. Christian Union, 24 (December 21), 615.
(Quotes the London Athenaeum's comment that The Portrait of a Lady is dull.)

63 ANON. "Mr. Howells' New Novel." Chicago Tribune, December 24, p. 9.
(Review of W. D. Howells's Dr. Breen's Practice.) Howells's American girls are "much more pleasing and natural" than James's, and his stories are simpler, his "poetic vein more pronounced."

64 ANON. Quoted critical reference. Cincinnati Commercial, December 27, p. 4.
(Reprint of an excerpt from John Hay's New York Tribune review of The Portrait of a Lady, 1881.71.)

65 ANON. "About and For Women." Memphis Daily Appeal, December 29, p. 2.
(Speaking of the girls of James's and Howells's novels, the St. Louis Globe-Democrat says that one cannot portray girls successfully and treat them always seriously, because even the best and most charming have something ridiculous about them.)

66 ANON. Review of The Portrait of a Lady. Colorado Springs Weekly Gazette, December 31, p. 4.
James has "acute reflections," a "power of keen analysis," and an ability "to lay so bare the secret workings of the human heart and mind," but lacks sentiment, enthusiasm, and real warmth. The plot is not deep, the characters are not remarkable, and the analysis at times is tiresome.

67 ANON. Critical reference. Literary World, 12 (December 31), 496.
(Review and assessment of the year's literature.) The Portrait of a Lady is not "immortal," but "the most careful and elaborate, though by no means the most pleasing, study in the art of writing a novel."

68 B., M. H. "No Romance All Real." Louisville Courier-Journal, November 6, p. 6.
(Letter to the Editor. A female reader, in response to the Courier-Journal editorial two weeks previous, disputes

the claim that James's and Howells's characters and situations are unlike the real world.) Their scenes are drawn from real life and observation, and their heroines are "flesh and blood . . . active, healthy women" in contrast to the "sentimental, lachrymose automatons" of earlier novels. The understatement of emotions makes characters more, not less, robust and realistic.

69 CLARE, IDA [pseud.]. Reviews of Atlantic Monthly. St. Louis Post-Dispatch, January 17, p. 2; November 12, p. 2.

(Earlier review calls The Portrait of a Lady "one of the best stories" ever penned by its author. Later review notes that the novel "develops wonderfully" with "almost a Ouida-like intensity in its sketchings of characters" who "seem very real and yet, somehow, totally unreal and impossible.")

70 CLARE, IDA [pseud.]. Review in Weekly Boston Letter. St. Louis Post-Dispatch, November 22, p. 2.

The Portrait of a Lady is the "most remarkable story of the year," but despite their appearance of life and animation, and however elaborately drawn, the characters "have no souls behind their mechanism by which to make them really independent . . . they are soulless."

71 HAY, JOHN. Review of The Portrait of a Lady. New York Tribune, December 25, p. 8.

The realism of the novel, the living quality of its characters, and the genius of its author make it not a light work of amusement, but a serious study of social conditions and "the moral aspects of our civilization." At the end "no one in it really prospers."

72 HAZELTINE, MAYO WILLIAMSON. Review of The Portrait of a Lady. New York Sun, November 27, p. 2.

(A fairly comprehensive assessment which praises James's powers of observation, his judgment, tact, and taste, as well as the entertaining and instructive quality of his books, but finds the range of emotions and subjects he portrays are limited because he confines himself to good society and has acquired of necessity a style which will register subtle rather than sharp distinctions. Hazeltine uses the language of art to describe this style which, though delicate and subtle, yet achieves "a power of expression" "vigorously and admirably displayed.") The portrayals of Madame Merle and particularly Osmond are admirable, and Isabel is an androgynous character possessing masculine traits but also "self-centered aspirations" which contribute to her downfall.

1881

73 HENRY, M. L. "Mr. James as a Patriot." New York Tribune, September 29, p. 3.

(Letter to the Editor. James is defended against charges of lack of patriotism leveled by American critics. M. L. Henry admires his "true estimate" and just treatment of "some of the finest, most substantial" American character traits and "fundamental virtues which often lie beneath most unprepossessing exteriors," and provides as examples, among others, Caspar Goodwood, Ralph Touchett, and Henrietta.)

74 J., M. C. "The Romance of Daily Life." Louisville Courier-Journal, November 6, p. 6.

(Letter to the Editor. A reader objects to the Courier-Journal's calling James's and Howells's novels and characters unnatural, lacking in human vitality.) These authors' characters are "true to nature" and "every-day life," the authors themselves are the most familiar fixtures in the popular consciousness of American fiction, and The Portrait of a Lady indicates that James's art has gained in "strength and force."

75 MORSE, JAMES HERBERT. Review of The Portrait of a Lady. Critic, 1 (December 3), 333-334.

James's character portrayal suffers from his excessively analytical method, and the characters "represent national peculiarities only in a gross way," the girls being recognizable in American social life, but "second-rate."

76 SCUDDER, HORACE E. "The Head of Medusa, and other Novels." Atlantic Monthly, 47 (May), 709-710.

(Review of Washington Square.) "Elaborate nonentities," including the dull and commonplace Catherine, people this book, whose almost "sole excuse for being" is its wit and ingenuity. The reader admires James's cunning instead of sympathizing with the heroine for her suffering.

77 SMALLEY, GEORGE W. "Mr. Henry James, Jr.--The Publishers." New York Tribune, December 19, p. 6.

(A discussion of the reception of The Portrait of a Lady by the British critical press, particularly [and quotes] the Pall Mall Gazette.)

78 STACKPOLE, HENRIETTA [pseud.]. "Isabel Has No Descendants." Louisville Courier-Journal, November 6, p. 6.

(Letter to the Editor. A reader differentiates between Daisy Miller and Isabel of The Portrait of a Lady on the basis of Isabel's "deliberate, logical way" of thinking, the "intellect and dignity" which enables her to control her emotions in a crisis.) These are positive rather than negative traits, not indicative of lack of soul or humanity. James's and Howells's books are among "the most charming . . . of this century."

79 TEMPLETON [pseud.]. Review in Weekly Boston Letter. Hartford Daily Courant, November 19, p. 1.
The Portrait of a Lady is James's "greatest novel" and up to a point his "most fascinating and attractive," but possibly owing to "the perversity of its creation," its "unhealthy charm" gets the better of the healthy, and what promised to be "one of the most delightful books ever written" ends as "a morbid study of character." Yet, its fascination, the "wonderful power" with which it is written, its literary finish, and the genius of its author are in all of American fiction bested only by Hawthorne.

80 TEMPLETON [pseud.]. "Mr. Henry James, Jr." Hartford Daily Courant, December 3, p. 1.
(Regular Boston letter. Description of James.) James will probably be lionized in social and literary circles while in this country, though his slighting of America may put off some people. The Portrait of a Lady is being much read and more talked about than anything else in current literature. Despite its unsatisfactory plot, it is his greatest work and shows first-rate talent, even genius.

81 TEMPLETON [pseud.]. "Mr. Henry James, Jr." St..Louis Post-Dispatch, December 16, p. 7.
(Reprint of parts of 1881.80.)

82 TEMPLETON [pseud.]. "Henry James, the Novelist." Cincinnati Commercial, December 24, p. 3.
(Reprint of part of 1881.80.)

83 WHITING, LILIAN. "Boston Days." Cincinnati Commercial, May 7, Extra Sheet, p. 4.
Mrs. Burnett's A Fair Barbarian may have served as a counterirritant to Daisy Miller and "soothed the wounded American sensibilities" because its heroine has a refined dignity Daisy lacked.

1882

1 ANON. Review of The Portrait of a Lady. Californian, 5 (January), 86-87.
James's choice of subject (American expatriates) and setting is a handicap, providing only a moral vacuum of decadence, and the secondary characters, excluding Ralph

and his father, Lord Warburton, Goodwood, and Pansy, are "a miserable, puny, pigmy race." Yet, James's novel is "a highly remarkable and moving tale," the characters have "real life" in them, and Isabel is morally exemplary, despite her lack of "any definite moral credo."

2 ANON. "Bits of Criticism," "The 'Thunderer' on Henry James." New York Tribune, January 1, p. 6.
(Quoted excerpt from the London Times review of The Portrait of a Lady, December 14, 1881.)

3 ANON. Brief reference. Indianapolis Journal, January 2, p. 7.
(The Portrait of a Lady is listed among recent acquisitions of the Indianapolis Public Library.)

4 ANON. "A Year of American Fiction." Louisville Courier-Journal, January 6, p. 4.
(Editorial.) James is "the first of American living novelists," The Portrait of a Lady is "unquestionably his masterpiece," and his powers of analysis and his artistic workmanship are praiseworthy, but his pessimism, his "cynical introspection," and his devotion to "evanescent and morbid portrait painting" removed from the "flesh-and-blood, everyday knock-about world" are regrettable.

5 ANON. "Literary Notes." Indianapolis Journal, January 13, p. 2.
The Philadelphia Times calls The Portrait of a Lady "the portrait of a novelist--by himself."

6 ANON. "The British Female." Omaha Republican, January 15, p. 5.
(Reprint of a New York Times item refers to the way James's subtle attack on the taste and style in dress of British women has caused "the better portion of the British public" to wince.)

7 ANON. Review of The Portrait of a Lady. Independent, 34 (January 19), 11.
The "merely literary merits" of the novel are commendable, but its heroine is unnatural, its Americans unrepresentative, its purpose (whether satiric or didactic) unclear, and its content unsatisfactory, with "no good heart in it."

8 ANON. Review of Catholic World. New York Freeman's Journal and Catholic Register, January 21, p. 3.
The Catholic World "notice of James's much-discussed 'Portrait of a Lady' is the best we have seen." (See 1882.12.)

9 ANON. Review of The Portrait of a Lady. Churchman, 45 (January 28), 97-98.

Isabel's career lacks credibility; all the marriages are unhappy, and hers suggests at the end polyandry; the conversations are long and pointless; and the whole is "a disappointing performance" according to either philosophical or imaginative criteria. None of the women is very attractive, "one is decidedly repulsive," and the whole work will have the unintended effect of "a satire on modern woman."

10 ANON. Note. Colorado Springs Weekly Gazette, January 28, p. 4.

The Portrait of a Lady is in its fourth edition, one of the reasons Houghton Mifflin had a happy holiday season.

11 ANON. "New Books." Charleston (S.C.) News and Courier, January 28, p. 2.

(Review of The Portrait of a Lady.) This is James's masterpiece, and "one of the most notable novels of the day," fully atoning for his past slights on his countrywomen and placing him among the best "modern writers of analytical and speculative fiction." It shows ripening and development, subtler insight, more thorough comprehension of human nature, and will be enthusiastically received. The lovely, natural Isabel, drawn "with exquisite delicacy," is "the ideal American girl," and the other characters are fine.

12 ANON. Review of The Portrait of a Lady. Catholic World, 34 (February), 716-717.

James cynically belittles things "supposed to be the particular pride of Americans" and he portrays manners rather than character, but he may be more unmerciful than unjust, and his "lotus-eating" Americans abroad may be less caricatures than accurate portrayals, typical of a generation which has lost its religion and thus its moral bearings.

13 ANON. Review of The Portrait of a Lady. Harper's Monthly, 64 (February), 474.

(The metaphor of the portrait is used to praise James and his delineation of character.)

14 ANON. Review of The Portrait of a Lady. Lippincott's, 29 (February), 213-215.

This novel does not show great contrast to its predecessors but reflects a steady development resulting in finer diction, closer analysis, and more careful attention to detail. James's instinctive avoidance of the commonplace, and his tendency to reflect and divine rather than see directly, cause the "absence of weight and reality" in his

1882

characters. The portrait of Isabel is a prime example of this method. (The reviewer combines the vocabularies of science and art to describe it.)

15 ANON. Note. Colorado Springs Weekly Gazette, February 4, p. 4.
(W. B. Closson is engraving a portrait of James for Houghton Mifflin.)

16 ANON. "Snobbery in America." Atlanta Constitution, March 10, p. 2.
(Editorial.) In Our Continent Judge (Albion) Tourgee is attacking the literature for which James is responsible and responding to his strictures in Hawthorne against American provincialism. There is "a grain of truth at the bottom" of James's "delicately fashioned criticism" of New England, he never intimated that America lacks material for novels, and he would not insistently deny that provinciality is the core of the world's most successful literature. James's culture is "a little burdensome," but he is not a snob, and he is proud that Ralph and Mrs. Touchett of The Portrait of a Lady are Americans, and so are we.

17 ANON. Quoted critical reference. Literary World, 13 (April 8), 118.
(A reprint of part of the Pall Mall Gazette review of The Portrait of a Lady, December 3, 1881.)

18 ANON. "Mr. James's New Novel." Atlanta Constitution, April 16, p. 4.
(Editorial review of The Portrait of a Lady.) It is doubtful whether, since Thackeray, there have been such profound and earnest studies of character as those in this book, though the comparison between James and Thackeray must be "as to extent and not as to results." The narrative is of emotions, and is evolved rather than told, with "a good deal of realistic fervor." The realism is so artistic as to border sometimes on the theatric. James achieves "the very flower and perfection of art" in painting his rascals Osmond and Madame Merle. His humor, showing the influence of French methods of thought, would be more delightful if it were less self-conscious. The book's one defect as a study of character is the absence of the element of tragedy, or "rage."

19 ANON. "The June Magazines." Atlanta Constitution, June 1, p. 4.
(Editorial review of Atlantic Monthly.) James's essay on Daudet is "very stilted," but it is not stupid, simply because James "never writes anything stupid."

20 ANON. Review of Guerndale and note on Henry Adams's Democracy. Our Continent, 2 (July 12), 27; 2 (August 2), 126.
(These notices commend these books' deviation from James's methods.)

21 ANON. Humorous item. Our Continent, 2 (August 23), 221.
(A spoof "interview" with James reveals Isabel Archer's postnovel "fate.")

22 ANON. Review of Virginia W. Johnson's An English 'Daisy Miller.' Nation, 35 (August 31), 183.
This author's portrayal of an American woman does not compare well with James's "skillful execution." Miss Johnson should have gathered proof from existing fiction that "Daisy Miller is one of a class universal in modern life, and not a special American type." James's "carefully worked out" portrayal of the Americans' reaction to Daisy's behavior "is the testimony from fact, not from personal opinion, that good society in America" does not permit such conduct.

23 ANON. "Authors and Publishers." Our Continent, 2 (October 4), 413.
Since dramatic power is the principal element lacking in James's stories, people are curious about the play he is working on.

24 ANON. "Items." Boston Evening Transcript, October 6, p. 6.
(Note.) The "numerous readers" of Daisy Miller and The Portrait of a Lady will be very curious about both the portrait of James and Howells's article about him, to be published in the November Century.

25 ANON. Editorial. New York Times, October 26, p. 4.
(Response to the Athenaeum's criticisms of W. D. Howells's A Modern Instance.) With George Eliot gone, James, Howells, and Thomas Bailey Aldrich "are creating a new method for novelists" and "shaping the romance of writing" today. Despite the Athenaeum's obtuse failure to understand them, they will influence English novelists at the close of the century.

26 ANON. "Mr. Howells on Mr. James." Boston Evening Transcript, November 7, p. 6.
Howells's November 1882 Century article on James is "somewhat disappointing." He is more frank about James's wonderful use of language than he is about James's failure to create "vital and recognizable characters." James's workmanship is captivating, but readers wonder about his

limited point of view and his negative attitude toward his characters. Some very inferior writers excel James and Howells in the "fascinating quality" of atmosphere.

27 ANON. "Literature." American, 5 (November 11), 74.
(Review of Elizabeth Stuart Phelps's Doctor Zay.) Despite James's effort and "perfection of method," The Portrait of a Lady failed to reach the high-water mark of American fiction. Its humor and social criticism were too elaborate for the literary fashion of the day. James's earlier books are his best.

28 ANON. "New and Old Novels." New York Tribune, November 12, p. 3.
(Editorial. A reaction to Howells's Century article which objects not to his "lavish praise" of James, but rather to his allegedly unjust comparison of dead authors like Dickens and Thackeray with writers "so characteristic of the intellectual attitude of the time," who have not yet stood the test of time.)

29 ANON. Notes. Our Continent, 2 (November 15), 605; 2 (December 6), 701; 2 (December 27), 797.
(Critical references to James, including a London Times remark on him as less American than Howells, and a London World quote mocking Howells's Century comments on James, Dickens, and Thackeray.)

30 ANON. "An American Novel." Atlanta Constitution, November 19, p. 6.
(Editorial review of W. D. Howells's A Modern Instance.) James and Howells "regard superficiality as an accomplishment," and succeed in making it effective. Their books are full of "humor and information," "grace and refinement." To show character not merely as an individual's emotions, but "in all its relations to life," would be "to take the confidential attitude" of Thackeray, which Howells repudiates for both himself and James.

31 ANON. "The American Point of View." Atlanta Constitution, November 26, p. 6.
(Editorial review.) In "The Point of View" James makes a very gentlemanly retort to the Americans who criticize his international attitude. The piece has irony, humor, intelligence, acuteness, and fine art, but the people who write the letters in it are "morally unhealthy," uninformed "noodles" lacking vigor and individuality. The conception, method, and intent of these letters are snobbish. Much of the criticism of James's alleged lack of patriotism is

itself provincial, and the question of whether America or Europe is better is moot, an imaginary controversy.

32 ANON. "Howells, James, and Stevenson." New York Times, November 29, p. 2.
(Quoted section from the London Saturday Review's discussion of the contrasting literary philosophies expressed in R. L. Stevenson's "Gossip on Romance" in Longman's Magazine, and in 1882.39.)

33 ANON. "A New England Instance?" Atlanta Constitution, December 17, p. 8.
(Editorial. Some comment on 1882.39.) The art of authorship flouted by Howells and "others of the James school" is "nobler, and higher, and more effective than literary art." Howells's and James's skill is great, their style is perfection, their humor is pleasing, and their knowledge of "the little superficialities of character is amazing," but "their books are not vital."

34 ANON. Obituary of Henry James, Sr. Nation, 35 (December 18), 555.
James, Jr., is a well-known and successful novelist.

35 ANON. "Literary Notes." Atlanta Constitution, December 24, p. 2.
Lord Otho Fitzgerald is said to have been the original for Lord Warburton of The Portrait of a Lady. (Item also appears in "The Bookshelf," Our Continent, 3 [June 10, 1883], 60.)

36 ANON. Review of W. D. Howells's A Modern Instance. Our Continent, 2 (December 27), 796.
James is a master of contemporary fiction.

37 BROWNELL, W. C. Review of The Portrait of a Lady. Nation, 34 (February 2), 102-103.
This is James's masterpiece and Isabel Archer is "the American girl par excellence." James has "displayed his patriotism and the national genius by inventing a new variety of literature," "romantic sociology," whose "truly original excellence" is "the imaginative treatment of reality." The Portrait of a Lady in particular is the "most eminent example" so far of "realistic art in fiction" because its substance is real, its presentation imaginative.

38 HENRY, M. L. "Mr. Henry James, Jr., and His Critics." Literary World, 13 (January 14), 10-11.
(Letter to the Editor. A reader defends James against

"the charge of unpatriotic sentiment" with assertions that his American characters tend to be admirable or individuals rather than types.)

39 HOWELLS, WILLIAM DEAN. "Henry James, Jr." Century, 3 (November), 25-29.

(In a general discussion and favorable assessment of James and his work, Howells addresses the problem of his endings, considers his analytic tendency to have increased to the point that in The Portrait of a Lady there is little to call dramatic, and compares James and George Eliot as having, respectively, an artistic and an ethical purpose.) Isabel and Eliot's Dorothea Brooke are "the most nobly imagined and the most nobly intentioned women in modern fiction," but Isabel, with her "beautiful dreams" rather than Dorothea's "grand aims," is "the more subtly divined of the two." (Howells expresses a qualified preference for the romantic over the realistic element in James's fiction, discusses his reserve and impartiality toward his characters, his acceptance in America, his fairness to Americans, and his "growing popularity," and praises his style. He makes the soon-to-be famous remarks on novel writing as "a finer art in our day than it was with Dickens and Thackeray.") The new school of fiction is the wave of the future and "its chief exemplar" is James, "who is shaping and directing American fiction" and possesses "a very great literary genius."

40 HUNTINGTON, H. A. "A Pair of American Novelists." Dial, 2 (January), 214-215.

(Review of The Portrait of a Lady.) Isabel has proud, headstrong, introspective tendencies, but is admirable. There is an absence of religious conviction in the novel, and James's subjects and point of view are limited, lacking in the basic and the elemental.

41 McMAHAN, ANNA B. "The American Heroine." Our Continent, 1 (April 19), 147.

With truth to reality as the criterion, among contemporary American fictional heroines none are satisfactory. Isabel Archer seems to have the character traits to enable her to do justice to her real-life counterparts, but her experiences are too narrow and ordinary (the result, ironically, of James's "realism") to develop that character.

42 MORSE, JAMES HERBERT. "Henry James, Jr., and The Modern Novel." Critic, 2 (January 14), 1.

(In a general discussion of James's work, and of its author as "realistic, almost materialistic," rather than spiritual and imaginative, James's technique is praised, but the vocabulary of mechanism is used to describe his view of human nature and his analysis of character.) He is acute and entertaining, but his books are wanting in "human sweetness and sympathy," in humor and pathos.

43 "NEMONA." "Our Novelists." New Orleans Times-Democrat, December 31, p. 14.

Many regard James as "the representative American novelist," and his books are a "distinct advance" over those of his mediocre predecessors, but in overall satisfactoriness he is second to Howells. His "brilliant novelettes," with their superior workmanship and style, please a large audience, but he does not focus enough on Americans and the novelty has nearly worn off his international theme.

44 P[HELPS], E[LIZABETH] S[TUART]? Review of The Portrait of a Lady. Penn Monthly, 13 (March), 233-234.

(The writer approves of the opening scenes but not of the ending, uses language of mechanism to describe the portrait of Isabel.) Isabel is intellectual but inconsistent, Madame Merle is "real" but Henrietta and Bantling atypical, Ralph is delightful, and the style is almost painfully finished and polished. James has yet to capture the essence of the American girl, despite his study of her.

45 SCUDDER, HORACE E. Review of The Portrait of a Lady. Atlantic Monthly, 49 (January), 126-130.

Isabel is "representative of womanly life today," and James's technical expertise is admirable, but the ending is ambiguous and the novel itself lacks "consistency with the world of reality." Its appeal for the reader is intellectual rather than emotional.

1883

1 ALLEN, JAMES LANE. "The First Page of 'The Portrait of a Lady.'" Critic, 3 (January 27), 27-28.

(A textual discussion of the novel's first scene which finds details too few, imprecise, and inconsistent, and therefore questions the perfection of the book's literary workmanship.)

2 ANON. Humorous items. Life, 1 (January 11), 16; 1 (January 18), 26; 1 (April 26), 197; 1 (May 10), 225; 1 (June 7), 272 (quotation from "G. T. L." in the London Saturday Review).

(Some general humorous and satirical comments on James, usually spoofing his alleged Anglomania and lack of regard for his own country.)

1883

3 ANON. "The New School of Fiction." New Orleans Daily Picayune, January 14, p. 3.

(Reaction to Howells's claim in 1882.39 that his and James's art is finer than that of Dickens and Thackeray.) Howells is right that his and James's greater objectivity and reliance on the reader to interpret for himself is an improvement over the intrusiveness of Thackeray, but the realists' method is not so much a finer art as it is "a more exact and catholic science." The artist should be true to the ideal rather than the actual.

4 ANON. "Migma." Our Continent, 3 (January 31), 156.

(Note. Reference to Daisy Miller, Miss Stackpole, and Mrs. Burnett's "Fair Barbarian" as having been avenged in Miss Broughton's new story.)

5 ANON. "From the Other Side." New Orleans Daily Picayune, February 4, p. 4.

(Editorial. Reaction to Louis John Jennings's January 1883 [London] Quarterly Review article on recent American fiction.) There is a degree of justice in what the critic says of tendencies in American fiction, but the same points apply to contemporary English fiction, too. Analysis is the "special tendency of the modern mind" in general, and distinctly American local color and "provincial picturesqueness" are harder to find than in the days of Cooper and Sims. James's and Howells's Europeanized Americans are less defensible. It cannot be said that James and Howells have produced "nothing of permanent value in literature," but neither is it true that they are better than Dickens and Thackeray, "who wrote with greater force and maintained a stronger hold upon the reading public than any English-writing novelist of today."

6 ANON. Quoted critical reference. Life, 1 (February 8), 68.

(Quotes negative comments on James and The Portrait of a Lady from Jennings's January 1883 London Quarterly Review article, finding it "Blind Right" in its "surmises." See also a cartoon, 1883.95, spoofing Howells's alleged effort to elevate James above Thackeray.)

7 ANON. Notes. Critic, 3 (February 10), 60-61.

(The first item calls L. J. Jennings's Quarterly Review essay "interesting," and notes its negative comments on James and Howells. The second item finds Margaret Oliphant's January 1883 Blackwood's article's criticism of Americans, including James, a shrill, oversensitive reaction to essays by Howells [see 1882.39] and C. D. Warner.)

8 ANON. "Nancy Beck, of San Diego." New York Times, February 18, p. 10.

(Review of The Siege of London.) James's sketches are always of literary interest, especially this gossamer, flimsy, diaphanous "not exactly pleasant" piece showing his wonderful, "peculiar skill" and "inimitable cleverness of touch." The construction of the romance has changed very much since Thackeray's Vanity Fair. This story is "retributive," because there is something ludicrous about Mrs. Headway's capturing the Baronet. It is for the "most fastidious," and its wholesomeness is up to the reader.

9 ANON. Review of The Siege of London, The Pension Beaurepas, and The Point of View. Boston Evening Transcript, February 23, p. 6.

When published in the Century "The Point of View" caused nearly as much comment as Daisy Miller, and the multitude who read only extracts from it in the newspapers can now enjoy the whole.

10 ANON. Notice of The Siege of London, The Pension Beaurepas, and The Point of View. New York World, February 28, p. 4.

(Account of where each story was separately published.)

11 ANON. "The Contributors' Club." Atlantic Monthly, 51 (March), 428.

(A defense of the value and distinction of contemporary American literature refers to "the keen analysis of The Portrait of a Lady.")

12 ANON. "The Novel of To-Day." Nation, 36 (March 1), 185-186.

A "curious international literary discussion" has been provoked by Howells's comments on Dickens and Thackeray, and there has been a "decline of the novel of 'purpose'" because of the nearly complete "emancipation of the downtrodden" during the last fifty years, the absence of any "tyrannical social system" on which to blame abuses, the prosaic nature of contemporary reform issues, and the airing the press gives to abuses. James shares the French valuing of art for its own sake rather than for a lesson it teaches.

13 ANON. Notes. Nation, 36 (March 1), 192-193.

(First item reviews the controversy in England resulting from Howells's and Charles Dudley Warner's essays in the Century. It mentions the London World's and Saturday Review's angry responses to Howells's essay, and the Blackwood's and Quarterly Review articles as pulverizing James and Howells and scattering their dust. The latter article is discussed at some length, and its invective, innuendo, false statements, ungenteel defense of throne and altar, and the "languid curiosity here" to know who wrote it are noted. Its author is revealed to be L. J. Jennings, London correspondent of the New York World and former "famous vituperative editor of the New York Times.") Jennings's one insinuation worth notice, that James and Howells wrote mutually flattering articles on each other for the Century, contains "no truth . . . whatever" since the Century essay on Howells was written and signed by T. S. Perry, a fact of which "Jennings must or might have known." (Second item refers to the British-dominated quarrel over the American novelists, and praises Th. Bentzon's February 1, 1883, article in the French Revue des Deux Mondes as a kind of retort to the British attack. The writer notes her praise of James's and Howells's "'profoundly interesting studies of contemporary life in America,'" implies that they give "an exact and realistic description of American life," and commends the article as meriting attentive reading.)

14 ANON. "Mr. James's New Volume." American, 5 (March 3), 330-331.
(Review of The Siege of London.) This is "as penetrating and entertaining" a work as any by this agreeable writer. The title story is highly original and lifelike. James's characters are individuals.

15 ANON. "American Fiction." Portland Morning Oregonian, March 4, p. 4.
The author of the January 1883 Quarterly Review article on American novels assails James and Howells with venom partly because of annoyance at the decline in English fiction. Howells was right that current fiction must be more introspective than that of Dickens and Thackeray, and both James and Howells, though overpraised, try to supply the demand. They are not equal to Hawthorne and George Eliot, but each has done "honest and excellent work" and is eminent in his own sphere. James is analytical and less creative than Howells, but does "fine and subtle criticism of life and manners." He and Howells are doing work as real and truly characteristic of its time as was the work of American writers of one or two generations ago. James's and Howells's work is as true to American society as the work of George W. Cable and Bret Harte is to "certain American localities." The Quarterly Review article is too hard on James and Howells.

16 ANON. "New Publications. A Slash at English and American Society." Cincinnati Commercial Gazette, March 4, Extra Sheet, p. 1.
(Review of The Siege of London, The Pension Beaurepas,

and The Point of View.) James's attention to details is microscopic and amazing, and he knows well human nature altered by society, but he has small acquaintance with "simple human nature." The question raised by Howells of whether James writes a finer novel than Dickens or Thackeray is a matter of taste. James's style has a polite but slightly biting humor, he thinks the "falsities of society" he describes are "the real business of life," and he is a "cynical man of the world" who makes his readers more suspicious of other people. All the Americans in "The Siege of London" are "poor stuff," and James seems trying to draw more distinctly European lines of caste.

17 ANON. "Mr. Henry James' Last Volume, 'The Siege of London.'" New York Daily Graphic, March 5, p. 27.

James excels at and particularly focuses on characters who are "invariably tawdry and vulgar," but some of whom are also "picturesque and moderately fascinating." "The Siege of London" is artistically perhaps the best thing James has done since Daisy Miller; it is concise and complete. In "The Point of View" James is more of a humorist than anywhere else.

18 ANON. "Late Publications." Philadelphia North American, March 7, p. 4.

(Review of The Siege of London, The Pension Beaurepas, and The Point of View.) These stories contain some of James's "most finished and skillful work." "The Siege of London" has more story than usual for James, and characters portrayed with James's "usual keenness of analysis and verbal felicity." Cultivated readers will get much pleasure from it.

19 ANON. "New Publications . . . Literary." Hartford Daily Times, March 9, p. 1.

(Review of Atlantic Monthly.) James writes "in his best vein" of "Tommaso Salvini," an article which will greatly interest this actor's admirers.

20 ANON. "Minor Notices." Literary World, 14 (March 10), 78.

(Review of Esther J. Trimble's A Hand-Book of English and American Literature.) James and W. D. Howells are "the two leading American novelists of today." (See 1882.103.)

21 ANON. Review of Harper's. Albany Evening Journal, March 12, p. 1.

In the April Harper's Mr. Curtis defends Howells and James "against the attacks of their irate American critics."

1883

22 ANON. "The Case of Mr. Howells." New York Tribune, March 18, p. 6.

(Editorial.) James and Howells are highly regarded among foreign critics, who have "recognized them as the principal representatives of a new school of fiction" with "certain fine and fresh qualities" lacking in contemporary English novels. There has been a sudden turnabout in the American press's opinion of James and Howells from seeing them as a credit to their country to revolting against them as "against two malign pretenders, whose books are at once an affront to American intelligence and a danger to American letters." The shift is "not quite so queer" in the case of James as in that of Howells, since part of the American press has always been hostile to James, refused to accept him as an American novelist, and doubted his "desire for patriotic fellowship." Thus the present outbreak against him is nothing new, since James has recently shown neither cynicism nor snobbism. The current fervor against him is attributable to the favor and friendship of Howells, possibly in particular as expressed in the remark about Dickens and Thackeray. The remark is "unfortunate" and Howells should not have made it.

23 ANON. Review of Atlantic Monthly. New York World, March 19, p. 2.

To an extent the first act of Daisy Miller, A Comedy supports Charles Dudley Warner's contention ("Modern Fiction") in the same (April) issue that ordinary talk is not worth writing or reading as dialogue. The British, however, are greater producers than Americans of "the insipid society novel."

24 ANON. "Literary." Hartford Daily Times, March 22, p. 1.

(Review of Atlantic Monthly.) The first installment of the play Daisy Miller adds attractions to the original which "will make it quite worth while" for all readers.

25 ANON. "Literature." Chicago Times, March 24, p. 11.

(Review of The Siege of London, The Pension Beaurepas, and The Point of View.) These are three of the brightest and keenest of James's "Americo-European studies." The "pungent medicine" James administers should "do some good" among Americans both abroad and at home.

26 ANON. "Fiction." Literary World, 14 (March 24), 90.

(Review of The Siege of London.) James can write fiction, but here he dwells too exclusively on the theme of the American girl abroad. "The Siege of London" is another version of Mrs. Burnett's A Fair Barbarian, and is a disagreeable episode agreeably written. "The Pension Beaurepas" is more pleasant. In general, James dissects and distorts, but nonetheless amuses, and people do read him.

27 ANON. "Arts and Letters." Springfield (Mass.) Republican, March 25, p. 4.

(Review of Atlantic Monthly.) The first act of Daisy Miller, A Comedy is not more dramatic than the novelette, but is keener and deadlier satire, perhaps because it is without the "gracious descriptions" and "fine analyses." Although the work is "not for the stage," the new form has sharpened the pungency of the satire, which was always more directed at Winterbourne than at Daisy, and has "deepened it into realism." As "an earnest work" the story definitely "gains by this new treatment."

28 ANON. "On the Reviewer's Table." Albany Evening Journal, March 26, p. 1.

(Review of The Siege of London, The Pension Beaurepas, and The Point of View.) A new story by James is an event in social as well as literary circles, and "The Siege of London" is "eminently readable" and "delightfully anti-American" with its choice "polite ridicule." It is charmingly told by a master of the "delicate badinage" heaped "gracefully and pitilessly" on Mrs. Headway. The skill and wonderful color and animation are delightful, but James should perhaps put his "great talents" to better use than the derision of his countrymen.

29 ANON. Our Continent, 3 (March 28), 413 [quotes Revue des Deux Mondes]; 3 (April 18), 508-509; 4 (July 11), 60-61; 4 (August 1), 159 [quotes Boston Literary World].

(Brief direct or indirect critical comments on James.)

30 ANON. Review of The Siege of London and comments on James, in Boston letter. Springfield (Mass.) Republican, March 29, pp. 2-3.

The English reviewers' outraged response to Howells's Century claim that his and James's art is finer than that of Dickens and Thackeray shows the English unawareness that their "ruling novelists" have been deposed by "a commonwealth of American authors." These Americans (presumably including James) live in and for the present and write "very admirable little stories and comedies for the amusement" of the hour. "The Siege of London" and the dramatization of Daisy Miller are "painfully good and droll." James already has a school of imitators. "The Siege of London" is, like all he writes, eagerly read, and it has all his "brilliant inconclusiveness" as well as many "admirable sayings and piquant" character traits. Yet, Hawthorne's idealistic great works will be remembered long after the realists of today are forgotten.

1883

31 ANON. "Literature/Some Reflections Suggested by Henry James' Last Work." Chicago Tribune, March 31, p. 9.
One pities James for his inability to eradicate from his work all taint of his kinship with Americans. He is very popular and deserves his honors, but he should portray more typical and attractive types of American women. "The Siege of London," "The Pension Beaurepas," and "The Point of View" are not stories "in the old-fashioned and exceedingly pleasant sense." James's style has "inimitable ease and strength" and he is a truly fine novelist, but his aims are "unworthy of his powers."

32 ANON. Review of The Siege of London. Dial, 3 (April), 280.
These stories "are all clever," especially "The Siege of London," and they exhibit "at their best" the author's "brilliant literary traits." James satirizes his countrywomen. When he outlives "certain conceits and vagaries" which presently interfere "with the fine and true development of his capacities," this "gifted writer" may produce a novel that will entirely satisfy his readers and reach the high mark they set for him.

33 ANON. "The Children's Century." St. Louis Missouri Republican, April 1, p. 4.
(Quoted reference. Item from Cincinnati Commercial-Gazette refers to James as "the popular novelist" who has called the nineteenth century the children's century.)

34 ANON. "Literature." San Francisco Chronicle, April 1, p. 6.
(Review of Atlantic Monthly.) James's article, much advertised, is "not particularly good reading."

35 ANON. "Recent Novels." Nation, 36 (April 5), 301.
(Review of The Siege of London.) In some ways this is James's best international sketch, illustrating "inimitable skill." Together "The Point of View" and "The Pension Beaurepas" form an amusing study of international life.

36 ANON. Review of The Siege of London, The Pension Beaurepas, and The Point of View. Detroit Free Press, April 7, p. 8.
James writes not novels, but studies. "The Siege of London" is one of his brightest efforts. Most of James's Americans, like those in the other two stories in this collection, find America "'hard, cold and vacant.'"

37 ANON. "American Women Abroad." Hartford Daily Times, April 10, p. 1.
(Item from London World refers to "the semi-Europeanized republicans, whom Henry James has satirized in many novels.")

1883

38 ANON. Review of The Siege of London. Churchman, 47 (April 14), 405.

James is always "clever, dry, satirical," lacking in sympathy perhaps, but a keen reader of American human nature. He has given his countrywomen many wholesome, if severe, lessons, and "The Siege" provides one of the most forcible.

39 ANON. "New Publications." New York Times, April 15, p. 6.

(Review of Mayo Williamson Hazeltine's Chats About Books, Poets, and Novelists.) Hazeltine gives "happy expression" to the criticism that James is slightly snobbish and weak in constructive power but a precise artist of flawless workmanship who makes the most of his meagre and shop-worn materials. James's works have "a cold glitter" fascinating to "a peculiarly cultured or satiated reader."

40 ANON. "Literary Style." San Francisco Chronicle, April 15, p. 6.

(Editorial.) The American "romancers" most to be commended for style are, perhaps, Bret Harte, James, and Howells. The latter two have sacrificed much of plot for the sake of style, a fault "much less observable" among contemporary English novelists, and absent in Thackeray. The future American prose writer "will have to cast his work in somewhat less finical molds" than those used by James and Howells, and not try to compensate for having little to say by covering it with "verbal ornament."

41 ANON. "Literary." Hartford Daily Times, April 19, p. 1.

(Review of Atlantic Monthly.) The second act of Daisy Miller "will have a lot of readers."

42 ANON. Albany Evening Journal, April 21, p. 4.

(Reprint of humorous poem from London Punch on Howells and James versus Dickens and Thackeray.)

43 ANON. Note. Literary World, 14 (April 21), 123.

(Refers to Julian Hawthorne's fiercely and ably taking up the "cudgel against Howells and James.")

44 ANON. Review of Century. "Some Century Papers." New York Times, April 22, p. 5.

James's May Century article on George Du Maurier is "appreciative and interesting." (Long quotations from it.)

45 ANON. "Idler and Poet." Hartford Daily Times, April 23, p. 1.

(Review of Century.) The May Century contains James's "charming little essay" on Du Maurier's caricatures in Punch.

1883

46 ANON. Review of Atlantic Monthly. New York World, April 23, p. 2.
The second act of Daisy Miller, A Comedy "is somewhat dull for a comedy" and "dramatic only in form."

47 ANON. "The Magazines." Indianapolis News, April 24, p. 2.
(Review of Atlantic Monthly.) The May Atlantic might almost be designated "a 'Howells and James' number, as both these popular writers are represented."

48 ANON. Humorous editorial item. Atlanta Constitution, April 25, p. 4, col. 2.
Henry Cabot Lodge says the "Daisy-Miller-Junior James business is worse than provincial, being rigidly and distinctly colonial." Up until now James had thought himself "a red-handed cosmopolitan with side whiskers and a frock coat."

49 ANON. "Recent Publications." New Orleans Daily Picayune, April 29, p. 8.
(Review of Century.) James's article on Du Maurier makes "very nice reading" despite James's working over some old Punch jokes.

50 ANON. "Notes on Art and Artists." New York Times, April 29, p. 12.
(Note on the illustrations for James's May Century article on George Du Maurier.)

51 ANON. Note. San Francisco Chronicle, April 29, p. 6.
The "female critic" Th. Bentzon has asserted in her Revue des Deux Mondes article on Howells that currently Americans author "the best novels written in English" and that Howells and James head the "new American school, whose realism is so delicate."

52 ANON. "Recent American Fiction." Atlantic Monthly, 51 (May), 706-707.
(Review of The Siege of London, The Pension Beaurepas, and The Point of View.) It is well known that James is "the most brilliant of the discoverers of Europe," and he has been a little negligent of Americans in America. The "brilliant little story" "The Siege of London" seems to have no "very deep meaning," but as "a sketch of superficial manners . . . is vivacious and very intelligible," with "capital" humor. James's subtlety has "never appeared to better advantage" than in "The Point of View," and its letters are fresh and clever, "so agile, so true to every wind of doctrine that blows, . . . that the reader is lost

in admiration." The singularly individual Marcellus Cockerel shows James's ability to create characters who sound like themselves rather than like their author.

53 ANON. "Literary Notes." New York Tribune, May 9, p. 6.
At his reading in Boston, James was introduced as "the Thackeray of America."

54 ANON. "Literary Notes." New York Tribune, May 14, p. 6.
It is said that in his paper in the forthcoming Century on the Carlyle-Emerson correspondence, James shows "a notably just, sympathetic and intuitive appreciation of the natures and the genius of the two men." James has "undoubtedly an exact and delicate touch in criticism."

55 ANON. "The New Magazines." New York Tribune, May 27, p. 8.
(Review of Century and Atlantic Monthly.) In his June Century paper on Carlyle and Emerson, James "shows his eminent graces as a critic." His "methods of analysis and reflection naturally belong" to such work, in which his style is its most "delicate and clear."
James is not at his best in the comedy Daisy Miller in the Atlantic. The play lacks humor, is dramatically impossible, has an "analytic, microscopical style" unsuited to the stage, and has a silly heroine and vulgar hero.

56 ANON. "New Publications . . . A Modern Romance." New York Tribune, May 29, p. 6.
(Review of F. Marion Crawford's Dr. Claudius.) The lovers' surroundings "are as refined" as even James could have conceived.

57 ANON. "The Bookshelf." Our Continent, 3 (May 30), 699.
Many people think James's criticism is better than his stories. (Possible reference to New York Tribune, April 28, 1883, p. 6.)

58 ANON. "Two Esteemed Contemporaries." Atlanta Constitution, June 1, p. 4.
(Editorial.) The New York Times should write a "serious essay" on "the follies of travelling Americans in Europe." It should announce that the original of James's Daisy Miller "was the daughter of a retired soap boiler" and that Mrs. Miller's first husband was a fat refiner. Almost all these Americans who visit Europe do it not from interest in the Old World, but because it is the fashion to go there.

59 ANON. New York Tribune, June 4, p. 6.
(Writer quotes the British St. James's Gazette on Mrs.

Burnett's Through One Administration with reference to its allegedly English passion, absent in James's "chilly heroines," and to its allegedly American motive analysis, dialogue elaboration, and character self-dissection.)

60 ANON. "Wanted--An American Novel" and "'A Temporary and Foolish Reaction.'" Literary World, 14 (June 16), 192.
(Two editorial responses to correspondents. The first item lists James among those who give hope of American talent if properly directed. The second item counters a reader's complaint about newspaper men's "'temporary and foolish reaction'" against Howells and James with the assertions that the latter have first-rate abilities but pursue purposes and use materials of a lower quality, that their work so far is unworthy of their fame and will not earn them a foremost place among novelists, and that any reaction to them which tempers wild, patriotic adulation into just, sober criticism is neither foolish nor temporary.)

61 ANON. "The Bookshelf." Our Continent, 3 (June 20), 797.
In an article in the Revue des Deux Mondes, M. Bentzon has called James the least humorous of American writers.

62 ANON. Humorous editorial item. Atlanta Constitution, August 8, p. 4.
James's now being in Boston "disposes of much current gossip" because any man who can stand Boston's climate in August "is just as good an American" as the man living in Chicago or St. Louis.

63 ANON. "Americanism in Literature." Our Continent, 4 (August 15), 219.
The American element in literature is simply "the American element in our thought," and James's work is very American despite his long residence abroad.

64 ANON. Quoted reference. Our Continent, 4 (August 15), 220.
(A quotation from the London Spectator, via the New York Tribune, observes James's "inner creed" to impose no duty but lucid observation and a low tone of expectation, and calls it a "particularly sad remnant of the old Puritanism.")

65 ANON. Humorous editorial item. Atlanta Constitution, August 23, p. 4.
James complained awhile ago that America has no ruined castles, but "[w]e invite Mr. James to inspect the ruins of the Kimball House [hotel that burned] by midnight."

66 ANON. "New Publications. The Comedy of 'Daisy Miller.'"

Boston Daily Advertiser, September 1, p. 4.
(Sentimentalized, almost melodramatic description of what happens in the original story.) After being the heroine of "a small tragedy," Daisy is now the heroine of "a worthless comedy." In this comedy the characters are as bad as in the story, without wit, and tiresome and disgusting. Their talk is either flat or coarse. Though the story, now with a happy ending, may be true to life, it is not worth telling. It is unclear why anyone would write about such "weak and mean" people, and why a "brilliant writer" like James, "an admirable critic, a keen observer, a man of wit and cultivated taste," would "waste his time" on such trash as this comedy.

67 ANON. Review of Daisy Miller, A Comedy. Cincinnati Commercial Gazette, September 8, Extra Sheet, p. 1.
James has "a photographic skill in portraying disagreeable people, and the many defects and bores of society" that in real life one would manage to avoid. James has keen wit and literary gifts, but apparently advocates the belief "that life is not worth living." Many of the characters are repulsive, "shabbily mean and narrow," and their dialogue is "unrefined chatter."

68 ANON. "New Publications." New York Times, September 9, p. 10.
(Review of Daisy Miller, A Comedy.) The original Daisy Miller was "amusing but very undramatic," with fine workmanship, delicate observation, and gentle satire. It reflected well "the needlessly self-conscious feeling of Americans abroad," and provides a lesson for American girls and a moral for American parents. James is better trained and more skillful than Oliphant in the comparable story "Altiora Peto," but in dramatizing Daisy Miller James has erred artistically, and his "hand has failed him." The characters talk too much and all alike, and the play would be dry both on the page and on the stage. James seems capable "of infinite advancement and improvement," and should now "cast his work on larger lines," a direction seemingly indicated by The Portrait of a Lady.

69 ANON. Review of John Hay's The Breadwinners (published anonymously). New Orleans Daily Picayune, September 26, p. 4.
James is "most at home in Europe" and his characters are "a lot of wealthy idlers, dilettantes, bric-a-brac hunters," and others "foreign to us" in origin, speech, modes of thought, and ways of living.

70 ANON. "Miscellaneous." San Francisco Chronicle, September 30, p. 6.

1883

(Review of Daisy Miller, A Comedy.) This play shows James's original purpose, it reads very well, and for lovers of James's style it is very entertaining, but it lacks action, the characters are monotonously clever and brilliant, and the original version of the story was better.

71 ANON. "New Publications." Hartford Times, October 2, p. 2.
(Review of Daisy Miller, A Comedy.) This play is "pleasant light reading," but nothing more.

72 ANON. "Fiction." Literary World, 14 (October 6), 331.
(Review of Daisy Miller, A Comedy.) Though this play is very entertaining, the earlier version of the story was better, despite dense readers' indignation at that original story's lack of patriotism. The original Daisy was more sympathetic than this one.

73 ANON. "Recent Publications." New Orleans Daily Picayune, October 7, p. 7.
(Review of Daisy Miller, A Comedy.) One wonders why James made a comedy, with "cheaply commonplace dialogue," out of his "startling storyette" Daisy Miller. Daisy will hardly know herself, but the comedy "may be a boon to amateur actors this winter."

74 ANON. "Literature." New York Herald, October 7, p. 9.
(Review of Daisy Miller, A Comedy.) This dramatization of James's "famous little story" lacks essential action, is too talky, and is not skillfully constructed. Yet, "it is written with a witty sprightliness, a picturesque truthfulness to the whimsicalities of his characters and a keenness of satire" that characterize James's "happiest moments." The play is "highly entertaining" reading but would "weary the spectator." The characters are more distinct, human, and lifelike here than in the story, but unfortunately we see too little of Mrs. Miller, originally "a clever creation."

75 ANON. "Ouida Speaks her Mind." New Orleans Daily Picayune, October 20, p. 4.
(A quoted excerpt from popular novelist Ouida's "excited attack on the realists" in the London Times, which finds history as legitimate a center of interest as James's heroines and their proposals.)

76 ANON. Review of W. D. Howells's A Woman's Reason. Literary World, 14 (October 20), 350.
James is "undoubtedly" a realistic writer, but one hopes he will not confuse art with "the mere reproduction of natural facts."

1883

77 ANON. "Weather-Wisdom in Fiction." New Orleans Daily Picayune, October 21, p. 2.

James is "above, or beneath, the influence of the weather" and of scenery. His work is "lacking in flesh and blood," with more power than charm, because his method is scientific, not poetic.

78 ANON. Note. New Orleans Daily Picayune, October 22, p. 2.

(Item from Louisville Post.) The decisions of James and the actor Lawrence Barret to live permanently in Europe "must be galling to Boston," where both "have been highly honored." Their expatriation suggests that these men cannot find here "the culture which their aesthetic souls desire."

79 ANON. "Recent Publications." New Orleans Daily Picayune, October 22, p. 2.

(Review of November Century.) G. W. Cable's Dr. Sevier and James's "The Impressions of a Cousin" will "attract instant notice."

80 ANON. "The War of the Critics." Atlanta Constitution, October 23, p. 4.

(Editorial.) There is "a hotly contested war" among literary critics over the relative merits of the idealists and the analysts in fiction. James's attitude toward his readers is as confidential as Thackeray's, but he explains emotions rather than actions and events, and his confidentiality is French and "a trifle affected" rather than English, genial, and unstudied in the manner of Thackeray. Some critics of The Portrait of a Lady cried out for something more vigorous, rounded, and vital. Perhaps the American novel of the future will unite the idealists' "vigor and freedom of movement" with the artistic portrayal and analysis of emotions associated with Howells and James. (Reference to James's "exquisitely phrased" travel notes in the Atlantic Monthly.)

81 ANON. "The Comedy of Daisy Miller." Overland Monthly, n.s. 2 (November), 554-556.

(Review.) This burlesque is a rather regrettable and ruthless thing to do to such a "delicate and conscientious" work as James's greatest success, the original Daisy Miller. That study's subtleties and its heroine's striking truth and comprehensibility have not translated into the play, with its conventional heroine and incredible, stock characters. Yet, despite the lost sense of reality, it has much that is "entertaining and clever."

1883

82 ANON. Review of Daisy Miller, A Comedy. Independent, 35 (November 15), 1451.
The original novelette had "life and light," but this version, with its "tame conclusion," destroys Daisy's character.

83 ANON. Editorial critical reference. Atlanta Constitution, November 16, p. 4.
James's Daisy Miller is "a mean attack on the American girl, as well as an indifferent literary production." Mr. Labouchere's article pictures our girls "much better than Mr. James did or can."

84 ANON. "Recent Publications." New Orleans Daily Picayune, November 25, p. 9.
(Review of Century.) James continues his "rather tiresome" "Impressions of a Cousin."

85 ANON. "American Authors." Detroit Free Press, December 27, p. 9.
(Physical descriptions of James, Howells, T. B. Aldrich, Julian Hawthorne, and others.)

86 ARDEN, ALFRED. "Open Letters./Recent American Novels." Century, 27 (December), 313-315.
The Siege of London is by no means James's best work, but is "interesting and able," like all his books. He gives small and roundabout but important lessons in etiquette. James's work is primarily didactic and realistic.

87 BIERCE, AMBROSE. Editorial. Wasp, 10 (February 17), 5.
James and Howells are "two eminent triflers and cameo-cutters-in-chief to Her Littleness the Bostonese small virgin" but who "have for some years been the acknowledged leaders of American literature"; "their measureless, meaningless and unimaginative novels," destitute of plot, purpose, and art, are staple subjects among the "'cultured'"; and "the Craze" has made them, rather than Homer, Goethe, and Hugo, required reading. The new school is not literature but a conspiracy in which the participants puff each other's reputations with mutually flattering essays, a factory and mill of which "the two finest products . . . are James and Howells," of whom neither can think and the latter cannot write.

88 BUNNER, H. C. "Open Letter," "New York as a Field for Fiction." Century, 4 (September), 787-788.
James's devotion is not to New York settings, but "to settling international complications of taste and affection."

89 COAN, TITUS MUNSON. "American Literature in England." In Studies in Literature. Ed. T. M. Coan. New York: Putnam, pp. 17-29, 33, 45, 51, 65.

(Reprint of an article in January 1883 Blackwood's Magazine.) The writings of James and W. D. Howells are as intelligible as those of their English contemporaries. Howells is less accomplished than James, and moves in a narrower circle, so is "a better type of the American novelist." "The Point of View" is "extremely amusing and interesting." Despite Howells's claims in 1882.39 about Dickens and Thackeray, "the old gods will outlive the temporary dazzling" of James's "fine style and delicate power of analysis."

90 CURTIS, GEORGE W. "Editor's Easy Chair." Harper's Monthly, 66 (April), 791.

(A general defense of James and Howells.)

91 HALE, EDWARD E. Letter to the Editor. Literary World, 14 (January 13), 10.

(Letter eulogizing Henry James, Sr.) Few living men write English as well as Henry James, Jr., but his father wrote it as well. In the subtleties of James's "charming stories" appear traits inherited from his father.

92 HAZELTINE, MAYO WILLIAMSON. "Henry James, Jr." Chats About Books, Poets, and Novelists. New York: Scribner's, pp. 347-360.

James's artistic workmanship earns him a not very wide circle of less-than-enthusiastic admirers. Washington Square discloses his capabilities and his inability to write "a vivid, forceful American novel." If any American now writing attends to workmanship, it is James, but he chooses narrow themes and commonplace characters. He can say precisely what he means, but not with intensity, creative power, or "pictorial vivacity." He has only a moderate gift of metaphor, and a weak constructive faculty, but he often makes very dexterous use of meagre materials.

93 HENRY, M. L. "A Non-Combatant's View." Literary World, 14 (June 30), 209.

(Letter to the Editor. Henry reacts to the charge of idolatry for admiring the works of James and Howells, refers to the controversy among their critics, and expresses confidence that in the long run extreme or injudicious opinions will not damage their reputations. She finds James not the American Thackeray but considers it unfair to "deny him his legitimate reputation, and his mastery in his own field" of character-painting, and places him and Howells first among American novelists. She concedes that their style, particularly James's, alienates some readers and calls for an eclecticism in taste.)

94 JENNINGS, LOUIS J. "American Novels." St. Louis Missouri Republican, February 4, p. 14.
(Quoted critical remarks. Long excerpt from Jennings's January 1883 Quarterly Review article's "Merciless Review of Aesthetic Pretenders" James and Howells.)

95 KENDRICK [pseud. for John Kendrick Bangs?]. "A Literary Combination." Life, 1 (February 22), 91.
(Cartoon. Spoofs Howells's alleged effort to elevate James above Thackeray.)

96 MORSE, JAMES HERBERT. "The Native Element in American Fiction: Since the War." Century, 4 (July), 371-375.
James and Howells are "our two cleverest writers," although they lack greatness in humor, passion, poetic spirit, fun, pathos, poise and mastery, intensity, spiritual power, and perception of the demonic forces in man. Both are materialistic, affected by "the scientific critical spirit," and "capable of passions only in a restricted way," but James is able to "conceive a deeper character and grasp its stronger individuality," as seen in Isabel, Madame Merle, and Ralph of The Portrait of a Lady, his culminating work. He gives all of its characters some of "his own caution and causticity," and they are analytical to the point of seeming "morbidly self-conscious." Both James and Howells have "wonderful success in reproducing what they see and feel," in depicting "with fascinating skill" "the superficial aspect of American life." The scientifically oriented analytic school has shown the follies rather than the virtues of American life, which provides plenty of rich material for the novelist of large scope. James has tried to do justice to it, but he is not sympathetic with the democratic motive of American institutions.

97 READ, OPIE. Editorial. Arkansaw Traveler, 3 (April 28), 4.
The inconclusive way Howells and James end their novels is "not art."

98 RIDDLE, A. G. "The American Novel." Literary World, 14 (June 30), 209.
(Letter to the Editor.) James and Howells are "markedly American," James coming from "a strain of men essentially American" and treating everything "in an unconscious, American way." The current tendency to exalt the analytic over the creative is a sign of mental weakness if not decline, associated with scientists. There will be a reaction against it.

99 RUNNION, JAMES B. "Howells-Harte-James." Dial, 4 (October), 128-129.

(Review of Daisy Miller, A Comedy.) James's dramatization of his well-known novelette "must be regarded as a mistake." It is "neither readable nor actable." The character of the original Daisy was "a great success," but the Daisy of the play is too hardened. Situation and incident have been neglected, and the dialogue seems monotonous and interminable. James's "brilliancy as an essayist and sketch-writer has been admired and enjoyed all over the world," and his ability as a novelist has never been questioned, but he lacks the dramatic instinct. Howells is making more progress than either Bret Harte or James "in the domain of fiction."

100 SMALLEY, GEORGE W. "Notes on Books." New York Tribune, April 9, p. 6.

(Comments on Jennings's article on James in the Quarterly Review.)

101 STODDARD, R. H. "Current Literature." Springfield (Mass.) Daily Republican, April 11, p. 10.

(Quotation from R. H. Stoddard in New York Mail and Express.) James and Howells are clever in imagining people with disagreeable characteristics, but these writers do not have the art of delineating characters evident in Shakespeare, Fielding, Sterne, Scott, Dickens, Thackeray, Cooper, and Hawthorne.

102 THOMPSON, MAURICE. "A 'Modern Instance' of Criticism." Indianapolis Saturday Herald, August 15, p. 4.

The "so-called analytical novelists," whose chief is Howells, "have done much good." James "has never probed so deep" as Howells's A Modern Instance, and, though skillful and charming, his books tend to be "superficial and artificial." He "represents a passing phase of intercontinental balance of social forces," is interested in "art and artificial life" rather than in nature, and writes inimitable and indispensable "great little novels." Both he and Howells have an insufficient grasp of local color, but they deserve their place "at the head" of living American novelists. All the "ill tempered nagging" and criticism of their books has served only to advertise them.

103 TRIMBLE, ESTHER J. A Hand-Book of English and American Literature. Philadelphia: Eldredge & Brother. Rpt. 1896. Rev. ed. 1898.

(Mentions James. See 1883.20.)

1883

104 Z., A. "A Code for Anglomaniacs." Life, 1 (April 26), 201.
(Humorous article.) Intending anglomaniacs should study James's works, which will make them snobs.

1884

1 ANON. "Modern Fiction." Critic, 4 (January 12), 15-16.
(Reprint of parts of Henry Norman's December 1, 1883, Fortnightly Review article referring to James and other American novelists.)

2 ANON. "Recent Publications." New Orleans Daily Picayune, January 13, p. 9.
(Review of Princeton Review.) Julian Hawthorne's article on "Agnosticism in American Fiction" is "well worth reading." It says, perhaps truly, that James and Howells have done more than anyone to make our literature respectable during the last ten years, and they have brought the texture of fiction to an unsurpassed fineness.

3 ANON. Review of Atlantic Monthly. New York Times, January 27, p. 10.
James's Provence sketch "relates to Arles, which assures one" that "it is readable."

4 ANON. "New Publications. . . . Henry James's Portraits of Places." Boston Daily Advertiser, January 29, p. 2.
James is "an excellent portrait painter" and an observer, but is "the least emotional and the least sympathetic of writers." He has "admirable command of his intellect, his wit, his tastes and the English language." He is above all a critic, and he is entertaining, "with a delightful sense of the ludicrous and the grotesque." The reading is pleasant, and the most interesting passages compare the people of different nations and cities.

5 ANON. "From Our Special Correspondent." Springfield (Mass.) Republican, February 7, pp. 2-3.
Review of Portraits of Places.) The fanaticism of certain writers "is vastly better, in moral effect, than the pococurante indifference and esthetic nervousness" of writers like James. His "epicurean reflections" lack earnestness and concern "for the multitude," except to scoff. His essays' information and graces of style "do not compensate" for his "indifference to patriotism and high aspiration." A book by R. L. Stevenson is "more agreeable," but has "the same light tone of too much persiflage."

6 ANON. Quoted reference. Critic, 4 (February 9), 67-68.
(Reprint of part of a January 19, 1884 [London] Saturday Review article, including a critical reference to James.)

7 ANON. "Descriptions of England." New York Times, February 11, p. 3.
(Review of Portraits of Places.) James is better at descriptions of places than at anything, and among his pleasantest descriptions are those of England. His picture of England is the other side of the coin from that provided by Henry George. James deserves "more than a respectful hearing," and "does the traveling world a service in gently making game of the preposterous guidebooks to art galleries which Ruskin writes."

8 ANON. Review of Portraits of Places. Independent, 36 (February 14), 204.
James's "finished style" gives this volume a "unity and unbroken interest." In these charming portraits everything seems perfect, and James's art "strikes far deeper than realistic description." It portrays inner life and customs. (Review of George Du Maurier's Pictures of English Society refers to James's May 1883 Century article on Du Maurier.)

9 ANON. Editorial item. Atlanta Constitution, February 16, p. 4.
James's sadly looking on his country as being without "society" is a "species of tory flunkeyism . . . very popular at the north."

10 ANON. "Literature. . . . Notes." Chicago Times, February 16, p. 10.
According to a rumor, James "got some of the material" for Washington Square from "the late Mrs. Catherine Dix."

11 ANON. Review of Portraits of Places. Cincinnati Commercial Gazette, February 17, Extra Sheet, p. 1.
These sketches are in James's "peculiar critical and descriptive vein."

12 ANON. "New Publications." Detroit Free Press, February 17, p. 16.
(Review of Portraits of Places.) James's admirers will find in the sketch of Venice "a massing of all his colors" in a rare literary mosaic. The English sketches have "peculiar brilliancy and power," but James is too English to be "superbly expressive and ideally just" about American subjects. The American chapters will be the least interesting to Americans, but the book glows with James's noted "florid allurements of style."

1884

13 ANON. Review of Julian Hawthorne's Beatrix Randolph. Springfield (Mass.) Republican, February 17, p. 4.
This book has a perception of "what is good in American national character," a perception that James lacks and Howells does not pursue.

14 ANON. "Literature. Portraits of Places by Henry James." San Francisco Chronicle, February 24, p. 6.
These portraits are painted "with rare skill" and James gives his subject life. There is no better model for literary workmanship than these sketches, a trained observer like James is rare "in these days of realism," and the only quality he shares with Zola is "his genius for photographic study." James shows more familiarity with Europe than with America, and has the objectivity of a foreigner toward the United States. "Nothing is lost upon him," and few could convey better the charm, brilliancy, and "homelike features" of the European scenes. Despite the elaboration, James's literary art makes these sketches never dull.

15 ANON. Review of Portraits of Places. Dial, 4 (March), 286-287.
This book is much more valuable than ordinary books of travel and most collections of pieces reprinted from periodicals. The excellence of James's "refined and graceful style" has long been recognized. In work of this sort he "is at his best," whereas his fiction always seems to lack completeness and his criticism to lack profundity.

16 ANON. Review of Portraits of Places. St. Paul Daily Pioneer Press, March 2, p. 12.
As long as James does "not insist on writing the American novel, or attempt it, he is to be encouraged as a literary itinerant."

17 ANON. Review of Portraits of Places. New York Herald, March 2, p. 17.
These pictures are not portraits, but impressions in the manner of the impressionist school of painting. Sometimes, though, as in "Occasional Paris," James draws more distinctly.

18 ANON. Note. Chicago Times, March 8, p. 12; March 15, p. 12; April 19, p. 13.
(Brief references to the characters and situation of "Lady Barberina" and to its forthcoming publication in the Century.)

19 ANON. "Portraits of Places." Literary World, 15 (March 8), 69-70.
(Review.) James describes these places charmingly, with

an eye for their often hardly noticeable aesthetic value and "inner sentiment." These sketches have a "note of individuality" and "an admirable simplicity and literary self-restraint." James's description of Niagara Falls captures its drama more distinctly than any other.

20 ANON. "Literature." Chicago Times, March 22, p. 12.
(Review of French Poets and Novelists.) This new edition of James's essays is "in the simplicity and refinement of its makeup the book of a gentleman." It is not necessary to tell readers how "delightful is the text," in which we see James, the critic, at his best.

21 ANON. Quoted reference. Critic, 4 (March 22), 139-142; 4 (March 29), 153-154.
(Reprint of Karl Hillebrand's March 1884 Contemporary Review article referring to James.)

22 ANON. "Books of the Week." Christian Union, 29 (March 27), 305.
(Reviews of Portraits of Places and French Poets and Novelists.) In Portraits of Places James does not try to be profound, but delicately and keenly observes and felicitously describes what would otherwise be commonplace. The very pleasant piece on Venice is one of the best things James has done. French Poets and Novelists is foremost among recent, light criticism. It lacks "penetrating insight and decisive judgment," but no critic writes more charmingly or intelligently. If James is not profound about "great interior experiences" and the "secret recesses of literary power," he is always "suggestive" on character, knows about form, and has "a fine instinct" for a work's whole externality.

23 ANON. "Briefer Notices." American, 7 (March 29), 393.
(Review of French Poets and Novelists.) These essays give a better idea of James's "clearness of thought and grace of style" than do his more popular fictions. It would be hard to find any modern writing "more masterly and complete."

24 ANON. "April Magazines." American, 7 (March 29), 396.
(Review of Atlantic Monthly.) James contributes another delightful article on French travel.

25 ANON. "Writing About Writing." New Orleans Daily Picayune, March 30, p. 10.
(Editorial.) Despite Howells's assertion that fiction has become a finer art than in Dickens's and Thackeray's

day, the latter authors were better than those in Howells's "improved school," and created more memorable characters.

26 ANON. "Recent Travel." Atlantic Monthly, 53 (April), 569-570.
(Review of Portraits of Places.) Though James declares himself a "cosmopolite," his experience is limited to European civilization. He describes things he likes "with the warmth of a richly sensuous temperament," and is an "exceptionally keen," artistic observer, an "impressionist." But, he is not interested in "landscapes which cannot be described by tones and effects," and the defects of civilization bore him. Artistically, this book has "grace, definiteness, full light," while its social attributes are "amiableness and a high regard for the agreeable."

27 ANON. Humorous editorial item. Atlanta Constitution, April 17, p. 4.
When in the May Atlantic Monthly James admits to having eaten two pounds of French butter at a sitting, he "would have us believe that his appetite is larger than his imagination."

28 ANON. Review of French Poets and Novelists. Dial, 5 (May), 16.
Although not profound, this very notable literary criticism is everything else it should be. It is delicate, sympathetic, subtle, and delightful, but reflects James's limitations in perception, his errors in emphasis.

29 ANON. "Literature. . . . Notes." Chicago Times, May 10, p. 12.
A new story by James "will present its analytic charms" in the June English Illustrated Magazine.

30 ANON. "A New Literary Enterprise." New Orleans Times-Democrat, June 8, p. 4.
(Announcement that the Times-Democrat and the New York Sun will publish James's "Pandora," as well as works by Howells and Bret Harte.)

31 ANON. "Sport/The Comstock Polar Fund." Life, 4 (July 31), 62.
(Brief humorous item spoofs the bulk and indefiniteness of James's novels.)

32 ANON. "New Publications. . . . Henry James on 'The Art of Fiction.'" Boston Daily Advertiser, September 2, p. 2.
(Review. Summary of the contents of James's article in Longman's Magazine, with a number of quotations.)

1884

33 ANON. "Recent Fiction in England and France." Critic, 5 (September 6), 115.

(Reprint of part of Mary Augusta Ward's August 1884 Macmillan's article, including the section on James, Howells, and American realism.)

34 ANON. "Literary Notices." St. Louis Missouri Republican, September 13, p. 10.

(Review of A Little Tour in France.) James is "a student of men and things," a "graphic writer" of impressions, and "more than a common tourist." He is humorous and "always picturesque," and his books are "delicious," this one "full of novel interest."

35 ANON. "Literature." New York Herald, September 14, p. 6.

(Review of A Little Tour in France.) James has done a book without a "pen picture of an unattractive American." Its readable descriptions provide something between the unsatisfactory extremes of guidebooks and hurried impressions, to serve a person of taste and intelligence.

36 ANON. "Recent Books." Christian Union, 30 (September 18), 284.

(Review of A Little Tour in France.) Like Portraits of Places, this book shows the best points of a style that is this charming writer's "supreme possession." It lacks the insight of English Notes, and the play of imagination of travel books by Gautier and D'Amicis. James studies landscapes as he does character, with "a very nice sense of discernment," a "keen perception" of the artistic, and a faculty for finding the right word. James gives more "color" than information.

37 ANON. Review of A Little Tour in France. Boston Daily Advertiser, September 19, p. 2.

James succeeds best in descriptive writing, he can turn facts into "sparkling brilliancy," and these fascinating, stimulating sketches "are models of literary taste and workmanship." James sees with "the eye of an artist, with the delicate perception of a man of culture, and with the comprehensive grasp of a practical observer."

38 ANON. Review of A Little Tour in France. New York Daily Graphic, September 20, p. 602.

James is "a charming descriptive writer" and "does justice to his subject," writing often with "enthusiastic admiration," humor, or "critical acumen." His views are "broad and independent," and it is because he sees Old World picturesqueness so warmly and truly that he "has so cold an eye for things at home."

1884

39 ANON. Humorous item. Wasp, 13 (September 20), 7.
(Spoof of James's alleged geographical ignorance of his own country.)

40 ANON. "Literature. Sketches in Provence by Henry James." San Francisco Chronicle, September 21, p. 6.
James's descriptions of his impressions are "charming" and "fine," and their sometimes slightly wearisome details are to good purpose. No Americans and few British rival James as a literary artist, and this book reflects "the rich and varied culture" of a man more at home in French literature and art than in those of his own country. The pictures of French towns are set forth with fidelity and brilliancy.

41 ANON. Review of A Little Tour in France. New York Commercial Advertiser, September 22, p. 3.
We must thank James for this pleasant and "unpretending volume," but it very much needs an index. The tour is both well devised and extensive, and one wishes for twice the number of pages describing it. The narrative is never dull, but James has "seen considerably more than he has felt."

42 ANON. "Recent Publications." New Orleans Daily Picayune, September 28, p. 10.
(Review of A Little Tour in France.) To say that James is "a charming writer" is unnecessary, and his "admirers place him at the head of American story tellers," although he seems to "love England more than America."

43 ANON. "New Publications." Saint Paul (and Minneapolis) Daily Pioneer Press, September 28, p. 12.
Perhaps there are enough people who have not traveled or read about Europe to make it profitable for the prolific James to write this book. James does not revise it, writes "carelessly, conceitedly, and shiftlessly," and will learn no rhetoric but his own, which produces a headache.

44 ANON. "Current Literature." New York Daily Graphic, October 1, p. 679.
(Quotes "a curious sentence" from A Little Tour in France which is a "remarkable" use of English.)

45 ANON. Review of A Little Tour in France. Boston Evening Transcript, October 4, p. 6.
James is "charming as a descriptive writer," and pictures scenery with distinctness and fidelity. He is a sentimental tourist who gives us his emotional reactions neatly and with "scrupulous care," but who sees the old ruins only as they

are, ravaged by nature and man. He might have tried to reveal a more touching sentiment by imaginatively restoring for his readers this ancient art to its original beauty, but he does not.

46 ANON. "Literature . . . Notes." Chicago Times, October 4, p. 12.
The name The Princess Casamassima suggests "all kinds of romantic episodes," and this story will be James's longest and most elaborate.

47 ANON. Review of A Little Tour in France. Cincinnati Commercial Gazette, October 5, p. 14.
This book of travel is "serenely observant . . . , with tendencies toward light social essays."

48 ANON. "A Miscellaneous Lot." Springfield (Mass.) Republican, October 9, pp. 2-3.
(Review of A Little Tour in France.) This book is "hardly a work of travel," and its charm is more in James's personality than in the intellect or learning he exhibits. Though "scarcely worth remembering long," the book has a style "so graceful, vivid, [and] picturesque," with "such humor and enthusiasm," that James "adorns everything he touches" and gives the reader "real enjoyment."

*49 ANON. Review of A Little Tour in France. Churchman, 50 (October 11), 405.
(Cited in Foley.)

50 ANON. "The Critic and Good Literature . . . Minor Notices." Critic, 5 (October 11), 173.
(Review of A Little Tour in France.) James's descriptive delicacy is indescribable. Though irritating and egoistic, these sketches blend imagination and humor, personal and national history, "honey and gall," into "one of the most persuasive and poetic [little books] of the time."

51 ANON. "Current Literature." New York Daily Graphic, October 15, p. 783.
James, Walter Besant, and now Maurice Thompson are among the distinguished people discussing the art of fiction.

52 ANON. "Recent Fiction." Independent, 36 (October 16), 1324.
James's story "A Light Man" is among "some excellent old friends" in the fifth collection of Stories by American Authors.

53 ANON. "Recent Fiction." Independent, 36 (October 16), 1324.

(Review of A Little Tour in France.) As readers know, James's best is "very good." Portraits of Places was "rich and delightful, with deep, mellow color, well laid on," the work of a master hand. A Little Tour in France's contribution to knowledge and criticism is small, and the pictures are by the way rather than in depth, but it gives refined, ennobling pleasure, shows James's interest in humanity, and contains polished and imaginative sentences.

54 ANON. "Mr. James's Little Tour." Literary World, 15 (October 18), 351-352.
(Review of A Little Tour in France.) Sensitive, cultured, and unusually sympathetic, uncritical, open, and self-effacing, James has never been more agreeable. He makes the most of the least things, and succeeds in really seeing France.

55 ANON. Quoted reference. Critic, 5 (October 25), 203.
(Reprint of a London Saturday Review item on "America as a Field for Fiction" notes Europeanized Americans' complaints on this subject, yet lists James among the American novelists who "have proved, and are proving, that America is far from a barren field for the novelist" who "will open his eyes and see for himself.")

56 ANON. "Literary Notices." St. Louis Missouri Republican, October 25, p. 12.
(Review of Tales of Three Cities.) James "is popular, and those who desire to keep up with current literature must read him."

57 ANON. Review of Tales of Three Cities. San Francisco Chronicle, November 2, p. 6.
These stories show "all of James' best qualities and some of his worst." They reflect "elaborate care and . . . rare skill in expression," and will be enjoyed by anyone "fond of minute analysis of character." "Impressions of a Cousin" is the worst of the three, too light and intangible, and with an unsatisfactory ending. "Lady Barberina" is the best, very entertaining and showing James's "felicity in character drawing" and comparison of American and European social customs. The third story is an elaborate study with a fine portrait of the young hero.

58 ANON. "Authors and Books." New York Daily Graphic, November 6, p. 31.
(Review of Tales of Three Cities.) Despite some minor and just criticism, James has a good reputation. Boston's peculiarities and narrow ways bring out the peculiarities

in James's style. He paints minutely and carefully, with "quiet sarcasm." Though sometimes trivial, his work is excellent. Two of these stories are clever and amusing.

59 ANON. "Current Literature." New York Daily Graphic, November 7, p. 39.
(Brief reference to a note in the Critic on the title of The Princess Casamassima.)

60 ANON. Review of Tales of Three Cities. Hartford Daily Courant, November 7, p. 1.
In all these stories James slyly gives his own impressions and keeps always his critical, superior attitude. The Boston story is slight, but subtle and "very keen." None of the stories has "absorbing interest," but all are "thoroughly enjoyable" to those who like "the highest literary workmanship."

61 ANON. Review of Tales of Three Cities. Philadelphia North American, November 8, p. 2.
"Lady Barberina" is the most attractive of these stories, "A New England Winter" is amusing, and "throughout the book is pungently written."

62 ANON. Review of Tales of Three Cities. Louisville Courier-Journal, November 14, p. 4.
The stories are in James's "characteristic vein," and in each "the most unpleasant aspects" of the city are "thrown into relief" by the presence of "a superior cosmopolitan critic among the characters."

63 ANON. "Recent Publications." New Orleans Daily Picayune, November 16, p. 7.
(Review of Century volume, November 1883-October 1884.) "Lady Barberina," the delightful "Impressions of a Cousin," and "A New England Winter" were among the chief stories that appeared last year in the Century.

64 ANON. "New Publications." St. Paul (and Minneapolis) Daily Pioneer Press, November 16, p. 12.
(Review of Tales of Three Cities.) James is generally considered one of America's leading authors, but his works give neither pleasure nor uplift, and he is no storyteller. He was better when he wrote Roderick Hudson. Knowing he cannot tell stories, James attempts "critical portraiture" of American society, but his mind and soul are too small for the task. He has never shown "a broad and generous view of human nature" or drawn a character to admire or respect, but has rather portrayed smallest, most narrow-minded

1884

and inconsequential people in the minutest way as typical Americans. We "have sunk low" if these pictures have any truth. In Tales of Three Cities James is at his worst. The stories "maintain one dreary, monotonous level," the characters are not worth the trouble and inspire the weary reader's "supreme indifference," and the studies are not finished.

65 ANON. "Recent Novels." Nation, 39 (November 20), 442.
(Review of Tales of Three Cities.) James is at his best here, but it will be fully appreciated by only an inner circle of readers. The point of view is kept steady, and James's special faculty of description gives not so much the scene itself as "the thought and sentiment wakened by it," and can make the familiar seem new.

66 ANON. Review of Tales of Three Cities. Cincinnati Commercial Gazette, November 23, p. 14.
The fact that James "is a cold-blooded cosmopolitan analyst of society does not rob his pen of brilliancy as well as sympathy."

67 ANON. Notice of Tales of Three Cities. Independent, 36 (November 27), 1514.
These stories have James's usual "polished freedom and well-tempered originality."

68 ANON. "James's Sketches." New York Commercial Advertiser, November 28, p. 3.
(Review of Tales of Three Cities.) These sketches have not much relation to the three cities where they are set, and none of them is complete or satisfactory. Much is suggested, but "nothing made out," yet these stories have the "delicacy and refinement of perception and nicety of touch" that distinguish James from his contemporaries. "A hint from him is often more telling than a full page from others, and his studies are more powerful than their finished pictures."

69 ANON. "Literature. Mr. Henry James' Latest Work, 'Tales of Three Cities.'" New York Herald, December 3, p. 8.
"The style is pleasing, the plots are very cleverly developed, the descriptions of places are well drawn and the delineations of character are close and really admirable." James's art "is well nigh perfect," but something like the "over-soul" is missing. "Lady Barberina" is an interesting tale. James puts the reader in "an invigorating, healthy atmosphere, and it is refreshing to study him after the weak milk-and-water stuff" that makes up much fiction.

70 ANON. "How We Do It.--No. 1./By Ennery Jeems (Ne E. J., Junior)." Life, 4 (December 4), 314-315.

(Humorous item. Spoof of "The Art of Fiction" and of James's and Howells's theories of novel-writing.)

71 ANON. Review of Tales of Three Cities. Minneapolis Tribune, December 7, p. 14.

With "matchless skill and dexterity" James refurbishes "worn out, worthless, useless feelings and characters of humanity" and sets them up for show as types of the race." Yet, they are still "only old clothes."

72 ANON. Review of Century. Boston Daily Advertiser, December 9, p. 2.

The Bostonians will present "some very strange people . . . [whom James] is said to treat with delightful and even sympathetic irony."

73 ANON. "The Situation." Atlanta Constitution, December 11, p. 4.

(In a political editorial, reference to "what the Junior James calls 'the point of view.'")

74 ANON. "Current Literature." New York Daily Graphic, December 12, p. 199.

The Bostonians will introduce the reader to some curious people. If James considers such as these to represent Boston, the ground there will be too hot for him ever to set foot on again.

75 ANON. "New Publications. Tales of Three Cities." Boston Daily Advertiser, December 13, p. 2.

James is one of "the most considerable" of the group of writers "at the head of" American fiction, and his style is perhaps "the best of his good gifts." Among his faults are the neglect of ordinary people's ordinary workaday life; his exclusion of people's great joys, sorrows, or struggles; and the lack of action in his nonetheless "very charming and clever books." "The Impressions of a Cousin" is the least attractive and nearest to dull of the three stories in this volume, and the descriptions in "A New England Winter" are "especially good."

76 ANON. "Literary Notes." Colorado Springs Weekly Gazette, December 13, p. 4.

One of the characters in Howells's The Rise of Silas Lapham "speaks of Daisy Millerism" before James's novel appeared.

1884

77 ANON. Note. New York Tribune, December 15, p. 3.
(Quotation from 1884.72.)

78 ANON. Note. Life, 4 (December 18), 345.
James's continuing to publish what he calls stories may be fun for him, "but it is death to the dwindling class of readers who still believe he has something to tell them."

79 ANON. Note. Colorado Springs Weekly Gazette, December 20, p. 4.
(Paraphrase of 1884.72.)

80 ANON. "How We Do It.--No. 2./By W. Dowells," Life 4 (December 25), 362.
(Humorous item. Makes fun of Howells's praise of his and James's fiction as finer than English fiction. Also spoofs Howells's portrayal of women.)

81 ANON. "Literature/Henry James' 'Little Tour in France.'" Chicago Tribune, December 27, p. 9.
(Review.) James's constant readers know he has "a mocking humor, and . . . more prejudices than convictions," but will share his impressions "while under the charm of his dazzling diction." James examines and finds something wrong with everything, and can be cruel though quiet in judgments of people, but writes so gracefully that the reader temporarily acquiesces. Sometimes he seems amused at his own inconsistencies.

82 ANON. "The Critic and Good Literature . . . 'Tales of Three Cities.'" Critic, 5 (December 27), 304.
(Review.) These stories are delicate, witty, brightly painted, "full of marvelous tricks and turns and reflections," of "paradox, contrast, and surprise."

83 FAWCETT, EDGAR. "Henry James's Novels." Princeton Review, 14 (July), 68-86.
(Praises, highly and at length, James and his works, and The Portrait of a Lady in particular as his best novel.) As a beginner, James was not raw, but highly individual, if sometimes dull. The beautiful Roderick Hudson has unforgettable characters, the famous American is fuller of vital experience, The Europeans is less good, and Daisy Miller is acute, vivid, and clever. James has had an "enviably brilliant" career, his admirers are more numerous than some newspapers "rather maliciously" suggest, and he deserves to be ranked first among contemporary English-writing novelists.

84 HAWTHORNE, JULIAN. "Agnosticism in American Fiction." Princeton Review, 13 (January), 1-15.
Americans are particularly susceptible to agnosticism, and James seems to have moved toward unmixed realism. As an American, he has a less tragic vision than Turgenev, and he tends to create unheroic characters and situations and to magnify the "petty and insignificant." (See 1887.32.)

85 H[ENRY], M. L. "Mr. James's Latest Fictions." Literary World, 15 (September 20), 308-309.
(Review of Tales of Three Cities.) James has lost his power to delight readers, and has become dull. His style is now too self-conscious and jerky, his sentences too complicated. Roderick Hudson was his best work.

86 M[ARTIN], E[DWARD] S. "Lady Messalina./By Jeems." Life, 4 (July 3), 6-7.
(Parody of "Lady Barberina.")

87 P., M. C. "Reviews." American, 9 (November 1), 57.
(Review of Tales of Three Cities.) Despite his finesse, acuteness, "dispassionate clarity," and dainty perfection of style, the fastidious, condescending James lacks sympathy, is cold, and is so remote from the life he portrays that he distorts it.

88 PAYNE, WILLIAM MORTON. "Recent Books of Fiction." Dial, 5 (December), 206-207.
(Review of Tales of Three Cities.) James has exhausted the international theme, but because his style is "so intrinsically good within its narrow limits" his new books are "sure to find many readers." His portrayal of Jackson Lemon as "a typical American gentleman" is "a piece of gratuitous vulgarity" hard to pardon. His literary criticism and travel writing are better than his fiction.

89 ROLLINS, ALICE WELLINGTON. "Woman's Sense of Humor." Critic, 4 (March 29), 145.
Isabel of The Portrait of a Lady is among "our finest heroines," all of whom lack humor.

90 TEMPLETON [pseud.]. "Boston Correspondence." Hartford Daily Courant, February 2, p. 1.
(Review of Portraits of Places.) These essays are fresher and more vivacious than James's most recent articles of travel, which are rather dull. The Italian, French, and English "portraits" in this volume are among James's most careful essays and contain much that is worth hearing, which "makes his book really brilliant." The papers on North American resorts are less worth preserving in book form.

1884

91 _____. "Boston Correspondence." Hartford Daily Courant, October 25, p. 1.
There is brilliant work in all three of the stories in Tales of Three Cities. "A New England Winter" contains "four of the cleverest pictures of Boston places and . . . manners" ever made. James's shorter stories are "unequalled in their way" in American literature, and lack the flaws of some of his more elaborate works. His pictures of modern life could be more good natured, but they will hurt only the thin-skinned, and this reviewer especially enjoys their spiciness.

1885

1 ANON. "Recent Fiction--I." Overland Monthly, 5 (January), 108-109.
(Review of Tales of Three Cities.) This experienced, "faithful student and correct annalist of human nature" knows what he is about, but has produced a dull book. James lacks a good ear, and all his characters sound like him. Given good situations with intensity and pathos, he is "too labored, too anxious, too resolutely objective," too unconcentrated. In others of his books, whether or not he is interesting is often a matter of taste, and anything he writes is in many ways excellent.

2 ANON. "Book Reviews./. . . Briefer Notice." Overland Monthly, 5 (January), 112.
(Review of A Little Tour in France.) Almost everyone knows of James's fame. He is either the first or the second (to Howells) among current American fiction writers. This book alone would show him to be "a master of expression," and the delightful sense of comradeship with him "is the greatest charm of a charming book."

3 ANON. "The Outlook in Literature." Christian Union, 31 (January 1), 3.
(The writer sees and approves of a divergence in contemporary American literature from the reigning "agnosticism" of James and Howells, from their portrayal of the smaller and less dramatic, the negative rather than the positive aspects of life.)

4 ANON. "Authors and Publishers." American, 9 (January 3), 202.
(Note.) James "does not always get sugar-plums from his critics." (Quotes the Athenaeum's adverse criticism of "Impressions of a Cousin.")

5 ANON. "Tragedy and Hysterics." Atlanta Constitution, January 4, p. 6.

(Editorial.) The bulk of the recent large volume of critical comment on American literature concerns the literary methods of James and Howells. James is considered too thin, Howells too flippant, and both too superficial, but to inspire so much discussion, there must be something piquant about what they do. In a literary treatment of a recent violent incident, Shakespeare could provide the tragedy, while James and Howells would provide the hysterics.

6 ANON. "Men of Mark." St. Louis Post-Dispatch, January 7, p. 4.

James "is said to resemble the Prince of Wales so strongly" that a palace guard called him "Your Royal Highness."

7 ANON. "About People and Things." Indianapolis Journal, January 10, p. 4.

(James was very pleased to be mistaken for the Prince of Wales by a St. James's palace sentry.)

8 ANON. Notes. New York Tribune, January 14, p. 6; January 31, p. 6; February 4, p. 6; February 7, p. 6.

The Bostonians's characters resemble some people in Boston, and the book "promises to be stronger than anything" James has done for years; the Boston Herald quoted, finds James's portrayal of Miss Birdseye "a gross violation of good taste"; the Chicago Tribune finds James's women "'so utterly flat and silly that they are devoid of interest,'" which "strictures are not without truth." James overworks certain types.

9 ANON. "By the Way. . . . Pocket Biographies. . . . Henry James." Life, 5 (January 15), 32.

(Ironic capsule biography says James knows Europe better than he knows America.) "It is wished that somebody would sharpen his 'point of view'--and then stick it into him."

10 ANON. "James the Greater and James the Less." Springfield (Mass.) Republican, January 19, p. 4.

(Editorial.) James's father should have been a novelist and James himself, though successful in writing "pessimistic fiction" and unable to actualize God, should have been a theologian championing "the doctrine of total depravity." Unlike his father, young James does not combine a serious purpose and an entertaining manner.

11 ANON. Reviews of Century. Boston Daily Advertiser, January 20, p. 2; February 23, p. 3; March 24, p. 2.

(Reviews of early installments of The Bostonians.) This

story promises "delightful things," the next month "portions out another lot of bitter food," and then furnishes "new elements of freshness and interest."

12 ANON. "Literary." Louisville Courier-Journal, January 23, p. 4.
(Review of Century.) In the February issue, The Bostonians contains "a characteristic group of the 'strong-minded' of both sexes."

13 ANON. "Recent Publications." New Orleans Daily Picayune, January 25, p. 16.
(Review of Century.) The first installment of The Bostonians appears in the February Century, and "all shaky Bostonians feel their reputations in peril and are praying that James's story will be worthy of its title."

14 ANON. "New Publications." New York Times, January 25, p. 4.
(Review of The Literary Remains of the Late Henry James.) The elder Henry James is not the author of Daisy Miller, but is rather another and more interesting personality than his son the novelist.

15 ANON. "New Publications." New York Times, January 26, p. 3.
(Review of Century.) The Bostonians contains "an interesting group of men and women of the strong-minded sort." James and Howells help make this issue remarkable for its contributors alone.

16 ANON. Reviews of Century. Boston Evening Transcript, January 29, p. 6; February 26, p. 6.
In The Bostonians James repeats the methods of Daisy Miller "in a larger way . . . and with infinitely more art." Because his characters are so easily identifiable with living people, his story will be talked about and James's readers' opinions of him made known. The next installment is less "bright and spicy" and seems "a trifle heavy," the descriptions "realistic enough, but . . . labored and . . . almost as tedious as the people described."

17 ANON. "A Contemporaneous Ghost Story." Life, 5 (January 29), 60.
(Spoof of Howells, mentions the inclusion in The Rise of Silas Lapham of "a type-writer and a reference to 'Daisy Miller' at a period when neither of these articles had come into general use.")

18 ANON. Note. Indianapolis Journal, January 30, p. 4.
"All Boston is down" on James for caricaturing in The

Bostonians, "his latest alleged novel," Miss Birdseye, "of whom James's birdseye view is considered as inaccurate as it is impolite."

19 ANON. "New Publications." New York Tribune, January 30, p. 6.
(Reference to Daisy Miller in review of a story in Lippincott's.)

20 ANON. "Literature. . . . A Score of Novels." Chicago Tribune, January 31, p. 9.
(Review of Tales of Three Cities.) Two of these tales are "inferior specimens" of James's work, but the reader still enjoys his graceful style and a "descriptive power . . . beyond laudation." "The Impressions of a Cousin" has "unpleasant vagueness" and "A New England Winter" is a little dull and very incomplete, but "Lady Barberina" is "supremely interesting and sparkles" with James's polished humor. It treats the international marriage with brilliance and "great originality."

21 ANON. Review of Tales of Three Cities. Detroit Free Press, January 31, p. 8.
James is not an impressionist, but rather gives us "little classics of finished elegance" and precision. He does not make the reader laugh or cry and "his people are detestable rather than lovable," but the reader "is overcome by admiration" for James and his delightful, "polished company" of characters, and feels for some of them a "mild contempt" that shows James drew them well. His satire "is so exquisitely fine that the slightest touch of it" gives insight into a character.

22 ANON. "Men of Mark." St. Louis Post-Dispatch, January 31, p. 4.
(Brief comment.) "All Boston is down on Henry James" for caricaturing Miss Birdseye in The Bostonians.

23 ANON. "Authors and Publishers." American, 9 (February), 283.
(Note on The Bostonians. Quotes the Boston Herald criticizing James's satirizing in Miss Birdseye a well-known Boston lady.)

24 ANON. "Editor's Literary Record." Harper's, 70 (February), 492-493.
(Review of Tales of Three Cities.) These stories are wise, incisive, and "very clever," with "subtle analyses of character and society," and a "nearly perfect style."

25 ANON. "Recent American Novels." Lippincott's, 35 (February),

215-216.

(Review of Tales of Three Cities.) James continues to reveal the deficiency in American social life. He treats not the inside, but "the mystery of externals" with "the most faithful realism," "exquisite judgment," and "wit and discrimination." The stories' substance is "thin, almost trivial," but they are "immensely clever." "Lady Barberina" is too hasty, and part is "a little crude."

26 ANON. "Choice Literature." St. Louis Missouri Republican, February 2, p. 8.

(Review of Tales of Three Cities.) Apart from the attraction any book of James's always has "for a large circle of readers," this book appeals to those who have not had his social opportunities.

27 ANON. "Eastern and Western Fiction." Springfield (Mass.) Republican, February 8, p. 4.

(Review of The Author of Beltraffio.) James "is seen to better advantage" here than in most of his other recent work because he is "less indirect and discursive" and affected, less "fabian . . . in his attack on the warring problems of life," and he "deals more sensibly with persons who really live." "Pandora" is James at his best, "and makes some amends for 'Daisy Miller.'" Pandora is more real than James's other women, and has "such an original flavor of American life" that she is "truly charming." Nothing "could be better in their way" than James's "photographic portraits." "The Author of Beltraffio" is as near to romance as James gets, and "The Path of Duty" and "The Four Meetings" are cynical but very skillfully told. There is little "truly American" in the inner spirit of these international stories, and there "could hardly be a stronger contrast" than that between James and the western writer E. Howe.

28 ANON. Review of The Author of Beltraffio. St. Louis Missouri Republican, February 15, p. 16.

James can almost effortlessly get at and commune with "the spirit of things," and give it "a body of harmonies." These short works are charming and in many ways "the most delightful of his studies." The clear understanding, the full, delightful "confidence between author and reader" is one of James's "great charms." Without apparent effort he achieves surprises and effects.

29 ANON. "New Publications/. . . Short Stories by James." New York Times, February 15, p. 4.

(Review of The Author of Beltraffio.) "The Author of

Beltraffio" is the most ambitious of these stories, but its events are "unnatural, the logical sequence . . . impossible." "Georgina's Reasons" is the most disagreeable, with a "risque and uncomfortable" subject and a base, wanton heroine whose being married is James's artistic error. When the involutions of "The Path of Duty" are uncoiled, "the strand you hold escapes you entirely." "The Four Meetings" is the flimsiest of the stories. James's crisp style, polish, deftness, and neatness do not necessarily overcome "the extreme insignificance" of his topics, which are "a very feeble fluid" held in "a very perfect shell."

30 ANON. Review of The Author of Beltraffio. Philadelphia Public Ledger and Daily Transcript, February 18, Supp., p. 2.
James is at his most brilliant and suave, and "the polish and evenness of his writing can hardly be surpassed." Pandora Day is interesting. That story's "excellent picture of Washington society" shows that James "is really at his best on home ground" and that the national theme, at home, is a new direction for his art through which he will reach an audience more receptive to "his wholesome satire." In "dramatic energy and seriousness of purpose" "Georgina's Reasons" is the most important of the stories, while "Four Meetings," though slight, is charming and has striking humor, irony, and pathos.

31 ANON. "Current Literature." New York Daily Graphic, February 20, p. 819.
(Note on The Author of Beltraffio.) These stories are all "clever and interesting," but "Pandora" is "exceptionally ingenious."

32 ANON. Short notice of The Author of Beltraffio. Indianapolis Journal, February 20, p. 5.
This volume contains four sketches in addition to "the biographical sketch of Mark Ambient."

33 ANON. Review of Edward Atkinson's social science essays. Springfield (Mass.) Republican, February 22, p. 4.
(Reference to The Bostonians.)

34 ANON. Note. Indianapolis Journal. February 23, p. 4.
James reputedly was himself the subject of the kind of burlesque of Boston found in The Bostonians when he lived there one winter recently, "kept the whole neighborhood in an uproar with his 'nerves' . . . [and] thus made life not worth living in his environment."

35 ANON. Brief reference. Springfield (Mass.) Republican,

1885

February 23, p. 4.
(Reference to "Henry James and other 'lit'erary fellers.'")

36 ANON. "New Publications. The Author of 'Beltraffio.'" Boston Daily Advertiser, February 24, p. 3.
(Relates Mark Ambient's "art for art's sake" philosophy to James's "The Art of Fiction" in the September 1884 Longman's Magazine.) "The Author of Beltraffio" is impressive, "Georgina's Reasons" is "essentially unpleasant" and "almost impossible," and "Four Meetings" is "one of the most beautiful things" James has ever done. Its idea and "the delicate pathos" of the central figure, an "exquisite miniature," are "beyond praise." The felicities outnumber the infelicities of James's admirable style, and the book is delightful.

37 ANON. Editorial item. Atlanta Constitution, February 25, p. 4.
James is evidently "paving the way never to visit Boston" again since the second installment of The Bostonians "is probably worse" for Boston than the first. Yet, it shows that James can sketch character.

38 ANON. "Books of the Week." Christian Union, 31 (February 26), 21.
(Review of The Author of Beltraffio.) Contrary to claims that James has declined in the last two or three years, these stories are equal to his best work. In one sense he is not and can never be popular, but in the exquisite painting of delicate shades of character, in word choice, in showing the "sudden glimpses of the deep passion" beneath conventional society, and in the honest fulfillment of artistic purpose without cheap tricks, he stands alone in English fiction. James has the "finer qualities" of the best modern French realists. With its bold theme and finished treatment, the title story is the best. "Four Meetings" is "sad and hopeless," and "Georgina's Reasons" is "unpleasant in subject and almost unwholesome in tone."

39 ANON. "Current Literature." New York Daily Graphic, February 27, p. 889.
(Review of The Author of Beltraffio.) All these stories are long-winded and "immensely clever." "Georgina's Reasons" is the most remarkable and the most repulsive. James has thought, artistic feeling, and knowledge of the world, but he splits hairs too finely and can become a bore.

40 ANON. Critic, 6 (February 28), 101.

In fiction "we are having really too much realism," as illustrated by uneventful installments of The Rise of Silas Lapham and The Bostonians. Critics "who insist on recognizing Miss Birdseye" are as unkind as the author who portrays her.

41 ANON. "Literary Notices." Hartford Daily Courant, February 28, p. 1.
(Review of The Author of Beltraffio.) These are some of James's cleverest stories, and despite their international theme and abundant analysis of character, they are among the best he has done. They have the "fascinating charm of his style and all the delightfully provoking manner of his inspections of people," and they show as well his cosmopolitanism and "ability to look on two sides of a subject," as with the American girl.

42 ANON. "Recent Publications." New Orleans Daily Picayune, March 1, p. 6.
(Review of Century.) In its second installment, The Bostonians is developing "very decided interest."

43 ANON. Review of The Author of Beltraffio. Boston Evening Transcript, March 6, p. 6.
James's stories "will bear a second reading" and deserve interest.

44 ANON. Review of The Author of Beltraffio. Detroit Free Press, March 7, p. 8.
James "holds out another handful of jewels from the mine of his thought," and indicates his power not so much by what he says as by what he makes us say to ourselves. He relates facts rather than tells stories. His deliberate creation of the "cold-blooded, selfish" Georgina seems to "indicate a loss of artistic power," and he must have known such a woman.

45 ANON. Review of The Author of Beltraffio. Cincinnati Commercial Gazette, March 8, p. 14.
James delights in analyzing selfish, "weak, silly, mean people," and runs on interminably about "shallow thoughts and trivial, sham emotions." He is especially "coldly critical" of American women, his men are not manly, and his women not truthful. Lately, only members of James's own set praise his "supercilious twiddlings."

46 ANON. "Literary Notes." St. Paul (and Minneapolis) Daily Pioneer Press, March 8, p.12.
(Review of The Author of Beltraffio.) Admirers of James, "if current criticism hasn't quite exterminated them," will

be glad to find this collection of his stories from the magazines.

47 ANON. Comments on The Bostonians. Springfield (Mass.) Republican, March 8, p. 4.
James "has met with strictures of much severity, North and South," for the early installments of his novel, which is "receiving a deal of discussion in the newspapers," partly because it appears in the Century. Because of the elements of caricature and satire in Miss Birdseye and Mrs. Farrinder, James "assuredly deserves no mercy in Boston." His portrayals reveal his "cynical way of looking at any high purpose," and he commits libel with "his thin aliases." Giving "'sensitive'" Verena the name of Sintram's "saintly mother in Fouqué's tale" illustrates the way "he habitually approaches spiritual things." Howells in The Undiscovered Country treated "a similar character in the opposite fashion, and much more fitly."

48 ANON. Review of The Author of Beltraffio. Nation, 40 (March 12), 226.
This collection shows James's "usual fertility of invention and his remarkable powers of description." "Four Meetings" is the most pleasing, and "The Author of Beltraffio" most weird. In considering it, one realizes that for most readers, moral considerations still outweigh artistic ones.

49 ANON. "Fiction." Literary World, 16 (March 21), 102.
(Review of The Author of Beltraffio.) This volume gives no new evidence of power and has a lower moral tone than James's other works. "Pandora" is the cleverest of the stories, and has "delightful humor." "The Author of Beltraffio" is disagreeable, and "Georgina's Reasons" is a revolting "study in depravity." It and "The Path of Duty" have the base sexual themes of French literature, treated with James's "morbid" analysis. The admirable "Four Meetings" abounds in "vivid social contrasts."

50 ANON. "Literary Notes." Boston Daily Advertiser, March 24, p. 2.
(Reference to James's May Atlantic Monthly review of Cross's Life of George Eliot.)

51 ANON. "Literary/New Publications." Chicago Inter-Ocean, March 28, p. 10.
(Review of The Author of Beltraffio.) James "seldom fails to interest his readers," and in two or three of these stories he is "at his best."

52 ANON. Note. Louisville Courier-Journal, March 30, p. 4.
A certain theory by Ignatious Donnelly might "squeeze a drop of human blood from Henry James' cold analyzations."

53 ANON. "Literature of the Day." Lippincott's, 35 (April), 424.
(Review of The Author of Beltraffio.) These stories contain none of James's best work. Though their manner is "fairly good," their matter often revolts rather than attracts the reader. Despite some affinities with the "art for art's sake" French school, James is not good at depicting "violations of the moral code." He is better using his "exquisite sense of humor" to make his "unrivalled" criticisms of more conventional life.

54 ANON. Editorial item. Atlanta Constitution, April 2, p. 4.
"An indignant Mississippian" objects to James's stereotyping of the Southern gentleman in The Bostonians.

55 ANON. "Literature/Stories by Henry James . . . Recent Fiction." Chicago Tribune, April 4, p. 9.
(Review of The Author of Beltraffio.) James's writing reflects objects with exquisite detail and added charm. Mrs. Ambient is a "very realistic study," and this is neither the first nor the last time James's "genius has played luridly about a most comfortless subject." "Pandora" is "genial and delightfully humorous," and "Washington society has never been touched by so able a pen." The "exceeding cleverness" of "Georgina's Reason" cannot "atone for the baseness of its subject." "The Path of Duty" shows "a maze of moral entanglement" with the art of "the modern French school." "Four Meetings" is a "strong, sympathetic, delicate" story of "exquisite pathos," and "by far the most perfect effort of the author."

56 ANON. "Literary Lines." San Francisco Chronicle, April 5, p. 6.
Though James denies caricaturing the living in The Bostonians, "the caps he made" must have fit "very snugly" to provoke such an angry reaction from Boston society.

57 ANON. "Recent Fiction." Independent, 37 (April 9), 459.
(Review of The Author of Beltraffio.) Recently, James's characters have become clear and sharp, but also disagreeable. "The Author of Beltraffio" is one of his "most strikingly brilliant and original" short works, with his usual "penetration of insight and subtle analysis of human nature." The heroine of "Georgina's Reasons" is a "moral monster."

58 ANON. Quoted critical reference. Louisville Courier-Journal,

1885

April 10, p. 4.
(Quoted item from American Bookseller says that) "James and Howells are favorites at the Hub [Boston], but 'no good' in New York."

59 ANON. "Answers to Correspondents." Life, 5 (April 16), 220.
(Brief item.) James is right that the public is tired, and if he took "a nice long rest" the public would be immensely refreshed.

60 ANON. "Aut Scissors Aut Nullus." Life, 5 (April 16), 223.
(Quoted from the Boston Post.) James looks like the Prince of Wales, and it is "not often that two men have such hard luck."

61 ANON. "By the Way." Life, 5 (April 23), 228.
(Note.) James is "taking his monthly rise out of Boston" (reference to the reaction to the early installments of The Bostonians).

62 ANON. Note. Colorado Springs Weekly Gazette, April 25, p. 4.
(Quotation from "a sharp article" on James in the Boston Spectator, in which he is alleged to make "'the serious mistake . . . of believing that the life of Fifth avenue and Beacon street is American life, or the only phase of American life worth writing about.'")

63 ANON. "Literary." Boston Commercial Bulletin, April 25, p. 2.
James is a critic first, a novelist second.

64 ANON. "Some American Writers." Sunny South (in Atlanta Constitution), April 25, p. 4.
(From the Boston Herald, "Pen Portraits of Some of Our Most Distinguished Literary Artists," including James.)

65 ANON. "'The Author of Beltraffio.'" Critic, 6 (May 2), 206-207.
(Review.) James has printed all his disagreeable, painful, and repulsive stories in one volume. They lack his usually delightful "delicate flavors, . . . refined delineation," and "savory ingenious talk." They are too much like the products of the "fast-decaying Frenchy school."

66 ANON. "Two Tales of One City." New Orleans Daily Picayune, May 10, p. 4.
(Editorial.) James and Howells, the "two most famous exponents" of the "advanced school of American fiction," are presenting in The Bostonians and The Rise of Silas Lapham "certain phases of life peculiar to American society."

James's title is misleading, since he gives us Bostonians "in revolt against the existing social order" to the exclusion of "more regular ways" of getting along. Howells's story refutes the charge that these are "the" Bostonians with his "coarse people [who] are not quacks" and his "cultivated people [who] are not enthusiasts." Howells is more human and has more sympathy for the struggles of the characters he analyzes than does James, whose art is very fine and who dissects with "scientific precision and composure," but does not take the reader into his confidence. We should thank him for showing the "naked meanness and utter imbecility" of the vulgar charlatans he portrays.

67 ANON. "The American Peerage." Life, 5 (May 21), 285.
(Humorous note. Spoofs James's Boston connections, love of England, "French" style, and tendency to be obscure.) James gets the "proud and hitherto unbestowed title of Lord Camera, Earl of Obscura."

68 ANON. Reprinted note. Critic, 6 (June 20), 298.
According to the Chicago Standard James's The Bostonians, and other novels, "are plainly marked with the personal characteristics of some of America's diversified population," although James's novel does not, like the others listed, draw its material "from a part of the country hitherto undeveloped, . . . from a literary standpoint."

69 ANON. "Mr. James's Method." Life, 6 (August 20), 108.
(Reprint of item from Rochester Union that reacts to and refutes Julia Ward Howe's remark to the Concord School of Philosophy [noted in the New York Commercial] that James's method "does immense damage to character." The Union says that the patience, endurance, and self-control required to get through his later novels elevate rather than debase the reader's moral tone.)

70 ANON. "By the Way . . . Literary Notes." Life, 6 (September 10), 144.
(Humorous poem about contemporary writers spoofs James's alleged desire to be English.)

71 ANON. Editorial item. Atlanta Constitution, September 26, p. 4.
Boston is as sensitive as any other section, but neither James nor George W. Cable should be criticized for his portrayals, respectively, of Boston and New Orleans. They are not obliged to "conform their works to ideals, exaggerations or affectations" but simply to fit "certain characters to certain incidents."

1885

72 ANON. Note. New Orleans Daily Picayune, October 18, p. 4.
London Life announces that James has returned to Europe, where "his novels, ridiculing Americans, are so greatly enjoyed."

73 ANON. Humorous item. Life, 6 (October 29), 250.
(Reference to "The Bostonians" as Ben Butler and Sullivan.)

74 ANON. "The Atlantic Monthly." Charleston (S.C.) Sunday News, November 29, p. 5.
(Note that The Princess Casamassima will continue in the Atlantic.)

75 ANON. "Home Items." Life, 6 (December 24), 365.
"A literary club is preparing to celebrate the early termination of the 'Bostonians' in the Century."

76 ANON. "The Art of Novel Writing." Atlanta Constitution, December 28, p. 4.
(Editorial.) Despite the flaws in the works of Scott, Dickens, and Thackeray, it is worth asking whether any of the more modern novelists have given us as much amusement or any truer pictures of human nature, or made us shed more tears of real sympathy. It is true that "we might have cried a little" over Ralph Touchett of The Portrait of a Lady if it had not been for James's "overwhelming sense of propriety."

77 N., C. F. "Henry James." New York World, August 30, p. 19.
James is distinguished and successful, he has written a few good stories and many poor ones, and his style lacks real wit. (Anecdote illustrating James's subtle sense of humor.)

78 P., R. "Novel-Writing as a Science." Catholic World, 42 (November), 277.
James is less cold, rational, and scientific than Howells.

79 PORTER, CHARLOTTE. "Open Letter . . . The Serial Story." Century, 8 (September), 812-813.
In The Portrait of a Lady, Isabel is an example of a type of modern heroine more individual, assertive, and self-possessed than her predecessors, and the change is due in part to the shift in emphasis from plot to "the life within" the characters.

80 WETHERILL, J. K. "Mr. James and Some Others." Critic, 7

(September 5), 109.
(A general commentary on James which commends his style, industry, accuracy, and ability to capture intangible aspects of character, but which considers him cold, his characters and descriptions lacking concreteness, and his whole endeavor not entirely productive.)

81 WHITING, LILIAN. "Crumbs of Boston Culture." New York Daily Graphic, February 6, p. 709.
The Bostonians's Miss Birdseye has caused great controversy in the Boston Herald and the Boston Evening Transcript. (Takes humorous attitude toward the controversy and toward Howells's description of James's art as finer than that of Dickens and Thackeray.)

82 WYLKOM, WAT. "Henry James." New York World, May 3, p. 23.
In person, James has the same "calm, cool, calculating air," the tendency to analysis and bloodlessness, the lack of spontaneity, and the "assumption of superfineness" that characterize his fiction. He so dreads "provincialism and crudeness" that he behaves unnaturally. His presentation of Americans, whom he does not understand very well, is nonetheless more complimentary than people claim. With its sustained interest and superb workmanship, Roderick Hudson is his best novel. Although many of his readers do not understand his "far-away, passionless, acute method," he is presently "the fashion and in ceaseless demand."

1886

1 ANON. "A Boston Magazine." Atlanta Constitution, February 1, p. 4.
(Editorial review of Atlantic Monthly.) The Princess Casamassima shows James in a very happy new vein, in which he threatens to upset Howells's theories by portraying "strenuous" human passions. James seems to be leaving Howells's realm of the superficial and to be moving into an area where he shows for the first time that he has some conception of character, but where the "trivial treatment which has hitherto been his chief characteristic will bring him speedily to grief."

2 ANON. Review of Century. Boston Beacon, February 6, p. 3.
Bostonians should accept James's denial that in The Bostonians "he meant to describe anybody in particular. . . . He is much grieved by the interpretation put upon his little venture, and the Beacon is one of the offenders."

1886

3 ANON. Review of Century, editorial item. Atlanta Constitution, February 8, p. 4.

The Bostonians is dreary. According to a second item, Verena is an "impossible creation" although a reader has applied her and Olive's situations to real life, and "there are no Verenas in Boston, any more than there are Basil Ransoms in Mississippi."

4 ANON. "The Literary World . . . Literary Notes." Albany Evening Journal, February 10, p. 3.

(Review of Century.) The Bostonians is concluded in this February issue, and most "readers will not be sorry."

5 ANON. Humorous item. Life, 7 (February 18), 104.

A man who can prove he has read The Bostonians was deluged with offers from dime museums, but will go on the lecture circuit instead. A fortune awaits him, since "the American public who got as far as the third chapter wants to know what it was all about."

6 ANON. "Some Magazine Notes." Atlanta Constitution, February 22, p. 4.

(Review of Atlantic Monthly.) Despite its affectation in style, this last installment of The Princess Casamassima indicates that it will be James's most important work. If James keeps up his grasp of important aspects of character not evident in his other books, this novel will be a "notable contribution" to fiction.

7 ANON. Review of The Bostonians. Boston Evening Traveller, March 19, p. 2.

Despite the furor created in Boston by the book's early installments, it contains "certain material that is not only of present interest but of an enduring value. The types of character in it exist, and they are portrayed to the life. They comprise a series of photographs of very unusual and curiously interesting individualities. While there is no coherency, or fusion, that would transform this meandering narrative into a novel, while the characters have no especial relation as actors in a drama, they are yet rounded, life-like, perfect portraitures of existing types . . . [though not] representative of the various movements" with which James involves them. It will be in many respects one of the "most permanent value in the series of artistically touched novels" by James.

8 ANON. Review of The Bostonians. St. Louis Missouri Republican, March 20, p. 7.

The Bostonians is too prolix and tedious, and its

excessive analysis suggests "an automatism of thought as pernicious as the realism of literary method" of which James is "the patron saint." Yet, James has more heart than Howells, and this work is characterized by a "wholesome philosophy, . . . cunning satire, . . . caustic sarcasm and . . . general atmosphere of robustness." For its potential effect on "those prurient, sickly, silly systems of technical philosophy" which have made parts of Boston society "a byword and a hissing among all healthful people" but have been "coddled into a growth as unnatural, unusual, and disgusting as a puff-ball," James "should receive the canonization of men and women everywhere who have a decent regard for common-sense."

9 ANON. Review of The Bostonians. Cleveland Daily Plain Dealer, March 21, p. 4.
Since tastes differ, "there are people who plod with satisfaction along the prosaic path . . . from the first page to the last of the bulky volume" of The Bostonians and would be disgusted by a more sensational story. Others "would fall asleep over it."

10 ANON. Review of The Bostonians. Detroit Evening News, March 21, p. 2.
The book is long, but James "works the story up to quite a dramatic ending, and we have no doubt the work will be greatly enjoyed in England."

11 ANON. Review of The Bostonians. Boston Beacon, March 27, p. 3.
James's characters are not very interesting or attractive, and most readers prefer a story with dramatic action to analysis of emotions and motives of such people, on which James wastes his literary skill. Yet, James is "easily the greatest of our modern American society novelists," his portrayals of Bostonians are "true to nature," and they reveal "the sentiments of men and women as they are," so if they are dull the fault is with society and not the novelist. This novel will live, and its literary mastership will be "prized and praised after the fault-finders of to-day" who read it carelessly like a newspaper, seeking something startling, are forgotten.

12 ANON. Note and review of The Bostonians. Indianapolis Journal, March 28, p. 9; March 29, p. 5.
In an item from the Boston Record, "the ghost of Henry James's 'Bostonians' is abroad in the land and will not be laid," and a "minor story writer" has written a sequel in which, because of her and her husband's poverty, Verena

returns to the lecture stage. "Everybody knew that Mr. James had made a story eminent for delicious dullness, but this is the first intimation we have had that it had a moral." In a brief review/mention, The Bostonians is one of a list of books in which "there is little . . . that will prove enduring, and none that will attract unusual attention."

13 ANON. Review of The Bostonians. New York Times, March 28, p. 12.

James has taken a small subject of minor significance and stretched it to a very great length, and is "enigmatical" about his purpose. The book is yet interesting in an esoteric way, is done with "wonderful art," and provides "many a tiny little picture, nothing being garish, all dainty, worked up to the most exquisite pitch of art," with passion "always circumscribed within decent and tidy limits." It is "an exquisite hothouse, where things might take on luxurious growth, only he trims and trims, and trails and tacks them neatly on a trellis."

Although James's "talent is a great one," he tends toward "excessive minuteness" and triviality, "dawdles over" small things. Miss Birdseye inspires sympathy and is "the saddest of all the sorry women who drag their fads" through The Bostonians.

14 ANON. Review of The Bostonians. New York Tribune, March 28, p. 6.

Despite the numerous patches of humor, The Bostonians is dismal and James's other works cannot compare with it in "monotonous and oppressive solidity." James has developed a "disagreeable subject" at inordinate length, filled his novel with unpleasant incidents and disagreeable personages who, with their crudeness, vulgarity and weakness," are "inexpressibly tiresome," and among whom there is no one who inspires "a spark of sympathy, nobody from whose counterpart in real life we would not flee as from a stupendous bore." The novel ends with "a violent and sensational scene" unjustified by previous events in the story.

15 ANON. "New Publications. . . . Literary Notes." New York Times, March 29, p. 3.

(Note.) The American supply of The Bostonians and F. Marion Crawford's Lonely Parish narrowly escaped going down with the ship the Oregon. (Noted also in New Orleans Daily Picayune, April 3, p. 4.)

16 ANON. Review of The Bostonians. St. Paul (and Minneapolis) Daily Pioneer Press, March 29, p. 4.

Olive, as well as Mrs. Farrinder, "is far more of an American type than Daisy Miller is," although James "has never thoroughly and successfully studied American women" and his recent attempts must have been "from the standpoint of England or Italy." The Bostonians, although at times "a little tedious," "contains some of his brightest writing" and "is very superior to the pretentious 'Portrait of a Lady,' which is singularly devoid of interesting situations, and can hardly be called a story." Although James is among "our most pretentious novelists," neither he nor others in this group, Howells and F. Marion Crawford, "has yet created a character which takes hold upon the popular mind like Becky Sharpe or Silas Wegg and scores of other English creations," nor have they equalled the work of Hawthorne.

17 ANON. "By the Way." Life, 7 (April 1), 186.
(Humorous note.) Few people have read the literary "swash and drivel" that fills The Bostonians. James must be reading his own productions to put him in the mental condition "that allows of his writing such stuff."

18 ANON. Quoted reference. Boston Evening Transcript, April 3, p. 6.
The conclusion (quoted) of the London Spectator's "neat review" (March 20, 1886) of The Bostonians finds it new and original but long and drawn out like Boston modes of thought.

19 ANON. Review of The Bostonians. Chicago Tribune, April 3, p. 13.
James "imagines that the keenness of his perception will make amends for the triviality of the object analyzed" in his "mental microscope," and his "realism is becoming sordid," although there are "moments of compensation" such as the description of the Tarrants' home. With respect to Olive, although James "may not think so, it is difficult to make altruism altogether ridiculous." The need to rescue the age from feminization is "[t]he moral of the book," but "the world will not greatly trouble itself" about whether James's "ideas of woman-suffrage are right or wrong" and "they do not of themselves constitute what is known as a novel."

20 ANON. Review of The Bostonians. Cincinnati Commercial Gazette, April 3, p. 13.
Although "intellectual Boston can see itself darkly in this mirror, and struggle with the impression that it is food for mirth," James's odd characters cannot be used to satirize the mass to the degree suggested. If "he can be dull in his microscopic search after motives, he can also

1886

give a brilliant turn to a personal description," such as that of Selah Tarrant. The novel "does not realize all that was expected, but it is racy of Henry James."

21 ANON. Review of The Bostonians. New York Daily Graphic, April 3, p. 311.
Every character except for Dr. Prance "is either a crank or an amiable fool." James nearly matches them, and in Verena he "has pretty nearly converted himself into the feminine gender, and has unconsciously written his own internal biography" since "he too prattles away in the most captivating manner," but at the end he seems to have "taken you nowhere, and brought you to nothing." He has entertained you and "dissected human motives, actions and contradictions, . . . [b]ut you have been listening all the while to the analytic introspections of a butterfly, who flutters and sips most prettily, and sweetly gives you the little all that a butterfly knows." Ransom's ideas are "a few antique opinions of a secondhand dude," James's "tittle-tattle" possibly in ridicule of woman suffrage is ineffectual, and this novel itself is "intellectual bric-a-brac."

22 ANON. Review of The Bostonians. Detroit Free Press, April 3, p. 8.
Despite its length and the ridicule and detraction James has received, The Bostonians "really is a readable and an interesting story which might almost have been written by a novelist without any peculiar or advanced views as to art in fiction." "A little judicious skipping . . . reduces it to practicable and entertaining dimensions." (Part of rest of review taken from 1886.13.)

23 ANON. Review of The Bostonians. Chicago Inter-Ocean, April 3, p. 10.
The Bostonians is, if anything, "more ponderous and heavy" than even the earlier works of its author, "who is not remarkable for his sprightliness." Its characters inspire neither tears nor merriment. Although many of the sketches "are very true to life, . . . more real than fictitious," and it has "fine writing, keen satire, and elegant portraiture," the book is dreary, dull, uninteresting, and unnecessarily long, with "disagreeable" pictures and sketches and "talks full of the vinegar of life."

24 ANON. Cartoon. Life, 7 (April 7), 218-219.
(Spoof of James's and Howells's novels as being without action or plot.)

25 ANON. Review of The Bostonians. Chicago Times, April 10,

p. 13.

James's books have "a high place among current works of fiction," and The Bostonians treats women's emancipation "with much justice" despite the overdrawn details and the characters, who are sketched "boldly and definitely," but are "too extreme to be life-like in any general sense" and occasionally border on clever caricature. The style is "always strong and pointed, if not rigidly artistic," but has too many adjectives, parenthetical phrases, long sentences, and grammatical errors in conversation. Yet, James's criticisms of people "are trenchant, acute, and often pungent," though the book is too long.

26 ANON. Review of The Bostonians. New Orleans Daily Picayune, April 11, p. 14.

James, "now an Englishman, to all intents and purposes," has "brought an aroused swarm of hornets about his head by his truth and satire" in this novel, which "is a remarkable book."

27 ANON. Review of The Bostonians. San Francisco Chronicle, April 11, p. 11.

When someone of James's "fame, merited or otherwise" enters upon the as yet "not too much analyzed" "undiscovered country" of "charlatans and . . . deluded would-be reformers . . . ," it is "a sign that others are likely to rush pell-mell" after him. Olive is "the most strenuous" character in the book, the plot is "entirely emotional," and the moral, if there is one, is "the incongruousness of women dealing with the ruder problems of life and the crudity of ideas and of practice which so-called social reforms would substitute for the maturity of customs and codes that are centuries old." That the new ways cannot be proven superior by "mere argument and assertion" is the "lesson" The Bostonians illustrates. James's style and "improprieties of language" in the speech of some characters "might be severely criticized," the "narrative is in the main made up of the merest frivolities," and it is to be hoped that the James-Howells school of fiction "is not the fiction of the future."

28 ANON. Review of The Bostonians. Louisville Courier-Journal, April 16, p. 4.

The Bostonians is "almost interminable and rather dreary" and "dragged itself through the Century."

29 ANON. Review of The Bostonians. Critic, 8 (April 17), 191-192.

The "afflicted and indignant city" of Boston is right in thinking that James "really meant some Bostonians, not Bostonians in entirety." He "intended to satirize objectionable Bostonians alone, and . . . it is unjust to say that he 'lacks feeling.'" The pictures of the Tarrants, Miss Birdseye, Mrs. Farrinder, and Olive are "all . . . remarkably well drawn," while Ransome, the Burrages, and Mrs. Luna are "more hackneyed characters." James "says nothing, . . . but says it with an art that is constant and charming," a "touch so fine that the reader is content to skip nothing." The story moves very slowly and is, "with its comparatively crude devices and inartistic close, . . . what one cares least for."

30 ANON. "News and Notes." Literary World, 17 (April 17), 137.
The Bostonians "has proved an entire failure," and many booksellers complain that James's popularity "has suddenly left him, much to their loss."

31 ANON. "Two Social Satires." Springfield (Mass.) Republican, April 18, p. 4.
(Editorial review.) The Bostonians is long and hard to get through, and "there are many better novels." The mockery in this satirical work "is excessively elaborate." James "has taken great liberties with Boston people and places . . . and treated the best Boston notions without respect, . . . in fact with a condescension which is temperamental" with James, "and which perhaps he calls cosmopolitan." Yet, he is "rather more severe toward Boston than to other places," since his Bostonians are all "cranks." Olive is "impossible to accept as a type," but "as an individual study she is most powerfully presented," and, like any other examination of insanity, she is "depressing in the last degree." Her part in the satire becomes "much too tragical, . . . overweights the tale, which becomes a treatise on alienism," and relegates the movement which is the object of the satire to a secondary position. The satire itself has "vigor and . . . partial truth," although the "real nobility" of the women's movement "is utterly scorned." The book "is as ably written" as any of James's others, despite "its great tedium, the exceeding absurdity of much of its detail, and the indefensible liberties of his portraitures."

32 ANON. Review of The Bostonians. Independent, 38 (April 22), 495.
The novel is long and of esoteric interest, since James delights "in writing what to the majority of flesh-and-blood men and women has no excuse for being so praised, and books that grow more and more arid and dull." This "long, prosy, carefully written" work "was not worth writing, and is unreadable," and will be admired by only a certain class of

readers. James "has undoubtedly put some of his very best work" into it, "an amount of care that a broad-minded critic appreciates with real regret." It "is as finished as an ice-castle on the Neva" and "warms us up just as much."

33 ANON. "Literary Links." Butte (Mont.) Daily Miner, April 25, p. 2.
(Note.) Among "the most popular magazine writers," Howells and James are the best paid, each having received $5,000 for his recent novel in the Century.

34 ANON. "Authors and Publishers." American, 12 (May 1), 28.
(Note.) The Boston Literary World says that The Bostonians has been an entire failure and that James's popularity has left him, much to the booksellers' loss.

35 ANON. Note. St. Louis Post-Dispatch, May 1, p. 11.
The Bostonians "has proved an utter failure, and many booksellers are complaining that Mr. James' popularity has suddenly left him, much to their loss."

36 ANON. Review of Lippincott's. New Orleans Daily Picayune, May 2, p. 14.
In the May Lippincott's (1886.81) Gossip Department James "is given a tremendous and viciously rude hauling over for the small offense of having written 'The Bostonians.'"

37 ANON. Review of The Bostonians. Nation, 42 (May 13), 407-408.
The Bostonians is elaborate and brings out a number of contrasts which "are pushed far, and bring out remorselessly much that is peculiar to the civilization of the day" so that "[e]very American reader will find in the book some reflection of his or her mind." Boston finds the book a distortion. Although James's portrayal may be related to a dislike of things Bostonian common outside New England, he "wisely eschews likes and dislikes" and avoids spoiling his best effects as he would if he, "observer and critic by nature and training," identified himself "with the puppets whom he so cleverly exhibits." In The Bostonians James is not at his best, the story "drags in places," and the conversations lack naturalness because of James's "passion for a sort of dramatic repartee." Yet, "the criticism and analysis and observation are so good" that one must admire if not always enjoy the book. James is "one of the first of American novelists," and he and Howells provide the best record of current American society, "in sketches which must ever remain a constituent portion of American literature."

38 ANON. Report on "A Lecture on Literature" by Professor

1886

Melville B. Anderson. Indianapolis Journal, May 19, p. 8.
According to Professor Anderson the "sympathetic analysts of human hearts" Howells and James "bring me into a closer sympathy with human nature, into a closer interest with the lives of men." Despite the widespread assumption that no one has read The Bostonians, it is, according to Anderson, "a keen analysis of human character." Although some say it has no soul and is "an anatomist flashing a cold steel scalpel over his subject," in Anderson's view "an anatomist may work for a good end, and I enjoy artistic work for the neatness with which it is done."

39 ANON. "Late Literature . . . Notes." Albany Evening Journal, May 25, p. 3.
(Review of Century.) The serials of Howells and James are "among the more notable features" of the November 1885-April 1886 volume.

40 ANON. Review of The Bostonians. Albany Evening Journal, May 28, p. 3.
The Bostonians is "an extreme example of the modern analytic novel," it is excessively long, the characters are not particularly interesting and most are commonplace, yet they are not typical Bostonians. They are not attractive, the "minuteness" with which they are treated makes them "still more wearisome to the reader," and the "general dislike" of this book "shows that the great public still craves fiction" with elements of "the heroic and romantic." Yet, "[a]mid the dreary waste" of this novel are "fine touches" showing what James could do if he were "not governed by a wrong theory of storywriting."

41 ANON. Note. Salt Lake Tribune, May 30, p. 2.
The London Times finds The Bostonians "'feminine in style, grasp and matter,' but many Bostonians are open to the same criticism, though, as the Times continues about James's book, they are not the less 'interesting and amusing.'"

42 ANON. "Delicate but Deadly." Atlanta Constitution, June 5, p. 4.
(Editorial.) Without mentioning their names, the New York Sun has recently made a subtle but deadly attack on our "Miss Nancy novelists," James, Howells, and George Washington Cable.

43 ANON. Review of The Bostonians. Literary World, (June 12), 198.
This long novel is somber and tedious, but upon a second

look the "apathetic Basil" seems more representative, Olive's "insane ambition begins to rise to sublimity . . . and her cruel disappointment assumes a tragic interest," while the "inconsequent and untrustworthy" Verena seems "the leading character in a comedy" whose closing scene is ingenious and "as amusing as anything on the stage." James's sudden ending is in this instance "very satisfactory," but although the English probably think James fairly represents "some phases of American life in his careful and highly elaborated novels," the "advanced women" and their men in this novel "have an atrociously exaggerated importance attached to them," they "are not worth the space they occupy," James "has made a lamentable misuse of his keen analytic powers" in portraying Olive and the "slow dragging of the reform," and "it is like bringing heavy artillery to bear on shadows." Verena, however, is "in some sense a success" and sometimes natural flesh and blood.

44 ANON. "Mr. Howells and His Critics." <u>Atlanta Constitution</u>, June 21, p. 4.
(Editorial.) James's biographical and critical essay on Howells in <u>Harper's Weekly</u> is very pleasant, polished, and has "a dainty coolness."

45 ANON. "Literary Notes." Detroit <u>Evening News</u>, July 18, p. 2.
(Review of <u>Atlantic Monthly</u>.) The <u>Atlantic</u> for August will be a "rare delight" for readers in that it is full of papers, stories, and poems "one likes to think over." <u>The Princess Casamassima</u>, the other serials, and the editorial miscellany are "all good, each in its way."

46 ANON. "An American Novelist in His Workshop," by "Henry Games, Jr." <u>Life</u>, 8 (July 22), 48-49.
(Humorous item. Letter from "Games" describes "Willyum Beans Trowells" at home and discusses "Trowells'" literary plans, with references to Games's "The Mossgrownians" and "Princess Cussihussiwussema.")

47 ANON. "A Hundred American Authors." <u>Critic</u>, 9 (July 24), 37.
(James is listed among the hundred "American authors perhaps worthiest of being read by their fellow-countrymen of the present day.")

48 ANON. "By the Way . . . Some Figures." <u>Life</u>, 8 (July 29), 60.
(Humorous note. Listing of exaggerated fictional sums that James and other writers allegedly receive for their writing.)

49 ANON. Detroit <u>Evening News</u>, August 15, p. 2.

1886

(An item reprinted from the Art Age refers to a young woman, well dressed and probably a Vassar graduate, as a "Daisy Miller.")

50 ANON. "Literary Notes." Detroit Evening News, August 22, p. 2.
(Review of Atlantic Monthly.) Serials by Bishop, James, and Craddock are part of the September issue, whose papers are, overall, "calculated to interest the intelligent reader."

51 ANON. "New Books. Princess Casamassima." Boston Evening Transcript, November 3, p. 6.
In The Princess Casamassima James makes a "new departure" from the "high life" and portrays the masses with "wonderful success." His admirable method reproduces "the point of view of real life," he compels readers to think (a disadvantage when the public still refuses to take fiction seriously), and he is too much an artist to anticipate the conclusion dictated by "the resistless logic of character." This book is an addition to James's list of "strong, original novels," and it has "wider scope" and "stronger grasp" than any of his works since The Portrait of A Lady. It is full of keen characterization, "brilliant, delicate touches," and, like all James's best works, "strongly dramatic elements" revealed by "an exquisite literary art."

52 ANON. Review of Julian Hawthorne's Confessions and Criticisms. Boston Beacon, November 6, p. 3.
On novels Hawthorne has some good views, and with regard to novels only, one can agree with him that James and Howells have done more than anyone else to make literature respectable during the last ten years. (See 1887.32.)

53 ANON. Review of The Princess Casamassima. Boston Beacon, November 6, p. 3.
This is easily James's best book. The story bears rereading, because whatever his shortcomings, James is the cleverest of living English-writing novelists. His books are good company, not offensive, condescending, or too explicit, and this story, taken from life, abounds in "really brilliant passages" of pathos. James the artist "allows things to settle themselves," his "presentation of the case is masterly," and this book is "one of the great novels of our time."

54 ANON. "World of Letters. . . . Some New Books." St. Louis Missouri Republican, November 6, p. 10.
(Review of Half-Hours with the Best American Authors.)

A literature that possesses such names as those of "Irving, Prescott, Bancroft and Motley in history, Emerson and Thoreau in philosophy, Hawthorne, Cooper, Holmes and James in fiction, Bryant, Longfellow, Poe, Lowell and Whittier in poetry, and others of no less merit in other branches of authorship, needs no advocate, but may . . . speak for itself."

55 ANON. "Old World News by Cable." New York Times, November 7, p. 1.
(Critical comment. Reference to part of the Athenaeum review of The Princess Casamassima as "rather cruel.")

56 ANON. "New Publications." Detroit Free Press, November 13, p. 8.
(Review of The Princess Casamassima.) Though very superior in many respects to James's other novels, this story is too long and wordy.

57 ANON. "Christina Light's Career." New York Tribune, November 14, p. 10.
(Review of The Princess Casamassima.) The Princess is a "theatrical eccentricity" rather than a character, and although charming and "extremely interesting," she is ultimately a mystery. James does not write of real socialism as if he believed in it, but cleverly describes its cheap imitation. The book "is strong enough to obliterate the effect of the unfortunate" Bostonians, which inspired resentment. The Princess is therefore "a novel of very decided rank," the work "of a rare and brilliant master" who displays more than his usual command of his subject, ability in construction, and purpose for his characters. Despite some loose ends, the book is "a beautiful and symmetrical piece of art" upon which James has spent "some of his brightest ideas and his most conscientious work."

58 ANON. "New Books." Charleston (S.C.) News and Courier, November 14, p. 5.
(Review of The Princess Casamassima.) This is the least successful of James's novels, with most of the faults but few of the merits of his previous works. The plot is inconsequential, and James carries character analysis so far that he sacrifices dramatic force. The Princess and Hyacinth are somewhat admirable, but too many of their actions are incomprehensible. The other characters' fates are left "in utter uncertainty."

59 ANON. "Books and Authors." Atlanta Constitution, November 21, p. 13.

1886

(Review of The Princess Casamassima.) This book is "a decided improvement" on "that immense mess of verbiage" The Bostonians, but "far below" The Portrait of a Lady. The princess, like all of James's characters, is a puzzle, and she is not worth solving. The reader can understand and sympathize with none of the characters except Millicent Henning, Madame Grandoni, and Vetch. James's little knowledge of his subject is superficial. He has missed an opportunity to portray "genuine human nature," which, according to his theory, is "melodramatic."

60 ANON. "Literature." Cleveland Daily Plain Dealer, November 21, p. 12.

(Review of The Princess Casamassima.) In this book James enters "a somewhat new field," but he still has his typically "lame and impotent conclusion to a long drawn out story." Despite his "ineradicable defects as a novelist," James has "a large clientage" who will enjoy this book as they have its predecessors, and we leave them to it.

61 ANON. "New Publications./A 'Slumming' Romance." New York Times, November 21, p. 12.

(Review of The Princess Casamassima.) This novel of slumming, this sinister, tiresome, "singularly unpleasant" romance, shows the decadence of a "once most distinguished" literary art. James overindulges his tendencies to be "retrospective and introspective" and displays a distinct "want of virility" in delaying the inevitable denouement and "perfuming" his subject.

62 ANON. "Literature of the Day." Chicago Tribune, November 27, p. 12.

Mr. Mallock is "the Henry James of the English." Possessing great gifts, "he yet contrives to disappoint his readers" and gives them "a pang" with every new book.

63 ANON. "Lagniappe." New Orleans Daily Picayune, November 28, p. 3.

(Brief quoted item from New York Graphic.) James "in his new story asks: 'What's the use of brains if you haven't got a backbone?'" The answer is "A good deal. A man with brains can hire all the backbone he wants at $1 a day."

64 ANON. "Recent Publications." New Orleans Daily Picayune, November 28, p. 7.

(Review of The Princess Casamassima.) This novel "has been universally admired," to the extent that one can admire James's "unravelings of social events." It finds "many readers who dote on his charming style."

65 ANON. "Books Reviewed." St. Paul Daily Pioneer Press, November 28, p. 12.
(Review of The Princess Casamassima.) Hyacinth is disappointing and the Princess a failure. The movement is slow, deliberate, and diffuse, leaving "a labyrinth of inferences," and the characters are very distinct, though they do not talk brilliantly. The books is not dull, but original and readable, with "a certain fascination." James should attempt an American novel as good.

66 ANON. "Literary Notes." Detroit Evening News, November 28, p. 2.
(Review of The Princess Casamassima.) Christina Light is "a spoiled child of the world," and James is "getting more human in his writing."

67 ANON. "New Publications. . . . Fiction." Portland Morning Oregonian, November 28, p. 2.
(Review of The Princess Casamassima.) This story is perhaps "the most serious piece of work" James has yet done, and has less "flippant cynicism" than his other books. It is "very readable," and those who have not already read it will enjoy it.

68 ANON. "Three American Novelists." San Francisco Chronicle, November 28, p. 6.
(Editorial.) Current American novelists are not nearly as good as Thackeray and Balzac. The Princess Casamassima is a strong novel, but too prolix, subtle, and analytical, traits growing on James's fiction since the vigorous American. The Portrait of a Lady was "nebulous and unsatisfactory." James's writing is cold-blooded and objective, with not very interesting characters. He has been misled by "false ideals," foreign point of view, and ignorance of his own country. Therefore, instead of writing the great American novel, he "lays no claim to permanent literary fame."

69 ANON. "New Books. . . . Latest Novels." Cincinnati Commercial Gazette, December 4, p. 13.
(Review of The Princess Casamassima.) This novel "is decidedly a rambling tale, microscopic in sentiment and description, cultivated and keen, but not leading up to anything or down to anything particularly."

70 ANON. "Literature. A Batch of New and Readable Novels." San Francisco Chronicle, December 5, p. 11.
(Review of The Princess Casamassima.) This is "a far stronger book" than The Bostonians. As in most of James's

novels, plot is secondary to character study and James "uses too many words." He describes his characters from the outside, and "his analyses of emotions and thoughts are frequently tedious and unnecessary," but the book's power "makes it readable" and it is one of James's best works.

71 ANON. "The Field of Literature. Some Recent Novels." Indianapolis Journal, December 6, p. 3.
(Review of The Princess Casamassima.) A taste for James's novels must be cultivated, and by people of leisure. Those who dislike his books dislike them very much, and will probably find The Princess Casamassima "tedious and wearisome." Yet, it has "many admirable points," including cultivated style, "felicitous flow of language," and, despite an air of unreality, less than usual of the sense that James's characters are his puppets. Lady Aurora, Miss Pynsent, and Hyacinth are "clearly drawn," "pathetic," and memorable, but the other characters are disagreeably erratic. The "vast amount" of mental and physical work put into making this book is unusual in a contemporary novel.

72 ANON. "Writers Who Lack College Training." Critic, 9 (December 11), 297.
(Article from St. Louis Globe-Democrat on the education of various contemporary authors.) Though James has not had university training, he is a purist who carries the "refinements of language" farther than any man of his time. He "analyzes and sub-analyzes" it and his characters, and is nearly a faultless stylist, but one eventually wearies of his "superfinenesses of expression," his "strained periphrasis" and excessive self-consciousness, and his eternal qualifying and distinctions. At first his work may delight, but it lacks "directness, force, [and] vitality," and its conscientiousness about verbal forms has a "ceremonious elegance" that "suppresses feeling and annuls enthusiasm." Howells has acknowledged James as his master in novel writing, though many prefer him to James.

73 ANON. "Notes." Critic, 9 (December 11), 298.
James has gone to Florence for the winter, and G. W. Smalley says in the New York Tribune that English opinion of The Princess Casamassima is "far more favorable" than the criticisms in the Athenaeum and the Academy indicate.

74 ANON. "Literature." Chicago Times, December 18, p. 10.
Despite "much sharp criticism," a new novel by either James or Howells "is eagerly welcomed by very large circles of readers." Many enjoy Howells's "finical" play of humor who do not like James's "acrid and over fastidious cynicism."

75 ANON. Review of The Princess Casamassima. Chicago Times, December 18, p. 10.

James treats his subject, socialism, in his "usual pungent and sarcastic manner," but with an "incompleteness and ambiguity" that leave the reader doubting the characters' motivations and the author's intent. The little "so-called hero" is pitiful.

76 ANON. "World of Letters. Henry James' Novel, 'The Princess Casamassima.'" St. Louis Missouri Republican, December 18, p. 10.

James is "a master of detail" who elaborates each picture with such fidelity and overattention that we see the characters too closely. This book is "attenuated, long-drawn out, full of incident and unimpassioned small facts," yet is also a tale of today, intrinsically exciting, with people "entirely too common" in real life "pictured with a bold, unwavering hand." James sometimes "rises to a sublime height of moral and philosophical reflection" and makes "an analysis of human life in certain conditions irresistible in its strength of logic and beauty of style." With all his "verbosity and weariness of detail," James also "possesses those high qualities of perception and sympathy," is "much more human" than Howells, and in the opening episodes more dramatic. Millicent Henning is more interesting than the "abnormal, ugly" princess, and, although there is something pitiful in Hyacinth's fate, James is "too true an artist" to indulge in special pleadings and simply relates the facts. James is "essentially a great writer," with a subject worthy of him, and has produced "a book of no ordinary quality" that is both instructive and entertaining, a "study in sociology" and a novel "of romantic and enduring interest."

77 ANON. "Brief Notices." St. Louis Post-Dispatch, December 18, p. 10.

(Review of The Princess Casamassima.) The lamentable financial and literary failure of The Bostonians has evidently shown James that the art of splitting hairs does not pay, and The Princess Casamassima shows considerable improvement over that novel. It has less "fine subtle argumentation," more attempt to tell the story straightforwardly for the reader, and vigorous treatment of the characters, but James still includes "superfluous analysis" and excess verbiage.

78 ANON. "Some New Books." Albany Evening Journal, December 23, p. 3.

(Review of The Princess Casamassima.) This book offers

"a pleasing contrast" to the "wearisome" Bostonians. Both the princess and Hyacinth are "interesting and well worth portraying." The material is fresh and "handled with great skill," "there are even some dramatic passages," and James shows his familiarity with London. This story is "one of the best and most brilliant" he has produced, and indicates that when he is "on the right track" he "can do great things."

79 ANON. "Recent Fiction." Independent, 38 (December 23), 1665.
(Review of The Princess Casamassima.) With "more breadth and virility" than one would expect, James has written in this novel "scenes of actual distinctness, almost robustness," which are often, like the characters, "particularly unpleasant." The "final tragedy" is graphic with the sensationalism of an illustrated weekly. Yet, James has not given up the "persistent attention to detail" that has flawed his later novels, and this book is much too wordy, with "slipshod" sentences and paragraphs, and an apparent moral philosophy of "profound, heartless indifferentism toward life, death," and everything that concerns humanity.

80 B., H. "London Letter." Critic, 9 (December 4), 283.
The Princess Casamassima is too well written and not obvious enough to be a success. Yet, it is better to fail with James than to succeed with Mr. Shorthouse.

81 BABCOCK, W. H. "Our Gossip Column." Lippincott's, 37 (May), 554-556.
(Review.) The Bostonians is too long and not a story nor a treatise. Ransom is "the character who most nearly approaches to a real living interest," but "it is impossible to believe in him." The Bostonians are "half-sane, half-decent, yet wholly prosaic and uninteresting," and hardly one "would be considered respectable . . . in any well-ordered community." They are not typical of real Bostonians, and, although James's early works were good, no one would read The Bostonians "unless from a sense of duty or in the absolute dearth of anything better."

82 BRIDGES, ROBERT [Droch]. "Bookishness/The Christmas Prayer of the Critic." Life, 8 (December 9), 365.
(Humorous letter to Santa Claus asks that James be given humor, pathos, genius, fancy, a "patent condensing verbosity damper," and, with the rest of the Boston School, "an abundance of common humanity.")

83 _____. "Bookishness. 'Process' Literature." Life, 8

(December 23), 398.
The "whole indictment against the clinical school of novelists is summed up" recently and admirably by William Hays Ward, who says "'We are in the age of the Reproductive Processists in literature and art, . . . a school which offers to do nothing but play the passive recorder of actions and emotions, in utter unconcern as to their moral quality. . . . [These writers] do not create ideally, and . . . [they] leave out such grand themes as justice, holiness and devotion.'" With this statement in mind, to "live up to the principles of realism" one should "revise his nomenclature" to include "such terms as the 'Howells Heliotype,' the 'James Photogravure,' the 'Zola Electrotype,'" and discuss their novels "as clever semi-mechanical processes" rather than literature. To "carry out the trade idea," there should be "vigorous competition" in which the "Howells' Heliotype company should underbid the James' Photogravure," until one company absorbs the other and "a great fiction monopoly" eventually is created, followed by a Congressional investigation.

84 EGAN, MAURICE F. Note. Catholic World, 43 (April), 130.
The Bostonians is "a dismal failure."

85 _____. Review. Catholic World, 43 (July), 560-561.
The Bostonians "has received a great deal of attention" but one gets the impression that nobody has read "this colossal and long-drawn-out analysis of minute emotions except the author himself." After the three hundredth page of "masterly inactivity" the fate of the hero becomes "a matter of indifference," and the ending rewards the reader "scantily."

*86 FAWCETT, EDGAR. "Henry James's Novels." Princeton Review, 14 (April), 59-68.
(Unlocated. Cited in Ricks.)

87 HAWTHORNE, JULIAN. "Lowell in a Chatty Mood." New York World, October 24, p. 9.
(Interview with James Russell Lowell.) Lowell likes "James personally very much," and liked The Bostonians, but thinks The Princess Casamassima James's best work and "could have run away with the Princess myself." Lowell feels James's "great virility" in The Portrait of a Lady and even more in The Princess Casamassima, but liked Hawthorne least of all James's works because James could not understand and get into sympathy with his subject.

88 HAZELTINE, MAYO WILLIAMSON. Review of The Bostonians. New

York Sun, April 4, p. 4.

In The Bostonians James "seems to have determined to repel, once for all, the hackneyed imputations of painstaking emptiness and strenuous superficiality," and this novel "is nothing if not earnest," its world "the converse of the world" of "commonplace characters and trivial aspects of life" allegedly found in his previous works. For James to "devote himself to the portrayal of such types" as are found in The Bostonians "was of itself a positive advance and a veritable honor . . . like the assumption of the toga virilis," the "resolve of an artist already proficient in genre painting to risk his fame in the grand style." He is not entirely successful, but never insincere or condescending to his subjects. Miss Birdseye "is alive," reveals "the presence of a master's handiwork," "touches the highest level of a novelist's achievement," and is "one of the most veracious, impressive, and memorable [portraits] in contemporary fiction." Olive is "less interesting," "less distinct," and "sexless," and James makes some important factual errors.

89 ME, GEORGE W. "By the Way . . . The Forthcoming Magazine./ Some Advice." Life, 8 (September 30), 192.

(Humorous item.) The editor of a new magazine should "eschew the primeval joke of the Editor's Drawer, dropping into his basket the while such delicate squibs as the 'Bostonians'" and cryptic poetry.

90 PAYNE, WILLIAM MORTON. Review of The Bostonians. Dial, 7 (May), 14-15.

Current American novelists give "a painful sense" of their limitations. The character types in The Bostonians are "so entirely abnormal as to prevent them from reflecting in any degree the character of Boston people, or . . . of any people as a class," and Ransom the Mississippian is "the only person in it who has much human reality." The book is "very long" and "eminently uneventful," and James not only is "wearisomely minute in his own analysis" but allows "his characters to imitate him in this respect," producing "a mass of analysis of trifling things . . . burdened by its own excessive weight, a collection of more or less felicitous expressions, . . . and a generally accurate use of English." If a novel "were merely an exercise in style, 'The Bostonians' would be a marked success."

91 _____. Review of The Princess Casamassima. Dial, 7 (December), 189.

This work illustrates James's merits and defects, which are "intimately bound up together." It would be hard to overpraise the "admirable finish" of his details, but the "main lines" of his work are nebulous, He has here taken a "new departure" from his usual and by now played out "vein of social trifling." If the admirable analytic quality of this book could be combined with the "admirable narrative quality" of Mr. Black's Sunrise, the product would be "one of the best of modern novels." Though The Princess Casamassima cannot be compared with "such delicate and inimitable trifles" as Daisy Miller, it should be foremost among James's longer, more serious works.

92 PESSIMO [pseud.]. "Authors' Children." Houston Post, January 28, p. 6.

(Item from Chicago Times.) Julian Hawthorne and James are among the very few authors who have inherited literary talent from their fathers.

93 RICHARDSON, S. D. "Henry James as a Novelist." Harvard Monthly, 2 (April), 59-68.

(A general assessment of James's work, which considers him and Howells the leading and most representative American novelists currently writing.) Evaluated on the criteria of the tenets of realism, James's descriptions are uninteresting; his characterizations "intensely analytical," tedious, and superficial; his plot "mechanism" lacking unity, purpose, and incident; and his intention to give "a true conception of human life" unfulfilled. His reflection of "good society" is too relentlessly accurate and thus distorts. His work embodies and he exemplifies a dominant spirit of his age, the preponderance of intellect over emotion and soul, and therefore he is not great.

94 ROGERS, W. A. "The Modern Novel." Life, 7 (May 20), [288-289].

(Cartoon. James and Howells are performing autopsy or brain surgery, hunting for nothing.)

95 _____. "Literature at Low Tide." Life, 8 (September 9), 148-149.

(Cartoon. The booth occupied by "Henry Games" at the writers' carnival is the "Thin-Type Gallery.")

96 SCUDDER, HORACE E. Review of The Bostonians. Atlantic Monthly, 57 (June), 851-857.

James, Howells, and F. Marion Crawford are presently "the most distinctly professional novelists in America," and faithfully entertain the public. James's book is not a serious study of the "woman question" but is "rather a study of the particular woman question in this book." The portrayals of Olive, Miss Birdseye, Mrs. Farrinder, and the Tarrants "have never been excelled" by James. Except for Miss

Birdseye, whose "pathetic nobility" James admired and portrayed with "personal tenderness," and who is "the one redeeming feature of the book" considered in its "humane aspects," the characters are "either ignoble . . . or . . . repellant [sic] for other reasons," and James "does not love them," although he is interested enough to analyze them. But when this interest leads him "to push his characters too near the brink of nature," one hesitates, as with "accepting the relation between" Olive and Verena "as either natural or reasonable." James's "exhaustive reflections" approach caricaturing the subject, the ending providing "an almost indecent exposure" of Olive's mind. James's manner is "almost too familiar" and his "reporting the mind" of "his baser characters" adds to "the general effect of slouchiness" in much of the book. The book's web is "spun" fine, it has a strong conception underlying it, the material is fresh, separate passages are clever, and Miss Birdseye's death scene is a "consummate success," but there is in the work a "sorry waste." Yet, James, Howells, and Crawford deserve public gratitude for making "positive additions to the sum of pleasure" in this world.

97 SHEPPERD, ELI. "An Alabamian's Opinion on 'The Bostonians.'" Boston Evening Transcript, April 1, p. 6.

(Letter to the Editor.) James's portrayal of the Southerner is so authentic that James must have encountered him somewhere. He shows genius in his portrayal of Verena and her parents, and tells his story as Ransom courts Verena, "without undue haste" or "uncouth exertion," "with sustained but not aggressive effort" and "well-grounded self-confidence," attaining the victory in "the splendid denouement, this sparkling last chapter, set like a jewel in the rounded whole of his story," which is itself "like a precious golden gem-set circlet," with "neither defined beginning nor end."

98 TEMPLETON [pseud.]. Review of Century. Hartford Daily Courant, January 4, p. 1.

The Bostonians lacks freshness and is James's least attractive novel. So far, The Princess Casamassima is better.

99 ______. "Boston Correspondence. . . . Literary." Hartford Daily Courant, February 27, p. 1.

(Review of Atlantic Monthly.) The "sufficiently odd" subject of The Princess Casamassima "might have been made more interesting," and the only entertaining character so far is Milicent Henning.

100 WHEELER, ANDREW C. [Nym Crinkle]. Review of The Bostonians. New York World, March 28, p. 12.

Members of James's school are not storytellers but "entertaining lecturers who discuss character." In The Bostonians James provides "a marvellously fine analysis of two women, and has signally failed in the creation and adjustment of the incidents, which, in the hands of a good storyteller, would have elicited and illustrated the motives and springs of action, which this author requires interminable pages of explanation to make clear." With "complacency and ingenuity," the characters neglect the action for metaphysics. James indulges his "hairsplitting tendencies" through "whole pages of subspeculation, side lights, surmises, subtle explanations" between "the intention and the consummation of the most inevitable and obvious acts," which, once committed, explain themselves. The novel becomes "a statement of processes, not an exhibition of results"; Verena "wears a disembodied air," is "bloodless," "a phenomenon rather than a type"; and James's English "is more copious than exact."

1887

1 ANON. "Books and Authors." Atlanta Constitution, January 2, p. 13.

(Review of Century.) In essays like his piece on the French actor Coquelin James shows his "peculiar style and methods . . . at their best."

2 ANON. "The Minister's Charge." Literary World, 18 (January 8), 4-5.

(Review of Howells's The Minister's Charge.) James is "a careful, almost an intuitive, observer" who holds himself above the characters whom he studies "with the elaborate patience of scientific research." Yet, he keeps "an even balance of values" and gives each person, motive, action, and speech "a definitely assigned place."

3 ANON. "The Princess Casamassima." Literary World, 18 (January 8), 5.

James has never produced a stronger work. This novel has "more flesh and blood" than any of his others, except possibly Roderick Hudson, and "the field is broader, the characters are more diversified, [and] the central theme is more clearly defined" than one expects in James's books. The narrative is "firmly outlined and well-rounded," the motives for action abundant, the movement steady if not always swift, and the climax distinct. James's method is still "hard and dry," and he portrays his impressions with as little emotion as possible, but his realism is "always delicate." He suppresses "the coarse and brutal elements of nature." He studies the effects of socialism on the individual rather than on the mass. Perhaps the most real character is Millicent Henning, Hyacinth's fate has pathos, and the "inevitable sequence" of his career is "a triumph of artistic comprehension."

4 ANON. "Books and Authors." Atlanta Constitution, January 9, p. 2.
(Review of Blackwood's Magazine.) The review of The Princess Casamassima in the December 1886 Blackwood's is "charming" and suggests that James "knows even less about English life than he does about" American life. For James there is "no real life" in this country, and The Bostonians shows that this "very charming writer" has "no real or even definite grip on America." It is no wonder that he exhausts his genius "on the trivial and the infinitesimal."

5 ANON. Note. Atlanta Constitution, January 16, p. 13.
Someone has written a parody sequel chapter to The Bostonians which compensates for James's indefinite ending and in which Ransom elopes with Mrs. Luna and Verena returns to Olive and the stage and then marries Burrage. Written by "Henrietta James" and cheaply priced, it "will probably have a larger circulation" than The Bostonians, since a last chapter with "a definite conclusion" is "much more interesting . . . than a great number of chapters with no ending."

6 ANON. "Books and Magazines." Boston Beacon, January 29.
(Review of Lippincott's.) Anonymous writers warn Mary N. Murfree, James, and others that "their work is not entirely satisfactory" to those who admire astonishing heroes, cry over novels, and want illusion rather than truth. Yet, truth is poetical, and fiction is "a somewhat precarious commodity."

7 ANON. "'The Princess Casamassima.'" Critic, 10 (January 29), 51-52.
This book is misnamed because the princess is first lost in "a snarl of interminable analysis" and then a foil for the "rare and charming" Hyacinth. This "socialistic drama" fails because of the jerky narrative caused by the serial form, and the "inconsequence and inconclusiveness" of the ending, but it is "endlessly delightful" to lovers of "interpretations, of emotions analytically examined, of hairs radiantly split." This novel is "an entrancing bundle of emotions and conversations, of eccentric freaks of the analytical imagination," and of conspirators "realistically handled." In it James "apparently bids definitive farewell to America."

1887

8 ANON. "Our Monthly Gossip." Lippincott's, 39 (February), 184.
(Discussion of Howells's remarks on Russian and American novelists.) "An uproar of dissent" arose over Howells's earlier statement (1882.39) that James's literary style is finer than that of any other novelist.

9 ANON. "Four New Novels." Epoch, 1 (February 11), 19.
(Review of The Princess Casamassima and Mary N. Murfree's [Charles Egbert Craddock] In the Clouds.) Christina Light was "an original sort of American girl." James has here taken a new departure, and his first three chapters suggest Dickens, but, unlike Dickens, he treats his material "in a remote and loftily critical way." Hyacinth and Millicent are "well and powerfully sketched," but the tale is too long and wordy. It has a "curious and exceptional interest," and James should research the "uncommon lives of 'common' people" in a more popular and sympathetic way. Miss Murfree's book "handles practical affairs with even more vigor" than James can muster.

10 ANON. "Book-Talk." Lippincott's, 39 (March), 359.
(Review of The Princess Casamassima and W. D. Howells's The Minister's Charge.) This novel is filled with clever, even brilliant, descriptions and conversations, but they inspire not much interest, and the characters simulate real life but are mechanical manikins. The situation would seem to have material enough for "stirring incident," a moral, conviction, or warning, but James merely observes with "the calm, superior air of one who has outgrown emotion and enthusiasm." One sighs for the methods of Dickens and Thackeray, which Howells considers "of the past." Howells is a humorist and "takes a more humane interest in his fellows" than does James, who has plenty of wit but almost no humor.

11 ANON. "Books and Authors." Atlanta Constitution, March 20, p. 14.
James and Howells write entertaining books, and have humor and a beautiful style, but, unlike H. Rider Haggard, they "touch neither the hearts nor the sensibilities of the great public." Haggard upsets their controversial "pet theories" about the novel, and is very popular. People do not go to novels for the trivialities and commonplaces of real life.

12 ANON. "The Gentleman in Modern Fiction." Atlanta Constitution, March 27, p. 8.
(Editorial.) James has never portrayed a Boston gentleman. The "only real gentleman he ever drew" was Mrs.

Touchett, who refused to associate with the other characters in The Portrait of a Lady.

13 ANON. "Books and Authors. . . . Gossip and Criticism." Atlanta Constitution, March 27, p. 13.
Maurice Thompson protests in the Independent against "analytical realism." According to him the "truth" the analytical novelists purport to give is "'unpicturesque and uninteresting,'" without uplift, and it inspires neither enthusiasm nor patriotism.

14 ANON. "Editor's Study. . . . Monthly Record of Current Events." Harper's, 74 (April), 829.
(Review of The Princess Casamassima.) The Princess Casamassima is "a great novel," James's greatest, and "incomparably the greatest novel of the year in our language." It has no faults, the drama works "simply and naturally," the "causes and effects are logically related," the "theme is made literature without ceasing to be life," the characters are striking, and the book has the "easy" breadth and generous scope of the best Russian work. James shows sympathy for his characters without gushing over them, and manages his notable knowledge of London well. His book is much better than W. H. Mallock's The Old Order Changes.

15 ANON. "Books and Authors." Atlanta Constitution, April 3, p. 13.
Rider Haggard and Robert Louis Stevenson have shown everyone but the critics that the public welcomes heroic, robust, healthy, picturesque fiction. The discussion between "the romancers and the trivialists" should be informative to young writers. Robert Browning will have Henry James and Sir James Steven for neighbors in De Vere gardens.

16 ANON. "The Decay of Sentiment." Atlantic Monthly, 60 (July), 75.
The triumphs of realistic prose "fail to lift their readers out of themselves" like the masterpieces of the past. We appreciate The Bostonians' "minute perfections," but can wait to finish it. Daisy Miller could never "charm a gouty leg."

17 ANON. "Fiction Outdone." Atlanta Constitution, August 7, p. 13.
(Brief reference in item from New York World.) While novelists of the new school are seeking with their little microscopes "molecules of human nature and experience," Nature turns out romances. "Real life is the worst antagonist of the realists." This Spanish-American international

episode would make James's or Howells's blood curdle "if it were told in fiction."

18 ANON. "Finance." Life, 10 (September 1), 124.
"Henry James always Howells when he is hurt. This is a joke that requires thought to be appreciated."

19 ANON. "Briefs About Books. . . . Literary Notes." Atlanta Constitution, September 11, p. 4.
The Chicago News calls the work of the analytical novelists "'the Flub-dub of mental vivisection.'"

20 ANON. Brief reference. Life, 10 (September 15), 1.
(Criticism of Howells's praise of Tolstoy.) When Howells tried "to dwarf the art of Thackeray by using Henry James as a unit of measure, Life fell upon him," as it has many times since, always for good reason.

21 ANON. "A Literary Controversy/Mr. Maurice Thompson Defends Himself Against the Abuse of a Boston Paper." Indianapolis Journal, September 18, p. 11.
Maurice Thompson refers to Howells's November 1882 (1882.39) statement that James's fiction is a finer art than Dickens's and Thackeray's. He also mentions Howells's praise of The Princess Casamassima, which Thompson finds a "society story" and "not American."

22 ANON. "A Passing Fancy." Atlanta Constitution, October 2, p. 14.
(Editorial.) The present "craze for Russian novels . . . is confined to a small circle" composed mainly of "admirers of the Howells-James school of literature."

23 BEERS, HENRY A. An Outline Sketch of American Literature. New York: Chautauqua Press, pp. 269-279. Rpt. 1888, 1889, 1890. Hunt, 1891, 1893, 1896.
James and Howells are "the two favorite novelists whose work has done more than anything else to shape the movement of recent fiction." Their novels are analytic and realistic. In clever sketches James sees both Americans and Europeans from a foreign perspective, and interprets them to each other not through sympathy, but through subtle contrasts. He maintains the "critical attitude." Roderick Hudson is not his most characteristic work, but is his "most powerful" in its grasp of elementary passion. As James's "faculty of minute observation and his realistic objectivity" have increased, so has his "uncomfortable coldness." His art focuses more on "mere manners," less on character and passion, and the heart is left out. Portraits of Places is

"among the most delightful" of travel books. The Bostonians is "the latest and one of the cleverest of his fictions." Howells is fonder of Americans, and his characters are more lovable.

24 BOYESEN, HJALMAR HJORTH. "Why We Have No Great Novelists." Forum, 2 (February), 615-622.
To be popular, novelists write for young women, and therefore are silent about "all the vital things of life." For example, the only "political incident" in all of Howells and James is in The Princess Casamassima.

25 _____. "Why We Have No Great Novelists." American, 13 (February 5), 253-254.

26 BRIDGES, ROBERT [Droch]. "Bookishness[.] . . . The Old and the New Style of Fiction." Life, 9 (February 3), 62.
(Reaction to Howells's remarks in February Harper's about American short stories.) American short stories deal with women's domestic world, "very few men of health, grit and force can see anything intellectual or manly in the weaving of stories for effeminate readers," and the "stalwart young men of to-day" have "a hearty contempt" for "the whole school of 'realists' who differentiate pretty little spasms of pride, envy or love, and imagine they are 'studying human nature.'"

27 _____. "Bookishness[.] What Books Are Made For." Life, 9 (June 23), 348.
The "whole modern school of Realists falls short of making good literature" because it does not make us forget troubles. Its "photographic methods, picturing only the visible and material realities of life, serve to intensify our sorrows, to add a pang to remorse, to make the hearthstone seem more desolate, and to raise the vision of a hopeless future."

28 _____. "Bookishness." Life, 10 (August 4), 62.
With The Bostonians James wrote himself into a two-year partial literary eclipse and semiobscurity, although during that time he published "probably his greatest work," The Princess Casamassima, which "would have made a fine reputation for an unknown man." In "the mere art of expression" James "has few living equals." His study of Hawthorne (1880) attests to his critical and literary skill, despite its offensive patronizing air. Some day "there will be a 'James revival,'" because such "consummate art of expression" will surely find renewed recognition. "His work is better than his Realistic theories."

29 _____. "Three Ghosts Who Met On Christmas Eve." Life, 10 (December 8), 325-326.

(Conversation among the ghosts of Dickens, Thackeray, and Hawthorne about the difference between their works and more recent fiction.) A man (James) has written a book to prove that Hawthorne is provincial. One wonders how many new editions of The Bostonians or The Minister's Charge or Silas Lapham "are printed for the Christmas trade." The recent writers write "from a mistaken point of view" when they put "individual life" above home and everything else. "Their hero or heroine is an intellectual prig," "self-conscious, suspicious, pharisaical," who "lives for his own advancement and dies discontented." The earlier writers remembered that home, not the individual man or woman, is the social unit and develops the best in people.

30 _____. "Bookishness[.] Something About a Little-Known Writer." Life, 10 (December 22), 361.

Mr. Deming has not sought fame and published a new book every year "filled with an affected knowledge of the world." As James would say, he "is thoroughly provincial." Breadth of view and knowledge of the world are admirable qualities, but "when gained at the sacrifice of sincerity, depth of feeling and simplicity of style, they are a heavy burden" for an author.

31 EGAN, MAURICE F. "A Chat About New Books." Catholic World, 44 (January), 554-559.

(Review of The Princess Casamassima.) James does not seem to think deeply on the issues beyond what he is writing, gives an impressionist view of socialism, and "does not pretend to see a remedy anywhere" for British social ills. Yet, that he has Prince Casamassima say that only the church can save the world "from humanity without a God" gives hope that American writers whose philosophy "begins and ends with Schopenhauer" will see the importance of the church to civilization. The Princess Casamassima is the best long work James has ever done. The princess has no heart, principle, constancy, or morality, but is "clever and interesting." The studies of the socialists "are exquisitely careful and true," the "play of character on character is direct," and, though there is no story, there is "little tiresome analysis" and none of James's obnoxious or tiresome affectations. It is "regrettable" that James "should prefer realism to idealization," and present his material with such indifference.

32 HAWTHORNE, JULIAN. Confessions and Criticisms. Boston: Ticknor & Co., pp. 61-70, 75-77, 87.

(Chapter 2 is a revision of 1884.84.) James and Howells "represent what is carefullest and newest in American fiction," and "every critic of American novelists must reckon with them" (see 1886.52).

33 LOGAN, ANNIE ROBERTSON (MACFARLANE). "Recent Novels." Nation, 44 (February 10), 123-124.

(Review of The Princess Casamassima and W. D. Howells's The Minister's Charge.) This novel shakes one's image of James as "the chief apostle of that restricted realism" which denies or ignores the influence of extraordinary people and incidents on the general course of things. James's "persistent desire to see the truth, and his marvelous ability for telling it" make him now a "realist" in the true sense. He shows "a versatility and power hardly hinted at in his former work," "his wit and sarcasm are agreeably tempered by a tenderness and even intensity of feeling" hitherto repressed, and he extends and stimulates our understanding of and sympathy for humanity. Millicent Henning is "typical," James may be accused of treating socialism frivolously but is actually earnest, and he may also be charged with "supersubtle" overanalysis, but writes in fact with "precision, elegance, and distinction" of style. A comparison of this book with Howells's The Minister's Charge shows many similarities, but James "has given us some comfort" while Howells makes us gloomier.

34 THOMPSON, MAURICE. "Studies of Prominent Novelists./. . . No. 3--William Dean Howells." Book News, 6 (November), 93.

With Howells's essay on James (1882.39), these two novelists gained British and American attention.

35 UNDERHILL, ANDREW F. "Lessons in Literature." Life, 9 (March 3), 120.

(Humorous item. In mock dialogue about Howells, brief reference to James's essay on Howells.)

36 _____. "Lessons in Literature." Life, 9 (April 14), 207.

(Humorous dialogue spoofs James's liking for England, his friendship with Howells, his tendency to analysis, the sometimes tedious length of his books, and their lack of plot.)

37 WELCH, PHILIP H. "From Advance Sheets." Life, 9 (May 12, 1887?), 262-263.

(Humorous item. Parody of James and Howells entitled "The Bostonese.")

1888

1 ANON. "Negro Myths. . . . May Magazines." Atlanta Constitution, April 29, p. 12.
(Review of Atlantic Monthly.) It is a relief that James brings the "very dull and almost intolerable" Aspern Papers to a close.

2 ANON. "Recent Publications." New Orleans Daily Picayune, May 6, p. 7.
(Review of Century.) James pursues "in his elegant dilettante fashion," his eminently social studies in the first part of "The Liar."

3 ANON. "Recent Publications." New Orleans Daily Picayune, May 27, p. 14.
(Review of W. D. Howells's The Minister's Charge mentions James's praise of it. Review of June 1888 Harper's mentions "Two Countries.")

4 ANON. "Reviews . . . Henry James's 'Partial Portraits.'" Critic, 12 (June 9), 278-279.
(Review.) The international copyright situation justifies the expatriation which provokes unfriendly comments on James's works. James's own critical essays have "an undeniable charm, if not precisely a fascination," half convincing even to the reader with an opposing point of view. It is James's personal bias that provides the charm especially in the Emerson essay, and less so in the one on Daudet.

5 ANON. "Literature." Louisville Courier-Journal, June 10, p. 20.
(Review of Century.) In the June Century James's "extraordinary contribution" "The Liar" is concluded. It is "utterly unworthy" of its author.

6 ANON. "New Publications/A Novelist's Criticism." New York Times, June 10, p. 12.
(Review of Partial Portraits.) With Matthew Arnold gone, it would be hard to find "so fine and full a gift of appreciation" as James shows in this excellent, disinterested criticism. As in his fiction, James renders his own impression "with all its detail," and his method is the same as Howells's. The literary skill of his stories overcomes the grotesque improbability of some of their plots. The essay on de Maupassant is "singularly skillful and thoughtful."

7 ANON. Review of Partial Portraits. Boston Beacon, June 16, p. 3.

James has not gone far enough in praising Emerson's contribution to American letters. Emerson's clear and direct language is preferable to "the current emphasis on artistry."

8 ANON. "Literature. Partial Portraits." Louisville Courier-Journal, June 17, p. 19.
Written by one who thoroughly comprehends the art of novel writing and appreciates it in others, these essays are charming. The most interesting is on Turgenev, and it is curious that a man like James, who so admires Turgenev and Daudet, also enjoys the works of Robert Louis Stevenson. (Quotation from Stevenson in praise of James.) These essays "are all extremely interesting."

9 ANON. "New Publications. . . . Partial Portraits." Detroit Free Press, June 17, p. 10.
Though interesting, the sketches in Partial Portraits are in almost every instance caricatures, "exaggerations . . . of salient characteristics," rather than proportioned pictures. James's "habit of . . . mind" makes such distortion inevitable.

10 ANON. Note. Portland Morning Oregonian, June 17, p. 1.
James's "Two Countries" in the June Harper's is "extraordinary," so "full of clever things about nothing that, lacking contrast, it becomes dull," and the "ridiculous calamity" that ends it excites an interest it does not deserve. The story's "air of unreality takes away all its sting."

11 ANON. "Mr. James's Criticisms. An Admirer of Art for Art's Sake. Partial Portraits." New York Tribune, June 17, p. 10.
These sketches are "more genial" than those in French Poets and Novelists, and "even more charming." However one may disagree with his methods, one must recognize the readability, "beauty and subtlety" of his critical style, and he is "at his best" in this kind of work. Yet, here as in his fiction, James is like a scientific specialist and lacks the power to synthesize. In fiction he dissects characters "brilliantly and incisively," and writes with humor, irony, and refinement, yet leaves an overall effect of vagueness. His criticism is fascinating, delicate, and subtle, but lacks "solidity and virility of belief." His views are elusive when we try to gather them "under some comprehensive head," but if any principle emerges, it is an amoral "relativity of art" which accepts all views, however depraved, that are faithful to reality and gracefully expressed. For example, he fails to point out the moral deficiencies of

French writers like de Maupassant, and to distinguish between negating moral teaching and accepting immoral teaching.

12 ANON. Review of Partial Portraits. Independent, 40 (June 21), 786.

These essays are "remarkably clever, remarkably brilliant," yet remarkably disappointing. They are richly suggestive, but inconclusive.

13 ANON. "Literary News." New York Daily Graphic, June 23, p. 874.

In the continuation of "A London Life" in the July Scribner's, James's account of "an American beauty married to a swell Englishman" is "just the information" for which many of us "are hungering and thirsting." James "is at his cleverest on his chosen ground."

14 ANON. "In the English Papers." Literary World, 19 (June 23), 203.

(Quoted favorable comment on James's criticism, from the Athenaeum.)

15 ANON. Review of Scribner's. St. Louis (Mo.) Republic, June 23, p. 12.

In the July 1888 issue James will begin a four-part story, "which promises well."

16 ANON. "Bits About Books." Atlanta Constitution, June 24, p. 18.

(Note. Quoted comments from the Athenaeum on James as novelist and critic.) "The Athenaeum rather aptly calls Henry James 'the novelist with an outlook on letters instead of on life.'"

17 ANON. "The Novel Writers' Vote." Louisville Courier-Journal, June 24, p. 12.

(Editorial.) In claiming to have read every American novel, Senator Hiscock is evidently seeking the support of a neglected class, the novel writers. One "may read an occasional novel by Howells or James" or others without feeling a martyr, but a politician who reads every American novel shows "patriotic devotion which entitles him to the Presidency."

18 ANON. "James and Haggard. Two Kinds of Realism." New York Tribune, July 1, p. 10.

(Review of The Reverberator.) James's characters seem caricatures and not believable. They are bloodless and languid.

1888

19 ANON. "Books and Authors. A Sheaf of Novels." Boston Daily Advertiser, July 3, p. 2.
(Review of The Reverberator.) The Reverberator has in common with Robert Louis Stevenson's The Black Arrow "great literary charm," but is unlike it in every other respect. James's book shows the truth that for many people life is not mainly incidents but is, rather, a series of states of mind. The plot is slight, but no words are wasted, and the story is entertaining, with humor and pathos. It is not merely an admirable and "clever social sketch," but is in addition a fairly dignified criticism of an aspect of modern life.

20 ANON. "Current Literature." Indianapolis Journal, July 5, p. 10.
(Review of Partial Portraits.) This collection presents "an interesting literary menu," and "The Art of Fiction" is in James's "characteristic style."

21 ANON. "Reviews." American, 16 (July 7), 184-185.
(Review of Partial Portraits.) These "delightful, suggestive, discriminating" essays are full of "careful insight and minute appreciation," "keen and penetrating" insight, given with "a studied, highly finished expression," fine strokes. Sometimes, though, the "very highly cultivated voice" sounds "thin, strained, and artificial" when it should be "more simple and direct."

22 ANON. "Henry James' Mr. Flack. This Boston Englishman Cruelly Punctures Our Conceit." Chicago Tribune, July 7, p. 10.
Revealing the ancient and ongoing antipathy of British toward Americans, the English critics like James because of his condemnation of Americans, while American critics express hostility brought on by James's defiance of "American amour propre." James has never portrayed a wholly pleasing American type, and now the "odious" George Flack is the "lowest degradation" to which James's "malevolent" skill can condemn the American type. This revenge on the American press should bring him satisfaction, but, though his portrait is clever, his book proves "the worthlessness of malice in ideal art" and in presenting such detestable Americans James has behaved about as nobly as Flack does. The English critics will find the story "true, pungent, admirable," humorous, and faithful to the American character.

23 ANON. "Mr. James's Partial Portraits." Literary World, 19 (July 7), 212.
(Review.) James's criticism both entertains and instructs, brings up "a multitude of new and suggestive ideas," and has

a distinct point of view. He misses the whole Emerson, but is better than George Eliot. The "unspeakably clever" way he handles the unsavory side of de Maupassant is "a triumph of suggestion." Perhaps the best chapter is on Turgenev.

24 ANON. "Henry James' New Story." St. Louis Globe Democrat, July 8, p. 22.
(Review of The Reverberator.) James is an acquired taste not popular with the general public. He has low expectations of human nature, and his characters are neither great, to be taken seriously, nor particularly well realized, despite their minute portrayal. (Plot summary.)

25 ANON. "Book Notes." New York Sun, July 8, p. 4.
(Review of The Reverberator.) The Dossons are "purely artificial studies of character, without force or originality." Their sort is not common in America, and George Flack is "an exaggerated but clever specimen." The French characters are more successful, and the hold of the head of a French family upon its younger members is "rather felicitously illustrated."

26 ANON. "Partial Portraits." Epoch, 3 (July 13), 456-457.
(Review.) James is one of the most thoroughly equipped literary men of the day, showing in these essays a "largeness of view, delicacy and fineness of perception, warm sympathy, and a power of generous appreciation" given even to writers with methods the reverse of his own. The study of Stevenson is "particularly good," and all writers and critics should read "The Art of Fiction." The book is the best collection of literary essays published in some time.

27 ANON. "Recent Literature. . . . 'The Reverberator.'" Chicago Times, July 14, p. 12.
Admirers of James will be disappointed, because despite the author's skill, the "minutely analyzed" people in this book are "not very interesting." Mr. Dosson is unusually mild and nonassertive for an American speculator, and Flack and Delia are the most nearly American. James introduces too many sentences with "well."

28 ANON. New Publications . . . A Study of Foreign Americans." New York Times, July 15, p. 12.
(Review of The Reverberator.) James presents "curious specimens" such as the "characterless" Mr. Dosson, who seems reduced to "imbecility" by his European experience, and who with George Flack shows "the lack of refinement common to average" Americans. Francie Dosson seems American only in her "superficial ways and speeches," has too little spirit

and individuality to be a type, and is much more "ignorant, listless, and obtuse" than most American girls. James satirizes and is at his best with the Proberts, who illustrate the truth that Americans who live abroad often acquire the bad qualities of foreign societies. This book has a moral directed at "pernicious" society journals. It is "able, though longwinded," and interesting enough without "having great sustained interest," but it is not very pleasing.

29 ANON. "'Partial' and 'Ignorant' Essays." Springfield (Mass.) Republican, July 15, p. 4.
(Editorial review of Partial Portraits.) James's titles and his style are "neat and carefully touched," what he says is "worth noting, but hardly worth discussing," and his "verdict is individual and sincere, but not broad" or reliable. He has the style, but not the comprehensive point of view of the cosmopolitan. His sketch of Du Maurier is charming, he says incongruously "clever and pleasant" things about Emerson, and does George Eliot less than justice because of a grievance against her. The "clearest and most pleasing portrait" is of Turgenev. James does not worship these writers, but nonetheless treats them with respect, criticizing "gently and courteously." His occasional "playful satire" is "vastly engaging," and he "entertains more than he instructs." The lazier essays of Richard Dowling are a relief after these more rigorous ones.

30 ANON. "Literary Notices." Hartford Courant, July 18, p. 2.
(Review of The Reverberator.) This is incidental rather than serious work, and will not enhance James's reputation, although it has "marks of his unquestionable genius."

31 ANON. "Reviews." American, 16 (July 21), 217-218.
(Review of The Reverberator.) The Proberts are presented with James's "utmost skill." He is too hard on American journalism, when the British papers are more offensive. Yet, although James's Americans are "blundering, dull, insensible to the finer phases of life," he gives them "the substantial virtues."

32 ANON. "James's Partial Portraits." Nation, 47 (July 26), 75.
(Review.) James's criticism is here very agreeable, alert, intelligent, and graceful, yet it discontents the reader with its substitution of personal impressions for conclusive judgments. James is perhaps excessively tolerant of France and hard on Emerson's New England.

33 ANON. Review of The Reverberator. Boston Beacon, July 28, p. 3.

This is "a terrible picture of American society journalism," but is also "a capital treatment" of the subject, and "extremely well done."

34 ANON. "New Books. . . . Latest Novels." Cincinnati Commercial Gazette, July 28, p. 6.
(Review of The Reverberator.) Almost all the Americans in this book are "absurd and vulgar." James is a literary tory who portrays his Americans "to please the English public," and although Flack is a caricature, Francie Dosson hardly rational, and her father "wooden," the most objectionable American in the novel is James himself. Perhaps the foreign reviewers will console him for his readers' disapproval.

35 ANON. "Literature. . . . 'Partial Portraits.'" San Francisco Chronicle, July 29, p. 7.
These essays are finished pieces of literary work, most of which open all sides of their subjects. As a novelist James is "too coldly analytic," lacks humor, and does not tell stories, but as a critic he has few faults. He is the ablest American literary critic, and applies the methods of Sainte-Beuve more skillfully than any other American. These portraits are clear, finely individualized, and suggest new possibilities in familiar works. The best of the group is the one on Turgenev. James treads on dangerous ground, however, when he expresses tolerance for the "lubricity" of the foul tales of de Maupassant, and advocates only aesthetic and not ethical judgments of literature.

36 ANON. "Books and Authors." Christian Union, 38 (August 2), 130.
(Review of The Reverberator.) This book has James's usual fine touch, delicate workmanship, "clever contrast of character," "faithful realism," and need for "a warmer human interest and a brighter humor." The reader is absorbed, but feels dissatisfied and that the characters are not true types. The satire is "very keen," but the facts are not credible.

37 ANON. Review of The Reverberator. Churchman, 58 (August 11), 173.
James has discovered a new, international motif for "the comedy of real life which he describes so delicately and well." The climax is witty but not farcical, the characterization skillful, the style faultless, and the workmanship the finest, but the work is somehow hollow and superficial, lacking any philosophy or standard but that of artistic perfection.

1888

38 ANON. "Gossip About Books." Minneapolis Tribune, August 19, p. 7.
(Comments on Hawthorne in review of Social Life and Literature Fifty Years Ago.) The author of the book being reviewed tries to refute James's and George Parsons Lathrop's adverse criticisms of the social and literary atmosphere in which Hawthorne and Irving were raised by showing that age's intellectual supremacy.

39 ANON. "The Reverberator." Epoch, 4 (August 24), 55.
(Review.) As good a critic as James should recognize that this book is "dull, commonplace, and often vulgar," the most unsatisfactory of all his works, and a failure. The story is uninteresting, the characters "odious and despicable," "feeble, flaccid, and lifeless." The heroine is stupid and weak.

40 ANON. "Literature. . . . 'The Reverberator.'" San Francisco Chronicle, August 26, p. 7.
The portraits in this book are "broad caricatures," and will be even more offensive to Americans than Daisy Miller was. The heroine is weak and insipid, lacking mental and moral backbone, common sense, and self-assertion. Her father is even worse, almost an imbecile. James has not observed such types as these, but has simply magnified certain traits to create characters "no nearer real life than some of Dickens' grotesque creations." The story moves sluggishly, and "great literary art has been wasted on a subject utterly inadequate." The "only artistic thing" in the book is Gaston's struggle between custom and affection.

41 ANON. Review of Scribner's Magazine. New York Daily Graphic, August 28, p. 454.
James concludes his "brilliant 'London Life.'"

42 ANON. "The Newest Books." Book Buyer, 5 (September), 313.
(Review of Partial Portraits.) This noteworthy and permanently valuable volume shows James at his delightful best, and goes far to prove true Stevenson's assertion that James is "the most distinguished," as well as the most promising, of American authors. The aptness of the characterization and the subtlety of the discernment are remarkable. The thought is fresh and the style charming.

43 ANON. "Book Reviews./Partial Portraits." Public Opinion, 5 (September 8), 483.
(Review.) These "clearly-cut images" of literary figures are valuable, "exquisite bits of literary work," and show James to be one of the best American critics. Yet, in

keeping with his sympathy with the "fleshly realistic" French school, his novels are often not morally uplifting.

44 ANON. "Books and Authors. Literature and the Literary People." Atlanta Constitution, September 9, p. 12.

The Kansas City Times says current fiction is full of "simper, insanity and gush, . . . platitude, idiocy and drivel," but not power or imagination.

The best American novelists are the old ones, but Poe and the very American Cooper have been forgotten, and Hawthorne will be. "Nambypambyism" is now the standard. James has had the audacity to declare himself the great American novelist, but he is no more such a novelist than a fallen pine cone is a great pine tree. He is not even a novelist at all. His books are insipid, his women hysterical, and his men nonentities.

45 ANON. "Henry James's 'Reverberator.'" Critic, 13 (September 15), 123.

(Review.) Reporters should read and digest this work of "delicate and inclusive art." James rarely writes with "so direct a moral" or with "a more stinging and yet graceful sarcasm."

46 ANON. "The Reverberator." Literary World, 19 (September 29), 313.

(Review.) James always seems to choose disagreeable subjects, but at least he does here a careful, artistic, "skilled and well-proportioned" job on them. The characters are consistent, but Francie and Flack may be more caricatures than real types. James has nowhere been more "successful in carrying out a certain purpose" than in this book, which is more worthwhile than most of his recent works.

47 ANON. "Partial Portraits." Atlantic Monthly, 62 (October), 564-568.

(Review.) As a critic, James is one of a "group of pleasant and elegant essayists who are the successors of men of larger calibre, if not of finer perception." His aims are modest in this volume, yet the essays on Daudet and Maupassant are up to the level of his others on French writers, which as a whole constitute the best criticism of the French "accessible to the English reader." As in that criticism, James is inconclusive because his mind is inductive. His criticism "is almost entirely concerned with surfaces" and its great detail and frequent changes of point of view give the reader "a blurred impression," but James has vigor, pleasant wit, and alertness of mind. Taken as personal impression rather than as final judgment, his criticism shows him "one of the most excellent of literary companions." The surprising "reality and sincerity of his appreciation of Emerson" reveal a "very unusual catholicity of taste." His "charming" pages on Daudet show James "in his best mood and spirit," and are "more agreeable" than his almost partisan justification of Maupassant.

48 ANON. "Recent Novels," Nation, 47 (October 4), 273.
(Reviews of The Reverberator and Pendleton's A Virginia Inheritance.) The characters and phases of life in James's novels are typical, as they are in this one. Perhaps his strongest book, The Princess Casamassima, "missed general appreciation" because its "strange incidents" offended readers' expectations in this regard. The treatment of the Dossons is "most admirable," and in portraying Flack James neither preaches nor scolds. Francie's fortunes are narrated with "incomparable ease, grace, and brilliancy." James shows indifference to his audience.

49 ANON. "The American Novel." Portland Morning Oregonian, October 11, p. 4.
(Editorial.) The American Dickens, writer of the great American novel, will come from the West because the "strain after effect has crippled the soul of Eastern romance production," and the Boston "coterie of literature . . . is too much affected by Anglo-mania, . . . flabbiness and poverty" of intellectuality, ignorance of soil, and "inability to appreciate the true manliness and womanliness of pure American character."

50 ANON. Review of Partial Portraits. Churchman, 58 (October 13), 458.
In these attractive, interesting, capital essays, James has an artist's perceptiveness, penetration, and linguistic power. He misses nothing he looks for.

51 ANON. Review of Aristocracy. Cincinnati Commercial Gazette, October 13, p. 6.
This "ruthless sketching from life" of the English aristocracy is a decided contrast to James's "flatteries" of them.

52 ANON. "Miscellaneous." North American Review, 147 (November), 599.
(Review of The Reverberator.) This book is "rather dull and commonplace."

53 ANON. "Some New Books. . . . Book Notes." New York Sun, November 11, p. 4.

(Review of The Aspern Papers.) Though insignificant in plot and with characters of moderate quality, "The Aspern Papers" is one of James's "finest achievements," and "a masterly study of human nature and emotions." James's genius has given the trivial plot "remarkable interest," the few characters "stand out with unmistakable clearness," the catastrophe is "sharply outlined," and the Venetian setting adds a special charm.

54 ANON. "New Publications. Novels and Tales." New York Tribune, November 13, p. 8.

(Review of The Aspern Papers.) In The Aspern Papers there is "scarcely any action," not an exciting situation, and almost monotonous dialogue. The old lady's niece is simple, curious, colorless, and almost soulless. Yet, James's "unequalled skill" makes these "scanty materials" into a story with quiet humor, much "admirable psychical analysis," and "a light and delicate interest, which gives pleasure by the refined and subtle dissection" of tiny things. "Louisa Pallant" is "a curious social study," but James throws doubt over and obscures the characters of mother and daughter, and was perhaps not himself decided about them. "The Modern Warning" is not pleasing, has an inexplicable ending, and is less artistic than the other two stories.

55 ANON. "New Publications. Book Notes." Boston Evening Journal, November 16, Supp., p. 2.

(Review of The Aspern Papers.) These stories are "delicate studies," and in "The Aspern Papers" James is at his best because his "critical manner" and "delicate analysis" have an appropriate theme and "an attractive and suitable subject." "The Modern Warning" has "depth and earnestness" and "brilliancy of characterization," despite the "extravagant ending" that "turns a serious piece of writing into a farce." These stories show that James "has a power and effectiveness of literary style unsurpassed in modern fiction."

56 ANON. "New Publications." Boston Herald, November 19, p. 3.

(Review of The Aspern Papers.) James's best work is in his delineation of character. He can make the most unpromising people interesting with just the right amount of elaboration, and a "finish and touch" both pleasing and unexpected. The title story makes good use of slight materials, and each one of these "admirable studies" has its "own special attraction."

57 ANON. "The Aspern Papers." Epoch, 4 (November 23), 290-291.

(Review.) James's works seem to open "an infinite vista

of subtle character study" which turns out to be a "clever trick." His theory of art is Greek, and he shuns action for the "graceful, icy pose." This book has dustier background and dimmer people than its predecessors, but its descriptions of Venice are charming. Too often, critics berate James for not presenting "a large and inspiring view of life," which he does not profess to do. His literary art has a high quality whose value no shortcomings can destroy. His novels, giving "the elaborated small views" of life, are worth serious attention and valuable to historians, psychologists, and social scientists.

58 ANON. Review of The Aspern Papers. Churchman, 58 (November 24), 643.
These stories are fascinating and exasperating, with unsatisfactory endings. They have a peculiar, delicate charm, a haunting and piquant flavor of unrealized adventure.

59 ANON. "Literary." Chicago Inter-Ocean, November 24, p. 11.
(Review of The Aspern Papers.) These are three of James's "best short stories."

60 ANON. "Talk about New Books." Catholic World, 48 (December), 402-405.
(Review of The Reverberator.) This book was worth writing and is worth reading, two things not always true of James's work. Yet, his technique is always admirable. Though read by "comparatively few," James is "talked about by almost everybody." In this clever piece of workmanship he deserves that the talk should be entirely favorable.

61 ANON. "Literary Notes." Hartford Times, December 7, p. 3.
In the December Century, James "writes with full knowledge and critical enthusiasm a paper of which the pregnant title is 'London.'"

62 ANON. Review of The Aspern Papers. Detroit Free Press, December 8, p. 3.
These "very interesting" stories are written in James's "own graceful style."

63 ANON. "Minor Notices." Literary World, 19 (December 8), 451.
(Review of The Aspern Papers.) These stories have that "air of high breeding," found in all James's works, which "lends attraction" to books of little substance. The Aspern Papers is a "delicate, refined, and long-drawn-out treatment of a slight incident. Lady Chasemore's suicide in "The Modern Warning" is shocking and not credible.

64 ANON. "Recent Publications." New Orleans Daily Picayune, December 9, p. 10.
(Review of Century.) James's article on London in the December Century "goes less to style" than is usual for him, yet it is readable. James treats London with a "man of the world air" and makes the reader feel of the world too.

65 ANON. "Literature in the Republican." Springfield (Mass.) Republican, December 9, p. 4.
James is one of a number of "noted writers."

66 ANON. "Recent Fiction." Independent, 40 (December 13), 1609.
(Review of The Reverberator.) This "brilliantly," often inimitably, clever and amusing satire has fewer of James's mannerisms and faults than much of his work, and many of his best traits. Flack deserves to be remembered and to marry Daisy Miller.

67 ANON. "A Charming Trip Over Old English Country Roads." Chicago Tribune, December 15, p. 12.
(Review of Social Life and Letters Fifty Years Ago.) James has aroused the anger of this anonymous Boston author, who wants none of James's sympathy for the "intellectual barrenness" of New England life fifty years ago. The author draws "rather ill natured comparisons between the social conditions" that produced Irving and Hawthorne, and those that produced Howells and James.

68 ANON. "Short Stories by James." New York Times, December 16, p. 19.
(Review of The Aspern Papers.) Without "the dramatic instinct and the habit of condensation, and with his tendency to spin subtle distinctions, James is not at his best in short stories. His strong point is neither plot nor characters, but charming, "delicate touches" skipped by the hasty reader. The old ladies in the title story are not credible, but the impressions of Venice are truthful. "Louisa Pallant" is "a more interesting character study." Although "The Modern Warning" is the weakest in plot, it has "a surprising number of acute observations" on "very irritating types" of Americans and English. The stories all have unsatisfactory endings, but also "a constant play of intellectual subtlety, now forced, now true, which makes up for all defects."

69 ANON. "Literature. . . . 'The Aspern Papers.'" San Francisco Chronicle, December 16, p. 2.
These stories have "the indisputable marks" of James's handiwork. Opinions on James's place as a writer of fiction

will differ, as always, but he has fallen into "some faults of style" in the "ablest" of these three stories, "The Modern Warning." A writer of his ability should avoid "such careless and slipshod work" and not rely on "his power of psychological dissection and mental analysis to carry him through."

70 ANON. "New Publications." Indianapolis Journal, December 17, p. 3.
(Review of The Aspern Papers.) James's admirers will enjoy these stories.

71 ANON. Review of The Aspern Papers. Hartford Courant, December 18, p. 2.
These "remarkable stories" are very good, with a subtle, penetrating flavor. James fascinates not only by style but also by his "remarkable handling of his subjects," his "probing of the depths of human motives," the excitement of his characters' unsatisfactory conclusions, and his delicate flattery of including the reader in his great knowledge of the world. James dissects his subjects, but not unpleasantly. The special charm of "The Aspern Papers" is in James's manner and delicate character delineation, while its plot is an illusion. "Louisa Pallant" is shocking, and with "a simplicity that is the highest art" James makes his moral point, a sermon on retributive justice like those of Tolstoy or his American followers. The failure of "The Modern Warning" accentuates the merits of the other two stories, and James has yet to know "the real American woman."

72 ANON. Review of The Aspern Papers. Christian Union, 38 (December 20), 737.
James is expert at getting all the meaning from an episode and a character. These stories are "supreme" in "minuteness of analysis and delicacy of touch." They concern the tragic "filament" in the labyrinthine soul of woman, beneath an external commonplace life.

73 ANON. "Literary Notes." St. Louis (Mo.) Republic, December 29, p. 12.
(Review of Atlantic Monthly.) The Tragic Muse opens the Atlantic issue "most worthily" and introduces us to "delightfully-drawn" English people.

74 ANON. "The Literary Wayside." Springfield (Mass.) Republican, December 30, p. 4.
(Review of Atlantic Monthly.) The Tragic Muse is "very foreign" and has "a riddling title" and an Englishman "of a too utterly utter type." One turns with interest from it to

a romance by Hardy, whose "bold and striking" art is "the strong literary feature of the magazine."

75 BRIDGES, ROBERT [Droch]. "Bookishness . . . Paul Patoff." Life, 11 (January 12), 20.

(Review of F. Marion Crawford's Paul Patoff.) This novel has the fault of "frequent, long and elaborate analyses of motives and mental conditions, in the manner of Henry James."

76 _____. "Bookishness[.] Mr. James's Estimate of Mr. Stevenson." Life, 11 (April 12), 208.

(Review of James's essay on Stevenson in the April Century.) James's literary essays always give pleasure. His word choice is exact and discriminating, his appreciation of verbal fencing is keen, and his praise is measured with "honest judgment." He reports with "rare accuracy" and sees more than other men, but while his "breadth of view makes him appreciative," its "multitude of details . . . tends to dwarf the importance of certain cardinal points." Because he is a cosmopolitan he did not satisfy the admirers of Hawthorne in his "very acute" study of that author and criticism of Hawthorne's "evident provincialism." Admirers of Stevenson will approve enthusiastically of most of James's generalizations, find them expressed with a hard-to-equal "delicacy and grace of style," and praise James's "generous sympathy" toward his subject, but they will be disappointed that James has somehow missed the highest and most significant quality in Stevenson's work, its "Moral Heroism."

77 _____. "Bookishness[.] Some Notes About New Stories." Life, 11 (June 7), 322.

James's "Two Countries" in the June Harper's has "a very subtile bit" of character study. As in James's other works, "the analysis is pressed to the minutest motive." James is "almost remorseless in his method of vivisection" and the results are "inevitable under his logic," but it is a pity that three such fine characters should meet catastrophe by following their consciences. James misrepresents the New York conscience in Lady Chasemore and her brother because, in the past decade, "the sensitive Puritan conscience" has been made more vigorous and robust by the broader and coarser life of material prosperity.

78 _____. "The Reverberator." Life, 12 (July 26), 48.

Given the "almost unanimous verdict" that The Reverberator is disagreeable, the reasonably perceptive reader will be surprised to find that it is enjoyable. Though Flack is not attractive, he represents a phase of journalism that James would not claim as the prevailing one. The other

1888

characters are "charming," James shows his admiration for the Dossons' "sincerity and honest simplicity" and satirizes them only good-humoredly, and Mr. Dosson is "a perfect delight." The "wonderful precision and flexibility" with which James uses phrases enables him to present a character in very few words. These characters are "well worth knowing." The ending is not a complete surprise and is unusually satisfactory for James.

79 _____. "Bookishness[.] Some Recent Books and Criticisms." Life, 12 (November 29), 302-303.

(Review of The Aspern Papers.) Each of these stories is an "unemotional study of a disagreeable phase of character," but if worth doing at all, they could hardly be done more skillfully. Anyone sensitive to literary form will find, to offset the "unsympathetic qualities," an exhilarating pleasure like that of watching "a daring and graceful skater" and being perhaps chilled but never bored. The "delicate force" of "The Aspern Papers" lies in the skill with which James entraps the reader into a "keen interest" in the hunt for the letters, and then into the "shame and humility" the hunter later feels. The reader understands "the weak point in human nature" that has led to so many literary sins.

80 _____. "Bookishness/Oracles and Critics." Life, 12 (December 13), 332-333.

(Quoted critical reference. Review of Charles F. Richardson's American Literature, 1607-1885.) One must have great faith in Richardson's "direct inspiration from Parnassus" to accept without dispute his judgments that James is not an artist, not a "'master in the older and larger and better manner,'" and not superior to Howells in ability, reputation, or mastery of style.

81 COLE, CATHARINE. "Miss Rives' Story." New Orleans Daily Picayune, April 22, p. 12.

(An attack on Amelie Rives's sensational The Quick or the Dead refers favorably to a number of other, more worthy, American works and writers.) James "does rare etching on thumb-nails or egg-shells."

82 FAWCETT, EDGAR. "Writing a Novel." Colorado Springs Weekly Gazette, December 1, p. 5.

Roderick Hudson is an exquisite story.

83 FULLERTON, WILLIAM MORTON. "Books and Authors. Balzac and Mr. James." Boston Daily Advertiser, December 10, p. 5.

(Review of The Aspern Papers.) Both James and Balzac, his master, delight in men and women and curiously observe humanity, but James has more limitations and his taste is "nicer, more exclusive." Although Balzac is a demigod, a "giant of letters," while James is "a literary artist with no superior," they are "more alike in their methods" than any other two writers of their eminence. Their work is "always interesting," often superlatively so, and "often perfect." Yet, in the "strongest contrast" to Balzac's exploration of "unsightly passions" in "Cousin Bette," James tells not of sin and evil but, with his inimitable peculiar art, writes polite, "charmingly engaging" tales of ladies and gentlemen. He uses Balzac's manner, but on a small rather than a large canvas. He has never been more delightful than in these three sketches, with which most readers are already familiar.

84 HOWELLS, W. D. "The Editor's Study." Harper's, 77 (October), 799-802.

The Reverberator is "thoroughly American," Francie Dosson is true, lovable, "a marvellous expression of the best in American girlhood." Flack is "perfect" of his type.

James has reached a maturity in his writing and a primacy among novelists. No one has had more to say to his generation about "certain typical phases," and he has "incomparably the best manner of saying it." Future readers will be amazed at James's now receiving only "feeble and conditional acceptance" by the best critics, and almost "ribald insult" from the common literary paragraphers. That magazine editors continue to print his best stories shows a continued interest in his work and is "a true measure of his popularity." The Aspern Papers, "The Liar," "A London Life," and others currently appearing are masterpieces.

85 M[ARTIN], E[DWARD] S. "Reflections." Life, 12 (August 9), 81.

(Note.) It is rumored that James, like Howells, has improved, and that "his latest works are edifying." It will be "a proud day for Life when both these gifted gentlemen, scourged from their maleficent theories, are found humbly putting in their sturdiest licks for the entertainment of their brethren."

86 PARKER, H. T. "Mr. Howells and the Realistic Movement." Harvard Monthly, 5 (January), 145-149.

James does not see the life of his time with Howells's "delicacy of discernment and power of delineation."

87 POOL, M. L. "Women and the Realists." Boston Evening Transcript, January 14, p. 10.

A certain class of readers, many grades above readers of the most popular novels, read Howells and James and are "fascinated by their skill" but exasperated by their realism. One such reader thinks James is not a genius, but very talented and a "morbid anatomist," an analyst whose characters are not warm-blooded. James must write within his limitations of vision.

88 SALTUS, EDGAR. "Morality in Fiction." Lippincott's, 42 (November), 712.

Bourget and James excel in pinning the evanescent emotion, but James is handicapped by Anglo-American prudery and "lulls his reader with minor chords."

1889

1 ANON. "Reviews . . . Mr. James's 'Aspern Papers.'" Critic, 14 (February 9), 61-62.

(Review.) James's works are usually like a "procession of Grecian masks" that move like automatons, but with fine form. The Aspern Papers is an exception in that the characters are vital and haunting, the best being Miss Bordereau. Louisa Pallant is "a brilliant bit of character drawing in the author's best vein," but the ending of "A Modern Warning" is "melodramatic and unnatural." James's plots are not important. The tales are "miniatures painted with the exquisite grace of a Fragonard."

2 ANON. "'Scribner's' for March." St. Louis Post-Dispatch, March 3, p. 22.

(Review of Scribner's.) James's "An Animated Conversation" contains witty, satirical discussion of "some interesting social topics from the international point of view."

3 ANON. "More Novels." Nation, 48 (April 25), 353.

(Review of The Aspern Papers.) James's work has "intellectual subtlety and supersensitiveness," and he is a first-rate craftsman. He stands or falls by "the refined accurate truth" of his interpretation of the thoughts and motives of his characters. In this volume the motives are very light, the interpretation is "admirable, cold, polished," with a worldly touch and no concessions to popular ideas of what is nice and proper. The stories will satisfy "exceedingly" the restricted class to which they appeal.

4 ANON. "Books and Authors. Stories by Henry James." Boston Daily Advertiser, May 14, p. 5.

(Review of A London Life.) These stories gain from being read at one sitting, James is almost unique as a novelist whose works give the reader even more pleasure on a second reading, and James's art is enjoyed most when known intimately. His "skillful suggestion of fine shades of meaning," his "precise indication of subtle shades of difference" in an "aptness of phrase . . . almost marvelous," and his extensive and well studied knowledge of human nature, all can delight. His limitations are that his attempts to portray tragedy are disastrous, since he seems to have lost the power to conceive of the depths below the surface of life. Yet, as in "A London Life," he can "describe the slight signs of the coming storm," and Laura is "extraordinarily well done, a clever study." "The Patagonia," which aims at tragedy, is the least successful story of the volume. James's telling it through the eyes of a passenger on the ship is a "dodge" that enables him to give only the surface of what occurs, and even his delightful descriptions, social analysis, fine characterizations, and amusing conversations do not make up for it. He is "at his best" in "The Liar," whose psychological problem takes on "an almost dramatic interest." "Mrs. Temperly," though very slight, is a delightful study. The details give the greatest pleasure in these stories, and the total impression is of least importance to James's admirers.

5 ANON. Review of A London Life. Indianapolis Journal, May 15, p. 3.
These are "good stories."

6 ANON. "Books and Authors./Recent Fiction." Christian Union, 39 (May 16), 638.
(Review of A London Life.) For awhile James seemed to be losing his readers' interest, but during the last year his stories have shown "decidedly more vivacity of style." The works in this volume are "fresh in style and interesting," and, though they will not add to his reputation, they will revive many of his former readers' interest in him.

7 ANON. "A London Life." Literary World, 20 (May 25), 178.
(Review.) James does better with stories than with novels since "his clever and elaborate touch" on details may obscure the matters that sustain a long work's interest. His "analysis is triumphantly clever" and his skill exquisite, but his works "lack human sympathy and heart," and are neither gay nor passionate. The sentiment is amateurish, the impression vague, and the dialogues are "too subtly simple and brokenly allusive." "The Liar" is by far the best story in this volume.

8 ANON. "New Books/Literary News." St. Louis (Mo.) Republic, May 25, p. 14.

1889

(Review of A London Life.) Such a volume of stories from "so popular an author, especially with the ladies, is sure to meet with a ready smile."

9 ANON. Review of A London Life. Boston Evening Transcript, June 15, p. 6.

James draws his characters well and in "The Patagonia" introduces a sensational act and a pathetic situation, but they do not move the reader because here, as elsewhere, James obscures his characters' real selves and makes them cold-blooded and passionless. "The Liar," and then "A London Life," are the best stories of this volume. "The Liar" is an admirable study, with an ending as nearly dramatic as anything in James. His stories seem unfinished, and suggest that he himself could not decide how his "self-conscious, analytical characters" would act at crucial moments.

10 ANON. Review of A London Life. Louisville Courier-Journal, June 23, p. 18.

Since James "has long since constituted himself a literary cable between this country" and England, it is scarcely necessary to say that these stories deal with "London society and the international social question."

11 ANON. "'Four Stories' by Henry James." Critic, 15 (July 6), 3.

(Review of A London Life.) James, like the Chinese, is a "most exquisite" caterer of "indelicate things." Despite some of these stories' "delightful style, their happy off-hand phrasing," they suggest "misplaced genius." James's genius is "too precious to be thrown away" on things like "A London Life," "The Patagonias," and "The Liar," in which this "great writer" exalts triviality or offers us poison.

12 ANON. "Native and Foreign Novelists." New Orleans Times-Democrat, July 21, p. 4.

(Editorial.) James makes "no appeal to deep feeling or wide sympathies," and his books lack humanity. His cleverness has a hard glitter, his characters are "pallid and tenuous," and his vision makes everything look small. His style has some felicities, but also an affected, "bastard Gallicism."

13 ANON. "Recent Novels." Nation, 49 (July 25), 77.

(Review of A London Life.) It is novel to have a James story in which we are more occupied with what the people do than with how they do it. Selina is done in James's best manner. He long ago "reached perfection in the art of insinuation" and one of the charms of his work is our imagining more than he tells us, but here, especially in "Mrs. Temperly," he does not tell us enough.

14 ANON. "Talk about New Books." Catholic World, 49 (August), 688-692.
(Review of A London Life.) James is at his best in this volume, and his best is very good. With each new work, his style becomes more facile and accurate, his sentences more limpid, picturesque, and clear. Readers object, though, that he sees too little. It is strange to find a clever man like James so dilettante, so amateurish toward contemporary life and thought, and so "neatly and decorously aloof from the questions" that concern the rest of us.

15 ANON. "New Publications." New York Times, August 12, p. 3.
(Review of A London Life.) The "wonderful cleverness" in the title story is mainly in the dialogue, but real people who talked that way would be insufferably sharp. James seems to "eschew happy topics" and happy endings. "The Liar" is one of his eccentricities, and "Mrs. Temperly" is so sketchy and ethereal that it is unintelligible.

16 BOYESEN, H. H. "The Hero in Fiction." North American Review, 148 (May), 594-601.
Given the American sympathy with the lowly-youngest-son-who-wins-the-princess type of hero, and our demand for his brilliant success, cheating him of his reward (as in The American) or making him unworthy of it (as in Roderick Hudson) is not satisfactory. James does not now know his country well enough to produce "two such types of our national life as Silas Lapham and Bartley Hubbard." Soaring in high British society, James looks down on America "with a sad, critical disapproval." Yet, he and Howells "represent the latest evolution of realistic fiction," their "unheroic heroes" are usually social types, and they may leave us "a National portrait-gallery" valuable to future historians.

17 BRIDGES, ROBERT [Droch]. "Bookishness." Life, 13 (February 7), 76.
(Review of Bret Harte's Cressy.) "The Path of Duty" is one of James's best short stories. Its victim of the ideal of self-denial "is drawn with such delicate satire that you almost pity him, and are suddenly conscious of the weak spot in your own armor."

18 _____. "Bookishness/Recent Stories by Henry James." Life, 13 (May 23), 300.

1889

(Review of A London Life.) As Americans gain "broader intelligence and wider experience" and a "fuller appreciation of form and finish in literature," they will more keenly appreciate the work James has done "and is now doing with finer grace and art than ever before." The fair-minded, attentive reader would admire this grace and faultless form in James's works, as well as their "'surprising depth of earnestness, a keenness of moral insight, an uncompromising attitude toward what is small and mean,'" and, often through the point-of-view character, a sense of how easily helpless human nature deceives itself.

19 _____. "Bookishness/Two Ways of Looking at a Book." Life, 14 (August 29), 118.
(Review of George Moore's Confessions.) George Moore is acute when he says of James that his scenes are developed "'with complete foresight and certainty of touch,'" but that his characters remain nebulous and live "in a calm, sad, and very polite twilight of volition.'"

20 CLARK, KATE UPSON. "Book Reviews." Epoch, 5 (July 19), 389.
(Review of A London Life.) No one of these stories is "thoroughly agreeable." "A London Life" is "especially obnoxious," with neither outcome nor moral. "The Patagonia" has "exquisite art," dramatic movement, and an uncharacteristic thrill at the end. "The Liar" is "clever to the point of brilliancy," and "Mrs. Temperly" only a fair sample of the work of perhaps our best writer of fiction. James's books lack really ardent lovers, and do not work enough against the dehumanizing effects of modern life and manners.

21 [HOWELLS, W. D.] "Editor's Study." Harper's, 79 (August), 477-478.
(Comments on A London Life.) It is the very accuracy of James's pitiless portrayals of Americans (which we perceive as caricatures) that angers his countrymen and women. He is a fine artist and pays "the penalty of being true."

22 LADD, GEORGE T. "The Psychology of the Modern Novel." Andover Review, 12 (August), 149, 154.
The "realistic school of writers" has been successful, and has a "class of readers who prefer the healthier intellectual and emotional quickening" of life as it is, rather than "morbid sentiments or unwholesome passions." Yet, sometimes Howells and James carry their realism too far and become tiresome, as in The Bostonians.

23 LANG, ANDREW. "Unhappy Marriages in Fiction." North American Review, 148 (June), 676-685.

One of James's characters has said that the great war of the world and of the future will be between men and women. One does not expect James's characters' marriages to be happy, since they contain a superfluous element of misery, their "international complications."

24 M., H. S. "Reviews." American, 18 (June 15), 138.
(Review of A London Life.) Drawn with "masterly touches," James's characters are accurately observed, in detail, and at this work "no one is keener, more delicate, more discriminating" in perception and expression than James, whose facility increases with the years. Where intuition or imagination is required, however, he is unsatisfactory.

25 OLIPHANT, M. O. W. "Success in Fiction." American, 18 (May 11), 62.
(Excerpt from Mrs. Oliphant's article in The Forum mentions James.)

26 RICHARDSON, CHARLES F. American Literature, 1607-1885, vol. II, American Poetry and Fiction. New York: G. P. Putnam's Sons, 1891, 1892, pp. 432-436. Rpt. Popular ed. 1893, 1895, 1896, 1898, 1902, 1904, 1910.
Distinguished for careful elaboration of style and for reticence, James has quietly influenced American literature. The Bostonians is the most typical of his works: "long, dull, and inconsequential," with a "dreary and narrow" method, but mildly pleasing and at times delighting with portraiture and scenes. Though a "faultless photographer," James lacks heart and his works are usually inconclusive. Roderick Hudson and The Portrait of a Lady are the best and Confidence the worst of his long books. If he is preeminently the American novelist who represents contemporary "life" and reality without artificial idealism, life nowadays is shrunken, shrivelled, "cold, thin, and incomplete."

27 SMYTH, ALBERT H. American Literature. Philadelphia: Eldredge & Brother, pp. 140-142. Rpt. 1894, 1896, 1898, 1900.
Howells and James are "the two men who best represent the American novel at the present time." Their books are photographic rather than artistic, and are expertly styled, but "monotonously clever," unsympathetic treatments of small subjects. James originated the international novel and was influenced by French literature. French Poets and Novelists is excellent criticism.

28 WALSH, W. S. "Book-Talk." Lippincott's, 43 (April 1), 605.
We have passed the "Howells and James fever," when a new book by either was "a holiday occasion," of greater importance

than "even a Presidential election." With their wit, "happy art of saying nothing," adroitness at showing humorous human foibles, their modernity and Americanness, Howells and James grew "in popular favor." Now, though, neither readers nor critics enjoy their books, and James is "deliberately refused" by a public who want Haggard, Stevenson, Amelie Rives, and Edgar Saltus.

1890

1 A., G. W. "Reviews." American, 20 (June 28), 213.
(Review of The Tragic Muse.) This is more a piece of social philosophy than a novel, yet it has "all the fascination of dramatic and emotional narrative." James is "a master of style," but perhaps no contemporary writer "so runs counter to the sympathies of intelligent readers." Here, his style is more direct, luminous, harmonious, felicitous, and humorous than ever before. In this "wonderful piece of literary insight and finish," James is precise and methodical in creating a picture which, though focused on a few people, seems to have great implications about modern life. Miriam is the greatest of James's literary achievements, "a consummate piece of literary art."

2 ANON. "Short Stories." New Orleans Daily Picayune, March 2, p. 12.
(Editorial.) James was "at his best" in the 1870s and early 1880s, more appealing than now. He had "a fine faculty for close observation and nice analysis." Since then his fame has grown, but so has his "bad habit of overrefinement and mannerism."

3 ANON. "The New Books." Detroit Free Press, April 26, p. 3.
(Review of Atlantic Monthly.) The Tragic Muse "drags its slow length along."

4 ANON. Review of Atlantic Monthly. Louisville Courier-Journal, May 3, p. 7.
The Tragic Muse closes in James's "usual undramatic manner."

5 ANON. "Some May Magazines." Indianapolis Journal, May 4, p. 7.
(Review of Atlantic Monthly.) At the close of The Tragic Muse, James's "leaving of several pairs of battered hearts to find what comfort they can in each other's company is highly realistic, though not at all tragic."

6 ANON. "Among the Magazines." Charleston (S.C.) Sunday News (and Courier), June 8, p. 5.
(Review of Harper's and Century.) James's translation of Alphonse Daudet's Port Tarascon in Harper's is "an admirable piece of work in its way."
The Century for June contains an installment of The Anglomaniacs, an international study of the kind Howells and James have made popular. This anonymous story may be attributed to one or the other of "these clever writers."

7 ANON. "Books and Authors. . . . The Newest Books." Boston Daily Advertiser, June 14, p. 5.
(Review of The Tragic Muse.) The publication of The Tragic Muse is "a real event," and it will rank among James's masterpieces. It is "a particularly acute study," and will be especially interesting to many for its picture of theatrical life and its critical remarks about the stage.

8 ANON. "New Publications. The Tragic Muse." Boston Evening Journal, June 14, Supp., p. 4.
This book admirably reproduces political, artistic, dramatic, and social aspects of English life and shows James's knowledge of England, but it resembles The Bostonians more strongly than any other novel because James's method and view of his character are similar in these works. James has a leisurely manner, the reader believes in the truthfulness of the whole novel, and, by the time he reaches the pleasant ending, the characters seem like old friends.

9 ANON. "Recent Literature." Chicago Times, June 21, p. 10.
(Review of The Tragic Muse.) It is mystifying why this novelist writes a story entirely about English society. James is right that one must be a little coarse and insensitive to "snub and slight" to be an eminent success. The book is written exquisitely, if a bit finically, and has James's "usual keen searching analysis of character and motive" and more than his usual prolixity of explanation. James refines away his stories' morals with excess analysis.

10 ANON. "Literature of the Day. . . . Henry James's Latest Novel." Chicago Tribune, June 21, p. 13.
(Review of The Tragic Muse.) The workmanship is clever, even exquisite, and the style is faultless, but James has written a very long novel about nothing in particular, and its subject is worth very little. He could write more than good fiction, "hitting smashing blows at the wrongs of the day or . . . telling some of the strong stories of this the most deadly earnest of all ages." To see such a writer working with trivial matter rather than with modern heroism and knavery is neither inspiring nor hopeful.

1890

11 ANON. "The Tragic Muse./Mr. James's New Departure." New York Tribune, June 22, p. 14.

James is moving away from the exasperating sense of inertia that "dulled the point and weakened the effect" of his other works, away from Gabriel Nash's aesthetic philosophy into a portrayal of "a strictly human basis" of intelligible, motivated action and definite "purposes fully worked out." The study of Miriam, though an exceedingly difficult task, is James's finest, "most perfect and coherent" work yet. He presents her and the other women more successfully and objectively than he does the men. The dialogue is, as usual, brilliant, and the charming style is not to be faulted.

12 ANON. "Literature. . . . 'The Tragic Muse.'" San Francisco Chronicle, June 22, p. 10.

The Tragic Muse has "the very quintessence" and perfection of James's usual "analytic, introspective, and philosophical" style, but his portraits are of real people and he tells a story. Miriam Rooth is "clearly individualized" and original. Gabriel Nash is also lifelike and clearly outlined, and suggests Oscar Wilde. James's numerous admirers will find in this novel "fresh evidence" of his genius.

13 ANON. Review of The Tragic Muse. Christian Union, 41 (June 26), 913.

In his recent stories, James seems to have recovered the freshness and hold on life he was losing in The Bostonians. A London Life was an improvement, and The Tragic Muse is even "stronger and better in every way." This novel is in many respects James's "best story" so far, and probably no American could convey with such "delicacy and refinement" the "nice gradations" of the artistic temperament. Yet, he tells his admirable story with too much distracting brilliancy and subtlety. The book's "intellectual quality" is very high.

14 ANON. "Literary." Chicago Inter-Ocean, June 28, p. 12.

(Review of The Tragic Muse. Essentially an abstract of the points made in 1890.11.) A hasty reading will not give the reader a "just estimate" of this book's merits. Despite the tiresomeness of Gabriel Nash, many of the characters are "warm-blooded, full of life and vitality."

15 ANON. "Literary News and New Books." St. Louis (Mo.) Republic, June 28, p. 10.

(Review of The Tragic Muse.) James's "many admirers will welcome a new book" by him.

16 ANON. "In the World of Books." Portland Morning Oregonian, June 29, p. 14.
(Review of The Tragic Muse. Unacknowledged reprint of almost all of 1890.10.) The "tasty dress" of these two volumes "will add greatly" to James's "popularity in society."

17 ANON. "New Publications. . . . Art in Romance." New York Times, June 29, p. 11.
(Review of The Tragic Muse.) James deals with art "artfully" in the broad sense, and the obvious purpose of the book extends rather than contracts its limits. His work "generally gives the feeling that he is personally acquainted with the facts," and is faithful sometimes to the point of weariness so that only its absolute truth can compensate for its "barrenness of fancy." He has dwelt among his material in everything but The Princess Casamassima, gives "intellectual information" fairly and accurately, further interests the reader already interested in a topic, and is "at home" in The Tragic Muse. More than in his other books, he "is interested right through," and in Nick Dormer he displays his "startling capacity for absorbing and giving out the truth." James shows rather than tells, and lifts, stirs, and wakens any lover of art. In Miriam James produces "the purest strain" he has yet created, the story is unusually "full of movement" for one of James's, and he has not presented such a "spectacle of conflicting forces" since The Princess Casamassima. His former work seems to have been a schooling for The Tragic Muse, which is, at least at present, a masterpiece in which James is neither too objective nor too personal. The book has a "composite individuality" with both variety and unity, and is an "inspiration."

18 ANON. "Among the Literary Fellers." Chicago Evening Post, July 8, p. 8.
James's translation of Daudet's "Port Tarascon" in Harper's is very admirably done. It is surprising that "so rigid a stylist" as James could so faithfully reproduce Daudet's "frolicsome style."

19 ANON. "The Literary World. . . . Summer Novels." Cincinnati Commercial Gazette, July 12, p. 10.
(Review of The Tragic Muse.) As is usual with James, the characters "are largely a study of human motives under the pressure of conventionality." James puts "very little downright human nature" in his novels, but "clips and prunes and shapes like a French gardener of the old school."

20 ANON. "New Books." New York Sun, July 12, p. 5.

(Review of The Tragic Muse.) This novel is a long essay, a sustained, brilliant, and charming discussion and fine analytical criticism of acting, painting, and aestheticism. Miriam becomes a second Rachel, and Gabriel Nash is a bore who deserves the condemnation he receives from most of the other characters. This book is "great reading in its way," but "Jack Sheppard" is a more exciting story.

21 ANON. "New Publications." Cleveland Plain Dealer, July 13, p. 5.
(Review of The Tragic Muse.) This novel is "of the true James type," and whether it is too long and talky depends on whether the reader is "a Jamesite or an anti-Jamesite."

22 ANON. "The Tragic Muse." Literary World, 21 (July 19), 231-232.
(Review.) James has a penetrating "acuteness of vision" and is "suggestive, provoking, agreeable," with "inimitable lightness of touch," despite his "fashionable slang." Yet, though the book entertains, he tends "inevitably toward disillusion," cares "only for the unimportant," and exaggerates "the defects of the photograph." The characters are finely finished, but the "muse" is artificial as well as clever. James's success, his "curiously brilliant surface," "leaves our real sympathies untouched" and lacks "real pathos, real power." He has finish, but not style, and is clever, but not great.

23 ANON. "Recent Publications." Indianapolis Journal, July 25, p. 3.
(Review of The Tragic Muse.) This "is one of the best of the author's novels, and in some respects the most satisfactory of any."

24 ANON. "The Tragic Muse." Churchman, 62 (July 26), 109.
(Review.) James is "the most purely intellectual of novelists," without human interest in his characters. He considers the primeval passions vulgar, likes delicate shading and abstruse distinctions, and "carries analysis to the vanishing point." He shows life dried, under a microscope, polished and framed under glass. The Princess Casamassima was his strongest and most moving work.

25 ANON. "Fiction for Idle Summer Days." Book Buyer, 7 (August), 289-290.
(Review of The Tragic Muse.) The characters are "an extremely interesting collection of types," carefully studied and portrayed. The study of Miriam Rooth is "the strongest piece of work" from James in a long time, and its subtle

touches, delicate shading, and "happy phrases" will "appeal with force to every refined taste." The other characters are "scarcely less interesting."

26 ANON. "Talk About Books." Chautauquan, 11 (August), 649.
(Review of The Tragic Muse.) The main character is portrayed with a skill that James has never equaled, that few modern writers have surpassed, and that makes the book the work of "a finely equipped genius." The story is James's best yet, and a piece of truly artistic literature.

*27 ANON. Review of The Tragic Muse. Godey's, 121 (August), 172.
(Cited in Ricks.)

28 ANON. "Literature/Henry James's 'Tragic Muse.'" Critic, 17 (August 2), 55.
(Review.) It is hard for Americans to have sympathy with as well as admiration for their "foremost living writer of fiction" when he so dazzles them with his characters' wit, imagination, and intellect that ordinary people cannot follow him. Though without much incident, this "studied and spirited romance" shows James's "rare and exquisitely polished skill as an essayist." The book's wit and "'super-subtle' analysis" illustrate his uniqueness as a personality in American literature.

29 ANON. "Literature." Louisville Courier-Journal, August 9, p. 7.
(Review of The Tragic Muse.) This novel is not a story, and the characters have only a vague and indefinite connection with each other. They perhaps are not intrinsically interesting, but with the "iridescent glitter" of James's wit playing over them, they "gain irresistibly in the reader's favor." By the end, these puppets inspire the reader's tenderness. The initial long conversation is full of "paradoxical and illusive flashes" in which James's wit "shines" to best advantage. Gabriel Nash's "'Hawthorne-like disappearance'" is compatible with the rest of his performance, Julia Dallow is more "delicately pictured" than Miriam, Biddy is delightful, and one could hardly better Mme. Carre.

30 ANON. Review of Rudyard Kipling's The Story of the Gadsbys. San Francisco Chronicle, August 17, p. 7.
Unlike Kipling, James spends three-quarters of his pages indulging in "the popular fashion of describing the emotions or the mental perplexities of his characters."

31 ANON. "New Books." Charleston (S.C.) Sunday News (and Courier), August 24, p. 5.

1890

(Review of Guy de Maupassant's A Coquette's Love.) De Maupassant owes his American vogue to James's essay which celebrates that Frenchman's "mastery of an art" which James himself "has toiled after in vain."

32 ANON. "The Bookshelf." Cottage Hearth, 16 (September), 294.
(Review of The Tragic Muse.) Though James has in a way surpassed himself here, and the atmosphere is fascinating, the story's long descriptions and conversations are tiresome.

33 ANON. "New Books." Lippincott's, 46 (September), 423.
(Review of The Tragic Muse.) James's characters are pleasant to meet, and some of the women have a "piquant charm" that makes up for the lack of incident. Miriam Rooth and Gabriel Nash are memorable, and James's "languid and luminous touch" makes small talk seem "very big."

34 ANON. "Book Reviews./The Tragic Muse." Public Opinion, 9 (September), 539-540.
(Review.) James's theme here has greater scope and contemporary importance than his previous ones, and he presents many of its aspects very clearly. Yet, his limitations in power keep him from treating it fully and convincingly. His portrayal has the keenness of the analyst, but "little of the warmth of daily life."

35 ANON. "Some Novels." Overland Monthly, 16 (October), 437.
(Review of The Tragic Muse.) This novel is "by far the most notable" currently being reviewed and it has won many readers and admirers. The opening, though, will please only "the most ardent lover of the naturalistic and plotless novel." The whole book is admirable for "its perfect polish and consummate naturalness." It has a definite conclusion, and an "artistic tone" that gives the work special interest. The minor characters are done "with great faithfulness," the best being Gabriel Nash.

36 ANON. "Recent Fiction." Nation, 51 (December 25), 505-506.
(Review of The Tragic Muse.) James's only English rival in the art of fiction is R. L. Stevenson. If James wrote more adventure stories, he would get "more applause than he does for his beautiful manner and exquisite style." There is some activity in this book, but Nick, Peter, and most of the subordinate characters are "less interesting for what they do than for what they think." James devotes his greatest energies to exhibiting the complexities of complex minds.

37 BOK, EDWARD W. "With the Book Folks." Indianapolis News,

July 16, p. 6.
A New York autograph dealer says that when James was the rage, his letters went for $2.50, but now do not fetch even 50 cents. (Noted also in Detroit News, July 18, 1890, p. 5.)

38 BRIDGES, ROBERT [Droch]. "Bookishness." Life, 15 (June 19), 354.
(Review of W. D. Howells's The Shadow of a Dream. Brief reference to James's phrase "the immitigability of our moral predicament.")

39 _____. "Bookishness." Life, 16 (November 27), 304.
(Review of Poems by Emily Dickinson. Reference to James's statement that however life may lay traps for us, we may find "'tolerably firm ground . . . in perfect art.'")

40 CLARK, KATE UPSON. "Book Reviews." Epoch, 8 (September 5), 77.
(Review of The Tragic Muse.) James has become "thoroughly English." Despite its "many brilliant passages," the expert scene management, and artistic character treatment, the book is too long, thin, and dull. James's vocabulary is extensive and his taste usually immaculate, but some of his innovative expressions are offensive.

41 DeKOVEN, ANNA FARWELL. "Pierre and Jean." Chicago Evening Post, May 10, p. 8.
(Review of Guy de Maupassant's Pierre and Jean.) James "is certainly responsible for a good deal of unnecessary articulation of dry bones," and Howells has been guilty of "as great a sin against taste and art" in the commonplaceness of his subjects.

42 [HOWELLS, W. D.] "Editor's Study." Harper's, 81 (September), 639-641.
(Comments on The Tragic Muse.) For a writer as modern as James, the story is merely the means to an end. The Tragic Muse, "a charming prospect of nineteenth-century life," marks "the farthest departure from the old ideal of the novel" and has only very ambiguous rewards for and portrayals of vice and virtue. Its modernity and "recognition of the very latest facts of society and art" is one of the most valuable, delightful things about it. At the end the characters go on, as in real life, and it is childish and primitive to demand more definite resolution. Miriam is "much more perfectly presented" than any other woman of her kind in fiction. The book has a "manifold excellence," with "nothing caricatured or overcharged, nothing feebly touched

or falsely stated," and a style sweet and musical. Its vision of London "aspects" is so fine, broad, true, and absolute that no Englishman has ever matched it.

43 JAMES, HENRY. "Henry James on Literary Art." Critic, 17 (October 4), 171.
(Quotation from speech of Gabriel Nash in The Tragic Muse.)

44 LANG, ANDREW. Old Friends, Essays in Epistolary Parody. London and New York: Longmans, Green, & Co., pp. 25-29. Rpt. 1892, 1893, 1913.
(Daisy Miller is a character in a brief, humorous sketch.)

45 PAGET, VIOLET [Vernon Lee]. "Lady Tal." Vanitas/Polite Stories. New York: Lovell, Coryell, pp. 10-11. Rpt. 1892; J. Lane, 1911.
Jervase Marion, a James-like character, vacations in Venice, "has the pleasure of understanding so much," and "loses the pleasure of misunderstanding so much more."

46 PAYNE, WILLIAM M. "Recent Fiction." Dial, 11 (August), 92-93.
(Reviews of The Tragic Muse and Henryk Sienkiewicz's With Fire and Sword.) This novel ranks high among James's works; it is second perhaps only to The Princess Casamassima, and far superior to either The Bostonians or The Portrait of a Lady. It has not much story, the characters are mostly "vulgar types," and their relations remain unsettled at the end, but they are all "distinctly individual, and the product of a very delicate art." The author's bits of dramatic criticism are almost the most delightful feature of the novel, surpassed only by Gabriel Nash, who alone would make the book more than worth reading. Despite the pages of "monotonous analysis," the "languid pace" and mannerisms, James's art is far superior to Howells's in that it offers "a definite form" the reader may count on. Any chapter of With Fire and Sword "easily outweighs the whole" of James's book of "fine-spun analysis."

*47 REINHART, CHARLES S. "Henry James." Harper's Weekly, 34 (June 14), 471-472.
(Cited in Ricks.)

48 [SCUDDER, H. E.] "The Tragic Muse." Atlantic Monthly, 66 (September), 419-422.
(Review.) This book shows that "the art of the novelist is acquiring a wider range" when it can show, interpret, and

attempt a generalization about a picture of human life and "the suborder to which it belongs." The "simple theme" on which James "plays with endless variations is profound enough to justify" all his labor, and he treats it with "great success," holding even the careless reader to the end with his "singularly interesting" disclosures of "the progress of human souls." The group of portraits is brilliant, and James's technique is not only consistent with "breadth of handling," but also "the facile instrument of a master workman who is thinking of the soul of his art."

49 SHERWOOD, MRS. JOHN. "American Girls in Europe." North American Review, 150 (June), 687.
Though it offended "some few Americans who did not understand it," James's "witty sketch" of Daisy Miller has helped and educated innumerable others.

50 WHARTON, ANNE H. "Some Tendencies of American Fiction." American, 19 (January 25), 293-294.
Few drawing rooms contain better talk than that of James's and Howells's women, who are lifelike and "very cleverly drawn." Yet, though the style affords pleasure, they are instances rather than types, and within a "narrower range of vision" than they at first seem. Although people consider realism the invention of some leading litterateurs of the day, including James, it was used by earlier writers as well.

51 YOUNG, ALEXANDER. "Boston Letter." Critic, 16 (May 17), 250; (May 31), 272.
The Tragic Muse will attract fresh interest when published in book form, and Lowell finds it "the most notable thing" James has done. The story has freshness and charm, and there are "comparatively few novels" of its kind in English. It is "vigorous."

1891

1 ANON. "The News in London." New York Tribune, January 11, p. 1.
(London letter. Review of a production of The American at Southport, England.) Mr. Archer, the well-known London critic, thought the play "most interesting," with "alert, telling dialogue" and good stage effect, and the audience felt so even more decisively. The play provoked great public curiosity and was received with enthusiasm. James is "at the height of his fame as a novelist," and his development of his evident "theatrical talent" will provide "no small enrichment of the stage."

1891

2 ANON. "American Fiction." Literary Digest, 2 (February 14), 430.
(Reprint of part of an article mentioning James in the January 1891 Edinburgh Review.)

3 ANON. "Briefer Notices." Public Opinion, 10 (February 21), 482.
(Review of Confidence.) The author's name, and the book's having passed through the seventh edition, are proof of its merit. It is an interesting study, and the bright, cultivated, sweet heroine is "an excellent example of her countrywomen," quite above the hoydenish and altogether objectionable Daisy Miller. The story is "well written and delightful."

4 ANON. "The Lounger." Critic, 19 (August 22), 91.
(Quotation from and discussion of James's New Review essay on Ibsen.) James is clever and discriminating, but overqualifies his sentences.

5 ANON. "Notes." Critic, 19 (September 19), 146.
At Southport, England, the play The American absorbed a country audience throughout, and they called James out at its finish.

6 ANON. "Henry James's New Play." New York Times, September 27, p. 1.
(Review of The American.) This play was a disappointment to a very distinguished audience. Only the "brilliant and pointed" dialogue merits praise. Incongruously filled with melodrama, the play will please least those who most enjoy James's "exquisite workmanship," and any popular success it has will be due to its artistic flaws.

7 ANON. "The Lounger." Critic, 19 (December 19), 351.
James has been corresponding with the actress Mme. Modjeska, who says that anything he writes would be "well worth reading." James and Modjeska would be a good artistic combination.

8 BEERS, HENRY A. Initial Studies in American Letters. New York: Chautauqua Press, pp. 185, 203-210. Rpt. 1899.
(Repeats remarks on James in 1887.23.)

9 HAWTHORNE, JULIAN, and LEMMON, LEONARD. American Literature: An Elementary Text-Book. Boston: D. C. Heath, pp. 250-256, 283.
James's works merit serious and respectful attention. French Poets and Novelists established him as "one of our

keenest and most agreeable critics." His early stories were romantic, and his distinctive innovation has been a narrative which subordinates plot and action to verisimilitude of setting and character. His style is self-conscious, but rich and delicately refined. He has wit, but not humor, is objective to the point of a jarring, coldly critical attitude, and dissects characters from without. He is afraid to "cut loose from observed fact," and his method is barren. Howells has less high imagination, but more poetry. James has influenced analytical novelists such as Edgar Fawcett, whose plots are more strongly dramatic than his. James is not unsuccessful, but will not likely become popular.

10 JAMES, HENRY. "A Critic on Criticism." Critic, 18 (June 6), 305.
(James is quoted.)

11 _____. "Current Criticism/No Room for Ibsen in England's Pantheon." Critic, 19 (October 31), 240.
(Quotation from James's New Review essay on Ibsen.)

12 MATTHEWS, BRANDER. "Concerning Three American Novels." Cosmopolitan, 11 (July), 380-382.
In fiction writing, James, Howells, and G. W. Cable are more than a match for the British Stevenson, George Meredith, and Thomas Hardy. The three Americans concern themselves with more wholesomely realistic and mature topics than the pseudoromantic, idle loves of the young. The Tragic Muse is in some ways James's "strongest and subtlest story."

13 PRESTON, HARRIET W. "Mr. James's 'American' on the London Stage." Atlantic Monthly, 68 (December), 846-848.
(Review.) Though the English Compton's portrayal of Newman is surprisingly good, this dramatization of one of James's "very best stories" has many defects and could have been much better. The first act "is tiresome and irrelevant." The death of the "pleasant young" Valentin, "one of the most profoundly tragic" scenes James ever wrote," here seems gratuitous, "futile and merely sensational." Other characters are colorless or overacted. James "may yet win a legitimate triumph" in the theatre, but whatever success this production may have will "unhappily be due to a sacrifice of all the distinction of the original tale," and to a replacement of "the keen though quiet wit of its dialogue" by "trivial catchwords" that make Compton's "American" vulgar.

14 WALFORD, L. B. "London Letter." Critic, 19 (October 24), 216.
The "very general feeling of respectful regret" attending the production of James's play is reflected in the "preternaturally mild and gentle" press notices. No one wants to

say an unkind word of the play or its distinguished author, but it bores its audiences.

1892

1 ANON. "Mr. Lowell Abroad." Critic, 20 (January 9), 27-28.
(Long quotation from James's very "readable" essay on Lowell in the January 1892 Atlantic.)

2 ANON. "Books, Writers and Readers." Chicago Evening Post, February 12, p. 4.
(Note.) James is rumored to be writing a comedy to be produced by Edward Compton. He is said to have written a play for Genevieve Ward.

3 ANON. "Today's Literature./'The Lesson of the Master,' by Henry James." Chicago Tribune, February 27, p. 13.
James is "the foremost American novelist," but in eagerly avoiding the commonplace he sometimes makes his plots too ingenious and far-fetched. His short stories have too little "free play of natural feeling" and too much of the influence of "the artificial restraints and conventions of European society." Too many of these "brilliant sketches" focus too much on problem and solution. "The Lesson of the Master" has "a real and permanent interest," and is "well told," with the "fine shadings and delicate appreciations" that make other writers feel "like raw clowns." It is "a masterpiece, unsurpassed in its kind," the best thing in the book. "Brooksmith" is "a sympathetic study," "The Pupil" cleverly sketches Bohemian life and emphasizes its least attractive features, "The Solution" is "too slight and farcical," "The Marriages" is "ingeniously depressing," and "Sir Edmund Orme" is not typical of James.

4 ANON. "Today's Literature. . . . Brief Mention." Chicago Tribune, February 27, p. 13.
(Review of second series of Paul Bourget's Pastels of Men.) These "Pastels" have more color, movement, picturesqueness, and dramatic effectiveness than James's stories, but they lack James's "delicate humor."

5 ANON. "In the Library." St. Paul Daily Pioneer Press, March 6, p. 12.
(Review of The Lesson of the Master.) James's work merits "thoughtful study," and his "faultless diction," clear vision, and "illuminating touch are always inspiring." Unfortunately his calm assurance, and the repose that is among the most artistic attributes of so finished and "admirably

poised" a writer, have the effect of indifference. Yet, in "The Lesson of the Master" the very presence of St. George gives the feeling that something tremendous is coming. The story is strong morally as well as artistically, and finely wrought out with James's usual masterly touches. The other story in the volume that merits special mention is "The Pupil," a "delicate, affectionate" study that appeals strongly to the imagination. The relation between the boy and his tutor is "a singularly lovely study of character," and one of James's charms is "his power to prove that his people really are as witty as he says they are."

6 ANON. "Stories by Henry James, Jr." Boston Evening Transcript, March 11, p. 6.

(Review of The Lesson of the Master.) Like all James's works, these stories are "elaborate in finish and interesting in subject."

7 ANON. Review of The Lesson of the Master. St. Louis (Mo.) Republic, March 12, p. 10.

These "dignified attempts" are very like James, with his "delicious naivete." His admirers will like them.

8 ANON. "Henry James' Stories." San Francisco Chronicle, March 13, p. 9.

(Review of The Lesson of the Master.) James's refined literary art is unique, and no one without leisure and patience should attempt to read him. "The Lesson of the Master" is "an admirable study of character," but only a variation of the idea in Mrs. Humphrey Ward's "History of David Grieve." The other stories in the volume are interesting, and reveal James's "consummate literary art" which in finish and precision "equals the finest work of the best French writers."

9 ANON. "Four New Novels." New York Times, March 20, p. 19.

(Review of The Lesson of the Master.) Lately James serves his readers skimpy meals of mental pablum, his excessive "dilettanteism and eclecticism" become oppressive, his recent stories have "no plain speech," his thinking is emasculated and sterile, and his work is so full of pianissimo, modulations, faint vibrations, sharp staccatos, and "tiny trillings" rather than any blares of trumpets, that he confuses and sickens the reader. "The Pupil" is "pathetic and told with art," Morgan is not natural, James's artifice in producing the climax is "too salient," and his works are becoming "thin, brittle, attenuated, impalpable." His style is perhaps purposely in contrast to realism, but it does us no harm.

1892

10 ANON. "Books, Writers and Readers." Chicago Evening Post, March 26, p. 4.

A soon-to-be-issued volume of stories by the late Mr. Balestier entitled The Average Woman includes a memoir by James.

11 ANON. "Henry James' Stories." Cincinnati Commercial Gazette, March 26, p. 13.

(Review of The Lesson of the Master. Paraphrases many points from 1892.8.) James's short stories are always interesting, sometimes more for the art than for the story, but they have too little conversation and perhaps too much "painfully minute character analysis." One may both admire James's subtlety and become impatient with it. His English and French are fine, and his flow of words has an exquisite smoothness, but sluggishness of the current sometimes irritates, and James's stories have a spirit of infinite gloom. St. George and Overt are "admirably drawn," Morgan's wit is abnormal, Pemberton's nature is weak but good, and the other stories "are equally artistic in their characterization of human misery." James could not have done a better job of giving the reader the blues, and these stories leave a bad taste in the mouth, but "there is a certain pleasure in the pain of it all."

12 ANON. "The Lesson of the Master." Literary World, 23 (March 26), 110.

(Review.) The title story is the best, though it and "The Marriages" have James's characteristic oversubtlety and inconclusiveness. Both stories are "well done" to a certain extent, and all in the volume are better than the average of James's recent work. His works "compel attention, and are full of masterly touches."

13 ANON. Review of The Lesson of the Master. New York Herald, March 27, p. 29.

This book will renew wonder that "a man who writes so well finds so little to write about." A man "well born and bred" should be able to find better work than "making fun of blunderers," and James should portray "hearts and heads" as well as good and bad manners.

14 ANON. "Novels and Tales." Book Buyer, 9 (April), 115-116.

(Review of The Lesson of the Master.) James possesses the "rare and admirable quality" of an individual style. These stories are "very delightful reading," and the title story "deals with an old question in a very fresh and original way." It contains many "happy characterizations" of clever people such as one meets in James's stories. These people are generally more clever than those one meets in real life, but their talk is bright and their companionship agreeable.

15 ANON. "The Lesson of the Master." Churchman, 65 (April 9), 460.
(Review.) James is at his best in these clever, "rare gems," cut cleanly "with exquisite nicety and finish." His pen strokes are "unmistakable and perfect."

16 ANON. "The Lesson of the Master." Louisville Courier-Journal, April 9, p. 7.
The title story is written in the "dawdling, desultory fashion" James seems to like lately, and James is like St. George. The ending "is marked out with that airy lightness of touch that is one of the chief charms" of James's stories, and is "so cleverly handled" that one almost forgives him "the tedious detail" and the wearisome, "wandering[,] commonplace dialogue of the beginning."

17 ANON. "The History of David Grieve." New Orleans Daily Picayune, April 17, p. 18.
(Review of Mrs. Humphrey Ward's The History of David Grieve.) Though "brilliant novelists," James, Howells, and F. Marion Crawford lack Mrs. Ward's "power of feeling."

18 ANON. Review of The Lesson of the Master. New Orleans Daily Picayune, April 24, p. 12.
These are good stories by "one of the English masters of the art of story telling." They have both "grace of style" and "depth of purpose."

19 ANON. "Recent Fiction." Nation, 54 (April 28), 326.
(Review of The Lesson of the Master.) This volume attains artistic perfection. James has the modern artist's impartiality toward his characters. For those who enjoy his "spectacle of pure intellect and artistic sensibility dominating commoner if not inferior qualities," this book will be "a source of pure delight."

20 ANON. "Comment on New Books." Atlantic Monthly, 69 (May), 711.
(Review of The Lesson of the Master.) Though James's English "is becoming more and more mannered," these clever stories serve the reader well. James "is always immensely clever," and "The Pupil" and the title story are "little masterpieces."

21 ANON. "Recent Fiction." New York Tribune, May 15, p. 18.

1892

(Review of The Lesson of the Master.) The title story is more decisive than is usual for James, and therefore "a very good story." It is among his best works, and although the others in the volume are not, they nonetheless have "acuteness, delicacy of touch, and subtle analysis."

*22 ANON. Review of The Lesson of the Master. Christian Union, 47 (May 20), 981.
(Unlocated. Cited in Foley and Ricks.)

23 ANON. "New Books and New Editions." New York Times, November 20, p. 19.
(Review of Daisy Miller.) In the context of James's recent, more involved work, this story seems even cleverer than when first issued. It is fun to read and is and will continue to be the most read of his books. Its truth "will be violently disputed so long as American ladies read." James handles his delightful subject tenderly and skillfully.

24 ANON. "Christmas Books." New York Tribune, November 21, p. 8.
(Review of Daisy Miller and An International Episode.) This praiseworthy holiday edition is for the thousands who find Daisy most "beautiful, amiable and innocent." McVickar's illustrations, however, are poor.

25 ANON. "'Daisy Miller' Rediviva." Critic, 21 (November 26), 294.
(Review. Comments on McVickar's illustrations in the new edition of Daisy Miller.)

26 ANON. "Daisy Miller." Public Opinion, 14 (December 17), 266-267.
(Review.) "Among our old friends" in new holiday editions is Daisy Miller, who taught Europe the difference between European and American girls.

27 BRIDGES, ROBERT [Droch]. "Bookishness." Life, 19 (April 29), 266.
(Review of F. Marion Crawford's The Three Fates.) James's "The Lesson of the Master" is one of three striking recent stories about the development of the literary temperament.

28 EGAN, MAURICE FRANCIS. "Some American Novels." American Catholic Quarterly Review, 17 (July), 622.
(Article on F. Marion Crawford's novels.) Howells and James are "ethical disciples of Flaubert rather than of Thackeray," but fortunately their realism is not like French naturalism. James dissects and etches, lacks Crawford's "great manner," and has more consistently good technique.

29 HAWTHORNE, JULIAN, and LEMMON, LEONARD. American Literature: A Textbook for the Use of Schools and Colleges. Boston: D. C. Heath, pp. 248-254.
(A slight reworking of 1891.9.)

30 HIGGINSON, THOMAS WENTWORTH. The New World and the New Book, With Kindred Essays. Boston: Lee and Shepherd, pp. 65-66, 84, 114, 118-119.
Although, without college, writers like James and Howells show a cleverness and genius, a "strength and delicacy of style," their essays are less richly and broadly allusive than those of an earlier generation. The London correspondent of the Critic has quoted an Englishman as saying that the main results of the Civil War were the development of Henry James and the adoption of Robert Louis Stevenson. James stayed far away from the war, but it probably affected him.

31 HUTTON, LAURENCE. "Literary Notes." Harper's, 86 (December), Supp. 1-2.
(Review of reissue of Daisy Miller and An International Episode.) The "storm of obloquy" that surrounded James on the initial publication of Daisy Miller now seems curious, since Daisy was neither vulgar nor at all the "'typical' American girl." The clever "International Episode" has "all the crystalline brightness" of James's most intellectual moments.

32 MATTHEWS, BRANDER. "More American Stories." Cosmopolitan, 13 (September), 630.
(Review of The Lesson of the Master.) Readers of these "very clever tales" may wonder whether James might have greater strength for his art if he came to America more often. Those who love his flexibility, subtlety, "delicate art," and "extraordinary sensitiveness to impressions" must regret seeing him write so constantly of the British rather than of Americans. He seems to have lost interest in his countrymen, and will lose touch with his country. This volume is one of James's finest, richest, and truest.

33 MURRAY, DAVID CHRISTIE. "Current Criticism." Critic, 20 (January 2), 13-14.
(Quotation from Murray's review of the play The American for the Contemporary Review.)

34 SHARP, WILLIAM. "Thomas Hardy and His Novels." Forum, 13 (July), 583.
Howells's realism is thin and James's is superficial, compared with Hardy's.

1893

1 ABBOTT, MARY. "Books of the Week." Chicago Evening Post, September 23, p. 12.

(Review of The Private Life.) These psychic stories are "so near fascination," yet so far from it, and have, despite their flaws, "some excellent James flavoring." James's characters make one feel comfortably, deliciously, and vaguely supercilious, but they remain too elusive, hard to figure out. "Lord Beaupré" has "something fine and vigorous" about it, in contrast to the effete title character, who is an "excessively amusing" caricature of his type and class.

2 ANON. "Some Holiday Books." Atlantic Monthly, 71 (January), 124.

(Review of Daisy Miller and An International Episode.) James "may be said to have been the first really to lay an Atlantic cable in literature," and he "very properly enjoys his honors" in this edition, which is among "the most notable holiday books of the season."

3 ANON. "Some Holiday Books." Atlantic Monthly, 71 (January), 124-125.

(Review of The Great Streets of the World.) These collected descriptions of the life on great streets of the world are written by seven authors, including James. The writers "struggle more or less successfully with the problem of a literary representation of humanity on the run," and make more of the people than of the architecture. The pieces may have been better displayed in their individual publication in the magazines.

4 ANON. Review of The Real Thing. Chicago Times, March 25, p. 12.

These stories are all "entirely characteristic" of James's "very familiar work." They are "excellent as character studies," and are interesting as that, rather than as what we usually mean by short stories.

5 ANON. "The World of Books." St. Paul Daily Pioneer Press, March 26, p. 16.

(Review of The Real Thing.) Three of these stories deserve "good ranking" in James's work. The first, "The Real Thing," gratifies "every artistic sense," and its completeness gives the reader a supreme satisfaction. The workmanship is "of the finest quality," and James has never done anything more telling than Miss Churm. "Nona Vincent" is the second of the three stories deserving special attention, and the third, "The Chaperon," is spirited.

6 ANON. "Stories by Henry James." New York Times, March 27, p. 3.

(Review of The Real Thing.) Four of these five stories would be understood by only the artist or literary man. James, the "subtlest of modern romance makers," writes for these people rather than for the general public, and treats "only those finer and more delicate things" that harass a conscientious man. James seems to feel that form is "the only really desirable thing in human existence." "Sir Dominick Ferrand" has "a strong bit of true life and blood in it," and is appealing since James "rather disdains the material side of things." James's art keeps the old story of hidden papers from being commonplace. In "Greville Fane" the satire on Mrs. Stormer is "bitter" but perhaps deserved. James has expatriated himself in "manner, taste, and subject," and in London or Paris his "nice dilettanteism . . . must bring keen delight," but only to a limited "charmed circle."

7 ANON. Review of The Real Thing. Philadelphia Public Ledger and Daily Transcript, March 31, p. 3.

James is "brilliantly clever, as usual." The pleasant "Sir Dominick Ferrand" is the one romance among "these analytical essays in fiction," and stands far "above its competitors."

8 ANON. Review of The Real Thing. New York Sun, April 1, p. 7.

The title story is "very amusing and delightful," concerning "beautifully worked up" perversities of the art world. Of the others, "Sir Dominick Ferrand" is "especially ingenious and delightful," with distinctive workmanship.

9 ANON. Review of The Real Thing. Providence Sunday Journal, April 2, p. 13.

Only people of "literary taste and artistic insight" will understand and admire these "clever and charming" stories. "The Real Thing" is the most ingenious, and "Greville Fane" is admirable, with deep-cutting satire.

10 ANON. "Books of the Week. . . . The Real Thing." Detroit Free Press, April 3, p. 8.

These are "five of the best short stories" of the voluminous James. The title story is a "pathetic sketch" which has "a nameless charm" made even more attractive by the reader's feeling that James stands "on the verge of the ridiculous."

11 ANON. "Book Notices./Fiction." Hartford Courant, April 8, p. 11.

1893

(Review of The Real Thing.) These stories are "very happy examples of the peculiar merits of this subtle analyst." In the title story the picture of the Monarchs has an admirable "delicacy and pathos," "Sir Dominick Ferrand" has more "interest of story," and "Nona Vincent" tells "capitally" of a young playwright. "Greville Fane" has a deftly touched note of pathos, and "The Chaperon" is the most representative of James and the least attractive, dealing more than the others in "shades and fine-spun social issues," but with a "happy conception." The "exquisite finish, felicitous phrasing, and the insight of the cosmopolitan observer" make James's work unusual and highly enjoyable, and, like Meredith's work, it is written for the few.

12 ANON. "Fiction. . . . The Real Thing." Literary World, 24 (April 8), 113.

(Review.) No novels and stories are more depressing than James's, "despite their excellent workmanship." He portrays small emotions, but not the joy of living. His imagination "vivisects but does not soar." Yet, his "creations always seem real."

13 ANON. "The Literary World. . . . Some Danish Stories." Cincinnati Commercial Gazette, April 15, p. 14.

(Review of The Real Thing.) James and Howells do not now have the vogue they enjoyed a few years ago, and even fewer readers read James than read Howells. James describes that modern subject "character," and those who want to study it "can not do better than to read" James. The title piece is "a marvel of brilliant analysis," but it cannot be called a story. The people who care for a study like "Greville Fane" must be "very limited indeed." It is "a far cry" from James to Fanny Burney, and in her day there was no such thing as conscious study of character.

14 ANON. "Literature/'The Real Thing.'" Critic, 22 (April 15), 230.

(Review.) These stories are "among the best things" James has ever done. They show as subtly as any others the charm of his style, a style of which he is "perhaps the greatest master" writing today in English. "The Real Thing" is "charming and touching," with a "deep artistic truth." "Sir Dominick Ferrand" is the strongest of the stories.

15 ANON. "Literature." San Francisco Chronicle, April 16, p. 9.

(Review of The Real Thing.) James has never written a "perfectly satisfactory long novel," but most cultured American readers think him "the most accomplished living short story writer in England or America." All these stories show his "supreme mastery" of that "most difficult" of literary arts. They give the mental pleasure of a well acted play, and have perfection of style, with no gaps or raggedness, none of the overelaboration that weakens James's long works. The title story is "an admirable sketch," with Mrs. Monarch's jealousy of the model in James's best vein. In "Sir Dominick Ferrand," the strongest story, James's treatment of an old theme is "as original as it is startling," with complications "genuinely dramatic." "Greville Fane" is "a remarkable study," and the other stories are "well worth reading."

16 ANON. "Some New Stories by Mr. James." Boston Evening Transcript, April 22, p. 7.

(Review of The Real Thing.) The title story is "hauntingly sorrowful," told with what in a writer of less correct form would be "a swaggering matter-of-fact style." It leaves a bitter after-taste, and is one of the "keenly-etched pictures" James is master of when his theme is "small and sordid sorrow." "Sir Dominick Ferrand" is the "most powerful" of the other stories, and recalls James's earlier works such as "The Romance of Certain Old Clothes," with its element of "dramatic interest of action." James's "clear, graphic touch and singular felicity of style make his choice of subject" secondary, but in this volume his subjects have "much originality and interest."

17 ANON. "Books, Magazines and Literary Chit-Chat. . . . The Real Thing." St. Louis (Mo.) Republic, April 23, p. 14.

James "is really a clever writer," but one must be in the mood to read him. The title story is the best of the volume, contains some of James's "happiest work," and is "worth the price of the book." The rest are "good, but not so striking," although "The Chaperon" is "novel in plot and treatment," reflecting James's merit of being "usually new."

18 ANON. "Books and Authors./Recent Fiction." Boston Daily Advertiser, April 27, p. 5.

(Review of The Real Thing.) These stories are "of real life," and the tales after the title story are "all in . . . James's best vein."

19 ANON. "Recent Novels and Short Stories." Book Buyer, 10 (May), 153-154.

(Review of The Real Thing.) It is unlikely that even the "extraordinarily clever work" James has done in the past ever surpassed the achievement of the title story of this volume. Both its workmanship and the interest and value of its character studies seem nearly flawless and give evidence of genius. James is not often "able to touch the deeper springs of human feeling," but he makes the reader feel very keenly the Monarchs' "pathetic helplessness."

20 ANON. Quoted comments. Book News, 11 (May), 419.
(Quotations from 1893.6, 8.)

21 ANON. "Talk about New Books." Catholic World, 57 (May), 284.
(Review of The Real Thing.) James here shows himself a man "whose literary reputation is secure," getting away with things that would condemn novices. These stories are "bits of study" whose charm is in the "delicacy and effortless pathos of their treatment." They give "luminous insight" into the world of artistic struggle.

22 ANON. "Talk About Books." Chautauquan, 17 (May), 485-486.
(Review of The Real Thing.) "The Real Thing" is a clever sketch, written in James's "distinctive style."

23 ANON. "Books of the Month." Cottage Hearth, 19 (May), 245.
(Review of The Real Thing.) These stories are in James's "most inimitable style," and the title story is memorable.

*24 ANON. Review of The Real Thing. Godey's, 126 (June), 771.
(Cited in Ricks.)

25 ANON. "Literary Notes." Harper's, 87 (June), Supp. 3, 162.
(Review of Picture and Text.) The pieces of criticism are "brilliant," and James has a high, even unique place among American essayists. All who care for the work of illustrators should study this "instructive and delightful" book.

26 ANON. "Recent Fiction." Overland Monthly, 21 (June), 660.
(Review of The Real Thing.) This book, which must have been written "in an immaculate library," is very much in contrast to some out-of-doors Western stories. The reader of James "knows just what he is getting" and does not need an "elaborate criticism" of James's work. If the reader enjoys it, he will not be swayed by a reviewer, and if he is new to James, he should take heart because these tales are not James's most characteristic.

27 ANON. "Literature. . . . Picture and Text." Louisville Courier-Journal, June 17, p. 7.
(Mainly quotations from James's essays.) In this "delightful little volume" each chapter is full and "unusually good reading," and the book will be interesting to magazine

readers and provide "peculiar entertainment" to people of artistic temperament.

28 ANON. "'Picture and Text.'" Critic, 22 (June 24), 417.
(Review.) James is "very entertaining in these essays," and is nowhere more at home, or more delightful, than when writing of Broadway.

29 ANON. Review of Picture and Text. St. Paul Daily Pioneer Press, June 25, p. 12.
James's book is "a pleasant and profitable addition" to the series, and, since it treats a special subject interesting to people of culture and leisure, it will prove attractive.

30 ANON. "Picture and Text." Detroit Free Press, June 26, p. 8.
It is "a good thing" to have these essays in collected form.

31 ANON. "Essays by Henry James." New York Times, June 26, p. 3.
(Review of Picture and Text.) James has not omitted many impressions, and the many recorded are "enchanting" and in his "delightfully-analytical manner." Few critics "have known so well how to praise" or so cultivated "the divine art of appreciation." In this volume "the praise is always convincing, the expression is always sincere," and if James has too much a predisposition to praise, it is never evident. The book is valuable as "a guide to contentment" and "teaches one to multiply the number and the variety of fine impressions."

32 ANON. "Books." Hartford Courant, July 1, p. 4.
(Review of Picture and Text.) These studies are written with an "elegance, insight and urbanity" that only James can provide. The introductory paper "Black and White" is charming, and "After the Play" is both keen and amusing.

33 ANON. "New Books./Brief Reviews of Important and Interesting New Publications." New York Sun, July 1, p. 7.
(Review of Picture and Text.) James talks "very delightfully about his friends, the artists," and his "flowing text" is charming. In this analysis "liking and admiration are the constant notes," and the book is "fine tribute and agreeable reading." Both its subjects and the general public "should be very much obliged."

34 ANON. Review of Picture and Text. Boston Daily Advertiser, July 5, p. 5.
"After the Play" is "a bright sketch," and this book "is

one of the most taking of this excellent series of little volumes."

35 ANON. "Stories." Advance, July 13, 544.
(Review of The Real Thing.) These are "skillful and reasonable" stories.

36 ANON. "Picture and Text." Boston Evening Transcript, July 15, p. 6.
The essays in this "bijou volume" are delightful, graphic, and clever, and James's name assures that they are "daintily finished, brilliant in phrase and abounding in keen insight." They are so well written that one often forgets the artists in admiring James's cleverness. The book not only "deals charmingly" with the artists in black and white, but is itself "a continuous series of exquisitely wrought pictures in black and white" that give more pleasure than do the original sketches or the landscapes themselves.

37 ANON. "Briefs on New Books/Appreciative Chats on American Artists." Dial, 15 (July 16), 47.
(Review of Picture and Text.) It is not necessary to speak of James's quality as an essayist. Even people who do not like him "must admit his painstaking fidelity to his models," and at worst, "he may serve to sharpen the reader's appetite for a bit of down-right Anglo-Saxon."

38 ANON. Review of Picture and Text. Philadelphia North American, July 22, p. 6.
(Partial listing of artists treated in the essays.) The paper on Sargent is attractive.

39 ANON. "Bookishness/Some Unrepentant Exiles." Life, 22 (August 17), 102-103.
(Review of Picture and Text.) James himself has not paid the price he says the cosmopolite pays: he still has a distinct function, and, "when the Americans in Europe get leave to send a delegate to Congress he will be the representative of their choice." He is such a good writer that the layman can understand almost every word of this volume of art criticism.

40 ANON. "Literature." Boston Commonwealth, 33 (August 19), 6.
(Review of Picture and Text.) James shows his "sure touch," keen sense of literary form, "thorough grasp of his subject," and sympathy with "art as art." "After the Play" is clever, James's criticism is appreciative, and the whole volume shows charmingly the real interest "genuine criticism of an adequately literary form" can have.

1893

41 ANON. "Recent Fiction." Independent, 45 (August 24), 1154.
(Review of The Real Thing.) In "point of insight, clever characterizations and subtile analysis," these stories are up to James's best level, but in addition to fine manners, they contain "mannerisms very disfiguring" to what would otherwise be a charming style. One would expect such a "careful and fastidious" genius to avoid "weak and unnecessary parenthetical phrases," worn-out formulae, and "formal self-consciousness."

42 ANON. "New Stories by Henry James." New York Times, August 27, p. 19.
(Review of The Private Life.) Cultivated readers anticipate James's books with pleasure at his personal quality as well as the literary art unequalled by any living American except perhaps T. B. Aldrich. James is among the best modern novelists, and his works exert a powerful and delightful immediate influence, but are not memorable. The successful "Private Life" and the admirable and pleasurable "Lord Beaupré" are "as finely wrought and as entertaining" as any James work since Daisy Miller and An International Episode. "The Visits," like "The Middle Years," is "far beyond the sympathetic comprehension" of most people.

43 ANON. "Literary Notes." Harper's, 87 (September), Supp. 4, 648.
(Review of The Private Life.) "The Private Life" suggests much to the thoughtful reader, is brilliantly treated, and contains two of James's best studies of gentlewomen. All these stories are clever and of crystalline clarity, but none is exciting, adventurous, or virile. James does not treat timely topics, but has unerring thought and observation, unusual cleverness, and an almost dazzling "brilliancy of method."

44 ANON. "Recent American Publications. . . . Essays, Criticism and Belles-Lettres." Review of Reviews, 8 (September), 354.
(Review of Picture and Text.) James discusses the artists "in a spirit of penetrating and irrefutable criticism," and makes "discriminating remarks" about contemporary drama.

45 ANON. "Literature." Boston Commonwealth, 33 (September 2), 6.
(Review of The Private Life.) George Du Maurier and James depict modern society as "accurately and vividly" as anyone, with "delicate humor" and art. "The Private Life" is delightful, "Lord Beaupré" is less precious, and "The Visits" is "a triumph of story telling by indirection, suggestion and allusiveness." James's style is "always delightful," but he overuses the impersonal pronoun.

1893

46 ANON. Review of The Private Life. Boston Evening Transcript, September 2, p. 6.

When these stories appeared in the magazines they elicited "unstinted praise" because they display "the keen analyst's peculiar literary power." The title story is "a suggestive fantasy, fascinating in its implied condition of things," with "a curious psychological study" in Lord Mellifont. "Lord Beaupré" is "a masterly delineation of human motives, persistently claiming the reader's attention to the very end." "The Visits" is "a short but strongly limned sketch " whose "closing paragraphs are absolutely harrowing."

47 ANON. "'The Private Life, and Other Stories,' by Henry James." Chicago Tribune, September 2, p. 10.

Whatever interest these stories may have as "human documents," they are "not exactly thrilling" as narratives. Lately James takes less interest in human nature as a whole, and more interest in its "rarer and more obscure phenomena." His stories' queer people suggest a museum of freaks. James uses all his power and finesse of style to give "a semblance of reality" and probability to the title story. The occult is not James's element, since his "temper is too skeptical, too analytical," although he not long ago wrote "a capital ghost story." "Lord Beaupré," a "masterpiece" of James's delicate irony, is more appealing, and is "worked out with admirable thoroughness." In the "sad little tale" "The Visits" the treatment is not sympathetic enough, reflecting James's trace of "Mephistophelian . . . indifference," his sense that to betray tender emotion when telling a story is not good form. Yet, the closing scene is beautifully done. In all, James's admirers will find him clever and half-epigrammatic, but his "artificial, 'society' manner" begins to "impair one's pleasure in his talent."

48 ANON. "The Private Life." Cincinnati Commercial Gazette, September 9, p. 14.

James gets "more and more skilled in drawing fine lines and distinctions finely," but this increased fineness does not recommend him to the public, and he "is far too subtle and delicate" for ordinary men to take pleasure in. (Summary of "The Private Life.")

49 ANON. "Fiction./The Private Life." Literary World, 24 (September 9), 291.

(Review.) "The Visits" has "a touch of real pathos and tragedy," but the other stories are more in James's "usual vein." They have unlikely situations and characters who are "intricate, illusive, phantasmal--as bloodless as paper dolls and very little more interesting."

50 ANON. "Stories by Henry James." San Francisco Chronicle, September 10, p. 7.
(Review of The Private Life.) This volume is "hardly likely" to add much to James's reputation, and not reprinting these stories would have been no serious loss to the reading world. The "undeniable cleverness" that characterizes all of James's work is not entirely lacking, but does not stand him in quite as good stead as usual, and this volume's "average level" is flat. In "The Private Life" and "The Visits" execution is "distinctly inferior" to conception, and even in the best story, "Lord Beaupré," James has not made as much as he might have of "comparatively new and really promising material." The irreverent may find further support for the idea that "a large part" of James's art is to be disappointing. Though "the initiated" may welcome this book and read it with pleasure, those who do not know James are better off with Daisy Miller and Washington Square.

51 ANON. Review of The Private Life. Advance, September 21, 708.
These stories are readable, but exasperatingly improbable, leaving unsolved mysteries.

52 ANON. "Notes." Nation, 57 (September 21), 213.
(Review of Picture and Text.) These essays have James's "leisurely circumlocution" and other qualities that mark the master's technique, but this "writing around a subject" can lead him astray of grammar as well as of meaning.

53 ANON. "Opinions of Henry James./Essays in London and Elsewhere." New York Times, September 24, p. 23.
These essays have done "good service" in the periodicals, and the vivid, "charming and graphic" impressions of London show that James has studied it "deeply and lovingly" and "thoroughly saturated" himself in its atmosphere. They will satisfy readers unfamiliar with London, and also the ones familiar with London who also have learned to like James's literary manner. Rarely since his "fine account" of George Du Maurier has James shown this highly gratifying "clearly defined personal quality" or "note," a term often "sadly misused" by "clumsy imitators" of James. Seeing a very human side of this "often cold and reserved" writer increases the pleasure. The essay on Lowell is admirable, though not a final appreciation, with many good phrases worth preserving. As a phrasemaker, James has few equals among writers in English, and is inferior only to Pater. James's essays on the French writers and Browning are characteristically good, but the ones on the "tiresome" Ibsen are not very luminous or interesting. The essay on criticism is

1893

interesting with a vengeance to book reviewers, who "have striven, against odds, to create a large public liking for the nice literary skill of Mr. James." The closing imaginary conversation seems hardly worth preserving.

54 ANON. Review of The Private Life. Boston Daily Advertiser, September 25, p. 5.
James's short stories are "always welcome," and these are in James's "usual attractive style."

55 ANON. "The Book Table. . . . Henry James' Essays." Detroit Free Press, September 25, p. 3.
(Review of Essays in London and Elsewhere.) Because of his mode of life and because he helped "start the realistic school" of novelists, few writers "have excited more contradictory criticism" than James. Some critics, mostly Englishmen, "pronounce Howells and James the most eminent of our modern American authors," but as Americans "we are not proud" of James and find that his attention to foreign places and authors in these essays offends American patriotic pride. Yet, in this volume he handles his subjects "in a masterly style, with wonderful perspicuity and force" and an unquestioned ability to analyze. Though one of James's enemies has claimed his stories need an interpreter and are misty and vague, these essays are "concise and interesting, and show great depth of thought and study."

56 ANON. "New Books/. . . Literary Notes." Indianapolis News, September 27, p. 4.
(Notice of publication of The Wheel of Time.) "Owen Wingrave" is "a psychologic study, united to an out-and-out 'ghost story.'"

57 ANON. Review of Essays in London and Elsewhere. Philadelphia Public Ledger and Daily Transcript, September 29, p. 2.
James's descriptions of London are graphic and clear cut, but are overshadowed by the "more powerful charm" of James's literary essays that accompany them. These essays have "nice discrimination and a positive felicity for distinguished phrasing," and the Lowell essay "alone would make the fortune of a lesser book." The portrait of the poet is "ample and noble," and he is presented as one would wish "for curious sightseers to view."

58 ANON. "Lowell's High Place/Defined by Henry James in his Collection of Essays." Chicago Tribune, September 30, p. 10.
(Review of Essays in London and Elsewhere.) James's essay on Lowell, to Americans the most interesting of the

volume, shows an "appreciation of virility and patriotism" surprising in James, who draws an "ingenious" contrast between Lowell and Hawthorne. James also seems to make an apology for his own life, and because he is so admirable a writer of English, one is glad when he seems ashamed of his "expatriation of sympathy," and one hopes that the "lofty sentiment" with which he ends the Lowell essay "contain the promise of a larger life of endeavor for himself." The second most interesting essay is on Fanny Kemble. Eventually, James's self-explanations and constant discrimination between "shades of triviality" become tedious and boring. (Much of review is about Lowell.)

59 ANON. "The Literary World./The American Language./Mr. Henry James on its Differences from Pure English." Cincinnati Commercial Gazette, September 30, p. 14.

(Review of Essays in London and Elsewhere.) James is always making "such nice distinctions, such clever implications" that are unintelligible, but one "can afford to wade through a good deal" for James's occasional lapse into the vulgarity of a "bright and suggestive word." In "An Animated Conversation" James hits himself and Howells hard with the implication that they write like women. He also suggests that the great writers in America have written in English rather than in American. The American language is to be found in the newspapers. Their readers, the American people, will insist that the great American novelist of the future write in American, though he will be condemned and ignored by critics using the English standard and he will have to found his own publishing house to get it printed.

60 ANON. Review of The Wheel of Time. New York World, September 30, p. 4.

These stories are "cameos of finished workmanship and exquisite taste." They are very unlike each other, with the first a "social sketch," the second "a bit of quaint humor," and the last "a creeping psychological study" which is "English, of course."

61 ANON. "Comment on New Books." Atlantic Monthly, 72 (October), 570.

(Review of Picture and Text.) This book "illustrates the illustrator," and collects James's "happy analyses" of the work of several artists. "After the Play" is "a clever talk of clever people about the theatre."

62 ANON. "Books on Varied Themes." Book Buyer, 10 (October), 288.

(Review of Picture and Text.) These papers "are all charming reading," like everything James writes. They give "a new insight into the art of the illustrator."

1893

63 ANON. "Books on Varied Themes." Book Buyer, 10 (October), 364-365.

(Review of The Private Life.) This book is not up to James's "usual mark either in theme or in workmanship." He has not usually confronted his readers with "such incomprehensible enigmas" as the characters in The Private Life. Only "the most sentimental and impressionable of readers will be able to sympathize with silly Helen Chantry" in "The Visits." "Lord Beaupré" is the best of the three stories.

64 ANON. "Literary Notes." Harper's, 87 (October), Supp., 3.

(Reviews of The Wheel of Time and W. D. Howells's Evening Dress.) Like Washington Irving, James has chosen to be an original writer, and he has succeeded at what he has attempted. The Wheel of Time is clever, has James's usual "crystalline clearness," and is equal to anything he has ever done. Despite their differences, we associate James with Howells.

65 ANON. Review of Picture and Text. Literary World, 24 (October), 355.

James does good work here. "After the Play" has his "peculiar and rather frigid cleverness," a certain "playful earnestness," and "considerable keen criticism." James's forte is conversation.

66 ANON. "French Writers." New York Tribune, October 1, p. 14.

(Review of Essays in London and Elsewhere and Picture and Text.) Essays in London's chief value is its discussion of Flaubert, Loti, and the de Goncourts. Taine's method is sound in James's capable hands, producing true, just, and charming portraits. James is observant, sympathetic, and "uncommonly entertaining."

67 ANON. Review of The Wheel of Time. Providence Sunday Journal, October 1, p. 13.

The manner may be "vastly superior" to the matter in these stories of delicate, elusive substance. Some will find them vague, but thoughtful readers will be strangely fascinated. No other living novelist can touch so finely and firmly the intangible perplexities and unpassionate emotions created by modern society. No other writer except Mrs. Oliphant "more often reaches the ultimate truth by some sudden flash of sympathy." If not sympathetic, James is "discreet and well-bred." "Collaboration" is the most pleasing story in a volume the cultivated should read.

68 ANON. Notice of The Wheel of Time. Albany Evening Journal, October 5, p. 8.

Though the first story is the longest, not everyone will think it the best.

69 ANON. Review of Essays in London and Elsewhere. Chicago Times, October 7, p. 12.

These essays are written in James's characteristic pleasant, refined style, and are finished. James gives "interesting personal reminiscences," and "a picturesque characterization" of many London spots.

70 ANON. "The Literary World. . . . 'The Wheel of Time.'" Cincinnati Commercial Gazette, October 7, p. 14.

James "appeals more to a certain exclusive class than almost any other English novelist." His publishers send out few editorial copies of his books, few people like him and buy him regularly, and he is so fine in "his allusions, his insinuations, his implications, that he is an enigma to an ordinary American." Yet, he sometimes hits on "a bright idea," and the reader always feels James "is trying to get at something really good."

71 ANON. Review of The Wheel of Time. San Francisco Chronicle, October 8, p. 7.

These stories are written in the style that is now "so familiar to English and American readers," and which, "except to the very elect, has become somewhat tiresome." James's habit of analysis is so pervasive that his characters must ask the reason for every action, and these reasons make up the bulk of his stories. James is "largely responsible" for the "reaction among readers of fiction in favor of stories of life and action."

72 ANON. "Mr. James and Other Story-Tellers." Springfield (Mass.) Republican, October 8, p. 6.

(Review of The Private Life.) James is very much himself in these stories, and "his tricks of speech," his theatrical situations arranged as are no one else's, and his "point of view, are strongly characterized." The conversation between Mary and Lord Beaupré is "more Sphinx-like than human beings not of the James type can conceive," and "The Visits" is "excessively irritating." "The Private Life" is "very smart and . . . very mysterious," and will be remembered by readers of the Atlantic.

73 ANON. "New Publications." Boston Herald, October 9, p. 5.

(Review of Essays in London and Elsewhere.) James's criticism is always moderate, and he expresses his subjects' "peculiarities and diversities" precisely. In this "wonderful study, hardly to be equalled in a lifetime, and written with that exquisite faithfulness in minute detail which is the despair of his imitators," James analyzes feeling as only he can, and makes London more real than a color picture could. Many of his books have been more widely read, but none is more worthy than this one.

74 ANON. "Henry James's 'Private Life.'" Critic, 23 (October 14), 236.
(Review.) James "has never done much better work" than these stories, executed with all his "wonderful insight into human psychology" and a literary skill and taste comparable with the best of the French. "The Private Life" and "Lord Beaupré" are "perfect," but "The Visits," though strong, is not so well done.

75 ANON. "Current Criticism . . . Mr. James on Literary Criticism." Critic, 23 (October 14), 247.
(Item reprinted from the New York(?) Evening Post finds James's complaints about critics and reviewers in Essays in London well founded.)

76 ANON. Brief review of The Wheel of Time. St. Paul Daily Pioneer Press, October 15, p. 15.
All of these stories are "of the 'society' order," and "Owen Wingrave" is "a psychologic study, united to an out-and-out 'ghost story.'" (See 1893.56.)

77 ANON. "The Week's Books. . . . The Wheel of Time." Detroit Free Press, October 16, p. 3.
James's "stock of short stories does not seem to be running out," and these stories are "very much like all the others he has written." They deal with English high-life, which is undoubtedly James's forte, since "he never took pains to find out much about American high-life." In "The Wheel of Time" James treats well the theme of the ambitious mother attempting to marry off her daughter. He "has not left us vaguely groping in the mist for an idea" as he sometimes does. Everything is "clear and concise."

78 ANON. "Literature . . . Essays in London and Elsewhere." Louisville Courier-Journal, October 21, p. 7.
These papers have very little connection other than that they are all essays. The entertaining one on London has "some pleasant descriptions" resulting from "considerable delicate observation." Without James's "very peculiar style" the book would be more readable, but despite "the frequent obscurity of his meaning," James's "criticisms are always sound." The essays on Lowell, Browning, Flaubert, and Loti are all worth reading. (Long quotation from essay on Loti.)

79 ANON. "'The Wheel of Time.'" Critic, 23 (October 21), 253.
(Review.) Several of James's volumes of stories are more interesting than many of his novels, and the keenness of his "analysis of the intricacies of action is a perpetual delight." The second story is "much ado about nothing," but "Owen Wingrave" has "a keen fascination." Nothing in this volume quite reaches the heights of The Princess Casamassima, "The Real Thing," or "The Visits."

80 ANON. "Notes on New Books." Philadelphia North American, October 21, p. 2.
(Review of The Wheel of Time.) James is "one of the most noted literary critics of the time" and the founder of a school of fiction "peculiar to modern intellectual development," and he fills "a place of the first importance in American literature." His and Howells's school advocates "pure art" and the subordination of plot to character delineation. Literally sticking to this method might fail to please the public, but "The Wheel of Time" shows that a middle course gives "charming results." It has a situation well suited to James's skillful treatment, and in a short space James has drawn in the lady and the gentleman "two portraits . . . striking in outline and finish." "Collaboration" is "full of originality," and "Owen Wingrave" pictures a career that inclines "to the gruesome and the tragic."

81 ANON. "The Literary Field./The Latest Fiction." Cleveland Plain Dealer, October 22, p. 7.
(Review of The Wheel of Time.) These stories "have the same qualities which commended" James's previous stories to their admirers: "perfection of style and independence of the taste that demands a love story with a wedding, present or proximate, at the end."

82 ANON. "The World of Books/Recent Essays by Henry James and Agnes Repplier." St. Paul Daily Pioneer Press, October 22, p. 12.
(Review of Essays in London and Elsewhere.) Essays will not go out of fashion as long as James lives to supply the demand. This book gives "a keener impression of novelty than any book of similar scope which has appeared for a long time," partly because James chooses recent topics, has a wholly original and pleasing style, and takes "infinite zest in his work himself," from a sheer love of the art and labor of writing. He is "perhaps the most shining" American example of this kind of work in the last quarter of the century. He has gone on living up to and never betraying his own excellent standards, has "criticized only where he could

admire," has allowed other people to preserve their standards, has laid down only laws that are general and whose application wounds no one, and has an audience not universal, but "grateful and appreciative." In this volume the "most personally characteristic" essay is on London, the one on Mrs. Kemble is "a captivating and enlightening analysis," the Ibsen critiques are interesting, and the piece on Loti is "particularly fine," with "a subtle and refined study" of aspects of the French school. That study is "the more trustworthy and satisfying because it deprecates" some "unfortunate" aspects which to many readers are "essential elements of French literature."

83 ANON. "Recent Fiction." Independent, 45 (October 26), 1453.
(Review of The Private Life.) James is the opposite of Kipling in everything, his style "is the very flower of fin de siècle conventionality," he excels in "ample spread of verbal trickery," and his phrasing is admirable. These stories are not of his best, and they have an alien, European, "dilettantish suggestion" as of an American romancer spoiled by studying the French realists. They are very fine, artificial, and finical.

84 ANON. "Henry James' Essays." Detroit Evening News, October 29, p. 12.
(Review of Essays in London and Elsewhere. Mainly a discussion of Pierre Loti.) One of the cleverest of James's essays in this volume is the one on Loti, who may have, as James thinks, an overdeveloped faculty of external perception and a resulting "perversion of the natural feelings."

85 ANON. "A Few Story-Tellers, Old and New." Atlantic Monthly, 72 (November), 695-696.
(Review of Annie Eliot's White Birches.) Annie Eliot has been a disciple of James, but seems now to "part company" with him and "assert her own individual power."

*86 ANON. Review of The Private Life. Godey's, 127 (November), 620.
(Cited by Clayton L. Eichelberger, United States Fiction: 1870-1910, p. 180.)

87 ANON. "Fiction. . . . The Wheel of Time, and Other Stories." Literary World, 24 (November 4), 367.
(Review.) James's "grace and distinction," his "charm of technique," are well suited to the short story. He treats his themes with "constant skill" and does not overelaborate. The pathos of these studies of life's incompleteness is relieved by "delicate humor" and "a genuine element of heroism."

88 ANON. "Literature/'Essays in London and Elsewhere.'" Critic, 23 (November 18), 315.

(Review.) Like Flaubert, James is a writer's writer. The essay on Flaubert is "shrewd and brilliant" and shows James at his best "as a detailed psychological analyst." These essays' chief defect is their lack of focus and climax. James's style is "an admirable expression of his individuality," and its very minuteness is happily adapted to his train of thought.

89 ANON. Review of The Private Life. Outlook, 48 (November 18), 906.

James's authorship assures these stories' "delicate and strong workmanship." Each is perfect of its kind. "Lord Beaupré" has "the strongest human interest and humor," and "The Private Life" the "highest psychological interest."

90 ANON. "Literary Notes." Harper's, 88 (December), Supp., 2-3, 164.

(Review of Essays in London and Elsewhere.) James's essay on London is refreshing, the best of his writings, and the best paper on London written in modern times.

91 ANON. "Essays in London and Elsewhere." Literary Digest, 8 (December 9), 115.

(Quoted excerpts from an unfavorable British review of Essays in London in the Spectator, and favorable American reviews in the New York Tribune, Philadelphia Times, and New York Times.)

92 ANON. "Essays in London and Elsewhere." Literary World, 24 (December 16), 444-445.

(Review.) James is so indirect and qualifies so much that he is clumsy, losing "perspicacity" and intellegibility. His critical essays on contemporary literature are better than those of any other living American author, but he is not "'vividly impressionable,'" nor does he rise to "'perception at the pitch of passion.'" He struggles, but "lacks certain qualities of the great artist."

93 BRIDGES, ROBERT [Droch]. "Bookishness/'The Real Thing.'" Life, 21 (March 30), 200.

"The Real Thing" is subtle and shows James's "exquisite method." Its "crowning achievement" is the indefinable way James makes the reader feel that the real thing is "higher and more significant" than art.

94 _____. "Bookishness/Knock-Down Effects in Life and Art." Life, 22 (August 3), 71.

1893

(Quotation from James's "After the Play," Picture and Text, that laments the contemporary audience's lack of regard for fineness.) What James's character says of the theater is also true of fiction. The current materialistic standard and demand for "knock-down effects" has helped to rid contemporary stories of much sermonizing and digression, but it has also "kept the multitude from fully appreciating that finer art which depicts the intricacies of character." This art "has reached one of its rarest phases" in James's own subtle work.

95 _____. "Overheard in Arcady." Life, 22 (November 2), 278-279.
(Satire. Characters from "The Lesson of the Master" and Daisy Miller discuss James and his art.)

96 CRAWFORD, F. MARION. "What is a Novel?" Forum, 14 (January), 592.
The literary history of the future will find it hard to explain that two writers as different as Henry James and Rider Haggard "find appreciative readers in the same year of the same century." Public opinion is divided on the artistic issue.

97 EGAN, MAURICE FRANCIS. "Books of the Week." Chicago Evening Post, March 26, p. 5.
(Review of The Real Thing.) Of all writers in English, James is "the most accomplished" at "making something out of almost nothing." He has been called dull only by those who want a story, and though he does lapse that way occasionally, he is "the first of the writers of prose de societé, and therefore entitled not to be brilliant all of the time." He is inimitable in relating an episode, but often exaggerates his characters' importance. "The Chaperon" is told "in a reticent manner" with an effort worthy of Flaubert "applied to English style," but "Nona Vincent" is less successful. James's being "so perfect and adept" at "making words more valuable and impressions realities" makes up for his expatriation, which is yet not denationalization.

98 F., E. "Two Books of Essays." Providence Sunday Journal, October 8, p. 13.
(Review of Essays in London and Elsewhere.) James is always "immensely stimulating," and he writes for the cultivated. His London descriptions are very vivid and felicitous. The most valuable essays are on the French writers, and although one may disagree with what James says, one must admire his "skill and sympathy" in saying it.

99 HARRISON, FREDERIC. "The Decadence of Romance." Forum, 15

(April), 217-224.

There are still delightful writers, and Howells, Besant, Ouida, Rhoda Broughton, Mrs. Burnett, and James "are as good reading as we need," but there is "no living novelist" who has achieved universal and accepted fame. Among the reasons may be the highly organized, "mechanical culture" of the age, whose "comfort, electric lights, railway cars, and equality are the death of romance." Writers like George Eliot, Meredith, R. L. Stevenson, Howells, and James are not as intensely involved with life as were their predecessors, and they look on its stage "from a private box."

100 LOGAN, A. M. "Henry James." Nation, 57 (November 30), 416-417.
(Review of Essays in London, The Wheel of Time, and The Private Life.) No writer of fiction has suffered more than James from being misunderstood, while none has more consistently directed his energy toward "the perfection of form and expression." The only one of these essays which may receive unqualified approval is the one on Lowell, in which James shows his "combination of affectionate sympathy with clearness of vision." The two volumes of fiction give the impression "of form without substance, of fine-spun elusive phantoms with no claim on emotional regard." In his perfection of rendering a given subject, James "has achieved unique distinction in English letters," but to be in what he calls the great tradition he must apply his "exquisite method" to subjects that are well "in the range of common experience, and that appeal with some passion to intelligence and emotion."

101 PAYNE, WILLIAM MORTON. Review of The Real Thing. Dial, 14 (June 1), 341.

James does not create new types or invest familiar scenes with new interest, so we enjoy his stories because of "the subtlety of his analysis and the polish of his style." The stories in this volume are typical of James's art, and readers who know his work will know what to expect and will not be disappointed.

102 _____. Review of The Private Life. Dial, 15 (October 16), 228.

"Lord Beaupré" follows the "lines of normal human activity," but the other two stories are "whimsical in the extreme, if not actually morbid." "The Private Life" is "hopelessly elusive," but has "a certain power of fascination," and ingenious delineation of the two main characters.

103 _____. "Recent Fiction." Dial, 15 (December 1), 344.
(Review of The Wheel of Time.) People have charged

James's short stories with sacrificing interest to subtlety of analysis, but his more recent stories have "distinctly gained in interest" while losing nothing in subtlety. "The Wheel of Time" is less striking than the other two stories, and written in a manner that by now must be a reflex action for James.

104 [SCUDDER, HORACE E.] "A Few Story-Tellers, Old and New." Atlantic Monthly, 72 (November), 695-696.

(Review of The Real Thing and The Private Life.) In the thirty years since James "began to delight cultivated readers," his subtlety has naturally grown "more impenetrable," his discriminations finer. He is better in long works, yet "remains today, in some respects, the consummate artist in miniature story-telling of this generation." The stories in these volumes "have an unmistakable individuality" and show James's "increasing power of penetration" rather than a widening range of observation. In this respect, his "vein of criticism of life" is "inexhaustible." "The Real Thing" is "a most ingenious satire" wrought "with good-humored skill." "The Private Life" is very elusive, yet its moral comes through clearly.

105 S[MALLEY], G[EORGE] W. "Mr. James and His English Critics." Critic, 22 (January 28), 52.

(Reprinted from London letter to the New York Tribune.) The play The American "was not unsuccessful," but it had less success than it deserved because of the British social and literary reaction against Americans. English critics of the play also could not forgive James's French methods. The British mood has changed, though, and James's next play should find a more congenial audience.

1894

1 ANON. "Mr. Henry James as an Essayist." Dial, 16 (January 1), 25.

(Review of Essays in London.) James has always seemed a better essayist than novelist because the "critical and analytical habit of mind" with which he is "so richly endowed" is "too self-assertive for the purpose of the story-teller." This volume is "rich in subtle observations and delicate critical shadings." Though the contents are "a little ill-assorted," all the essays except the very shortest ones are little masterpieces. The essay on Lowell is perhaps the "finest appreciation" we have of him, and the French writers, especially Flaubert, "are handled with sure sympathy and real penetration." No one has excelled James at interpreting recent French writers for English readers.

2 ANON. "Literature./. . . Henry James's Essays." Boston Commonwealth, 33 (January 6), 6.

(Review of Essays in London.) The essay on London is "a fine special plea" in justification of James's expatriation. The Lowell essay is "very pleasant" and just, the portrait of Fanny Kemble is "vivid," and the papers on French writers are "brilliant and subtile" analyses.

3 ANON. "Book Notices." Methodist Review, 76 (March-April), 335-336.

(Review of The Private Life, The Wheel of Time, and Essays in London.) James is essentially a critic, more English than American, and his stories are "his poorest productions," lacking "the stirring and passionate interest of real life." Because of their "essential feebleness" and their obtrusive, too elaborate art, they do not hold our attention. James's style is a feat, but it is much less radiant, rich, strong, and culturally "ripe" than Lowell's. All these essays are "well worth reading," but only the one on Lowell will excite much interest.

4 ANON. "Literature." Independent, 46 (March 1), 273-274.

(Review of Essays in London and Elsewhere.) Here, James's presumably latest thought is scanty, and his latest style is difficult and overwrought. His literary theory combines "a certain parenthetical timidity" with "studied indifference." With a subject lending itself to verbal trickery, the essay on London is the best. The critical papers are noncommittal and not informative, yet James's "literary wiles" delight us.

5 ANON. "Comment on New Books." Atlantic Monthly, 73 (April), 568.

(Review of The Wheel of Time.) "Collaboration" makes the "keenest impression."

6 ANON. "Notes." Boston Commonwealth, 33 or 34 (April 14), 7.

In Harper's Weekly, James slights the potential literary talents of illustrators, but, with his gaze "always toward highest things," he overlooks the "pretty good" stories already written by American artists.

7 ANON. "Living Writers of Fiction." Dial, 16 (June 16), 351-353.

(Review and comparative evaluation of nineteenth-century European and American fiction.) No one has yet, or seems likely to, become the Great American Novelist. Neither James nor Howells nor F. Marion Crawford may claim the title. Among living novelists, Bret Harte and Dr. Holmes probably come the closest.

1894

8 ANON. Review of Theatricals: Two Comedies. Detroit Evening News, June 17, p. 10.

Although these plays "were constructed with a view to representation," perhaps "their greatest value" will be as "highly dramatic novels," to be enjoyed "in a seat that costs nothing."

9 ANON. "Two 'Rejected' Plays." New York Times, June 17, p. 23.

(Review of Theatricals: Two Comedies.) Rumors that James wrote these plays for Daly's company, and for Ada Rehan, "have frequently been printed." Miss Rehan was probably the actress James intended for them, but it is easy to see why the manager, possibly Mr. Daly, refused to risk money and produce them. Despite James's "earnest attempt" to write "comedy pure and simple," these plays are "clearly, if not far, above" and far apart from the larger public's taste. In this respect they are like James's novels and all the literary and artistic qualities of his personality. Yet, the plays are "very clever," and seeing the "exquisitely dainty and fanciful" comedy "Disengaged" presented would please his admirers as much as does reading his other works. This play gives "rare and uplifting" pleasure, is "full of motion," and has "sufficient dramatic action" and "delightfully good" character drawing. Although James too often uses old comedy writers' catch phrases, it is a pity that New York and London have no theatres for "just such plays." "Disengaged" will more surely please readers than will the more sombre "Tenants," which suggests "L'Adventurière" and Oscar Wilde's "Woman of No Importance." James's play is superior in subtlety, wit, and "delicacy of touch," especially to Wilde's "cheap vlugarity."

10 ANON. "Two Comedies by Henry James." Chicago Tribune, June 23, p. 10.

(Review of Theatricals: Two Comedies.) The cablegrams (to the newspapers?) have often suggested that James was writing a play for Ada Rehan, but the parts she excels in are younger women than Mrs. Vibert. The plot of "Tenants" is "Frenchy" in every sense, and could serve for an emotional drama like "Sowing the Wind." "Disengaged" is dainty and frivolous, and Mrs. Jasper reminds one of the heroine of "A Scrap of Paper." As a dramatic writer James lacks objectivity, and theatrical personages must be examined "through the telescope, not the microscope."

11 ANON. Review of Theatricals: Two Comedies. Detroit Free Press, June 25, p. 3.

These plays "are as entertaining in their way as anything" James has published.

12 ANON. "Theatricals: Two Comedies." Nation, 58 (June 28), 491.
(Review.) Some of the reasons these comedies were not acceptable may have been the distribution of "the good things" among a number of characters, a weak motive in one play, a confused plot in "Disengaged," lack of dramatic and theatrical action and sympathetic quality in both, and dialogue demanding exceptionally brilliant delivery. As literature the plays have excellence and will pleasantly entertain the reader, but dramatically they are less successful.

13 ANON. Review of Theatricals: Two Comedies. Chicago Inter-Ocean, June 30, p. 10.
Readers know that James has cleverness and facility with dialogue, can compress much thought into a single sentence, and can be pungent almost to the point of wit, but James does best with dialogue in the context of a narrative. His skill is in "telling a story clearly and describing a character accurately," but he is neither adept nor a "takingly clever amateur" as a dramatist, and his power as a storyteller is not heightened by the dramatic form. The two plays are "commonplace enough," and have sprightliness and interest, but do not adequately repay the time spent reading them. James has used "in the most matter-of-fact and conventional way" material that could have made "much more captivating and really actable plays." He has left his characters in "unattractive outline," and committed "absurdities of characterization" by not, like the novelist, telling us things about them. His comedy is rather flat and sometimes almost silly. In "Tenants" one line is overworked and the relations between the characters are curious, but that play is better than "Disengaged," a more conspicuous "attempt at smart writing." One wonders, painfully, whether Harper's published these plays because of the name of their author.

14 ANON. "Theatricals." Literary World, 25 (June 30), 202.
(Review.) "Tenants" and "Disengaged" might be very interesting on the stage, but their charming conversation needs the accompaniment of "look and tone."

15 ANON. "The Book Table." St. Louis Post-Dispatch, July 1, p. 23.
(Review of Theatricals: Two Comedies.) These plays are good, and playable, comedies "of high order, with the short, crisp epigrammatic style that is the essence of a good play."

16 ANON. Notice of Theatricals: Two Comedies. Albany Evening Journal, July 3, p. 5.
(Virtual reprint of 1894.11.)

1894

17 ANON. "Henry James as a Playwright." Springfield (Mass.) Republican, July 5, p. 4.

(Editorial review of Theatricals: Two Comedies.) When James published his play "The American" he caused "a general surprise" which intensified when it was "reasonably successful." In some ways no contemporary novelist is "so well fitted for dramatic writing." James has marvelous skill in manipulating dialogue, and only its "incredible cleverness" detracts from its realism, but for drama James must omit "keen" bits of comment and thus lose much of his power. It has been long since he wrote anything remotely suggesting his American origins, but that choice is an artist's privilege, James knows the English upper classes as few authors do, and his defection is our loss and England's gain. His hold on the general American reading public has diminished accordingly, and where he and Howells once exerted equal influence, James now exerts hardly any, though "cultivated readers" enjoy his "clever English sketches." "Tenants" has "one of the clever women of the world" James "paints so well," and "several effective situations," but the action drags a little and the play is pointless and "far too fin-de-siècle." "Disengaged" is "only a trifle," but entertaining. Mrs. Jasper and Mrs. Wigmore are "vividly sketched," the men "a little more indistinct."

18 ANON. Review of Essays in London. Philadelphia North American, July 9, p. 6.

Here is "much incisive and original discussion." James's critical sense is keen, brilliant, but always even-tempered. The essays on Lowell and Mrs. Kemble are fine.

19 ANON. "Literature . . . Two Comedies by Henry James." San Francisco Chronicle, July 22, p. 7.

(Review of Theatricals: Two Comedies.) Most readers know that anything James writes "must have something worth reading and admiring," but he is not likely to arouse sympathy for his failure to get these plays produced. His stage directions do not compliment the intelligence of either actors or readers, and he evidently thinks he has "written above the brain capacity" of theatre people and, implicitly, of the public. "Tenants" is stiff, formal, and stilted, with characters like "elegant automata" and affected speeches that are yet "excellently written" and express "many clever ideas." "Disengaged" is different. It has a "very light" theme, people "of the Henry James order," and much "finicky" work that is lost in staging, but is also bright, witty, and full of action, interesting to James's admirers but not as effective with the general public as his work and its meaning deserve. The general audience would find it "too fine on the point," and, since the number of people with taste for such "dainty trifles" is limited, James may not expect to be produced until he "writes comedies of some stronger or more generally attractive quality."

20 ANON. "Briefs on New Books." Dial, 17 (September 1), 125.
(Review of Theatricals: Two Comedies.) Reading these plays is like an "exacting game," the dialogue is amusing and "has the usual ultra-delicate flavor," the action is difficult to discover from the "enigmatic utterances" and is "usually preposterous," and the characters are "extraordinarily conventional and colorless." These plays have interest, but James's other work has so much more that the plays will never be "great favorites."

21 ANON. "New Publications/Henry James as a Playwright." New York Times, December 15, p. 3.
(Review of Theatricals: Second Series.) James's reasons for publishing these plays are "plausible and elegantly expressed," but few readers would agree with his secret opinion that they merit performance. They are somewhat farcical in idea but not in treatment, with slender but well-proportioned plots, humor too subtle for the stage, "exquisite workmanship," elliptical dialogue requiring intellectually alert readers, and lack of theatrical perspective.

22 ANON. "Mr. James' Drop to Drama." Brooklyn Daily Eagle, December 23, p. 6.
(Review of Theatricals: Second Series.) "Nothing could be nicer" than James's method of portraying social or artistic circles, and lately he puts "the sublimated social interests of some of his frivolous cultured people into dramatic form."

23 KIRK, S. "Contemporary Essays." Atlantic Monthly, 73 (February), 267-268.
(Review of Essays in London.) James might have increased his reputation by sacrificing a little subtlety and pursuing writing as a less fine art, but if he had, we would have had "less literature." For James "the way to get a literature is not to advertise for it as original or American, but to learn to look at things truly, and to write as well as possible." All of James's work is a kind of literary criticism, involving "processes of analysis, comprehension, and restatement." He has been successful in applying these processes to life itself, though his work lacks "the supreme gift" of dramatic power. James's criticism is not superior to his novels, and he turns his ever-abundant cleverness "to more and more account." This volume is not brighter, but more

mellow than Partial Portraits, and the criticism is balanced, sympathetic, and unexaggerated. The essay on Ibsen "is probably the most complete and illuminating" yet written about him, but James's treatment of London seems "a little perfunctory."

24 LOOMIS, CHARLES BATTELL. "Announcement!" Life, 23 (March 29), 206.

(Humorous item. In a list of works that would be "absolute novelties by famous authors" appears "Seven Murders in Seven Minutes, A story without an Englishman," by Henry James.)

25 RUTHERFORD, MILDRED. American Authors, A Hand-Book of American Literature from Early Colonial to Living Writers. Athens, Ga.: Franklin Printing and Publishing, pp. 568-570. Rpt. 1902.

James's ideas "are not truly American," and Daisy Miller is "an exaggerated picture of . . . an exceptionally silly" girl, but James is "a most admirable critic." He is considered the leader of the "neorealistic school," the originator of the international novel, and a representative of "the analytical and metaphysical school of novelists." Readers often think his stories end too abruptly.

26 THAYER, WILLIAM R. "The New Story-Tellers and the Doom of Realism." Forum, 18 (December), 470-480.

People laughed at Howells's claim that his and James's fiction is a finer art than that of Dickens and Thackeray, but he told the plain truth. Yet, if Kipling can create an illusion in a paragraph, and Howells or James requires ten pages, their "Epidermism" is an inferior means of literary expression. Realism has been a phase indicating the decadence rather than the regeneration of fiction. In its era, fiction "has been enslaved by scientific methods" and the imagination has been supplanted by lower faculties. More certainly than eight years ago, however, realism is waning and Epidermism has found "its true habitat in the sensational daily press."

27 VEDDER, HENRY C. "Henry James." American Writers of Today. New York: Silver Burdett, pp. 69-86. Rpt. 1895, 1898, 1899, 1910.

James is "brilliantly equipped" to be a novelist, Boston loves him, and he cannot be ignored, but he lacks familiarity with America. In his earlier works he was "a preacher of social righteousness." The American and Daisy Miller are "realistic in every detail," but, dwelling on unpolished Americans, they tell half truths. The angry response to

Daisy Miller was therefore not wholly unjust. James has elsewhere drawn more polished European Americans, but not "the genuine American." The charming Princess Casamassima is an improvement over earlier works in that it does not try to teach a lesson about Americans. James usually eschews plot and heroic action, but parts of this novel are almost romantic. His short stories are as workmanlike as any, and can be too self-consciously clever. He is the leader of the American school of realists, and his refined, broad-spirited criticism is preferred by many to his fiction. James divorces art from morality in theory, but not in practice. By general agreement, he "ranks among the first of living novelists and critics," and is recently a successful playwright. His style is gentlemanly, clear, easy, and flexible.

28 WATKINS, MILDRED CABELL. American Literature. New York: American Book Company, pp. 182-184.

James and Howells are now "at the head of the new schools of realistic and analytic fiction." Daisy Miller was much read and talked about, but not much liked by American girls. A Bundle of Letters and French Poets and Novelists are good. James is analytic and writes conversations wittier than real ones.

1895

*1 ANON. Review of Terminations. Harper's, 91, Supp. 3, 648. (Unlocated. Cited in Ricks.)

2 ANON. "Notes." Nation, 60 (January 3), 18.

(Review of Theatricals: Second Series.) These plays have literary merit and their "polished and witty dialogue" will please the intelligent reader, but they are inherently feeble as plays, in "both conception and construction." Plots and characters are "curiously artificial, unlifelike, and extravagant," unworthy of James's "reputation and undisputed abilities."

3 ANON. "Henry James's Play Fails." New York Times, January 6, p. 5.

(Brief United Press item.) Though "splendidly mounted and well acted," Guy Domville was weak and without technique, a "stupendous failure." After the "hopeless" third act, James faced the jeering crowd with "scornful coolness."

4 ANON. Review of Theatricals: Second Series. Chicago Tribune, January 12, p. 10.

1895

Two plays "by literary men," James's "Guy Domville" and Oscar Wilde's "An Ideal Husband," received "'black eyes' from the rude populace of London last week." Wilde has had successes and so can afford a failure, but James "has no such reason to bear his ill luck with equanimity." Neither "The Album" nor "The Reprobate" is interesting enough in plot or vivacious enough in style to call for a description. James fails as a playwright simply because "he is an analyst and is not constructive nor dramatic."

5 ANON. "The Drama/'Theatricals.'" Critic, 26 (January 12), 38.
(Review.) The comedies "Tenants" and "Disengaged" are amusing and clever in their polite conversation and character sketches, but they lack such essential qualities as "action, progressive dramatic interest and plausibility of motive." Neither will add much to James's reputation as a dramatist, but they are pleasant reading and promise better things in the future.

6 ANON. "Notes." Critic, 26 (January 12), 40.
(Quotes New York Tribune and [1895.3] United Press cablegram account of "the failure" of Guy Domville, in which the second act dragged, "'the third was hopeless,'" and James faced the hoots and hisses with a gaze of "'scornful coolness.'")

7 ANON. "Henry James as a Playwright." New York Times, January 13, p. 4.
(Editorial.) Although James has worked hard, developed, and improved as a dramatist, his humor is too delicate, his plays too subtle, for success in the theater. He has kept his individuality and his plays have "a great literary charm" absent from the works of any other contemporary English dramatist except Pinero. Yet, his plays do not compare as literature with his other works, which always find "a good market." James has kept up his reputation as a novelist. No "intelligent person" will "make sport of his little discomfiture."

8 ANON. "Insults to James." St. Louis Post-Dispatch, January 13, p. 24.
"London is still discussing the sensationally hostile reception" received by "Guy Domville." (Detailed AP account of the audience response. See 1895.3, 6.)

9 ANON. "Henry James's Play." New York Times, January 27, p. 14.
(Quotations from two notices of Guy Domville by "the distinguished London critic" William Archer. Archer praises

the play as a whole, especially the first act, and criticizes the abusive audience.)

10 ANON. "Mr. James's Plays/They Are Not For The Stage." New York Tribune, January 27, p. 20.
(Review of Theatricals: First Series and Second Series.) These volumes show "how badly a man of talent can write" when he attempts what he is unqualified for. They have no action, interesting characters or situations, or felicitous expressions, only "depressing prattle" about insignificant matters.

11 ANON. "Mr. James as Dramatist." Dial, 18 (March 1), 156.
(Review of Theatricals: Second Series.) These plays are similar to those in James's first series, and one wonders whether, if produced, they would have had "as striking success as that attending" his "recent play at the theatre of his patron saint." James's comments are amusing, and make the volume more interesting. Though it is "rather mean to be sniffy" about anything by James, it is irritating that "when he can write such captivating things he should write such stupid ones."

12 ANON. "Fiction." Critic, 26 (March 2), 159.
(Reference to republication of Washington Square as part of a series promising "an inexpensive library of some of the best books published in recent years.")

13 ANON. "Theatricals." Literary World, 26 (March 9), 76.
(Review of Theatricals: Second Series.) It is curious that these "unactable comedies" should be published about when James's only acted play has been "hissed off the boards." These plays have "brilliant dialogue and clever epigram," but are "essentially undramatic."

14 ANON. "Literary Notes." New York Tribune, March 13, p. 8.
The Bookman tells of an American man of letters who finds James's plays unactable, unreadable, and unspeakable.

15 ANON. Review of Washington Square. Independent, 47 (May 30), 737.
This is one of James's "smoothly written, superanalytical, nothing-if-not-literary and upon the whole mildly pleasing novels." Like his other works, it seems artificial, intended to project "cosmopolitan breadth" but achieving only "a most refractory provinciality." James seems to write down to his countrymen, but does not fool them with his almost affected emphasis on breeding. He has "generally admirable diction" and is a self-conscious, "supremely clever literary

artisan," thoroughly "un-American in all his sympathies and aspirations." As a fiction this book is commonplace, but "as a verbal figment it is admirable."

16 ANON. "Mr. James in a Sombre Mood." New York Times, June 26, p. 3.
(Review of Terminations.) These stories have none of the "graceful gayety" of "The Private Life" or the comedies. They are subtle and elegant, but all but the few who relish whatever James writes will think them "uncommonly dry." The liveliest of these unlively stories is "The Coxon Fund." In "The Middle Years" and "The Death of the Lion" James writes "sadly and somewhat bitterly," and from experience, about "the difference between popularity and merit in literature." "The Altar of the Dead" is "still graver," a "strangely subtle yet scarcely satisfying tale." Overall, the workmanship is "beyond compare," except for one obvious error.

17 ANON. Review of Terminations. Chicago Times-Herald, June 29, p. 12.
James has grown more and more finished and lately leaves much to the imagination, but nothing to his readers' taste. Archly, he flits like a butterfly "from flower to flower of rhetoric." He is "elegant, but far from simple." James "deserves credit" for his high moral stand in "The Death of the Lion," whose style is "exquisite," with "touches of the finest humor." "The Altar of the Dead" is "a beautiful tale of sadness, repression, and forgiveness," and the sympathy of the characters is "most touching and lovely."

18 ANON. "Stories for Summer." Chicago Tribune, June 29, p. 10.
(Review of Terminations.) "The Altar of the Dead" is somber, even for James. (Plot summary and long quotations.)

19 ANON. Review of Terminations. Portland Morning Oregonian, June 30, p. 13.
In his "Literary Passions," Howells implies what seems to be true, that people either love or hate James, with no rational reason. James's individuality is "nowhere more strongly marked" than in these "sorrowful stories," because he does not feel, and does not let his readers feel, sorrow for his dissected characters. These people are "so analysed" that they lose all outward shape. James is clever, but "a shade among shadows."

20 ANON. Review of Terminations. Boston Daily Advertiser, July 6, p. 5.
In these stories the reader "happily misses" James's pessimism, and gets "graceful and artistic though serious

studies of character" in James's own style. They are impressionistic yet powerful, "genuine literary gems."

21 ANON. "Terminations." Detroit Free Press, July 8, p. 8.
The title is as ambiguous as what James writes, and if by "Terminations" he means farewell, "of course we shall all be sorry," though his unfavorable portrayal of Americans embarrasses and angers. "The Altar of the Dead" is "unquestionably the best" of these stories, though it has James's characteristic "air of indefiniteness." It is well written, has two ideal characters whose human nature keeps them from being "booky," and is beautifully spiritual and sad yet not pessimistic. Except for the humor in "The Coxon Fund," the stories are "a trifle gloomy and depressing."

22 ANON. "Terminations." Literary World, 26 (July 13), 218.
(Review.) James amuses himself by mystifying the public. These stories have even more than his usual "subtlety of style," but their plots are lucid. "The Death of the Lion" and "The Middle Years" have simple, sympathetic character sketches and suggest a return to James's "earlier and pleasanter, if less pyrotechnically clever, literary form." "The Coxon Fund" is confusing, and "The Altar of the Dead" uncharacteristically romantic for James.

23 ANON. Review of Terminations. New York World, July 13, p. 6.
Anyone but "an enthusiastic admirer" of James would find "The Death of the Lion" and "The Coxon Fund" "prosaic and tedious," dull. The other two stories, however, are "somewhat uncommon in conception, exquisitely tender and pathetic," "delicate and delightful portraitures of life from the sombre side."

24 ANON. Review of George Moore's Celibates. St. Paul Daily Pioneer Press, July 14, p. 18.
The third story of this book is in James's vein, but lacks his "exquisite paraphrases of feeling." Also, James is never indelicate, while Moore "is never anything else."

25 ANON. Review of Terminations. St. Paul Daily Pioneer Press, July 14, p. 18.
These stories have an "undertone of exhaustion" behind James's usual exquisite manner, are somewhat fantastic and morbid, and have an "overworked and lifeless" air, with little youth and hopefulness. They have artistic purpose, but not a wholesome or inspiring effect. "The Death of the Lion" has "certain grand outlines," and "The Coxon Fund" a "spasmodic brilliancy," but overall this volume will hardly add to James's reputation, even among his "most ardent admirers."

1895

26 ANON. "Mr. Henry James's Latest." Colorado Springs Weekly Gazette, July 18, p. 3.
(Review of Terminations. Because of "a little prejudice" against James, this reviewer has read this volume with care and tried to revise his judgment of one whom Howells "considers the greatest master of contemporary fiction.") Nonetheless, these stories are "dreary," nothing happens in them, and one wonders why they were written. "The Death of the Lion" and "The Middle Years" are just alike and do not succeed in being pathetic. "The Coxon Fund" is dreary and unreadable, with parts hazy and vague, but it has in it an idea that a "bright writer" might have made into something.

27 ANON. "Some New Novels." New York Tribune, July 21, p. 24.
(Review of Terminations.) James makes an unsuccessful effort to be exhilarating, and the vivacity is forced because his mood has become sad, his theme tragic, while his style has grown more "finical and thin," with the tone of tea table chatter. "The Death of the Lion" is almost bathos, its hero boneless, and its characters dull, "vulgar types, too vaguely drawn to be typical," their souls thrown away for the sake of talk. The delightful Frank Saltram never really satisfies the imagination of the reader, but rather is smothered in a mass of trivial talk. James has been synthetic only once or twice in his career, and here his line of analysis is futile, barren, inflexible, and dull.

28 ANON. "Notes." Nation, 41 (July 25), 63.
(Review of Terminations.) "The Altar of the Dead" outranks the other two stories in originality of conception and delicacy of imagination, and shows James's ability to find the right word. The other two stories will leave people wondering "why so exquisite a literary art" has not yet found a subject worthy of it.

29 ANON. "Henry James's Theatricals." Boston Evening Transcript, July 27, p. 10.
(Review of Theatricals: Second Series.) The "whimsical and quaint humility" of the "unique" introduction are disarming, and with witty paradoxes James makes "a clever and brilliant apologia" for managerially "'unavailable'" plays. "The Album" and "The Reprobate" are "well worth reading," "graceful little semi-satirical extravaganzas, immensely witty, immensely undramatic," that hit at "the social types and foibles of the hour." The characters talk charmingly and are good company, even though they do not "do" on the stage.

30 ANON. Reprinted review of Terminations. Cincinnati Commercial

Gazette, July 27, p. 13.
(Reprint of 1895.23.)

31 ANON. "Terminations." San Francisco Call, July 28, p. 21.
(Review.) None of these analytical stories has much incident, but the literary grace of the master of this art charms the reader. The moral of each story has an air of pessimism and mournfulness whose "subtle suggestiveness" is among the charms of the book. The volume will not increase James's fame, but it will retain "the wide circle of readers" of the "delicacy of sentiment and felicity of phrase" which have made him, in his domain, without a rival in English.

32 ANON. "Literature . . . 'Terminations.'" Critic, 27 (August 3), 67-68.
(Review.) Though always an analyst, James could now hardly be called a mere realist, because since Daisy Miller his "perceptions have broadened and deepened," his power of expression has strengthened, and his "vision has become too acute, his sympathy too rich," to be confined by a single theory. To convey "the involutions of so reflective, fastidious, and critical a brain" requires a complex style. In this volume, each tale has "something interesting." "The Altar of the Dead" is "improbable and evasive," with inscrutable characters, yet it compels our interest and its emotions are universal.

33 ANON. "New Books." Churchman, 72 (September 7), 262.
(Review of Terminations.) These stories have a "curious episodical character." Each is "a single idea, wrought out with exceeding care and felicity of touch." Rather than having no endings, these stories seem to be all ending. They are fragmentary, but clean. The "most artistically conceived" is "The Altar of the Dead."

34 ANON. "Comment on New Books." Atlantic Monthly, 76 (October), 565.
(Review of Terminations.) These stories have qualities of "Henry-Jamesiness," including "infinite elaboration, exquisite care, and utter disregard of his reader's time." "The Death of the Lion" and "The Middle Years" have a rather drowsy "atmosphere of refined satire" dear to many and even welcome in an age when letters are no longer "polite." In "The Altar of the Dead" the reader goes "into a sombre and fantastic land where Daisy Miller never came."

35 ANON. "The Best Recent Novels." Independent, 47 (November 21), 1579.

1895

(In review of the year's best fiction, comments on Terminations.) Henry B. Fuller's master is James. In Terminations, James "strikes a distinct note of romance," and his style, "always attractively parenthetical," has long, involved, breathless sentences. These stories are "of peculiar interest for their matter, their spirit and their manner."

36 BRIDGES, ROBERT [Droch]. "Bookishness/The Recent Stories of Henry James." Life, 26 (July 4), 8-9.

(Review of Terminations.) One must admire James's style, but his recent work also has depth and pathos. For "subtlety, poetical expression, delicate fancy and inherent pathos," James may never have excelled "The Altar of the Dead."

37 FITCH, GEORGE HAMLIN. "Some Books and Their Authors./Features of the Work of Henry James, One of the Foremost of Living Literary Artists." San Francisco Chronicle, June 23, p. 4.

(Portrait.) James will never be a popular author, but, like Meredith, he has "a small but enthusiastic following" who believe him "the ablest literary artist of his time." The "great body" of readers do not like his style or works because he writes for the few, his essays have too much elaboration and too many allusions, and his novels are weakened by too much qualification, explanation, analysis, and description. Yet, because he portrayed better than anyone the effect of Europe on certain types of Americans, one cannot neglect him. Daisy Miller, his most conspicuous but not his best work in this field, was too impersonal and unsympathetic, but now seems mild. The lack of humor and of the dramatic faculty are the "vital causes" of James's weakness as an author. His plays are a waste of time to read and have a weak dramatic framework, halting action, and no real life. His "most valuable work" is his essays on authors, which are "among the best" produced in the second half of the nineteenth century. "A Passionate Pilgrim," with its absurd plot, unappealing hero, and ineffective ending, illustrates James's method in the short story. No one has divined better than James the egoism and selfishness of creative natures. Among the novels, Roderick Hudson is "a singularly luminous sketch," and The Portrait of a Lady is the most finished. Since Stevenson's death, James is "the ablest conjurer with words" in English, but he misses Stevenson's "genuine poetry." James's lack of humor and of the "personal note" will forever keep him from being loved as much for himself as for his work.

38 L., J. B. "Books of the Week." Chicago Evening Post, July 6, p. 5.

(Review of Terminations.) James is more a critic of life than a storyteller, and appeals to reason rather than fancy. He is a master of style and in "The Middle Years" holds the reader spellbound. The stories are "curiously penetrating," with pathos and "melancholy charm." "The Altar of the Dead" shows the least finished literary art.

39 LATHROP, GEORGE PARSONS. "Short Stories by Henry James." New York Herald, June 30, Section 4, p. 5.
(Review of Terminations.) This volume is very different from Daisy Miller. No other writer in English could develop "The Death of the Lion" successfully. The involutions of James's style detract considerably from the "freshness and force of his inventions."

40 ROLLINS, A. W. "Ad Absurdum." Critic, 27 (September 28), 193.
Although the world found Daisy Miller an unkind treatment of the American girl's wretched manners, it is "one of the great compliments to the sincerity and moral sweetness of American girlhood."

41 SMITH, JOSEPH. "The Denationalized Native." Life, 25 (June 6), 379.
(Mock interview with a fictitious James-like novelist, "Washington Plummerby, the famous American writer and critic, who has lived abroad for the past thirty years.")

42 WAUGH, ARTHUR. "London Letter." Critic, 26 (January 26), 70-71.
The display by the ill-disposed Guy Domville audience was "unusual and very reprehensible," and James showed "genuine pluck" in facing them. Although the play had James's subtlety in developing motive and "much that delights the literary sense," it was unsatisfactory and, as everyone by now knows, "a regrettable failure." James should try again to achieve the success "to which his talents so eminently entitle him."

43 WELLS, CAROLYN. "In the Literary Klondike." Life, 31 (February 10), 107.
(Humorous descriptions of the "gold-claims" of various authors.) James's claim is large and carefully worked. His sentences are so heavy that they drop to the bottom of the stream, and he "pounds and polishes them till they're right up in shape."

1896

1 ABBOTT, ELIZABETH. Chapter 12, "Modern Novelists." In American Literature Papers. Boston: Lathrop Publishing, no pagination.
James and Howells are generally thought to be "our best novelists," though neither is dashing or lively. They will not continue to be widely read long after they are dead, because of the forgettable subjects they write of.

2 ADAMSON, ROBERT L. Review of Atlantic Monthly. Atlanta Constitution, March 29, p. 32.
The April Atlantic is "unusually good," and contains the opening chapters of "The Old Things," one of James's "delicate and yet dramatic delineations of character."

3 ANON. "Literary Gossip." Chicago Evening Post, June 6, p. 5.
(Review of Atlantic Monthly.) James's "interesting serial" The Old Things continues.

4 ANON. Review of Embarrassments. Boston Evening Transcript, June 13, p. 6.
These studies are sketched in James's "usual minute and clever manner."

5 ANON. Reprinted review of Embarrassments. Louisville Courier-Journal, June 20, p. 7.
(Reprint of 1896.4.)

6 ANON. "Recent Fiction./Henry James's New Book." New York Tribune, July 5, p. 24.
(Review of Embarrassments.) James has never been more clever and subtle, but this volume exaggerates his characteristic defects of "excessive retrospection," overcomplication, "almost vicious predilection for style," and "tyranny of sheer cleverness." Despite its charming style, "The Figure in the Carpet" is "an unprofitable, exasperating tale" with a very disappointing ending. In "Glasses" the portrait of Geoffrey Dowling is "splendid realism," and a "masterpiece of characterization." Some sentences "flash with the brilliancy of true wit," but the compositions as a whole do not match "the perfection of the details."

7 ANON. "The New Books of the Week." Philadelphia Times, July 5, p. 7.
(Review of Embarrassments.) James's stories grow "more recondite and more attenuated," but preserve "a distinguished individuality." These have an inconclusiveness, a "sense of baffled penetration." James probably has a diminished

audience which nonetheless finds in him unique artistic and intellectual qualities.

8 ANON. "Two Good Books." New York Commercial Advertiser, July 11, p. 16.

(Review of Embarrassments.) James's elaborate thinking and style need plenty of space, and he is not a writer for "the frivolous, the superficial or the dull-witted." His plots are often "frivolous and puerile," but he gives them an at first awesome "air of ponderous gravity" and has admirably beautiful syntax. In "The Figure in the Carpet" the pleasures of James's scholarly style do not make up for the dreary pages of dull, meaningless complications that confuse the reader and leave him uninterested and indifferent. Though leisurely, with "ponderous" machinery, the best of these stories is "The Way It Came" (plot summary). "Glasses" and "The Next Time" are lighter, but good examples of James's "mellifluous, graceful storytelling." It is not so much what he says as it is "his exquisite manner of saying it" that makes James "one of the most brilliant exponents of light literature" in this century, and "the Addison of his day."

9 ANON. "Embarrassments." Detroit Free Press, July 13, p. 7.

These "characteristic" stories which make up the "much heralded 'new novel'" by James all exhibit his "delicately analytic method" and emphasize not "mere incident," but the influence of events on character. They appeal less to those who want to be amused than to those who seek "the charm of literary style, a delicate irony," and subtle humor. James is like a "naturalist who discovers a miniature world in a drop of water" and lets us look through his microscope. Though he sometimes proses and is often thought dull by the unappreciative, his studies of "life's reciprocal influences" lay before us "the meanings and the depths of the psychological tragedies of human existence."

10 ANON. Review of Embarrassments. Boston Daily Advertiser, July 23, p. 5.

Though this book is not American, but "thoroughly and essentially English," American readers will enjoy it. "Glasses" is one of James's best character sketches, "remarkable in its interpretation and understanding of feminine thought." It and "The Next Time" are "absolute gems of their kind," with "fine, delicate, discriminating and polished" phrases. If James's theory of the novel is correct, they will rank among the best literature of the century.

1896

11 ANON. "Literature/'Embarrassments.'" Critic, 29 (July 25), 52-53.

(Review.) In style, these stories are very similar and harmonious. Yet, the characters are original, with "an exquisite flavor" we get from very few living writers.

12 ANON. "Henry James's Latest." Colorado Springs Weekly Gazette, July 26, p. 10.

(Review of Embarrassments.) A "small and highly select" group will welcome a new book by James, "delight in his fine-spun texture, and enjoy his style," but this reviewer has never been able to see why anyone should read James who does not have to. After a reading of the first story in this collection, this volume seems to support that impression. One would "wantonly insult" James by suggesting that his story has a moral, but if it does not, there seems no justification for his having written it and he appears to have been just filling space. Mr. Flowers's Arena novels on the initiative and the referendum would be better reading. (Plot summary of "The Figure in the Carpet.")

13 ANON. "New Publications." Philadelphia Public Ledger and Daily Transcript, July 26, p. 9.

(Review of Embarrassments.) James has gained his most enduring fame as a short-story writer, and no other author is so skilled at giving slight and obscure ephemera the "weight of serious moral problems" by the "sheer power of a literary art of compact style and minute analysis." The portrayal of real life scarcely occurs to James, and he does not appeal to our sympathies, espouse a creed, reform, preach, or inflame. We are left with nothing to haunt or reassure us, and we take no genuine interest in his pale, ghostly characters, but he has, in his own words, "'the talent for seeing the heroic in the familiar, and for exalting the trivial'" with details. The pleasure and stimulus of his works is "solely to the intellect, to the sense of order and fitness." "The "incomparable" style is "not always lucid, but rich, varied and stately of movement," with a complex diction. The mere power to appreciate "this elaborate and brilliant style is a distinction," and James's "fine, rare mixture of epigram, satire and worldly philosophy" makes other reading seem flavorless, "slovenly and dull." These stories are "consummate examples" of James's method which reaches literature's "most artful form and perfection of technique." They are not for the casual reader.

14 ANON. "Recent Fiction." Independent, 48 (July 30), 1037.

(Review of Embarrassments.) From James we expect "mild and polished," rather than great, delight. His stories excel his novels, and these are among his best. Written with great care, they "show how near a good style may come to the flimsiest preciousness." They will appeal to dilettanti.

15 ANON. "Recent Fiction." Nation, 63 (July 30), 91.
(Review of Embarrassments.) Style and form count for very much with James, with his "verbal niceties and felicities," his "crisp compactness varied by such leisurely lingering over evanescent detail." James plays with his mysteries "deftly and delicately," and "his very elusiveness and indefiniteness of effect somehow prove his mastery."

16 ANON. "Book Reviews . . . Embarrassments." Public Opinion, 21 (July 30), 152.
(Review.) Reviewers like to use reviews of James to tell how literature should be written. The stories in this volume are too discursive, lack incident. "Glasses" and "The Next Time" are too attenuated. Yet, James has produced much "excellent work" in the past, and will do so again.

17 ANON. Quoted comments. Book News, 14 (August), 616.
(Long quotation from 1896.7.)

18 ANON. "Some Sketches By Henry James." New York Times, August 2, p. 23.
(Review of Embarrassments.) These sketches are neither disappointing, like The Private Life, nor are they completely reassuring. They have so little subject that their interest is "as exclusively as possible technical," and therefore they will not be popular. "The Figure in the Carpet" is improbable and not one of James's successful treatments of the literary life. No one but a writer would be interested in it or "The Next Time," but "Glasses" has a more human interest.

19 ANON. "A Leaf from the Past/. . . Has Done Nobler Work." San Francisco Call, August 23, p. 23.
(Review of Embarrassments.) It is strange that a writer of such "conceded ability" prefers to write these uneventful, analytical, evanescent stories rather than a good standard novel with an object and purpose, like The Bostonians. The stories are "sparkling and forceful" and show James's command of English, but they will add little to his reputation.

20 ANON. "New Books./. . . Mr. James's New Volume." Boston Evening Transcript, August 25, p. 6.
(Review of Embarrassments.) "The Way It Came" is "a genuinely good story" with "motive, point and a climax,"

told "in terse and admirable English." It holds the reader's interest. "The Figure in the Carpet" is "a very bad story" whose "grace of style" makes its "absence of substance" the more exasperating.

*21 ANON. "Four Stories." Hartford Times, August 29, p. 13. (Review of Embarrassments.)

22 ANON. "Talk About Books . . . Other Fiction." Chautauquan, 23 (September), 783.

(Review of Embarrassments.) These are unique stories, in which James has "artfully analyzed human motives and emotions with a style as charming as it is original and lucid."

23 ANON. "Henry James as Critic." Hartford Courant, September 4, p. 6.

(Editorial. Response to a September 1896 Bookman article on James as a critic.) A liking for James's novels is a taste which, once acquired, can be extravagant. James is an influential American critic whose essays have "refinement, culture, keenness of perception," polished and roundabout expression, and "psychologic fantasticality." His "practical disavowal of conscience in literature" and his seeming to be "an aesthete at the expense of naturalness and manliness" have kept him out of touch with the broad reading public. He provides not portraiture, as the Bookman suggests, but "intensely subjective impressions." A "student of human nature in his way," James "lacks broad humanity" and has "a sense of . . . the drawing room" in all he does.

24 ANON. "Notes." Churchman, 74 (September 19), 338.

(Review of Embarrassments.) These stories are suggestive, interesting, and tantalizing, but do not have endings. They are "the idealization of failure," with "everything like results" eliminated.

25 ANON. "New Novels." New York Tribune, September 27, Sect. 3, p. 2.

(Review of The Other House.) This story excites interest, amuses, and has a bustling, theatrical quality that keeps curiosity at a peak. However, when this quality yields to that of the analytical essay, it becomes a hair-splitting conversational novel, like so many of James's others. Both James and Mrs. Ward are analytical and "excellent talkers" whose talk is "a stimulus and a pleasure" if not an inspiration.

26 ANON. "Books and Authors/Henry James' Personal Romance." St. Louis Post-Dispatch, October 4, p. 32.

Though James shies away from wedlock, the great romance of the life of this "apostle of bald realism" was Constance Fenimore Woolson, "a leader of romantic fiction." He was her "devoted slave" in life and the "principal mourner" and "man-of-the-family" following her death.

27 ANON. Review of The Other House. New York Herald, October 17, p. 14.

James's new book is "very clever," and its "careful workmanship" will be for many its chief charm. The story is "simple and attractive," the characters "original and well-drawn," the incidents "natural and clearly described," and the dialogue "crisp and to the point." This "meritorious" work has neither padding nor "vulgar sensationalism," and, though it does not inflame the reader with enthusiasm or overwhelm him with "vivid descriptions of stirring scenes," it will certainly add to James's reputation. It gives "many a jewelled sentence and happy thought," and James charms but never stimulates. He shows hidden chambers of the human heart, delights with his use of language, and is unsurpassed in "the art of writing fiction." When disturbance is abhorrent, the "well bred placidity" of James and this book is welcome.

28 ANON. Brief notice of The Other House. New York Sun, October 17, p. 7.

Naming James as the author of a book gives it "commendations enough."

29 ANON. Review of The Other House. Chicago Inter-Ocean, October 31, p. 11.

James is "a dramatist and an artist, as well as a prince among the writers of romance." This story is "intensely dramatic," full of surprises, and "wonderfully analytic in interesting characters," but James's digressions into eloquent analysis on "the verge of intensely interesting" episodes are frustrating and the "distinguishing feature of the story." James allows one of his "novel" characters, Tony, to "dangle . . . in midair" at the end, and after "all its artistic literary work, the story itself is not satisfactory, or at all cheering."

30 ANON. "Reviews of Books./Noteworthy New Fiction." New York Times Saturday Review of Books and Art, 1 (October 31), 4.

(Review of The Other House.) James is enviably interested in his craft, even in public failures like Embarrassments. The Other House is a success in England

and assuredly will be here. It is a masterpiece, one of James's best works and one of the best modern novels, with a good story as well as technical virtuosity, and an ending presenting a human tragedy "forcibly and movingly." Because of some bad, unnecessarily difficult writing, the reader must work hard to understand the book.

31 ANON. "Books for the Week." Chicago Evening Post, November 7, p. 5.
(Review of The Other House.) This novel is a step backward, in the right direction, because something exciting happens, as in James's early books. His descriptions are "nagging and small," he juggles phrases showily, he is "explicit to a fault," and he makes "misfit epigrams." Yet, the characters live. The book is "strange, intensely introspective," very diverting, and more memorable than some better stories.

32 ANON. "Among the New Books./Henry James' Latest Novel is a Stirring Tragedy." Chicago Tribune, November 10, p. 3.
(Review of The Other House.) The innocent title hides a surprising amount of action. The characters are so strong that they may have overpowered James into committing "the rankest heresy" and violating all his precedents by having them actually "do things." Rose Armiger is sometimes "less than human" because even James cannot create a woman who can do what she does and still be human. Her story sometimes repels, but is faultlessly unified, and fascinating. James is a "painter of miniatures," a critic, a creator, and above all an artist, so despite flaws in his materials and situations, or unlikeable characters, his treatment is flawless and the characters "live and breathe in a style quite unusual for the figures of a realistic cameo." (Plot summary.) James handles the motives well, and Rose's departure at the end is "dramatically, if not morally, satisfying."

33 ANON. "Literature." Congregationalist, 81.2 (November), 725-
(Review of The Other House.) James illustrates disagreeably his psychological expertise in a book with little incident and a "merciless frankness" in dissection that leaves little to the imagination. An unnatural, repulsive climax leaves the characters in an "apparently hopeless mess" that shows James's lack of "the sense of artistic fitness."

34 ANON. Review of The Other House. New York Observer, 74 (November 12), 756.
James can make these "bright little sketches . . . exceedingly taking." His style is "always clear and pleasant," and his books "have a charm that his many readers" recognize and "greatly enjoy."

35 ANON. "Literary Notes." New York Tribune, November 13, p. 8.
(Quotation from Blackwood's.) A carping critic in Blackwood's says the mother in "The Old Things" is more New York than English. James does not speak American at all and perhaps does not even remember his native language.

36 ANON. "A Man Who Was Liked Too Much." San Francisco Call, November 15, p. 21.
(Review of The Other House.) This "fine story" consists "almost entirely of clever conversations" and contains "fine bits of description." James's "brilliant way of saying things makes the book worth the perusal."

37 ANON. "Book Reviews." American, 25 (November 21), 315.
(Review of The Other House.) James has won eminence as a novelist, "which implies commercial success." Yet, despite the "self-complacency" of fine stylists like him and Meredith, "fineness may not necessarily be greatness." In this book, James condescends to become "readable by the common herd," shows more of the storyteller and less of the artist, makes incident and character count, and lets his people talk like real ones. The public will congratulate him. The tragedy gleams through "the light and pleasing web of his narrative" without destroying its charm, until the revelation at the end. If James continues to combine the natural with the artistic, he will be "classed among the greater masters of his craft," from whom he now stands apart.

38 ANON. "A New Novel by Henry James." San Francisco Chronicle, November 22, p. 4.
(Review of The Other House.) Whether or not one accepts his principles of writing, with "all their limitations of interest," given James's point of view this story "unquestionably maintains a high level of excellence, and amply proves that James "is an accomplished master in the art of fiction" as he conceives it. The workmanship is "most careful," the style is choice but at times perhaps "a trifle overwrought," and the dialogue is "clear-cut and epigrammatic." The excess of minute analysis and conversation, whose only purpose is to show "the play of subtle motives and the fluctuations of feeling," remains, but James "spares no pains to do his best," and this book is likely to rank high among his works.

39 ANON. "'The Other House.'" Critic, 29 (November 28), 335.
(Review.) This book is "an event of the first order," a "masterpiece." In this gripping and powerful work James confronts passion more directly than before, yet subtly and

artfully links motive with event. He will become popular, universal. Except for Rose Armiger, "the argument of the whole thing is absolutely flawless." The technique is "really marvelous," an application of a perfected short story method to the novel with "an almost startling success."

40 ANON. "Mr. Henry James's 'Theatricals.'" Critic, 29 (November 28), 340-341.

(Review of Theatricals: Second Series.) James's striving for rapidity of action and directness of speech has hurt these plays' literary and dramatic qualities. Their chief weakness is "manifest unreality," since the characters' speech does not match their manners or habits, and their actions are "purely theatrical," without natural motive. James would have done better to follow his own instincts.

41 ANON. Review of The Other House. Current Literature, 20 (December), 486-487.

These characters are perhaps "as odd a collection" as ever assembled by a novelist. James so carefully avoids the conventional and commonplace point of view that the result seems strained, with a suggestion of "unreality and stagecraft." The dialogue is disjointed, epigrammatical, and difficult, and the characters sometimes lose their firmness of outline, perhaps reflecting a Dutch influence. The story is "surprisingly and absorbingly interesting," and shows how a clever and skillful writer can make an unpromising plot and unrealistic characters seem probable. James was better, if less skillful, in the delightful Portrait of a Lady.

42 ANON. "Recent Fiction." Independent, 48 (December 10), 1693.

(Review of The Other House.) This book has James's usual admirably careful style, minute character study, and "valuable distinction," but its artificiality, "verbal artisanship," and "dilettantesque regard for conventional social pessimism" excite little genuine interest. The characters are "thin blooded, muscularly degenerate," repulsive, and unmagnetic people, "politely introduced."

43 ANON. "Current Fiction. . . . The Other House." Literary World, 27 (December 26), 476.

(Review.) As in his other later works, James is like a literary juggler of "highly colored impressions." When he tries to portray "overwhelming passions" rather than the mild emotions, "heaven save his readers." Tony is poorly drawn and unconvincing, and the plot "is really revolting in its cold-blooded lack of moral sense."

1896

44 BANKS, NANCY HUSTON. "'The Way It Came.'/Henry James's Newest Book Deals in Subtle Things." Salt Lake Tribune, June 21, p. 15.

(New York Letter, review of Embarrassments.) These days, when writers' reputations go up and down so fast, only a few ever achieve near an established reputation. Of these few, none "stands more firmly in his original place" than James. Despite their objection that his stories come from nothing and go nowhere, critics agree that the manner of coming and going is "eminently artistic and peculiarly fascinating." From the first James has seemed more English than American. The stories in this volume show no change in or falling off from "his characteristic methods and inimitable style," which is "as fine in literary quality and as psychological" as ever. The only difference is in the greater distinctness of outline of the "strangely pathetic" "Glasses," which has "a clear-cut motive," and of "The Way it Came," which is "still more dramatic and convincing," though it deals with a very elusive subject. (Long quotation from "The Way it Came.")

45 _____. New York Letter, review of The Other House. Salt Lake Tribune, October 18, p. 11.

In this book James has made "a sudden, wide and rather startling departure." The Other House has James's usual subtlety and the "exquisite literary grace" that has long made him the "unrivaled master of style among American writers," but this new book lacks, among other things, the "fresh, refined humor" pervading The Portrait of a Lady, The American, Daisy Miller, and nearly all of his earliest works. This story has a motive and theme wholly unlike those of its predecessors, and James's art always seemed too delicate for the "strong meat" of the "immorality and crime" at the heart of this work. The beginning "strikes the sensational as its keynote," and "with the lightness of a drawing-room farce" the story moves through "strenuous development" to "an appalling denouement" that the reader is unprepared for with his "new motive." That the book "is not dull or commonplace goes without saying," since James wrote it, but it is unlikely to increase his hold on his American audience that "has been so faithful" through all his years of "enlightened absenteeism." (Long quotation.)

46 BROWN, EDITH BAKER. "A Literary Journal. . . . The Other House." Bookman, 4 (December), 359-360.

(Review.) In the last few years James's art has declined, and steadily retreated from life. His recent stories are dreary and "lack the vital spring of art," as well as the poetic quality, the delightful, penetrating humor, of his best earlier work. Those early works had a vigor of life rather than of the artist's studio, while The Other House is artificial in construction, and is until the closing chapters like a play "without the necessary excitement of action" and "direct and speaking passion," "a drawing-room farce interminably and dully prolonged until the last scene." The book has one moving and "supremely beautiful" scene between Tony and his beloved, and James's usual subtle character portrayal, but "it trifles with its theme," does not "hold the sympathies with the conviction of life," and in its "general failure in emotion has spoiled a conception which might have been poetic."

47 HAPGOOD, NORMAN. "Henry James." The Bachelor of Arts, 3 (October), 477-488.

James's irony, subtlety, and style suggest "the airiness of irresponsibility." The abundance and fineness of his distinctions make us feel the futility of the world he describes. Yet, James is more than a "fascinating and cultivated satirist." "The whole that gradually appears is deeply typical of life, with much of its mystery." Literal, inelastic people limited to set classifications find him "remote, unreal, indefinite, inconclusive." He has range as well as precision, endurance as well as acuteness, and his subjects set forth completely "some essential springs of the mind." His art represents, but does not directly copy, life. His work lacks exuberance and a vivid sense of the physical, but his distinguished value is in his "perception of the shapes of the moral world." For him form and idea are inseparable. His metaphors are both baffling and convincing, and in drama he loses his charm and "misses the living touch." In his critical essays his inability to strike directly becomes repetitiveness, and his delicacy becomes squeamishness. He "narrows his vocabulary by overworking his fresh and apt words." Inhabiting both the world of art and the world of sympathy, James has been a needed education for Anglo-Saxons.

48 MACDONNELL, ANNIE. "Living Critics. IX--Henry James." Bookman, 4 (September), 20-22.

James's fiction suggests the critic, and his criticism the novelist. His methods in fiction are "mainly those of the critic," and when he writes serious criticism he is always seeking "the man or woman underneath the books." His foreign experience, light touch, and swift expression "have given him a reputation for a cosmopolitanism which he does not possess and does not aim at possessing." He has a Teutonic habit of mind, likes seriousness to be expressed rather than merely implied, considers the English superior interpreters of character, and makes "astounding judgments." His portrait of the French mind is "very appreciative, very fine, very forcible." Within "certain limits," James has given us a "marvellously true" version of Gautier, Hawthorne, and Balzac, with "no fumbling." James "is not merely the fine literary artist fastidiously carving and colouring," but has, "with more faithfulness than most," been fulfilling his vow to be "'infinitely curious and incorrigibly patient'" in judging the works of other men's minds. (See 1916.89.)

49 MORSE, JOHN T., JR. Life and Letters of Oliver Wendell Holmes. Boston and New York: Houghton Mifflin, 1:243. Rpt. 1897, 1899.

James was in the Saturday Club.

50 PATTEE, FRED LEWIS. A History of American Literature, With a View to the Fundamental Principles Underlying Its Development: A Textbook For Schools and Colleges. Boston: Silver Burdett, pp. 240, 429-432. Rpt. 1897, 1899, 1900, 1903. Rev. ed. 1909.

James is the founder and the best-known representative of the American realistic school. Few books "have raised such a storm of protest" as his early novels. For him, a novel is only "a study in sociology" and deals in externals. He has not yet portrayed a typical American gentleman or tourist, and his best work is in short stories and critical sketches, many of which place him "near the head of the American school of critics." His work's "chief charm" is in the "exquisite finish" of its style, a wit, grace, and refinement that hold the reader's attention despite the lack of incident.

51 RICHARDSON, CHARLES F. A Primer of American Literature. Boston: Houghton Mifflin, newly rev. ed., pp. 93-94. Rpt. 1897. First ed. 1878, 1880. Rev. ed. 1883, 1884, 1885, 1887, 1888, 1891, 1892, 1893, 1894.

James's early long novels are "like highly finished statuettes, clear-cut and cold." The Europeans and Washington Square show a relative lack of finish. Some of his short stories have a "warmth of human sympathy," even pathos. The Bostonians is his "ablest and most representative" work, and within "self-assigned limits" it shows "an honesty of portrayal not less marked than that of the sympathetic delineators of American folk-life."

52 SCUDDER, H. E. Review of Owen Wister's Red Man and White. Atlantic, 77 (February), 265.

In "The Real Thing," one of his subtlest stories, James touches most firmly the interesting truth that the actual is not necessarily the real.

1896

53 STOCKTON, LOUISE. "The Treatment of the Plot." Critic, 29 (July 25), 51-52.
No negative and natural plots can be more irritating than James's. He unravels his many-colored tassel and throws it down in a way that is like life, but not entertaining.

1897

1 ANON. "Comments on New Books." Atlantic Monthly, 79 (January), 137.
(Review of The Other House and Embarrassments.) Although James is "commonly reported" to have been unsuccessful as a playwright, The Other House shows his power "of developing a great tragic character," Rose Armiger. The story is "under the breath," the air "charged with electricity" up to the end, when "the storm bursts with a terrific momentary energy." Embarrassments is a group of the kind of brief tales which for many readers have come to represent James and place him among the "'decadents.'" If "super-subtlety of theme" and very "carefully wrought" expression constitute decadence, this volume puts James "inextricably in the decadent ranks." "Glasses" is the "most definitely powerful" story in the book.

2 ANON. "Book Reviews. . . . Henry James's Last Novel." Overland Monthly, 29 (January), 106.
(Review of The Other House.) This novel is "nothing more than a bundle of clever talk between a lot of clever people," is very much like a play, and would be a hit as one. It is very little like Daisy Miller. James sacrifices "interest to literary finish," the reader feels the book's unreality, Rose Armiger is too artificial to move the reader's emotions, and Tony Bream is too weak. Yet, the story is "bright, light, and artistic."

3 ANON. Reprinted comments on What Maisie Knew. Indianapolis Journal, January 4, p. 4.
(Reprint of humorous item from Chicago Post making fun of the title of What Maisie Knew and of James's subjects.)

4 ANON. "About Books and Writers." American, 26 (January 9), 29.
(Notes.) As literary art, The Other House probably "outranks all novels in English" of 1896. Daisy Miller is one of the few American women that live in books, and she is not as noble as she should be.

5 ANON. "Within the Sphere of Letters . . . The New and Enlarged Chap Book." Springfield (Mass.) Republican, January 17, p. 11.

(Review of the Chap Book.) This number of the Chap Book "contains several good things," including a serial by James that "promises well" (What Maisie Knew).

6 ANON. "Within the Sphere of Letters./ Topics of Passing Interest." Springfield (Mass.) Republican, January 17, p. 11.

(Quoted critical comments on The Other House.) The "most ridiculously inadequate" of the reviews of The Other House appeared in 1896.43. It "was bad enough" to give James's book "a bare mention" in the column of minor notices, and to rate the other current fiction higher, but the review itself is "excruciatingly funny." (Reprint of all of review.)

7 ANON. "Sir George Tressady and Other Fiction." Nation, 64 (January 28), 71.

(Review of The Other House.) The ending is an assault on the nervous system. The "technical devices are so skillful that things appear to arrange themselves without direction or supervision." James's people talk very cleverly, and readers who demand events get not only the catastrophe but also "the beauty and skill of the approach." Though robust young novelists may scorn James's concern for subtleties, they should study him to acquire a method "invaluable for the expression of any sort of a literary genius."

8 ANON. "North and South." New York Tribune, January 31, Part 3, p. 2.

(Review of The Spoils of Poynton.) To do what James does with inanimate objects is a significant feat. This book lacks the brilliant patches of The Other House, but is more substantial and will last longer. It has well sustained power, an uncharacteristic suggestion of poetry, poetic fitness at the end, and best of all, an "unconstrained spirit of vivacity." The humor is not smooth, the narrative is "often jerky and obscure," but James shows vividly his "consummate skill" as "absolute master of his material and his style."

9 ANON. "Talk About Books." Chautauquan, 24 (February), 630-631.

(Review of The Other House.) The diction is dignified and pure, and a less clever writer might not have developed the unique situation as skillfully.

10 ANON. "The Book Table . . . The Spoils of Poynton." Detroit

Free Press, February 15, p. 7.
James's novels require leisure and are like paintings whose details are elaborated at the expense of "strength and forcefulness." Especially in this book, with its "almost inconsequent plot," James writes of minutiae with the methods of the "critic and analyst of character." He "has spun a more than ordinarily agreeable novel, full of touches of somewhat whimsical humor, as if he thoroughly enjoyed the situation he has created."

11 ANON. "The Book World." Boston Evening Journal, February 20, p. 7.
(Review of The Spoils of Poynton.) This story has James's "remarkable dialogue and graceful style," some "brilliant and memorable plays of thought," without the subtleties of The Other House. The revelation of Owen's love for Fleda is "one of the most powerful things of the kind in recent fiction," and will refute the claim that James cannot describe lovers.

12 ANON. "Books for the Week." Chicago Evening Post, February 20, p. 5.
(Review of The Spoils of Poynton.) This is "a long, turgid, inexpressibly dreary" waste of words, emphatically lacking in ideas, imagination, and action, and dealing with "unresponsive trifles."

13 ANON. "Current Literature." Chicago Inter-Ocean, February 20, p. 10.
(Review of The Spoils of Poynton.) Readers of the Atlantic Monthly will remember this charming story, with its memorable and "beautiful descriptions," and its "profoundly interesting" dialogue. James interweaves comedy and tragedy "with masterly skill," the narrative is always good, the incidents are full of "life and movement, ripple and sparkle," and James has "seldom done a more polished" piece of work.

14 ANON. "Henry James." New York Times Saturday Review of Books and Art, 2 (February 20), 1.
(Review of The Spoils of Poynton.) Lately, James spins scant material finer than ever, here with no appeal to laughter, tears, or the universal "romantic taste." Though he aims to study characters, we care little for them. James writes exquisitely and treats Mrs. Gereth with irony and sympathy. Most readers will not understand her and James's views, but the one in 10,000 who does will delight in the subtlety, refinement, and piquancy, and that will be sufficient reward for both him and James.

15 ANON. "New Books." New York Sun, February 20, p. 7.
(Review of The Spoils of Poynton.) Though lacking the "passion and intense human interest" that distinguished The Other House from many of James's other works, this book is nonetheless "a very notable achievement." In less skillful hands, its motif could become trivial, but "by sheer force of his art" James holds the reader's attention to the end, despite his "microscopic and supersubtle analysis of motives" and "ceaseless working around and about an idea." He confronts us with a pulse-quickening situation that reveals his characters as not automata, but flesh and blood. The book is neither cheerful nor very hopeful, but it "contains that true note of tragi-comedy" which is "perhaps the dominant note in life."

16 ANON. "Books, Authors and Art./James's 'Spoils of Poynton.'" Springfield (Mass.) Republican, February 21, p. 13.
Who but James could make "so delightful a story from such attenuated materials"? Although it is a minor work, James has seldom had "a more characteristic subject" or "given us cleverer writing." His art succeeds in showing the overwhelming nature of the passion for the beautiful, and in convincing the reader of the beauty of the objects that in this case inspire it. The analysis of Fleda Vetch's "brave, honest, sensitive little soul" is "altogether admirable," and there is "hardly another living novelist who is capable of it." Having Poynton burn is "melodramatic and banale," and the restitution of the treasures is "somewhat illogical and not quite credible," despite the "superrefinement of psychology" intended to explain it. This novel will not, like The Other House, appeal to "a large audience," but those who like "delicate analysis and cunning literary work will find it one of the noteworthy books of the new year."

17 ANON. "Among the New Books./'The Spoils of Poynton' is Typical of Henry James." Chicago Tribune, February 22, p. 3.
This book shows James at his best and at his worst. Those who like his "perfect literary miniatures," his "dearth of action" and "deluge of analysis," his remarkable, "superhumanly" clever women and his "gawkish," scarecrow-like men who are merely their foils, and "all the appurtenances of the subjective novel," will enjoy The Spoils of Poynton. The others, "the vast majority," will find it not as interesting as the "less typical" The Other House. The story concerns the mind and feelings rather than things and acts. Now that James, like a modern doctor, has illuminated the inside of characters, we can see the "curious process" of dissection done with "marvelous skill," and be interested

if we like clinics. Technically, the book is a perfect work of art that portrays mental and moral struggles vividly. The ending is futile and disappointing enough without the burning of Poynton, but in discouraging readers' enthusiasm and optimism James is no doubt "true to his creed of realism."

18 ANON. "Books and Authors/Books of the Week." Outlook, 55 (February 27), 610.
(Review of The Spoils of Poynton.) In this "curious study of motive and character," James is as "delicately analytical, as deliberate in manner, as subtle in suggestion," as he has ever been, with "a keen humorous sense" throughout.

19 ANON. "Henry James's New Novel." Brooklyn Daily Eagle, February 28, p. 10.
(Review of The Spoils of Poynton.) This book has not much plot and does not appeal to the emotions, but it amuses and entertains, charms and delights with its "absolute finish," its "simple and forceful style." It is another triumph of "artistic excellence," an anatomist's dissection, but it leaves little impression in a way that suggests James is not a great novelist.

20 ANON. Review of The Spoils of Poynton. Cleveland Plain Dealer, February 28, p. 13.
For readers of the exciting romances of Rider Haggard, Stanley Weyman, and S. R. Crockett, The Spoils of Poynton is not a story. Yet, James makes it interesting, handling "the slightest materials" so deftly that the manner of telling, the "skillful weaving," pleases even if the result is too flimsy for practical use.

21 ANON. Paraphrased critical comments on The Spoils of Poynton. Indianapolis Journal, February 28, p. 12.
A writer in the London Mail finds James's "clear, delicate, dainty style" a relief after the "over emphatic method" of so many contemporary writers. He finds in James's work nothing spasmodic, sharp, or crude, but, rather, clear, evenly flowing writing. He says the lack of plot is even an asset, and in any event, is more than atoned for by the finish of character drawing and richness of detail in a story that "brings rest and refreshment to a jaded mind."

22 ANON. "The Spoils of Poynton." Boston Evening Transcript, March 10, p. 9.
The appreciation of James is becoming "more and more a typical thing." The "cultured class" talks in epigrams,

James's constant readers are no doubt those accustomed to social "'habit and observance,'" the "real enjoyment of his books" is a kind of test of familiarity with "good breeding," and James catches the tone of those "supreme" social circles more successfully than do Ouida's descriptions of furniture.

23 ANON. "Book Reviews/The Spoils of Poynton." Public Opinion, 22 (March 11), 312.
(Review.) James is at his best portraying Mrs. Gereth's embarrassment and conflict. He elaborates, but not, as in some of his other works, to a fault. The story is not dull, includes curious studies of human nature, and will interest the minority who can appreciate something other than romance.

24 ANON. "Henry James' Latest Novel." San Francisco Chronicle, March 14, p. 4.
(Review of The Spoils of Poynton.) This novel will probably confirm many readers' belief that James will never "repeat the brilliant successes of his earlier work." Like The Other House, it is clever, but it is "overwrought, often tiresome and . . . unconvincing," and suffers from tedious "unnecessary analysis and amplification." Occasionally James produces "a few thoroughly interesting pages," an epigrammatic sentence, or a neat turn of phrase, but, despite the effective ending, the story drags and is depressing. That a writer with such an admirable sense of style should develop the "countless mannerisms and affectations" of James's latest work, is unfortunate. This novel is not as full of them as was The Other House, but it has too much artificiality, strain, and effort, too many words with "forced and unnatural meanings."

25 ANON. "Some Recent Fiction." Literary Review, 1 (March 15), 41.
(Review of The Spoils of Poynton.) The plot is disappointing, but the style is very enjoyable. James is caviare to the multitude and delights students of expression, here even more than usual. The focus is on things rather than on people.

26 ANON. "New Books." Churchman, 75 (April 17), 608.
(Review of The Spoils of Poynton.) This novel shows that, with all his accomplishments, James lacks one of "the fundamental requisites" of the great writer, a sense of humor. He should satirize these characters' distorted motives rather than treat them seriously. As in most of James's books, the inconsequential people saying bright things and acting "in a purposeless and absurd manner" convey a sense of

futility. James is a master of literary wit in "a highly finished and artificial" style, but if he could handle "human nature as well as he does words, he would be the great artist of the day."

27 ANON. "Current Fiction./The Spoils of Poynton." Literary World, 28 (April 17), 126-127.
(Review.) The story concerns an "ignoble squabble," the ending is typical of James, and the reader remains "calmly indifferent" because the spoils and the characters "seem equally bloodless, unreal, and uninteresting."

*28 ANON. Current Literature, 21 (May), 388-389.
(Unlocated. Cited in Ricks.)

29 ANON. "'The Spoils of Poynton.'" Critic, 30 (May 1), 301.
(Review.) This book gives "keen pleasure" and is itself "a piece of decorative art," perhaps the only "wholly adequate and sympathetic study of the collector's passion" in fiction. Fleda is one of James's finest conceptions, the love scenes have "extraordinary force and fire," and the lovers are "human and real." As James gets cleverer, he becomes more convincing, and here he gives almost overwhelmingly "an intimation of perfection."

30 ANON. "Literary Notes." Life, 29 (May 27), 438.
(Humorous item.) James's admirers "will welcome the promised Abridged Edition of his Works, in a hundred neat volumes."

31 ANON. "The Lounger." Critic, 30 (June 26), 445.
(Quotes and gives qualified support to Henry Harland's statements in the June 5, 1897, Academy praising James as a short-story writer.)

32 ANON. "Recent Fiction." Nation, 65 (July 1), 18.
(Review of The Spoils of Poynton.) Given a certain sympathy for the collector's passion, Mrs. Gereth, whose expression of that passion is perfect, is "an impressively tragic figure." Her defeat seems more terrible than that of Fleda Vetch, whose renunciation is not credible. Yet, the fancy and phrases of which Fleda is woven "are good enough to afford a rare pleasure."

33 ANON. Review of The Spoils of Poynton. Independent, 49 (July 29), 980.
This story is not James's best, but it is entertaining--delicious whey for "people who can enjoy mere art." It has James's usual "distinction of style" and delightful literary

quality "tenuously drawn" through long sentences. A public cloyed with "coarse-grained and flamboyant" fiction will soon be ready for such work by a "'great little novelist.'"

34 ANON. "What Our Authors Are Doing." Life, 30 (August 5), 108.
(Humorous note.) James has gone to the mines of Siberia, where he will "spend the next six months polishing a sentence he has been at work upon since Christmas."

35 ANON. "Books of the Week/. . . Notes." Chicago Times-Herald, August 28, p. 9.
James's Harper's essay on George Du Maurier is "ineffably boring." Despite the keenness of James's criticism, the "absence of informality and sparkle" are forbidding, and the indirectness, circumlocution, and lack of paragraphing are trying.

36 ANON. "Rich Ore, but Hard to Work." Life, 30 (September 16), 233.
(Note.) James's language is good, and skillfully employed, but to get at the sense and meaning of it requires much exertion.

37 ANON. "What Maisie Knew." Literature, 1 (October 23), 19.
(Review.) This book will hardly enhance James's "great reputation." It proves that a novel may lack plot, amusement, excitement, and humor, yet still be worth reading. Even James's special, educated public may long for more wholesome fare than these characters' bewildering immoralities, unpleasant situations, and unpromising story. Sir Claude is agreeable, and Mrs. Wix the best drawn character, "thoroughly human and lifelike." There are subtle touches of humor and truth in some descriptions that show James at his best. With its analysis and elaboration, this "serious study" is difficult reading.

38 ANON. "Books of the Week/. . . Henry James' Masterpiece." Chicago Times-Herald, October 30, p. 9.
(Review of What Maisie Knew.) Although some parts drag, this book is never really tiresome, as some of James's others are. In volume form, the story seems more sharply striking, "more remarkable than ever." A study of "a large and important," hitherto unstudied class, the book relates "not only possible but credible" events. Though labeled indecent, it is "a very giant of a commentary on a fearful modern evil," the "first dignified and unshrieking protest" against "easy divorce and easy morality." It is a novel with a purpose which is yet "artistically concealed."

1897

39 ANON. "Henry James' New Novel." Brooklyn Daily Eagle, October 31, p. 16.
(Review of What Maisie Knew. Portrait.) This notable work by a famous writer is deeply interesting. It has no plot, but the skill with which James reveals the adults' foulness is admirable. The interview between Maisie and the captain is as fine a bit of satirical writing as James has ever done. The book will appeal "to students of literary expression."

40 ANON. "Books of Week." Providence Sunday Journal, October 31, p. 15.
(Review of What Maisie Knew.) This novel has James's "delicate workmanship," but is "a hopelessly sordid and vulgar story," a tragic situation made grotesque. Yet, its dullness should "make it innocuous."

41 ANON. "New Books." Indianapolis News, November 3, p. 5.
(Review of What Maisie Knew.) This story has little incident, conversation, or sensational effect, and demands an intelligent, perceptive reader. James tells it with sympathy, tenderness, and fine insight revealing a little girl's soul, but he uses too many words. The book is an admirable, though not a "'realistic,'" study of life as felt by a rich imagination. It will "add largely" to his reputation.

42 ANON. "A New Novel by Henry James." New York Commercial Advertiser, November 6, p. 12.
(Review of What Maisie Knew.) Though it treats a "distinctly unpleasant" theme, and is certainly not for the young, this book "contains some of the keenest, most profound analysis" this subtle novelist has yet produced. James "has handled a most audacious subject in a masterly fashion," shown "consummate art" in portraying the entire action from Maisie's point of view, and "revealed a depth of power" and an originality beyond anything in his other works. The influence of the symbolists is evident, and James is to be thanked for Mrs. Wix, who will "go down in history" with Dickens's Sairy Gamp. Although one must censure this novel for its surfeit of immorality, the book will sell, and its "marvellous insight" makes it "the foremost study of child psychology in contemporary fiction."

43 ANON. "New Books." New York Sun, November 6, p. 6.
(Review of What Maisie Knew.) The skill with which James "successfully treats a difficult and most unpleasant theme" is proof of "the rare quality" of his art. Given its world of "sordidness and selfish vice," treated coldly and intellectually like "a brilliant exercise in psychological

analysis," this book can never be very popular, but with the limited audience to which James "now more obviously than ever makes his appeal," it will rank among "his most notable achievements."

44 ANON. "Review of New Books/A Study of Child Development by Henry James, and Some Other New Novels." Portland Morning Oregonian, November 7, p. 12.

(Review of What Maisie Knew.) It is extraordinary that James could have lived with this "almost inconceivably disagreeable" subject long enough to write so many pages. If "the presentation of vice in ugly colors constitutes a moral story," this book is "highly moral," but "art surely has some better purpose, and morality some more hopeful issue than to administer disgusting lessons."

45 ANON. "East and West." New York Tribune, November 7, Supp., p. 8.

(Review of What Maisie Knew.) James builds an environment with "masterly precision," then puts in it anemic "people so hopelessly artificial, so abysmally vulgar, that all verisimilitude disappears." Maisie is plausible, and she and Mrs. Wix are sympathetic. The dialogue is vivacious and sometimes captivating in its rapidity and cleverness, but too much in the book is squalid and sordid.

46 ANON. "Henry James." San Francisco Call, November 7, p. 23.

(Review of What Maisie Knew.) The vile improprieties in this book are shocking, "yet so delicately put, so masterly written, with such infinite tact, humor and pathos," that one appreciates its subtlety and dexterity, its beauty of detail, and its "tender humanity." James is "a living master," and his books appeal to "the few who feel their exquisite delicacy," their uniqueness in English. His works have a rare, "peculiar value," and living, unforgettable characters. This is "a great book." (Portrait.)

47 ANON. "Books and Authors/Books of the Week." Outlook, 57 (November 13), 670.

(Review of What Maisie Knew.) Here, James keeps "his usual subtlety of analysis," but not his "usual distinction of manner." The study is not untruthful, but it is disagreeable and tedious, with an "eminently unpleasant subject."

48 ANON. Review of What Maisie Knew. St. Louis (Mo.) Republic, November 13, p. 4.

James "maintains his usual subtlety of analysis," but loses "his usual distinction of manner" and has "an unpleasant subject." Yet, the study of the meaning of Maisie's experience is "certainly an agreeable one."

1897

49 ANON. "Books, Authors and Art./Prof. Peck on 'Fonetik Refawrm.'" Springfield (Mass.) Republican, November 14, p. 15.

(Satire.) Sentences are being cut very short this fall. James, "one of the best-groomed men of letters in London," has removed "over a bushel of 'ands' and 'buts'" from his new novel.

50 ANON. "Recent Publications/The New Books." New Orleans Daily Picayune, November 17, p. 6.

(Review of What Maisie Knew.) This book is unlike James's previous work, and was "widely read and very generally and enthusiastically commended" during its serialization. It has James's "exquisite delicacy of style" and confirms his "high reputation as a master of analysis," but it lacks some of his "usual distinction of manner."

51 ANON. "Among the New Books./Henry James' Study of the Moral Effects of Divorce." Chicago Tribune, November 22, p. 8.

(Review of What Maisie Knew.) Reading this book is like riding the crest of a wave after being in the trough of the sea of fiction. The merciful lack of certain undesirable qualities makes its "positive excellences come as an afterthought." James can instruct as well as entertain, but does so less obtrusively than do most of his fellow writers. Mrs. Wix is delightful, "there are no tragic notes," and the climax as well as the details are wrought convincingly from the situation and characters. James's book is both "'important'" and a success.

52 ANON. "Literary Notices." Hartford Courant, November 25, p. 13.

(Review of What Maisie Knew.) When James changes "his moral atmosphere," he does not change his style, which is "impossible to parody" and "frequently so obscure as to be unintelligible." James does not recognize the effect of immorality on his characters, but, with his wit "as delicate as ever," is interested only in "how they behave and dress," so that his improper people differ little from his respectable ones. Yet, he treats his subject "with great delicacy" and writes nothing really improper.

53 ANON. "Books and Bookmakers . . . 'What Maisie Knew.'" Louisville Courier-Journal, November 27, p. 7.

Of the two classes of American realists, one, including James, pioneered realism, lived and wrote in a favorable environment, was "rewarded with early and genuine appreciation," and wrote of "the higher walks" of urban or foreign society. The second class of realists are the rising

American novelists, who also love naturalness, but have succeeded under less favorable auspices and so write of the masses. This "satirical study" by James is not lacking in sympathy because it deals with the wealthy, and is even harsher than the second class of realists in its "hatred of wrong and vice." Since James's readers are "generally the intellectual," the ordinary reader may wish this story had been "clearer and more dramatic"; the second class of realists would have been "strong and unsparing" in some of the scenes. A "leading American critic" commends James for his handling of "very dubious and delicate subjects," but lovers of James's "earlier and more powerful stories" hunger for "the same strength" in this latest book.

54 ANON. "Henry James's New Work, 'What Maisie Knew.'" New York Times Saturday Review of Books and Art, 2 (November 27), 9.
(Review.) Throughout, this book has exquisite workmanship, "marvelously skillful manipulation of words." At first one enjoys it, but by the inconclusive end, one wonders if it was worth the effort. The characters are queer and horrid, and James is concerned only with details, but the book is not "morally squalid."

55 ANON. "'What Maisie Knew.'" San Francisco Chronicle, November 28, p. 4.
This is "a peculiar book," unlike James's other works. It has his "old charm of style," but "the subject and the treatment are novel and not pleasant," leaving "an impression of sordidness and meanness." The "incomparable" literary art is the equal of anything in James, and is the only thing that makes the story tolerable.

56 ANON. "Chicago Items." Book News, 16 (December), 289.
(Review of What Maisie Knew.) The subject is revolting and the style tortuous, but this magnificent book is "one of the most remarkable" in English in years. No one but James could have developed Maisie's character so subtly. Her picture's "wonderful delicacy" is "beyond praise."

57 ANON. Current Literature, 22 (December), 505.
(Long quotation from 1897.43.)

58 ANON. "Some American Novels and Novelists. . . . Some American Novelists Abroad." Review of Reviews, 16 (December), 727.
(Review of What Maisie Knew.) James uses American methods and shows "superior subtlety and refinement of craftsmanship." Here, his vulgar material, his uninteresting, "drearily nasty" characters, are not worthy of his "extremely able treatment." Yet, despite the stifling atmosphere,

this is "a remarkable study of the mind and character of a child." (Portrait.)

59 ANON. "The Literature of the Year." Congregationalist, 82.2 (December 2), 860.
(Review of What Maisie Knew.) James illustrates his "peculiar artistic ingenuity," but does himself no honor in a book both tedious and revolting. He has sunk incredibly low to show his adroitness.

60 ANON. "Within the Sphere of Letters./The Proposed 40 Immortals." Springfield (Mass.) Republican, December 5, p. 12.
Despite his expatriation, it is odd to see James included in the London Academy's list of proposed members of an English academy.

61 ANON. "What Maisie Knew." Literary World, 28 (December 11), 454-455.
(Review.) Both this book and James's paper on Du Maurier are regrettable. James is undismayed by the events of his "inconceivable plot," and seems cold and utterly without generous human sympathy. The style is "jerkily incoherent," and the contents are "repellant to taste and feeling, to law and gospel." The novel is incredible in a writer whose work has been morally "beyond reproach."

62 ANON. "Recent Fiction." Independent, 49 (December 16), 1660.
(Review of What Maisie Knew.) Despite its insipid title, this is one of James's best works. Although it is "bloodless and effeminate," with "minute analysis of very disagreeable and . . . uninteresting experiences and aspirations," as well as an often foglike style, it will fascinate certain cultivated readers of "hot-house literature." It is "worth studying" as "exotic, strenuously forced," specialized fiction, "carefully sterilized" whey.

63 ANON. "Book Reviews/What Maisie Knew." Public Opinion, 23 (December 30), 855.
(Review.) This book has "the most delicate humor" and "the truest pathos," and shows "a most admirable" side of James's genius. He risks coarseness, but avoids it. His approach to the hackneyed and thankless subject of divorce is relatively original, and his power to portray "the soul of a child" compares with that of Zola and Barrie.

64 APPLETON, EVERARD J. "Book News for the Busy Book-Worm . . . Henry James--Hack Writer." Cincinnati Commercial Tribune, November 28, p. 27.

(Review of What Maisie Knew.) This novel is "undoubtedly the worst piece of work" James has ever done, very poor and silly, "indescribably worthless," and the most foolish, dreary, and tiresome novel this reviewer has encountered in the last ten years. It is flabby, padded, and dull, and ends in "a mental bog of nonsense." That this book was written by the author of Daisy Miller is surprising and extremely disappointing.

65 BRIDGES, ROBERT [Droch]. "Bookishness/Why 'Maisie' Isn't Worth While." Life, 30 (December 9), 518.
(Review of What Maisie Knew.) James never invented a better situation for his complicated art than this one, but this book is "one of the most vague, disagreeable and enigmatical productions" of James's usually "pellucid mind." The analysis, innuendo, and irony are "spun to the breaking point," to the vanishing point, and the book is "intelligently, artistically, analytically dull."

66 CABLE, GEORGE W. Comments on The Other House. Current Literature, 21 (May), 388-389.
(Reaction to an anonymous quotation that defends James against charges of untruth to human nature in The Other House. Quotation says that James knows these things better than the rest of us do.) What is resented is not the improbable, but the incredible and sensational, the failure to be true to art as well as to nature.

67 E[DGETT], E[DWIN] F[RANCIS]. "Writers and Books." Boston Evening Transcript, January 14, p. 19.
(Quoted critical reference. Long quotation from Joseph Conrad's praise of James in the North American Review.)

68 _____. Review of Irving Browne's The House of the Heart. Boston Evening Transcript, November 3, p. 10.
Some humorous verse from this book implies that James's works are not dry.

69 _____. "Literary Statesmen and Others." Boston Evening Transcript, November 24, p. 10.
(Review of Norman Hapgood's "Literary Statesmen and Others.") This book assesses James and others aptly and justly with very fine and "fine-spun" criticism. (Quotation about James.)

70 ERIE, MERVIN. "The Spoils of Poynton." Bookman, 5 (May), 258-259.
(Review.) This book "is no trifle," and in portraying the woe produced by bric-a-brac, James "deserves infinite

credit for seeing life in its true relations." The details of his workmanship "deserve close scrutiny," he seriously "keeps both eyes" on his object without stopping occasionally to tickle his readers, and is usually too interested in his subject to worry about being "true to his constituency."

71 F., E. "A Dozen Novels." Providence Sunday Journal, February 21, p. 15.

(Review of The Spoils of Poynton.) Critics now war over James less fiercely than they once did, and his "intellectual subtlety has conquered" even those who disapprove of his literary methods. Only an ardent Jamesian will enjoy this novel completely. Containing almost no passion, it contrasts very much with the intense and breathless Other House. Though it addresses the mind rather than the heart, it will greatly delight those who can appreciate the fineness of James's satire, "the keenness of his wit and the minuteness of his observation."

72 HAPGOOD, NORMAN. "Henry James." Literary Statesmen and Others: Essays on Men Seen From a Distance. Chicago: Herbert S. Stone & Co., pp. 193-208. Rpt. 1898. New York: Duffield, 1906.

James's writing has an ironical attitude and "the airiness of irresponsibility." The fineness and abundance of his distinctions increase our sense of the futility of the world he describes. He builds forms from a "mass of apparently surface touches that are adequate expressions of the deepest and most lasting experiences," creating a whole that is "deeply typical of life, with much of its mystery." Literal, inelastic readers find him "remote, unreal, indefinite, inconclusive," and he lacks exuberance and the ability to "paint vividly the physical world." His "rare, distinguished genius" is that of the artist as psychologist, and the personal, abstract idea, inseparable from his form, is what gives life to his work. He cannot represent "directness and simplicity of feeling," his fiction is better than his criticism, he overworks "his fresh and apt words," he "has been a marked man of his time," and he "has done a good work in it." (Reprint from 1896.47.)

73 HYDE, GEORGE M. "Mr. James's 'Adorable Subtleties.'" Book Buyer, 14 (April), 303-305.

(Review of The Spoils of Poynton.) Throughout, this "is a tale of thrilling psychological interest," but the last fifty pages "are vibrant with the fresh, almost reckless improvisation" of The Other House. The concluding scene has a "delightful irony," and "a lurid value not wholly unlike that of the Stonehenge scene" in Hardy's Tess. James's characters did not seem puppets, abstractions, or abnormal. The story has an "atmosphere of moral picturesqueness," and its theme, which only seems trivial, "was invested with an exquisite human interest." In unmasking the characters, James seems to sweep as with a searchlight, "the remotest nooks of the human soul." His story "is as complete and harmonious as a mosaic," with no uneven edges or loose ends, and no straining or mechanical effort, though the "gossamer web" of his style is sometimes "rudely shaken by ill-chosen words and figures." Those who "decry the purely artistic attitude" and "clamor for the picturesque" confess their "intellectual penury" when they fail to credit James's "triumph of taste" in elevating the commonplace "by the sheer force" of his art. Overall, one should be "universally sensitive to excellence," to that of Turgenev, Meredith, and James as well as that of Kipling, Hardy, and Mérimée.

74 NEWELL, ALFRED C. "Signs of the Times in Old and New Fiction." Atlanta Constitution, November 21, p. 20.

Contrary to what "some of the later-day faddists" believe, the days of Dickens and Thackeray are not over, and there is coming "a big literary reaction" in the older novelists' favor. The "freakism of the searchers-for-something-new is going to frazzle out," and there is "no permanent place for 'sexual fiction' in literature." Not since the time of Fielding and Smollett have "such vile contributions been shoved on the market" in the name of art--analytical, realistic art. The "remarkable" James's What Maisie Knew is an example of the work of this school, which is "doomed." Its "very real modern novelists are nothing more than reeking excrescences--soon to be cast off by healthy literary action."

75 PAINTER, F. V. N. Introduction to American Literature. Boston: Leach, Shewell, & Sanborn, p. 253. Rev. ed. Boston: Sibley & Co., 1903, 1911, 1916.

James originated the international class of fiction, and is "a leader of the realistic school of novelists."

76 PAYNE, WILLIAM MORTON. "Recent Fiction." Dial, 22 (January 1), 22.

(Review of The Other House.) This book is "the most readable" that James has produced in years. It is in effect a play in three acts, and the presentation of the visual details of the "scene" is very important and "so well done that adverse criticism is hardly possible." Yet, the action "is not altogether natural, and the tragic climax finds us inadequately prepared." This artistic flaw in the plot transforms "into crude melodrama what starts out to be a successful comedy of manners."

77 _____. Review of The Spoils of Poynton. Dial, 22 (May 16), 311.

In a "well-regulated novel," the young man would have married Fleda Vetch. This book is "written with the most delicate literary art," but remains "about as cold-blooded and unattractive as it is possible for a work of fiction to be."

78 SANBORN, ANNIE W. "New Books." St. Paul Daily Pioneer Press, March 21, p. 15.

(Review of The Spoils of Poynton.) If James's mission is "fine handling of sordid situations" and turning them into "backgrounds for nobility and delicacy," he "is more than a dilettante at life," as well as at literature. The effect of this novel is striking, yet "richly subdued" and "delicately indicated." This extreme refinement has developed so that the motive of Daisy Miller now seems obvious and those who resented that work "unconscionable boors." Only "a perfectly sure hand" could have kept the subject of The Spoils from becoming vulgar and boring. The beauty of the story is in the admirable Fleda, where James reveals "fine insight and rare finish." To have seen within and portrayed such a person, who lives her life as a whole rather than in patches, is an achievement, and women may thank James for having imagined her. This aspect of the story is subtle, but "saturating in its affluence."

79 _____. "New Books." St. Paul Daily Pioneer Press, November 7, p. 18.

The question of what Maisie knew remains unanswered at the end. In outline the story is as sordid as one of George Moore's, but in treatment, with James's "incomparable hair-splitting and wire-drawing," it is "astonishingly refined." Under the spell of his "fine interest in anything human," we find the "pathetic" little Maisie worthwhile and her environment absorbing. Mrs. Wix is "a masterpiece" worthy of Balzac, and no one less subtle than James could convey Sir Claude's charm, grace, and spiritual vitality. The characters uphold the accusation that James portrays commonplace people, but out of their "unbeautiful lives" James has woven a fabric with as much a proportion of the beauty of "pure aspiration and honest sacrifice" as the average soul achieves. People like Maisie, Sir Claude, and Mrs. Wix may not be worth knowing and would never read or understand James's books, but they owe James a debt for finding them out and giving them their due.

80 W., R. "Letters from the People./Henry James and the Mayoralty." Springfield (Mass.) Republican, October 29, p. 6.

(Satirical letter to the editor.) To correct the Boston impression that James is running for Mayor of New York, this writer has interviewed James, who aspires only to the House of Lords or the French Senate, and is unlikely to run anywhere but in the magazines. A mugwump must have started the rumor, since "no other political personage" is likely to have heard of James.

81 WELLS, CAROLYN. "A B C of Literature." Life, 30 (July 22), 68.

(Humorous verses about authors.) James "expounds lofty motives and aims," and has "sentences long," "arguments strong," and "the most unpronounceable names."

82 WILLIAMS, TALCOTT. Review of The Spoils of Poynton. Book News, 15 (April), 389.

This book shows "how completely method can get the better of the man." Here there is nothing but method, used so skillfully that it gives the effect of a reality which vanishes on close scrutiny.

83 WOOD, J. S. "A Recent Critique on Howells." Bachelor of Arts, 4 (April), 343.

James has been absorbed by London, and his later work "only shows fineness and polish, not ideas," because he has felt only the influence of refined London society.

1898

1 ANON. "'What Maisie Knew.'" Critic, 32 (January 8), 21.

(Review.) Though sometimes slightly tedious, this novel is "one more master-piece from a pen that produces little else." Of James's recent series of "remarkable experiments in themes and methods," it is the most "startling" achievement, "one of the most astonishing literary tours de force of the present generation." The "skill and tenderness" with which James handles the "unheard-of plot" go far toward compensating for "the atrocity of having devised it."

2 ANON. "Books of the Week./. . . Minor Mention." Chicago Evening Post, January 29, p. 5.

(Review of January Cosmopolis.) James's story is the best fiction in this issue.

3 ANON. Review of What Maisie Knew. Bookman, 6 (February), 562.

This novel refutes Christie Murray's recent "superficial" judgment that James could provide "supreme enlightenment" about the workings of the human heart, but does not. This novel is "all about the human heart," and is "full to overflowing of eager, tender interest" in Maisie's. Her growth is a sight "pitiable and beautiful," yet James "keeps his sense of fun," knowing that she will "come through with an unbroken and gentle spirit."

4 ANON. "As Howells Sees Fiction." New York _Sun_, February 6, p. 3.

(In interview, W. D. Howells notes James's remark that the novelist is one on whom nothing is lost.)

5 ANON. "Ten Novels." _Nation_, 66 (February 17), 135.

(Review of _What Maisie Knew_.) The fact that Maisie "never excites an emotion of compassion or pity" may indicate that she is "neither natural nor probable," but "an arbitrary, artificial construction." The method is experimental and cannot be called a failure, and in phrase James is "unusually brilliant," but he falls into obscure diction, too often mistaking it for subtle thought.

6 ANON. "Literary Gossip." _Life_, 31 (April 2), 281.

(Humorous item.) James's proposed trip around the world "is not, as we had at first feared, in search of vigor." It is likely that "this most conscientious of our authors is off in search of a word."

7 ANON. "About Books and Writers." _American_, 28 (June 11), 384.

(Response to James's article in _Literature_ on American literature.) That James "has no very intimate knowledge of or love for" American literature is evident in his "singularly cold and distant" remarks about it. He is "truthful according to his lights," but he should find out more about his country and then make "humble apologies to Howells, _et al_., and the playwrights."

8 ANON. "Literary Pickups." (New York) _Book Notes_, 1 (July), 29.

(Note.) James was wise not to serialize _In the Cage_, since his stories do less well in serial form than those of "any other recognized writer."

9 ANON. "Our Authors." _Life_, 32 (July 7), 13.

(Humorous item.) The "superb coldness" of James's style will be benefited by the climate of Mt. Blanc, where James will write "a novel of passion" whose scenes "will be laid in Boston and the Klondike."

10 ANON. "Gossip of the Authors." Life, 32 (July 28), 65.
(Humorous item.) James writes about eight words a month, and both he and George Meredith write their stories backwards.

11 ANON. "Fiction." Literature, 3 (August 20), 158-159.
(Review of In the Cage.) The whole story is told "with a subtlety and insight" in which James is unrivaled. Yet, though exquisite, it is cherry-stone carving and excessively elaborated. The scene between the heroine and the Captain is not very convincing, but managed "with considerable skill." The final scene is admirable and shows the "tragedy of humble and defeated lives" with unusual "quiet force."

12 ANON. "Brief Comment on This Week's Books." Life, 32 (August 25), 152.
(Humorous item. Reference to James's carefulness and attention to detail.)

13 ANON. "Literary Notes." Life, 32 (September 8), 187-188.
(Humorous item.) James's "great novel" What Maisie Knew has been catalogued among the books of reference in the library of the British Museum for the use of people over twenty with a doctor's prescription.

14 ANON. "'In the Cage.'" Chicago Evening Post, September 24, p. 5.
(Review.) James can perform "very cleverly in many different ways," though What Maisie Knew was disagreeable. Here, "brilliant" passages and sallies relieve whole chapters of "more or less tedious ruminations." The heroine's point of view is captivating and the story has "a positive fascination."

15 ANON. "Henry James's Latest Puzzle." Chicago Tribune, October 1, p. 7.
(Review of In the Cage.) James keeps his characters in a fog in this "introspective, analytical puzzle." It is "after the well-known James manner," only "a little more puzzling and obscure than usual." Having the young lady sit on the park bench with the Captain is "a daring amount of action" for one of James's novels. Lovers of fog at sea or "deliberate obscurity" in a picture or story will delight in this work.

16 ANON. "Books, Authors, and Art./Mr. James's 'In the Cage.'" Springfield (Mass.) Republican, October 2, p. 15.
James is read only by other novelists, and his characters often have the instincts of the novelist. The girl in this

book, for example, has the novelist's lively interest in people and social relations, and makes the conversion of facts into romance. In its "naive and hazy view of liaisons" the book resembles What Maisie Knew, and its "delicate portrayal of a sensitive and perceptive spirit in an alien environment" suggests The Princess Casamassima. This book also has "a real note of tragedy" in the blighting of the hopes of the two women, and a "delicious contrast" between social classes. It is "a subtle and finished study" of some "phases of English society," and the "keenness of its discernment of a small but fine nature makes it a work of art," but one regrets that James "does not employ his powers on more important material." Also, it is surprising to see such a scrupulous writer misuse "whom."

17 ANON. "Books, Authors and Art./Mr. James's 'In the Cage.'" Springfield (Mass.) Republican, October 5, p. 15.
(Review.) James, like "his greater exemplar Meredith," is "preeminently the novelist's novelist," and some say only they read him. It is "uncharitable" to speak of James as diffuse and wordy, but he does mix metaphors. Except for The Other House he nowadays writes only minor works. This is "an unsurpassed study of trifles," a brilliant use of meager materials.

18 ANON. "Mr. James's Imaginings." New York Times Review of Books and Art, 3 (October 8), 660.
(Review of In the Cage.) The enigmatic James formidably tries to make as much as possible out of as little as possible. All of his works are a boon to cultivated people, and his "literary charm is still potent," but his writing is growing more obscure.

19 ANON. "The Exceeding Cleverness of Mr. Henry James." New York Tribune, October 9, Supp., p. 14.
(Review of In the Cage.) James is subtle, pathetic, lucid, delightful, amazingly precise, and supremely clever in "nearly the most brilliant piece of writing" he has ever done. Yet, he wastes his time and ability on dull, offensive matters and trivial, base motives.

20 ANON. "In the Cage." Detroit Free Press, October 10, p. 7.
This novel shows out of what "slight material an author can build a book." The story is "deliberately and delicately" suggested rather than related. It is the art and "delicate intricacies of the pattern" James carves, rather than the content itself, that must reward the reader.

21 ANON. "In the Cage." Boston Evening Transcript, October 12,

p. 10.
James has hit upon "an ingenious method" of "kindling his imagination and that of the great clientage which delights to tickle itself with the fertility of his complex mind." Yet, the reader's mind "rebels at being poised upon such minute bearings," and most readers want "some verisimilitude, some real quality in the thing to be analyzed," in addition to "mere delight in the analysis." In the Cage will delight one who accepts James's "extravagant hypothesis," it is perhaps his "most refined work," and it has a style that is lucid rather than in James's involved later manner. Yet, the girl seems actually to be James, since her fantasy "is beyond any other human being's conception."

22 ANON. "The Two Magics." Literature, 3 (October 15), 351.
(Review.) "The Turn of the Screw" is "astonishing" and shows James's "subtlest powers." Although James is "one of the most interesting of writers," he is not the most lucid, and leaves "everything unexplained." "Covering End," though in James's literate style, is "as conventional as an ordinary stage comedy," full of familiar types, and an antidote to the "gloom and gruesomeness" of the other story.

23 ANON. "Magic of Evil and Love./An Extraordinary New Volume from Henry James." New York Times Saturday Review of Books and Art, 3 (October 15), 681.
(Review of The Two Magics.) After In the Cage's "painfully elaborate treatment of an almost worthless subject," these stories are "doubly surprising and gratifying." "Covering End" is richly humorous and exquisitely witty. "The Turn of the Screw" is "a deliberate, powerful, and horribly successful study" of evil, without being gross, grotesque, or didactic. It is "one of the most moving" and most remarkable works of fiction in many years. This gifted author's moods have changed over the years from that of the satirist and subtle humorist.

24 ANON. Notice of In the Cage. Detroit Evening News, October 16, p. 23.
(Brief reference to the plot.) The girl's "love affairs are not well regulated."

25 ANON. "The Newest Books." St. Louis Post-Dispatch, October 22, p. 4.
(Review of In the Cage.) James is "always diverting, but never thrilling."

26 ANON. "Fiction./A Masterpiece by Mr. Henry James." New York Tribune, October 23, Supp., p. 14.

(Review of The Two Magics.) "The Turn of the Screw" is great because it "crystallizes an original and fascinating idea in absolutely appropriate form." With it the author of a dozen fatuous works takes his place among literary creators. If James had begun earlier in this brilliant vein, where his genius resides, he could have been great. "Covering End" is forced, infelicitous, "a tissue of the wildest and most farcical impossibilities," a disgraceful companion to the ghost story.

27 ANON. "The Two Magics." Detroit Free Press, October 24, p. 7.
After James's "elaborate treatment of an inconsequent subject" come these two "quite distinct stories." "Covering End" has James's "spontaneity and graceful fancy," humor, and "remarkable powers of expression." "The Turn of the Screw" equals, "but is wholly unlike," Stevenson's Dr. Jekyll and Mr. Hyde in dreadfulness, and "holds a deep and moving moral." It is "a horrible successful study" of the influence of evil.

28 ANON. "Books and Authors." Outlook, 60 (October 29), 537.
(Review of The Two Magics.) James has written "nothing more characteristic in method and style" than "The Turn of the Screw." This tale is "altogether on a higher plane both of conception and art" than the common ghost story. It illustrates "a profound moral law," but the story itself "is distinctly repulsive."

29 ANON. Review of In the Cage. Time and the Hour, 8 (October 29), 10-11.
One man "of taste and feeling" has said he would rather have written such a book than to have led a conquering army or triumphed in the forum. For him, its "delicacy of thought and expression," its "triumph of keen analysis over crude activities," express "the fine flower of culture." For many others, however, it is too fine spun, oblique, trifling, and lacking in incident.

James's methods are "the amusement of elegant leisure," and in the improbable dreamland he here portrays, "things are unmoral." The style is more conventional than usual, though still difficult.

30 ANON. Review of In the Cage. Portland Morning Oregonian, October 30, p. 22.
This work has "fine analytical and emotional descriptive writing," but is "a disappointing novel." James "lavishes his rich powers upon this inadequate and unworthy-of-him plot," but "the exquisite beauty of the workmanship" is some compensation. This book is "cold and classical, . . . destitute of a note of human interest."

31 ANON. "In the Cage." San Francisco Chronicle, October 30, p. 4.
James wastes "enormous cleverness" on "a vulgar and commonplace subject." He "has never displayed greater literary art," but the story does not reward one for the time spent reading it.

32 ANON. "Mr. James's New Novel." Springfield (Mass.) Republican, October 30, p. 8.
(Editorial review of In the Cage and The Two Magics.) In the Cage is "finely wrought." "The Turn of the Screw" is gruesome, but its horror is mitigated by its "delicate and elusive" telling. "Covering End" would be trifling except for the clever character portrayal and the originality of treatment.

33 ANON. "Book Reviews . . . The Two Magics." Overland Monthly, 32 (November), 493.
Readers "who like the weird will be fascinated" by the "remarkable" "Turn of the Screw." James's style "has become as interesting as a Chinese puzzle" and reminds one of Meredith, except that James's combination of "riveting . . . the reader's attention on every sentence" and holding him absorbed with sensationalism is "unique among story-tellers." "Covering End" faintly reminds one of Daisy Miller, but the ways and speech of James's characters "have grown more intricate" since the time of Daisy Miller.

34 ANON. "The Two Magics." Book Notes, 1 (November 1), 331.
(Brief quotations from reviews of The Two Magics in the Chicago Inter-Ocean, the Nation, and the Springfield (Mass.) Republican.)

35 ANON. "New Books." Indianapolis News, November 9, p. 5.
(Review of The Two Magics.) James "retains his own magic" and charm for those who enjoy "searching delicate humor, subtile analysis of emotion and motive," vivid character portrayal, and "invariable good temper." Those who do not are unfortunate.

36 ANON. "The Two Magics." Literary World, 29 (November 12), 367-368.
(Review.) The hint of gruesomeness in "The Turn of the Screw" is vividly fulfilled, and one can only admire James's portrayal of child life. "Covering End" makes an old tale charming. Our great and genuine enjoyment of the book is more in the way the stories are told than in the stories themselves.

1898

37 ANON. "The Two Magics." Portland Morning Oregonian, November 13, p. 22.

"The Turn of the Screw" is "a thrilling and natural story, . . . meritorious because it crystallizes an original and fascinating idea in an appropriate form." It is "no vulgar ghost story" with "sudden shocks" or "clanking chains." "Covering End" is "a tissue of wild and farcical impossibilities."

38 ANON. "Some of the Year's Best Fiction." Independent, 50 (November 17), 1424.

In the Cage "represents plenty of good literature and not much else."

39 ANON. "Henry James' Latest Social Study." San Francisco Call, November 20, p. 28.

(Review of In the Cage.) Opinions will differ about this book. It is neither easy to read nor full of incident, and not "a very high class literary production." Yet, it is well worth reading, leaves a lasting impression, and has a charm when certain paragraphs are reread. James's unusual style of word painting is truthful, strong, and "very vivid."

40 ANON. Review of The Two Magics. New Orleans Daily Picayune, November 27, p. 10.

This "most fascinating tale" has well-drawn and lifelike characters, "brilliant and entertaining" dialogue, and the delights of James's style. Not since The Bostonians delighted readers has he given us anything "more subtle and clever" or fitting his "peculiar charm."

41 ANON. Critic, 33 (December), 450-451.

(Portrait by Will Rothenstein.) James is preeminently independent and pursues perfection in his art, so his peculiarities make the slipshod hostile and confound even his supporters. Yet, he has become one of our greatest men of letters and gives us a "'pleasure so rare.'"

42 ANON. "The Recent Work of Henry James." Critic, 33 (December), 523-524.

(Review of In the Cage and The Two Magics.) Lately, James seems to experiment with intricate problems more for his own joy than for his readers' edification. These two books are examples of this "literary rarefaction," so super-subtle as to be almost impalpable. In In the Cage James makes from very tenuous material a more "firm, rounded, finished product" than could any other living writer. This "marvellous piece of work" replaces facts with intuitions in a way that convinces the reader. "The Turn of the Screw" is "the most monstrous and incredible ghost story" ever written, yet this "imaginative masterpiece" also convinces and binds the reader by its spell. "Covering End" is almost "dramatically perfect" and ready for the stage.

43 ANON. "Books and Magazines." Pittsburgh Leader, December 2, p. 13.
(Review of In the Cage.) No one but James could have written this remarkable story. Its "highest quality" is James's sympathetic handling of his subject; he is respectful and impartial, not snobbish.

44 ANON. "The Season's Books." Outlook 60 (December 3), 881.
James has said that John J. Chapman's Causes and Consequences is one of the most thorough and intelligent American analyses of Emerson.

45 ANON. "More Novels." Nation, 67 (December 8), 432.
(Review of The Two Magics and In the Cage.) The contemporary popularity of James and Kipling, writers who are so different, suggests the influence of democracy on the production of literature. James has never used colloquial English with better literary effect than in these two volumes. He converts "into vivid, exquisite, immensely amusing pictures of life stuff that has long been the property of formal and tedious philosophers."

46 ANON. Review of In the Cage. Independent, 50 (December 15), 1791.
This is "a very vulgar story" dressed up to look stylish, "a dish of ill-smelling stuff carefully garnished with good literature."

47 ANON. "Current Notes." Time and the Hour, 9 (December 24), 10.
James's preface to Pierre Loti is interesting for its praise of Loti's travel descriptions.

48 BARRY, JOHN D. "On Books as Christmas Gifts." Ainslee's Magazine, 2 (December), 516-519.
(Review of In the Cage and The Two Magics.) In the Cage's subject is unique and its manner is "involved and fantastic." Equally involved is the style of the "very up-to-date and absorbing" Two Magics. A James novel is not a safe gift, but "he has ardent admirers."

49 BATES, KATHARINE LEE. American Literature. New York: Macmillan, pp. 128, 266, 319, 321-324. Rpt. 1900, 1904, 1910, 1911; Chautauqua Press, 1897, 1907.

1898

(Quotation from "The Art of Fiction." Full-page portrait.) Despite James's "fastidious finesse" and Howells' "warmer humanity, no really great American writer has emerged since the Civil War. Though James is criticized for lack of patriotism, he is not particularly hard on Americans and objects mainly to their vulgarity. The main interest of his books lies in his "microscopic observation of men and manners," his "labyrinthine discussion of problems of conduct" as matters of taste, the beauty of his detail, and the accuracy of his workmanship. Roderick Hudson and The Tragic Muse are two of his "richest books." Both his satire and his seriousness are well bred, and although some think his style overwrought, others like its "fine fascination." James converses with his own wit, his work is intellectual and self-conscious, and his general manner is "cold, watchful, analytic," but sometimes the language takes on "a strange and solemn glow" and he achieves at rare mements "the ethereal and the passionate."

50 BRIDGES, ROBERT [Droch]. "Bookishness/Cosmopolitan Literary Juggling." Life, 31 (April 9), 298.

(Review of Henry B. Fuller's From the Other Side.) Fuller gets the kind of pleasure from playing with the technique of a short story that is evident in James's best work. James has made it superfluous for any other American writer to "prove how cosmopolitan he is by sketching Transatlantic conditions."

51 _____. "Bookishness/Henry James as a Ghost Raiser." Life, 32 (November 10), 368.

(Review of The Two Magics.) James has frequently given his readers shivers by his coldness in treating intense emotions, and now tells a tale of terror "extremely well." His images are fleeting, but things of artistic beauty. "Covering End" would make "a beautiful one-act play," and James treats its situation "lightly and gracefully."

52 ESCONDIDO [pseud.]. Review of In the Cage. Book News, 17 (September), 19.

A "more delightfully whimsical little romance" has not come along in years. The telling is so "exquisitely adroit," with a delicacy that yet maintains emotional intensity. It is the work of a man "who knows his world and accepts it wholesomely."

53 HALE, EDWARD EVERETT. James Russell Lowell and his Friends. Boston: Houghton Mifflin, pp. 201-202. Rpt. 1899, 1901.

James was a member of the Saturday Club.

54 HOWE, M. A. DeWOLFE. American Bookmen: Sketches, Chiefly Biographical, of Certain Writers of the Nineteenth Century. New York: Dodd, Mead, pp. 258-259. Rpt. 1902.
(James is quoted briefly on James Russell Lowell.)

55 HYDE, GEORGE MERRIAM. "What Maisie Knew." Book Buyer, 16 (February), 66-68.
(Review.) Maisie is "morally at home in atmospheres which . . . would be appalling and awkward for anyone" but James to analyze. In his treatment of this "monstrous" situation James occasionally rises to the level of farce. He has "exhausted the psychological and satirical possibilities of his premises," and his "vision has penetrated to the tragic irony of things without wholly compassing their awful tragedy, which is well." James apparently enjoyed writing the story, but the "cryptic style," with its vague sentences and "the monotony of the author's hair-splitting refinements --a kind of morbid intellectuality," are regrettable. Probably quite unintentionally, he has written "a fine purpose novel." He "might have preached for hours and not produced such convincing moral effects."

56 LANIER, H. W. "Two Volumes from Henry James." American Monthly Review of Reviews, 18 (December), 732-733.
(Review of In the Cage and The Two Magics.) In the Cage is a "dreary monotone" of "laboriously intricate analysis and complex psychology." In contrast, the "horribly absorbing" "Turn of the Screw" shows James's "delicate, subtle psychology" to best advantage. Its horror puts conventional ghost stories to shame, and it is "the finest work" James has ever done, with a beautiful, fascinating sense of completeness, of finish.

57 MABIE, HAMILTON W. Review of In the Cage and The Two Magics. Book Buyer, 17 (December), 437.
James has lost none of that "cunning of craftsmanship" reflecting both "the subtlety of his mind and the refinement of his methods," but his method may have been "pushed too far for the highest interests of his art." The conception of In the Cage is "so tenuous" that nothing but James's art saves it from "utter flatness." Whereas others would have made of it "a brilliant tour de force," James gives this "extraordinary piece of work" a certain reality, but perhaps of art rather than of psychology. The human interest of this story is "less deeply felt" than the intellectual interest. "The Turn of the Screw" is "one of the most appalling ghost stories ever told," and its shock is not to the senses, as in most ghost stories, but to the imagination. (In review of Paul Bourget's Antigone and Other Portraits of

Women, Mabie notes that Bourget makes more concessions than James to his readers, has a less concentrated style, uses less ellipsis, and has "an easier and fuller" narrative movement.)

58 NOBLE, CHARLES. Studies in American Literature. New York: Macmillan, pp. 360, 366. Rev. ed. 1907, 1910, 1912.

Closely associated with, yet different from Howells, James is "one of the most finished and artistic" of modern writers. He says bright things in "the most inimitable way," his scenes and characters are detailed studies, with "fine delineations," and his conversations are perfect of their kind. His best work may be stories like Daisy Miller, "Tales of Three Cities," and "The Wheel of Time," but, though his work lacks incident and passion, it is "all strong." Though it will not be widely popular, literary students will like it.

59 PANCOAST, HENRY S. An Introduction to American Literature. New York: Henry Holt, pp. 178, 199, 244, 309, 311, 313, 314. Rpt. 1900, 1905. Rev. ed. 1912.

James left the "ideal and romantic beauty and grace" of A Passionate Pilgrim for works full of a "strikingly realistic" cleverness and penetration.

James and Howells are the recognized leaders in the realistic movement.

60 PECK, HARRY THURSTON. The Personal Equation. New York & London: Harper's, pp. 4-5, 118-119.

James's criticism of life is narrow and focused through an opera glass, rather than "the accurate and cosmic view of a sociological astronomer." George Moore is not wholly unfair when he says (quoted) that James fails to speak the "one magical and unique word" and that his characters never do anything decisive.

61 SANBORN, ANNIE W. "New Books." St. Paul Daily Pioneer Press, October 9, p. 19.

(Review of In the Cage.) This book is disappointing in its lack of story, and, more seriously, in its being a study "less worthy and less illumined by flashes of the divine element in man" than is usual for James. Mudge is "nearly the most distinct and amusing person in the book," and his marriage to the girl would be more consoling if she "herself had aroused a keener interest."

62 _____. "New Books." St. Paul Daily Pioneer Press, November 6, p. 26.

(Review of The Two Magics.) It is "a significant tribute"

to James's genius that these stories contain an excess of those two qualities essential to fiction, imagination and restraint. "The Turn of the Screw" is unmatched for "boldness of imagination and suggestion, and delicacy of treatment." The heroine of "Covering End" is "as intuitive and fine" as James himself, and though the "plan and motive of this story" are slim, the richly abundant setting and "brilliant visual effect of the whole" are in their way "a superb triumph." Our senses experience its characters "with a really thrilling completeness."

63 WELLS, CAROLYN. "In the Literary Klondike." Life, 31 (February 10), 107-108.

(Humorous comparison of writers to gold-miners.) James's mine is "large and carefully-worked." Though his heavy sentences drop to the bottom, he "pounds and polishes them till they're right up in shape."

1899

1 ACKERMANN, EDWARD. "Book Reviews." Book Notes, 2 (January), 48-49.

(Review of In the Cage and The Two Magics.) Many novels are greater than In the Cage, but few are cleverer. The subject is trivial and the plot scant, but the thought is subtle and the workmanship is exquisite, "perhaps the best" yet from this clever though not popular author. The morbid Turn of the Screw also has style and subtlety, and "Covering End" is delightful, with "brilliant dialogue."

2 ANON. "Chronicle and Comment." Bookman, 8 (January), 407.

(Quoted critical comment.) Writing for the Academy, Henry Harland says that James constantly attempts the impossible and constantly achieves it.

3 ANON. "Book Reviews/Mr. James Turns the Screw." Dixie, 1 (January), 59-60.

(Review of The Two Magics.) James is "perhaps the one anomaly of American art," and continues to shock readers. Yet, his skill and subtlety keep his horrible subject within the bounds of art and near those of propriety.

4 ANON. Review of The Two Magics. Sewanee Review, 7 (January), 124.

In these characteristic stories James should be less subtle, but his character analysis deserves much praise and his treatment of the supernatural is unique.

1899

5 ANON. Review of In the Cage. Literary Review, 3 (January-February), 15.
This subtle, exquisite book has "extraordinary power and reality," if not much plot. It is a psychological study as romance which "has never been excelled and probably never equalled."

6 ANON. "Literature." Independent, 51 (January 5), 73.
(Review of The Two Magics.) Though charming in style, nearly perfect in art, and showing James's genius, The Turn of the Screw is inexpressibly disgusting and evil.

7 ANON. "Books and Their Makers." Ainslee's Magazine, 3 (February), 112.
(Review of In the Cage and The Two Magics.) "The Turn of the Screw," one of the "most curious and subtle ghost stories ever written," has provoked much talk. In the Cage lacks "animation and interest." James's style has lost "clearness and simplicity."

8 ANON. "Talk About Books." Chautauquan, 28 (March), 630.
(Review of The Two Magics.) James skillfully paints the intangible and excites the reader.

9 ANON. "Mr. Howells's 'Ragged Lady.'" New York Times Saturday Review of Books and Art, 4 (March 18), 164.
(Review of Howells's book.) Though associated with Howells in the 1870's in their reaction against sentimental or artificial style, James was less merry and engaging then, and now diverges from Howells to explore the force of goodness through "repulsive channels" of vice and intrigue.

10 ANON. "Books, Authors And Arts/Some Clever Short Stories." Springfield (Mass.) Republican, April 2, p. 19.
(Review of book by Edith Wharton. Many references to evidence of James's influence on her.)

11 ANON. "Literary Pickups." Book Notes, 2 (May), 314.
(Review of The Awkward Age.) Here James shows his ability to analyze motives and to write brilliant, epigrammatical conversation.

12 ANON. "Something to Read." Indianapolis News, May 3, p. 5.
(Review of Sarah Jeanette Duncan's Hilda.) This author emulates James's "long and abstruse metaphysical discussion."

13 ANON. "Books of the Week./Typical Novel by Mr. James." Chicago Tribune, May 13, p. 10.
(Review of The Awkward Age. Portrait.) James is in a

sense "the Browning of fiction," with "the same obscurity of omission and commission." In The Awkward Age James "has given free rein to his passion for analysis and ultra refinement of phrase," and for all its intimidating length, the novel has "not enough action . . . to move a butterfly's wing."

14 ANON. "Books of the Day." Chicago Times-Herald, May 16, p. 9.
(Mentions the keen analysis in "Europe.")

15 ANON. Brief reference. Cincinnati Commercial Tribune, May 21, p. 31.
James and Joel Chandler Harris are two "of the best known American writers."

16 ANON. "Fiction./Mr. Henry James and his Literary Method." New York Tribune, May 21, Supp., p. 13.
(Review of The Awkward Age.) James is not a great writer, nor is he always clever, and he neglects issues for art. The novel fails to realize its situation's potential and is neither good portraiture nor good literary art, but rather is tortuous and trivial, lacking imagination, invention, knowledge, feeling, experience, life, and sympathy for life. The characters lack depth.

17 ANON. "Books of the Week/A New Novel by Mr. Henry James." Providence Sunday Journal, May 21, p. 15.
(Review of The Awkward Age.) This very talky book has a distinct story and a potentially "fine subject" with a "strong human interest," but contents itself with "mere virtuosity." James deals with his characters indirectly, and the way they discuss and analyze each other becomes wearisome.

18 ANON. "Books of the Day . . . Literary and Art Notes from Abroad." Boston Evening Transcript, May 24, p. 12.
(Note on James's plans to write "delightful travel sketches.")

19 ANON. "New Books." Indianapolis News, May 24, p. 5.
(Review of The Awkward Age.) James is obscure, his confusion and redundancy are worse than ever, and he elaborates at amazing length. Despite his literary skill, the trivial plot has little action and is "dull and deadly."

20 ANON. "Books of the Week./. . . Mr. James' 'Awkward Age.'" Chicago Evening Post, May 27, p. 5.
(Review.) In this interesting story, James paints characters "delicately and subtly," but they all sound like him and his style is "runaway."

1899

21 ANON. "Henry James's Latest Novel." New York Times Saturday Review of Books and Art, 4 (May 27), 349.
(Review of The Awkward Age.) James's admirers may falter through so much exquisitely subtle intricacy, on such a dull subject, but they will be glad to have read the book to the end for its dry, fine, elusive qualities. There is neither buoyant comedy nor heights and depths of tragedy. Although James's people are initially interesting, only Daisy Miller has been clearly memorable. Here, the characters are depraved, but nothing in the book shocks or uplifts much.

22 ANON. "The Awkward Age." Detroit Free Press, May 29, p. 7.
This novel is "a satire on all the phases that London society presents to those who understand it." The most delightful figure is Mr. Longdon. The story "reflects, as intimately as a mirror, the small lights and shadows of daily life," and has James's usual "delicate perception, . . . microscopic detail," and "subtle comedy and tragedy." Yet, for a reader without "a keen perception of literary art and style" this book is "prosy if not dull."

23 ANON. "Books of the Day . . . A New Henry James Story." Boston Evening Transcript, May 31, II, p. 12.
(Review of The Awkward Age.) James's artistic development would have been healthier if he had not expatriated himself. His later books have "a smothered effect," a "perfumed artificiality," and a trivial quality" that suggest the need for "some fresh, virile and tonic air." This book has "no obvious tragedy," and, though delicate, fanciful, and often clever, it is too long. The people never speak plainly or directly, and "juggle their adverbs" atrociously. In some of the descriptions, the imaginative, artistic touches appear with the old charm. With "two or three exceptions," James's "permanent reputation will depend not on his story telling," but on his travel sketches, essays, and "delicate local color." He does have "a genuine acquaintance" with the "smart" circles he writes about, and he "has chosen to divert his fine genius" to these "social studies," however "unimportant they may seem."

24 ANON. "Books of the Day." Chicago Times-Herald, June 1, p. 9.
(Review of The Awkward Age.) People who like James when he is "most thoroughly himself" will revel in this novel's "infinitesimal analysis" and "minute observations." The conversation is "sometimes bright and sometimes tedious."

25 ANON. "Books of the Week/Novels and Tales." Outlook, 62 (June 3), 314.
(Review of The Awkward Age.) The characters are not

"distinctly outlined in our minds," but the plot development is good. The book has James's usual subtle characterizations and his "exemplary English," but it is more like a psychology text than a work of literature.

26 ANON. "Literature./A Few Good Books for the Summer." Independent, 51 (June 8), 1565.
For those who "enjoy nothing so much as being thoroughly bored," there is The Awkward Age.

27 ANON. "The Newest Books." St. Louis Post-Dispatch, June 10, p. 4.
(Review of The Awkward Age.) In this "dramatic satire" James portrays current English social life "with all the wealth of observation, keen insight, and artistic power" which only he can bring to a subject. Mr. Longdon is "very charming." The book "is full of delicate comedy" and tragedy, and shows "an infinite keenness of perception of the small lights and shadows of our daily life, beautiful effects which only a literary artist could produce." (Echoes many phrases and ideas from 1899.22.)

28 ANON. "'The Awkward Age': A Satire on English Morals." Brooklyn Daily Eagle, June 11, p. 19.
(Review.) The English are much less sensitive about this portrayal of girlhood than the Americans were about Daisy Miller, who was charming and very American. The Awkward Age gives a "broader, finer" and much better picture of life as a whole than did What Maisie Knew, but its contents are thoroughly disillusioning. Not everyone likes James's style, but he is fascinating to writers because he is able to express inexpressibly delicate shades of meaning.

29 ANON. "'The Awkward Age.'" San Francisco Chronicle, June 18, p. 4.
This novel is "a characteristic bit of work" for James, "an elaborate attempt" to solve a problem which he does not finally solve. It is written with "all his accustomed skill," and the reader with leisure will enjoy it.

30 ANON. "Questions of the Hour." Life, 33 (June 22), 531.
(Brief reference.) Literary journals' contests to determine what literary men should constitute an American academy of letters are inconclusive. Voters are governed by the "fancy of the passing moment," and Laura Jean Libbey, Richard Harding Davis, and "Old Sleuth" vie in the number of votes received with Howells, James, Kipling, Fiske, and Warner.

1899

31 ANON. Review of The Awkward Age. New York World, June 24, p. 6.

Although this novel "may be a very life-like portrayal of English social life," the reader who prefers creations "with blood and bones" will find it "rather flabby and dispiriting," full of talk. The talk is natural, "often very bright," and sometimes witty, but perhaps not worth the effort required to read it. The study of Nanda is interesting, but "the details of her acquisition of knowledge seem unnecessarily exhaustive," although they are not as dull as some authors such as Howells would have made them.

32 ANON. Review of The Awkward Age. Bookman, 9 (July), 472-473.

Readers looking for a story, a problem, or studies of character all have "excellent grounds of complaint" against this book. Some will enjoy it, yet still doubt whether it was "worth the trouble of writing." As in What Maisie Knew and The Two Magics, James here studies "degeneration," but deals with it "so lightly and so politely, that you are convicted of priggery if you take it seriously at all." No other living writer could labor so patiently and delicately to make a fine point, "deal so sensitively with fine shades," and "analyse the slight so subtly, so wittily." The details have "infinite grace" and the observation "genuine fun," but the overall effect is "clumsy and even wearisome." James includes "too much good stuff" and "works a delicate thing to death."

33 ANON. "New Books." New York Sun, July 1, pp. 6-7.

(Review of The Awkward Age.) This book is an account of the conversations of a group of "superfine" people in London, a series of "long and very clever but exceedingly placid dialogues" that hint that "directness is vulgarity." No one knows better than James "how not to be vulgar." Some passages in the novel suggest George Meredith's "intrepid manner of expression," and these characters prize "the power of talking above all the other gifts of life." (Long quotations.)

34 ANON. "On the Library Table . . . The Awkward Age." Minneapolis Tribune, July 16, Part I, p. 4.

James seems "a greater artist than ever" with each new story, and "paints his characters so delicately and subtly" that one thinks they "cannot be improved, until the next appears." His characters' ideas "always match their deeds," and many of the people in this book sound alike. As in What Maisie Knew, the story is "a study of a girlish mind . . . brought into contact with the hard facts of a pitiless world."

35 ANON. "The Awkward Age." Literary World, 30 (July 22), 227.
(Review.) This "thoroughly disagreeable study" is a big dose of "analysis, intricacy, dry cleverness, and disheartening suggestiveness." James's observation and knowledge grow ever keener, and his "critical exactness is marvelous," but he drains "all the blood and warmth and goodness out of people" and leaves only their dry sins of disease rather than of passion.

36 ANON. "Book Reviews." Critic, 35 (August), 754-756.
(Review of The Awkward Age.) James "continues to surpass himself with regularity and ease," and for "subtlety and acute insight" this novel is ahead of all his other works. He studies "with his customary lucidity and exhaustiveness" parts of London society that other authors treat with awkwardness, embarrassment, and incompleteness. Nanda is his "supreme creation," his most absolute and beautiful evidence of the "essential nobility and high-mindedness" of the "nice girl."

37 ANON. "More Fiction." Nation, 69 (August 24), 155.
(Review of The Awkward Age.) These characters talk wonderfully, but too much, and have thin blood and acute nervous susceptibility. As a literary performance, this book is "very brilliant and fascinating," but it shows how in polishing a manner for perfection one may get "adrift from nature and lapse into the most artificial mannerism."

38 ANON. "Some Recent Novels." Churchman, 80 (September 2), 266.
(Review of The Awkward Age.) There is probably "no better analyst of character" writing in English than James, and no one manages conversations so well. Yet, his art is so subtle that it will likely defeat his purposes. Here, he makes us loathe the society presented.

39 ANON. "Books, Authors and Arts./Mr. James's 'The Awkward Age.'" Springfield (Mass.) Republican, September 17, p. 15.
This book will stagger even James's "sincerest admirers," and will not be among his six or twelve best works. It is like an enlarged photograph, "a typical specimen of his later work magnified most potently" to emphasize the "triviality of theme," the "riskiness of incident," the "ultra-refinement of language," and "a style so tortuous, so superfine, so elliptic," that Meredith's "seems almost like English in comparison." Yet, one may still ardently admire James as "one of the cleverest and wittiest" of current writers, who has "handled certain kinds of fiction with a finer technic, a completer skill," than any other living writer in English. This book is abundant in these qualities;

the "dialog never drags, and flashes with frequent wit." The people have the bloodless yet lifelike "drawingroom reality" possessed by all of James's characters, but the only entirely admirable one is the "charming" Mr. Longdon. Mr. Mitchett is sympathetic, and "very much alive," but Vanderbank is commonplace. Both young girls "are to be pitied," and the rivalry between mother and daughter for Van's love is "the least pleasing part" of James's theme. Despite the fine technique and quotable passages, the impression the book leaves as the "marvelous details fade from memory" is "a little barren." The story does "not begin to match" "The Turn of the Screw," or The Other House, in which James "struck a deeper, fuller note than he has lately aimed at."

40 ANON. "Howells on Writers Old and New." Chicago Times-Herald, October 23, p. 6.
(Editorial.) With his "mincing prettiness," James should only questionably be included among Tolstoy, Zola, Kipling, and Hardy. Scott, Thackeray, and Dickens are also above him. What Maisie Knew contains "finical writing and filthy suggestion."

41 ANON. "The Passing of Howells." Chicago Inter-Ocean, October 29, p. 16.
(Editorial.) The recent war has made yesterday's visions become realities, and caused "the romantic renaissance." People now demand "the power of a Kipling rather than the gilded touch of a Howells or James."

42 BANGS, JOHN KENDRICK. "A Roaring Romance." Life, 38 (June 1), 455.
(Review of F. Anstey's Love Among the Lions.) James might have found in the "'psychological moment'" wherein the heroine decides she must be married in a circus lion's cage, "ample material for an interesting discursion" of four or five hundred pages of "his charming, but somewhat puzzling, periods."

43 BRIDGES, ROBERT [Droch.]. "Bookishness/The World as Seen by a Subtile Telegrapher." Life, 33 (January 19), 46.
(Review of In the Cage.) James's style is "the most complex and subtile of modern writers in English." He is always "a consummate artist" and the working out of this story's idea is "an artistic triumph," but the "superrefinements of his reticulated phrases" limit the reader's enjoyment, strain his eyes, and enable him to catch James's meaning only "faintly through a mist."

44 CARPENTER, MILLIE W. "Heights and Depths of Henry James." New York Times, August 12, p. 540.
(Letter to the Editor.) A "vivid light" of criticism has been thrown on James's recent work, his "lovely, later, frost-picture pieces" which are fine, imaginary, not moral, and unlike his more open-corridored earlier books. These late books quicken the pulse with intellectual life, have heights and depths, and are events to be thankful for. (Points out similarities between Grandcourt in Daniel Deronda and Osmond in The Portrait of a Lady.)

45 _____. "'The Awkward Age' Again." New York Times Saturday Review of Books and Art, 4 (September 23), 622.
(Letter to the Editor. Response to 1899.47.) Some of the adjectives the "Cynic" applies to The Awkward Age are as displeasing as the book is. The novel's publishers and the editors of Harper's Weekly must not have thought it vile. Whatever the morals of James's books, their art is admirable.

46 CROSS, WILBUR. "The Contemporary Novel." The Development of the English Novel. New York: Macmillan, pp. 263-268. Rpt. 1900, 1902, 1903, 1905, 1906, 1909, 1911, 1914.
James is a literary impressionist and psychologist, an exponent of the "artistic presentation" of real life. The morality in his books is "higher" than in the old novels.

47 CYNIC [pseud.]. "'An Infamous Book'--Our Old Friend 'The Cynic' Says So." New York Times Saturday Review of Books and Art, 4 (August 19), 550.
(Letter to the Editor. Response to 1899.44's praise of The Awkward Age and James's other late works.) The Awkward Age is as detestable, vile, salacious, and erotic a work of fiction as has been written in the nineteenth century by an Englishman or an American. Yet, the characters are not openly wicked. Fortunately, the young people who read it will not understand it or will find it dull.

48 _____. "'The Cynic' Replies to 'Montblanc.'" New York Times Saturday Review of Books and Art, 4 (September 9), 596.
(Letter to the Editor. Response to 1899.53 disparages the feminine intellect.)

49 FISHER, MARY. A General Survey of American Literature. Chicago: A. C. McClurg, pp. 379-382; 2nd ed. 1901.
James's work would be delightful if his half-contemptuous, "unsympathetic, disillusioned attitude" did not make him at times "the least satisfactory of novelists." His overanalysis of character deprives the reader of his own interpretation. The disagreeable Bostonians is a clever satire. An

"exceptionally fine" critic, James is shrewder than Stedman and better on realism than Howells.

50 HOWELLS, WILLIAM DEAN. "The Latest Avatar of American Girlhood." Literature, n.s. 2 (July 28), 57-58.
James's portrait of Daisy Miller startled us into a new awareness of the American girl's qualities. Its rejection, as much as its acceptance, stamped it as "the most typical, if not the average, American girl." Americans failed to do justice to Daisy's charm, innocence, courage, and self-reliance. Copies of her abounded in fiction, but her type could not last.

51 KNIGHT, LUCIAN L. "The Literary World." Atlanta Constitution, June 11, Mag. Supp., p. 9.
(Review of The Awkward Age.) Admirers of James's "versatile and easy pen" will "cordially welcome" this book. Some of the portraitures are done in his best style, but the work itself lacks "brilliant interest" and is sometimes "rather dull and tiresome." James's greatest drawbacks are being "too analytical," and not terse and to the point enough. This work may please his old friends, but will probably not make him new ones.

52 McLEAN, M. D. "Henry James's Latest." Boston Sunday Post, May 21, II, p. 4.
(Review of The Awkward Age.) The Awkward Age is "very long and psychological," the quality that made What Maisie Knew fascinating and In the Cage depressing, and The Two Magics maddening. One can have too much of even James's clever subtlety, so that the news that his next work, "Europe," will be in his earlier manner, is a relief.

53 MONTBLANC [pseud.]. "A Word With 'the Cynic.'" New York Times Saturday Review of Books and Art, 4 (September 2), 591.
(Letter to the Editor. Response to the "Cynic's" letter criticizing The Awkward Age.) The Awkward Age is less good than M. W. Carpenter says (1899.44) and less wicked than the "Cynic" says (1899.47). The way its characters sneak around in their affairs is true to life, "an unretouched photograph."

54 _____. "'Montblanc' to 'The Cynic.'" New York Times Saturday Review of Books and Art, 4 (September 23), 634.
(Letter to the Editor. Implication that James is "a relatively clean" author. See 1899.48.)

55 PAYNE, WILLIAM MORTON. "Recent Fiction." Dial, 27 (July 1), 21.

(Review of The Awkward Age.) If drawing rooms were the world, one would have no reasonable ground for dissatisfaction with James's novels. He has never produced a book better than this one, but the pages of drawing-room talk and incident, though "delightfully finished and subtle" in the manner of cherry-stone carvings, are "inexpressibly" wearisome. They have "little to do with anything that makes life really worth having." There is no outcome, and the characters are not particularly interesting.

56 PRATT, CORNELIA ATWOOD. "The Evolution of Henry James." Critic, 34 (April), 338-342.

Critics recognize that James is "far and away the most finished prose writer" of our generation, but they do not always emphasize his "more vital qualities" coming from his refusal to compromise his art. He has grown rather than dried or slackened, and his example contains "an immense moral lesson for the young artist." He began with a "lucid, quiet, elegant" style and considered his subjects "with suavity rather than with fervor." Since 1890 his work's connotation has been "richer and its execution more brilliant than ever before," and he now "arouses enthusiasm rather than admiration." In the stories of the early 1890s, he began to exercise his breathtaking craftsmanship on the problem of saying the unsayable. As feats of execution, his novels of the late 1890s exceed anything in the language. James has focused on the "Thing Itself" he wanted to express, and thus produced works of "extraordinary vividness, . . . completely seen," detached and independent, performances "audacious and brilliant."

57 ROYCE, CAROLINE HALSTEAD. "An Appeal to 'The Lady from Philadelphia'--With Apologies to Mr. Bok." New York Times Saturday Review of Books and Art, 4 (September 16), 610.

(Letter to the Editor.) The likeness noted by Millie Carpenter (1899.44) between James's Gilbert Osmond and George Eliot's Grandcourt is "exceedingly real and interesting." The "Cynic's" claim (1899.47) that What Maisie Knew (The Awkward Age) is wicked in every line is excessive, but the book never had "any sufficient excuse for being."

58 SANBORN, ANNIE W. "Books." St. Paul Daily Pioneer Press, June 11, p. 20.

(Review of The Awkward Age.) To the extent that it achieves James's intention, this book is "a supreme work of art." Despite the mannerisms and "incredibilities of speech," James has with notable precision created a "prodigious" effect. The reader is not bored by enforced looks of London society at large, but rather sees more luminously "within a microscopic range." Mr. Longdon is "most lovable," and he and Mr. Mitchett are "inexpressibly and unexpectedly fine of nature." James has produced Nanda with "a completeness, a fidelity to scientific probability, and an optimism as to the survival of fitness" that almost reconciles the reader to the sacrifice of her individual happiness to the development of her type. The symmetrical arrangement of the characters on a moral continuum from Mr. Longdon's "conventional decency" to Harold Brookenham's vulgar parasitism, with Nanda's kindly, intuitive, radiant goodness in the center, is "especially masterly." James is "delicate without prurience," and "explicit . . . without salaciousness," and has shown that "the departure from the old domestic ideal" of morality in favor of "greater extremes of sensation" has brought people to a choice between turning back and plunging "to perdition." This book has "a moral writ large in every trenchant line."

1900

1 ANON. "General Gossip of Authors and Writers." Current Literature, 27 (January), 21-22.
(Reprint of Kenneth Herford's account for the Detroit Free Press of his visit to James. Description of James's life at Lamb House, emphasizing his neatness, kindness, and generosity.)

2 ANON. "Notes." Sewanee Review, 8 (January), 112-113.
(Review of The Awkward Age.) Despite his fine "psychological analysis of character and brilliant management of conversation," James has so overcultivated his special gifts that he has lost any gift of narrative he ever had. The Brookenham set is too clever, and the story too complicated.

3 ANON. "Literary Notes." New York Tribune, January 20, p. 10.
(Paraphrase of and quotation from James's North American Review article on French literature.) The article is "occasionally wearisome," and James's style does not improve with the years. Forcing it into the French mold has made him "both finical and obscure," "dull and tortuous."

4 ANON. "General Gossip of Authors and Writers." Current Literature, 28 (August), 148.
(Brief description of James's life in Rye as placid. Information from Saturday Evening Post?)

5 ANON. Note. Boston Sunday Post, August 12, p. 18.
(Announcement that The Soft Side will be published in

the fall.) Although the general public would not agree, James's earlier manner was better than his "later mood." Yet, this book supposedly "promises well."

6 ANON. "A Baffling Analyst./Mr. Henry James and His Twelve New Problems." New York Tribune, September 29, p. 10.
(Review of The Soft Side.) Never were there "more complex and baffling narratives" than these. Every line savors of literary detachment, technical preoccupation. The characters are puppets never clearly seen, their potentialities are not exhausted, they lack the vital human spark, and they are not really significant or typical. The endings are inconclusive, and the stories have an obscurity, an incertitude. James lacks the greatest gift of making action flow from a living character, and his analysis is to an extent self-defeating.

7 ANON. "Literary Note." Detroit Free Press, October 1, p. 4.
The Soft Side will provide James's admirers with "a good opportunity" to study his style, since the themes are varied, and the style is "by no means uniform." (Brief description of James's house at Rye, and his method of composition using secretary and typewriter.)

8 ANON. "New Books." Washington Post, October 1, p. 10.
(Review of The Soft Side.) These stories show at their best James's "characteristic perfection of style and method," his manner.

9 ANON. "Henry James' Subtle Tales." Chicago Tribune, October 6, II, p. 10.
(Review of The Soft Side.) For many readers these stories will seem bland and dreary, but their "fineness of style" is not commonplace, and is "a subtle concoction" with "temptations and delights," although James often seems to think style alone is enough. These tales are "typical examples of the exquisite perfection" of his art which hangs on a "frail thread of human interest." One of "the cleverest and most deliciously humorous" is "The Third Person," told with "consummate art." In "Miss Gunton of Poughkeepsie" James returns to his "fine and delicate analysis" of international episodes. In it he treats love scenes with a "delicacy and subtle refinement" few authors could match, and for which readers "can never be sufficiently grateful." It is always "the art of the telling rather than what is told that holds the reader's attention."

10 ANON. "New Books." New York Sun, October 6, p. 7.
(Review of The Soft Side.) This volume "will be welcomed

cordially" by "that select circle of readers" to whom James makes his appeal. One or two of these stories "seem, in their exquisite art and delicately subtle characterization, to touch the highest point yet reached" by this romancer who is a writer's writer. The psychological depth of the apparently slight "The Great Good Place," the "strange, uncanny fascination" of "Maud-Evelyn," and "the firm and certain stroke that lays bare . . . the hidden depths of human meanness in 'Paste,' all make one wonder more than ever" at James's skill. The "altogether delightful" story "The Great Condition" seems, of its kind, "an almost flawless piece of literary art."

11 ANON. "Books of the Week." Providence Sunday Journal, October 7, p. 15.

(Review of The Soft Side.) James has become the victim of his own cleverness, reaching a subtlety so extreme that his language is too involved for ordinary readers to follow. These stories present "some social and psychological problems of interest," but do not attempt elaborate study of character or social philosophy. They are agreeable, written "easily and pleasantly," with "a happy suggestiveness." "The Real Right Thing" is an admirable example of James "at his best."

12 ANON. "Some Recent Fiction." Chicago Evening Post, October 10, p. 5.

(Review of The Soft Side.) James portrays nothing so feelingly, so understandingly, as artists' devotion to art and to each other. Of the stories with this theme, "John Delavoy" is the best. One of the ghost stories has an "absurd psychological situation," and "The Great Condition" is "the prettiest of mature love comedies." James always provides enjoyable "verbal felicities," but his style is too complicated. Probably no living American writer furnishes "a keener intellectual treat."

13 ANON. "Lights and Shadows." Chicago Evening Post, October 10, p. 5.

The heralded return of James to Boston to live indicates that city's effort to "regain lost prestige" by acquiring this cultural asset. Perhaps Cook County can outbid Boston and secure James for itself, "but the returns would not justify the expense and trouble" and James is too devoted to London to return here.

14 ANON. "Recent Fiction." Churchman, 82 (October 13), 450.

(Review of The Soft Side.) James is read more for his well-known manner than for matter. These china-paintings seem always about to tell something, with delightful, carefully moulded structure. These and other realists' characters are so ordinary they are unreal.

15 ANON. "Books of the Week." Outlook, 66 (October 13), 423.
(Review of The Soft Side.) As usual, James is subtle, without solving anything. The stories are full of close observation, keen analysis, and James's delicacy of skill and style, but they are "too subtle, too psychological, too analytical."

16 ANON. "Henry James, the American Novelist, Says He Will Not Leave London." Chicago Times-Herald, October 14, II, p. 1.
(Portrait and brief biographical sketch.) James "is said to be English in almost all respects," and will not, as rumored, leave London to live in a Boston suburb.

17 ANON. "Books, Authors and Arts./Henry James's Short Stories." Springfield (Mass.) Republican, October 14, p. 15.
(Review of The Soft Side.) The newspapers rumor that James will return to America and possibly live in Massachusetts. He might find life here crude, but it would be good for his art and possibly carry it out of "the pretty little circle" where it has revolved for the past ten years "without making progress." James has had, perhaps, the "surfeit of prosperity" that is one of the dangers of success. Among "the most delightful" of these stories is "The Tree of Knowledge," which has a "most clever" ending. "Maud-Evelyn" attracted "much attention" when it appeared in the Atlantic Monthly, and the "singular little story" "The Abasement of the Northmores" has a curious, yet "very human" motive. "The Given Case" is exasperating, and "Paste" is "rather trifling," with interesting psychology but difficult reading. One hopes that not only famous authors like James, who "have their own way with publishers," but also less established writers will be able to cultivate the long short story.

18 ANON. "'The Soft Side,' by Henry James." Chicago Inter-Ocean, October 15, p. 9.
These stories have unsatisfactory endings, leave a bad taste, and disappoint the readers. With his charming literary style, James leads readers pleasantly along with "interest and romance" and "leaves them lost in uncertainties," thus trifling with them "more unscrupulously" than any other "great writer of romance." This volume is "a good illustration of total literary depravity."

19 ANON. "Masterpieces by Henry James." Boston Journal,

1900

October 19, p. 5.
(Review of The Soft Side.) For "ingenuity, subtlety, and richness of phrasing" these stories "are not surpassed in current literature." James's imagination is "rivaled only by the records of the societies for psychical research and he vitalizes these fancies with that same power of realizing the unreal" mastered by Dante. These stories' weaknesses are superficial and do not reduce their charm or force.

20 ANON. Review of The Soft Side. New York Commercial Advertiser, October 20, p. 8.
Most of these stories are in James's later manner, with which this reviewer is "growing decidedly impatient." It is "unlikely that any of our readers are not familiar" with James. "The Great Condition" is "remarkably good," and its situation, "worked out to the very last detail" with all James's subtlety, makes it "extraordinarily interesting." "Paste" and "The Tree of Knowledge" are "very well worth reading," but "The Great Good Place" is "pure twaddle" and the other stories are not particularly appealing. Readers with the James habit will read this volume anyway, and those "who do not generally read him can well afford to buy" it for the sake of "The Great Condition." (Plot summary of that story.)

21 ANON. "The Soft Side and . . . the Hard Side." New York Herald, October 20, p. 12.
"No contrast could be greater than that between the veteran" James and "the brilliant boy" Stephen Crane. James "easily maintains his position at the head of American letters," that is, if he is still an American and not a cosmopolitan. James represents the leisure valued by "the immediate past," and Crane "the strenuous life" that fits "the contemporary mood." James cuts with a rapier and makes Crane, who hews with a broadsword, seem "almost rowdyish." The Soft Side vividly illustrates the subtlety of James's thought, the "elaborate ingenuity of his style." The "delicate finesse of his art" seems "to reach the vanishing point" and leave only a fragrance which abides "even if the meaning is elusive." As ever, his dialogue is "as free as slang, as fine as art."

22 ANON. "Henry James's 'The Soft Side.'" New York Times Saturday Review of Books and Art, 5 (October 20), 717.
(Review.) These stories could have been written only by James. The analyses of motive and situation are done with James's surpassing skill and charm, his "supreme literary art," but sometimes its very distinction makes his style

hard to understand. He includes little material and few facts, and gives the reader a confusing, tangled mass of threads, woven with "almost miraculous ingenuity," and an inconclusive ending. With his "unrivaled powers," James should do more that is really worth doing.

23 ANON. "The New Books." New Orleans Daily Picayune, October 21, II, p. 9.

(Review of The Soft Side.) Without addressing "the vexed question" of James's position as a writer, one may say that this book is "noteworthy" and that despite certain obvious defects, its stories "present a singularly uniform average of excellence." They show James's usual "highly intellectual attitude and exquisite literary ability," as well as a certain aloofness and critical detachment that makes his observations seem accurate. His characters are not impressively real, but "have the value of carefully finished portraits." "The Great Good Place" has "vivid analysis," "Europe" is more definite and has "a climax of real power." James "is always suspected of writing allegories into his stories," and may have in "The Tree of Knowledge." "Miss Gunton," in contrast, "contains nothing elusive in its subtle delineation" of the American girl abroad. It has "a good deal of humor," and the breaking of the engagement is "delightfully imagined."

24 ANON. "The Soft Side." Boston Evening Transcript, October 24, p. 12.

In its last development, James's genius is that of "the cameo artist or the miniature painter" which on "the broader canvas of the novel" may be fatiguingly "fine-spun and even finikin." Each of these sketches illustrates his methods perfectly and is "completely delightful, stimulating and provoking to the fancy." To be admitted to the company of these subtle, sensitive, articulate characters is "enormously flattering." The title The Soft Side suggests how, "in the alembic of the master," the "stiff and ungentle traits of human nature are fused into . . . sympathetic harmony," a "charming texture." It is doubtful whether "the modern mind, fastidious and exacting as it is, could find more delightful feasts" than those in this volume. "The Great Condition" is the easiest for the beginner who seeks "the liberal education" that James "imparts to those who follow him," and the final explanation is "delightfully ingenious." "The Great Good Place" is "perhaps the most deftly fascinating" of the stories. Because of the "completeness" of James's art, excerpting and quoting from "the elusive, airy refinements" of his manner are not effective. Members of "the James cult" may be assured that this book contains "some of his best work."

1900

25 ANON. "Henry James' New Book." Detroit Free Press, October 27, p. 11.

(Review of The Soft Side.) Reading one of James's novels is like "traveling through a mirror-lined labyrinth," a "good deal of profitless" and baffling exercise despite the brilliancy and promising-looking openings. None of the stories in this volume have definite conclusions. James deserves "credit and praise" for the atmosphere, the "rare bits of description," and "a manner so distinctive," but his failure to "get somewhere or do something" is exasperating.

26 ANON. "New Stories by Henry James." San Francisco Chronicle, October 28, p. 24.

(Review of The Soft Side.) The title of the volume only remotely describes its contents. The stories are typical of James in that they are clever, but in the "perverse and exasperating" manner of his later work, with remorseless elaboration and overhandling of simple themes, and a "refined and manneristic" style that obscures meaning. These "peculiarities" are regrettable, especially when, as in "The Tree of Knowledge," they "mar our enjoyment of a really touching study of character."

27 ANON. "Library Table: Glimpses of New Books." Current Literature, 29 (November), 626-627.

(Review of The Soft Side reprinted from London Speaker discusses the relation of gesture to meaning in James's works, and praises The Soft Side as his best volume of stories since The Lesson of the Master.)

28 ANON. "Books of the Week." Outlook, 66 (November), 711.

(Review of A Little Tour in France.) These notes are "charming and leisurely." Author and artist "bring out delightfully" the features of the French towns.

29 ANON. Review of The Soft Side. Independent, 52 (November 1), 2638.

James is a master of words, but there can be too much of style, like any other good thing. These stories are nearly perfect pieces of work, but their art is infinitesimally fine, like cherry seed carving. James's genius has "nothing large, virile, compelling," and though his "dapper, natty . . . finely articulated" work charms us, it needs "the sound of a genuine, unhindered human voice to break the fine mechanical monotony."

30 ANON. "New Books of the Week." Indianapolis News, November 3, p. 12.

(Review of The Soft Side.) These stories are "a treat," pleasing in their delicate characterizations and exquisite literary art, but they are strange, the style is tortuous and confusing, and the characters are impersonal rather than flesh and blood. James is "a conscientious student of human nature."

31 ANON. "Books and Authors." New York Times Saturday Review of Books and Art, 5 (November 3), 750.

(Review of A Little Tour in France.) A reprint of a twenty-year-old work should not be passed off as a new work. No one is better fitted than James to express the "subtle, inimate attraction" of the Loire valley.

32 ANON. "The Soft Side." Minneapolis Tribune, November 4, Part 3, p. 8.

These stories' scenes and characters are aloof from "the sunny side of life." They are neither didactic nor dramatic, and have no purpose but to "depict in choice English some episodes in the lives of quiet, refined people whose claims to distinction" are other than wealth, "military prowess or political success." In "an age of sensational and war-like fiction," of Marie Corellis, Rider Haggards, and Stephen Cranes, it is "refreshing" to enter James's "select society of heroes and heroines." Now that James has left novels for short stories, he has been compared to medieval monks skillfully and patiently carving pictures on cherry stones. James's art of the miniature painter appeals to the few, since many wonder "how amid the storm and stress of modern life a virile intellect can find time for such finely spun and even 'finical' work." Yet, one is thankful to be led sometimes away from carnage, squalor, and commercial noise to the "quiet pastures" of uneventful lives. Miss Gunton is a "rather improved" Daisy Miller, and each interesting story has "its peculiar excellence and charm." The "'fit though few'" members of the James cult think, in disagreement with the general public, that James is the greatest living writer in English. His audience is "much smaller than that of the more sensational novelists," but readers who care for how a story is told will heartily appreciate everything he writes, and in its way his art "is perfect."

33 ANON. "A Literary Note." Life, 36 (November 8), 374.

(Brief humorous reference.) James is both obscure and prolific.

34 ANON. "Literary Notes." Albany Evening Journal, November 10, p. 9.

(Review of A Little Tour in France.) James has recently been so exclusively a psychological novelist that readers may forget that some of his best work is travel writing.

35 ANON. "Educational./. . . Literary Notes." Church Standard, 80 (November 10), 35.

(Review of A Little Tour in France.) James "has devoted himself so much to psychological fiction that the public has largely forgotten that some of his most felicitous writing" is in travel sketches.

36 ANON. "Literary Notes." Newport (R.I.) Mercury, November 10, p. 7.

(Review of A Little Tour in France.) Despite his devotion to psychological fiction, some of James's "most felicitous writing" is in travel descriptions. These sketches will please lovers of both literature and "the graphic art." (Very similar to 1900.35.)

37 ANON. Review of A Little Tour in France. Cleveland Plain Dealer, November 11, Part 3, p. 3.

(Notes the addition of illustrations to the original text.)

38 ANON. Review of The Soft Side. Congregationalist, 85 November 17, 703.

As usual, these stories "are masterpieces of analysis of mental operations," with "little or no external action." In one or two, James loses himself, and the reader, in his mental ramblings.

39 ANON. "New Books." St. Paul Daily Pioneer Press, November 18, p. 28.

(Review of The Soft Side.) These stories have James's "well-known style, with the lack of plot, the abundance of realistic detail, and close character analysis . . . so subtle" that it becomes at times incomprehensible, and "the involved and complicated sentence structure." Those who care for James like him very much, and "will admire the cleverness and subtlety of these tales." Those who do not like him are also ardent, and "will be repelled" by these stories' difficult style and lack of movement.

40 ANON. "Literature . . . Fiction." Independent, 52 (November 22), 2803-2804.

(Review of the year's best books includes The Soft Side.) In these tales reflecting "the last refinement of story-telling," subtlety "feeds on subtlety, until literary illusion becomes bewildering tenuosity." These "cups of shadow-soup," with their involuted sentences, have a feminine flavor and do not stimulate "a virile brain."

41 ANON. Review of new edition of Daisy Miller. New York World, November 24, p. 8.

This volume is "a most pleasant" reminder of "the early days of the American girl abroad." There has been "really nothing better in its way" since Daisy Miller first appeared, and she "is as true to life to-day" as when the portrait of her "attractive personality" was first "drawn so skillfully" and her "charming story" told.

42 ANON. "Holiday Books." Providence Sunday Journal, November 25, p. 15.

(Review of A Little Tour in France.) James's racy humor and "keen eye for the beautiful" make this "one of the most pleasing and popular works on the subject," and one unlikely to become out of date because of its charming style.

43 ANON. "More Fiction." Nation, 71 (November 29), 430.

(Review of The Soft Side.) In his devotion to the word, James "loses interest in the common aspects of life and in its broad issues," and becomes so obscure and aloof that he alienates his public.

44 ANON. "Some Collections of Short Stories." Review of Reviews, 22 (December), 767.

(Review of The Soft Side.) These stories show James's characteristic "wonderful distinction in style," subtle analysis, and perfect method. Despite criticisms that he neglects matter for form, he will never lack readers to appreciate "such exquisite delineations as 'Paste' and 'Maud-Evelyn.'"

45 ANON. "Holiday Books/. . . Henry James in France." Chicago Evening Post, December 1, p. 20.

(Review of A Little Tour in France.) James sees richly, much more than the untutored observer. Though written years ago, this book's value "is undimmed."

46 ANON. "Rambles in France." Literary World, 31 (December 1), 251.

(Review of A Little Tour in France.) Both James's and Clifton Johnson's books on France furnish "delightful reading," but James's is the more "intellectual and scholarly."

47 ANON. "Best Fiction of the Year." Chicago Evening Post, December 8, p. 6.

(Editorial.) In many considerations of and referenda on

1900

what are the best novels of the year, James, Howells, and Mark Twain "are passed over, while the most sensational of the American successes are not even represented."

48 ANON. "Holiday Books." Congregationalist, 85 (December 8), 859.
(Review of A Little Tour in France.) These sketches are graphic and graceful, superficial but "full of real interest."

49 ANON. "Other Gift Books." The Living Church (Milwaukee and Chicago), 24 (December 8), 247.
(Review of A Little Tour in France.) Despite (Richard?) Le Gallienne's accusation that he lacks virility and vitality, James is "genial, hearty, and wholly sane," though not florid. Here he has much of the "drop of blood" Le Gallienne found wanting, and many of the descriptions are memorable. James's vision is clear and constant, and his means of expression is always perfect, and perfectly mastered. He has an audience that stands for the verities rather than for the subtleties of literature.

50 ANON. "Miscellaneous." Standard, 48 (December 8), 433.
(Review of A Little Tour in France.) Any journey with James is "enchanting." He offers vivid impressions rather than technical lore. He is "observant, humorous, sympathetic," and readers will love and delight in this book.

51 ANON. "Among the New Books." Chicago Tribune, December 12, p. 13.
(Review of Daisy Miller.) New printings of this "deservedly famous" story appear "with charming regularity." Daisy is as delightful as any of James's females, and is "a sweetly pathetic bit of real femininity," but she may no longer be an authentic type.

52 ANON. "Life's Hall of Fame." Life, 36 (December 20), 532.
(Brief humorous reference. James, Chauncey Depew, DeWitt Talmage, Mark Hanna, and Theodore Roosevelt are mentioned as among the many candidates for admission to the fictitious "hall of fame.")

53 ANON. "Review of New Books." Chicago Times-Herald, December 25, p. 13.
(Review of A Little Tour in France and Daisy Miller.) In A Little Tour in France, the "minute quality" of James's method is visible, as is his emphasis on the psychological dimension of places. As a work for tourists, this book is a classic. Daisy Miller is also a classic, the "once and

for all" treatment of the American girl abroad, with many unsuccessful imitators. A copy should accompany every young American girl going abroad.

54 BRONSON, WALTER C. A Short History of American Literature. Boston: D. C. Heath & Co., pp. 284, 346. Rpt. 1901, 1903, 1905, 1906, 1908, 1909.

James is in his way a realist, "analyzing character and motives with great precision and subtlety," making portraits with a fine, microscopic finish. His style is "quietly vivacious," with "happily turned phrases," but he makes one wish for "broader horizons and a freer stride."

55 C., J. B. "Recent Fiction." Louisville Courier-Journal, October 20, p. 5.

(Review of The Soft Side.) No writer puzzles the mind as James does. He is "wholly intelligible" to the introspective, but to the "practical, observant world" he is "strangely vague." "The Great Good Place" will attract the attention of "the successful man in any class of life." "Europe" and "Maud-Evelyn" are sure to be popular because of their glimpses of "the intangible under world and outer world." The other tales are in James's style and manner, that of the medical student dissecting for nerves, except that James hunts "for tense and hidden workings of the mental machinery."

56 CLAPP, HENRY AUSTIN. "New Books and Those Who Make Them./The Soft Side." Boston Daily Advertiser, October 27, p. 8.

James's "Great Good Place" will not be acclaimed by "the religiously orthodox," and is "cool and dim" when compared with Mrs. Oliphant's "The Little Pilgrim," but it "has extraordinary delicacy and refinement" and shows James's "gift of subtle suggestiveness at its best." These stories have little to do with the ordinary conditions of life, and "gray cerebral matter and nerve tissue," rather than the blood for which James has no taste, are the materials for his "fine work." "The Given Case" is told "with exquisite finesse," "fine strokes of wit," and "clever observations of character," but is confusing. "The Third Person" is "faintly humorous," and "John Delavoy" has "extremely fine minuteness of detail" and satire that is "keen and bitter" yet fair. This volume contains "scarcely a passion," and it is "not news to anybody" that James is "'caviare to the general'" and does not appeal to the masses. His "many admirers" speak less of what he does than of how finely he does it, and he often puts a "severe and highly objectionable" strain on even an attentive mind. Almost no one but James "would have hit upon" the chief idea in "Miss Gunton," and "absolutely" no one else could have carried it out "to such an artistic and delightsome conclusion," one that will make "crude Americans everywhere" rejoice.

57 GILDER, JEANNETTE L. "Miss Gilder's Literary Letter." Chicago Tribune, October 14, p. 50.
(Review of and quotations from James's introduction to Century Classics edition of The Vicar of Wakefield.) James's introduction is different from the usual in that it says the book is far from a model story.

58 HORTON, GEORGE. "Stories By Henry James." Chicago Times-Herald, October 3, p. 9.
(Review of The Soft Side.) James fills out simple plots "with minutest ingenuity." There are probably 10,000 incurable Jamesites in America. This volume contains two or three stories "in his best vein" and several others "entirely unworthy of his reputation." It is disappointing to see a writer of James's rank do a stale and weak version of de Maupassant's "The Jewels." He can do very badly when he "sets his genius at the task."

59 HOWELLS, WILLIAM DEAN. "Editor's Easy Chair." Harper's, 102 (January), 318-320.
James has "supremely the gift of getting at himself," and he has an original view of life, expressed with a delicate and perfected method. Such "beauty and distinction" are not appreciated enough nowadays.

60 [KERFOOT, J. B.] "The Latest Books." Life, 36 (October 18), 306.
(Review of The Soft Side.) These stories deal with the peculiarities of queer people. A number of people like James's English, but the majority do not. James uses many commas, but several of these stories are "worth translating."

61 _____. "The Latest Books." Life, 36 (December 20), 530.
(Review of A Little Tour of France.) The convoluted "celebrated James style" of the preface makes an interesting comparison with the book, written sixteen years ago in plain English. (Comments on the illustrations.)

62 MCLEAN, M. D. "Books of the Day." Boston Sunday Post, September 30, p. 20.
(Review of The Soft Side.) These are entertaining, "capital stories, subtle bits of character study" in James's "most attractive manner." They are easier to understand than any of his other recent work. The book will not add to his reputation as What Maisie Knew did, but it will win back

readers who had given up trying to follow this master storyteller's dissecting and "psychological mazes."

63 PECK, HARRY THURSTON. "This Decade's Immortal Books." Ainslee's Magazine, 5 (February), 12-16.
In fiction, as in all literature, the 1890's have been the most sterile decade of the century. James's "most characteristic" and enduring work was written "more than ten years ago." Although he still shows the qualities of "a master of social psychology," he "never reaches now" the level of The American, The Europeans, and "The Point of View."

64 SHIPMAN, CAROLYN. "Many Points of View." Book Buyer, 21 (November), 299-300.
(Review of The Soft Side.) One questions whether the issues James treats are serious or insubstantial. His "power to analyze a situation to its fullest psychological extent" has not diminished, and his characters are still little more than puppets. These stories contain much cleverness, but much of it confuses or evades the reader. In addition to the "artistic perfection" already obtained, the reader asks James for "real heart behind the automatic hearts" of his characters. Yet, The Soft Side has "a degree more of human interest" than Terminations had.

1901

1 ANON. "A Short Guide to New Books." World's Work, 1 (February), 442.
(Review of The Soft Side.) James "unravels psychological complications with his extremest irony and subtlety." These stories are "good brain exercise," "too brilliantly clever not to be interesting," but "somewhat bloodless and overrefined."

2 ANON. "Vampires." New York Tribune, February 9, p. 8.
(Review of The Sacred Fount.) The Awkward Age and The Soft Side disappointed hopes raised by "The Turn of the Screw" that James would eschew trivialities for creative imagination. In The Sacred Fount he treats something like the supernatural with as little imagination as possible. What he tries for is almost unbelievably irrelevant, and the impish, analytical James deals in "'the palpable obscure.'" The novel contains not life, but only figures juggled in a pattern.

3 ANON. "Books of the Week./. . . Mr. James' Unrevealed Secret."

1901

Chicago Evening Post, February 9, p. 5.
(Review of The Sacred Fount.) In 300 "hairsplitting pages," James does not reveal this book's secret. The bored outsider feels unable to breathe the rarefied atmosphere of subtlety. At the beginning James sets his witty characters forth in vivid, refreshing terms, with "inimitable, amazing art," but the subject may not be worthwhile.

4 ANON. Notice of The Sacred Fount. Chicago Tribune, February 9, p. 10.
This novel "is said to present a series of somewhat remarkable character studies of a group of English men and women. . . ."

5 ANON. "Books of the Week . . . Of Three Notable Novels That Open the . . . International Spring Season Two Are American." New York Herald, February 9, p. 12.
(Notice of The Sacred Fount.) "Despite their long residence abroad and their devotion to English themes," Henry James and John Oliver Hobbes are American not only by birth, but also in "their training, their instincts, and their literary methods." With this "good beginning," one hopes that more American authors "will establish . . . international reputations."

6 ANON. "Books of the Week . . . Opening of the Spring Season Looked . . . Upon with Anxiety by English Publishers . . . Living Writers with Great Sales." New York Herald, February 9, p. 12.
(Note.) "Among living writers the greatest sales go to Marie Corelli, Hall Caine and Guy Boothby." Novelists like James, Joseph Conrad, Maurice Hewlett, and Henry Harland have readers enough "to make the publishing of their books a successful financial operation."

7 ANON. "Henry James in a Fresh Analysis of 'Polite' Society." New York World, February 9, p. 8.
(Review of The Sacred Fount.) To make clear the point that in the society of this book it is "everybody's business to be concerned" with everybody else's business, James writes a "great deal of conversation and social analysis." The book has no incidents, but the relationships among the people are the basis for "a disgraceful lot of dogging and inquisitioning," and the story is told "in an egotistic first person" by the worst busybody of them all. The "numerous followers" of James "in his analytic paths" will find this novel "decidedly worthy of pursuit."

8 ANON. "Henry James' New Novel." Brooklyn Daily Eagle,

February 16, p. 7.
(Review of The Sacred Fount. Portrait.) A new novel by James is an event. He is "so great an artist" that, as in The Spoils of Poynton and What Maisie Knew, he can charm, delight, or fascinate the reader with his literary power and finish, despite a thin or commonplace plot. This book has little plot or incident and does not show James at his best. Its "vampire" idea is clever and well exploited, but it does not fit well with James's "intensely modern" atmosphere. He carries to an unfortunate extreme his recent tendency to create "fantastic situations" that concern problems "outside the range of ordinary human interest." So, despite its "mastery of technique" and faultless style, the book "misses its mark" and seems labored.

9 ANON. "Books of the Week." New York Herald, February 16, p. 11.
(Notice of The Sacred Fount.) The Sacred Fount is among the expected novels "by well known writers."

10 ANON. "Henry James./His New Work, 'The Sacred Fount.'" New York Times Saturday Review of Books, 6 (February 16), 112.
(Review.) This book tells no story, does not attempt to delineate character, is nearly eventless, and has in it "something revolting." It is only questionably true to life or worthwhile, James spends his "brilliant gifts" on a "niggling work," and his style, the Jacobites notwithstanding, is too stylish.

11 ANON. "Poor Literary Outlaws." Washington Post, February 22, p. 8.
(Editorial. Reference to the "irreproachable" James's The Two Magics as one of the books banned from the Boston Public Library.)

12 ANON. "In the Literary World . . . Mr. Henry James' New Novel, 'The Sacred Fount.'" Detroit Free Press, February 23, p. 11.
To read a James novel is a solemn and somewhat dismal thing, but to approach this one is "a matter of unusual seriousness." It has no story or character portrayal, but only "a psychic problem presented on the point of a hat-pin and turned round and round," leaving the reader bewildered. This book seems the product of "painstaking but fruitless toil," evidencing James's ingenuity and "admirable workmanship," but of dubious value to anyone.

13 ANON. Review of The Sacred Fount. Literature, 8 (February 23), 144.
Plenty of people will admire the cleverness and obscurity

of this most Jamesian of books, but it is not among his best. James puts more mind into his subtleties than Howells does, and with a little text, a brief remark, he includes "a wilderness" of analytical, exegetical comment.

14 ANON. "Books of the Week . . . Novels of the Present Season Show a . . . Large Catholicity in the Popular Taste." New York Herald, February 23, p. 15.
(Brief review of The Sacred Fount.) That "little miracle of jewelled phrase" The Sacred Fount "has gone into its second edition sooner than has been usual" with James's later books. It "baffles and perplexes most of its readers," but is therefore "exciting discussion among them," and "discussion is the life of bookselling."

15 ANON. "'The Sacred Fount.'" Boston Sunday Post, February 24, p. 30.
(Review.) This first important book of the spring has a brilliant main theme and, for Jamesians, a fascinating beginning, but is confusing, has no ending, and contains little incident. It is well done, but not nearly as worthwhile as What Maisie Knew. Although other writers reach a far wider public, James is perhaps of all current authors "the most secure in his position and his following," a "devoted few."

16 ANON. "Literary Matters./A Puzzling Novel by Henry James." Detroit Evening News, February 24, II, p. 17.
(Review of The Sacred Fount.) This is one of the most puzzling books published in a long time, with no plot or characterization in the usual sense of the term, but only minute analysis of actions and psychological study of "influence and motives." The characters are not lovable or attractive, nor is their society complimentary to the English. The complex style has in places "the true ring" of James's "high conception of art" and yet is marred by "colloquialisms, vulgar expressions," and peculiar sentence construction.

17 ANON. "The Latest from Mr. James." Providence Sunday Journal, February 24, p. 15.
(Review of The Sacred Fount.) Since the remarkable Princess Casamassima, James's always complicated and artificial but exquisite style "has suffered an extraordinary deterioration" into obscurity and chaos. Always "needlessly analytical," James now has a mania for analysis. Worst, his recent "mystical strain" makes him even harder to understand. The affairs in this book seem unreal and obscure.

18 ANON. "Books, Authors and Arts." Springfield (Mass.) Republican, February 24, p. 15.
(Review of The Sacred Fount.) This novel will stagger some of James's "most unflinching admirers," and may make them question his sanity. Even with poor material James achieves "a sort of success" by his literary virtuosity. Here, the subject is potentially good, but James treats it too realistically. Despite the many "good things" it contains, the book is so indirect and so hair-splitting, with such a tortuous, involved style, that it is hard to understand and does not repay the exertion required to read it.

19 ANON. Review of A Little Tour in France. Church Standard, (Philadelphia), 80 (March 2), 624.
James seems "immensely better as a descriptive writer than as a novelist." In this "really delightful" book he is at his best, with an observant eye, a reflective mind, a rich memory, and a smoothly flowing style.

20 ANON. "The New Books/. . . Fiction." Congregationalist, 86 (March 2), 353.
(Review of The Sacred Fount.) This book is "too intricate and intense for most readers," and "intolerably dull" for more. It is "good labor wasted on a trivial and somewhat unwholesome theme."

21 ANON. Review of The Sacred Fount. Outlook, 67 (March 2), 554.
James "has probably never written anything more elusively subtle," but the effort required to follow his "delicate distinctions and suggestions is hardly repaid." The talk is ludicrously incredible.

22 ANON. "Books, Magazines, and Authors." Atlanta Constitution, "Sunday Magazine," March 3, p. 6.
The Two Magics is among books rejected by the Boston Public Library. James's "later works are rejected because they 'hide plot, expression, style, clearness and force under a rubbish heap of senseless words.'"

23 ANON. "Books/Novels, Romances and Short Stories." Cleveland Plain Dealer Sunday Magazine, March 3, Part III, p. 8.
(Review of The Sacred Fount.) This book is "much ado about nothing," and the right person "to chronicle the frivolous and scandalous gossip in a 'bright' way" is James. The style is either his brightest or his most wearisome, depending on whether the reader admires or dislikes it, and "there is no middle ground among his readers."

24 ANON. "A String of Wrong Deductions." San Francisco Chronicle,

1901

March 3, p. 28.
(Review of The Sacred Fount.) Readers may wonder what purpose this book has other than as an exercise in logic. It is not a story, but rather the "carefully wrought out personal narrative" of the "distempered fancy" of one of the characters. The psychological reasons offered in support of this "caprice" are "pointed and sometimes puzzling, but are carried to a somewhat wearisome length."

25 ANON. "Among the New Books./A Puzzle." Chicago Tribune, March 5, p. 13.
(Review of The Sacred Fount.) This novel will almost certainly be controversial because it fully justifies "every adverse criticism" passed on James's work by those who do not like his methods, and it has puzzled his admirers into wondering whether he is purposely fooling them. Though the style is "limpidity itself" compared with that of some of his other works, the fundamental inconsistency of plan makes the book so unreadable that one wonders why it was written.

26 ANON. "Books and Their Writers/ Henry James at his Vaguest./ 'The Sacred Fount,' His Latest Work, Is Also His Most Characteristic." Louisville Courier-Journal, March 9, p. 5.
Only a few years ago "the American field of fiction was . . . so barren that new books by James and Howells were annual literary events, eagerly awaited and widely discussed." Year after year James set forth realistic but rather uninteresting, workmanlike, properly drawn, tinted, and grouped characters "who passed their entire time in introspection and positively indecent meddling with others' inner consciousness," yet never did or said anything worth remembering. Throughout these years the critics praised James's analysis, lucidity of style, and perfection of form. The "leading critics and novelists" disapproved reading too much Thackeray, Dickens, Dumas, or Scott, and most Americans followed Howells or James instead of Hardy or Meredith. Then, the coming of a change, of "really fine novels" by Stevenson, Kipling, and others who scorn pettiness and trivialities, "shrivelled" the work of James and Howells to "its true proportions." James has become very English, but "his fame still rests chiefly on that truthful satire" Daisy Miller. Critics still praise his style and subtlety, and will no doubt do so for The Sacred Fount. In that book, characters apply superlatives and elaborate analysis to "the most trivial thoughts" and events, while James "dwells complacently on his subtlety." The one critic competent to handle James's case was Thackeray.

27 ANON. "Literature./A Mysterious Novel." Independent, 53

(March 14), 619-620.
(Review of The Sacred Fount.) What James does is "never very impressive," and his manner of doing it is the chief thing. Here, he intends to "demonstrate a theory of art" rather than tell a story. His refusal to speak directly to the reader is confusing and mortifying. The story, merely the occasion of "literary decorations," advances through telepathy and is full of a reprehensible vagueness. James consistently tempts his characters' worst motives, but they are "too well bred to compromise themselves." James does gracefully and audaciously nearly everything "we condemn in other writers." More people will buy this book than will read it, since readers are more interested in a story itself than in the science of writing it.

28 ANON. "Library Table: Glimpses of New Books." Current Literature, 30 (April), 493.
(Review of The Sacred Fount.) This book is "probably the literary event of the month," but an exasperating one in which James has "out-Jamesed himself" in complexity, subtlety, and "brilliantly tedious" dialogue.

29 ANON. "Appraisals of New Books." World's Work, 1 (April), 667.
(Review of The Sacred Fount.) This is one of James's "books about nothing," full of "fine-spun, transparent gossamer." It reminds one of Clarissa Harlowe, but the comparison does not favor James because, although Richardson was a "sentimental psychologist" with a "microscopic" scale, his interest was "in human life." The Sacred Fount, on the other hand, "belongs to the experimental laboratory" and is preoccupied exclusively with operating "delicate mechanisms" to measure "atomic weights." It is in a "by-path of literature," because literature, unlike this novel, "deals with human, not scientific, interests, and . . . presents life as in the grip of necessity."

30 ANON. "Aut Scissors Aut Nullus." Life, 37 (April 18), [332].
(Anecdote quoted from the Argonaut shows James wittily getting the better of an author critical of James's work.)

31 ANON. "Talk about New Books." Catholic World, 73 (May), 249.
(Review of The Soft Side.) James seems to write about nothing. Yet, the individual moves, looks, and situations are of intense interest, the whole structure is "a marvel of invention and skill," and "as a paragon of style" these stories are "a valuable and serious contribution to literature."

32 ANON. "New Novels." Churchman, 83 (May 4), 552.

(Review of The Sacred Fount.) Howells's "fearless support" and the devotion of a small but waning circle of admirers have kept for James the reputation of "a consummate artist in fiction" for the few, despite charges of obscurity and "lack of the true American spirit." Praised for his style, "subtle skill" in character analysis, and powers of minute observation, he has held ground with the critics, but lost it with the reading public. In this novel, he tries to make "nothing out of nothing." Though the talk is clever and subtle, the reader understands neither the relations between these "decadents," nor why he should take them seriously.

33 ANON. "Collections of Short Stories." Literary World, 32 (June 1), 92-93.
(Review of The Soft Side.) Here are James's familiar "graphic, carefully sketched, laboriously polished, bloodless automata," with their "perplexed explanations" that never explain, and their "interminable and subtle conversations which convey nothing." The opening story, with its hint of the satisfaction of feeling, "is a pleasing exception to the rest of the volume."

34 ANON. "Talk about New Books." Catholic World, 73 (July), 538-539.
(Review of A Little Tour in France.) This is "one of the most delightful books of the season," with delicate and artistically perceptive descriptions and psychological observations that give the very air and color of France.

35 ANON. "The Lounger." Critic, 39 (October), 305.
(Satirical reference to James's obscurity, in notes on authors submitted by "Mr. F. Wells, a humorous bibliophile of Boston.")

36 ANON. "Life's Personal Column." Life, 38 (October 31), 345.
(Brief humorous reference to James's long, puzzling sentences.)

37 ANON. "Announcement." Life, 38 (November 21), 415.
(Humorous item. Mock-announcement of books needed by "a long-suffering public.") A book that would gratify the public is A Plain Tale by James, written in real English with short intelligible sentences and an easily understood plot.

38 BURTON, RICHARD. "The Henry James Myth." Writer, 14 (January), 5-7.
(Reprinted from The Philosopher.) Whatever faults critics

may find with James's work, they usually praise his style. Yet, as quotations from The Two Magics show, James does not satisfy the criterion of clarity. In his earliest novels he was "a master of lucid, high-bred, cogent English."

39 CHAMBERLIN, JOSEPH EDGAR. "Books of the Day . . . Henry James's New Novel." Boston Evening Transcript, February 13, II, p. 12.

(Review of The Sacred Fount.) This book is most extraordinary, and "seems insane," though its author is not. James attempts "to apply a high order of mysticism" to a series of flirtations that show how English customs differ from American, "to our advantage." One must expect mysticism in any serious work by a man of James's "inheritance, education and genius." Yet, his Swedenborgian father would have taught him that "the application of seership to the purposes of an analytical society novel would be 'disorderly'" and the road to madness. The book's style, both elaborately polished and colloquial, is interesting, but the characters do not speak good English. This novel cannot be recommended "as a valentine for the young."

40 CLAPP, HENRY AUSTIN. "New Books and Those Who Make Them. . . . The Sacred Fount." Boston Daily Advertiser, February 23, p. 8.

No one, not even an admirer of James's genius, can read this book without a disagreeable mix of "amazement, consternation and irritation." Whether a self-parody or an "audacious trick" on the public, the book is "unique, a curio, a literary prodigy without precedent," based on "tomfoolishness." Its weak "thimble-rig game might be interesting, if anything ever led to anything," but "the insignificance of it all is exceeded only by its tiresomeness." The style is "generally terrible," though it has James's usual "splendidly lucid intervals" and air of "serene, refined, conscious distinction." His "very bad manner" of late seems designed to "alienate his warmest admirers," and the worst part of this book is the smashing of "the whole flimsy structure" at the end. It is an affront to the reader to be dragged through so much for nothing. Howells has said that James has found himself, but it is to be hoped that he soon loses that self and resumes "that strong artistic personality" which even at its "most delicate fineness was incapable of triviality."

41 DEAN, MARY. "Three Books Reviewed by Mary Dean." Indianapolis News, April 13, p. 5.

(Review of The Sacred Fount.) A new James book acts "like enchantment" on those for whom he writes, but this is a minor work. The beginning and the setting are good, but the talk is not and the style is almost unreadably involved.

42 FITCH, GEORGE HAMLIN. "Book Chat." San Francisco Chronicle, March 24, p. 24.
(Review of James's introduction to Oliver Goldsmith's The Vicar of Wakefield.) James's introduction is irritating throughout because despite his disclaimers, he damns Goldsmith with faint praise. Lovers of "genuine fiction" will always delight in the characters in Goldsmith's "immortal story," while "his commentators will be forgotten."

43 H., A. E. "Talk About Books." Chautauquan, 32 (January), 454.
(Review of A Little Tour in France.) We see these scenes and the images they evoke as "in a delightful dream," and the travel sketches have a "distinctive literary quality."

44 HARKINS, E. F. Little Pilgrimages Among the Men Who Have Written Famous Books. Boston: L. C. Page, pp. 91-105. Rpt. 1902; as Famous Authors, 1906.
Although a cosmopolitan, James is as loyal an American as Bret Harte. He has been overcriticized for expatriation, since his cynicism is well founded, his satire is "more or less truthful," and he himself is "gentle and unassuming." Daisy Miller provoked bitter talk, but many authors have been "condemned unjustly for telling the truth," and the great novelist is a photographer rather than an idealist. The Spectator's remark that although James has attained great perfection in a certain specialized kind of writing he does not tell human stories, is the "last word" on James's art. James has acquired "his extraordinarily brilliant style" through great effort.

45 HOWELLS, WILLIAM DEAN. "Mr. James's Daisy Miller." In Heroines of Fiction. 2 Vols. New York: Harper's, 1:164-176.
James has created "more finely yet strongly, differenced heroines than any novelist of his time," and Daisy Miller is his most famous. No other novelist has approached him in appreciation of women and ability to suggest their charm. He belongs to the post-Civil War period of "keen, humorous" national self-criticism in fiction, when people both resented and adored his portraits of American women. Since then, he has done work that is better and maturer, but not so unique as his international stories. Readers are less refined than in Daisy Miller's era, but they would probably react to it less negatively if it were published today. In their "somewhat baffling failure" to immediately accept James, the "ignorant masses of educated people" do not recognize "one

of the greatest masters of fiction who has ever lived." Yet, "no American writer has been more the envy and ambition" of young writers seeking distinction. Daisy Miller has a "perfection of . . . workmanship," and "never was any civilization offered a more precious tribute than that which a great artist paid ours" in the title character.

46 [HOWELLS, W. D.] "The Editor's Easy Chair." Harper's, 102 (January), 318-319.

Of all authors now writing in English, James has supremely the gift of getting below the surface. His view of life is original and his effect on the reader is like that of an essence or fragrance. Many of these stories are so good in their way that "one could not imagine anything better." No author has "more fully perfected his method," whose "consummate art" is unobtrusive. No other method in the history of the language "has so clearly embodied a literary intention of such refinement, or so unerringly imparted a feeling of character."

47 _____. "Editor's Study." Harper's, 102 (April), 809-810.

(Quotes and paraphrases parts of James's North American Review article on the Italian novelist Matilde Serao.)

48 _____. "Editor's Study." Harper's, 102 (May), 974.

James is "the subtlest of literary critics and the most eminent master of subjective fiction," but Howells is preferable. The psychological complexities of James's late works are bewildering, but richly reward study, especially for a select audience. Many more readers continue to love him, but prefer his earlier books.

49 MASSON, TOM [THOMAS L.] "The Toilers. A Literary Extravaganza." Life, 37 (June 6), 479-480.

(Gilbert and Sullivan style mock musical about writers. James sings a "Song of Myself." Cartoon of James.) James is "a stylist pure" with long sentences, many commas, and dull and unbeautiful plots which all must endure for the sake of the cultured few who love his true art.

50 MCGINNIS, MABEL. "The Numbers./(With apologies to Henry James)." Life, 37 (June 13), 511-512.

(Parody of James.)

51 NEWCOMER, ALPHONSO G. American Literature. Chicago: Scott, Foresman, pp. 294, 298-299. Rpt. 1902, 1904, 1906, 1908, 1911, 1913.

James's name has long been coupled with Howells's. Americans have often resented James's portrayals as

1901

inaccurate or unfair, but James is not quite American. In his realistic method, he has gone beyond Howells, tirelessly reporting trivial conversations and minutiae. His hostile critics think he too cleverly analyzes the heart out of his characters, but his cult of admirers finds his work the perfection of the novelist's art. His style is "polished, witty, in a way brilliant."

52 PECK, HARRY T. Review of The Sacred Fount. Bookman, 13 (July), 442.

James has become "morbid and somewhat decadent," and "is beyond all question in a bad way." Telling what this book is about is difficult and not worthwhile. James tells it with "endless talk," innumerable innuendoes, "subtle speculations about nothing," and "morbid analysis." Many of his books are "a joy and a delight," but lately "he is woozy."

53 PRATT, CORNELIA. "Recent Novels Reviewed." Critic, 38 (April), 368-370.

(Review of The Sacred Fount.) This is another of James's "incredible feats." It is gossip sublimated, "incorporeal, dazzling," but lacks the implied "intimate relations with the world of ethics" that usually enrich James's works. The story is so hard to follow that it strains "even a willing intelligence to the breaking point" and is unfair to the reader.

54 SHIPMAN, CAROLYN. Review of The Sacred Fount. Book Buyer, 22 (March), 148.

People like James's fiction either very much or not at all. This novel "provides much food for thought" and is written in a style which a critic might say "involves too much thought." Whatever one may think of James's "increasing mannerisms of style," no one "interested in human nature can fail to care for what he has to say."

55 W., W. I. [pseud.]. "Kickers' Column." Life, 38 (November 7), 368.

(Letter to the Editor in defense of Jews.) The decline of literature from Longfellow, Hawthorne, Howells, and James to the recent historical romancers is much greater than the decline of the theater.

56 WELLS, CAROLYN. "Verbarium Tremens." Critic, 38 (May), 404.

(Satirical poem about the obscurity and "the dizzy heights of diction" in The Sacred Fount.)

1902

1 ABERNETHY, JULIAN W. American Literature. New York: Maynard & Merrill, pp. 178, 200, 281, 287, 425, 445-448. Rpt. 1903, 1905, 1907, 1908, 1910, 1911, 1913.

(Quotes James on Emerson, Hawthorne, and Lowell. Quotes Howells's April 1901 North American Review praise of James.) James is a superior critic, and French Poets and Novelists exhibits "scholarly care in analysis and interpretation." The leading representatives of realism are Howells and James, its "true high priest" in the common estimation. James carries it "to the perfection of a special science," and in his early novelettes set forth international contrasts with consummate skill, but "a cold disregard" for the feelings of Americans, who raised "a sensational storm of protest." His books have no plot, action, or conclusion, but contain real facts and brilliantly witty conversation. His skill is perfected in his short stories, where he "holds a unique mastery." His work's finish is "faultily faultless," and "too exquisite for wide popularity."

2 ANON. "Our Personal Column." Life, 39 (February 6), 115.

(Brief reference.) James and other writers were present at "a nice dinner . . . recently given to Mr. Ernest Thompson-Seton." (Fictitious?)

3 ANON. "Our Personal Column." Life, 39 (February 27), 163.

(Humorous reference.) James is considering the editorship of the Congressional Record, which is "far too simple and interesting as it stands."

4 ANON. "A Matter of Style." New York Times Saturday Review of Books, 7 (June 21), 424.

(Editorial. Reference to 1902.29.) James "has ceased to be the master of style and has become the slave of it," but he has never been guilty of "the commoner tricks of fine writing." Howells is superior to him as a master of style.

5 ANON. "Writers and Books." Boston Evening Transcript, August 23, p. 12.

Of several novels to be published soon by Scribner's, perhaps the most important will be The Wings of the Dove, in which James "deals in characteristic fashion with a great moral problem."

6 ANON. "Mr. James's New Novel." Springfield (Mass.) Republican, September 7, p. 19.

(Review of The Wings of the Dove.) This is James's most important book in recent years, and first real novel in some time. To his usual "unbounded cleverness" it adds a slender thread of human interest, and, with a story neither vague nor meager, it gives the reader much to chew on. The descriptions have "a veil of obscurity" and Milly is vague as well as sympathetic, but this strange story contains much to admire and is a work of art.

7 ANON. "Mr. James on Love." New York Tribune, September 13, p. 10.

(Review of The Wings of the Dove.) In his later works, James's "taste for the subtle and the curious" becomes an obsession. This "intensely fastidious amateur of the emotions" also searches keenly for the bizarre, the "strange motive." This story shows how he has lost his bearings and obscured "his vision of the truths of human nature." The book is talky, with a complex, indirect style, but by a "multitude of infinitely delicate and immeasurably subtle touches" James achieves a somewhat comprehensible effect. Milly is charming, one of his most picturesque characters, but in general his people are "pictures instead of living beings," despite their artistic charm. Here, James caricatures love and caricatures himself "in the form and style of this astonishing production."

8 ANON. "Mr. Henry James at Length." New York Sun, September 13, p. 8.

(Review of The Wings of the Dove.) The "peculiarities" of James's style show nowhere more markedly or abundantly than in this book. For James the word "vague" means "a manner . . . laudable and distinguished," in contrast "to the simple vulgarity of an explicit manner." He has "peculiar and most deliberate fun with the English language," and writes "fat disorderly" paragraphs "stuffed with parentheses and studiously involved and distorted phrases."

9 ANON. "'The Wings of the Dove.'" San Francisco Chronicle, September 14, Supp., p. 4.

This is a "complex novel of English social life." It is difficult reading, since "introspective analysis . . . takes the place of dialogue and action," but once James's ideas and style have lost their strangeness, interest awakens and increases. While it has its charm, the book is not satisfying. Its vagueness is "continually disconcerting," and its "complexity of thought and expression" require of the reader too much mental work, too much digging to derive the pleasure.

10 ANON. "Henry James's New Novel." Springfield (Mass.) Republican, September 16, p. 11.

The New York Tribune severely criticizes The Wings of the Dove for its abnormality. (Quotation from the Tribune.)

11 ANON. "The Wings of the Dove." Detroit Free Press, September 20, p. 11.

Being able to read Henry James with enthusiasm has become "a sort of hall-mark of culture in literary circles," implying an appreciation of fineness and subtlety, and an intellectual sensitiveness. Those who enjoy "microscopic dissection, acute psychological analysis, and a gradual culmination to an unexpected climax" will think this book "the most significant example" of James's "literary dexterity," but "the multitude who read for entertainment" will find it obscure. Despite James's "niceties of expression" and his literary art, his elusive, remote motive and long sentences are exasperating. Though his idea is "delicately worked out," the "impression of over-elaboration, over-ornamentation, remains." James's characters are too clever to be real, and the plot is "subordinated to character analysis." Being what they are, his characters must act as they do, and "the secret springs of action are so minutely portrayed" that minds seem "laid bare" under the "intellectual scalpel" of a "skilled psychologist."

12 ANON. "Henry James on Love." New York Tribune Weekly Review, 1 (September 20), 13.

(Review of The Wings of the Dove.) James is "an intensely fastidious amateur of the emotions" who abhors the obvious, avoids direct statements, and writes of morbid situations and odd people who do little. By very delicate and subtle touches he achieves in some way "a comprehensible effect," and Milly is one of his most picturesque figures, but in general he makes charming pictures rather than flesh and blood human beings. He caricatures both love and himself, and has lost his bearings regarding "the truths of human nature." (Reprints 1902.7.)

13 ANON. "Henry James and Other Story Writers." Cleveland Plain Dealer, September 21, Section 3, p. 6.

(Review of The Wings of the Dove. Portrait.) The "thin thread of narrative" goes through "a bewildering maze of conversations, reflections, and half-formed sentences." For those who like "romance of action" this novel will lack a story. Yet, some fascination draws the reader on after the first three chapters. Measured by the standard of most other novelists' work, James's novels are "flat, stale and, unprofitable, yet he always has a large reading public and among them a considerable proportion of devoted admirers." His style is "frequently atrocious," despite the claims of his devotees, and its undeniable charm for those with the taste for it. As usual, although his characters are interesting, they are "rarely really nice," and they talk all around a subject rather than approach it directly. For a James story this is a good one, but, like his others, it is "caviare to the general."

14 ANON. "Books and Men Who Made Them/Some Guesses at Henry James' 'The Wings of the Dove.'" Chicago Inter-Ocean, September 22, p. 7.

Anyone who understands James's recent novels must have begun early in life and worked hard. James's books are verbal labyrinths with characters who are spooks, not human enough to be good or bad or even cast a shadow, despite their bad morals. Their "plannings and doings are about as exciting as a diagram." The value of James's complex style is that it hides his violation of the proprieties, since without flesh there is no frailty.

15 ANON. "Recent Fiction." Churchman, 86 (September 27), 364.

(Review of The Wings of the Dove.) James's work demands serious treatment, but this book presents uninteresting characters, swamps action in motive, and is over elaborated. James "has never drawn so heavy a bill upon the credit of his first achievements."

16 ANON. "New Publications/Henry James's Latest Obscurities." Philadelphia Public Ledger and Philadelphia Times, September 27, p. 11.

(Review of The Wings of the Dove.) This long, puzzling book subjects the disciples in the "James cult" to a more severe test than ever before, and makes The Sacred Fount seem "clarity itself." James tells us not stories, but about people who grow less real and "more and more like disembodied motives and emotions" who all talk like James. From the clearness, precision, and discriminating dialogues of The Portrait of a Lady, James's style has grown extremely fluid and his themes more recondite and less important. Yet, he has always had the artist's assurance of his craftsmanship, "absolute command of his medium," clearness of insight, certainty of perception, and "easy mastery" of his "queer psychology." In minute detail, James has never excelled some of the work in this book, the minor figures are "marvelously done," and the book "abounds in penetrating flashes and single impressions of convincing force," yet is is dull and leads to "no appreciable result" except the "occasional enjoyment of a penetrating phrase."

17 ANON. "London Literary World." Washington Post, September 29,

p. 10.
(Note.) Stephen Crane and James are "complete opposites in almost every detail."

18 ANON. "The Wings of the Dove." Book News, 21 (October), 68-69.
(Review.) This novel has "extreme refinement of human emotion," elaboration of detail, and "cold, calculating" intellectual keenness, but it is unduly long and lacks passion, sentiment, and dramatic action. James is a master of character creation, exactness, and technical execution, but he lacks creative genius and force.

19 ANON. "Henry James' Novel." Chicago Record-Herald, October 4, III, p. 3.
(Review of The Wings of the Dove.) To read this long, difficult book requires "patience and devotion," intellect and culture, and to make a pastime of James takes scientific training and work in "the fine mathematical measurements of psychology." This book has a "perpetual fussiness," but though caviar to the multitude, James is near perfection, "according to his method, in rendering an episode of the soul." Criticisms that his "sensitive penetration" has "form without substance," that his people are phantoms, cannot apply to this book, which has plot and a deeply significant moral drama about real people in a real place. Although James delicately expresses "shades of thought and variations of motive," and he is "still the vivisectionist" who discovers "unsuspected nerve fibers of tremendous importance to the student of life," he might make "nobler characters."

20 ANON. "Books/'The Wings of the Dove' and Other New Works." Boston Sunday Post, October 12, p. 18.
(Review.) The obscure Sacred Fount made James hard to defend and alienated some of his "elect few" devotees. The Wings of the Dove is characteristic James, "subtle and psychological," yet it is intelligible. It should be read by those who like "the essence of modernity."

21 ANON. "Literary News Notes. . . . Anglo-American Love Affair." Cincinnati Commercial Tribune, October 20, p. 8.
James's famous story "An International Episode," in a new edition, is "a capital comedy."

22 ANON. "Recent Novels." Nation, 75 (October 23), 330-331.
(Review of The Wings of the Dove.) This hard-to-follow story is "a study of the abysmal in human consciousness." The situation seems monstrous, but James saves us from moral

indignation and nervous shock by swathing it in the speculative and conjectural.

23 ANON. "The New Books./. . . The Wings of the Dove." Indianapolis News, October 25, p. 6.
(Review.) James's style is very involved and difficult, and the ending fails us, but the story is "thoroughly interesting" and the book fascinates with its beauty, splendor, and wonder without being really noble.

24 ANON. "Writers and Readers." Reader, 1 (November), 1.
(Portrait by Will Rothstein. Quotation from London Times review of The Wings of the Dove.) James has changed since Roderick Hudson and Daisy Miller. On The Wings of the Dove the critics agree only that it "is worth long and elaborate discussion."

25 ANON. "Literature/Mr. Henry James." Independent, 54 (November 13), 2711-2712.
(Review of The Wings of the Dove.) James shows his age and his addiction to contemplation as he neglects incident for subjective experience, loses sight of his object, and eludes the reader in "long, dull paragraphs of emotional tergiversation." His overrefined procedure fails to accomplish its purpose, has only a technical interest, and illustrates the futility of art for art's sake.

26 ANON. "The Novels of a Season." Outlook, 72 (December 6), 789.
(Review of The Wings of the Dove.) James's only master has been his art, his only passion perfection. His early work was fine and penetrating, his style "close and fastidious," but also "clear and deeply expressive," with great human interest. Now his tendency toward subtlety and complexity, the psychologist in him, has superseded the artist. Here, the characters are realized with "marvellous skill" and the story is full of delicate touches, but the motive is improbable and the style is too involved, obscure, congested, reflecting the misdirection of a great talent.

27 BURTON, RICHARD. "Bjornson, Daudet, James: A Study in the Literary Time-spirit." Literary Likings. Boston: Lothrop, pp. 122-129. Rpt. 1903; Boston: Copeland & Day, 1898; Maynard & Small, 1899.
James is excessively refined, unlured by the flesh, a devotee of art for art's sake who "applies agnostic analysis to the psychological states of human beings." His aestheticism, his "man-milliner fussiness," have helped lead him to prefer subtleties over "elemental interests and passions."

His "subtle indirection of style and tenuity of thought" have lost him readers. Roderick Hudson is a "superb romance," with "largeness, moving power, and sense of impassioned life." The American is "very rich, vital," from James's "heyday of power." The works that follow it are successful, but show "a great artist" being "slowly moulded by his philosophy" and his times into "an unfriendliness with life." The increasing inconclusiveness of plot reflects "the agnostic in literature" and combines with "indirection of manner, increasing attention to subtleties of detail, and a keener edge of cynicism" to produce "the present James." His fiction shows the influence of the "Time-spirit."

28 C., J. H. [pseud.]. "The Gazette Literary Page." Colorado Springs Weekly Gazette, October 19, p. 17.
(Review of Owen Seaman's Borrowed Plumes. Portrait.) This collection of "parodies on the works and style of several well-known writers of fiction" includes one on the "peculiar style" of James (quoted).

29 COLBY, FRANK MOORE. "The Queerness of Henry James." Bookman, 15 (June), 396-397.
James has "written furiously against the proprieties for several years," and "[a]ny other man would be suppressed." Never "did so much vice go with such sheltering vagueness." Although his novels deal with "unlawful passions," they make "chilly reading" because the vices, passions, and characters are so bodiless and bloodless. Whatever these books' moral purport, "they may be left wide open in the nursery." In his earlier works James's "world was small, but it was credible--humanity run through a sieve, but still humanity." Since then, however, his interests have dropped off, he sees fewer things in the world, and his characters grow "more meagre and queer and monotonous."

30 _____. "In Darkest James." Bookman, 16 (November), 259-260.
(Review of The Wings of the Dove.) For a large class of people, James is ridiculous. In this book he shows signs of partial recovery from the excessive introspection of The Sacred Fount and The Awkward Age. We see "the same absorption in the machinery of motive and in mental processes the most minute," but, as in James's early work, this novel presents "conditions as well as . . . people," and "men and women . . . in describable homes" rather than "merely souls anywhere." For James, "analysis is the end in itself," and in what he chooses to focus on he is indiscriminate to the point of self-indulgence. His obscurity is unfair to the reader, yet, despite his "wearisome prolixity, he often

1902

succeeds in producing a very strange and powerful effect." (See 1904.47.)

31 FITCH, GEORGE HAMLIN. Comments on Hawthorne in review of George E. Woodberry's Nathaniel Hawthorne. San Francisco Chronicle, October 12, p. 4.

The few professional authors, including James, who have written studies of Hawthorne have failed. Woodberry continually harks back to the note of Hawthorne's "provincialism" harped on in James's "remarkable" sketch. Everyone admits that James is a consummate literary artist, but no one believes he will ever have a place beside Hawthorne in American letters. Yet, he patronized and condescended to the writer whose work is so far beyond his own, in the manner of foreigners toward Americans, and failed utterly to comprehend Hawthorne's genius.

32 FULLER, HENRY B. "Latest Novel of Henry James is Typical Example of His Art." Chicago Evening Post, August 30, p. 4.

(Review of The Wings of the Dove. Portrait.) James has not become less obscure; he still makes readers grope and guess through his subtleties. His technique is Whistlerian. His earlier books are fine, but he has become too refined, impalpable, and intangible.

33 GORREN, ALINE. "Mr. Henry James and the Human Will." Reader, 1 (November), 88-90.

(Review of The Wings of the Dove.) This book shows that James's later manner is his final one. He puts not much faith in the conscious human will as a mover of events, but deals, rather, in obscure, sporadic, subconscious motives to perhaps an excessive extent. His second sight about these impulses is the mark of his final manner. The characters in his late books tend to be idlers with morbid passions, and if they were more moral, these books would be even more interesting, with more staying power.

34 HOWELLS, WILLIAM DEAN. "Mr. James's Masterpiece." Harper's Bazaar, 36 (January), 9-14.

(Reprint of the Daisy Miller chapter from 1901.45.)

35 LAWTON, WILLIAM CRANSTON. Introduction to the Study of American Literature. New York: Globe School Book & Co., p. 298. Rev. ed., World Book Co., 1914.

James seems somewhat rootless. His devotion to psychological analysis makes him view humanity with more "pathological microscopy" than "ordinary human sympathy." He has genius and unique methods, deserves attentive study, and crosses from literature into science.

36 MCADAM, R. W. "Under the Lamp With Late Books." Atlanta Constitution, September 14, "The Sunny South" (Magazine Supp.), p. 8.

(Review of The Wings of the Dove.) This "no little heralded" book is long but enigmatic, must be absorbed bit by bit for the reader to "extract its hidden essence," and has nothing "so full-bloodedly vulgar" as thrills for the reader. Those who enjoy it must be too "ennuyé," passé, and anemic "to take love seriously" or expect passion. James very subtly may "pique our imagination and tantalize our expectancy," but he never succumbs to our "crude desire" for the tangible, and he is "a pastmaster of artistic circumlocution, which is to say he is a society realist." He "will appeal satisfyingly" to those with "relish for infinitesimal analysis that evades conclusions," and votaries of characters are intentionally not strong, but they are "well wrought of their type." James's "individualistic play upon language" is sometimes "truly original," but however clever he is, he is still wordy and his book "loosely written," which is "one of the charms of unconsciousness." The story contains "rare bits of description."

37 MOWBRAY, J. P. "The Apotheosis of Henry James." Critic, 41 (November), 409-414.

The Wings of the Dove is the late James in its most extreme form yet, a falling away from his earlier books. This work is obscure, remote from life, effeminate, and "hardly Saxon."

38 NORRIS, FRANK. "An American School of Fiction?/A Denial." Boston Evening Transcript, January 22, p. 17.

If James had stayed in America, he "would have been our very best writer." He would have applied his "finish of style" and "marvellous felicity of expression" to concrete, vigorous, "simple direct action" instead of to the "vagueness and indecision that so mars and retards" his work.

39 PEATTIE, ELIA W. "Henry James' Sordid and Ineffective English Romance." Chicago Tribune, September 13, p. 18.

(Review of The Wings of the Dove.) James, our "one great American novelist," is an Englishman. He has spent much time on this book, and accomplished little. He uses admirable material, but has no characters "with any vigorous, honest, hearty purpose," no one "to strengthen the moral supineness of lackadaisical bewilderment of the others," no one who is "reliable, truth telling, effective, and abiding." Also, Maeterlinck "would be abashed" to find "his own verbal folly flung back at him" in such a rude way. James's world is thin, his characters move among shadows, his creation is a transparent, flimsy fabric, and his atmosphere is "elusive and indefinable," but he is, vexingly, of the first class, his "delineations are remarkable," and his character description "always threatens to awaken interest." He has "instilled his curious and exquisitely fine psychology" into the "vicious and degenerate" English theme of greed for inherited money. That James left his country "was a grief," and that he "deserted" its ideals is an even greater one. He creates a situation where "the American mind does, indeed, break down," and he has taken "almost infinite pains" to introduce "'each aspect of the case.'"

40 PERRY, BLISS. *A Study of Prose Fiction*. Boston: Houghton Mifflin, pp. 10, 89, 92, 192-193, 284, 316-317, 326. Rpt. 1903.

Many James pages are "acute beyond belief," amazingly and admirably subtle, yet "oversubtle, perverse, and in the end pointless and ineffective." Though indirectly, James expresses a moral attitude. He knew the theory of fiction better than Hawthorne did, but *The Marble Faun* is greater than *The Portrait of a Lady* because Hawthorne is a better story-writer. James is an accomplished critic.

41 SCHUYLER, MONTGOMERY. "Subtle Mr. James." *New York Times Saturday Review of Books*, 7 (October 4), 658.

(Review of *The Wings of the Dove*.) For fewer readers than ten years ago, the appearance of a new James novel is "the most interesting event in current fiction." In recent years he has required more and more of his readers, and very few would pronounce *The Sacred Fount* a success. *The Wings of the Dove* does not follow his recent formula of all workmanship and no subject, but though he tells a story he is still too subtly analytical and obscure. The characters are real and worthy of all the elaboration James lavishes on them. The book is one of his "high successes."

42 SEAMAN, OWEN. *Borrowed Plumes*. New York: Holt, pp. 153-171.

(Acknowledged parody of James. See 1902.28.)

43 SEARS, LORENZO. *American Literature in the Colonial and National Periods*. Boston: Little, Brown, p. 428. 2d ed. 1905; 3d ed. 1909.

James is the most prominent of the American writers who have lived long enough in London "to set forth with tolerable justice the traits of both branches of the Saxon race," while being accused of "emphasizing unfortunate peculiarities."

44 SHUMAN, EDWIN L. "Autumn Announcement Book Number." Chicago Record-Herald, October 4, III, p. 1.
Whether one will like The Wings of the Dove will depend on "one's ability to tolerate James's peculiar analytical methods."

45 W., E. C. "Henry James' New Book." Louisville Courier-Journal, September 13, p. 5.
(Review of The Wings of the Dove.) For those who admire James's style, this story "will stand out as one of his strongest works." The action is slow, the characters "are analyzed and reanalyzed," and their tortured utterances weary the reader. The plot "works out in an interesting way," and with at times some "dramatic force." As a whole the book will "please the James followers."

46 WILLIAMS, TALCOTT. "Howells and Henry James." Review of Reviews, 26 (October), 446.
(Review of The Wings of the Dove.) Howells and James lead the "recognized group of novelists" who publish each year. The "unique effect of woven words" in this book is exasperating in that it gives "the shimmering sense of the cinematograph" which seems to be, but never is, real.

1903

1 ALDEN, W. L. "Mr. Alden's Views." New York Times Saturday Review of Books, 8 (October 24), 751.
(Reference to James's "Life of Story" in the headline, but no discussion of it in this letter from London.)

2 ANON. "Critic and Author." Living Age, 236 (January 3), 61-63.
(Reprint of an Academy article commenting on James's essay on Balzac for a new translation of "Memoirs of Two Young Brides.")

3 ANON. "Howells on James./The Later Work of the Author of 'The Ambassadors' Described by his Contemporary." New York Times, January 3, p. 12.
(Paraphrases and quotes from 1903.112.)

4 ANON. "The Genius of Henry James." Harper's Weekly, 47 (February 14), 273.
Complex and highly individual writers like James, of "uncommon psychological subtlety," "original creative faculty," and innovative manner and method," often wait years for their genius to be duly appreciated. Yet, James has attained

a kind of apotheosis as the subject of three recent critical articles in magazines. (Summarizes, quotes from, and praises a favorable article on James in the January 1903 Edinburgh Review. See 1903.95.)

5 ANON. "The Novels of Henry James." Literary Digest, 26 (February 28), 300-301.
James's name is "so prominent in current magazine literature" that Harper's Weekly (1903.4) has declared his attainment of something like an apotheosis. (Quotations from 1903.10 and 1903.112.)

6 ANON. "Books and Reading." New York Evening Post, March 2, p. 6.
(Short review of The Better Sort.) Most readers will find James's "later cryptic manner" easier to tolerate in stories than in novels.

7 ANON. "Books and Authors/Special Types," Boston Daily Advertiser, March 4, p. 8.
(Review of The Better Sort.) At one time, James was unrivaled as writer of short stories in English. His portraits' "breadth and fine finish," his "unerring sense of the inevitable word," and his "acute understanding of the social order, were fountains of delight." His works of that period, before he entered his own world and became more psychological than his brother, "are his monuments." He is now "the apostle of an orchid race" as surely as Howells is "the apostle of mediocrity." James is "often finical in his passion for precise expression, and carries refinement to the point of dissolving substance," but "his brilliant technique and the gray beauty of his somewhat spectral creations have their spell," giving us "clouded visions of a new and weirdly fascinating race of beings." At times his dialogue has the old and "fondly remembered dash," but "more frequently it eddies vaguely." James can, when he chooses, define character "swiftly, neatly, and conclusively." "The Beast in the Jungle" is "the most powerful, subtle, and reasonable" of the stories in this volume, and the others are done with James's "unmistakable method."

8 ANON. Review of The Better Sort. Atlanta Constitution, March 7, "The Sunny South" (Literary Supp.), p. 12.
These stories offer "a very unusual opportunity" to study James's "remarkable talent at short range" with the advantage of a variety of subjects and characters.

9 ANON. "The Better Sort. By Henry James." New York Commercial

Advertiser, March 7, Second Section, p. 5.
James "goes a degree higher in the realm of pure mathematics" than do other novelists who "have the art of working out psychological problems" by "algebraic formulas." He "deals with the infinitely small variants of human passions" and a book like The Wings of the Dove is as difficult as a "treatise on quaternions or the theory of determinants." His short stories give, "with far less tension, his characteristic quality, his flashes of brilliant irony, his deliberately obscure phrases, which a little thought shows to be luminous with pent up meaning." The stories in this volume "are all on the same level of excellence," and "Broken Wings" has in it "a real tragedy."

10 ANON. "The Novels of Mr. Henry James." Living Age, 236 (March 7), 577-595.
(Reprint of 1903.95.)

11 ANON. "Fresh from the Book Shelf/. . . Fictional Rambles About Boston." Indianapolis News, March 7, p. 8.
(Review of Frances Weston Carruth's Fictional Rambles in and About Boston refers to places in Boston "made famous through the novels" of Howells, James, Arlo Bates, J. F. Cooper, and others.)

12 ANON. Review of The Better Sort. New York World, March 7, p. 8.
It is remarked that James is "less difficult in these tales than in his novels."

13 ANON. "Henry James at Home." Indianapolis Journal, March 8, p. 2.
(Discussion of James's house at Rye.) Some relegate James's work to the "realms of fiction" but others exalt it "to the heights of philosophy." The interest in his work by "that best of critics," the critical reading public, "is as keen as ever," and James has the nowadays rare quality of not seeking "public clamor."

14 ANON. "Fiction." New York Tribune, March 8, Supp., p. 11.
(Review of The Better Sort.) James usually writes about queer people in the backwaters of life, who engage in "morbid analysis of very queer and generally contemptible," petty emotions. These stories show him at his best and at his worst. "The Beast in the Jungle" is "admirable in conception and masterly in technique, a little triumph." In "The Birthplace," "The Tone of Time," and "The Beldonald Holbein" James's method also "shines effectively," though "far less brilliantly." The others, however, give the

"sickening oppression" of "spiritual squalor" among little, unreal characters, and seem wasted efforts. James's style is tortured, he uses cliches, and his failures outnumber his successes, which will nonetheless establish his fame.

15 ANON. Review of The Better Sort. New York Tribune Weekly Review, 2 (March 14), 12.
(Reprints 1903.14.)

16 ANON. Review of The Better Sort. Cleveland Plain Dealer, March 15, Section 4, p. 2.
These stories are generally more readable than some of James's later novels because they have fewer long passages leading to nothing, and "more matter and less art," which is "a decided gain for the average reader."

17 ANON. "Mr. James's Many Writings." Philadelphia Public Ledger and Philadelphia Times, March 15, p. 20.
(Paraphrase and quoted critical comments from Edinburgh Review on James's industry and the style and fresh atmosphere of his fiction.)

18 ANON. "Books, Authors and Arts./Mr. James's New Short Stories." Springfield (Mass.) Republican, March 15, p. 19.
(Review of The Better Sort.) American critics have rediscovered James, and recently leveled at him a crackle of hostile criticism that is unworthy of its target and misses both what James has done and what he has tried to do in changing his work. Occasionally a critic like Howells in the North American Review (1903.112) or Harriet W. Preston in the Atlantic (1903.124) or the writer in the Edinburgh Review (1903.95) hits the mark. Except possibly for Meredith, James is "the most original of important living novelists," and his difficult style is almost supremely suited to the task he has made his own. The "sinuosities and convolutions" provide a necessarily "intricate and delicate tool" for James's pursuit of "refinements of intellectual analysis." He has shaped language "to meet a new and extraordinary demand," he is "simply unrivaled by any other novelist" in his particular field, and, whether or not his work will prove as important as his admirers believe, it is a "new and extraordinary kind of art." These tales may not be James's best work, but they are characteristic, show "remarkable conformity between the material and the development," as well as James's usual "skillful indirectness" and his "remarkable gift" for revealing essentials without stating them. The finest story of the volume is "The Beast of the Jungle," a fantastic "allegory of deep significance" with "real tragic power" and a "touch of the weird and

bizarre in the most ordinary surroundings." "Broken Wings" and "The Beldonald Holbein" are light and felicitous. "The Special Type," "Mrs. Medwin," "Flickerbridge," and "The Story in It" are trivial or unimportant, but "The Birthplace" is "really amusing," if flawed, satire.

19 ANON. "James's Latest Stories/Another 'Turmoil of Presences' by Our Great Literary Obscurantist." Philadelphia Public Ledger and Philadelphia Times, March 20, p. 20.

(Review of The Better Sort.) James's works are like Whistler's in that their vague haziness has "infinite possibilities of drama" that make other pictures seem mere "theatrical effects." James is "obscure, exasperating, absurd," and indirect, but his characters are more memorable and alive "with all the mystery of life" than are many which are "clearly defined and completed." The satire in "The Birthplace" is unusual for James, touches "thought and convictions rather than conduct," and is "extraordinarily and cruelly effective." The last story of the volume treats its subject with penetration, authority, and grim humor, but too much complication. One likes James either very much or not at all, his manner serves his purpose completely, and nothing "just like" these inimitable later stories "has been done by anybody." They "stand apart from the general current of English or American fiction."

20 ANON. "Mr. James's Latest Short Stories." Chicago Evening Post, March 21, p. 16.

(Review of The Better Sort.) James has "a very rare and penetrating insight into the finer aspects of modern social relations." The genuine James reader revels in his difficult style, but his unnecessary involutions show little consideration for the more indolent multitude. The best of these stories is the delightful "Flickerbridge," almost a masterpiece of manners and high comedy.

21 ANON. Review of The Better Sort. Detroit Free Press, March 21, p. 12.

However James "may rank among critics" who are supposed to know literature, this critic finds him "tediously prolific over unimportant affairs," and hopes for something better than The Wings of the Dove. These stories have James's usual "microscopic analyses, endless explanations and modifications." Probably the strongest is "The Beast in the Jungle," which has the "deepest psychological meaning." The reader may wonder what is the use of such "depressing, elusive" stories that "deal with the ignoble traits of human character," have nothing encouraging or sympathetic in them, and always obscure their "'true inwardness'" with words.

1903

22 ANON. Reprinted critical item. Salt Lake Tribune, March 22, p. 27.

(Reprinted item from New York Tribune on names in fiction.) James is the only current author who finds appropriate and distinctive names for his characters without feebly imitating Dickens. The Better Sort "is full of good names" which are "very Jamesian, but very natural," even when detached from the text.

23 ANON. "'The Better Sort.'" San Francisco Chronicle, March 22, p. 18.

James "was once a delightful writer," but the qualities that made him "deservedly popular" and "a favorite with the public"--skillfully imagined and executed plots, interesting situations rendered intelligibly, knowing what he wanted to say, and saying it well--have given way to an "over-refinement of style," unreadableness, and a lack of coherence. This volume is "a monument of the depths to which talent can be brought" and is "the quintessence of decadent refinement." James should place himself under the direction of the German Emperor to regain "frankness, simplicity, and directness of style."

24 ANON. "Literature." Independent, 55 (March 26), 741.

(Review of The Better Sort.) Under his affected literary manner, James lacks the sense of proportion. He distinguishes the insignificant and makes tragedies of small emotions. His sentences are like "algebraic puzzles," and the reader does not become attached to characters who are amoral subjects for literary dissection.

25 ANON. "The Books of The Week/Better or Worse?" Public Opinion, 34 (March 26), 410.

(Review of The Better Sort.) These stories concern subtleties and mental attitudes rather than gross acts. The contents more than repay the reader for struggling through the fog of James's style. "The Beast in the Jungle" has art. (See 1903.66.)

26 ANON. "The Better Sort." St. Paul Daily Pioneer Press, March 28, p. 8.

(Portrait.) Although James is "generally conceded" to be "the founder of the realistic school of fiction in America," his "manner of dealing wholly with externals and his flattering method of leaving the reader to draw his own conclusions" have "degenerated into a degree of analysis and mere photographic description that is intolerably enigmatical" and "meaninglessly vague," all but unintelligible. James's cold, correct, classical earlier style has been replaced to an extent by a tortured, entangled one whose success and literary excellence are questionable. Elizabeth L. Cary's statement (1903.101) that James's "misty suggestiveness" leads the reader eventually to a "'rich and true outline'" is poetic, but overestimates the average reader's insight. Of these stories "The Beldonald Holbein" "will appeal most forcibly to those who enjoy exaggerated character sketches," but the others are too long and difficult.

27 ANON. "A Review of Current Literature/. . . The Better Sort." Indianapolis News, March 28, p. 8.
(Review.) These stories have depressing endings and James's difficult, "curiously involved literary style." Yet, getting through his labyrinths can be exhilarating, and no one can do quite as well as James at the kind of psychological analysis in "The Beast in the Jungle." These stories have much "delightful, decorous high comedy," wit, and clever situations.

28 ANON. "Henry James and The Better Sort." Literary World, 34 (April), 73.
(Review.) James's works raise the question of whether even his extreme cleverness can be greatness. The Better Sort stops "just short of greatness." It is "brilliant, fascinating, haunting." As in James's other books, the characters delight because they are inexhaustible, with infinite possibility, never quite known. Yet, because they lack souls and we admire but do not love them, James's books are not great. "Broken Wings" is more human than the other tales, "The Papers" is "a joy and a delight," and "The Birthplace" is wonderful for its "extraordinary subtlety." Whether readers like the book will depend on whether they like James, but he is at his most agreeable here.

29 ANON. "Henry James." Harper's Weekly, 47 (April 4), 552.
James is better known than his brother William, and is "one of the keenest analyzers of character among living writers." Despite his "involved and analytical method," he "commands the attention of an enormous public on both sides of the Atlantic," including readers of popular novels. The Ambassadors is "in many respects his greatest work." (Large portrait.)

30 ANON. "The Work of Henry James." Springfield (Mass.) Republican, April 5, p. 27.
(Portrait. Article in honor of James's sixtieth birthday, with a review and some assessment of his career.) Mrs. Craigie ("John Oliver Hobbes") and James have portrayed fashionable London better than most native English

writers. Though James went abroad and Howells stayed home, and their names are no longer linked as they were, they both learned from Turgenev. Some Americans criticize James's expatriation, but he is so well suited to London that it has not hurt his fiction. Although his novels may never be popular, "his fame has steadily grown" and people have recently begun to realize what an important figure he has become. Now that Hardy and Meredith have stopped writing, he is perhaps "the most distinguished" novelist in England. Daisy Miller may have been his only popular novel, Christopher Newman is "a notable creation," and The Bostonians is dull but clever. Since 1890 James's new, highly original development has perplexed some of his old admirers.

31 ANON. "Henry James at Threescore." Springfield (Mass.) Republican, April 19, p. 19.
(Portrait from the North American Review.) In the last twenty-five years James's face has grown "stronger, richer and more subtly intellectual."

32 ANON. "Library Table: Glimpses of New Books." Current Literature, 34 (May), 625.
(Note.) James's mastery of "subtle and delicate analysis of character," of the psychology of emotions, and of some "deceptive qualities of style" have gained him a unique position in English letters, but do not save him from his greatest fault, "lack of physical action." Yet, one can forgive even that in the author of The Portrait of a Lady and The Bostonians.

33 ANON. "Library Table: Glimpses of New Books." Current Literature, 34 (May), 625.
(Review of The Better Sort.) These stories show the "distinguished author at his best." They portray a world in which nothing happens and the characters' actions are only mental. James's style and "delicate and refined analysis" will alienate the average reader.

34 ANON. "The Point of View." Scribner's, 33 (May), 636.
James, Howells, and George Meredith, like the more distinguished Zola and Kipling, deal mainly "with the actual, or with the logic of the actual."

35 ANON. "The Literature of the Day/. . . Fiction." Congregationalist and Christian World, 88 (May 2), 640-641.
(Review of The Better Sort.) The James cult acclaims this volume, but for most readers James's "subtlety and metaphysical analysis" do not compensate for his shady characters, dreary situations, prolixity, and confusing style.

36 ANON. Review of The Better Sort. Outlook, 74 (May 16), 184.
Here is James's later manner at its best in "admirable studies" of character subtleties and complexities. They are less obscure than The Wings of the Dove, and the style is better, full of "those delicate touches and shadings" of which James is a master.

37 ANON. "The Literary Guillotine/VII/James versus Eddy." Reader, 2 (June), 33-40.
(Humorous article. Account of "trial" in the "Literary Emergency Court," a mock lawsuit brought by James against Mary Baker Eddy "'for infringement of his patent obscure sentence.'" Mark Twain is the judge. Much discussion of James's style. See 1903.126, 133.)

38 ANON. "Notes on New Novels." Dial, 34 (June 1), 374.
(Review of The Better Sort.) Here, James returns to his older, and better, manner. The characters show the usual "subtlety of analysis," but they lack in good part the "involution of thought and phrase" bewildering to many readers. Because of this "greater simplicity of style and treatment," this book may be recommended to a larger circle than anything James has written in the last five years.

39 ANON. "More Novels." Nation, 76 (June 4), 460.
(Review of The Better Sort.) James's command of the art of writing stories needs no comment, and beneath his "elaborate ease of manner" is a structure and the control of elements necessary to produce the desired effect. Happily for the general public, these stories' endings are not "irrationally ambiguous," and the characters' morals are more settled than in Maisie. James provides a spectacle of "mental and spiritual fencing and skirmishing" unlike that of any other English-writing novelist. He finds human relations "fascinating in proportion to their delicacy and mystery." His capacity for observation and brilliant representation, and his "mastery of some dominant human motives," are amazing.

40 ANON. "Four Recent Novels." New York Evening Post, June 6, p. 6.
(Review of The Better Sort.) James's command of the art of writing short stories, his control, extraordinary facility, and assurance, need no comment. Here, the undiluted emotions of the characters and the unambiguous endings seem to be concessions to popular opinion. James is intimate with what "really goes on between people whose make-up is not primitive."

1903

41 ANON. "Summer Fiction." World's Work, 6 (July), 3700.
(Review of The Better Sort.) Even ten years ago a list of books by James, Howells, Mary Wilkins Freeman, Charles Egbert Craddock, F. Marion Crawford, Thomas Nelson Page, Bret Harte, and Frank Stockton would have meant "a literary feast," but contemporary fiction is so uniform in merit that this literary aristocracy currently shows "no greater creative vitality" than the facile, "unlaureled story-tellers who not long ago lagged far behind them." The "elect" will find in the "delicately attenuated" stories of The Better Sort the pleasure that James's "later manner can give an alert mentality." Readers who like stories to be "told" rather than "subtly hinted" will miss "a delightful but difficult exercise" if they bypass this book.

42 ANON. "Notes About Books and Authors." Chicago Evening Post, September 12, p. 12.
(Note on The Ambassadors.)

43 ANON. "'The Birthplace.'" New York Times Saturday Review of Books, 8 (September 26), 658.
(Exploration of a possible factual source for "The Birthplace.")

44 ANON. Comments on The Ambassadors. Reader, 2 (October), 430.
The Ambassadors is "emphatically a work of noble literature" in which James shows his sense of life's unexplainableness and largeness. In his perceptions of these qualities "and their union with some distinctly human narrative, he is probably the greatest novelist that ever lived."

45 ANON. "W. W. Story." New York Times Saturday Review of Books, 8 (October 10), 706.
(Review.) This volume has "an embarrassment of riches." In his "delicate, crepuscular style," James "has succeeded so perfectly in recreating" Story's environment, and shown "with so much skill" his place in American culture, that quotation is difficult.

46 ANON. "Books and Authors/W. W. Story." Boston Daily Advertiser, October 12, p. 8.
(Review.) James "might have been the great American novelist," but he chose to live in England and "surpass most English writers of this generation in analysis of the true blue Briton." He is "a subtle, searching critic," with "sound judgment and penetrative vision," a charming personality. The book treats its subjects "brilliantly, pungently," and shows James's "highest interpretive effort."

47 ANON. "A Gifted Amateur." New York Times Saturday Review of Books, 8 (October 17), 738.
(Editorial. Comments on William Wetmore Story.) James's biography of Story is "interesting and delightful."

48 ANON. "A Precursor./Mr. James's Book on W. W. Story." New York Tribune, October 17, Part II, p. 2.
(Review of William Wetmore Story.) This amiable book is not the worse for its indefiniteness of form, and the social history to which James makes "tantalizing, elusive allusions" would be entertaining to read. James still pursues "the evanescent, innermost Shade of Meaning," with "a vast expenditure of explicative energy," but sometimes fails to find it. When he does hit it squarely, however, the illumination is splendid. His style "grows atrocious in its tortuous analysis," but the book provides "keen enjoyment."

49 ANON. "New Books./Mr. James's Account of W. W. Story." New York Sun, October 17, pp. 5-6.
(Review.) The book is thorough, entertaining, and delightful, and no one could have set forth the material better.

50 ANON. "Topics of the Week." New York Times Saturday Review of Books, 8 (October 24), 749.
(Comments on The Ambassadors.) This novel has elicited "some admiring, some coherent, and some bewildered reviews" in England. One needs to be completely under the influence of James's "subtle charm" to thoroughly enjoy the book. Yet, it is "a notable essay in philosophical fiction" with profound insight into character and a delicate and elusive humor which "relieves the sombreness of minute analysis."

51 ANON. "The Sculptor Story." Nation, 77 (November 5), 365-366.
(Review of William Wetmore Story.) Readers will either drop this book in despair or find it the most attractive of the season. Though his remoteness from America causes errors, James is at his best here. He does not exaggerate about Story, but is rather lukewarm and is usually ready to be critical of America.

52 ANON. "Literary Briefs and Personals." Standard, 51 (November 7), 15.
James is "in the front rank of writers," and many consider him "the foremost living English novelist," but few people know that he began as a painter and changed his course "with hesitation."

53 ANON. "Story About Edith Wharton." Indianapolis Journal,

1903

November 8, III, p. 2.
(Anecdote reprinted from Washington Post about Wharton and James.)

54 ANON. "Story and His Friends/Henry James's Delightful Volumes of Letters and Reminiscences of the Sculptor." Philadelphia Public Ledger and Philadelphia Times, November 8, p. 22.
James's reminiscences "mingle in a delightful way" with those of the letters. He reconstructs a vanished society with "the imagination of the novelist," the temper of the social historian, and "the rare perception of a critic." He has followed and understood aesthetic as well as social change and has woven it all together with "a delicate literary art" which is "inevitably winning," if sometimes tantalizing, and which gives to this work appropriate "distinction and charm."

55 ANON. "Books and Authors . . . An American Embassy." Boston Daily Advertiser, November 14, p. 8.
(Review of The Ambassadors.) In his distaste for appealing to the frivolous, James "has become excessively subtle" and so exclusive that one must almost suffer "to feel his fine attraction." Always "a close critic of life," he formerly had the pieces of his stories fall "into close, rapid order" and was "clear, persuasive and entertaining." Now his characters have overelaborate conversations, but he maintains his originality, "rare finesse," ease, flexibility, "masterly precision," and his "queer concreteness" with its "mysterious reality peculiarly his own." This book is "an exceedingly refined study" which displays aspects of Paris and London society "with the freedom of perfect familiarity and much skill."

56 ANON. "William Wetmore Story." Churchman, 88 (November 14), 599.
(Review.) A "professional dissector of souls," James is well qualified to write this interesting book, which contains "very keen analysis."

57 ANON. "A Versatile Career." Congregationalist and Christian World, 88 (November 14), 698-699.
(Review of William Wetmore Story.) This "unusual biography" is "in its own method a remarkable success" and reveals much about James himself. James's complex style rewards the deliberate reader with "carefully studied and animated pictures." (Portrait.)

58 ANON. "An International Novel." New York Times Saturday Review of Books, 8 (November 14), 818.

(Review of The Ambassadors.) It is good to see the inventor of the international novel return to this theme with more comprehensive vision and riper art. Here, unlike in the earlier novels, Europe gets the better of America. James's subject is not striking, but his story is delightful and not morally corrupting.

59 ANON. Review of The Ambassadors. New York World, November 14, p. 8.

In this book, the "action is timed to the psychologic moment," but, as is usual with James, "nothing of the psychology runs to waste." An English review mentions "'the immeasurable importance of the trivial'" in James's works, but "numerous people . . . delight in following" him "on his excursions among the metaphysics . . . just for the pleasure of seeing him get safely back to the point."

60 ANON. "Books of the Year." Independent, 55 (November 19), 2740.

The Better Sort indicates that James "has reached the period of literary dotage where the distinguishing qualities of his style, the oddity of his method, have become almost meaningless idiosyncrasies."

61 ANON. "Books of the Week . . . London Book Gossip." Chicago Record-Herald, November 21, p. 15.

George Meredith and James, "an indefatigable worker," have published books "only at long intervals."

62 ANON. "Books of the Week . . . Flood of Novels in England." New York Herald, November 21, p. 13.

(By cable from London.) Few male novelists "of any note" turn out novels "at a rapid rate." Hardy, Meredith, James, Anthony Hope, Barrie, Conrad, and Stanley Weyman, all take considerable time producing their works.

63 ANON. "With Books and Authors." Atlanta Constitution, November 22, p. 10.

(Review of The Ambassadors.) Admirers of James's "peculiar style and literary quality" will find this book a treat. It is a study of men and women such as only James can make, "developed with great originality of motive" and marked with the characteristic finesse of "the mature work of one of the most successful living novelists."

64 ANON. "'The Ambassadors'/Henry James's Latest Novel Well Sustains His Reputation." Philadelphia Public Ledger and Philadelphia Times, November 22, p. 13.

To read James one must "accept both his purposes and his

1903

methods" and "float with him," responsive "to his elusive intimations." While "the general impression" in this novel is of vagueness, "the particular impression is of absolute life likeness and complete personal portrayal." James's characters are entertaining but all talk with the same "elliptic phrases," the reader "wanders hopelessly among parentheses," James is concerned not with conclusions but with the older civilization's effect on the younger, and the advantage of reading him is that "everything is there if the reader can supply the requisite perception."

65 ANON. Item on George E. Woodberry's America in Literature. Springfield (Mass.) Republican, November 22, p. 19.
American writers' "recognizable dependence on France" is surprisingly slight and is perhaps seen only in James.

66 ANON. Comments on The Better Sort. Public Opinion, 35 (November 26), 681.
(Review of the year's literature reprints some of the remarks from Public Opinion's review of The Better Sort.)

67 ANON. Review of The Ambassadors. Public Opinion, 35 (November 26), 680.
James's reputation is long established, and The Ambassadors is of genuine value, "the best effort" of his later period. It is a "thoughtful, scrutinizing," yet humorous study, elaborated with "fine distinctions, delicate shadings, and microscopic observations."

68 ANON. "'The Ambassadors' A Study of Two Codes of Morality." Chicago Evening Post, November 28, p. 33.
(Review.) This difficult book is finer than The Wings of the Dove. It is "a rare treat," not exactly a masterpiece, but "a thing of exquisite beauty and a joy forever" to the elite of fiction readers. James is wonderful, "amazingly ingenious and subtle," and reveals so much in the simple and commonplace. For the study of man, James's is the right method to reveal what lies behind our daily transactions.

69 ANON. "The Eternal Comedy of Manners Played Again in Henry James' New Book 'The Ambassadors.'" Philadelphia North American, November 29, 7th Section, p. 6.
A new novel by the "distinguished author" James "means scarcely so much" today as when Daisy Miller was published. The Ambassadors shows James's "refinement of style, prolixity . . . and indefiniteness," but it is "a minor triumph of mentality" reflecting a "passion for careful and critical

analysis of character." It contains fanciful persiflage, "minute and tasteful personal description," and "critical and convincing analysis of motives" that leaves little to the imagination. James is part of "a school of literary regeneration," there are great possibilities "in the novel for serious purposes," and James's "method of character delineation" has produced "substantial results." The denouement in this story is "long delayed" but spirited and fantastic, James has left "nothing undone," we come to know Strether and Miss Gostrey "down to the finest fibre of their eccentric natures," and it is well worthwhile to follow James's "keen analysis" of them to the end, if only to admire his "tactful skill." His "philosophy of literary indirection is contagious as well as alluring." The "game" of rambling through James's "endless pages of rippling fancy" is worth it as a mental exercise.

70 ANON. "Novels and Stories." Providence Sunday Journal, November 29, p. 21.

(Review of The Ambassadors.) The author of The American, The Princess Casamassima, and The Tragic Muse was an artist of "wonderful subtlety," of "rare discrimination and delicacy," but lately James's style has become so elaborate and his discriminations so minute that his books are too hard to read and must with regret be given up. This novel's theme "might have been made profoundly interesting," but its method, as applied to fiction, is "essentially false."

71 ANON. Note. Indianapolis Journal, November 30, p. 7.

William Wetmore Story "has been in so great demand that three editions have already been ordered."

72 ANON. "What to Read. . . . The Ambassadors." Book News, 22 (December), 395-396.

(Review.) This ingenious intricacy, with its "perfect symmetry" and its "precise measurements of form," shows that James's cleverness "surpasses the wonderful" and that he is "soulless scientific" rather than poetic. We derive no good from these novels of "cold-blooded, steel-cutting psychology," which "leave us completely unsatisfied."

73 ANON. "New Books." Harvard Graduates' Magazine, 12 (December), 214-217.

(Review of William Wetmore Story.) James cannot tell a story, but sees things as "blurred and uncertain." His style is "literary foppery," "the most affected, indirect, and wearisome" in English since Lyly. James condescends toward American life and incessantly, egotistically, thrusts himself into the foreground.

1903

74 ANON. "Recent Fiction." Literary World, 34 (December), 348.
(Review of The Ambassadors.) This long book will appeal to a very small class, "the knowing," for whom it will be "a marvel, a perpetual and high delight." James again proves himself "the master hand," and with Joseph Conrad and Edith Wharton insures the fate of English fiction. The story's scheme is "delightful," though nothing "'happens.'" The joys of the character work, the subtle charm, are "worth a hundred plots." James has never drawn "more real, more delightful, more finished" characters than Strether and Maria Gostrey.

75 ANON. "The Portrait of an American." Living Age, 239 (December), 595-603.
(Reprint of a review of William Wetmore Story from November 1903 Blackwood's Magazine.)

76 ANON. Comments on American and English fiction. Springfield (Mass.) Republican, December 1, p. 11.
(After a quotation from Howells about the English invasion of American fiction and their possibly writing the great American novel.) "On the other hand, the English novel of the day seems to be getting itself written by Henry James and Henry Harland."

77 ANON. "The Christmas Bookstalls." Boston Evening Transcript, December 2, II, p. 18.
(Summary review of The Ambassadors.) All the characters "outdo Burke in their capacity for refining, and as a school of word play the conversations are unequalled."

78 ANON. Review of The Ambassadors. New York Commercial Advertiser, December 5, 3d section, p. 1.
Aside from Joseph Conrad's Falk, "the most noteworthy" piece of recent fiction from across the Atlantic is The Ambassadors. Its characters "are thoroughly and refreshingly American," and to epitomize it simply and straightforwardly would "do violence" to James's "whole literary creed." As in real life, our knowledge of these characters is hedged by uncrossable barriers, and in James's later novels we "see life through a haze of uncertainty." If the book can be summed up at all, it is "a study of the insidious influence of the French standards upon a New England conscience."

79 ANON. "Cream of the Season's Fiction. 'The Ambassadors.' By Henry James." Detroit Free Press, December 5, Part 2, p. 2.
Ethel Barrymore, supposedly "a great admirer of James," has said that this book "could easily have been written in five pages," but she is glad he did it in two volumes.

"Other enthusiastic admirers of this literary dilettante" will agree with her, and those "who enjoy the subtle, the elusive, in literature" will find The Ambassadors as good as anything James has ever done, better than What Maisie Knew. A reader needs much time and "a clear conscience" to get through this most recent novel, which shows James's art "at its highest," and has "subtly ironic humor and delicate excursions into the realm of the deeper feelings." The first ambassador is the most delightful, "a failure in execution, but correct in instinct, and everywhere thoroughly human after his kind."

80 ANON. "Fiction." New York Times Saturday Review of Books, 8 (December 5), 892.
(Review of The Ambassadors.) This is "the most successful long story" James has written in years. The plot is coherent up to a point, and the ending is puzzling. Though "psychological and analytical," the novel is absorbing for those who prefer "virility to prettiness in their fiction," and it is always interesting.

81 ANON. "Holiday Books." New York Times Saturday Review of Books, 8 (December 5), 886.
(Review of William Wetmore Story.) Story's life is interesting enough to a wide circle even without James's pen, but James's knowledge and fine art of expression increase the book's value.

82 ANON. "A Precursor." New York Tribune Weekly Review, 3 (December 5), 15.
(Review of William Wetmore Story.) This "just discernment" is not the worse for its indefiniteness of form, and the volume provides "keen enjoyment." With the years James has not "slackened his pursuit of the evanescent, innermost Shade of Meaning," but his style "grows atrocious in its tortuous analysis."

83 ANON. "Mrs. Duncan's Latest Stories." Springfield (Mass.) Republican, December 5, p. 24.
James's method makes a "curious combination" with the "country and subject matter of Rudyard Kipling." By James's method, this critic means not the prose style of "that much-debated master of fiction," but rather his "detached point of view and the elaborate examination" of the characters' motives. Mrs. Duncan exhibits this method more than she does James's "manner" and style.

84 ANON. Remarks on Henry Harland (Sidney Luska). Springfield (Mass.) Republican, December 5, p. 24.

With "The Cardinal's Snuff-Box" Harland "combined his Parisian delicacy of touch, which perhaps comes from a reverent study of Henry James, with a more popular vein of light romance and sentiment, and the great world responded in a day."

85 ANON. "Reviews of New Books." Washington Post, December 5, p. 13.
(Review of The Ambassadors.) Despite reviewers' sneers, James is "still recognized as the greatest living English novelist." This book is also great, except that it is often vague and incoherent, and James emphasizes the frailties of men and women.

86 ANON. "'The Ambassadors.'" San Francisco Chronicle, December 6, p. 8.
This book is not clear, interesting, or entertaining, and in these respects "falls deplorably below the accepted standards." Few readers will have the patience to unravel its tangle.

87 ANON. Review of The Ambassadors. Advance, 46 (December 10), 731.
The author of this clever story is noted for his entertaining manner, and rarely draws a poor or uninteresting character.

88 ANON. Review of The Ambassadors. Cleveland Plain Dealer, December 13, Part 5, p. 10.
This story has James's characteristic "literary peculiarities," which are merits or defects depending upon whether the reader has developed a taste for them.

89 ANON. Review of William Wetmore Story and His Friends. Springfield (Mass.) Republican, December 16, p. 11.
Anatole France's "taste for the unclean" seems lately to be affecting James, who has "wit enough to cover up his indecencies." In this book James figures more prominently than do his ostensible subjects, and his facts are sometimes inaccurate. He does not appreciate everything about Story, but allows us the means to see Story's merits. Neither Story nor James "takes quite the correct attitude" toward America, and a family memoir by Horatio and Henry Greenough, without "the overpowering pretensions of the James literature," puts the artist in "truer relations to his native land." Story's own letters put to shame James's contorted sentences with their "needless subtleties and parentheses." James's "uncouth" way of writing comes from "30 years of success in writing." Yet, the book has admirable aspects, and, though

occasionally "fantastic," "is anything but a failure, and even passes with many as a fine success."

90 ANON. "Books of the Week/Masterly Novel by Henry James." Chicago Record-Herald, December 19, p. 15.
(Review of The Ambassadors.) James's admirers will think this a great book. It is hard, but a masterpiece. Maria Gostrey is original, lovable, and unforgettable. Although one may justifiably object to the piecemeal exposition or the involved style, the book is "powerfully affecting." It has wit, humor, pathos, imaginative power, keen insight, poetically brilliant style, and a harmoniously splendid canvas.

91 ANON. "Our Boston Literary Letter." Springfield (Mass.) Republican, December 23, p. 11.
(Review of The Ambassadors.) This novel contains "the quintessence . . . of the indirect," and is filled with more "Chinese puzzles in language" and "ingenious and back-handed subtleties" than any other novelist could produce. Strether and Waymarsh are "impossible" Americans, the plot is "slender," the catastrophe is "indefinite," and James writes "for his own amusement, . . . to show what fine company he has kept, and how little peace of mind" he has gotten from an "uprooted life."

92 ANON. "Henry James' Latest." Louisville Courier-Journal, December 26, p. 3.
(Review of The Ambassadors.) In these "latter days" of James's "most finely spun method of dealing with motives obvious and recondite" he covers "every shred of thought, feeling, and even elusive imaginings" that concern his chief characters. The tangled relationships in this novel mitigate the pleasure of James's admirers and the pain of his enemies, since "there is much to delight" even the latter, but the end leaves us still in a maze. In The Sacred Fount and The Wings of the Dove James seemed to find much attraction in morally questionable people. He seems particularly anxious to portray the "craft, worldliness and materialism" currently gaining sympathy. The "baffling of assiduous force" has tragic or pathetic elements, dramatic possibilities, but the Woolett people's pilgrim fathers would strongly disapprove of some of the talk and situations in this book. James is very skillful here, but his "sophisticated cosmopolites" often "make one sigh for the deeper, more serious" and enduring touch of "The Altar of the Dead," the "Unfinished Madonna" (sic), and others from when James was more of a New Englander. The diction of The Ambassadors is an advance over that of his last two novels, "more fluent, not so mathematically precise," riper, richer, more poetic, yet still subtle

1903

and exact. Yet, "the master" who has helped to clarify American writers' English exasperatingly performs "some of his old capers" with English and carries over "twaddle and jargon into what should be literature."

93 ANON. "Books of the Week. . . . William Dean Howells Says That it is Good to be Alone." Indianapolis Journal, December 28, p. 6.
(Interview with Howells by George Lovejoy, reprinted from the New York Commercial Advertiser, mentions James.)

94 ANON. "The Year in Literature." Boston Evening Transcript, December 31, p. 21.
(The Ambassadors is listed among a dozen novels of "presumably enduring value" published in 1903.) William Wetmore Story is the subject of "two markedly significant biographical volumes" by James.

95 [BATTERSBY, H. F. P.] "The Novels of Mr. Henry James." Eclectic, 140 [3d series 9] (April), 541-559.
(Reprint of article from January 1903 Edinburgh Review. See 1903.4, 5, 10, 18.)

96 BLAKE, TIFFANY. "Mr. Henry James's Notable Biography." Chicago Evening Post, October 17, p. 6.
(Review of William Wetmore Story. Portrait.) This notable biography is more interesting than any other of the year. Its canvas is well filled with "an embarrassment of riches," rendered with "admirable skill."

97 BOYNTON, H. W. "Books New and Old." Atlantic Monthly, 92 (August), 278.
(Review of The Better Sort.) James's method "is a little too calmly intellectual" for his sobriety to amount to somberness. His detachment from emotional situations is not caused by indifference, but by "his abnormal preoccupation with secondary motives and events." Although these stories are not always "pretty or agreeable," they are neither cynical nor aimless. The opening story is "especially straightforward and distinct," with "nothing super-subtle in its development."

98 _____. "Books New and Old." Atlantic Monthly, 92 (August), 278.
(Review of Alice Duer Miller's The Modern Obstacle.) Several interesting recent novels have approached "the Jacobean method" in "sophistication, in subtlety, in sedulous avoidance of the obvious."

99 BROOKS, FLOYD D. "The Year's Literature." Living Church, 30 (November 21), 92.

William Wetmore Story is among the year's books that have permanent interest and value. James's fiction is among the work of the year with "more than fleeting interest."

100 BURTON, RICHARD. Literary Leaders of America. New York: Chautauqua Press, p. 314. Rpt. Scribner's, 1904, 1911, 1914.

Since 1860, realistic fiction has advanced remarkably, and Howells and James more than any others started the present school.

101 CARY, ELISABETH LUTHER. "Henry James." New York Times Saturday Review of Books, 8 (March 21), 184.

(Review of The Better Sort.) Some of these fruits of genius defy description. They celebrate the genius of goodness. "Nothing is more real" than the life James plunges us into, and he leads us toward the invisible and mysterious by way of the concrete and tangible, innumerable details. The stories hold us, the characters' activities are varied, amazing, and entertaining, and James transcends the details to discern their significance. Creating a beautifully unified impression through "the perfect relation of infinitesimal parts," he shows "the real and true outline of the thing seen." His "elaboration of method so disturbing to the impatient" increases the "delicious sense of mystery," but it takes a certain temperament not to resent the tortured syntax. (See 1903.26.)

102 DODD, LEE WILSON. "Tentative Verses." Life, 41 (June 25), 585.

(Parody of The Wings of the Dove.)

103 DOUBLEDAY, J. STEWART. "Reviews." Reader, 2 (June), 88-89.

(Review of The Better Sort.) James is "the foremost American novelist," and is here at his best. His work will stand the test of time, and no fiction writer has given the world anything intrinsically better than this mild, mature, unified volume. After finishing it, readers will want only James. In his "purity of aim, and intuitive, artistic justice," he is like Holbein. He is "very American" in his intensity, and "refreshingly un-American in not being diffuse." The style is as lucid as is possible in a book still interesting on a third or fourth reading.

104 DOUBLEDAY, J. S[TEWART]. "Reviews." Reader, 2 (November), 619-621.

(Review of The Ambassadors.) People should be cultured and over thirty to enjoy this book. Only Goldsmith, Jane

Austen, and Hawthorne have written such "naturally felicitous and delicately beautiful" English. The plot of this "excellent novel" is original and enchanting. The book is informed with a "beautiful, generous, delicate, successful irony," and has more humor than James's previous works. The question of Mme. de Vionnet's morality "is handled with completeness as well as delicacy," but Strether is a weak point. James is alone among novelists in making the places he portrays seem to spring from a "convincing tradition."

105 FINLEY, JOHN. "Letters and Life." Lamp, 27 (November), 333-337.
(Review of William Wetmore Story.) This book is more evocation than chronicle, depiction, or analysis, and James's evoking of a "vanished society" is entrancing to anyone with imagination and enough sense of direction to get through James's bewildering, "labyrinthian" sentences. A "pious feeling" pervades the pages, and to read the book "is to become an ardent Jacobite." It is "one of the best of books with which to begin or end or find one's way through a pragmatic day."

106 FITCH, GEORGE HAMLIN. Review of Joseph Conrad's Lord Jim. San Francisco Chronicle, April 12, p. 18.
Conrad "appears to have fallen under the influence" of James and to have reached "the false conclusion that psychology and analysis must be introduced lavishly in any story to make it a work of literary art."

107 _____. Review of Edith Wharton's Sanctuary. San Francisco Chronicle, November 22, p. 8.
At times this book shows "an overelaboration of motive, a dangerous approach to Henry James's method of self-analysis," but Wharton's book has "a masculine clearness and force that lifts it above the nebulous romances of James and sets it apart among the best creative work of the period."

108 GILDER, JEANNETTE L. "W. W. Story and His Friends./Henry James' Interesting Volume of Letters." Chicago Tribune, October 3, p. 12.
(Review.) This book is "unique among biographies," and contains "an embarrassment of riches."

109 GLASGOW, ELLEN. Comments on The Wings of a Dove included in Anonymous, "Views of Readers on Recent Books." World's Work, 5 (January), 3028.
James's book is "a wonderful elaboration of a slight idea--an exquisite word embroidery of an insignificant pattern."

110 HENNEMAN, JOHN BELL. "The Natural Element in Southern Literature." Sewanee Review, 11 (July), 351, 360.
The Bostonians was among the high quality works of American literature appearing in the Century's first decade.

111 HIGGINSON, THOMAS WENTWORTH, and BOYNTON, HENRY W. A Reader's History of American Literature. Boston: Houghton Mifflin, pp. 161, 246, 249, 250, 251.
James has great powers, but a nearly "fatal instinct" for superrefinement in life and art. His later method is so "subtle and detached" that he seems not at home even in his own country.

112 HOWELLS, W. D. "Mr. Henry James's Later Work." North American Review, 176 (January), 125-137.
Readers who like James tend to have a feminine fineness and sensitivity, and he is supremely gifted in divining and portraying women, but he has "imagined few heroines acceptable to women." Nothing could be more perfected than the method of James's last three novels, and no book since Hardy's Jude the Obscure equals The Awkward Age's "intensity of . . . naturalness." (Imagined dialogue about James and his characters. See 1903.3, 5, 18; 1916.83.)

113 KENNEDY, NATHALIE SIEBOTH. "Mr. Howells' Latest Fiction." Chicago Evening Post, October 24, p. 8.
(Review of Howells's Letters Home.) Howells may not be a literary deity, but the literary deities such as James and Meredith call for us to tiptoe.

114 KERFOOT, J. B. "The Latest Books." Life, 41 (April 9), 322.
(Review of The Better Sort.) This is "the most important of the unusual number of collections of short stories" recently issued. In it James reacts so markedly from his extreme manner that in sections one "forgets the method in enjoyment of the matter." The change is good for both author and readers.

115 _____. "The Latest Books." Life, 42 (December 11), 604.
(Review of The Ambassadors.) Here is James "at his great best and at his little worst, to take or to leave." It is the novel of analysis "raised to the nth power." The book is long, with few events, yet it accelerates the reader's attention and interest and leaves him "aglow with the enthusiasm of a perfect art."

116 MARBLE, ANNIE. "William Wetmore Story and His Friends." Dial, 35 (November 16), 348-351.
(Review of William Wetmore Story.) These volumes "should

gain unusual attention among the noteworthy publications" of the season because they contain the first adequate information about the life and work of one of the most gifted of representative Americans, as well as "new and rare glimpses" of those who created the best literature and art of the Victorian period. James edits this book with unerring "discrimination and taste," but his style has a peculiar and deplorable haziness. Yet, however individuals may regard his "rhetorical manners," his writing "bears a literary stamp of positive and permanent influence."

117 MASSON, TOM [THOMAS L.]. "Our Country./Literature." Life, 42 (December 11), 613.
(Brief humorous reference.) The United States has had a literature of its own ever since James went to London.

118 MILLER, ALICE DUER. "A Few Novels." Lamp, 27 (December), 467-469.
(Review of The Ambassadors.) This book will "bring into line" any of James's old admirers who "may have been wavering" since The Sacred Fount. In it he not only provokes the reader's interest but also answers the question, says "the definite word" missing from his recent fiction. James neither narrates nor interprets, but merely describes; he does not moralize, but only presents. He writes not only of the emotions and conscious mental processes, but also of "those almost sub-conscious states of mind" which, though often fleeting and trivial, are "the basis of our mental life." The average reader is unprepared to read of such things, and would probably prefer to remain vague about them. Except for "the inevitable obscurity" which such a subject entails, the narrative is rapid and lucid and the story itself "more vivid and more vital" than much of James's later work. His style is a "perfect instrument," and this book is "as brilliant a work of art as the best" of James, as fine and finished, but a little easier and wittier, with more narrative interest.

119 O'CONNOR, MARY. "Books of the Week." Chicago Record-Herald, October 10, p. 13.
(Review of William Wetmore Story.) This "master synthesis" has the James stamp on every line he wrote. The "refractive quality of his intellect" shows, and he tells the tale "in his own peculiar delicious fashion."

120 PEATTIE, ELIA W. "James' 'The Ambassadors.'/Four Hundred Large Pages in Which Little Happens." Chicago Tribune, November 21, p. 13.
James is "our most distinguished if our most expatriated

novelist," treats his theme with "dignity and repose" and "unrivaled deliberation," and can ignore a trivial or hurried audience as he has a provincial one. James is one of "the three or four Americans" whose books can be judged by international standards, and he has the "accustomed air" of sophistication. In this in many ways base and unlovely story are "almost intrusively intimate" glimpses into people's "fickle souls." Although it lacks in some degree all of the elements of a noble book and irritates the reader, this "perplexing masterpiece" has "touches of the master," and the "variety of its knowledge and independence of expression," its "richness of experience," make it "a great book." From James's incoherence, "provoking affectations," and "elaborate mistiness emerge unforgettable figures of men and women" whom the reader envies for their sensibility, intuition, and comprehension. We "provincials are disturbed" by James, who is no longer one of us and seems not to regret losing our innocence, dullness, and coherence to gain his "evasive philosophy," "patronizing cynicism," and "iridescent eloquence."

121 _____. Review of Edith Wharton's Sanctuary. Chicago Tribune, November 21, p. 13.

Wharton treats her theme "almost as subtly" as James would if he ever did "anything so obviously touching and redolent with sentiment." By her candor and "lack of embarrassment before the moralities," Wharton makes herself "a more significant artist than James." Her style, too, is "circuitous," but she arrives "at a comprehensible goal" and does not leave her stories "'up in the air'" as James does. Perhaps James thinks himself "at such moments a realist," but "the more orderly part of his audience" wishes he would "strike an understandable balance."

122 _____. "Few Notable Books in 1903." Chicago Tribune, December 26, p. 7.

The Ambassadors "made us like life less. The savor and joy has been in the lesser books," by authors other than Conrad, London, Moore, and James.

123 PHILLIPS, MARIE ALICE. Review of William Wetmore Story and His Friends. Atlanta Journal, November 8, p. 6.

This book "justifies the highest expectations." It is skillfully written and contains letters of great value.

124 PRESTON, HARRIET W. "The Latest Novels of Howells and James." Atlantic Monthly, 91 (January), 77-82.

(Review of The Wings of the Dove.) James's and Howells's works of the 1870s, A Foregone Conclusion, Roderick Hudson, and The American, mark their "highest achievement in fiction." Since then, James has written some "acute and penetrating if rather finical criticism." His "mystical inheritance," his habit of "minute analysis," and his inborn though "deeply overlaid" Puritanism all constitute an "un-English" temperament that handicaps him as a novelist of English manners. He is too complex and introspective, not open and direct enough, to write a good novel of English life. In The Wings of the Dove James tries "to shake off the nightmare" of the "uglier fancies" of his fiction of the late 1890s, and "return to a less dubious method." Though the book has a plot, the reader will probably not get through the "clouds of refined and enigmatical verbiage" to finish it. Kate has more "ardor and abandonment" than most of James's "bloodless heroines," but Densher is unconvincing as a man fascinating to women. (See 1903.18.)

125 SCHUYLER, MONTGOMERY. "Henry James's Short Stories." Lamp, 26 (April), 231-235.

(Review of The Better Sort.) James is in revolt against the conditions imposed on him by readers and seems to flout his public. Yet, a reader is safer from his excessive refinements in his short stories than in his novels. James's method of amplifying and documenting makes the "incredibilities" of his unsuccessful works (such as The Sacred Fount) not more convincing, but only more palpable. It aims not at selection, but at reproduction. In the present volume of stories, however, this gifted and accomplished writer accepts limitations, avoids the tendencies that keep people from appreciating him, and has produced virtually "a collection of masterpieces." What the aspects of life treated by these stories have in common is that they are "so philosophically because so genially observed." In none of his books has James "interposed fewer obstacles" to the reader's appreciation of him, and in none "has he vindicated more completely the position which all readers of English should be glad to accord him as a master of English letters."

126 SHUMAN, EDWIN L. "In Realm of Books." Chicago Record-Herald, December 11, p. 9.

(Review of The Literary Guillotine.) One of the funniest chapters in this anonymous parody of a number of well-known writers has James suing Mary Baker Eddy "for infringing his 'patent obscure sentence.'" Because she was writing obscurely when he was "simple and understandable" in Daisy Miller, she wins the case. (See 1903.37, 133.)

127 SMITH, JOSEPH. "The Present State of Literature." Life, 42 (October 1), 332.

(Brief humorous reference.) Among the signs that the literary outlook is alarming is that James "is foggy in several languages."

128 STILLÉ, KATE BLACKISTON. "The Better Sort." Book News, 21 (April), 557.
(Review.) These "bright, cold jewels" are by a "polished, exotic," accomplished, and disappointing artist who "plays with sacred things" but "points no guidepost," and "whose ideals have lost vitality." James is half-hearted in his work, indifferent toward his characters, and losing his nationality and robustness.

129 TERRY, PEARL. Review of The Ambassadors. St. Paul Daily Pioneer Press, December 19, p. 9.
Throughout his career James's works "have been more widely criticized than those of any other author of the period." His early novels were criticized for presenting caricatures instead of types. The extreme controversy over his later works centers on the style which in addition to being as tortuously involved, cold, "classically correct," passionless, and focused on externals as ever, is now painfully "pedantic and affected." The Ambassadors is an exaggeration of the tendencies of James's earlier novels, which substituted "analysis, photographic description and endless conversations" for plot and incident, left much to the reader's intuition, and showed character through manners alone. It is useless to compare James to others because he stands alone, whether as "the founder of the realistic school in America and the greatest living American novelist to-day," as his admirers claim, or as merely one who paralyzes the English language. That James is not for the average reader should not be held against him, since the great public are not always the best critics, and a reader who studies James "will be rewarded" at least with mental training.

130 TRENT, WILLIAM P. A History of American Literature, 1607-1865. New York: D. Appleton, pp. 364, 590. Rpt. 1905, 1908, 1914.
(Brief references to Hawthorne.) One may agree with James that Hawthorne did not make all he intended of The House of the Seven Gables.

131 WELLS, CAROLYN. "The Book-Shop Girl." Life, 41 (March 5), 198-199.
(Humorous article. Woman comes into book shop looking for Frank Norris's The Pit, and salesgirl sells her The Wings of the Dove instead. References to its length and to the length and obscurity of James's sentences, and an implication that the buyer has been duped.)

1903

132 ______. "The Book-Shop Girl." Life, 41 (April 23), 374-375.
(Brief humorous reference.) The stories in The Better Sort are the better sort of stories, but they aren't light. James is not a featherhead.

133 [WHITELOCK, WILLIAM WALLACE.] The Literary Guillotine. New York: John Lane, pp. 34-59.
(Satire on a number of well-known and popular authors. James and Mary Baker Eddy dispute James's patent on the "obscure sentence" which nonetheless contains "a palpable though obfuscated idea." See 1903.37, 126.)

134 WOODBERRY, GEORGE E. America in Literature. New York: Harper & Bros., p. 193.
Our recognizable dependence on France is, perhaps, only to be seen in Henry James.

1904

1 ANON. Reader, 3 (January), 122.
News of James's planned visit to America will "set excitement boiling in the cult." (Humorous references to James's expatriation, his style, and his possible impressions of America.)

2 ANON. "The Work of the Book World[,] Biography . . . A Rare Biography." World's Work, 7 (January), 4369-4370.
(Review of William Wetmore Story.) This is a rare biography, "with a finish." With "subtle touches" James brings "personalities . . . into high relief," makes them live again, and also shows the dawning of American awareness of the complicated world of art and esthetic social development. The material is "highly interesting," and James clothes "reminiscence with imaginative charm," keeps "backgrounds unobtrusive without loss of their color and meaning," and "interprets . . . sympathetically" to give the reader "swift and welcome recognitions."

3 ANON. "Notes on New Novels." Dial, 36 (January 1), 22.
(Review of The Ambassadors.) This book is long, but has something of James's earlier manner mixed with "all the keenness of analysis of his superior age and all the subtlety of treatment his advancing art makes possible." His style is less involved than in his other recent writing, but it is still "far too intricate" to permit skipping passages. Strether and Maria Gostrey are the most engaging characters, the situation permits James to display "his finest qualities," and this novel "will no doubt rank with his more notable achievements."

4 ANON. "In the Literary World . . . The Defects of Genius." Indianapolis Journal, January 3, Part 3, p. 6.
(Item from London Mail.) Robert Louis Stevenson "used to hush his family fireside with the warning that 'Henry James is going to speak,' which must have been embarrassing to a singularly modest man of genius."

5 ANON. "In the Literary World." Indianapolis Journal, January 17, Part 3, p. 9.
(Reference to The Ambassadors.) James is "the chief" of the "lesser" authors than Hardy and Meredith, and The Ambassadors shows him "at once in his best and most difficult manner."

6 ANON. "Reviews of Some of the New Books . . . The Ambassadors." Indianapolis Journal, January 18, p. 7.
Most people who like James find the beginning of this novel "quite out of the common" and the author "at his best." Yet, the rest of the book raises the question of whether James is impartially contrasting "rigid" American moral standards with the "loose" views of some foreign circles, or demonstrating "deftly" the advantage of "loose morals" under some circumstances. His handling of the subject "is subtle and extremely Jamesesque," and apart from the moral question he presents "a remarkably clever series of psychological studies." His art shows chiefly in the delineation of the effect of Paris on Strether. Like all of James's stories, this one leaves the reader "in the air," but, unlike some, it also makes the reader wonder about the characters' futures. The book is not too long if one likes James.

7 ANON. "Recent Fiction." Churchman, 89 (January 30), 150.
(Review of The Ambassadors.) This book deals with extremely contrasting standards of life. Chad's sister alone is undisturbed by Paris and keeps "her clear vision of right and duty." The book is "delicately wrought out," and "not without a moral purpose," regardless of its effect.

8 ANON. "The Lounger." Critic, 44 (February), 99.
When Howells and James started their careers, "their names were nearly always coupled," but since then James "has changed his style entirely" while Howells "has changed very little." James writes for a small audience, and Howells for a large one.

9 ANON. "Topics of the Week." New York Times Saturday Review of Books, 9 (February 6), 81.
(Response to 1904.50.) Herbert Croly's article is very

1904

interesting and worth reading. It is impossible to gauge precisely the effects of James's expatriation on his art, but he "has done honor to Americans at home" and we welcome his rumored visit.

10 ANON. "Literature and the Fine Arts./Unwholesome Fiction." Standard, 51 (February 6), 14.
(Review of The Ambassadors.) For some people, a James novel is an event, and he has never shown his power of characterization more strikingly than here. Yet, his characters tend to be complex, uncertain, halting, confused, with tortuous movements and contradictory emotions. The book's fascination is not in the story, but in "the play of character and the analysis of mood and temperament." James's books convey uncertainty about moral standards, "consciousness of the futility and narrowness of most lives, a kind of amused cynical contempt of things in general," a whole effect that is weakening as well as broadening. This story does not stiffen the moral fiber, and beneath its "fair and pleasant exterior . . . is decay and rottenness."

11 ANON. Review of The Ambassadors. Congregationalist and Christian World, 89 (February 27), 302.
As a story "the book gets nowhere," but the persevering reader will be rewarded with intimate pictures of Paris, an unsolved moral problem, and characters who, "upon reflection, grow clear."

12 ANON. "'The First American Stylist of His Generation.'" Literary Digest, 28 (March 19), 401-402.
(Long quotations from and summary of 1904.50.)

13 ANON. "Woolett Revisited." New York Times Saturday Review of Books, 9 (September 3), 592.
(Editorial.) James's homecoming is of graver interest to him than to us, since through his works Americans know him as well as if he had stayed here. Yet, his opinion of Americans will be attended seriously, and if the "trained and sensitive perception" of this "consummately finished man of the world" is not pleasantly surprised by "Woolett," we will be disappointed. Working people honorably engaged in life's serious business are more likely to be agreeable and stimulating society than are royalty or the leisured Parisians of The Ambassadors.

14 ANON. Notes. Harper's Weekly, 48 (September 10), 1375-1378.
James's return to America is an occasion of considerable public, as well as literary, interest, since people wonder what his impressions will be. (Anecdotes about James's

shocked response to the changes in New York and about his first actions upon arrival. Comments on how New York has changed since James left it.)

15 ANON. "The Return of Henry James." Literary Digest, 29 (September 10), 318.

(Long quotation from article in New York Evening Post on James's return to the United States, his subtle, circuitous style, and his influence on Kipling.)

16 ANON. "Topics of the Week." New York Times Saturday Review of Books, 9 (September 10), 601.

James's later books have not been simple in either theme or treatment, but The Wings of the Dove and The Ambassadors have been much discussed and probably had more readers than some of the "most highly esteemed" works of his middle period, such as The Princess Casamassima and The Tragic Muse. James is more of a "literary topic" than at any time since Daisy Miller and An International Episode, and a new work by him free of his recent "indirection and persistent symbolism" would be widely read.

17 ANON. "The Return of the Native." Outlook, 88 (September 10), 112-113.

In "refinement, delicacy, and subtlety" James is America's most accomplished man of letters. He has sought perfection and avoided commercialism, but in his devotion to technique he has lost "the true vision," the contact with life, and the "spontaneity of the highest creative mood." In contrast to the "charm of sentiment and of style" is his early work, his recent style has become a maze of subtle distinctions and qualifying clauses obscuring the thought. As a writer of manners, social motives, and character molded by social conditions, James "stands pre-eminent among American writers," but he will not be able to understand his country, to which he returns, unless he puts his heart into his work.

18 ANON. "The Return of the Native." Life, 44 (September 29), 309.

(Humorous item. Comment that things have changed very much since James was last in America, praise of New York, and interest in what James will have to say about it.)

19 ANON. "H. James Has His Eye on Us." Life, 44 (October 20), 375.

(Humorous discomfiture at the thought of James examining and recording his impressions of America.)

20 ANON. "A Review of the Important Books of the Year."

Independent, 57 (November 17), 1136.
(The Golden Bowl is listed.) James is to the literary world what William Astor is to the social order. Yet, we still own him, a considerable responsibility since most people understand only the titles of his novels.

21 ANON. "Mr. James' 'Golden Bowl'--With a Crack In It." Louisville Courier-Journal, November 26, p. 5.
(Portrait.) Frank Moore Colby's essay "In Darkest James" is brilliant. The Golden Bowl is "seriously a work of art," but its "finely microscopic" stitching suggests the patient work, intricate design, and waste of time, eyesight, and mind of a queen doing fancy needlework. Even such work would have a more plainly visible design than that of James's novel, which can be seen only here and there through "a mess of ornament." The book is "a most audacious puzzle" with twisting, intricate lines, and solving James's problems provides a "sort of fascination." The book has remarkable literary workmanship and that "sure fineness" that only James can give. The characters are "highly finished," but also too complex, indirect, underhanded, and parasitical. James's mannerisms increase with each novel, his sentences are "unnecessarily tortuous," he is "too fond of the dark," and he includes much "complicated emotional analysis" in proportion to everything else in the novel.

22 ANON. "Books of the Week . . . Sir Edward Burne-Jones and His Reminiscences--Output of Gift Books in London. . . . Mr. James' Latest Impressions." New York Herald, November 26, p. 12.
(Note.) The report that James is planning "a series of articles" on "his impressions of America revisited" is untrue. Although he has "received many requests" for such articles, he has not accepted any. He will write his impressions, but may not publish them as a book right away.

23 ANON. Springfield (Mass.) Republican, November 29, p. 11.
(James is mentioned among "well-known writers.")

24 ANON. "The Golden Bowl/Henry James." Book News, 23 (December), 275-276.
(Review.) James's style and work "no longer catch the general reader" and are not "better than ever." The prince is lifelike, and the long account of Maggie's development "is done perfectly," but style predominates too much over substance.

25 ANON. "The Christmas Book Wave." Current Literature, 37 (December), xvii.

(Comments on The Golden Bowl.) James's and Howells's audiences are "far smaller" than their fame would suggest. Many people lack time to read them, but consider them "tests of a man's standards" in current literature. James and Howells thus "suffer financially from too exalted reputations."

26 ANON. "Notes Among the Publishers/New Books & Magazines." Springfield (Mass.) Republican, December 1, p. 11.
In the November 27 Harper's Weekly George Meredith says that America has produced good writers, including the "'admirable'" James, but not yet any great ones.

27 ANON. "Mr. James./His Latest Study in Fiction of Americans Abroad." New York Tribune, December 3, p. 10.
(Review of The Golden Bowl.) This book is "absolutely original," with as "bizarre a motive" and as "curious developments" as any novel in memory. The public is divided between those who adore and those who dislike James and his singularity. A "pronounced streak of morbidity" runs through his later work. The characters in this one are "unnatural and uncomfortable" puppets, minutely interpreted. Though they never really explain anything, they confuse the reader with "infinitesimal fractions and shades of ideas." James's method is not at its witty, insightful, veracious best. It is thin and bloodless, and if this is consummate art, it lacks soul.

28 ANON. "A Review of the Season's Books." Outlook, 78 (December 3), 865.
(Review of The Golden Bowl.) This book is "a marvel of subtle adroitness" in a style practiced by a master craftsman with a "consummate skill" compounded of "rare psychological insight" and "extraordinary feeling" for words. Yet, the book's "grave defects" include being too circuitous, "too heavily laden with description, comment, and suggestion," with analysis carried so far that it hinders the story.

29 ANON. "By-Ways of Literature/. . . On American Criticism." Springfield (Mass.) Republican, December 3, p. 15.
Good current literary criticism seems to get "swamped in the huge mass of reviews" and books published. Yet, a "really notable" essay, such as by Howells or James, receives plenty of recognition. Younger writers may or may not be able to take these men's place.

30 ANON. "New Books./Henry James's Latest." New York Sun, December 3, p. 7.

1904

(Review of The Golden Bowl.) All the characters are Henry Jameses. The portrait of Charlotte makes us rejoice, as does the Prince, with all his "indirections, hesitations and attenuations." He is "a good man aside from the dialogue," Maggie "has delighted us," and the entrance of the Principino at the end is "a charming finishing touch to a generous and characteristic story" in the familiar James manner.

31 ANON. "Golden Bowl: Henry James." Boston Evening Transcript, December 7, p. 25.
(Brief notice.) This book describes "the processes of thought and the small incidents" connected with the characters' relationships. The characters discuss the matter "in every possible light" and they "'ring' and 'sound' instead of speak."

32 ANON. "American Criticism." New York Times Saturday Review of Books, 9 (December 10), 889.
(Review of a Wampum Library volume of American critical essays, edited by William Morton Payne, which includes James's 1880 North American Review article on Sainte-Beuve.)

33 ANON. Review of The Golden Bowl. New York Tribune Weekly Review, 4 (December 10), 11.
(Reprint of 1904.27. Cited in Foley as "very bitter comment," p. 102n.)

34 ANON. "If I Were Henry James." Springfield (Mass.) Republican, December 16, p. 11.
(Humorous poem.) James's stories have little plot or incident, and "work by indirection."

35 ANON. Review of The Golden Bowl. Cleveland Plain Dealer, December 18, Section 6, p. 2.
This story is told in James's characteristic "leisurely way of indirection and implication instead of the direct and vigorous narrative of some other successful novelists." The novel is also "Jamesy" in that the characters assume the others do not know what they know, and they all engage in "actual or constructive lying after the manner of the polite society in which the James characters always move."

36 ANON. "International Society As Mr. James Sees It." Chicago Evening Post, December 24, p. 4.
(Review of The Golden Bowl.) This strange, original novel, like all of James's, is "wonderful," but parts of it are tedious, it fails to fulfill its promise, it lacks the charm of The Ambassadors, and the Americans are not credible.

37 ANON. "About Authors." New York Times Saturday Review of Books, 9 (December 24), 927.
(Note.) The fact that The Golden Bowl is in its third edition suggests that James's growing popularity is due either to "an increase in the number of literary workers" or to the reading public's "irresistible curiosity," rather than to "any intrinsic element in his work."

38 ANON. "Mr. Henry James'. . . . Latest Puzzle." New York Herald, December 31, p. 12.
(Review of The Golden Bowl.) This book makes demands on the attention, and nowadays "the Master" can be approached only in an attitude of worship, "solemnly, seriously, reverently." Stripped of all that gives it distinction, The Golden Bowl treats a rather common situation which "in any other hands" would be vulgar. James's method has never been more "thought burdened" or "more removed from the common viewpoint." He presents the "vulgar details" through a veil of "delicate prisms" whose many facets give glints and glimpses of the characters that pique curiosity and lure the fancy. Since the significance of these glimpses would be "lost on grosser intelligences," James flatters the reader. His characters "always speak best for themselves."

39 ANON. "Some Staccato Thoughts Suggested by the American Fiction of Our Present Day." New York Herald, December 31, p. 12.
American fiction is "practically where it was" in the 1890s. James and Howells "remain its protagonists," and "from the dilettante point of view," The Golden Bowl and The Son of Royal Langbrith are "the finest" American fiction of the last year. Yet, many current tendencies, including the election of President Theodore Roosevelt, suggest that Americans endorse the "strenuous life" ignored by its literature, while "our novelists remain untouched by the forces . . . seething around them," focus on "trivial details," and do not "appeal to the great mass of American readers." English writers like Mrs. Humphry Ward, Kipling, Hardy, Conan Doyle, and Rider Haggard give better voice to "the mental struggles of the age" than do the "dainty ineffectualities of our own authors."

40 B., A. F. "From Readers. 'The Golden Bowl' and Henry James's Attitude Toward the Average Reader." New York Times Saturday Review of Books, 9 (December 31), 938.
(Letter to the Editor.) Some critics seem too stupid or hasty to understand James. Howells is right that the masses of educated people do not yet know that James is "'one of the greatest masters of fiction who has ever lived.'" The

Golden Bowl is not lucid like The Europeans, but it is easier to read than The Ambassadors. James has "a vision for all the humors of the world," and The Golden Bowl is "vastly more entertaining" than many popular novels. It is "deeply interesting and moving," a "serious, sincere work of a great master," but is not among the hundred most popular books of the season and may be too fine spun for the average reader.

41 BEACH, BURTON T. "Henry James's Novel Published at Last." Chicago Evening Post, November 19, p. 6.
(Notes on The Golden Bowl.) James has wisdom, but does not understand contemporary American youth of either sex, confusing it with that of forty years ago. Yet, this is a notable story because all the "wise and prudent" will find in it "some wonderful mystery" hidden from the less sophisticated.

42 BOYNTON, H. W. "'The Golden Bowl.'" New York Times Saturday Review of Books, 9 (November 26), 797-798.
(Review.) The limited boundaries of James's audience were fixed long ago, and nothing would be less likely to extend them than a book like this. It presents James at his worst, as The Better Sort presented him at his best. This novel has a "restless finicking inquisitiveness, a flutter of aimless conjecture," and James's manner is at best "a kind of physical deformity," a "mincing awkwardness." His characters inhabit a "land of dubiety." Yet, the final scenes contain many "pleasant human touches."

43 BRAGDON, CLAUDE. "The Figure in Mr. James's Carpet." Critic, 44 (February), 146-150.
James is "too great to be ignored, . . . yet too ignored to be great." Though he may have "lost in popularity he has gained in power" and put his talent to "increasingly finer uses." His "seemingly difficult and obscure" style is adequate to convey his meaning, but his critics "cannot forgive him his supreme virtue" of demanding his readers' attention and assuming their intelligence. His later manner is elusive, like music, and some of his late stories are immoral. James's and Meredith's fiction is philosophical and psychological, but James is not preeminently an ethical and philosophical writer. The "figure in his carpet" is "only the pattern of his wonderful mind," he is "the most incorrigibly modern" of novelists, and he tells the truth.

44 BROOKS, SIDNEY. "Henry James at Home." Harper's Weekly, 48 (October 8), 1548-1549.
(Portrait. Description of Lamb House.)

45 CARLETON, EMMA. "From Readers./A Consideration of the Ethics of Mr. Henry James." New York Times Saturday Review of Books, 9 (January 9), 26.

(Letter to the Editor.) "Prolonged admiring contemplation of artistic foreign manner" has spoiled James's morals, as reflected in The Ambassadors. Yet, he is so fascinating, ingenious, and artful, that he obscures from his readers what he is really doing.

46 CARY, ELISABETH LUTHER. "Henry James." Scribner's, 36 (October), 394-400.

The art created by James's "enlightened and fortified intelligence" is mature and demands a certain maturity and analytical ability in the reader. James is patriotic in the depth of the "temperamental refinement" of his Americans, who "represent their nation on its most exquisite side," "maintain their integrity" amid demoralizing influences, and encourage a "wholesome idealism." Because of James's reverence and concern for the aesthetic emotion, he is impatient with aspects of American life that devalue, deprive, or dissipate it. Yet, though his world contains "a vast amount of art," and almost no "primitive passion," it has much ordered, civilized sentiment and little artificiality. In it reality prevails and "the beauty and dignity of virtue [are] still preeminent." James is both realistic and mystical, his "equal sensitiveness to the visible and the invisible" give his works their moral worth, and he counts for the sturdiest morality. Unfortunately, his style is so difficult that future generations may not understand him, and "a greater mishap in literature could hardly be imagined."

47 COLBY, FRANK MOORE. "In Darkest James." Imaginary Obligations. New York: Dodd, Mead, pp. 321-335. Rpt. 1905, 1906, 1910, 1913.

James's books have violated proprieties for years, but his style is so difficult and his characters so fleshless that no one knows or cares. He is absorbed in "the machinery of motive" and minute mental processes, but his obscurity does not prevent enjoyment. (See 1902.30; 1904.21.)

48 COLSON, ETHEL M. Review of The Golden Bowl. Chicago Record-Herald, December 29, p. 8.

James's "constitutional admirers" will rejoice in this book, but others will grow "weary of pondering psychological abstractions" in a novel with virtually no action. The characters all talk alike in beautiful sentences. Even Maggie is "attenuated, shadowy and unreal." James needs faith that his readers "can construe an ordinary situation" without a diagram. The "purely academic style" is appropriate to James's psychology of "super-refinement" and "intellectual hair-splitting."

49 COOPER, F[REDERICK] T[ABER]. Review of The Ambassadors. Bookman, 18 (January), 532-534.

The "obscurity" and "queerness" of James's recent work is less in the manner of telling (with its mannerisms, "verbal mist," and "inexplicable syntax") than in the tale itself. James gives "as clear a statement as he can of a much befogged condition of facts." Though this novel is easier reading than James's last three or four, he "never gives you straightforward facts, but merely a series of impressions." This book has "all the tantalising vagueness of real life," and no one but James could have written it.

50 CROLY, HERBERT. "Henry James and His Countrymen." Lamp, 28 (February), 47-53.

(Recounting and analysis of James's expatriation in the context of his planned return to America.) The price of James's experience of Europe has been his detachment from his "plain primary heritage." No matter where James lives he is "above all deliberately and decisively the individual artist." He emphasizes those social traits that Americans at home most lack. In dwelling on the "finer proprieties of domestic life" which are more "authentic and definite" in England than here, James has eschewed the subjects of action and achievement that fascinate and engross contemporary Americans. He has placed his characters "in houses and rooms which illuminate and intensify their personalities." His expatriation and "his exclusive and consistent loyalty to his personal faith and vision" leave him "wholly separated from . . . [the] main stream of American literary fulfillment" of "the desire to give a vigorous and thrilling version of American life," its typical actions. Yet, what James's literary fellow-countrymen "need above all is some infusion of his incorruptible artistic purpose" and "freedom from stupefying moral and social illusions." His achievement "so extraordinary and so individual" is its own justification and should be accepted on its own merits. (See 1904.9, 12.)

51 E[DGETT], E[DWIN] F[RANCIS]. Review of The Ambassadors and The Golden Bowl. Boston Evening Transcript, December 21, p. 18.

It is hard to assign James his exact place in modern English literature. Sometimes his genius seems unrivalled and his writing inspired, while at other times he resembles literary tyros or is obsessed with "literary unrighteousness." His style is alternately clear and obscure, his form verbose and succinct, his manner straightforward and eccentric. "Unquestionably the most introspective of modern novelists" in English, he has not gained a large popular following, but has sought "an exceptional and unique" position in the literary world, and has achieved eminence, a "high rank" as the spokesman of "a small and select audience . . . influential enough to exalt his reputation far above the fame of his more popular fellows." These two latest novels show the "extraordinary mannerisms which have been growing upon him" since Daisy Miller made him familiar to novel readers. He is doing for fiction "what his father did for philosophy." Many of his earlier works indicate that he speaks "more as a cosmopolitan than as an American," and in The Ambassadors and The Golden Bowl he in addition writes of humans with extreme detachment, as from some "inaccessible planet." James loses himself in "a maze of thought," his characters are not clear, and he assumes too much reader insight, but when he leaves his psychological and verbose manner, he can write "definite and compact description." Nothing in these books "is not worth while from some point of view." James may not be as readable as Scott or Thackeray, but he knows what he wants to say, even if he cannot always say it in the usual language of his countrymen.

52 ELTON, OLIVER. "The Novels of Mr. Henry James." Living Age, 240 (January 2), 1-14.
(Reprint of article from [London] Quarterly Review, October 1903?)

53 _____. "The Novels of Mr. Henry James." Eclectic Magazine, 142 (February), 215-228.
(Reprint of article from October 1903? [London] Quarterly Review.)

54 G., J. [pseud.]. "A Literary Nightmare." Life, 43 (June 2), 534-535.
(Brief reference?)

55 GILDER, JEANNETTE L. "Some Recent Biography and Autobiography." Critic, 44 (February), 175-177.
(Review of William Wetmore Story.) This book is "unique among biographies" and shows us James's personality as well as Story's. Much of it is quotable, and little can be skipped.

56 HARRIS, MRS. L. H. "Novels and Novelists." Independent, 57 (November 17), 1132.
Although to many James seems to have reached the "high estate" of being able to ignore the average reader, some of

the "real meaning" beneath "the chastity" of his writing appeals scandalously to "the most wicked and commonplace of his readers."

57 HAWTHORNE, JULIAN; LAMBERTON, JOHN PORTER; YOUNG, JOHN RUSSELL; and LEIGH, OLIVER H. G., eds. The Masterpieces and the History of Literature: Analysis, Criticism, Character, and Incident. 10 vols. New York: Hamilton Book Co., 10:351-352. Rpt. 1906. New York: E. R. DuMont, 1902, 1903.

James steers away from great passions to portray things as they appear on the surface. Roderick Hudson has "a firmer grasp of elementary passion" than his subsequent works do. The American is considered his best book, and the controversial Daisy Miller his most popular. James is at his best in the short story, the master of a sometimes too apparent art. (Published in 1898 as The Literature of All Nations and All Ages. Philadelphia: W. Finley; Chicago, Philadelphia: E. R. Du Mont, 1900, 1901, 1902.)

58 HOWE, M. A. DeWOLFE. "Some Nineteenth Century Americans." Atlantic Monthly, 93 (January), 80-81.

(Review of William Wetmore Story.) James's image of Story's friends as "ghosts" "is forced perhaps into a duty too constant and obvious," but he is often "anything but obvious," and the book is full of "humor, insight, delicacy of perception and expression." His style sometimes baffles and estranges, but overall the book is a faithful picture of a "delightful" subject.

59 [HOWELLS, W. D.] "The Editor's Study." Harper's, 107 (January), 323-324.

(Comments on William Wetmore Story.) This biography's "high literary quality" is enjoyable, and its excellence heightens "all that we most desire in a work."

60 KERFOOT, J. B. "'The Ambassadors.' A Question./With Apologies to Henry James." Life, 43 (January 7), 22.

(Parody of The Ambassadors.)

61 K[ERFOOT], J. B. "Life's Guide to Summer Reading." Life, 43 (June 2), 537.

(The Ambassadors is listed among current books by "those who have something to say and the skill to say it well.")

62 LOGAN, ANNIE R. M. "The Ambassadors." Nation, 78 (February 4), 95.

(Review.) The enduring fundamental differences between Europeans and Americans are "much more elaborately and profoundly studied" here than in James's early books on the international theme. In his "very extended realistic representation," James strives "for the vain appearance," showing how an incident appears to a number of observers. He may as a result overdo it and be too explicit.

63 PEATTIE, ELIA W. Review of The Golden Bowl. Chicago Tribune, December 3, p. 10.

Nothing happens in this "slow moving, unpleasant" story. The heroines are "convoluting, evasive, loquacious, but uninforming." The characters in general are effete and useless, although the Prince can be almost lovable, as at the end. Much of the book is done with James's "most exquisite form of portraiture"--fine and minute, with restrained sympathy and an elegance attained by no other American writer.

64 WENDELL, BARRETT, and GREENOUGH, CHESTER NOYES. A History of Literature in America. New York: Scribner, pp. 397-398. Rpt. 1907, 1909, 1911.

The complete artist, James has grown increasingly difficult and subtle. To appreciate his "delicate shades" and the "exquisite refinement of both his perception and his style" requires effort but is rewarding. His subtlety is both his chief grace and his chief effort, and no contemporary English novelist is more masterly.

65 [WISTER, OWEN.] "The Contributors' Club/Mr. James's Variant." Atlantic Monthly, 94 (September), 426-427.

(Comments on The Ambassadors.) The Ambassadors is a post-Darwinian rendering of an ancient story, Don Juan. In keeping with the temper of the age, James dispenses with the supernatural and the moral. The old rather than the young man is the hero. James "'has reduced the English language to a fine spray, in which . . . the delicate colors and patterns gradually appear to our delighted eyes.'"

1905

1 ABERNETHY, J. W. "From Readers./A Utilitarian View of Henry James and Other Subjects." New York Times Saturday Review of Books, 10 (March 18), 170.

(Letter to the Editor.) The question of James's greatness is a problem. Howells and others maintain a "vague conviction, or current literary superstition" that James is great, but works failing the tests of popularity and intelligibility are unlikely to achieve greatness. Though James's books may be high-mindedly devoted to "certain principles of esoteric literary expression," a kind of "Della Cruscan preciosity," they add little to the spiritual wealth of mankind.

1905

2 ANON. Review of The Golden Bowl. American Monthly Review of Reviews, 31 (January), 116.
This novel is "so pregnant with fundamental brainwork, so rich in suggestiveness, and so accomplished in execution." It is clearer and therefore more vital than the other books of James's middle period.

3 ANON. Review of The Golden Bowl. Bookman, 20 (January), 418-419.
This book "has stimulated some excellent reviews." It is similar to its predecessors, and by now James's mannerisms are well known to people who have never read his books. Yet, the "lack of contrast and variety in his characters" results from his method and range of interests rather than from his mannerisms or his subtlety. He "is interested in mental processes that are common to all kinds of minds," and any record of the thoughts of even the simplest "would be a fearful and intricate narrative." James's "characters look alike because they are pulverised, and one hour in their lives seems as good as another." Half of this novel "consists of notes" which should have been destroyed and of details whose bare mention misleads us with "a sense of their importance."

4 ANON. "Some New Fiction." World's Work, 9 (January), 5766.
(Review of The Golden Bowl.) In no other book has James "succeeded in hiding, beneath a shimmering mist of words, so many strange, repellent, unspeakable things."

5 ANON. "Recent Publications . . . The New Books." New Orleans Daily Picayune, January 1, Part 3, p. 9.
(Review of The Golden Bowl.) One would expect to find James at his best in a book like this one. Many will think it shows him at his worst, since it is finicky and nervous, "lacks sympathy," and is not warmed by any genuine "heart feeling." Whether or not it does contain his best work, it is at least absolutely and unimpeachably original. James is too true an artist to overdescribe. As a study of international contrasts this story is perfect, but reading it is like drinking a "dazzling foam," a mouthful of delicious nothing.

6 ANON. "Books, Authors and Arts./Plea for the Artist in Fiction./Henry James's New Vogue./The Popularity of 'The Golden Bowl' and Some Reflection Thereon." Springfield (Mass.) Republican, January 1, p. 19.
(Poses a hypothetical admirer's defense of James's work against common criticisms of his dialogue, characters, and style.) In spite, or perhaps because, of James's "studied

avoidance of the popular," the circulation of his books "has been increasing at a remarkable rate," and his fame is "great and growing." His "elaborate, intricate, hesitating style" is really "a wonderfully delicate instrument," a "miraculous prism" that breaks common light into a spectrum revealing curious and interesting things. Both James's style and the fashionable and not very moral society he portrays suit very well his subtle and analytical purpose, in which endeavor he is unrivaled. His books have no "message" except the beauty of good manners, and they represent "keen, patient, polished, endlessly curious intelligence." His conversations are not padded, and all "flow out of" and "affect vitally" the immediate point. Other novelists recognize the difference between this "consummate art" that calls for "the highest mental powers," and mere fakery, and they read James "with cordial envy." No English novelist has so richly pictured the "splendors of a great aristocracy" as James has with an art which "evades the disillusionment of bald realism," suggests invisible things, and appeals with "the vague, sweet charm of poetry."

7 ANON. "Henry James' Latest Novel." San Francisco Chronicle, January 8, p. 8.

(Review of The Golden Bowl.) As "an eminent critic" of James has said, the important question is not "whether we like or detest his method, but whether he has put it to good use," and the critic thinks the method is "not at all at its best" in The Golden Bowl. (Quotation from the critic to the effect that the book is thin and bloodless, without emotional warmth or sympathetic purpose.) If this book is art, it is art without soul. The quoted "severe judgment" may warn the unwary, but it cannot affect "the idolatry" for James and his work by those "who understand or pretend to understand them."

8 ANON. "Books, Authors and Arts./Some Eminent New Books./Mr. James's 'The Golden Bowl.'" Springfield (Mass.) Republican, January 8, p. 19.

The Golden Bowl shows James at neither his best nor his worst, and the people who like him will like it, while "the perhaps greater number who dislike him" will not. American reviews have been "rather hostile, while the popular demand for the book has been surprisingly large." This novel is characteristic of James's later style, as "elaborately and beautifully woven" as The Ambassadors and The Wings of the Dove, but with a story of less "essential interest." James's "somewhat finicky" style is "hard reading" only if read too rapidly. The art and enjoyment of the book are not in a rush of events, but in the whole detailed picture, of which

1905

each detail "becomes a vital part," to be built upon and returned to as in real life. The fullness of detail gives a greater sense of reality than would otherwise be possible. The "ceaseless, prismatic play of metaphor" almost surpasses even Meredith's, and is where the imaginative quality of James's work appears most strikingly. James's treatment of art objects is "rich and suggestive." "By far the strongest part of the book," strong enough to repay the reader for many pages of relative triviality, is the awakening and growing feeling, awareness, and resourcefulness of the "too amiable, too self-sacrificing princess."

9 ANON. "The Golden Bowl." Independent, 58 (January 19), 153-154.
(Review.) James has produced "another two volumes of abstruseness, another long discussion of a situation appropriate only for scandal mongers," disguised with "heavy respectability" and subtlety. Yet, "the very greatness" of his work always demands that we read him. James believes in the moral virtues of Americans, and the characters' reserve averts disaster, but it makes the book monotonous to the careless reader.

10 ANON. "Notes." Nation, 80 (January 19), 53.
(Correspondent writes on James's January 9 lecture "The Lesson of Balzac" to the Philadelphia Contemporary Club.) James's delivery is mellow and effortless, "entertaining and not too obscure." His audience was attentive, and the copies of Balzac are all gone from the Philadelphia libraries.

11 ANON. "The Qualifications of a Great Critic." New Orleans Daily Picayune, January 22, II, p. 6.
(Editorial.) James, Howells, and Lowell are great critics who were not failures as artists.

12 ANON. "Mr. James and His Readers." Life, 45 (January 26), 107.
(Humorous comments on the lack of incident in James's novels, and on the time and effort it takes to read them.)

13 ANON. "Henry James's Golden Bowl." Nation, 80 (January 26), 74.
(Review.) The story is short, bitter, and "elaborately concealed." No one but James could write it in English "without grossness or vulgarity," and it illustrates "the appalling power for moral disintegration, if not corruption, implied in the possession of immense wealth."

14 ANON. "Mr. Henry James on Balzac." Book News, 23 (February),

485-487.

(Portrait, and summary of "The Lesson of Balzac.") James is "the most prominent of living American novelists," and has "with doubtful wisdom" been called the Dean of letters. He is not entirely successful as a speaker, but is then "far more human and likeable," more poetic, emotional, and witty, than he is as a novelist.

15 ANON. "The Golden Bowl." Reader, 5 (February), 380-382.

(Review.) This mixture of "ugly and charming aspects" has a strange theme. Despite the analysis and psychology, the "white heat" intensity of the love story shows through many times. Though shocking in some of its implications, "it yields treasure to the courageous reader." The characters are well done, like "masterpieces in the great galleries of the world," and never has the art of description seemed more like painting. The book is for the seasoned James reader, and James gives like no other writer "a sense of the complexity of life, a particularly vivid realization of the dominant note in the life of the particular case under scrutiny."

16 ANON. "Visit to America." Reader, 5 (February), 360.

(Observations on James's personality, appearance, way of life, activities in America, and misadventures in the theater.)

17 ANON. "Mr. Henry James./His Life in London and at Rye." New York Tribune, February 12, Supp., p. 6.

(Account of James's methods of housekeeping and composition. Photograph portrait from the Reader.) James looks upon his homeland with eyes more English than American, and his comments on it are anticipated with curiosity and a "cheerful cynicism." Since his last visit, he has probably changed more than his point of view has.

18 ANON. "Recent Fiction." Churchman, 91 (March 4), 334.

(Review of The Golden Bowl.) Not surprisingly, this book has been much discussed. In its "triumph of subtle analysis" and "extraordinary though somewhat outré brilliancy," the character study is masterful, but the situation is so shocking that reading the book will be unprofitable.

19 ANON. Note. Critic, 46 (April), 307.

The "steadily increasing number" of James's "discriminating admirers" will value the chance to hear him deliver "The Lesson of Balzac." His novels' appreciation of "the finer elements of American character" has "confirmed him in the regard of his countrymen."

1905

20 ANON. "Henry James." Outlook, 79 (April 1), 838-839.
James is a New Englander modified by foreign influences. He has made himself "a little master" of "social and spiritual portraiture," recording especially the "relative" rather than the "absolute" character, and focusing on "the most elusive changes" people and new environments make on character. He is thus a lesser artist than Balzac, Thackeray, and Tolstoy, who give us "great primitive or natural types." The works of James's youth are "fresh, clear, and beautiful," but the recent changes in his art suggest limitation. No American has been better equipped or "made a more exacting study of his materials and his methods."

21 ANON. "Henry James." New York Times Saturday Review of Books, 10 (April 8), 224.
(Editorial.) W. C. Brownell's Atlantic study of James (1905.81) is the most important yet, surpassing even the monumental Edinburgh Review article of three or four years ago. The Golden Bowl was "a crucial ordeal" for James's admirers, and his April North American Review article on New England is his least intelligible work. Brownell is right that James may perfectly express a thought without communicating it, that while his artistic attitude is immaculate his product is ineffective, and that his subordination of imagination to microscopic observation is regrettable. James has used his undeniable powers as conscientiously and artistically as any novelist, but he disappoints the diminishing number who continue to read him.

22 ANON. "Topics of the Week." New York Times Saturday Review of Books, 10 (April 15), 241.
The London Academy suggests that, having done George Meredith, the Germans will now try to translate James's later books into German. A reader objects to the "trivialities" in other Times readers' letters criticizing James's later books, because those late works are more original than the beautifully done earlier ones. (Mentions the date James will speak in Brooklyn on "The Lesson of Balzac.")

23 ANON. "New England: An Autumn Impression. By H---y J---s." Life, 45 (April 20), 457.
(Parody of James's North American Review article on New England, with phrases like "almost sophisticated dinginess of destitution." See 1905.25.)

24 ANON. "Life's Sunday-School Class." Life, 45 (April 27), 482-483.
(Humorous article. Members of the "class" are James, Hall Caine, Marie Corelli, "Winnie" Churchill, "Gerty"

Atherton, Cyrus Brady, and S. Weir Mitchell, popular writers.) James is from Boston, thinks he is too good for the rest of the writers, and speaks in big words and stilted phrases.

25 ANON. "What Mr. James Saw." Boston Evening Transcript, May 3, p. 19.
(Review of James's second article on "New England, An Autumn Impression," in the May North American Review. Long quotations.) This article is as "Henry Jamesish" as the first, and is written in a style "which is the delight of some and the unbounded irritation of others." Life's parody of James's April article (see 1905.23) is "a very witty and on the whole faithful condensation."

26 ANON. "Miscellaneous." Advance, 49 (May 4), 563.
(Review of The Golden Bowl.) This "deservedly popular" author's latest work is thoroughly interesting, "will surely prove a success," and is the equal of his other books.

27 ANON. "Books and Authors." New York Sun, May 17, p. 7.
(Comments on "The Lesson of Balzac.") James, the "literary lion of the hour," the "apostle of the complex," reads his lecture aloud so pleasingly, so soothingly, that one ceases to wonder what his involved sentences mean or to care if they mean anything.

28 ANON. Note. Boston Evening Transcript, May 24, p. 21.
(Refers to James's lecture on Balzac, his publication of English Hours, and his visit to his brother William.)

29 ANON. "Literary." Life, 45 (May 25), 597.
(Brief humorous reference.) Gertrude Atherton has dedicated a book to James, and it serves him right.

30 ANON. "Notes About Books and Authors." Chicago Evening Post, June 3, p. 4.
(Mentions James's Balzac lecture, English Hours, and his visit to brother William. Reprint of 1905.28.)

31 ANON. "Henry James Flays the Press/Blames It for 'Untidy, Slovenly' Language." Boston Evening Transcript, June 9, p. 3.
(Report on "The Question of Our Speech.") Criticizing newspapers, James "repaid the press for all courtesies extended to him." Then he horrified his audience with his warning that they would be able to speak perfectly only with great effort.

1905

32 ANON. "Shock for Mr. James." Chicago Record-Herald, June 9, p. 5.
James, now classified as an Englishman, has returned here to study "American types." In an address on "The Question of Our Speech," he shocked his audience of Bryn Mawr graduates by saying Americans do not pronounce vowels properly. The entranced graduates "just gasped" at his opinion of American schools and newspapers.

33 ANON. "Our Speech Untidy, Says Henry James." New York Times, June 9, p. 9.
(News article on James's Bryn Mawr lecture on American speech, with some summary and quotation.)

34 ANON. "James Attacks Papers and Schools./Says They Keep Speech Untidy--Says the Former Roar Like Maniacs." New York Tribune, June 9, p. 1.
(Quotation from "The Question of Our Speech," delivered at Bryn Mawr's commencement.)

35 ANON. "Speech and Manners." New York Sun, June 11, p. 8.
(Editorial. Comments on James's commencement address at Bryn Mawr on American speech.) James is justified in pointing out Americans' untidiness of speech, and he did "a good service" to the graduating class. Yet, he "could have extended his criticism" to speech in upper circles of English society, as well as to Anglo-American manners in general. Women should pay particular heed to his comments on vocal tone.

36 ANON. "Literary Notes." Chicago Record-Herald, June 17, p. 7.
Despite the fog of the style of "Impressions of New England" in the North American Review, it is clear that James admired American scenery, found the American businessman ubiquitious, and thought the women finer-textured than the men. Howells's "London Films" are clearer and more direct than James's impressions, showing "how far apart these realists have drifted in phraseology and mental habits."

37 ANON. "The Old Howells Again." New York Sun, June 17, p. 7.
(Review of W. D. Howells's Miss Bellard's Inspiration.) Howells's appreciation of James has told on him. A few of his sentences seem intended to show that if "tangling up a simple idea in a complicated sentence" is art, Howells can do it, too.

38 ANON. "Books and Authors." Philadelphia Public Ledger and Philadelphia Times, June 23, p. 6.
(Quotation from Howells's recent "graceful tribute" to James in an interview.)

39 ANON. "A Novelist's Impression of American Men and Women." Literary Digest, 30 (June 24), 929.

(Comments on "New England: An Autumn Impression" in the June North American Review, including long quotation from James's remarks on the contrast between American men and women. Quotation of New York Sun's reference to "the fog" of James's idiom.)

40 ANON. "Henry James's Impressions of New England." Current Literature, 39 (July), 97-99.

(Review, with quotations, of James's "New England: An Autumn Impression," in the April, May, and June North American Review. Photograph of James, with caption stating that his New England articles and Balzac lecture are attracting attention, especially in literary circles.) New England seems as puzzling to James as James is to his readers. The June installment is "hopelessly subjective."

41 ANON. "Notes on Books and Bookmen." Chicago Evening Post, July 19, p. 4.

James's lecture on Balzac "has stirred up" a very lively discussion. It will be published with his interesting study of Balzac.

42 ANON. Note. Atlanta Constitution, July 23, p. 2.

James's recent lecture on "The Question of Our Speech" has "stirred up such a lively discussion" that it will be published with "his interesting study" of Balzac.

43 ANON. Comments on "The Lesson of Balzac." New York Tribune. 4 (July 29), 12.

This "brilliant man of letters" talks around a great subject without making us feel the expected illumination. Most disappointing is James's allowing himself to adore Balzac by patronizing other classics.

44 ANON. Reader, 6 (August), 334.

James has for twenty-five years remained "one of the most interesting and provocative figures in American literature." He does not try to suit others, and has indulged himself in "the delicate, astute psychology of triflers," in small things, while Americans are "fond of large things." James has always laughed at Americans, sometimes so that we could hardly understand him. Yet, though he is "not a light-bringer," he is nonetheless an American. We "expect and desire him to attain immortality" and are proud of "his sheer, amazing cleverness." (Photograph by Alice Boughton.)

45 ANON. "Readers and Writers." Reader, 6 (August), 336.

(Quotations from James's Cambridge, Mass., lecture on Balzac, with comments.) This lecture was "a truly marvelous exposition of the art of the novelist as exemplified in Balzac." It had "masterful sentences" and "highly interesting generalization."

46 ANON. Review of "The Question of Our Speech." Boston Evening Transcript, August 2, p. 17.
(Summary of parts of the article published in the August Appleton's Booklovers' Magazine.)

47 ANON. Comments on "The Question of Our Speech." New York Tribune Weekly Review, 4 (August 5), 12.
James's own use of "dialect," his complicated style, make his criticisms of our speech ironic. Yet, his argument is justified, to the point, and "pure gold."

48 ANON. Review of "The Question of Our Speech." New York Tribune, August 6, Supp., p. 14.
(Reprints 1905.47.)

49 ANON. "Some Writings of the Day . . ./Mr. James on American Speech." Springfield (Mass.) Republican, August 6, p. 19.
(Review of The Question of Our Speech and The Lesson of Balzac.) James's criticisms of American speech have caused "much gasping and explanation," but they should be taken to heart because "he is a great critic of these things." Yet, he is needlessly alarmed over the destiny of English, which suffered more in the Celtic isles than it has here. Newspapers revitalize it more than do James's "beautifully polished writings," and he probably overestimates the immigrants' influence.

50 ANON. Editorial. New York Evening Post, August 9, p. 6.
James's criticism of American speech habits "has started a really interesting discussion" in the Indianapolis News and elsewhere. (Here, the controversy is treated somewhat satirically.)

51 ANON. "The Late Magazines." New Orleans Daily Picayune, August 13, III, p. 11.
(Review of Atlantic Monthly.) "No literary study could be more appropriate for a fiction number" than James's "notable paper" "The Lesson of Balzac."

52 ANON. "Literary Small Talk." Advance, 50 (August 24), 210.
(Note on James's return to America and his enjoyment of nature.)

53 ANON. "Bookishness." Chicago Evening Post, August 29, p. 4.
(Note.) James's recent activities have created a "polite popularity" for his work. Elisabeth L. Cary's soon-to-be-published book on him is one of a number of attempts to fix his rank as an author.

54 ANON. Review of The Question of Our Speech and The Lesson of Balzac. New York Sun, October 21, p. 8.
In the lecture on speech is James's own language in "its most mischievous and perplexing confusion." His eulogy of Balzac deserves "far more attention," but should have been written in his less affected earlier style.

55 ANON. Review of English Hours. Boston Evening Transcript, November 1, p. 19.
These picturesque scenes are presented "with a rare imagination and a sincere artistic touch."

56 ANON. "Why Not?" Life, 46 (November 2), 517.
(Brief humorous reference. Suggestion that James is vague.)

57 ANON. "Books New and Old." Boston Evening Transcript, November 3, II, p. 12.
(Review of The Question of Our Speech and The Lesson of Balzac.) The lecture on American speech "was widely quoted and discussed" when delivered in June. In the Balzac lecture, James "gives sound reasons" for his admiration of that writer, but also is aware of his defects.

58 ANON. "Other Books." New York Sun, November 4, p. 10.
(Review of Harald Höffding's The Problems of Philosophy, with a preface by William James.) The contrast between Henry James's tangled style and William's simple, "crystal clear" style, is very interesting.

59 ANON. "Books, Authors and Arts." Springfield (Mass.) Republican, November 5, p. 23.
(Review of The Lesson of Balzac in volume form, with paraphrase and quotation.) Reading James aloud often solves the difficulties of his style. His views on Balzac are "very interesting," illustrated with a "dazzling variety of metaphor" able to express subtle qualities "that can be felt, but hardly defined."

60 ANON. "Briefs on New Books./Brilliant Essays by Mr. James." Dial, 39 (November 16), 311.
(Review of The Question of Our Speech, and The Lesson of Balzac.) One takes a special "interest and delight" in

reading these lectures in book form, where they are easier to understand than when heard. A "logically balanced structure" and "fine shadings of thought and diction" characterize James's criticism. The more notable of the two essays is "The Lesson of Balzac," with its "concentrated vigor, its elucidation of the novelist's art, and its nicety of phrase." These essays will "raise a divergence of opinion," as does all of James's work, but "all will recognize the stimulating intellectual quality."

61 ANON. "Life's Retreat for the Prominent." Life, 46 (November 16), 592-593.
(Satire.) James and Gertrude Atherton are elected patron saints of a new building erected for prominent authors. (Reference to and imitation of James's style. Sketch by C. Budd.)

62 ANON. Review of The Question of Our Speech and The Lesson of Balzac. Chicago Evening Post, November 18, p. 6.
Those who want literature "to inform and complete life," rather than "to amuse primarily or to wheedle," will be glad to see this book. James is a supreme critic, very "sensitive to the values and variations of personality." His sensitivity to American speech is "neurotic as well as intellectual," but "The Lesson of Balzac" is "balanced, chastened, perfected yet informal," as noble a tribute as we have in English to Balzac and to the art of fiction.

63 ANON. "Literary News & Criticism/Holiday Books of Travel by Mr. Henry James & Others." New York Tribune, November 18, p. 5.
(Review of English Hours.) James seems afraid to state plain facts straightforwardly but must show his originality with conceits. Yet, the older essays contain such good travel writing that we can forgive his later tortuous style.

64 ANON. "Miscellaneous." Advance, 50 (November 23), 613.
"The Question of Our Speech" and "The Lesson of Balzac" are "important addresses."

65 ANON. "Here and There." New York Tribune Weekly Review, 6 (November 25), 11.
(Review of English Hours. Reprint of 1905.63.)

66 ANON. Review of English Hours. Advance, 50 (November 30), 647.
This well-known author's visit to America has drawn Americans toward him.

67 ANON. "This Bubble World." Life, 46 (November 30), 637.
(Brief humorous reference. Quotes Louisville Times as reporting that James wants to eliminate colloquial modes of expression.) Maybe James is afraid his novels "will some day be translated into English."

68 ANON. Review of English Hours. A.L.A. Booklist, 1 (December), 127-128.
(Listing of contents.)

69 ANON. "Belles-Lettres . . . James--English Hours." Critic, 47 (December), 572.
(Review.) James "is like his simple original self in this charming book," which is as delightful as any of the season.

70 ANON. "Holiday Publications." Dial, 39 (December 1), 381.
(Review of English Hours.) Readers of James's recent novels, unless they are among "the small minority who have fallen uncritically under the spell of his vagaries of style," will turn with relief to James "at his best, exhibiting at once his keenest and most lucid analytical genius" in essays from his "splendid prime." The "artistic motive" of "finding the interesting beneath the commonplace" is ever-present. Lately James has been dissecting "some very faded and unpromising primroses," but in contrast, these essays have a "tonic freshness" that carries the reader along rather than bewildering him "about everything and nothing" as James's late novels do.

71 ANON. Review of English Hours. Detroit Free Press, December 2, Part II, p. 2.
Most of these impressions were written before James "became so microscopic in his detail," and "need not be the less popular on that account."

72 ANON. "Our Assimilation." New York Times, December 3, p. 6.
(Editorial.) James's North American Review article "New York and the Hudson" is one of the most remarkable to appear in a periodical in a long time. His previous, too highly refracted, impressions have disappointed his admirers, been caviar to the general, and failed to "'catch on' to the American idea." In the most recent article, however, he does catch on and shows his belief in the American power to assimilate the foreign masses. He is "both a seer and a thinker, an observer and a philosopher," with a union of the faculties of observation and reflection "unique among living writers" of English.

1905

73 ANON. "Writers and Books." Boston Evening Transcript, December 9, III, p. 7.
(Review of Elisabeth Luther Cary's The Novels of Henry James.) More "an analyst of character than a writer of fiction," James lends himself to "energetic comment and dispute" and has a singular literary style, and therefore is "more talked about than a hundred of his popular contemporaries." Cary touches too lightly on James's "extraordinary style," and is often as obscure and wordy as the master himself. (See 1905.86.)

74 ANON. "English Hours." Churchman, 92 (December 9), 962.
(Review.) James is a "minutely analytic observer."

75 ANON. "English as She Is Spoke." Public Opinion, 39 (December 9), 764-765.
(Review of The Question of Our Speech and The Lesson of Balzac.) James makes his sound contentions with precise, "finicky persistence," and George Ade's rough idioms are preferable to his "pallid niceties." The lecture on Balzac is "much more vital," but still limited in appeal.

76 ANON. "Elizabeth Luther Cary's Study of Henry James." Louisville Courier-Journal, December 23, p. 3.
(Review. Summarizes the contents of Cary's "sympathetic" Henry James, A Study.) Cary is interesting on the play of James's imagination, but she should have been "as exhaustive and illuminating on the subject of his philosophy of life." (See 1905.86.)

77 ANON. "English Hours." Nation, 81 (December 28), 528.
(Review.) The style of the earlier essays contrasts with that of the later ones, but throughout the sketches the keynote of James's interest is the "air of history" he finds in the scenes.

78 ANON. "Answers to Henry James./His Criticism of the American Manner of Speech Brings Canadian Retort." New York Times, December 29, p. 6.
At the Modern Language Association meeting, Leigh R. McGregor of McGill University answered James's criticism of American speech, suggesting that his standard for defining "'people of culture'" is too high.

79 ANON. "Reply to Henry James." New York Tribune, December 29, p. 6.
James was "pilloried" at the Modern Language Association meeting at Haverford College for his criticisms of American English. The consensus was that Americans speak as well as,

if not better than, the British. Leigh R. Gregor of McGill College in Canada read a paper replying to James.

80 BRAGDON, CLAUDE. "A Master of Shades." Critic, 46 (January), 20-22.

(Review of The Golden Bowl.) A new book by James is "an event of importance," especially since the eclipse of Meredith, Hardy, Kipling, and Barrie leaves him as the only remaining first-class Anglo-Saxon novelist. In "craftsmanship and sureness of intention" his work is far superior to the average. James is the Sherlock Holmes of "secret places of the human spirit," revealing in this "remarkable novel" the emotions lurking beneath the finest and most finished surfaces of modern life. Like "all men of original genius arrived at maturity" James is interested in this inner reality, and he thus also reflects his father's Swedenborgianism.

81 BROWNELL, W. C. "Henry James." Atlantic Monthly, 95 (April), 496-519.

James's career has been markedly happy and honorable, and he has stuck to his ideal rather than merely try to please the public. If his substance has sometimes been thin, it has always been thoughtful, and never superficial. For James nothing seems trivial, and his "copiousness . . . is the result of his seriousness." Yet, though his attitude is "immaculate," his product is "ineffective." A scientifically disinterested curisity characterizes his later work, but he and his philosophy of life elude the reader. He is "perhaps the most individual novelist of his day" and yet reflects its current tendencies. He "has created a genre of his own" and made a distinctive contribution. His observation "has grown more and more acute" in pursuit "of a more complete illusion of nature," and now he "has reversed the relation between his observation and his imagination." Yet, "his realism does not leave a very vivid impression of reality," or always create effects closely corresponding "to actual life and character." Finding nothing too insignificant for artistic treatment, James's "interest in life [is] so impartial and inclusive as to approach aridity." In the "search for the recondite" he minimizes the passions and fails to deal directly with "the elemental," so that his books lack "large vitality" and miss "the typical, the representative," which is "the basis of both effective illusion and significant truth." Taken together, James's characters "constitute the lease successful element of his fiction," and his portrayal of human nature is limited, incomplete. His style is elaborate, scrupulous, yet elliptical, obscure. Though he has founded a school, and has many imitators, he has not produced a masterpiece of the first order, and thus his achievement is not commensurate with his "unmistakable powers." (See 1905.21.)

82 BYNNER, WITTER. "A Word or Two with Henry James." Critic, 46 (February), 146-148.
(Interview, with long quoted comments by James on New York, Boston, Henry Harland, and journalism.)

83 C., A. B. "The American Voice/Some Comments on the Criticisms of Mr. Henry James." New York Times, September 10, p. 6.
(Letter to the Editor. Discussion of American intonation stemming from James's criticisms of American speech.)

84 CARLETON, EMMA. "From Readers." New York Times Saturday Review of Books, 10 (January 14), 26.
(Letter to the Editor.) The appearance of The Golden Bowl and its "numerous following of magazine and newspaper criticisms" suggests amusingly and discouragingly that the evasive master James has created for himself "a school of evasive critics." The Golden Bowl is "not a high achievement" and is ethically "far out of plumb," while The Ambassadors ends with "a notably warped situation." One wishes James would "make us one of his old-time magic books under clean, blue American skies," while people grieve at the shrine of the gifted author of "The Altar of the Dead," The Spoils of Poynton, and The Tragic Muse who now exhibits such "artistically, politely vicious literary behavior."

85 _____. "The Middle West." New York Times Saturday Review of Books, 10 (January 28), 54.
(Satirical discussion of The Golden Bowl by residents of the Middle West.) The Golden Bowl is the "wooziest" book James ever wrote.

86 CARY, ELISABETH LUTHER. The Novels of Henry James: A Study. New York: G. P. Putnam, 215 pp.
James has an influence and "belongs indefeasably to our consciousness." He showed himself early to be concerned with form, perceptive, responsive, accurate, and imaginative," and he has always been a good American in that he is both fresh and ripe of mind. He alone among contemporaries tried to produce "a picture of international social relations," with patience, authority, and "an infinitely serious purpose." His art is dignified, mature, highly developed, and conscientious. Though he neglects wild, natural settings, James has made his interior landscapes as romantic and unfamiliar as those of Robinson Crusoe. As a critic, he is consistent. As a novelist, he combines fine observations with an interest in moral states, tactile values with

"the greatest possible amount of spiritual truth," the temper of the dreamer and mystic with that of the observer and analyst. The American is perhaps the most representative of his early works. No writer has been "more haunted by the compatibility of gentleness with the firmer qualities of the spirit," and his Americans have a particular innocent charm. James's strong sense of the poetic in human nature is balanced by a remarkable feeling for the details, "the genius of places." He has a rare perception of "the positive aesthetic value of moral and intellectual visions." Although his characters often do not spring to life immediately, they are alive. James interprets their shades of feeling "with precision and subtlety" and distills their essence without dissecting them. In scenes from What Maisie Knew, The Awkward Age, and The Golden Bowl, James shows "the magic of genius" by surprising "sentiment at its source," and, at "moments of great moral significance," moving "the heart with pity." His psychological exploration leaves us with a childlike sense of wonder. His style is somewhat obscure, but from the mass of his work we get both "an exhilarating sense of life" and the sense of a "judicial" moralist who sees the beauty of goodness and teaches us unobtrusively from "a profound and definite sense of moral values." For him taste combines with conscience and has "both intellectual and moral force."

87 _____. "Balzac and James." New York Times Saturday Review of Books, 10 (May 27), 337-338.

James's lecture on Balzac was given "with the air of high comradeship," a "very fortunate note to strike." James's art is intricate and defies labels, but it represents modern life, provides "nothing less than reality," and gives the adventurous mind the excitement of entering undiscovered regions. To future generations, his work will seem "the most important achievement in fiction of the period it so subtly reproduces," and to attentive present readers it gives new insight and pleasure. The Golden Bowl is a brilliant, pitiless, pitiful study whose development of its theme is as far as possible from the hackneyed.

88 CONRAD, JOSEPH. "Henry James: An Appreciation." North American Review, 180 (January), 102-108.

While exciting romances appeal to youth, the problems of conduct in James's books quicken our mature years. His characters are great and heroic in that they make the acts of renunciation whose necessity is the only "secret behind the curtain," and whose commission is our "most potent and effective force." James is a great artist and "the historian of fine consciences." (See 1905.110; 1916.76.)

1905

89 _____. "Current Comment." New York Times Saturday Review of Books, 10 (January 7), p. 12.
(Long quotation from 1905.88.)

90 COSMOPOLITAN [pseud.]. "From Readers." New York Times Saturday Review of Books, 10 (May 13), 314.
(Letter to the Editor.) Harry Hall's April 22 letter praising James is one of the signs in the Times Saturday Review of "healthy-minded Americans acquiring a taste for European decadence." James is very enjoyable, and his "fine mental gymnastics" make other writers seem insipid, but his very cleverness, brilliancy, and art distort moral issues and tend to discredit his "high purpose." (See 1905.95.)

91 No entry.

92 DUNBAR, OLIVIA H. "Henry James as a Lecturer." Critic, 47 (July), 24-25.
(Review of "The Lesson of Balzac.") James is a "supremely competent authority" on the novel and has "high seriousness of vision," yet is "radiantly free" from academic formulae. His memorable, "wonderfully lucid and structurally solid" lecture always offers "high intellectual entertainment." (See 1905.114.)

93 FIELDING, H. M. "Henry James, the Lion." Reader, 5 (February), 365-367.
(Photograph by Vander Weyde. Account of James's social, leisure, domestic, and working life in London and Rye.) James is lionized, has many imitators, and has, with Kipling, "done more to color the poetic and prose stream of their day than all the other poets and novelists put together."

94 FRANCE, WILMER CAVE. "Mr. Henry James as a Lecturer." Bookman, 21 (March), 71-72.
James's subtlety and indirection estrange men and appeal to women. In his long sentences he shows a fondness for adverbs "amounting to mania." His essay on Balzac is rich and thick with images, and he seems especially to like water imagery, as evidenced also in The Golden Bowl.

95 HALL, HARRY M. "From Readers./The Effect of Henry James on an Inquiring, Unprejudiced Mind." New York Times Saturday Review of Books, 10 (April 22), 266.
(Letter to the Editor. A West Virginia reader's response to the Times editorial, 1905.21.) James is in disrepute, with his books packed away in libraries or selling cheap. Yet, this reader bought and enjoyed The Golden Bowl, a "good story." To describe minutely the complex interactions of

normal minds takes "a new kind of thought," and future generations will see James as the father of the effort to accomplish "the stupendous task of the present century--to show the real mental processes that may possibly speak for a life beyond the grave." It is confusing to find so beautiful a book pronounced an unrealistic failure by literary authorities. (See 1905.90.)

96 _____. "From Readers./Further Remarks on the Influences of Henry James and the Danger of Moral Decadence." New York Times Saturday Review of Books, 10 (May 27), 346.

(Letter to the Editor. Hall's rueful reiteration of his liking for James, despite his critics.) James, Edith Wharton, and their disciples are not decadents or moral polluters. Milly Theale is "the loveliest of all women," and her martyrdom is the greatest in literature.

97 INQUIRER [pseud.]. "American and English Writers." New York Times Saturday Review of Books, 10 (February 4), 74.

(Letter to the Editor. Response to Richard Le Gallienne's list of the ten greatest living American authors, which lists James third.) The list is "exceedingly well considered," with the possible exception of James, whom some would not consider American.

98 IRWIN, WALLACE. "After Reading a Chapter by Henry James." Critic, 46 (March), 220.

(Parody. Humorous poem imitates James's style and suggests that he exhausts his readers.)

99 KERFOOT, J. B. "The Latest Books." Life, 46 (December 21), 780.

(Review of 1905.86.) Despite its arbitrary analytical divisions, this book has passages that perfectly articulate "the basic spirit of James's writings."

100 _____. "The Latest Books." Life, 46 (December 21), 780.

(Review of English Hours.) These commentaries are "full of quality and color," and constitute "an interesting and unarbitrary sampling" of James's "progressive attitude toward life and his own art."

101 LITTLEFIELD, WALTER. "News of the Book World." Chicago Record-Herald, July 15, p. 8.

Elisabeth Luther Cary's proposed "sympathetic dissection" of James's novels for the general reader will be a task "of monstrous difficulty," since James writes mainly for other writers, who may call him "Master" in either praise or irony. His thought is obscured to most in "a maze of rhetorical tropes" which provoke "the admiring dismay of critics."

1905

102 LOOMIS, CHARLES BATTELL. "Mr. Henry James and His Literary Style." New York Sun, May 19, p. 6.
(Letter to the Editor.) James's present, "willfully obscure" writing lends itself to parody, but his interesting lecture on Balzac was delightful and not nearly as obscure as the New York Sun literary note suggested. He "laughs in his sleeve at his devotees," but in his lecture this "brilliant American" was sincere.

103 _____. "An Attempt to Translate Henry James." Bookman, 21 (July), 464-466.
James always means what he says and is "sincere in his pursuit of trifles." For the "complex souls" who enjoy him he weaves his involuted, difficult style, but the commonplace reader does not enjoy it, and there are bogus Jamesites who dote on him but only pretend to understand him. Yet, despite his "fogginess of expression," James "by virtue of his best work must ever loom large in English literature."

104 McGILL, ANNA BLANCHE. "Henry James, Artist." Poet Lore, 16 (Winter), 90-96.
Earlier, James was dedicated to art. Now he is a "psychic analyst," and at its best, his style offers as engaging a "fitting of symbols to ideas" as anything in modern prose. He provides both a close rendition of outward appearance and an analysis of motive. He "stands almost alone" in his command of both description and narration. James's characters are not limited in range, but include "nearly all kinds and conditions." Some of his women may come to stand for representative types from the nineteenth century.

105 MARBLE, ANNIE RUSSELL. "Henry James: An Appreciation." Dial, 39 (December 16), 441-442.
(Review of 1905.86.) Miss Cary, like other James admirers, thinks his fiction enriches and quickens the minds of its readers. She "justly lays stress upon the staying quality" of the images of such women as "Maisie, Nanda, Maggie, and Maria Gostrey." With "discrimination" she says that James "does not dissect his characters, but rather . . . builds them up synthetically and slowly, to gain large effects."

106 MASSON, TOM [THOMAS L.] "Mary's Little Lamb. In Different Keys." Life, 45 (May 4), 514-517.
(Parody. The nursery rhyme rewritten in James's prose style, and also in the styles of James Whitcomb Riley, Mr. Dooley, Rudyard Kipling, and George Ade. Sketch of James by James Montgomery Flagg.)

107 MILLER, ALICE DUER. "The Golden Bowl." Lamp, 29 (January), 583-585.

(Review.) James has not given us "the finer possibilities," the "moral aspect," of his situation, but rather has brought out what is not "the most important or the most interesting" aspect. The Golden Bowl is "a detective story in the mind, a psychological dime novel" in which love of truth degenerates into mere curiosity. The subject is French, but the treatment shows a puritanical distaste for physical fact. The senses are entirely ignored and the book "confines itself almost wholly to the region of synthesized thought." We miss the "perfect verbal reproductions" of The Awkward Age and "the descriptions, lovely as poetry," in The Ambassadors, although there are "a couple of perfect sketches of people." An example of James's "extremest method," this book has no exciting interest and will appeal only to those who are fascinated by an intellectual exercise in psychology.

107a MILLER, DAISY [pseud.]. "From Readers. . . . Henry James." New York Times Saturday Review of Books, 10 (March 4), 138.

(Letter to the Editor. This response to 1905.117 includes a "Mary Had a Little Lamb" parody of James's style.) Not James's enemies, but his friends who loved his older "keen analysis" object to his later methods and tortuous style.

108 MOSS, MARY. "Some Significant Tendencies in Current Fiction." Atlantic Monthly, 95 (May), 696.

(Review of The Golden Bowl.) The characters are alive, compelling, and unforgettable, but James is a hermit, removed from earth and hovering "in a wonderful, labyrinthine dimension of his own." He is "a precious, morbid phenomenon, too exceptional for healthy discipleship."

109 N., E. "James and his Characters." New York Times Saturday Review of Books, 10 (January 28), 54.

(Letter to the Editor.) James's characters are so entertaining that we sometimes too readily forgive their vices. In his recent books James has "misunderstood the admittedly peculiar taste of his public." Roderick Hudson, The Princess Casamassima, and The American were better than these late, offending, sometimes tainted works.

110 O., M. U. "Joseph Conrad and Henry James." New York Times Saturday Review of Books, 10 (February 4), 74.

(Letter to the Editor.) Judging from his North American Review appreciation of James (1905.88), Conrad apparently plans to enter upon "the same futile word play" James began ten or twelve years ago. Although their worthwhile parts are admirable, James's books contain too little, if anything, worth understanding. The most charitable view of his attitude toward the public is that he is willing to supply a demand. Emma Carleton's comments in the New York Times (1905.84) were the best on the subject, and the James cult suggests the tale of the Emperor's new clothes.

111 OPTIMIST [pseud.]. "Current Comment. . . . Henry James." New York Times Saturday Review of Books, 10 (February 18), 107.
(Letter to the Editor.) The writer of 1905.117 champions James with only "the most threadbare defenses of all realistic-pessimistic literature," and James lacks the courage, the sincerity, and (being American) the excuse of its usual exponents. If he stayed home, he would meet mainly "decent, sane, and sound people." The great majority of Americans prefer optimistic to pessimistic literature, and the world is the worse for the decadence in James's books.

112 PEATTIE, ELIA W. "New Books by Howells and James." Chicago Tribune, November 11, p. 9.
(Review of English Hours.) Years ago, critics associated the names of Howells and James, and noted that they had sent American letters in a new direction. Now critics "almost oppose one to the other" with respect to subject and treatment. Yet, both English Hours and Howells's London Films are very engaging, and evidence "that trained, humorous, wholesome, compassionate, gay imagination" which these authors have to a degree that has kept both of them from "touching actual greatness." In their novels, both writers have been "trivial, clever," dealing in small ideas rather than in "great, grave, and heroic ideals." Yet, the two books under review deserve "nothing but applause." James is provocative, and his "reminiscences are far more affectionate" than Howells's.

113 PULLIAM, O. S. "From Readers." New York Times Saturday Review of Books, 10 (April 22), 266.
(Letter to the Editor. A St. Louis reader's response to 1905.21.) James's North American Review article is "clear, beautiful in style," and of a piece with all his late work. Unlike English critics, who understand James better and defend him, American critics have failed to see his overall purpose. They demand too much physical action, instead of its hidden springs.

114 Q., J. M. "In Workroom and Study." Portland Morning Oregonian, July 9, p. 34.
(Some summary of and excerpts from 1905.92.)

115 ______. "In Library and Workshop." Portland Morning Oregonian, August 13, p. 34.
(Note that, having returned to England, James enjoys long walks and prefers "the study of nature to that of mankind." Reference to his "Impressions of New England" in North American Review.)

116 ______. "In Library and Workshop." Portland Morning Oregonian, August 27, p. 34.
James's recent literary and other activity has given him a "'polite popularity,'" and encouraged critics to try to "fix his rank as an author." Elisabeth Luther Cary's forthcoming book is "a serious study" of this kind by an "enthusiastic" James admirer.

117 R., E. M. "From Readers./Another Contribution to the Discussion of the Merits of Mr. Henry James." New York Times Saturday Review of Books, 10 (February 11), 90.
(Letter to the Editor.) Writers of recent letters to the Times seem James's enemies, with Philistine opinions as old as Daisy Miller. Since "The Author of Beltraffio" James has taken literary risks to the great gain of both himself and literature, and has given us his three greatest novels--The Awkward Age, The Wings of the Dove, and The Ambassadors. They are works of "delicate art" and "marvelous realism" that expound life wonderfully. His scale is small, but he is specific; his characters are not all "terrible people," as some critics suggest, but are of a great variety of types. In his day James's impression of life "has never been excelled in veracity, completeness, and finish." (See 1905. 107a, 111.)

118 SCHUYLER, MONTGOMERY. "English Hours." New York Times Saturday Review of Books, 10 (December 2), 826.
(Review.) This must be a work "of no small interest," and the illustrations are unusually harmonious with the text.

119 SESSIONS, ARCHIBALD LOWERY. "For Book Lovers." Ainslee's Magazine, 15 (May), 156.
The Golden Bowl and Howells's The Son of Royal Langbrith were among the 1904 novels that added something "of permanent value to literature." They are good stories whose publication was notable because of their authors.

120 SHUMAN, EDWIN L. Review of English Hours. Chicago Record-Herald, December 2, Book Supp., p. 1.
This charming book delights us with felicity of phrasing and distinction of style, and should get nothing but praise.

The young readers who wonder at praise of James's style will see the reason in these "clear, limpid, melodious sentences."

121 SMYTH, ALBERT HENRY. "Henry James on American Speech." Book News, 23 (July), 856-857.
James's criticisms of American speech have caused "much argument," and, coming from a "master of a felicitous style," they are important. In indicating a whole people James does "a very difficult and dangerous thing," but what he probably really objects to is the stridency of American voices. (See 1905.125.)

122 TABER, FREDERIC COOPER. "Euphemistic Reticence." New York Times Saturday Review of Books, 10 (January 28), 54.
(Item from the Bookman discusses the subtlety with which James portrays improprieties in The Golden Bowl.)

123 W., M. I. B. "From Readers." New York Times Saturday Review of Books, 10 (January 14), 26.
(Letter to the Editor.) To give either "unmitigated praise" or condemnation to James's work shows lack of critical faculty and judgment. His involved twisted literary style "is incontestably open to severe criticism," but he is "a man of genius" with "a wonderful gift of analysis" and deep insight into human hearts and minds. His "fine thoughts" and characterizations make his artificial, "abominable poses" all the more exasperating to his admirers.

*124 WILLIAMS, TALCOTT. Review of English Hours. Book News, 24 (December), 324.
(Unlocated. Cited in Foley and Ricks.)

125 [WILSON, WOODROW] et al. "Henry James on 'Newspaper English.'" Current Literature, 39 (August), 155-156.
(Comments.) James's remarks at Bryn Mawr on newspaper English "have evoked widespread interest, are generally resented." (Quoted responses to the speech from the New York Evening Mail, Baltimore Herald, 1905.121, and Woodrow Wilson in the New York Herald.)

126 WYNNE, MADELINE YALE. "Books and Authors/The American Essayist." Chicago Evening Post, December 2, p. 4.
(Review of English Hours.) This book will be read "more as a study of James" than of England. His surrender to London's charm is "delightful." The details are significant and interrelate to enhance the meaning of the whole. The book is full of quotable "things that sum up and epitomize."

1906

1 ANON. "James--The Question of Our Speech. The Lesson of Balzac." Critic, 48 (January), 90.
(Review.) James's criticisms of American speech are reasonable and his advice "salutary," but he overestimates Balzac.

2 ANON. "The New Books. . . . By and Concerning Henry James." Review of Reviews, 33 (January), 121.
(Review of English Hours, The Question of Our Speech, and 1905.86.) James is at his best in the "impressionistic sketches" of English Hours, rather than in some of his "much more lauded novels." Cary's introductory chapter characterizes James's work "in excellent broad lines." "The Question of Our Speech" "incurred a storm of newspaper criticism" when James delivered it in the spring.

3 ANON. "Henry James." Independent, 60 (January 4), 44.
(Review of 1905.86.) Cary expresses "a sane reverence" for James's genius, follows his growth with "intelligent zeal," and goes deeply into his manner and purpose.

4 ANON. "Henry James." Independent, 60 (January 4), 44.
(Review of English Hours and The Question of Our Speech.) The essay on London in English Hours is James at "his very best." "The Lesson of Balzac" and "The Question of Our Speech" are of his "tantalizing best," with "much charm in the fine arabesque of words by which he half conceals the real Balzac." (Satirical response to "The Question of Our Speech" and its "aspersions" on the "vox Americana." Implied disapproval.)

5 ANON. Review of Elisabeth Luther Cary's The Novels of Henry James. St. Paul Daily Pioneer Press, January 6, p. 8.
At last "the great uncultured are to have a chance at Henry James!" It is good that Cary did not try to translate The Ambassadors or The Golden Bowl into English. (Includes quotation from the publisher.)

6 ANON. Review of Elisabeth L. Cary's The Novels of Henry James. Cleveland Plain Dealer, January 7, Magazine Section, p. 7.
This book is "not so much a criticism as a comment" on James's "point of view and the inferences he draws from life." (See 1905.86.)

7 ANON. "Essays and Other Literary Studies." Cleveland Plain Dealer, January 7, Magazine Section, p. 7.
(Review of The Question of Our Speech and The Lesson of

Balzac.) The newspaper synopsis of James's June address on American speech "produced a storm of newspaper comment." Whatever may be thought of James's own quality as a novelist, his "Lesson of Balzac" is "full of literary charm."

8 ANON. "Book Reviews . . . England in a Fog." Public Opinion, 40 (January 13), 59.
(Review of English Hours.) This book is hard to understand and shows us England through an "ethereal haze," but for those with some prior knowledge of the subject, it is good reading.

9 ANON. "Books of the Day/English Hours." Reader, 7 (February), 336-337.
(Review.) Among the many reasons to like this book are its luminous style, its subject, and the author himself. James writes with affection, pride, and a sense of fascination with London. The book is "crowded with vignettes of rare and elusive charm," and is "a source of solid and well-defined satisfaction."

10 ANON. "In Henry James Style." Life, 47 (February 22), 251.
(Long, involuted sentence from Men and Women is identified as in James's style.)

11 ANON. "Why, Oh, Why?" Life, 47 (February 22), 240.
The editor of the North American Review should send a rescue expedition to fetch James's still good thoughts out of the big woods of language in which he wanders.

12 ANON. "Howe's Travels." Life, 47 (March 22), 362.
(Briefly compares E. W. Howe's accounts of his travels with James's impressions of America, which are not "comprehensible to an average intelligence.")

13 ANON. "The Lounger." Critic, 48 (April), 298-299.
James's article in the February 1906 North American Review is hard to understand, and a quoted paragraph is as confusing as anything Meredith could write.

14 ANON. "Henry James on Protection." New York Times, April 1, p. 10.
(Editorial.) In recounting his impressions of his native land, James does not often comment on public questions. In his "exceedingly interesting paper on Boston" in the North American Review, he finds that the economic protection laws give the shops a sinister atmosphere that makes him uneasy.

15 ANON. "This Bubble World." Life, 47 (April 5), 425.

(Brief humorous reference to James's writing a cookbook with a plot.)

16 ANON. "Unpleasant." Life, 47 (April 12), 466.
(Reference to and humorous elaboration on a James comment on the Boston Public Library.)

17 ANON. "This Bubble World," Life, 47 (April 26), 519.
(Brief humorous comment on item from the Chicago News to the effect that James calls himself a frustrated American.)

18 ANON. "The Book-Buyer's Guide . . . Belles Lettres . . . English Hours." Critic, 48 (May), 470.
(Review.) This book will give "even the most hardened reviewer . . . geniune pleasure." James's eyes have pierced the London fog to what lies beyond. He assesses what he sees, lets its charm pervade the book, and has himself a charming style.

19 ANON. "Mr. James and English Speech." Outlook, 83 (May 5), 16-17.
James demonstrates the truth of the principle that art is a matter of manner rather than of material. There is much ground for his "severe criticism" of American spoken English, but his own written English is far from exemplary. He is either the worst writer of English in history, or so loves the esoteric that he is turning the language into a learned dialect. (Quotations from James's North American Review article.)

20 ANON. "Mr. James Should Clothe His Thoughts." Life, 47 (May 31), 593.
A Dr. Jastrow is pleased with James's recent piece on Philadelphia in the North American Review, but James cannot be a great writer when he is not even a good one. He is "the very worst living writer who can get his copy into print," and although he has good ideas, he uses language to obscure rather than to convey them.

21 ANON. "Not a Literary Cakewalk./The London Globe Says That Henry James's Style Might Be Worse." New York Times, August 10, p. 5.
The London Globe responds to a critic's remark that James "gropes his way through the English language like a blind man tapping with a stick," by noting that some other novelists dance through the language as if they were doing a literary cakewalk.

22 ANON. New York Times, September 2, Pictorial Section, p. 1.

1906

(Photograph by Vander Weyde.) James, Thomas Wentworth Higginson, and Israel Zangwill are "well-known authors whose writings have wielded a powerful influence in their respective fields."

23 ANON. "Sorrows of a Newport Reader." Life, 48 (September 6), 262.
A Newport correspondent of the (New York?) Evening Post was disappointed that the probably valuable substance of James's impressions was hidden by his excessive verbiage. The writer for Life agrees.

24 ANON. "Our Foolish Contemporaries . . . Poor Henry." Life, 48 (September 27), [348].
(Quoted humorous reference. Joke from Philadelphia Press says that people who do not like James's novels are divided into those who do not understand him and those who do.)

25 ANON. "Aut Scissors Aut Nullus . . . Foundation Almost Completed." Life, 48 (October 11), [414].
(Quoted humorous reference. Joke from London Tribune refers to a new book by James and to his long sentences.)

26 ANON. Humorous item. Life, 48 (November 1), 498.
James's language is obscure, but many think he deserves the benefit of the doubt.

27 ANON. "A Movement to Reform the Speaking of English/W. D. Howells, Henry James and Others Interested in Newly-formed Society to Study Spoken English with a View to Correcting Careless, Slipshod Utterance." New York Times, December 16, pt. 3, p. 4.
(Opinions of a number of writers and professors, including quotations from a James article to be published in Harper's Bazaar.)

28 ANON. "The Case of Spoken English." New York Times, December 18, p. 8.
(Editorial. Response to the James remarks on American English quoted in the December 16 New York Times.) James "can find no polite language adequate" to express "his contempt for American enunciation." The explanation of "our vocal barbarism" is more in thoughtlessness and carelessness than in James's theory that we are suspicious of refinement. Some very good work may be done by the new Society for the Study of Spoken English.

29 CAWEIN, MADISON. "With Howells Abroad." New York Times Saturday Review of Books, 11 (November 30), 789-790.

(Review of W. D. Howells's Certain Delightful English Towns.) Howells's kinship to James is unmistakable, though Howells has more wit and humor. Howells's criticisms of American speech have more authority than James's do.

30 HENDERSON, ARCHIBALD. "Aspects of Contemporary Fiction." Arena, 36 (July), 1-6.
James's books are very hard to understand, his emotions are intellectualized, and his characters are only half human. He is "a master-impressionist" who deals in "faint, elusive ambiguities" and aims "to catch the strange, irregular rhythm of existence, to set up an immense correspondence with life." He is "uncompromisingly realistic," and can be "finely graceful" and "heart-searching."

31 JAMES, HENRY. "Henry James in Washington." Life, 48 (September 13), [297].
(Quotation from James's June 1906 North American Review article on Washington illustrates his complicated style.)

32 _____. "Henry James on American Women." Life, 48 (November 1), [521].
(Quotation from James's "The Speech of American Women," Harper's Bazaar, November-December 1906.)

33 JENKINS, WILBERFORCE. "The News of the Day." Life, 47 (March 29), 389.
(Humorous April Fool's poem mentions James.)

34 [KERFOOT, J. B.] "The Latest Books." Life, 47 (June 28), 788.
(Review of The Question of Our Speech and The Lesson of Balzac.) The Question of Our Speech contains little substance and many words, but The Lesson of Balzac would alone fix its author's claim to critical standing.

35 SELDEN, CHARLES A. "Podunk Revisited (A la Henry James)." Life, 47 (May 31), 659.
(Parody of the style of James's impressions of America.)

36 VINCENT, LEON H. American Literary Masters. Boston: Houghton Mifflin, p. 297.
(Reference to the similarity between Nathaniel Hawthorne and Neil Paraday of James's "admirable story" "The Death of the Lion.")

37 YBARRA, T. R. "If Henry James Should Go to Coney Island and Be Moved to Write About It." New York Times, June 17, Part 3, p. 3.
(Parody of the style of James's impressions of America.)

1907

1 ADAMS, FRANKLIN P. "The Literary Zoo/'Bedbooks.'" Life, 50 (December 26), 783.
(Poem.) James's are among a number of books that help the insomniac to sleep. (Also, quotation to this effect from the New York Sun.)

2 ANON. "Explained." Life, 49 (January 17), 74.
(Joke. Item from Lippincott's refers to James's long sentences and to his never having written a historical romance.)

3 ANON. "The Literary Zoo/Heroes." Life, 49 (January 17), 82.
(Humorous verse reprinted from the Century makes fun of the "hero of Henry James," who "tells what he thinks he thinks he thinks.")

4 ANON. "The Human Zoo . . . Auto Versus Art." Life, 49 (February 7), 197.
(Humorous brief mention.) "Henry James is stranger than fiction."

5 ANON. "The Human Zoo . . . Answers to Correspondents." Life, 49 (February 7), 197.
(Humorous item. Advises James that he can learn English by taking out naturalization papers and trying a good public school.)

6 ANON. "'The American Scene,' . . by Henry James." New York Herald, February 16, p. 13.
(Quotes some of James's comments on New York.) James's study of American boots and teeth is a "curious instance" of his "peculiar passion for meticulous analysis."

7 ANON. "Drift of London Literary Talk." New York Times Book Review, February 16, p. 100.
The London reviewers have said The American Scene lacks originality, and they compare it with H. G. Wells's recent book about America. It is hard to tell which book is praised more, because the reviewers seem, as in the past, so hypnotized by James's style that they obscure their opinions with vague language.

8 ANON. "New Books./Mr. James's American Impressions." New York Sun, February 16, p. 7.
(Review of The American Scene.) This book rewards the tenacious and indomitable reader, despite the effort required to read it. James takes himself both seriously and with

humor, and writes of "subtle and evasive" rather than "grosser matters." Some of his impressions "are fairly salient" and can be grasped and remembered. James can be "of distinguished interest when he pleases."

9 ANON. "News and Views of Books." New York World, February 16, p. 8.

(Review of The American Scene.) James expresses "a fine true thought" to the effect that floods of immigrants "shock" one's sense of national unity. His book has searching analyses, and "wonderful chapters of observation" that are almost stories of discovery, but his sentences are puzzles. He should write more simply and clearly.

10 ANON. "The American Scene--." Albany Evening Journal, February 20, p. 3.

This book is "most delightful." Critics may object to the "confusing prolixity" and "irritating subtlety" of James's later writings, but a simplified James would not be James. He is artistically concerned with human life itself, and the book will satisfy both poetic and practical readers. It contains much "picturesque description," but more "keen analysis."

11 ANON. "Writers and Books." Boston Evening Transcript, February 20, p. 19.

(Review of The American Scene.) This is "only superficially a book of travel" and reveals "the strong characteristics of thought and style" that make James unique in English literature. He "penetrates the heart of the entire American scene" and shows us ourselves as we are, as we want to be, and as we do not want to be revealed. This book is as imaginative as his novels and yet "a record of stern and undeniable fact."

12 ANON. "Books and their Writers, Impressions of an Artist./ Henry James' Beautiful Convolutions Around American Scenery, Cities and People." Louisville Courier-Journal, February 23, p. 5.

(Review of The American Scene.) Being abroad has quickened James's "thought and sensitiveness," and he says good things as no one else could. One is "beguiled and baffled" by this book, but after persevering finds "suddenly the sense of a delightful picture, of special atmosphere, a combination of color" inseparable from the thing described. Though he may seem obscure and involved, in the final effect this "past-master of phrase" is "clarity itself."

13 ANON. "The New Books." Chicago Inter-Ocean, February 23, p. 7.

(Review of The American Scene. Very brief summary of contents.)

14 ANON. "In Library and Workshop." Portland Sunday Oregonian, February 24, p. 51.

(Note on The American Scene.) Among James's "most widely known and most popular" books is his little tour in France, a fact that "adds great interest to" his recent tour of and forthcoming book about America. The book is written with "felicity of phrase and beauty of language," "broad philosophy and constant distinction of style."

15 ANON. "Among the Newest Books . . . Side-Trips With Henry James." Boston Daily Advertiser, March 6, p. 7.

(Review of The American Scene.) James artistically analyzes Americans, who are "a plain people, a race of hustlers rejoicing in the strenuous life." We may look to him for "a better understanding of ourselves," and although his elaborateness sometimes "palls upon us" and his book is "rich in protests against things he did not like," it is the work of a literary artist and parts are "exceedingly penetrative."

16 ANON. Review of The American Scene. Hartford Courant, March 6, p. 19.

James's sentences are too long and confusing, and "he insists on talking most about that of which he knows least." His fine language and ornate style are too empty of content.

17 ANON. "A Man Without a Country." Outlook, 85 (March 16), 622-623.

(Review of The American Scene.) In contrast to the vivid, refreshing, deliciously glowing English Hours, this book overwhelms and bewilders with its "convolutions of phrase." One misses "the charming felicities" expected from James. He occasionally says something, but does not focus enough, and at the end leaves the reader in midair.

18 ANON. "'The American Scene.'" San Francisco Chronicle, March 17, p. 9.

When James wrote The Portrait of a Lady and The American, he was master of a "beautiful style--clear, limpid and perfectly intelligible" to ordinary people. His style is now too involved and obscure. Also, he returns to his country with foolish "preconceived ideas" based on "English or French slanders." His descriptions of American cities are fine, but they would be far better if they did not require such close attention. The book is "interesting despite its style, because it contains the conclusions of one of the keenest of modern observers, who is absolutely unprejudiced."

19 ANON. Review of The American Scene. New Orleans Daily Picayune, March 18, p. 14.
James's sentences are too long and involved, and he has "psychologized away" feelings, being less concerned with "the deep-seated central emotions" than with peripheral ones. His paragraphs are built like the skyscrapers he criticizes, but the chapters on Southern cities are interesting to the Southerner who wants to see himself viewed "disinterestedly, entirely from the outside."

20 ANON. "Books." St. Paul Daily Pioneer Press, March 18, p. 5.
(Review of The American Scene.) James is a "distinguished novelist" and the "foremost living exponent" of the art of using language "to conceal rather than to convey thought." His style is so difficult and complex that those who claim to admire him must also "believe they can fathom the unknowable." The style of this book is less involved than that of his recent novels, but the thoughts are more involved. Yet, the volume has "occasional brilliant touches" that show James's "marvelously keen perceptive powers," his near genius for description when he does not elaborate too much, his precise analysis of society, and his "powerful use of metaphor." His impressions of America are hardly flattering, but when he is complimentary it is with a generosity that softens the sting of his criticism. James does not provide much concrete information about the places he writes of.

21 ANON. "The Literary Zoo." Life, 49 (March 21), 402-403.
(Brief reference to James's remarks on the subject of Theodore Roosevelt's literary style.)

22 ANON. "Henry James on America." Nation, 84 (March 21), 266-267.
(Review of The American Scene.) In sympathetic insight, some foreign observers have been more American than James, but no writer on America "has made shrewder observations" or gathered up certain facts under "more illuminating labels." The American Scene is a work of "marvellously keen and subtle analysis" which "transfixes the defects and shortcomings of American civilization with unerring thrusts," but its vision is "too personal, too microscopic," to be a synthesis. James's descriptions of scenery are charming, vivid, and discriminating, and his treatment of the South is "especially subtle and sympathetic."

23 ANON. "The American Scene." Churchman, 95 (March 22), 428.
(Review.) Discursive, elusive, sometimes oversubtle, with a complex style, this book "has much to pique the fancy." James appears to write with insight, but on places one knows well he seems "the victim of auto-suggestion."

1907

24 ANON. "The Mazes of Henry James." New York Times Saturday Review of Books, 12 (March 23), 178.
(Reprinted comments from London Athenaeum.) The American Scene is like a maze, and is in this respect worse than James's novels.

25 ANON. "A New Book of Bepuzzlement:/Henry James on America." Springfield (Mass.) Republican, March 24, p. 23.
(Review of The American Scene.) This book is puzzling, its obscurity has become a joke, and it requires more effort than one usually devotes to a travel book. James likes what remains of the older America of his youth, and he is not dazzled by bigness or opulence.

26 ANON. "Literary News and Reviews/An Impressionist on America." New York Evening Post, March 30, Supp., p. 6.
(Review of The American Scene.) Here, James often writes like an American, yet is "a curiously alien observer" who is saturated with the conventions and ideals of an older civilization and prefers the past to the new and untried. The book's critical analysis is "marvellously keen," subtle, and accurate, but its vision is "too personal, too microscopic," to provide a positive synthesis. The book is one of the most fascinating rather than one of the greatest works on America. James is "fundamentally incapable" of understanding the average American, and treats him like a child with a dreary, common outlook.

27 ANON. Review of The American Scene. A.L.A. Booklist, 3 (April), 98.
This book contains "occasional exquisite bits of description," but is mainly "a laborious, detailed" accounting for and interpretation of James's impressions. It is "full of psychological subtleties" and involved expression, "baffling to the average reader."

28 ANON. "Casual Comment." Dial, 42 (April 1), 214.
(Note.) James's literary methods "recall those of Walter Pater." Both writers elaborate, pad, and polish a preliminary "sketch." In The American Scene, James clothes the "bony structure" of sentences with "the rounded fairness and grace" (or "the clumsiness and heaviness") of "abundant adipose tissue."

29 ANON. "Travel." Congregationalist and Christian World, 92 (April 13), 503.
(Review of The American Scene.) The "lover of intricate moods and analytical social studies" will enjoy these "interesting reflections." James's prose is difficult, and he would resent being considered to write for the plain man.

30 ANON. "The Literary Zoo./The Literary Competition." Life, 49 (May 9), 662.
(Humorous item. James allegedly offers a prize to anyone who shows that James's sentences "can be written as easily wrong-end-to as they can be written sidewise.")

31 ANON. "Sanctum Talks." Life, 49 (May 16), 680-681.
(Humorous article. Fictitious conversation between James and Life in which James says that his style is a gimmick and a sham. Caricature sketch of James.)

32 ANON. "Henry James as a Literary Sphinx." Current Literature, 42 (June), 634.
(Review of The American Scene. Article quotes various critics addressing the still unsolved "problem of Henry James" in comments on The American Scene from the London Times, London Literary World, Academy, San Francisco Argonaut, New York Times Saturday Review, British Weekly, Spectator, London Outlook, Athenaeum, and London Daily Mail.) Despite critical acclaim, James has only a limited circle of readers, and many critics who think the early work great do not praise his later writings. The American Scene very vividly reveals his "peculiar genius," in all its strengths and weaknesses.

33 ANON. "The Literary Zoo . . . Us and the English." Life, 49 (June 6), 758.
(Brief reference.) The half-English, half-American James talks about "tidy language," but Americans are more concerned that their language be stunning.

34 ANON. "The Literary Zoo . . . James." Life, 49 (June 6), 751-753.
(Comments on "The Manners of American Women.") Young people would do well to ponder James's cultured criticisms. James seems to respect their mentality, and to condense James's prose into a few "crisp sentences" would be a good exercise in composition for the young American woman.

35 ANON. "Hughes His Choice, Says W. D. Howells." Boston Herald, June 10, p. 2.
(Interview with W. D. Howells.) Howells's speaking of James and Mark Twain together is "inexplicable." Howells finds James's style inapt but natural to him, and what he has to say worthwhile.

36 ANON. "Manners of Our Women." New York Times, June 20, p. 6.
(Editorial. Response to James's Harper's Bazaar article on American women.) James writes his criticisms of American

women "in his later and more cryptic manner." The hotel bred American girl may be a nuisance, but she is not a representative "type of American feminine manners." James is not likely to help American women learn social conduct from European ones, and he does not get "anywhere near the root of the matter." American girls "are vastly superior in many ways to the English girls and quite their equals in modesty and intelligence."

37 ANON. "Our Own Times." Reader, 10 (July), 215-216.
(Review of The American Scene. James's The American Scene and Howells's Through the Eye of the Needle are very different, and each is "supremely, even exaggeratedly, typical of its author." Howells makes the complex simple, and James makes the simple complex. The American Scene is an analysis, so concerned with James himself that it is, like Howells's book, impalpable.

38 ANON. "The Literary Zoo . . . Browning--James." Life, 50 (July 4), 13.
(Humorous item. James, like Robert Browning, is obscure.)

39 ANON. "Literature/Euphues and His America." Independent, 63 (July 11), 95-96.
(Review of The American Scene.) Like John Lyly's "Euphues and his England," The American Scene is a monument not so much to truth or history as to rhetoric. The objects that do of themselves absorb James are "rarely characteristic of contemporary America," with which he is "entirely out of sympathy." His discoveries are hackneyed.

40 ANON. "Henry James's Americanism." Literary Digest, 35 (July 20), 96.
(Quotation from H. G. Dwight's article on James in the Putnam's Monthly, 1907.59.) Since James revisited America and rather caustically wrote his impressions, many have condemned him for un-Americanism. Dwight takes the opposite tack, asserting James's Americanness.

41 ANON. "The Literary Zoo . . . Pure Literature Law." Life, 50 (August 1), 133.
(Brief humorous reference.) In the context of "truth in labeling" adulterated books, James's recent book contains "One-half per cent saturated solution of simplicity. Rest unknown."

42 ANON. "The Literary Zoo/Fiction." Life, 50 (August 22), 222-223.
(Brief mention.) Some of James's works may be among the

best fifteen of the last twenty years, since he has only within recent years "fallen a victim to his own style."

43 ANON. "Light on Darkest James." Nation, 85 (October 17), 343-344.

Like Marivaux, James writes in the style of conversation, but his true subtleties are of thought. James's books are obviously not meant for the general reader, but fine writers appreciate them.

44 ANON. "The Literary Zoo/One Hundred and Fifty of the Best Novels of the Past Twenty Years/Part III." Life, 50 (October 24), 482-483.

(The Ambassadors is listed.)

45 ANON. "The Glorified Snobbishness of Henry James." Current Literature, 43 (November), 526.

(Quoted critical comments. Fairly neutral quotation from and discussion of Michael Monahan's article in The Papyrus declaring James a snob, an obscurantist, and a despiser of his own country.)

46 ANON. "Chronicle and Comment," "Current Criticism of Henry James." Bookman, 26 (December), 357-358.

It is "supposed to be vastly amusing to the public that certain persons find Henry James altogether incomprehensible," and readers of newspapers have very likely come to expect a James joke at regular intervals. Fortunately, this fad will pass, as will the Jacobites who write articles congratulating themselves on being among the fine minds who can understand James. His real admirers know he is "the most uneven of writers" who "hems and haws" and records "all his mind's processes, including its false starts." His style has thus "divided literary paragraphers into two classes: hooligans and hypocrites." No one has written discriminatingly of James since W. C. Brownell in the Atlantic a few years ago. (See 1905.81.)

47 ANON. "Henry James to Explain Himself." New York Times Saturday Review of Books, 12 (December 7), 776.

(Announcement of New York edition.) Many will say that no one except James is quite capable of the "herculean task" of explaining his fiction. The announcement that his early works have been translated into the language of The Golden Bowl promises "a most entertaining view of the evolution . . . of a great author's art and genius." The publishers are to be thanked.

48 ANON. "A Sly Hit." Life, 50 (December 19), 759.

1907

(Reprinted anecdote from the Washington Star about James's witty letter to a social-climbing jam manufacturer.)

49 ATHERTON, GERTRUDE. "The Best Book I Have Been Reading." Life, 49 (March 7), 344.
(Letter to the Editor. Atherton's "old favorites" include several of James's works.)

50 BICKNELL, PERCY. "The New Books/Home Impressions of an Expatriated American." Dial, 42 (March 16), 176-177.
(Review of The American Scene.) The "Daedalian mazes" of James's "wonderful prose" make the reader both delight and despair. This book is "strewn with the happiest phrases," and teems with "passages of exquisite artistry" which are a joy to lovers of the "gracefully elaborate," the subtly expressive and suggestive in English prose. James gives us not so much his impressions, as "his impressions of his impressions" or of what they ought to be.

51 BURTON, RICHARD. "The Bellman's Bookshelf." Bellman, 2 (April 20), 476.
(Review of The American Scene.) James's subtle, attenuated ideas and complex style are difficult and demand the reader's attention. His diction is as interesting as anyone's, and his manner is "outrageous, yet delightful," compensating for its aggravating rulebreaking with enough magic, music, and "most penetrating thought" to make the reader gasp with pleasure. The book is full of figurative language, and contains some of the keenest and kindliest social criticism of America ever written, by one with a particularly good vantage point. The pages on the American drummer are alone worth the price of the book.

52 C., E. "Mr. Henry James Again." New York Times Saturday Review of Books, 12 (June 29), 420.
(Letter to the Editor. "A Defense and an Appreciation of Henry James.") Despite all the things Americans have said about James over the years, they raise "a great commotion of protest" over his "frank report" of his impressions of America. His phrase "'the age of trash triumphant'" applies to the present "with a most artistic fitness." A man with the genius to write the intellectually appealing and "delectable" books James does has the right to avoid excessive American publicity by living abroad. Much of the criticism against him proceeds from meagre knowledge of his books. People emphasize Daisy Miller while forgetting the glorious "Pandora," really the great American novel and proof of James's "genius and his love of country."

53 CARY, ELISABETH LUTHER. "Henry James." New York Times Saturday Review of Books, 12 (April 6), 221.

(Review of The American Scene.) James writes too many of his books about Americans to have lost interest in his countrymen, and he treats them "with such a tender and beneficent justice" that he must find them "a peculiarly rewarding type." His present impressions of America are "amazingly interesting," including his sense of the ethnic variety of our society. His "remarkable truthful fiction" deals most largely with social questions, and here he makes many "wise comments" on New York life. He writes with a "rich and fantastic humor," and it would be hard to find anywhere in literature "more delicately synthetic and vital" portraits of our national heroes.

54 COOPER, FREDERICK T. "New Books Reviewed." North American Review, 185 (May 17), 214-218.

(Review of The American Scene.) This book is bound by "a continuity of thought and mood" with William Wetmore Story and The Ambassadors, perhaps James's "supreme achievement in fiction." These works reveal James's chief preoccupation and recurrent literary subject--the relation between America and Europe. The American Scene is intensely subjective, and although no one has ever written "subtler, keener, more luminous studies" of American cities, James's delicate intuition and just assessments are those of the aloof observer who finds that his earlier decision to leave America was the right one. It is James's thought, rather than just his style, that is difficult.

55 CORYN, SIDNEY G. P. "Henry James and America." San Francisco Argonaut, 60 (March 9), p. 504.

(Review of The American Scene.) James's works give "peculiar delight," and here he says many good things which might even be helpful if written in the language of the common people. His style is very complex and he glances at America "superciliously from a very superior . . . point of view." The book will arouse no resentments, and will probably be widely read.

56 D., F. J. E.[F?]. "Light on Darkest James." New York Evening Post, October 12, p. 4.

(Editorial.) Mr. Gill's "Henry James and His Double" (1907.61) is very acute and revealing about "the alleged and now proverbial obscurity" of James's style. Yet, James's true subtleties "are those of thought," which match his style. He has won the admiration of fine writers, who "marvel at his command of the fit word, the exact phrase, the fatally correct shading." He may find "in their approval more contentment than he would in the laudations" of the masses who find him obscure.

57 DE MEUIL, ALEXANDER N. "The Trash Novel of Today." St. Louis Post-Dispatch, March 9, p. 5.
If Howells and James are trying "to reconstruct humanity," they "will have to use more effective and alluring weapons than their miniature etchings."

58 DWIGHT, H. G. "Henry James--'In His Own Country.'" I. Putnam's, 2 (May), 164-170.
(Review of responses to James's return to America quotes or refers to items in the Critic, North American Review, Scribner's, New York Times, Bookman, New York Sun, and Atlantic Monthly.) James's return to America has provoked little public demonstration, but much printed comment on one "whose cryptic utterances and incomprehensible exile so little deserved" such publicity. The consensus is an uncertainty about what to make of him, and Americans are "neither willing to acclaim him nor able to ignore him." He arouses their "combative instincts" so that much of the commentary has been negative, especially after The Golden Bowl, much denounced for immorality and unintelligibility. Yet, James is "one of the few speakers of the day worth listening to."

59 _____. "Henry James--'In His Own Country.'" II. Putnam's, 2 (July), 433-442.
(Long quotation from New York Sun.) One of the reasons James has been so slow coming into his own has been the impossibility of making a final estimate of his voluminous and varied work. His American reputation hangs largely on Daisy Miller. His high quality and productivity show unusual "fecundity of mind and constancy of purpose." His later manner is a speaking manner, and his novelty is less of manner than of matter. His individual quality is best brought out by comparing him with a man like Kipling, but he is very hard to categorize. James was "the first English writer to reflect certain tendencies of European art," and the first American man of letters to be "a citizen of the world." He is "as truly and typically American" as Hawthorne, Harte, Whitman, or the contemporary "strenuous young men," though of a different type. He has gone farther "than any of his contemporaries" in relating the every-day to the mysterious, and has never settled for second best or stopped developing.

60 GILDER, JEANNETTE L. "Among the New Books. . . . Henry James' Book of Impressions of Our American Cities." Chicago Tribune, February 2, p. 9.
(Review of The American Scene.) A new book from James

is an important event in American literature, for "we still claim him as an American." The impressions in this book cannot always be understood, but parts contain much of James's "early charm." His chapter on the Bowery is interesting because James and the Bowery "seem as far apart as the poles." James likes principally the Philadelphia streets and is shocked by the New York skyscrapers.

61 GILL, W. A. "Henry James and His Double." Atlantic Monthly, 100 (October), 458-466.

The main source of the remarkable similarities between James and Marivaux "seems to be the wonderfully subtle and discriminative quality of their intelligences." Both men assert a "self-conscious individualism" in their criticism and teach the doctrine of "the absoluteness of 'the particular, given case.'" Both have "a distinct philosophical gift," and both use metaphors, but James goes farther with his metaphors, as in The Golden Bowl. The two authors' styles are similar. (See 1907.56.)

62 GUITERMAN, ARTHUR. "The Literary Zoo/Rhymed Reviews." Life, 54 (November 25), 753.

(Poem. Rhymed review of Julia Bride praises it as clever, perhaps worth telling, and understandable.)

63 HACKETT, FRANCIS. "Books and Bookmen/America Revisited." Chicago Evening Post, February 23, p. 7.

(Review of The American Scene.) This "exquisite study of American uncivilization" is not particularly tender or patriotic, but it is honest. James critically sought the best in America.

64 JENKINS, WILBERFORCE. "The Literary Zoo/The Unattainable." Life, 49 (June 13), 802.

(Humorous poem.) The latest book of "Hennery James" is almost impossible to understand.

65 KERFOOT, J. B. "The Latest Books." Life, 49 (March 14), 388.

(Review of The American Scene.) This book is very abstract and more a study of Henry James than of America. It is wonderful and delightful, but such a refined, "incorporeal essence" of James that it is "hardly worth while."

66 LARNED, W[ILLIAM] T. "The Literary Zoo/Lo, the Poor Novelist!" Life, 50 (September 19), 330-331.

(Brief reference.) It is whispered in literary circles that some of James's later fictions do not sell more than 500 copies.

1907

67 L[ARNED], W[ILLIAM] T. "The Literary Zoo . . . Topics for Women's Clubs." Life, 50 (December 19), 741.
(Brief humorous reference. A suggested topic is "Why is Browning like the bass clef in a Henry James dialogue?")

68 LEARNED, MR. & MRS. A. B. "The Literary Zoo." Life, 49 (January 3), [40].
(Brief reference.) Many critics have been impatient with the dilution of James found in many of Kipling's later stories.

69 LITTLEFIELD, WALTER. "In Realm of Books." Chicago Record-Herald, February 16, p. 7.
(Quotes and paraphrases part of The American Scene.)

70 M., E. "Book Reviews and Notes." South Atlantic Quarterly, 6 (July), 313-314.
(Review of The American Scene.) James is "frankly out of sympathy" with "'the eternal American note.'" His "style, like his thought, is baffling." Its "mingling of cold analysis with a dreamy sentimentalism" is unusual. Yet, because his "criticism is extremely disinterested rather than wisely sympathetic," intelligent Americans should read his book. He might be right.

71 MACKAY, ISABEL ECCLESTONE. "The Literary Zoo/The Glamor in It." Life, 50 (July 11), 51.
(Humorous poem.) In this poem about writers, James is identified with "Words, words--just words."

72 MARSH, EDWARD. "Henry James's 'The American Scene.'" Bookman, 25 (March), 188-190.
(Review.) Most readers experience some kind of disappointment in James's latest book. These readers are of two types: the "self-sufficient critic of Oshkosh" who liked Daisy Miller but was disgusted by The Sacred Fount, and the James enthusiast. The former will finally give up altogether on James, with his "wearisome verbiage" and "empty affectation of subtlety." On this kind of critic "neither pity nor regret need be wasted," but the "truer estimate" by the James enthusiast deserves more "sympathy and forbearance." Such a person will feel that in this book something present in the novels is lacking. Yet, this work is "an intensely human document," and James's subjectivity, his American birth and foreign experience, and his possession of "the finest and ripest intelligence . . . ever" among English writers of fiction, "devoted to a lifelong study of the interaction of character and environment," make him particularly well suited to his task. Understanding him is

difficult, especially when he writes of New England, while he is surprisingly at his best on Richmond and the Bowery. Yet, the book has lucid intervals and "is not an impenetrable and unrelieved bog of obscurities."

73 ROBERTS, KATE LOUISE. "One Hundred and Fifty of the Best Novels of the Past Twenty Years. Part I." Life, 50 (October 3), 383.
(Letter to the Editor.) A list of the best novels of the past twenty years would bar some of the best works of modern writers such as James.

74 ROBERTSON, CARL T. "Mr. James' 'Impressions.'" Cleveland Plain Dealer, March 3, p. 7.
(Review of The American Scene. Portrait.) This book is full of "ponderous and drooping sentences and limitless verbiage," and is notably "distressful, tiresome, unprofitable." It has an air of condescension toward America, and James's books are no longer read in this country. This one does not give pleasure or instruction, and is superficial, pompous, "overbearingly egotistical, . . . unfriendly without being frank, critical without basis or logic."

75 SHUMAN, EDWIN L. "In Realm of Books." Chicago Record-Herald, February 23, p. 9.
(Review of The American Scene.) To enjoy this difficult book, one must admire the intellectual subtleties and long, complicated sentences of James's novels. Although his ideas are elusive, James is at his best here, with an artistic temperament, exquisite word choice, and a style "rich in delicate fancy." He has neither "eye nor interest" for the ideals of democracy and the deeper sociological problems beneath the American unloveliness he disapproves.

1908

1 ANON. "Notes." Nation, 86 (January 2), 11.
(Response to first two volumes of New York Edition.) The prefaces will form a biographia literaria of uncommon interest and significance, but they are written in James's most exasperating clause-clogged style.

2 ANON. Note on New York Edition. Boston Daily Advertiser, January 10, p. 8.
(Quotation from preface to The American.) Readers who strive to get at "the meaning of Jamesesque fiction will not get much satisfaction" from James's explanations, since they, too, "exhibit clogging qualifications."

1908

3 ANON. "Scribner's Edition of the Novels and Tales of Henry James." Louisville Courier-Journal, January 11, p. 5.

(Review of New York Edition.) The American has had "much greater vogue" than Roderick Hudson, and James's own criticism of it is "far severer" than anyone else's. The prefaces are unnecessarily frank and self-critical, but are truthful and sincere. The Portrait of a Lady is "celebrated."

4 ANON. "On Revised Versions." New York Times Saturday Review of Books, 13 (January 18), 30.

(Editorial.) Admirers of James's early books will find his "unprecedented attempt" to rewrite them in his later manner "quite unsuccessful." The man who wrote The American is not the same man who has rewritten it.

5 ANON. "Comment on Current Books." Outlook, 88 (January 18), 145.

(Review of New York Edition.) The publication of this edition is "an event of unusual interest." James's essays and travel impressions show "his rare power of analysis, closeness of observation, and charm of style" at their best. The prefaces add to American literary history, since they concern "one of the most significant figures in our fiction." News of James's revisions "will distress some of his most loyal readers," who prefer the early to the later James.

6 ANON. Review/Notice of New York Edition. New York Herald, January 26, Literary and Art Section, p. 1.

In this edition of everything James "is willing should survive him," his essays tell how he developed his stories.

7 ANON. "News and Views of Books." Chicago Evening Post, February 12, p. 4.

(Note.) James's novels "seem to oppress" George Meredith, who also finds The American Scene to be more a tour of James's inside than of America.

8 ANON. Note on interview with George Meredith. Boston Daily Advertiser, February 21, p. 8.

Meredith thinks that James's account of America in The American Scene is "'really a tour of Henry James's inside,'" since James is so concerned with how sights impressed him rather than with the sights themselves.

9 ANON. "News and Views of Books." Chicago Evening Post, February 25, p. 4.

(Note.) One or two reviewers have complained of the prefaces to the New York Edition, and in referring to James's "bumptiousness" and "flapdoodle," the New York Sun is neither just nor discriminating.

10 ANON. "Mr. Henry James on His Own Art." New York Times Saturday Review of Books, 13 (February 29), 111.
(Review of New York Edition, vols. 3 and 4.) In the revised Portrait of a Lady the modifications rarely interfere with the story as they do in The American, but many of the changes are not improvements. In 1881 this book was "the most ambitious, the fullest, the most various view of human nature" that James had yet attempted, and the consensus of readers agree that his ambitious portrayal of Isabel was worth it. The preface was also "extremely well worth doing," but surprisingly, James deprecates Henrietta Stackpole.

11 ANON. "Literary Notes." San Francisco Chronicle, March 1, p. 10.
(Response to the first installment of Julia Bride in Harper's.) This is "brilliant work" in James's "vein of twenty years ago."

12 ANON. "Notes." Nation, 86 (March 5), 215.
(Review of New York Edition, vols. 3-6, with liberal quoting from prefaces.) Despite the exasperating style, the prefaces continue to be interesting.

13 ANON. "Henry James on the 'Casamassima'/In Introduction to His Recension of the Novel Author Tacitly Concedes Its Failure." New York Times Saturday Review of Books, 13 (March 7), 128.
(Review of New York Edition.) The Princess is not alive, is "not realized," in spite of James's and our efforts. James evades this problem in his introduction with a delightful iridescence and is enlightening on his other works. Overall the novel is most delightful, as well as most difficult, with fortunately few revisions.

14 ANON. "S. R. O. For James Talk/Women of Exclusive Clubs in Wild Scramble to Hear Novelist Lecture." Chicago Evening Post, March 10, p. 7.
There is great demand for seats at the lecture given by the creator of Daisy Miller and many other fascinating characters. (Brief summary of James's activities in Chicago.)

15 ANON. "'No Real Daisy Miller.'" Chicago Evening Post, March 11, p. 4.
An audience of 300 attending "The Lesson of Balzac" heard James say in answer to a question that Daisy Miller is a type rather than an individual portrait. (Brief account of some of James's activities in Chicago.)

16 ANON. "New Edition of Henry James." Louisville Courier-Journal, March 14, p. 5.

1908

(Review of New York Edition.) The Portrait of a Lady has been for many readers the James favorite, and he himself loves it but has made it more brilliant with revisions. His revisions have not, as some critics think, marred his earlier works, but have polished them to better match his later ones.

17 ANON. "Writers and Books/The Literary World of Today." Boston Evening Transcript, March 18, p. 19.

(Review of New York Edition.) These prefaces sound "a strong personal note," with a "lively biographical touch," and show the powerful influence of place on James. The prefaces form these volumes' principal interest, and have "that imaginative and introspective feeling" which has given James's fiction its "high literary position" despite its shortcomings. In the prefaces James "does for himself what he does for his characters in his novels," describing surroundings and analyzing motives.

18 ANON. Note on the New York Edition. Boston Daily Advertiser, March 20, p. 8.

In the preface to The Portrait of a Lady, James expresses his theory that "the story must grow out of the characters," and comments on Turgenev (James quoted on Turgenev).

19 ANON. Review of New York Edition. Literary Digest, 36 (March 21), 418.

In James's late novels, people "convey more the impression of life than of books," his conversations become more colloquial than in his earlier works. The prefaces are rich and suggestive, the most valuable feature of the edition.

20 ANON. "Princess Casamassima." Louisville Courier-Journal, March 21, p. 5.

(Review of New York Edition.) Less widely read than The Portrait of a Lady, this novel yet has several distinguished qualities. James is "unusually fine" in the preface, which "is full of deep thought, of subtleties which delight instead of baffling," and attempts even more than usual to express shades of meaning exactly and pleasingly. Appreciation for James will increase, and this poet and "artist of the inner life" will eventually receive his due amount of praise.

21 ANON. "James's Complete Works." Philadelphia Public Ledger and Philadelphia Times, March 21, p. 9.

(Review of New York Edition.) James is a "prominent American novelist" with a "definitely calculable public" who will welcome this edition. Without James "America would stand very much lower in the literary scale," and such an edition of his works "will tend visibly to increase the general appreciation in which he is so deservedly held by discriminating people" at home and abroad.

22 ANON. "Writers and Books/The Literary World of Today." Boston Evening Transcript, April 1, p. 21.
(Comments on New York Edition, vols. 3-6.) The prefaces provide an unusual opportunity to see "the intellectual processes of a creator of imaginative literature." If for no other reason than this, the new edition of James's works would have more "interest and importance than the customary reprint of famous novels." (Quotation from and paraphrase of passages from the prefaces.)

23 ANON. "With Authors and Books." Chicago Record-Herald, April 4, p. 8.
(Review of New York Edition.) This edition is justified by the illuminating analytical prefaces and "the human interest of the earlier stories." The Portrait of a Lady and The Princess Casamassima are written in "the lucid and charming style" of which James was once master. The prefaces discuss them frankly, instructively, and objectively. James's ideas about them will delight those with the patience to untangle his complicated sentences.

24 ANON. "Henry James./The New Collected Edition of His Novels and Tales." New York Tribune, April 5, pp. 6-7.
(Review of New York Edition. Portrait.) The prefaces are very useful, but long and overexplanatory, and James takes himself and his work so seriously that he is somewhat humorous. His work is brilliant and sometimes absorbingly interesting, but lacks gusto and a certain fullness and richness of beauty. James writes out of "a peculiarly cultivated and critical mind" that treats life not with passion, but with a purely intellectual interest in it as merely material for literature. For the magic of genius, he substitutes a kind of sublimated industry. He has versatility, an intense awareness of the rules of his craft, a tidy mind, and a conscience. He "is nothing if not the man of letters."

25 ANON. "Books of the Season." Chicago Evening Post, April 16, p. 6.
(Review of New York Edition.) The prefaces are minutely detailed, with discussions of technique primarily applicable, and indispensable, to a study of James's work. He has never been "more richly suggestive" as a critic.

26 ANON. "Notes." Nation, 86 (April 23), 376.

(Review of New York Edition.) The preface to The Tragic Muse is somewhat less interesting than the earlier ones.

27 ANON. "New Edition of 'Tragic Muse.'" San Francisco Chronicle, May 3, p. 54.

(Review of New York Edition, vols. 7 and 8.) The preface says much that is "shrewd and penetrating" about the difficulty of "adjusting any relations" between the life of the stage and the life of society. Although one may disagree with some of James's ideas, one must admire "the art of his exposition." The Tragic Muse is "as good to-day as when it was written, and as true to life." James shows "remarkable skill in painting the life of the theater" in "this fine story."

28 ANON. "Writers and Books/The Literary World of Today." Boston Evening Transcript, May 27, p. 21.

(Review of Views and Reviews.) James is "a world-renowned figure in the literary world, and a personality of influence and power." These reviews reveal much about the development of his imagination and style. The 1865 review of Whitman is unfair, "rabid and violent" in disapproval, and not to James's credit. Of this collection of reviews, only the latest, on Kipling (1891), is akin to the work of the present James "whose name rules our contemporary literature." Some people will like the earlier reviews as "wholly unlike the proverbial Henry James" and therefore "to be read enjoyably." Other readers, who like the later James, will appreciate this chance to see into "his prentice days and prentice work."

29 ANON. "Analyzing the Novel." New York Times Saturday Review of Books, 13 (May 30), 306.

(Review of New York Edition, vols. 9 and 10.) The prefaces show James's "ample if whimsical mind," but he is "too personal, too involved, generally too delightfully vague, in formulating his theory of fiction to be of any use to any but the most advanced student of the art." The Awkward Age is carefully constructed.

30 ANON. "Notes." Nation, 86 (June 4), 511.

(Review of New York Edition. Quoted excerpts from prefaces to volumes 9 and 10.)

31 ANON. "Literary Small Talk." Chicago Evening Post, June 23, p. 4.

James's phraseology, if not itself stimulating, spurs the cleverness of others. One critic has called Julia Bride "'the debut of the serial conundrum.'"

1908

32 ANON. "Our Foolish Contemporaries/Henry James and Life." Life, 52 (July 30), 124.
(Reprinted anecdote from Saturday Evening Post.) Perhaps James has escaped the "storm of anecdotes" that surrounds most "well-known authors, particularly of the best-selling variety." Perhaps the anecdotes could not break through the "barricade of sentences that surrounded him."

33 ANON. "Notes." Nation, 87 (August 6), 115-116.
(Review of New York Edition. Response to volumes 11 and 12.) The prefaces are, as usual, devoted to James's "suggestive criticisms of his own writings."

34 ANON. "New Edition of 'Views and Reviews.'" Louisville Courier-Journal, August 8, p. 5.
(Review.) These reviews reflect how James's style has become more complicated over the years. An early review shows clearly and directly his dislike for Whitman.

35 ANON. "A Shelf of Essays." Outlook, 89 (August 8), 810-811.
(Review of Views and Reviews.) It may not be fair to an author "whose critical oversight of his own work is so constant and keen" to collect these "fugitive papers" of James's apprentice period. Though newspaper and magazine reviews have only a "fleeting" value, James's comments on Whitman are interesting, some of his criticisms show "acute judgment," and the early style makes one regret James's loss of it.

36 ANON. "Henry James." Philadelphia Public Ledger and Philadelphia Times, August 22, p. 11.
(Review of New York Edition, vols. 9-12.) The prefaces provide "a most wonderful example" of James's recent, "extremely fluid" style. They are not easy reading, though it is "delightful" to hear James's reflections on his work. The Awkward Age is "one of the very finest of his penetrating comedies," and its preface is particularly interesting. The Ambassadors and The Golden Bowl are "very important novels" by "this strangely fascinating novelist." Those "who delight" in him will rejoice in the chance to reread "a long list of books that stand wholly by themselves."

37 ANON. "Writers and Books/The Literary World of Today." Boston Evening Transcript, August 26, p. 17.
(Review of New York Edition, vols. 9-12.) "Surely nothing more weird and strange" than these prefaces "has ever been offered to the reading public." As would be expected, James analyzes minutely his own states of mind, and the exploration apparently gives him "the keenest delight." Prior

to the publication of The Awkward Age (1899), which his publisher said was very poorly received, James had already had "sufficient warning" of "his meagre influence over the populace." He "lost no respect for his work" simply because the public neglected or disapproved of it.

38 ANON. "Chronicle and Comment." "The New Edition of James." Bookman, 28 (September), 12-13.
(Review of New York Edition.) These volumes provide "fine ecstasy" for the "ardent and avowed disciple" of James, and will strike even the unregenerate as dignified and interesting. James is unquestionably a figure of importance in English fiction, and "one of the keenest of critics." The prefaces taken together promise to be "one of the most interesting of personal documents," and the edition makes available some of "the most curious and entertaining" of James's earlier works. It is not often that such an edition of the works of a living writer "can be justified on so many valid counts."

39 ANON. "Who's What/In and Out of America." Life, 52 (September 3), 237.
(Humorous item.) James makes fog of a high quality and criticizes America to the King's taste. His motto is "To the Stylist All Things Are Meaningless."

40 ANON. "Henry James Will Break His Silence/Novelist, in New Edition of His Works, to Add Biographical Sketches." Cincinnati Commercial Tribune, September 13, p. 14.
James is "among the few novelists who have never been interviewed," and he "has always refrained from explaining passages in his books." Therefore, the proposed historical and biographical prefaces to his new edition "should be appreciated by his many admirers."

41 ANON. Review of Views and Reviews. Dial, 45 (September 16), 171.
(Summary of contents.) This unexpected addition to James's available works "gives us distinct cause for satisfaction."

42 ANON. "Volume XI of Scribner's James." Louisville Courier-Journal, September 26, p. 5.
(Review of New York Edition.) For years to come, the retrospection and self-analysis in these prefaces will be avidly read. Despite the initial "haziness of impressions" they are fascinating and always worth reading. What Maisie Knew is "a great achievement," and although it and the other stories have unconventional endings, they will be "eminently artistic" to the "literary epicure."

43 ANON. "Notices." Methodist Review, 90 (September-October), 839-843.
(Review of Views and Reviews.) James's "marvelously elaborate, subtle, labyrinthic" style "fascinates and entangles his host of readers today." His earlier style was "admirable for clearness and charm." (Quotes James on a number of writers.)

44 ANON. "Volume XII of the New James." Louisville Courier-Journal, October 3, p. 5.
(Review of New York Edition.) Though condemned by a few critics, this edition of "the great novelist" has been well received by thoughtful readers. The Turn of the Screw is still impressively uncanny and mystifying, arousing "the keenest" sympathy for the governess. It is "a monument of all that is frightful," but also "finished" and worth careful study.

45 ANON. "Henry James' Works." San Francisco Chronicle, October 11, p. 10.
(Review of New York Edition, vols. 11 and 12.) What Maisie Knew is "perhaps the most artistic" of James's tales, and its complications are treated in his "best style." The prefaces "furnish good reading," since they reveal much about the conception and development of these stories.

46 ANON. "'The Emotionalist.'" San Francisco Chronicle, November 29, p. 10.
(Review of Stanley Olmstead's The Emotionalist.) Olmstead seems in this novel to be "a faithful disciple" of James. He "meditates and speculates, soliloquizes and proses and philosophizes, after the manner of his master."

47 ANON. "Views and Reviews." Independent, 65 (December 3), 1312.
(Review.) These essays still "have a real interest," are not marred by James's late style, and show what book reviewing can and must be. It is pleasantly surprising that so individual a writer is so tolerant and eclectic.

48 ANON. "Notes." Nation, 87 (December 17), 601.
(Review of New York Edition.) The most interesting passage in the preface to "A Bundle of Letters" is a reminiscence of James's life in London.

49 ANON. Review of W. D. Howells's Roman Holidays and Others. Nation, 87 (December 24), 633.
Howells avoids the kind of psychologizing that makes James's travel essays too heavy or "too wire-drawn and

recondite." Howells's moralizing or psychologizing is in "an offhand, touch-and-go fashion" very different from James's. Neither writer can experience "a careless rapture" because both are too busy "taking stock of their impressions."

50 COLSON, ETHEL. "With Authors and Books." Chicago Record-Herald, July 29, p. 8.
(Review of Views and Reviews.) The most interesting thing about this volume is the contrast in style between the clear early and confusing late essays, which contrast will sharply astonish "many James students, admiring and otherwise." Though for years James has provided the critics much interesting material, he was unsparing "in his own early criticisms of other writers."

51 DITHMAR, EDWARD A. "'The Tragic Muse' in New Edition." New York Times Saturday Review of Books, 13 (April 11), 199.
(Review of New York Edition, vols. 7 and 8.) The Tragic Muse ages well, and is "still fresh, charming, vital." It is "one of the most absorbing and exhilarating of the modern novels" not in the "loose, baggy monster" class. The preface is "rich in thoughts about art" and "uplifts the mind, takes one into a rarefied atmosphere of fine thinking," and is very distinguished. James's latest conviction is that "the only true honors of real art" are those of contraction and concentration, and his style is very difficult.

52 E[DGETT], E[DWIN] F[RANCIS]. "Books of the Day/The New Henry James." Boston Evening Transcript, January 8, p. 16.
(Review of New York Edition.) James has observed humanity so much and so long that his large output of fiction is justified. His name "represents the most sincere purpose and the most earnest achievement in imaginative literature." His "peculiarities of style and phrase" have helped make him "one of the most thoroughly discussed and wrangled-over novelists of the age." His preface to Roderick Hudson is an answer to "those who believe that 'art for art's sake' is a shibboleth to be deprecated and execrated."

53 FITCH, GEORGE HAMLIN. "New Edition of Henry James and Other Books." San Francisco Chronicle, January 26, p. 10.
(Review of first two volumes of New York Edition.) Although the best American critics think James "stands at the head of living American novelists," the great reading public would not agree because of his "involved style" and "many mannerisms." James has presented "more types of the purely national character than any of our other writers," and his stories have "a certain breadth and distinction" in "strong contrast" to those of most other American novelists. James's

comments on Roderick Hudson are "keen and convincing," and his idea of romance in the preface to The American is very interesting and worthy of study. The original style of The American and The Portrait of a Lady is "far superior" to that of the revisions and of his later stories, although his recent stories show greater art in the development of character.

54 _____. "Modern Egypt and Other Books." San Francisco Chronicle, March 29, p. 10.
(Review of New York Edition, vols. 3-7.) The most noteworthy features of these volumes are the prefaces, which are characteristic of James's later manner and yet clearly written. One "is struck afresh with the perfect art" in character development displayed in those "old favorites" The Portrait of a Lady and The Princess Casamassima. The latter work "is beautifully done," and it would greatly benefit "the readers of this generation" if they "cultivated a taste for these novels . . . so rich in all the qualities that the novels of breathless adventure lack so lamentably."

55 _____. "Some of the Midsummer Books." San Francisco Chronicle, August 2, p. 10.
(Review of Views and Reviews.) It is "a revelation" to read James's "clear, incisive criticism" of George Eliot, and much of this volume is "of genuine interest" in that it shows how James's early critical writing prepared for his creation of fictional characters. The essay on Whitman is especially good. A man like James "could find no vantage ground on which to stand" with Whitman, and yet, "with great ingenuity," James "brings out everything that is weak, mawkish and theatrical in Whitman's verse." The essays are written in a clear style that most readers prefer to James's later manner with its possibly "greater literary culture."

56 GALBRAITH [pseud.]. "Geo. Meredith At Eighty." New York Times Saturday Review of Books, 13 (February 8), 65-66.
(Interview with George Meredith.) Meredith reads a James novel a year. The American Scene is more of a tour of James's insides than a tour of his homeland.

57 HACKETT, FRANCIS. "James on James." Chicago Evening Post, January 11, p. 4.
(Review of New York Edition, vols. 1 and 2.) James has genius, and his greatness as a novelist rests on "his mature work in particular." His attitude toward his early works is "surprisingly fresh." A few readers will share his faith in the supreme worthiness of the creative passion.

1908

58 _____. "News and Views of Books." Chicago Evening Post, January 29, p. 4.

(Comments on New York Edition, vols. 1 and 2.) Ardent Jacobins object to James's revisions of Roderick Hudson and The American. Some revised paragraphs are clearer and more accurate than the originals, and the revisions show the "fine and beautiful discriminations" of a delicate literary conscience. Yet, overall, "the original versions are better unified and more normally articulated." The prefaces are as noteworthy as any criticism James has done.

59 _____. "Books and Bookmen/Mr. James's Art." Chicago Evening Post, September 16, p. 7.

(Review of New York Edition.) Many dislike intensely James's methods and manners, his "bisection of a molecule." He is accused of tortuous obscurity and, more seriously, of pettiness. He does not dispense either moral medicine or sociology, or deal with public issues, but he accurately tells important truths about everyday life. He has "a steady and luminous appreciation" of character, an "exquisite sense of the relativity of standards." He observes so carefully and so avoids uncouth definition that his vice is disintegration rather than classification. His caring less for the thing done and more for the mood, manner, and motive, alienates those who lack his curiosity about the game of life and who cannot forgive his analyst's insusceptibility to "large and generous enthusiasms."

60 HALE, EDWARD E., JR. "The Rejuvenation of Henry James." Dial, 44 (March 16), 174-176.

(Review of New York Edition.) It is a matter of opinion whether James should have revised his early works as he has. He undoubtedly wrote better English thirty years ago than he does today. As the years passed his "feeling for expression became more precise, more refined, perhaps even more delicate," he remained "modern," and "he strove to get closer to the texture, the movement, of his own thought." All of this was "a fine ideal," but it was fleeting and came to mock him. The prefaces in this edition "will be a delight to all Jamesians."

61 HAMILTON, CLAYTON. The Materials and Methods of Fiction. New York: Baker & Taylor, pp. 25, 35, 55, 76, 116, 134, 147, 169, 177. Rpt. Chautauqua, 1911; Doubleday, 1912.

(Quotes James on a number of aspects of contemporary fiction.) A passage from James's genial "Art of Fiction" has cast "a vivid light" on the relation between character and incident and sums up the tendency of "the best contemporary novelists" to make description narrate. Lately, James has written for the supercivilized. It is hard to imagine how "the full force" of The Turn of the Screw's "cumulative mystery and terror could have been created with greater economy."

62 HAWTHORNE, HILDEGARDE. "Henry James As Critic." New York Times Saturday Review of Books, 13 (July 11), 385.
(Review of Views and Reviews.) This volume gives the reader "a keen delight" in observing James's growth, and the early essays' flow of style is "exquisite, ripe," smoother than it has ever been since. James's thought was always complicated, and the "clarity of the views, the justice of the criticisms," are surprising. Like Kipling, James showed a clever, precocious, maturity of judgment in youth.

63 HORNE, CHARLES E. The Technique of the Novel: The Elements of the Art, Their Evolution and Present Use. New York: Harper's, pp. 150, 187.
(James and Howells are the Americans mentioned among some "noted writers of recent years.")

64 KELLY, FLORENCE FINCH. "'The Whole Family' and Its Troubles." New York Times Saturday Review of Books, 13 (October 24), 590.
(Review of cooperative novel The Whole Family with chapters by James, W. D. Howells, Mary Wilkins Freeman, Mary Heaton Vorse, Mary Stewart Cutting, Elizabeth Jordan, John Kendrick Bangs, Elizabeth Stuart Phelps, Edith Wyatt, Mary Raymond Shipman Andrews, Alice Brown, and Henry van Dyke.) James's section is the most characteristic, and "sets forth the young man's ideas, prejudices, and desires searchingly, acutely, delicately, and gets nowhere with it all." He and Howells are "the star performers" among the participating authors.

65 PEATTIE, ELIA W. "Henry James Rewrites Earlier Novels into His Later Style." Chicago Tribune, January 18, p. 9.
(Review of New York Edition.) When the news that he would revise his "buoyant," "facile," "fascinating and perfectly coherent" early works raised eloquent protests about "falsification of history," James must have been amused at the public sense of proprietorship toward them. Those early novels were "the most mobile, elegant, cosmopolitan achievements" Americans had produced up to that time, they "marked, undeniably, a step in our literary history," and their popularity was a credit to their audience. Later, when James's nuances became too subtle to understand and incoherent, and his characters' eccentricities became futilities, he inspired "brotherly indignation" for hurting our feelings and offending

our ideals. James is "scorn proof," so that one may attack him freely, but one cannot be vexed with a man who is so frankly fascinated with the products of his youth. A serious and confident artist, James is not inartistic in "going behind the scenes" in his "remarkable" prefaces, and in this "defective edition" he merely refurbishes Roderick Hudson and The American rather than greatly changing them. Yet, it is shabby and annoying that he himself does not know the "key" to the mysterious behavior of his characters. As Balzac exploited people's foibles and Zola their passions, so James "has made a specialty of their disappointments," frustration, and futilities, which do not appeal to a wide audience.

66 _____. "Reviews of Current Publications. . . ./Henry James Enjoying His Earlier Literary Incarnations." Chicago Tribune, March 7, p. 9.
(Review of New York Edition.) Despite readers' fears, James "has retained sufficient sense of honor . . . not to lead these innocent and charming creatures of his earlier books into the tortuous paths of his later manner." The Portrait of a Lady and The Princess Casamassima "remain lucid, vivid, charming, and full of gay and rich romance." James may like them "almost as well as you or I, though this, of course, is going rather far," and he can be depended upon to reconsider and amend his earlier books "without harming them." The prefaces to these two volumes are more kindly and sociable than those of the previous volumes of the edition, but some of their advice is so self-evident that it hardly needs to be given. James is like a Theosophist who returns to an earlier incarnation and finds himself "enchanted by a simpler ans sweeter phase of his illimitable career."

*67 PHILLIPS, LeROY, ed. Introduction. Views and Reviews by Henry James. Boston: The Ball Pub. Co.
(Cited in Ricks.)

68 REPPLIER, AGNES. "Place aux Dames." Life, 51 (February 20), 193.
(Brief reference.) James, an "acute and unemotional writer," has praised Englishwomen.

69 SCHUYLER, MONTGOMERY. "Henry James Done Over." New York Times Saturday Review of Books, 13 (January 11), 13-15.
(Review of vols. 1 and 2 of New York Edition.) No living writer is more fit than James to prepare prefaces to his own work, and the preface to The American has "a subtle and delightful discussion" of realism and romance. The earlier

versions of his works are better than the revised ones, which "tend to obfuscate characters, weaken the passion, slacken the action, and attenuate the interest."

70 SHUMAN, EDWIN L. "With Authors and Books." Chicago Record-Herald, July 1, p. 10.
(Review of New York Edition.) The preface to The Tragic Muse is "more nebulous and less interesting than those on the previous novels." This novel began James's lapse into his "later manner" which, with its "exasperating overrefinement and finicking attenuation of every idea," has "smothered his real artistic powers." The prefaces are pleasant and not the least attraction of this edition which will be "of supreme interest" to James's admirers. The introductions' best part is James's "spirit of complete detachment." His analysis of each story's technique is "wonderfully keen and helpful."

1909

1 ANON. Review of Views and Reviews. A.L.A. Booklist, 5 (January), 14.
(Gives subjects of essays.)

2 ANON. "Official Action Just Taken Contemplates American Federation." New York Times, January 24, Part 5, p. 1.
(Portrait.) James is among the illustrious members of the Academy of Arts of the National Institute of Arts and Letters.

3 ANON. "The Movement to Advance Arts and Letters in America." New York Times, January 24, Part 5, p. 2.
(Brief biographical sketch of James appears with those of other "representative" members of the National Institute of Arts and Letters.)

4 ANON. "Among the Books . . . The Novels of Henry James." Philadelphia Public Ledger and Philadelphia Times, January 30, p. 6.
(Review of New York Edition.) This edition makes an interesting comparison with the original texts of James's works, and reminds one of the problem of James's "true place" as a storyteller. He is one of the most highly sensitized of contemporary novelists, with "delicacy of apperception," but to some extent his faculties have been wasted and he has not achieved broad effects. Yet, no one who reads more than newspapers and magazines can ignore James, who is "the nearest approach to a 'final' critic of

our crude new civilization and the types it has evoked." He, "more than any other, has appreciated and expressed that 'interest of contrasted things,' in types and in traditions, which remains the great concern of your social novelist."

5 ANON. "Some New Books of February." "Henry James' Novels and Tales." San Francisco Chronicle, February 7, p. 10.
(Review of New York Edition, vols. 13 and 14.) In The Reverberator, the results of Francie Dosson's indiscretion are brought out in James's best style. James "has never done anything better" than the sketch of Lady Barberina's type in the preface to volume 14.

6 ANON. "With Authors and Books." Chicago Record-Herald, February 19, p. 6.
(Review of William Hamilton's The Red Mouse. Reviewer criticizes Hamilton's style by asserting its similarity to James's.)

7 ANON. "Reticence in Fiction." Chicago Evening Post Friday Literary Review, March 19, p. 4.
(Editorial. Reference to 1909.65.) James's authorial self-effacement did not become reticence.

8 ANON. "Notes." Nation, 88 (April 8), 359.
(Review of New York Edition.) In the prefaces to volumes 15 and 16, which seem "rather pumped," James uses his "most prolix and cryptic style" and takes himself with "great seriousness."

9 ANON. "Stories of Henry James." Philadelphia Public Ledger and Philadelphia Times, April 10, p. 15.
(Review of New York Edition, vols. 15 and 16.) The prefaces are "a commanding feature" of this edition, and, though difficult, are "most enticing" to "the follower of the later James." "The Author of Beltraffio" is "one of the most characteristic" of James's tales.

10 ANON. "Scribner Edition of The Tragic Muse." Louisville Courier-Journal, April 11, p. 5.
(Review of New York Edition.) James knows the full secret of the value of unity in fiction. He gives "his best labor" to these admirable prefaces, which contain "interesting explanations and literary inspirations" and are "models of forceful English."

11 ANON. "Notes." Nation, 88 (April 22), 410.
(Review of New York Edition.) In the prefaces to volumes

17 and 18, James "takes himself with portentous seriousness" and dwells interminably on "the details of unimportant matters."

12 ANON. "Notes." Nation, 88 (April 29), 439.
(Review of New York Edition.) The introduction to The Wings of the Dove is prolix.

13 ANON. "The Lounger." Putnam's, 6 (May), 254.
(Review of "Disengaged," benefit performance at the Hudson Theatre in New York.) James is not a playwright, and some say he is not a novelist, with all his obscurity. His comedy is almost farce, very poorly constructed, and hard to follow, yet it is "interesting and amusing." It might do well for special matinees in Boston.

14 ANON. "A Few Biographical Facts." Book News Monthly, 27 (May), 640.
(Biographical sketch of James's life before 1870.)

15 ANON. "Books and Authors/Literary Notes." Boston Daily Advertiser, May 14, p. 8.
(Review of or note on New York Edition, vols. 17-20. Quotation from preface explaining the motive behind The Wings of the Dove.) Many people "for the first time now understand."

16 ANON. "Magazine Critique/. . . Mr. James' Right to Be James." Chicago Evening Post Friday Literary Review, May 14, p. 5.
(Comments on 1909.83.) Though in many ways good, Krans's article misreads James's approach to ethics and mistakenly criticizes him for lack of boldness when he is an etcher.

17 ANON. "Books Received." Chicago Record-Herald, May 15, p. 11.
(New York Edition is listed.)

18 ANON. "Life's Great Marathon Race/Preliminary Arrangements Are Now Being Completed/Everybody Enthusiastic." Life, 53 (June 10), 823.
(Brief parody of James's style.)

19 ANON. "Life's Great Marathon Race." Life, 53 (June 24), 884.
(Brief humorous mention. James and other writers are listed among the participants.)

20 ANON. "Notes." Nation, 89 (July 1), 11-12.
(Review of New York Edition. Discussion of and quotation from preface to The Ambassadors.)

1909

21 ANON. "Meredith on James's Inside." Boston Evening Transcript, July 3, Part 3, p. 4.
(Note.) Shortly before his death, George Meredith wrote that James's The American Scene is in substance "'not a re-visiting of America, but a tour of James's own inside,'" of how he felt when he saw this or that. (See 1908.7, 8, 56.)

22 ANON. "Recent Belles-Lettres." Chicago Evening Post Friday Literary Review, July 23, p. 6.
(Review of 1909.87.) Professor Northrup "achieves the distinction of not being unjust" to James when he tells us that "innocuous 'criticism'" that James is trivial and abstruse does not even touch him.

23 ANON. "Literary Small Talk/. . . Henry James on Biography." Chicago Evening Post Friday Literary Review, August 6, p. 7.
(Quotation from Will H. Rideing in McClure's quoting James on biography.)

24 ANON. "Notes." Nation, 89 (August 19), 159.
(Review of New York Edition.) The preface to The Golden Bowl provides a "discussion of literary method" which is at least frank, if not simple.

25 ANON. "The Novels and Tales of Henry James." Chicago Evening Post Friday Literary Review, August 20, p. 6.
(Review of New York Edition.) The prefaces are "invaluable," and indispensable to enjoying James fully. It would be hard to choose between the original works and this edition, which shows how James's taste has become more dainty, exacting, and conscious.

26 ANON. "Portland Place." Chicago Evening Post Friday Literary Review, August 20, p. 1.
(Reproduction and discussion of the frontispiece for volume 2 of The Golden Bowl, with James quotation.)

27 ANON. "Letters and Art . . . Why Mr. James 'Revised.'" Literary Digest, 39 (August 21), 275-276.
James's announcement a year ago that he would revise his works raised an outcry among admirers of his earlier works who were baffled by his later ones. In the preface to The Golden Bowl his discussion of his revisions is typically introspective, addressed more to himself than to the public. (Long quotation.)

28 ANON. "The Censorship." Chicago Evening Post Friday Literary Review, August 27, p. 8.
(James is among "the most eminent authors in England"

who expressed their disapproval of the censorship of plays. James's letter is printed.)

29 ANON. "Mr. James Puts It Well." Life, 54 (September 9), 345.
(Praises James's criticism of the censorship of plays in England.)

30 ANON. "The Novels of Mr. Henry James." Living Age, 262 (September 11), 691-696.
(Reprint of London Times review of New York Edition.)

31 ANON. "Literary Small Talk/. . . Henry James on London." Chicago Evening Post Friday Literary Review, September 17, p. 8.
The English critics note James's and Pett Ridge's differing views of London. (James quoted.)

32 ANON. "Literary Small Talk/Rewritten Novels." Chicago Evening Post Friday Literary Review, September 17, p. 8.
In the London Saturday Review, Filson Young thinks no one, including James, should rewrite novels, and George Moore (quoted) found reading James as strenuous and unnourishing as chewing cork.

33 ANON. "Henry James in Brief." New York Sun, October 9, p. 6.
(Review of Julia Bride. Description of and comments on the story parody James's style.) Mr. Pitman is "a delightfully entertaining character . . . whom it is a favor to know." It is unnecessary to say that the story is told with an art both "nice and lingering." The reader feels "genuinely sorry" for Julia.

34 ANON. "Henry James' Latest." Louisville Courier-Journal, October 9, p. 5.
(Review of Julia Bride.) The situation is original and well handled by this "master weaver of social snarls" and author of the "inimitable" Portrait of a Lady.

35 ANON. "A James Fantasy." Salt Lake Tribune, October 10, p. 36.
(Review of Julia Bride.) James's "obscure style" is charming to some people, but "extremely baffling to the ordinary reader." Anyone finishing this book will know little more about its contents than he did when he began.

36 ANON. "'Julia Bride.'" New York Times Saturday Review of Books, 14 (October 16), 613.
(Review.) James is sarcastic and a little unsympathetic in a less than pleasant story with "sordid features" and

complex language. Yet, it will reward patient readers and delight James's admirers.

37 ANON. "Late Works of Fiction." New York World, October 16, p. 9.
(Review of Julia Bride.) The basis for this story "involving so much of New York possibility" is "cleverly conceived," and the study would be "intensely interesting" if not for James's complex, obscure style.

38 ANON. "Mysterious Henry James." Boston Herald, October 23, p. 9.
(Review of Julia Bride.) This book contains some of James's best analysis. It is sometimes clear, sometimes obscure, but always subtle. Its theme is characteristic of James and provides "luscious material" for his genius. People who do not like his method will not finish it.

39 ANON. "'Julia Bride'/Characteristic and So Quite Psychological Novel by Henry James." Chicago Inter-Ocean, October 23, p. 5.
The style of this "quite clever psychological novel" is obscure and puzzling, but not without music and "a certain tenuous and phantasmal beauty." It contrasts with the "brisk and luminous" manner of James's early works. After pages of "twaddle" the story ends where it began, yet to comprehend this typically Jamesian tale shows superior intellect in the reader.

40 ANON. Review of Julia Bride. New Orleans Daily Picayune, October 24, Part III, p. 15.
This story is heavier than its light plot suggests, and it is told with all of James's "obscure simplicity and elaborate delicacy."

41 ANON. "The New Books." Outlook, 93 (October 30), 515.
(Review of Julia Bride.) The situation is complicated enough for James's "subtle and delicate method." The story has his "characteristic complication of motives and style," and ends "nowhere."

42 ANON. "Fiction." Churchman, 100 (October 30), 628.
(Review of Julia Bride.) This typically "very minute analysis" of states of feeling in a not-very-interesting situation is "exceptionally lucid" for James.

43 ANON. "Among the New Books." Detroit Free Press, October 30, p. 8.
(Review of Julia Bride.) This story is a social and psychological comedy in James's very difficult style.

44 ANON. "Julia Bride." Philadelphia Public Ledger and Philadelphia Times, November 6, p. 9.
(Review of Julia Bride.) Despite an Athenaeum reviewer's "acerbic" condemnation of James's recent writings as studies of "'a lot of corrupt and luxurious idlers,'" Julia Bride "will give pleasure" to James's admirers. It "abounds in the psychological nuances" in which James delights.

45 ANON. "Six Masters of Prose." New York World, November 20, p. 8.
(Review of W. C. Brownell's American Prose Masters.) Fellow critics may quarrel with what Brownell says of James, but he may be right when he finds (as do readers who are frank with themselves) that James's "second manner" was his best and that recently he has sacrificed too much "in the use of an unusual talent" to build "his intensely artificial and intricate style." (See 1905.81, 1909.67.)

46 ANON. "A Henry James Story." Chicago Evening Post Friday Literary Review, November 26, p. 1.
(Review of Julia Bride.) This story seems less about Julia herself than about the impression she made on James's mind. Yet, he is aloof and unprejudiced in this plotless work which makes no point but rather suggests and reflects a situation.

47 ANON. "A Guide to the New Books." Literary Digest, 39 (November 27), 962.
(Review of Julia Bride.) This book is in James's "characteristically involved style," ironically the result of his trying too hard to be intelligible. The story is "too much of a psychological puzzle to prove either instructive or entertaining."

48 ANON. "New Books." New York Sun, November 27, p. 10.
(Review of Italian Hours.) James is "at his very best here," partly because much of the book was written years ago when he had "enthusiasms and vivid sensations" and a less subtle and tangled style.

49 ANON. "Henry James." Bookman, 30 (December), 322.
(Review of Julia Bride.) The critical battle over whether, having done one thing well, James should be allowed to do anything else, has been raging for a dozen years. He is "the supreme example, the awful warning of the danger of attempting to do something better than one's best." Julia Bride would be considered "a slight but sufficiently pleasant" story if James had written none of the books that follow The Tragic Muse. As it is, "weary critics" feel

compelled to read it. James might have gone on writing Daisy Millers all these years, instead of trying to find some way of expressing what very few people regard as worth expressing.

50 ANON. "New Books Reviewed." North American Review, 190 (December), 836.
(Review of Julia Bride.) James gives us not plots or endings, but "careful analysis of emotion," which should satisfy us. This "piece out of life" is "wonderfully done," with memorable characters. James "knows more, feels more delicately, notes more finely than other writers," and has a style to match his method.

51 ANON. "Books and Authors/The Maneuvers of Julia." Boston Daily Advertiser, December 1, p. 8.
(Review of Julia Bride.) No one doubts that James knows people, is "a keen student of human nature." Complaints in recent years are that his elaborate style so shrouds his findings that many readers "are discouraged and abandon the chase."

52 ANON. "Picturesque Travel." Churchman, 100 (December 4), 843.
(Review of Italian Hours.) One seldom finds "more keenly discriminating or more sympathetic descriptions" of Italian cities.

53 ANON. "Other Volumes of Travel." Congregationalist and Christian World, 94 (December 4), 786.
(Review of Italian Hours.) These sketches appeal to the intellect and pique close attention but are not obscure. James is an accomplished observer of human nature with a "mincing dance-step" of a style.

54 ANON. "News and Views the World of Books . . . Book-Room Talk and Tips." New York World, December 4, p. 8.
(Review of Italian Hours.) In the early 1870s James wrote "simple and delightful English," and these early essays have "spontaneity, graphic quality and charm." They convey "ideas instead of a headache," and suggest that James must now have moments of regret that he has "bartered his English for a mess of style."

55 ANON. "Literature." Nation, 89 (December 9), 569.
(Review of Italian Hours.) This handsome volume is free from the "involved ambiguity of hesitation" that makes James's later writings, like The American Scene, "a task rather than a pleasure." One of the attractions of his impressionistic manner is its arbitrariness, and the text is romantic.

56 ANON. "'Italian Hours.'" Chicago Inter-Ocean, December 11, p. 5.

(Review.) This is "an interpretation rather than a description." The illustrations are not in Joseph Pennell's best manner.

57 ANON. Review of Italian Hours. Chicago Record-Herald, December 11, p. 8.

Most of these papers, from the early 1870s, are written in James's "simplest and most pleasing style." Yet, the art interest prevails, a warmer human interest is missing, and although James shows himself capable of deep feeling, it in this instance "fades into mere intellectual dilettantism." To lovers of Italy and admirers of James's "chaste, artistic style," this book will be a "treasure-trove."

58 ANON. Review of Italian Hours. Literary Digest, 39 (December 11), 1073.

James is best and most at ease when contemplating beautiful objects. His sketches are fresh, even original.

59 ANON. "Books of the Day." Philadelphia North American, December 11, p. 16.

(Review of Italian Hours.) This "gifted author's sympathetic descriptions are wondrously reproduced pictorially" by Pennell in a volume "fascinating" to Mediterranean travelers.

60 ANON. Review of Italian Hours. Independent, 67 (December 16), 1352.

The combination of these two masters, author and illustrator, was "exceedingly happy" and has produced a "charming" book.

61 ANON. "Italian Hours/Jo Pennell's Superb Illustrations Embellish Henry James' Great Work." Philadelphia Public Ledger and Philadelphia Times, December 18, p. 13.

(Discussion of Joseph Pennell's illustrations.) "It is altogether a superb book."

62 ANON. "Books, Authors and Art./History, Travel, and Fiction./ Henry James's Papers on Italy." Springfield (Mass.) Sunday Republican, December 19, p. 38.

(Review of Italian Sketches.) James's essays do not need the embellishment of the illustrations, nor do they need any pretense that they are more recent than they are. James is "in the enviable position" of being "a classic in his own lifetime, an artist with 'periods,' each of which has its claims and its partisans." Therefore James has not here

1909

tried for modernity, but for the "'face of things as it mainly used to be.'" Both he and Howells dealt a generation ago with Italy in "what was then an ultra-modern spirit," and if the intuitive rather than scientific approach of these two distinguished, "cultivated amateurs" seems less modern now, "the advantage is not all on the side of the new age." These essays have "the wonderful preservative virtue of style," they are "interesting as a record of things irrecoverably lost," James makes personal judgments reinforced by "keen and wary scrutiny," and what distinguishes his impressions is his "exceptionally delicate and precise" literary art.

63 BAYSWELL [pseud.]. "New York Book News." Chicago Evening Post, March 19, p. 4.
(Note on a charity performance of "Disengaged" at which "the audience was notable," fashion and brains seeming "to come to a tangent on the occasion of James.")

64 ______. "New York Letter." Chicago Evening Post Friday Literary Review, July 23, p. 6.
(Quotes publisher's praise of Julia Bride.)

65 BEERBOHM, MAX. "Henry James/Max Beerbohm in Saturday Review." Chicago Evening Post Friday Literary Review, March 12, p. 6.
(Excerpt from London Saturday Review.) Though James learned from the French not to be an intrusive author, much of the "immense delight" of his books, moral rather than aesthetic, comes from the man himself. His later method is unique, and gives us information gradually as real life does. His art has followed "the right line of progress," and though he eschews primitive emotions, his works have human feeling, especially "passion of conscience." Despite his self-suppression and irony, he shows clearly his reverence for the noble and horror for the ignoble.

66 BLAKE, WARREN BARTON. "Mr. James and Mr. Pennell in Italy." Dial, 47 (December 1), 450-451.
(Review of Italian Hours.) One does not quite say that this book is "'only a most delightful tour of Henry James's insides'" rather than of Italy, but it might have more spontaneity. Yet, perhaps spontaneity is "more than one has a right to ask from so masterly an analyst of men and of places."

67 BROWNELL, WILLIAM C. "Henry James." American Prose Masters. New York: Scribner's, pp. 339-400.
(Revision of 1905.81.)

68 BULLOCK, SHAN F. "London Letter." Chicago Evening Post Friday Literary Review, August 27, p. 4.
The letters from James and from Thomas Hardy that John Galsworthy read to the censor reform committee concerning the censorship of plays were "worth his whole personal evidence." James was "sublime," with long sentences and "polysyllabic incoherence."

69 _____. "London Letter." Chicago Evening Post Friday Literary Review, November 5, p. 4.
(Mentions James as among the "prominent men" who asked the press not to discuss J. M. Barrie's divorce.)

70 CANBY, HENRY SEIDEL. "The Americans From Bret Harte To The Nineties." The Short Story in English. New York: Holt, pp. 306-315, 271-272, 346.
James is a consummately skilled master of the serious American short story. He unfailingly keeps hold of his situation, but he is not always intelligible or interesting, and often neglects the imagination and the heart. His world is too restricted for an arch storyteller, and he is "unduly diffuse," elliptical, and obscure. His stories have been more successful than his novels at studying and analyzing "incomparably subtle and complex situations," but both show depth of insight. James's very advanced experiments in psychology render "an inestimable service" to those who see life's complexity. He may have been the first writer in English to "put realism into an impressionistic short story," to treat an interesting situation by avoiding sensation, to portray the subtle interrelations of our civilized people. He and Kipling "have advanced the art to conquests before unthought of." Despite his changes in style, his later stories are essentially similar to his early ones, and The Turn of the Screw is his most interesting.

71 CARY, ELISABETH LUTHER. "Henry James: An Appreciation." Book News Monthly, 27 (May), 641-645.
(Reviews the character portrayals in James's works.) James has youth's curiosity about "the minds and souls of those about us and the undiscovered country within ourselves." He is very interested in creating characters who live their own lives almost independently of their author. The portrayal of the complex inner lives of the people in The Princess Casamassima is a great triumph, and in this and other early stories James presents "the intimate life of the soul." The "amazingly rich cake" of the later novels is "a mixture of homely ingredients in common use, but somehow transfigured and made rare and delectable." The Awkward Age is one of James's "most nearly perfect creations," and

the self-revelation in the preface leaves the critic with nothing left to do. It shows how important organization and mental labor are to creativity. (Portrait.)

72 E[DGETT], E[DWIN] F[RANCIS]. "Writers and Books/The Literary World of Today." Boston Evening Transcript, May 1, Part 3, p. 5.
(Review of New York Edition, vols. 17-20.) The prefaces in this edition "have been regularly scoffed at and derided in some quarters" for "their egotism and their devotion to apparent trivialities," but these very aspects have given them "the utmost appealing interest" to some other readers. The prefaces give "the clearest possible insight into the methods of one of the leading novelists of the age." Daisy Miller was a "harmless story," and a long quoted passage from its preface is pure James but neither indefinite nor obscure. The theme of The Wings of the Dove is worthy of the discernible skill with which this "philosopher-novelist" handled it, though the book was not popular.

73 EDGETT, EDWIN FRANCIS. "Writers and Books/The Literary World of Today." Boston Evening Transcript, August 18, p. 17.
(Review of New York Edition, vols. 20-24.) The prefaces included in the edition are "highly individual and characteristic." The "ultra modern" James is identifiable with the earlier one, and his "scientific" researches have always been "enhanced in value and interest" by his "lively and sensitive imagination." Yet, the contemporary James's "peculiarities of mood and manner" and increased "passion for the literary analysis of life" make him very different from the James of the 1870s and 1880s. This edition of James "should mark an epoch in the American literature" of the period of transition between centuries. One regrets only the omission of so much of his important work, including The Bostonians and The Europeans, and James's revision of his earlier style.

74 E[DGETT], E[DWIN] F[RANCIS]. "The World of Fiction/Novels and Romance and Their Incessant Appeal to the Reader." Boston Evening Transcript, November 17, p. 22.
(Review of Julia Bride.) This book is impossible to describe or summarize, it has "a glamor of reality that is by no means realism," and it leads the reader through "introspective ways." For those who like him, James has not lost his verbal cunning.

75 FITCH, GEORGE HAMLIN. "Joaquin Miller's Poems and Other Books." San Francisco Chronicle, May 23, p. 10.
(Review of New York Edition, vols. 17-21. Summary of

some history of the original publication of Daisy Miller.) Daisy Miller first brought James many readers, and "many sharp criticisms on his European attitude" toward a recognizably "very faithful type" of the young American woman. Lovers of James's earlier direct and lucid style will regret the changes in the original text, and in The Wings of the Dove James's "peculiar methods of bringing out character and motive are shown in the highest measure." His greatest literary faults are his overuse of adverbs and his repetition of certain words and phrases.

76 _____. "'The White Prophet' and Other Books." San Francisco Chronicle, September 12, p. 6.
(Review of New York Edition, vols. 20-24.) In the preface to The Golden Bowl James says some characteristic things about revision of his works, and many readers will disagree with his claim that his early novels show traces of a lack of literary art. The "great novel-reading public" prefers his early work because it lacked the "extreme sophistication" of his later novels. The style of the preface is very difficult, a "fair specimen" of James's later manner, and unmistakably his.

77 _____. "New Holiday Books and Others." San Francisco Chronicle, December 5, p. 6.
(Review of Italian Hours.) This book contains some of this famous novelist's best work, with his best descriptive style and vivid, "remarkably clear" impressions. He shows here better than in his novels, which are sometimes made tedious by "refinements of motive and conduct."

78 GAINES, C. H. "Harper's Bookshelf." Harper's, 119 (October), xi.
(Review of Julia Bride.) James's "tremendous verbal felicities," keen perceptions, and bedazzling style have led many to regard his art as a mystery. Though his style can be elaborate, Julia Bride is "a masterpiece of clear delineation." (Small portrait.)

79 GRAY, BLAKENEY. "Henry James a la Jigsaw/A Literary Discovery." Life, 54 (August 5), 164.
(Humorous poem on sawing one of James's pages apart and mixing up the pieces so that they make an understandable plot.) James conceals his meaning.

80 HAMILTON, CLAYTON. "The Promise of New Playwrights." Forum, 41 (April), 342-343.
(Review of "Disengaged." Notice of performance of "Disengaged" at the Hudson Theatre in New York on March 11,

1909.) This play is a "commendable accomplishment," but does not promise James a successful future in the theater. It is spirited, "neatly constructed," and brilliantly written, with adroit dialogue and intellectual action carried on "with rare rapidity and dash," but it appeals too exclusively to the intellect to be popular with theater audiences.

81 HOWES, ABBY WILLIS. A Primer of American Literature. Boston: D. C. Heath, p. 138.

James's "fine distinctions in mood and character" gain him "the unqualified approval of a small cultured audience" who think him "a skilled master," but "a great number of readers do not understand him," or find him tiresome.

82 KERFOOT, J. B. "The Latest Books." Life, 54 (November 11), 676.

(Review of Julia Bride.) James's subject is treated with "infinite skill, a sort of dehumanized humor, and the rarified verbal atmosphere of ten thousand feet above sea level" which one must adjust one's mental state to fit.

83 KRANS, HORATIO S. "The Novels of Henry James." Book News Monthly, 27 (May), 633-640.

James and Howells changed American fiction. James patiently elaborates details and charms with a "marvelous descriptive faculty." Nowhere else in fiction is there "so firm, clear, just, comprehensive and subtle an appreciation and analysis of American character, in its most essential and distinctive traits." However crude, James's Americans have "endless inner refinements of kindness and conscience."

The late as well as the early novels have his "careful artistry, the quiet irony, the cool, unpleasantly aloof detachment, and the insatiable curiosity" that includes insignificant details and often inconsequential analysis. This fiction lacks freshness, "stylistic resource," bold strokes, drama, moving incident. Yet, James has been "strikingly original" in subjects and method, the inventor of the "artistic society novel" of minute observation, refinement, analysis, and subtlety. His books give "lessons in good morals and good manners." (See 1909.16.)

84 LARNED, W[ILLIAM] T. "The Literary Zoo/Every Man His Own Critic." Life, 54 (October 28), 572.

Among the unfortunate results that would occur if authors and critics tried only to please the public would be that James would contribute the "Daily Short Story" to the Evening Mail.

85 MARSH, EDWARD. "Henry James: Auto-Critic." Bookman, 30

(October), 138-143.

(Review of New York Edition.) This edition is a "nearly perfect" consummation of James's art and work. In his prefaces he has done "the unexpected, the unique thing," and produced a series of documents "without a parallel in literature," a "complete, thoroughgoing analysis" of his own craft by "one of the great masters of the game." James's critical acumen, wealth of observation, and "apposite illustration" of his art compel his detractors to concede that he is a great critic, if not a great novelist. In "the face of neglect or ridicule that would have checked any but an enthusiast," he has over the years been "singularly consistent." He goes "deep, as does every great novelist," but differs from Thackeray, Dickens, and Meredith "in the fullness and richness of his exposition of a whole set of relations commonly ignored by the novelist."

86 METCALFE, [JAMES S.] "Mr. Henry James on the Stage." Life, 53 (March 25), 401.

(Review of matinee performance of "Disengaged.") James's characters' speeches are "not entirely unintelligible," and are sometimes even funny. His method of construction is bewildering.

87 NORTHUP, CLARK SUTHERLAND. "The Novelists." A Manual of American Literature. Ed. Theodore Stanton. New York: G. P. Putnam, pp. 192-196.

James is controversial, has "an ardent, if not a large following," is "caviare to the general public," and is "one of the most striking figures among American novelists." He has shown "increasing subtlety and attention to finish." What Maisie Knew is unpleasant, and The Wings of the Dove has been called James's "most remarkable book." Judged by his best works, such as Roderick Hudson, The Princess Casamassima, and The Other House, he is a great artist. His style is not that of a master, but it has excellent qualities. Criticisms that he abstrusely writes of "petty ambitions of worthless Americans" do not even touch him. He does not preach, but he is in earnest and "the effect of his exposition of life is wholesome." Even if he becomes unintelligible in the future, the "great works" of his middle period will long delight many readers. (See 1909.22.)

88 PEATTIE, ELIA W. "Among the New Books." Chicago Tribune, September 4, p. 11.

(Review of New York Edition, vols. 20-24.) The prefaces impress the reader with "the vitality which James' creations possess for him." Characters that for others blur together have for him "a distinct personal essence," and he views

1909

the process by which they were created "with a detached admiration . . . both naive and amazing." The "sublime impudence" of his self-commendation would "shock every admirer away from him" were it not for his humility before his own attainments and his thankfulness for inspirations. This unique attitude may well be "regarded with satiric delight" during periodic James literary revivals in the years to come.

89 _____. "Among the New Books." Chicago Tribune, November 13, p. 13.
(Review of E. B. Dewing's Other People's Houses.) The characters are presented in a manner that James might commend, but their desires are more ardent and their acts more determinate than those of most of James's characters.

90 _____. "Among the New Books." Chicago Tribune, November 13, p. 13.
(Review of Julia Bride.) People no longer link the names of Howells and James. James and Julia Bride are much more subtle than the readers who follow this amazingly circuitous story.

91 _____. "Among the New Books." Chicago Tribune, November 27, p. 12.
(Review of Italian Hours.) James "never wanted to understand the American, or to get at the idealistic core of him," and he does not seem to admire "the violently constructive game of life." Yet, his writings on Italy are "felicitous" in their response to beauty and pathos. Enlivened by "the human element," these articles are, it is no surprise to the public, quite delicious.

92 QUENTIN, JOSEPH M. "Books." Portland Morning Oregonian, October 17, Section 5, p. 9.
(Review of Julia Bride.) This book is "academic, polished and humorously gentle," "safe, without being dull." All is "proper and American," with a "near-Boston atmosphere," a culture that makes the reader smile, and "no false note."

93 ROBERTS, W. J. "Old Rye: Its Literary and Artistic Associations." Book News Monthly, 27 (May), 645.
(Picture of and reference to James's house at Rye.)

94 ROBERTSON, CARL T. "On the Bookshelves." Cleveland Plain Dealer, February 7, p. 7.
(Review of The Whole Family.) This book with a chapter written by each of twelve "distinguished literary men and women," including James, is both funny and serious. There

is a real plot, and everyone "has taken everyone else more or less seriously" and cooperated. Even James "gambols polysyllabically and ponderously like a happy adolescent elephant, but generously abstains from hurling a wet blanket over what has gone before." The timid may skip his chapter. Whoever "got these big folks to consent" to do this book deserves much credit, but Mark Twain should have been included. (The other authors are Mary Heaton Vorse, William Dean Howells, Mary Wilkins Freeman, Mary Stewart Cutting, Elizabeth Jordan, John Kendrick Bangs, Elizabeth Stuart Phelps, Edith Wyatt, Mary R. S. Andrews, Alice Brown, and Henry van Dyke.)

95 ______. "On the Book Shop Shelves." Cleveland Plain Dealer, November 27, p. 6.

(Review of Italian Hours.) Those who like James like him, and those who do not do not. In this imposing book he provides very invigorating mental gymnastics to those with a taste for it. He is "much better" in his travel sketches than in his fiction. His involved style can be fun, and the chase after James's ideas, which he "is honestly trying to express," can be exhilarating, like a game. James "knows what is worth looking at," and few of the complainers about his admittedly difficult style could develop such an unmistakably individual style themselves.

96 SCOTT-JAMES, R. A. "Henry James' Preciosity." Chicago Evening Post Friday Literary Review, November 26, p. 6.

James's pride and aloofness from the common help to explain why his works have not gained the popularity they have deserved. (Supporting quotations from Italian Hours.)

97 SHELLEY, HENRY C. "The Book in London." Boston Evening Transcript, October 16, Part 3, p. 6.

(Note on Fortnightly Review.) In "Henry James and His Double" in the Fortnightly Review, W. A. Gill makes "a convincing case" for the close resemblance between Marivaux and James, noting especially "the wonderfully subtle and discriminating quality" of both men's intelligences. Both James and Marivaux have "a distinct philosophical gift."

98 SHUMAN, EDWIN L. "In Realm of Books." Chicago Record-Herald, February 20, p. 6.

(Review of New York Edition.) The "confessions and analyses" of James's prefaces are often more interesting than the stories. They show that he proceeds from "a central situation lighted on all sides and developed in the form of a picture" with minute "psychological stippling" of details. Those who enjoy his "static and intricate studies of minds and manners" will prize this edition.

1909

99 ______. "With Authors and Books." Chicago Record-Herald, September 23, p. 8.
(Review of New York Edition.) In the prefaces, the style is needlessly involved, and James's egotistical self-regard is in questionable taste. Yet, his judgment that The Ambassadors is his best work is correct, and the prefaces' exposition of the novelist's technique will be of value to budding writers.

100 SIMONDS, WILLIAM EDWARD. A Student's History of American Literature. Boston: Houghton Mifflin, pp. 336-337.
James's novels are associated with Howells's as "the best work of the American realists." James gives us "the extreme application of realistic theory" and "wonderfully minute" analysis of character and motive. His American audience is relatively small, and the international books like Daisy Miller aroused protest here. James is most admired for his artistic skill, and his keen wit and "general brilliancy of style" are evident in his short stories.

101 SMITH, GEORGE JAY. "After Reading Henry James." Life, 53 (June 17), 846.
(Humorous poem about reading The Golden Bowl parodies James's style.)

102 WALLACE, G. "Henry James as Caviar." New York Evening Post, December 1, p. 8.
(Letter to the Editor.) Most readers do not really understand James. He will long remain "caviar to the general," but he has "the glory of having concerned himself with the most difficult of modern character analysis, and of having produced masterpieces of literature."

*103 WILKINSON, WILLIAM CLEAVER. Some New Literary Valuations. New York: Funk & Wagnalls.
(Cited in Ricks.)

1910

1 ANON. Review of Julia Bride. American Monthly Review of Reviews, 41 (January), 124.
This "remarkable analysis of a social situation in the true James fashion" is an elaboration on an incident, without much plot or movement. It is "masterly, but not particularly sympathetic reading."

2 ANON. "The New Books." Outlook, 94 (January 1), 41-42.
(Review of Italian Hours.) Meredith's statement that

The American Scene was more a tour of James's insides than a tour of his native land is more applicable to James's later manner than to his early style, and applies to only a few chapters in this volume. The contrast between early and late styles shows, but here James is "always interesting, always picturesque, always full of suggestion."

3 ANON. "Julia Bride." Independent, 68 (January 6), 51.
(Review.) This story, in James's "most delightful and characteristic manner," is not for workers but for those with the leisure to "cultivate their delicacies and spiritual manners to the remotest decimal point." It concerns "the exquisite niceness of superfine people," and is "a textbook in snobbery written with the most discriminating sensibility."

4 ANON. "Literary Small Talk/. . . 'The Abject Actual.'" Chicago Evening Post Friday Literary Review, January 21, p. 7.
(Quotes James's "salient observations" on life after death, from the "discreet columns" of Harper's Bazaar.)

5 ANON. "Editions." A.L.A. Booklist, 6 (February), 227.
(Review of Italian Hours.) This volume contains "distinctive examples" of James's earlier and later manner.

6 ANON. "The New Books./Travel and Description." American Monthly Review of Reviews, 41 (February), 250.
(Review of Italian Hours.) This volume contains "exquisite and sympathetic descriptions."

7 ANON. "New Books." Harvard Graduates' Magazine, 18 (March), 425-426.
(Review of Italian Hours.) James is "foremost among the traveling Impressionists" and excels, equal to anyone, in this kind of work. The essays show his development as a stylist and how the sights affect his imagination. They will be read because he wrote them.

8 ANON. "Popular Birthdays/Here's How." Life, 55 (April 14), 678.
(Brief comments on James, with small pictures.) James's style is mysterious, his sentences are obstacles, and his "subtle delineations of character . . . are not for us," yet, without knowing why, "we have a boundless admiration" for him.

9 ANON. "Our Foolish Contemporaries . . . Poor Thompson." Life, 56 (July 14), 80.
(Reprinted anecdote from New York Tribune that quotes James's preference of small over large families.)

1910

10 ANON. "A New Storm Center in London." Life, 56 (August 11), 225.

(Brief mention. In a quotation from the New York Times James is mentioned among those included in the British Academy of Literature. The Life writer thinks they are good selections.)

11 ANON. "Books and Authors . . . More Stories by Henry James." Boston Daily Advertiser, November 5, p. 8.

(Review of The Finer Grain.) Like his brother, James is "highly psychological." The long, complicated sentences resulting from his "passion for minute analysis" make his works not for the great majority of readers. For his comparatively few "very loyal admirers, he has much charm," and "no writer of this English generation rivals him in understanding of feminine character."

12 ANON. "Books and Authors/Mr. Ingleside's Circle." Boston Daily Advertiser, November 5, p. 8.

(Review of E. V. Lucas's Mr. Ingleside.) "As usual, Mr. Lucas keeps his characters in touch with topics of the day. They talk of Rider Haggard and Henry James; of the era of the automobile; the sloppiness of much fiction; the postcard craze; the use of actresses' names and faces in booming toothpowders, and so on."

13 ANON. Review of The Finer Grain. Literary Digest, 41 (November 5), 819-820.

"The Round of Visits" and "Crapy Cornelia" reflect James's last visit to America. His work has always been notable for the contemporary note. "The Bench of Desolation" resembles The Wings of the Dove and shows how a master may reuse a single situation.

14 ANON. "News and Views in The World of Books . . . Books of Short Stories." New York World, November 5, p. 6.

(Review of The Finer Grain.) James is "quite himself" in these stories, and the book needs no other recommendation for readers who can follow his "cruel and unusual sentences."

15 ANON. "English Critics Find Much to Praise Among Novels Fresh From the Press." New York Herald, November 12, p. 15.

(Quoted critical comments on The Finer Grain from the London Mail, London Standard, and (London) Saturday Review to the effect that James's late style is difficult.)

16 ANON. "Notable Books of the Year." Independent, 69 (November 17), 1091.

(Review of The Finer Grain.) James deals with only the

human material "subject to the highest ornamental polish." He writes like both a woman and a man, and for a leisure class. Only he could describe the difficult, "delusive" aspect of his stories.

17 ANON. "The Season's Short Stories." Congregationalist and Christian World, 95 (November 19), 749.
(Review of The Finer Grain.) This volume contains James's later faults of "conceited obscurity," cringing before royalty, and "obsession" for illicit loves. The genius of "The Liar" and "The Altar of the Dead" has fallen into the inanities of "The Velvet Glove," and James dodders in the style of the later Balzac. Yet, "Crapy Cornelia" and "The Bench of Desolation" have the "indescribable charm" of James's earlier work.

18 ANON. "New Books and Their Makers/New Novels." Detroit Free Press, November 19, p. 6.
(Review of The Finer Grain.) These stories concern "those finer feelings that do not belong with the coarsegrained of humanity." As with James's writings in general, they are "distinguished for their deeper insight and particularity of detail."

19 ANON. "Word Juggling Mars 'The Finer Grain.'" New York Herald, November 26, p. 16.
(Review.) The fine literary art of an accomplished writer has degenerated into "mere word juggling." These stories are very difficult, their style maddening.

20 ANON. "Books" "The Finer Grain. By Henry James." Portland Morning Oregonian, November 27, Section 5, p. 9.
(Review.) It is because of James's "magic name" that such difficult, "prosy and uninteresting" stories get published. Such dullness is the reason "this once popular novelist is no longer popular."

21 ANON. "Fiction." A.L.A. Booklist, 7 (December), 164-165.
(Review of The Finer Grain.) These stories are in James's "most involved manner." They will be delightful to his admirers and unintelligible to the general reader.

22 ANON. "Current Fiction." Nation, 91 (December 1), 522-523.
(Review of The Finer Grain.) The style of this book is almost self-parody. Never has James's substance seemed "so attenuated, his manner so uselessly finicking." The stories are less tales than disquisitions about shadowy incidents.

23 ANON. "Current Fiction." New York Evening Post, December 3,

Supp., p. 8.
(Review of The Finer Grain.) The style of these stories becomes self-parody. Never has James's "substance seemed so attenuated, his manner so uselessly finicking."

24 ANON. "The Finer Grain/Stories in Henry James's Characteristic Manner." Philadelphia Public Ledger and Philadelphia Times, December 17, p. 12.
(Review.) Behind James's involved phraseology is usually a gem of thought or subtle humor unobscured by his curious mannerisms. The title story shows his indebtedness to Balzac. It and "The Velvet Glove" are more substantial and critically interesting than the others, which are more in James's "normal style and vein."

25 ANON. "Five Henry James Stories." Salt Lake Tribune, December 18, Last Section, p. 12.
(Review of The Finer Grain.) These stories have the usual "elusive, subtle quality" that makes James's stories hard, baffling reading. Yet, for the few with the time and patience, this book is more rewarding than most.

26 ANON. "New Books./Some Stories by Henry James." New York Sun, December 24, p. 7.
(Review of The Finer Grain.) The style of this "properly esteemed author" is very smooth, unhurried, and deliberate. This book gives a pleasure that fulfills expectations.

27 ANON. Review of The Finer Grain. Louisville Courier-Journal, December 31, p. 5.
With its double subtlety and fineness, this book will reward people of psychological bent who like chasing elusive motives.

28 BAILEY, MINNA KENNEDY. "In the World of Letters/Some of the New Books. The Finer Grain, by Henry James." St. Paul Pioneer Press, November 20, Section 3, p. 5.
This book will delight the James cult, and bore the rest. Only by being a close student of James can the reader endure not only his style but also his way of seeing "human relations in such an ethereal light, replacing all directness with subtlety and all frankness of emotion with a vague glimmer of feeling." He makes "the healthy-minded . . . sigh for the elemental."

29 FULLERTON, MORTON. "The Art of Henry James." Living Age, 265 (June 11), 643-652.
(Reprint of article from April 1910 [London] Quarterly Review.)

30 FURST, CLYDE. "American Prose Masters." Sewanee Review, 18 (October), 483-486.

(Review of W. C. Brownell's American Prose Masters.) Brownell's study of James is "a masterpiece of penetration and discrimination," perfect in its appreciation of the fecundity, sensitiveness, and contemporaneity of James's work. Yet, Brownell is too critical of his alleged narrowness, meticulousness, and elusiveness. James does not neglect "the province of the heart," and many feel his genius periodically enriches the world with new material and new representation drawn from a new return to nature.

*31 HACKETT, FRANCIS. Review of The Finer Grain. Chicago Evening Post Friday Literary Review, December 2, p. 1.

(Foley found this a "most flattering" review which called the stories first-rate products of a neglected genius and defended James against Arnold Bennett's criticisms, p. 130n.)

32 HARVEY, ALEXANDER. "The Literary Zoo./The Need of Worse Writers." Life, 56 (November 17), 879-881.

(In the context of the idea that good writers should employ bad writers to express their ideas originally, Harvey would enjoy hearing that James had hired a school boy to do his writing while James himself furnished the plot.)

33 _____. "The Literary Zoo . . . Writing About Nothing." Life, 56 (December 1), 956-957.

(Comments on The Finer Grain.) James shows his brilliance by making himself arresting when he has really nothing to say. These stories are for this and other reasons "quite irresistible" and are to be inhaled more than read.

34 _____. "The Literary Zoo . . . The Quest of the Wrong Word." Life, 56 (December 15), 1123.

(Brief mention.) The wrong word in James's "most characteristic passages" always has "its piquancy," but Gertrude Atherton can pick an "exquisitely and perfectly wrong" word out of thousands.

35 HARVEY, GEORGE. "New Books Reviewed." North American Review, 191 (May), 698-699.

(Review of Italian Hours.) The pictures, text, and informing spirit are all beautiful, reflecting both the enjoyment of youth and the golden, ripe serenity of "a wise and perfect maturity." These hours are "of the rarest stuff of life," testifying that the best of life is living and that the moment is valuable for its own sake.

36 IRVING, CARTER. "Henry James and His Art." New York Times

1910

Saturday Review of Books, 15 (November 5), 614.
(Review of The Finer Grain.) Like his characters, James's feeling and thinking have been refined too delicately for the grossness of the subject of human life. These stories show "the fatal effect of the microscopic habit." James's overuse of pet words blurs meanings and shocks the fastidious. In the "weirdly conceived and remarkably developed" "Bench of Desolation," James is "at his most interesting and memorable," if not at his best.

37 KERFOOT, J. B. "The Latest Books." Life, 55 (April 28), 771.
(Review of Gertrude Hall's The Unknown Quantity.) With full appreciation of James, one regrets seeing younger, serious writers adopt "the idiosyncratic forms of circumlocutions."

38 _____. "The Season's Books . . . The Guide." Life, 55 (June 23), 1150-1151.
(Listed is In After Days, by Howells, Higginson, John Bigelow, Elizabeth Stuart Phelps, Julia Ward Howe, H. M. Alden, W. H. Thompson, Guglielmo Ferrero, and James. Note says that their views of the future life tell little about immortality, but much about human nature.)

39 _____. "The Latest Books." Life, 56 (December 29), 1200.
(Review of Edith Wharton's Tales of Men and Ghosts.) The great trouble with the "super-civilized" literature of James and Edith Wharton is that it tends to fade away so that nothing remains but its supercivilization.

40 LARNED, W. T. "The Literary Zoo . . . Words, Words Words." Life, 55 (January 27), 181.
An essayist has noted that James is by turns as precious as Walter Pater and as democratic as Chimmie Fadden.

41 _____. "The Literary Zoo . . . Kansas Takes to Psychology." Life, 55 (January 27), 179-180.
(Brief reference.) The James boys Frank and Jesse are no longer better known in Kansas than are the New England James "boys" William and Henry.

42 _____. "The Literary Zoo . . . Poe's Taste in Poetry." Life, 55 (February 3), 223-225.
(Discusses the debate between James and Hamilton W. Mabie on Poe.)

43 L[ARNED], W[ILLIAM] T. "The Literary Zoo/Our Academy of Immortals." Life, 55 (February 3), 221.
(Brief mention.) James is among the writers and artists

chosen for the American Academy of Arts and Letters, and Larned agrees with the choice.

44 ______. "The Literary Zoo . . . For a Five-Inch Book Shelf." Life, 55 (March 24), 534-539.
Among those works that should appear on any five-inch book shelf of "Little Harvard Classics" are the novels of James, "translated and condensed."

45 ______. "The Literary Zoo/Bad News From Boston." Life, 55 (June 23), 1154.
(Brief reference. In the context of changes in the Atlantic Monthly, Larned would not like to see James using "the fine-tooth comb of his style in straightening out the kinks of the negro question.")

46 LUCAS, E[DWARD] V[ERRALL]. Mr. Ingleside. New York: Macmillan. Rpt. 1913.
(Characters mention James.)

47 M[ARTIN], E[DWARD] S. "Colleges and Writers." Life, 56 (October 20), 657.
(Brief mention.) James, like Kipling, Dickens, Mark Twain, Conrad, and other very talented writers, never went to college.

48 [MATHER, FRANK JEWETT.] "Two Frontiersmen." Nation, 90 (April 28), 422-423.
Mark Twain and Henry James are probably the greatest American writers of the end of the nineteenth century, and have more fully satisfied their native gifts than have any of their contemporaries. Though they have gone as far as possible in "diametrically opposed directions," they are both frontiersmen. James is the "scrupulous analyst" of a spiritual frontier less robust than Twain's real one. James is the prophet of the gentle, brooding, discursive type of American who lacks simplicity and constructive energy. Future literary historians will probably choose Twain rather than James as this period's great representative American writer.

49 P., L. "Books of the Day, . . . The Finer Grain/Henry James at the Head of a List of Recent Fiction." Boston Evening Transcript, December 21, p. 20.
(Review.) James "has taught us to catch glints of the rich and rare in what we had always supposed crass and common." Though his discriminations grow finer and finer, these characters are exceptional and companionable and remain fresh on rereading.

1910

50 PEATTIE, ELIA W. "Among the New Books." Chicago Tribune, December 3, p. 9.
(Review of The Finer Grain.) These stories are circuitous, their meanings are obscure, and the characters communicate too indirectly.

51 PIER, FLORIDA. "The Gentler View/Pale Adventurers." Harper's Weekly, 54 (December 10), 35.
(Review of The Finer Grain.) Lately, James substitutes meagre, faded old New England gentlemen for the "glowing" young heroines who used to be his main characters. Through them James gives us "a lesson in fine manners that we gladly, if a little yawningly, follow."

52 QUINN, ARTHUR HOBSON. "Some Phases of the Supernatural in American Literature." PMLA, 25:132-133.
Some of James's earliest stories resemble Hawthorne, but his "later and most powerful" supernatural story, The Turn of the Screw, does not.

53 RANSMEIER, JOHN C. "Recent Publications/The New Books." New Orleans Daily Picayune, December 4, Part 3, p. 10.
(Review of The Finer Grain.) These stories suffer from James's usual lack of definiteness, a failure of either perception or expression. Despite its admirers and its intrinsic interest, his style is to most readers "irritating, confusing, and needlessly obscure." Yet, he has a claim to consideration as an impressionist, and he is "undoubtedly . . . in the ranks of accepted writers."

54 SHUMAN, EDWIN L. "With Authors and Books." Chicago Record-Herald, November 1, p. 8.
(Review of The Finer Grain.) This volume is characteristic of James's "later, tantalizing phase." To be interested in these wearisomely detailed, descriptive stories requires deliberate effort. Yet, James is a finished artist in the carving of cherry stones. The situations are interesting, but because he treats them psychologically and intellectually rather than dramatically and sentimentally, the characters are shadowy pawns whose game fails to touch the emotions.

55 WHITE, WILLIAM ALLEN. "Books and Authors/Literary Notes." Boston Daily Advertiser, November 4, p. 8.
(Quoted critical comment.) A quote from William Allen White in the Emporia (Kansas) Gazette expresses rage at the idea that James's latest short stories have "any virtue." White says that although James "is considered, by the highbrows, as one of the great writers of this time," workingmen are "the greatest book buyers of this country" and they read authors they can understand, rather than James and Whitman.

1911

1 ANON. "Some Excellent Short Stories." American Monthly Review of Reviews, 43 (January), 120.
(Review of The Finer Grain.) James's volume is one of "three delectable dishes" from Scribner's. James dispenses "subtilized caviare," but it would be hard to find any writer, in any time, with a superior observing and analyzing intelligence, a more "observant and complex mind." (In review of Edith Wharton's Tales of Men and Ghosts, comment on her debt to James.)

2 ANON. "Henry James." Book Buyer, 35 (January), 231.
(Quotes the London Athenaeum's comments on The Finer Grain.)

3 ANON. "For the Reader of New Fiction . . ./The Finer Grain." Book News Monthly, 29 (January), 333-334.
(Review.) The polish and finish of James's works are appealing and stand out in modern fiction. This volume contains "fine psychological" studies "worthy of careful reading." The most striking is "Mora Montravers," whose ending is interesting and commendable. All the stories "show a pleasing familiarity with the really best things of life."

4 ANON. "Life's Family Album/A Confidential Guide to J. B. Kerfoot." Life, 57 (January 5), 60.
(Brief humorous reference. Kerfoot, Life's book reviewer, has an invisible edition of James.)

5 ANON. "New Books Reviewed." North American Review, 193 (February), 302.
(Review of The Finer Grain.) In his middle years James attained a perfect manner for his subtle, psychological subjects, but lately the complexity of his style is irritating. "The Bench of Desolation" is "the finest and the most Jamesian" of these stories, its exquisiteness faintly suggesting the "absolutely perfect" "Altar of the Dead." James modifies his usual aloofness toward his characters with "a humorous and gentle tenderness."

6 ANON. "Life's Family Album/T. S. Allen." Life, 57 (April 13), 746.
(Brief reference. In this mock interview, Life artist Allen lists James with Life writers John Ames Mitchell, E. S. Martin, James Metcalfe, J. B. Kerfoot, and Andrew Miller as his favorite authors.)

7 ANON. "Judge Chesterfield's Letters to His Son." Life, 58

(September 7), 383.
(Brief reference. In this satirical piece, Chesterfield advises that reading James should be left to puzzle-solvers and to women.)

8 ANON. "Lies." Life, 58 (September 21), 468.
(Brief humorous reference. One "lie" says that James has become a sign painter.)

9 ANON. "Gossip of Authors." San Francisco Chronicle, October 15, p. 6.
(Note.) In his new book with "the characteristic but not too esoteric title" The Outcry, James "may be counted upon for a striking discussion" of the issue of who should possess great art, a question "exercising England" and the rest of Europe.

10 ANON. "Books and Authors/The Portraits of Their Ancestors." Boston Daily Advertiser, October 21, p. 8.
(Review of The Outcry.) James "wraps . . . with circumambient prose" the feeling that great works of art belong to a nation rather than an individual. The "most downright statement" in the story is a criticism of America.

11 ANON. "Literary Notes." Louisville Courier-Journal, October 21, p. 8.
(Note on the situation in The Outcry.)

12 ANON. "Half a Dozen Stories." Outlook, 99 (October 21), 405-406.
(Review of The Outcry.) This very interesting, "immensely clever story" gives "an intellectual, but hardly a literary, pleasure." Its style is "the language of ultimate inference," hard to follow.

13 ANON. "News and Views of Books . . . Mr. James Obscures Anew." New York World, October 21, p. 10.
(Review of The Outcry.) This story is worth telling and could be a "delightful comedy" if not for James's "mistreatment of the English tongue," his too elaborate style, the monotonous quality of the conversations.

14 ANON. "The Literary Review/Newest Books/Latest Magazines." Detroit Free Press, October 28, p. 11.
(Review of The Outcry.) This novel's purpose is serious, but James's sentences are cryptic, unkind to English, and an outrage in a writer of his reputation. The characters all talk so much like James that "the James cult must have been as contagious as measles in little England," and the story

might be clever if not written in James's "peculiar 'dialect.'"

15 ANON. "New Books./The Experience of a Devourer." New York Sun, October 28, p. 8.
(Review of The Outcry.) James "has great fun with the characters" and must have been "in a happy mood" when he wrote the story.

16 ANON. "An 'Outcry' from Mr. Henry James." New York Times Saturday Review of Books, 17 (October 29), 687.
(Review of The Outcry.) Here, James is "at his worst and his best." With its opportunities for stating "with infinite refinement" the "intricacies of impulse and complex mental process" of refined idlers without "crude primary motives," the theme is exceptionally well suited to James's taste. It is worthy of him, and he handles it with ingenuity, humor, sharpness, and perspicacity. Yet, despite his fine phrases and "crisply expressive, admirable flashes," James's obsession with certain words keeps him from expressing himself exactly.

17 ANON. "The Outcry." Independent, 71 (November 2), 982.
(Review.) Here is "an infamous debauch of adverbs, challenging comparison" with James's other works. The book is "colossal in its indirection."

18 ANON. "English Notes on Recent Books." New York Herald, November 4, p. 8.
(Note on The Outcry.) The Outcry "is receiving much attention from the English press on account of its subject, as well as its author." (Quotation from the London Academy on The Outcry.)

19 ANON. Review of The Outcry. Detroit News, November 5, Women's Section, p. 15.
This book is written in characteristic James style, "but perhaps some people will enjoy it."

20 ANON. "The Magazines, and Native and Foreign Contributors." St. Paul Pioneer Press, November 5, Third Section, p. 10.
James cannot be listed among American writers "because he lives abroad so much."

21 ANON. "Some of the New Books This Week/'The Outcry.' by Henry James." St. Paul Pioneer Press, November 5, Third Section, p. 10.
(Review.) "People may be classified as those who read Henry James' novels and those who don't." He has "many

exasperating mannerisms," but also some "preeminent virtues." In this book "his virtues reduce his defects to comparative insignificance." The Outcry "is equal to the possibilities of its theme," is "high comedy, firmly wrought, and of delicate proportions."

22 ANON. "Current Fiction," Nation, 93 (November 9), 444-445.
(Review of The Outcry.) This story is like a play, in effect "a social comedy in three acts," "excessively 'well-built,'" with machinery of the stage "totally indifferent to the new cry against coincidence." Bender, like the other characters, is in outline a conventional stage figure, but James makes him live more than any of the others, who are yet "sufficiently amusing."

23 ANON. "Reviews of New Books." Hartford Courant, November 10, p. 15.
(Review of The Outcry.) "Octave Thanet or Owen Wister would have made a fairish magazine short story of this pretentious book." The characters all speak James's "peculiarly involved language."

24 ANON. "Literature." New York Evening Post, November 11, Supp., p. 7.
(Review of The Outcry.) This novel is constructed like a play. Bender, like the other characters, is "in outline a conventional stage figure," but he has more life than the other "still sufficiently amusing figures."

25 ANON. "Life's Commonplaces Dealt with in Books of the Week." New York Herald, November 11, p. 8.
(Review of Arnold Bennett's Hilda Lessways.) Sometimes this book resembles James's earlier work, "in which those fine distinctions which enable close students of human life to distinguish one Bostonian from another were remorselessly revealed." But James was dealing with a society in which, at the time, subtleties counted, while Bennett cultivates "the most barren literary soil," the provincial life of Great Britain.

26 ANON. Review of The Outcry. New Orleans Daily Picayune, November 12, Part III, p. 10.
This is "one of the best pieces of analytical work" James has done in years. He "has handled his theme very cleverly," developed his situation in "his characteristic, persistent and effective way," led up to the crisis skillfully, portrayed characters "distinctly and yet delicately," and excelled in analysis of character and motive.

27 ANON. "A Henry James Novel." Salt Lake Tribune, November 12, Magazine Section, p. 9.
(Review of The Outcry.) In this book James is less obscure than is usual in his analytic stories, and the characters are more distinct. The James cult may not like it as well as some of his others, "but the general public will like it correspondingly better."

28 ANON. "Henry James's New Book." Literary Digest, 43 (November 18), 924.
(Review of The Outcry.) In this novel James is "more up to date" than ever, and he was never guilty of missing "a point of great contemporary interest." The dialogue is puzzling, but the book is "an amazing tour de force" and shows James's "tremendous sense for the theater."

29 ANON. Review of The Outcry. New York Herald, November 18, p. 10.
This story is entangled in an obscuring maze of adverbs. Lord Theign is one of those unrealistic and "intensely conservative noblemen" James delights in. Given the author's subject and skills, the book "should have been much more interesting."

30 ANON. "'The Outcry.'/Henry James Writes a Comedy on the Commercialization of Art." San Francisco Chronicle, November 19, p. 6.
(Review.) James's "art of using language to obscure rather than wholly to conceal thought is one in which this most thoughtful of all modern novelists has no equal," and one which would have made him "a striking success as a political orator." Unlike Meredith, "James achieves obscurity by omitting nothing," yet he also "is a master of Meredithian metaphor," has "seductively puzzling plots, and in character analysis is without a peer among contemporary novelists." The Outcry is "a delightful comedy" whose dialogue, though in Jamesese, is "often brilliant." The book is James's best in the last two decades, and assures the enjoyment of the attentive reader.

31 ANON. "Fiction." A.L.A. Booklist, 8 (December), 174.
(Review of The Outcry.) This story has all James's "delicate humor and gift for keen analysis," with a style less involved than usual.

32 ANON. "For the Reader of New Fiction . . ./The Outcry." Book News, 30 (December), 278, 288.
(Review.) James "has been justly called the greatest modern master of analytical fiction," this study in wellbred

conversation shows him in "one of his best humors," and because his imitators can never match him in this vein, his books are welcome. He enjoys using "unusual adjectives."

33 ANON. "The Latest Books and Literary News." Chicago Inter-Ocean, December 2, p. 5.
(Review of The Outcry.) This book is more "fanatically Henry Jamesish" than James has ever been before. Although his devotees may read and like it, people "who are fond of real English, real stories, can't."

34 ANON. "New Books/Other Books. New York Sun, December 2, p. 11.
(Review of 1911.48.) "There is no accounting for tastes and there may be people who will enjoy reading every day in their lives a scrap" of James's writing.

35 BALLINGFORD, J. BOUNDER. "Coronation Postponed." Life, 57 (June 15), 1155.
(Brief reference. In this satire, James was present at a dinner given by the literary men of England.)

36 BURTON, RICHARD. "The Bellman Bookshelf." Bellman, 11 (December 2), 722.
(Review of The Outcry.) One hardly knows how to react to this "supersubtle" study by a "practically British" author. Its meaning leaks through language which has more "indirection, finesse, involution" than anything in English letters before Browning.

37 CLARK, WARD. "Henry James's 'The Outcry.'" Bookman, 34 (December), 434-435.
(Review.) A few years ago outbursts of abuse and ridicule greeted each of James's successive books, culminating in The Golden Bowl. Yet, surprisingly, he now with calm assurance "holds his place secure, if apart, among the masters of fiction." In those earlier days it took courage to defend him, but now "the burden of proof is thrown upon those who still blindly deny his patent if limited genius." James's "social comedy is an artificial creation," like Wycherly's or Sheridan's, and he himself practically concedes certain of his faults. His manner and mannerisms are "the inevitable accompaniment of his real accomplishment," which is to bring out "the subconscious or semi-conscious motives and emotions" beneath the thought of a highly strung, finely organized society. The Outcry is not one of James's great works, but it may extend his influence to some who have not read him since Daisy Miller. Its comedy is "mellower, cheerier" than that of The Spoils of Poynton,

and it is on the whole more "human" than some of James's works. It is "capital social comedy" which does not go deep into personal or social life, but "plays charmingly on the surface" with genial humor rather than brilliant wit.

38 GUITERMAN, ARTHUR. "The New Inferno." Life, 58 (October 26), 706.
(Brief humorous reference. In the new inferno, Colonel George B. McC. Harvey sits "in woe immersed" reading Henry James.)

*39 HALLECK, REUBEN POST. History of American Literature. New York: American Book Co.
(Cited in Ricks.)

40 LEE, RUTH. "Life's Suffragette Contest . . . XXIX/With Apologies to Mr. Henry James." Life, 57 (January 5), 14.
(Humorous item. This short statement on why a man should not marry a suffragette parodies James's style.)

41 M[ASSON], T[HOMAS] L. "The Literary Zoo . . . The Higher Fiction." Life, 57 (March 23), 592.
(Sarcastic comparison of the "lower," descriptive, materialistic fiction illustrated by A Tale of Two Cities, with the "higher" fiction of James, illustrated by a complicated excerpt from The Finer Grain.) The "Higher Fiction" avoids simple statements of facts, deals in mental situations, and gives its characters the form of algebraic equations.

42 METCALFE, [JAMES S.] "Drama/Not Putting Our Best Foot Forward." Life, 57 (February 9), 308.
(Review of Edward Sheldon's "The Boss.") Metcalfe agrees with criticisms he imagines James would make of this melodramatic play and its lack of culture and refinement. James is no longer intimately acquainted with American life.

43 P., L. "The Outcry/Henry James's Unsatisfied Yearning for the Stage." Boston Evening Transcript, November 11, p. 9.
(Review.) The Outcry is like a play in three acts, and reflects James's unsatisfied yearning for the stage. As a play it would be too slow and uncompelling, but as narrative it is "the most spirited thing" James has done in recent years. Despite James's usual adverbs, the speech is plainer than usual, and "sparkles" with his characteristic quiet wit. The comedy is "sprightly, timely, aglow with the verbal richness" for which we turn to James almost alone among the moderns. Though he may never again produce such a notable "social epic" as The Ambassadors, he continually surprises

and delights and never disappoints us. May he continue to write, and may we, like the crowd in Goethe's Faust, continue to demand and read him.

44 PEATTIE, ELIA W. "Fiction Reviews/Literary Gossip." Chicago Tribune, November 4, p. 11.
(Review of The Outcry.) This "romance about pictures" does not really have a conclusion, reading it requires an "undue amount of concentration," and Lady Grace's sterling character is "the one high light--the one reassuring note."

45 QUENTIN, JOSEPH M. "Books." Portland Morning Oregonian, December 10, Section 5, p. 9.
(Review of The Outcry.) James "comes into literary prominence again" with this new book in "that high-flown department" of analytical fiction. The fine literary work and fairly interesting plot show that the quasi-Englishman James can "come back" from the vein of his soporific efforts of recent years. The book "has a welcome call and is worth a careful reading."

*46 SELDES, G. U. "Henry James: An Appreciation." Harvard Monthly, 53 (December), 92-100.
(Unlocated. Cited in Ricks.)

47 SHUMAN, EDWIN L. "With Authors and Books/Henry James and Others." Chicago Record-Herald, October 28, p. 11.
(Review of The Outcry.) Here, James has simplified considerably his "elusive and rather difficult psychological manner." As usual, the plot is a "seductive puzzle, piquing curiosity" amid the "play of fancy and Meredithian metaphor." James is unsurpassed by any living writer in cleverly bringing out psychological subtleties, and his dissection of motives is "delightful, true, even humorous." The characters are not memorable, and they all talk like James; the story is not great, but it is "a small gem of its kind."

48 SMALLEY, EVELYN GARNAUT. The Henry James Yearbook. Boston: R. G. Badger.
(Introductory statements by the editor and W. D. Howells praise James. See 1911.34.)

49 THOMSON, JOHN. "'The Outcry' By Henry James/Fine Protest Against the Sale of Heirlooms of National Importance." Philadelphia Public Ledger and Philadelphia Times, November 6, p. 6.
(Review.) The theme "is finely brought out" in this book, and the characters are drawn with "a subtle realism." The "firm basis of fact" in which this "literary gem" is set

"adds vastly to its interest," and despite James's "usual obscurities" of style, "the refinement of his diction" and the polished sentences make the book "a finished product of modern literature."

1912

1 ANON. "The Outcry." North American Review, 195 (January), 141-143.

(Review.) This novel is really "a charming drama." James's art is so finished and fine, "his perception so subtle, and his irony so quietly comprehensive," that his work is "caviare to the general," but happy are those who can enjoy his excellence, power, and art. James compliments his readers by appealing to their intelligence and imagination. Though people object that James is too little emotional and too fearful of the common and commonplace, his "marvelous power of elimination" and distillation make his realism superior to that of mere accumulation of detail.

2 ANON. "The Season's Best Fiction/Some Novels of Distinction." American Monthly Review of Reviews, 45 (January), 122.

(Review of The Outcry.) Less cryptic than usual, James provides "a delightful social comedy." His "language alone gives an education."

3 ANON. Joke. Life, 59 (January 4), 62.

James is "hopelessly involved."

4 ANON. "Other Stories." Congregationalist and Christian World, 97 (January 6), 23.

(Review of The Outcry.) This story has a lucid plot, comprehensible sentences, and charming characters. Lady Sandgate is one of James's "most alluring and touching women."

5 ANON. "Recent Fiction and the Critics." Current Literature, 52 (February), 235-236.

(Review of The Outcry.) All James's stories have "a certain importance" as studies of English character. In this book James is often "innocently the victim of the cliché," and reviewers think this novel was originally a play. It is filled with complexities, mysteries, strange notes, and unrealistic conversations, yet overall it seems "absolutely true to life." (Quotations from reviews in the London Outlook, New York Evening Post, Chicago Tribune, and Academy.)

1912

6 ANON. Review of Joseph Conrad's Under Western Eyes. Current Literature, 52 (February), 236.
James makes "the sophisticated people of England" comprehensible to the great world west of them.

7 ANON. "'The Outcry.'" San Francisco Call, February 4, p. 7.
(Review.) One need not be an expert on James's "strange and curious" style to understand this book. The dialogue is less Jamesian than the "stage directions" between speeches, which are James "at his very worst." Though the argument against American art stealing is unconvincing, this "pleasant little comedy" can, with skipping, provide "a certain heavy intellectual enjoyment."

8 ANON. "Mr. James and Mr. Howells." New York Times, April 4, p. 12.
(Editorial. Comments on James's North American Review seventy-fifth birthday letter to Howells, with quotation (see 1912.18.) Twenty years ago, James's and Howells's names were coupled, but now they are thought to contrast since James has "widely departed" from his earlier line of development while Howells has stayed with his. Therefore, James's simple, sincere appreciation of Howells's work is very interesting, and as clear, convincing, and just as any.

9 ANON. "Journalism and Literature." Life, 59 (May 16), 1047.
(Brief reference. Ironic suggestion that literature has become so realistic that a hyperbolic journalism is the sole outlet for the literary imagination.) Thomas Hardy, James, and H. G. Wells write novels whose "every elusive word . . . is absolutely and irrevocably true."

10 ANON. "Henry James and Others on Browning." Literary Digest, 44 (June 1), 1159-1160.
(Notes, quotation, and comments on British response to James's talk on The Ring and the Book for the May 7 Browning centenary.) James is so commonly "a butt for journalistic witticisms that the enthusiasm of the London reporters over this address is worth recording." (Quotes favorable comments from the Pall Mall Gazette.)

11 ANON. "Intimate Interviews." Life, 60 (July 25), 1486.
(Humorous article. James "interviews" himself, discussing his intricate style, his subtlety and ambiguity, and his "highbrow intellectual art attitude" as "abnormal habits" grafted upon his "exceedingly simple nature." Caricature by James Montgomery Flagg.)

12 ANON. "If Mr. Henry James Had Written 'The Ring and the Book.'"

Literary Digest, 45 (September 21), 467-468.
(Discussion, with long quotations, of James's May 1912 centenary address on Browning to the Academic Committee of the Royal Society on Literature.) In his treatment of The Ring and the Book, James makes "a superb application" of the theory expounded in his New York Edition prefaces.

13 ANON. "From the Bookman Mail Bag." Bookman, 36 (October), 176-177.
(Reader's request for a résumé of the story of The Golden Bowl, and specifically the answer to whether Mrs. Rance was in the billiard room. The editors reply.) In guessing at implied improprieties in this book, the reader "is more apt to fall short of the author's own imaginings than to surpass him."

14 BEERBOHM, MAX. "The Mote in the Middle Distance." A Xmas Garland, Woven by Max Beerbohm. New York: E. P. Dutton. Rpt. in The Question of Henry James, A Collection of Critical Essays. Ed. F. W. Dupree. New York: Henry Holt, 1945, pp. 40-43.
(Parody of James's style.)

15 CAIRNS, WILLIAM B. A History of American Literature. New York: Oxford University Press, pp. 231, 463, 470. Rpt. 1916.
James and Howells are "the two most distinguished living American novelists." They study and portray things "as they are."

16 GRETTON, M. STURGE. "Mr. Henry James and His Prefaces." Living Age, 272 (February 3), 287-295.
(Reprint of article from the January 1912 Contemporary Review.)

17 HOLLIDAY, ROBERT C. "Henry James, Himself/Showing that a Clerk Can Look at a Celebrity to Some Purpose, and Presenting a Great American." New York Evening Post, October 26, Supp., p. 1.
(A New York bookstore clerk describes a number of James's visits to his shop. Emphasizes James's intense interest in the books, his earnestness, and his democratic respect and deference toward the clerk himself.)

18 JAMES, HENRY. "By Mr. James/A Letter To Mr. Howells." North American Review, 195 (April), 558-562.
(Letter. Reprint of James's letter to Howells regretting his inability to attend Howells's birthday celebration. Reminisces over their years of literary acquaintance and praises Howells's work. See 1912.8.)

1912

19 McINTYRE, CLARE. "The Later Manner of Henry James." PMLA, 27, 354-371.
(By comparing the original and revised editions of four James novels, McIntyre explores causes for the increasing obscurity of James's originally clear style.) In his later manner, James substitutes the general for the particular. His sentences show a foreign influence, and an attempt to write conversationally. All the characters talk alike. The Portrait of a Lady is "one of the finest of modern novels," but The Golden Bowl is vague in expression and more words often mean less thought. Only James's most extreme supporters would say his more obtrusive style is a gain in "sense and vigor."

20 PERRY, BLISS. The American Mind. Boston: Houghton Mifflin, pp. 51, 56-57.
Long ago James and Howells attained "an unmatched artistry" in the international novel. James will portray "with unrivalled psychological insight" the Europeanized American of the 1870s and 1880s, and thus contribute to our national self-definition.

21 PITKIN, WALTER B. "What Is a Short Story?" The Art and The Business of Story Writing. New York: Macmillan, pp. 34-37, 40. Rpt. 1913, 1914, 1915, 1916.
(Discussion of the contrast between The Turn of the Screw and O. Henry's The Furnished Room. The Aspern Papers is mentioned as a typical novelette.)

22 TABER, HARRY PERSONS. "The Jabberwocky of Authors." Life, 60 (August 22), 1654.
(Humorous poem reprinted from Evening Mail mentions James.)

23 TRENT, W. P., and ERSKINE, JOHN. Great American Writers. New York: Henry Holt, p. 244.
(Reference to James and Howells as "eminent contemporaries" of Mark Twain whose position in American literature is different from his.)

1913

1 ANON. "Books of the Week." New York Globe and Commercial Advertiser, March 15, p. 8.
(Review of A Small Boy and Others. Quotations from the descriptions of James's meetings with General Winfield Scott and Thackeray.)

*2 ANON. New York Times Saturday Review of Books, 18 (April 20), 236.
(Unlocated. Cited in Foley and Ricks.)

3 ANON. "Small Boy And Others." Philadelphia Press, April 21, p. 11.
(Review.) This is "truly a most interesting book," with "fascinating appreciations" of books and the stage, and "delightful" glimpses of William that generously acknowledge the older brother's "superior intellectuality."

4 ANON. "General Literature." A.L.A. Booklist, 9 (May), 375.
(Review of A Small Boy and Others. Favorable quotation from Publishers' Weekly.) Despite its "involved and difficult style, the work will interest a considerable body of readers."

5 ANON. "Henry James Remembers." Louisville Courier-Journal, May 3, p. 5.
(Review of A Small Boy and Others.) This "mellow, richly human" reminiscence will delight some (the elect) and confuse many. The details blur the general effect.

6 ANON. "Literary Criticism and Book News." New York Tribune, 13 (May 3), 10.
(Review of A Small Boy and Others.) James is "reticence itself," and abounds in "delicate suggestion" while leaving the facts to take care of themselves. The book has charm, and the reader is sustained through difficulty and much bland psychological minutiae by loyalty to "so fine a type of the literary conscience," a devoted artist deserving "admiration and respect."

7 ANON. "News and Views of Books," "As A Boy in Old New York/ Henry James Tells Delightfully of What He Saw and Heard." New York World, May 3, p. 6.
(Review of A Small Boy and Others.) James "still can write delightful English" in chapters "charmingly clear and direct." "Any number of readers" would welcome more James reminiscences.

8 ANON. "Painting James's Portrait/For Sake of Novelist, Sargent Breaks His Recent Determination." New York Times, May 4, Part 3, p. 2.
(News item on John Sargent's deciding to paint James refers to their friendship, and to James's "interesting essay" on Sargent published in the early 1880s.)

9 ANON. "The House of James." Boston Herald, May 17, p. 4.
(Review of A Small Boy and Others.) In the "stately and

gracious sentences" of "his best and most astonishing manner," James records impressions with the right amount of elaboration, yet keeps the boy's point of view. He writes of real and fictional people with "lively indirection."

10 ANON. "Essays and Miscellany . . . Two Boyhoods." American Monthly Review of Reviews, 47 (June), 761.
(Review of A Small Boy and Others.) James's story is well told and has an appeal. His achievements "have fulfilled the promise of youth."

11 ANON. "Literature and Art." Current Opinion, 54 (June), 489-490.
(Quoted excerpts from and commentary on A Small Boy and Others, with photograph. Also, quotation from London Athenaeum and from R. A. Scott-James's remarks on James in "Literature a Fine Art," English Review, April 1913.) A Small Boy is a volume of "super-realistic memoirs." As What Maisie Knew has shown, James is "past master of the psychology of childhood." James's place as "our foremost artist in words is undisputed," yet Americans find his books increasingly hard to read.

12 ANON. "New Books Reviewed." North American Review, 197 (June), 863-864.
(Review of A Small Boy and Others.) James has genius in "his own peculiar and individual field." He writes autobiography in a very teasing fashion, in "perversely flashing and colorful impressions" that require the reader to imagine practically all the reality. The view permitted of William James is too vague, but the glimpses of General Winfield Scott and Thackeray are more satisfactory.

13 ANON. "Three Old Boys." Independent, 75 (July 3), 43-44.
(Review of A Small Boy and Others.) This book has "rare reminiscences," beauty, and "provoking dislocation as to individualities." James repaints scenes more successfully than he evokes the image of himself and his distinguished brother. The picture of himself as a child is shadowy, "a flitting phantom." Starting with rich fancies, James "failed not to reach the hard ground of fact in fiction." Both he and John Muir "have done remarkable pioneer work for America." His style has "handsom vocables" but is labyrinthine.

14 ANON. "The Boyhood of Henry James." Nation, 97 (July 24), 79-80.
(Review of A Small Boy and Others.) This book is hard to follow, since James is as intricate as ever, and this narrative is "literally incomparable." James writes with

"a pontifical majesty" and lately a "princely indifference to readers." Despite the "occasional brilliant flashes of characterization," the passages of "cold humor," and the felicitous phrases, it is regrettable that James should have spent time on "such trivial fond records as these."

15 ANON. Review of A Small Boy and Others. Bookman, 37 (August), 595-598.

James has the fine literary gift necessary to evoke the youth of one so precocious as himself, and he does it "with a freedom wholly delightful." The figure of the small Henry James is remarkable and engaging, and the pictures of places are equally "entertaining, bright, vivid."

16 ANON. "The Hundred Best Books of the Year." New York Times Saturday Review of Books, 18 (November 30), 672.

(Includes and comments on A Small Boy and Others.) This "very delightful book" of "charming memories" has James's "zeal for analysis and exact statement," but does not attempt an accurate, chronological account. It is well worth reading, and gives vivid glimpses of the author, his father, and William.

17 BICKNELL, PERCY. "Mr. James's Memories of Boyhood." Dial, 54 (May 1), 372-374.

(Review of A Small Boy and Others.) As a work of art, this book seems of "the Impressionist school," with suggestions of Pre-Raphaelitism and perhaps other more recent trends. The book "is a piece of exquisite artistry," with all the characteristics of James's style "raised to their highest power." Even "the less ardent admirers" of this style "cannot but feel the charm" of this remarkable autobiography.

18 COLBY, F. M. "The Book of the Week." Harper's Weekly, 57 (May 3), 18.

(Review of A Small Boy and Others.) James is obscure and, as many reviewers have noted, he loses his reader. He in effect had no boyhood, and observed and analyzed social types and groups even when very young. His social observances and standards are secondary ones, and his phantomlike characters never set off "against an ultimate reality." All conclusions about James are rash, he is the "pons asinorum of current criticism," and the only critic in America who has written adequately of him is W. C. Brownell. (Portrait.)

19 E[DGETT], E[DWIN] F[RANCIS]. "The Newest Henry James/'A Small Boy and Others' Begins in Biography, Ends in Autobiography." Boston Evening Transcript, April 2, p. 2.

1913

(Review.) The autobiography of this "super-realist" is "discursive, reflective, introspective, analytic," and has more to do with states of mind than with external events. It is "of rare quality," and "in its completeness and in every detail" an "extraordinary account" of James's personality and career, "unlike any other autobiography ever written." These qualities make up for the meagreness of the glimpses of William.

20 FORD, JAMES L. "Variety of Themes Are Covered in the Week's New Books." New York Herald, April 5, p. 9.
(Review of A Small Boy and Others.) A simplification of James's "involved and exuberant style" is the only thing needed to make this book "delightful reading."

21 GILDER, JEANNETTE L. "Henry James' Autobiography." Chicago Tribune, April 5, p. 8.
(Review of A Small Boy and Others.) Despite the complexity of James's style, this is "a most unique and delightful fragment of autobiography," unlike any other ever written because it is in his "peculiar later method." Though difficult, the book is "full of good things" and rewards the reader's effort.

22 K., J. "The New Books." Churchman, 107 (May 10), 610.
(Review of A Small Boy and Others.) These are "charming reminiscences" in James's "characteristic style." He tells his memories "with the sympathy and reverence which are the duty of all who write of childhood."

*23 KILMER, JOYCE. Review of A Small Boy and Others. New York Times Saturday Review of Books, 18 (April 13), 217.
(Unlocated. Cited in Foley and Ricks.)

24 LARNED, W. T. "Who's Really Who in Letters." Life, 62 (July 17), 134.
(Brief mention. James is listed among the forty American novelists of note in the Century Dictionary of Names.)

25 LONG, WILLIAM J. American Literature: A Study of the Men and the Books That in the Earlier and Later Times Reflect the American Spirit. Boston: Ginn & Co., pp. 457, 460.
James and Howells are prominent among recent novelists. James's characters are almost too small to be called heroes and heroines.

26 MABIE, HAMILTON WRIGHT. "American Novelists." Mentor, 1 (August 4), 1-4.
James's flexible, mature-sounding style, able to convey

"fine distinctions and delicate shadings of thought," was something new in American fiction a generation ago. His early stories arrested attention with their "insight into character" and their fine workmanship. They had the romance of human temperament, not of incident, and James brought out character by "analysis and description," rather than by action. In recent years, his habit of analysis has grown so that his stories' movement is impeded, and his style has become complex and obscure. Few writers have been more acutely penetrating or have painted character more delicately, and James is among the small group of American writers with real distinction.

27 MACY, JOHN. The Spirit of American Literature. New York: Doubleday, Page, pp. viii, 16, 79-81, 96, 149-150, 209, 298, 324-339.

James is "one of the best critical minds of our time." His essay on Lowell is good, and his study of Hawthorne is excellent, but he exaggerates the inadequacy of the American environment as material for fiction. His, Poe's, Hawthorne's, and Howells's stories are "admirable in manner," but thin and lacking "large vitality." There are better storytellers than James, but none more interesting or intelligent. Ignorant of Americans at home, he does not really make international comparisons either. The contrasts he so "minutely and faithfully studies" are between individuals rather than national types. Although his view of a limited range of humanity is "intense and exquisite," he has lost touch with large, common human nature. He is not a philosopher but a craftsman, and almost morbid in his dislike of vulgarity. He lacks a good ear, and thus undervalues Poe's verse. His stories often do not sound true because the critic in him overshadows the novelist and his mind is better than his narrow subjects. His famous obscurity results from his dealing as clearly as possible with the least known, most complex fraction of human experience. His works contain remarkable dramatic scenes, and although timid with passion, he worships what is fine in humanity.

28 M[ASSON], T[HOMAS] L. "Some Horrible Books." Life, 61 (March 27), 621-622.

(Brief mention. As opposed to elementary physical horrors, this writer takes "greatest pleasure in the refined excellencies" of some of James's "more subtle cruelties.")

29 MATTHEWS, BRANDER. "American Character in American Fiction." Munsey's, 49 (August), 794-797.

Howells's The Rise of Silas Lapham, James's Daisy Miller, and Mark Twain's Huckleberry Finn had a popularity not so

1913

immediate and spectacular as that of some best sellers, but "far more durable." Their characters continue to interest after many readings.

30 NORTON, CHARLES ELIOT. Letters of Charles Eliot Norton. Ed. Sara Norton and M. A. DeWolfe Howe. Boston: Houghton Mifflin, 1:80, 340, 395-396, 422-423.
(A number of brief references to James.) In a 1908 letter, James's recent works are enigmatic in character as well as in style, especially compared to the ideals suggested by his own nature.

31 PERRY, T. S. Review of A Small Boy and Others. Yale Review, n.s. 3 (October), 186-189.
This record is charming, interesting, and "curiously complete." It is an "inner history" whose "incidents are almost nothing," and is somewhat like Stendhal's Vie de Henri Brulard. James is at his best, with "humor, gentle pathos, and amused intelligence." Some readers may dislike his style, but it makes a "delightful" work richer and better, more complete. Rarely does a book arouse "such increasing sympathy."

32 SHUMAN, EDWIN L. "With Authors and Books/Henry James' Memories." Chicago Record-Herald, April 19, p. 5.
(Review of A Small Boy and Others.) The long sentences of "henryJamesese" are by turns "charming, tantalizing and exasperating." (Brief biographical sketch and portrait.)

1914

1 ANON. "James on Young Novelists." New York Times, March 22, Part 3, p. 2.
(Response to James's London Times Literary Supplement article on young English novelists, with a number of short quotations.) James's "influence on the younger school of English novelists is perhaps greater than any other living writer." He is polite, but "not carried away with enthusiasm" for their work.

2 ANON. "Chronicle and Comment." Bookman, 39 (April), 117-120.
(Review of Notes of a Son and Brother.) In all the "charming circle" portrayed here, so "characteristic of a closed period in the development of our national manners," William James is the "brightest light," the figure bearing "the authentic stamp of genius." We see glimpses of the others of the James circle "through the fine haze of retrospect" that the author interposes.

3 ANON. "Henry James on His Rivals/The Reticent American, in Candid Mood, on Wells, Galsworthy and Others." Boston Evening Transcript, April 1, p. 22.
(Introduction to criticism by James.) In this reprint of part of a James essay in the London Times, he makes a "remarkable" contribution as "one of the greatest of the old" group of writers commenting on "the promise of the new." Also notable are James's unusual outspokenness and his surprising sympathy with the ideals of the revolt of the younger writers.

4 ANON. "Some of the Best Books Found During Past Year/Fiction and Serious Works Named by Notable Citizens." New York Sun, April 4, Part 2, p. 1.
(Note on Notes of a Son and Brother. Brief partial summary of contents.)

5 ANON. "Henry James' Reminiscences." Louisville Courier-Journal, April 20, p. 6.
(Review of Notes of a Son and Brother.) Though it initially seems a maze, this book fascinates in matter and manner. James is "a specialist in subtlety."

6 ANON. "General Literature." A.L.A. Booklist, 10 (May), 355.
(Review of Notes of a Son and Brother.) James "gives a characteristically subtle analysis" of the influences on his career.

7 ANON. "More Light on the History of Mr. Henry James's 'Visiting Mind,' in the Second Volume of His Autobiography." New York Tribune, 74 (May 2), 10.
(Review of Notes of a Son and Brother.) In parts of this book James's humorless, too resolute pursuit of the truth becomes "almost unbearably wearisome," but the rest has some interest and charm deriving in part from his "perversely beguiling manner." His memories are discursive and "delicately modulated," and he can be extraordinarily winning and full of atmosphere when he has a really substantive topic he cares about. His clever, fastidious savoring of intellectual experience is neither creative nor informed with the passion of great imaginative writers, but "it has a certain energy of its own, a certain original point, and it makes, successfully, its own peculiar appeal."

8 ANON. "Books and Authors." Boston Daily Advertiser, May 8, p. 4.
(Note on Notes of a Son and Brother. Quotes "apt character sketches" of John La Farge and William Hunt.)

1914

9 ANON. "Self-Revelations of a Great Novelist/The Extraordinary Autobiography of the Extraordinary Mr. James." Current Opinion, 56 (June), 457-458.

(Review of Notes of a Son and Brother.) None of James's recent novels has been received "with such enthusiastic approval" as greeted this volume. (Brief quotation from London Outlook, New York Tribune, Blackwood's, and 1915.37.) References to James's own recent criticism of other novelists in the London Times, and to his style, with a long quotation in which he discusses Edith Wharton. Sketch of James by William James.)

10 ANON. "Short Reviews." Harvard Graduates' Magazine, 22 (June), 696.

(Review of Notes of a Son and Brother.) This work "eddies, digresses, regrocesses and meanders," but is much more interesting than A Small Boy. James's "style seems to be fast disintegrating," with a "hectic pursuit of adjectives" and a loss of coherence and clarity.

11 ANON. "The Story of the Jameses." Independent, 78 (June 1), 366-368.

(Review of Notes of a Son and Brother. Full-page portrait by Sargent.) This autobiography has a leisurely pace, and is "delightful reading." Through breaks in James's "cloudy style," one gets "fascinating glimpses of interesting people." but James omits many facts that would help orient the reader.

12 ANON. "The New Books." Churchman, 109 (June 27), 842.

(Review of Notes of a Son and Brother.) This delightful book shows how the "urge toward art" acted on the James children and made of Henry "the greatest writer of English now living." This volume is "the most true and important, autobiographically," of any in this "remarkable series." It creates between author and reader a greater "closeness of approach" than could "any amount of admiration" for his "skill and comprehension" as a novelist.

13 ANON. "Brandes's Despair of Us." Literary Digest, 48 (June 27), 1546.

("Europe's Greatest Critic" Georg Brandes is quoted as saying that James, almost a personal friend, is the one American author whose work he admires. Yet, he finds in James the excessive reserve characteristic of American and English writers.)

14 ANON. "Suffragette Ignorance of Henry James." Literary Digest, 48 (June 27), 1545-1546.

James has maintained "a dignified calm . . . in the face of the feminist assault upon his portrait." Many of his admirers, however, are not so calm. (Quotes at length an admirer's protest in the London Academy.)

15 ANON. "Literature/Memoirs By Henry James." Nation, 99 (July 2), 16-17.
(Review of Notes of a Son and Brother.) In this book the "simplest thought . . . must go halting to the reader on heroic stilts." The long sentences are too filled with the "shadowiest dubieties" and the "faintest qualifying afterthoughts" of a moment of consciousness, rather than with any objective account of men and events. Many of the phrases suggest too much aestheticism and a certain egotism.

16 ANON. "Literary Section/. . . Important Biography." Congregationalist and Christian World, 99 (August 20), (no pagination).
(Review of Notes of a Son and Brother. Reference to James's "tortuous and convoluted style of thought.")

17 ANON. "A New Literary Order." Life, 64 (October 8), 619.
(Humorous item.) When the literary map is rearranged, the works of Edith Wharton and Henry James should be barred from the suburbs, where they engender an intolerable feminine highbrowism.

18 ANON. "Henry James' Book Has Fine Quality." Philadelphia North American, October 24, p. 12.
(Review of Notes on Novelists.) These essays present James in his "best and highest literary estate." The "minuteness of detail and pressure of involved statement" which make his fiction difficult are here an advantage, as James analyzes his subjects exhaustively. The Browning papers are "the most notable tribute of talent to genius extant in modern literature." The essay on the new novel is "discerning, happily phrased, nicely discriminating and sagely prophetic." Overall, in "extended, smoothly flowing paragraphs," James "exhausts the resources of a rarely discriminative mind possessed of an amazingly expansive vocabulary."

19 ANON. "'Notes on Novelists' Is a Series of Essays by Mr. Henry James." New York Herald, November 6, p. 6.
(Review.) One of the most interesting chapters is "The New Novel." James's critical work has "a permanent quality . . . that makes it well worth preserving."

20 ANON. "Belles Lettres." Independent, 80 (November 16), 243.
(Review of Notes on Novelists.) Much of this book's

interest and value comes from James's revelations about himself and the movement of his style from "'silver'" to "turgid." His appraisals of writers are "thoughtful and acute."

21 ANON. "Brilliant Criticism of Other Novelists in Fine Big Book by Henry James." Detroit Tribune, November 29, III, p. 13.
(Review of Notes on Novelists.) Nothing finer than these delightful, stimulating, idea-packed essays can be found in contemporary criticism, and it would be hard for anyone else to combine James's "clarity of thought with his labyrinthian expression." He writes brilliantly of Arnold Bennett, and, being neither too old-fashioned nor too modern, in general outshines contemporary critics.

22 ANON. "Essays and Criticism." American Monthly Review of Reviews, 50 (December), 763.
(Review of Notes on Novelists.) This volume is "one of the most satisfying" among recent essay collections. The essay on D'Annunzio is the best, and in it James has excelled all of that writer's other critics.

23 ANON. "The Art of Fine Writing." Life, 64 (December 17), 1128.
(Brief mention.) James, Huneker, and Maeterlinck practice the art of fine writing, but it takes a woman to do it as it ought to be done.

24 BICKNELL, PERCY F. "The New Books./Glimpses of a Gifted Family." Dial, 56 (April 1), 289-291.
(Review of Notes of a Son and Brother.) These fuller memorials of James's famous family members "have been awaited with no little eagerness." This book contains "a wealth of matter . . . presented with all the elaborate artistry" dear to James's readers. It is "a remarkable piece of autobiography and one of the most notable works of the season." Its characteristically Jamesian style "is a wonder and a delight to the reader fond of intricacy, of delicate shadings, of occasional tangled involutions."

25 BREDVOLD, LOUIS I. "Essays on the Novel." Dial, 57 (November 1), 332-333.
(Review of Notes on Novelists.) The subjects of these essays are sketched "with fine insight, with generous though discriminating appreciation, with the charm and felicity" to which James's readers have long been accustomed. For James the novel itself is "a manifestation of the critical spirit."

26 COLBY, F. M. "The Book of the Month." North American Review, 200 (October), 632-635.
(Review of Notes of a Son and Brother.) James's obscurity

of style is often not justified by complexity of thought. Many pages of his later books "read like very awkward first draughts, mere drag-nets of material," insignificant details and mental processes. Yet, this "drag-net method" may also bring up "many strange and shining things." This book portrays "delightful figures who gain a certain color of romance" from James's vague blur of words.

27 D., N. P. "Books of the Week." New York Globe and Commercial Advertiser, March 21, p. 10.
(Review of Notes of a Son and Brother. Brief partial summary of contents.)

28 E[DGETT], E[DWIN] F[RANCIS]. "Henry James/The Intimate." Boston Evening Transcript, March 11, p. 24.
(Review of Notes of a Son and Brother.) Neither this volume nor A Small Boy and Others is the less important or interesting for its "discursiveness and its incoherence." This book is "notable for its graphic portrayal" of personalities and for its "revelation of a mind that leaves nothing unobserved and . . . sees nothing . . . unworthy of comment."

29 _____. "Henry James the Critic." Boston Evening Transcript, October 21, p. 24.
(Review of Notes on Novelists.) The most analytic of writers, James "defies analysis" and is very original. He is one of a few novelists who are also good critics, and his criticism reveals much about his own mental processes. These essays are notable and thoroughly representative of one who is not a popular novelist but nonetheless is "one of the masters of modern fiction."

30 FURST, CLYDE. "Book Reviews." Sewanee Review, 22 (January), 111-114.
(Review of A Small Boy and Others.) This book is essentially literary criticism and a record of the development of James's imagination, rather than simple autobiography. It illuminates his works almost as much as his recent prefaces do, but tells little about his brother William. It is to be very much hoped that he will write a sequel.

31 KILMER, JOYCE. "Henry James at School." New York Times Saturday Review of Books, 19 (March 15), 117-118.
(Review of Notes of a Son and Brother.) This latest volume of an important and remarkable series makes the reader feel intimate with the author and his family. Various parts are pleasant, graphic, and "delicately beautiful," with "accurate and sympathetic character studies," especially of

John La Farge. James shows "that sometimes illuminating, sometimes obscuring attention to detail" that "distinguished him as a novelist," and here his discursiveness is a virtue.

32 LITTELL, PHILIP. "Henry James as a Critic." New Republic, 1 (November 21), 26-28.
(Review of Notes on Novelists.) In his novels, James uses various devices for waiting to reveal his characters, and in this book his devices for delay are his long, complicated sentences. As everyone knows, James does "marvellous things" with his "high manner," and here he uses it to reveal, as never understood before, the essential truth about each of the novelists he discusses. He also shows the "figure in his own carpet," "a body of aesthetic doctrine" that young novelists should consider. James's insight fails on Lawrence and Arnold Bennett, but, without resorting to formulae, he raises important questions about the novel.

33 MATTHEWS, BRANDER. "Seven Books of the Month." Bookman, 40 (December), 460-462.
(Review of Notes on Novelists.) James here gives us "the intimate criticism of a most expert fellow-craftsman." As with Sainte-Beuve, his dominating quality is his "insatiable curiosity," and he explores an author's work thoroughly to discover his secret, his essential quality. Some of James's best critical essays are missing from this volume. Overall, contrary to what readers have perhaps come to expect, the style is "neither recondite nor involute," and the writing shows more enjoyment and zest than do some of James's "more recent and more attenuated novels." James does drop occasional Gallicisms and Briticisms.

34 METCALF, JOHN CALVIN. American Literature. Richmond, Va.: B. F. Johnson Publishing, pp. 427-429.
James is "a more subtle and thoroughgoing realist" than Howells. His fiction is unique, the fanciful treatment of realistic situations. His method is scientific and metaphysical, with little plot or action. His art may be overrefined, his "acute and fastidious dissection of character" may be chilling, his "subtlety tends to end in enigma and his analysis in obscurity," and his late books display "a bewildering metaphysical tangle" and "involved diction." His international novels are "cleverly done," with perfect technique, "faultlessly urbane." James is "an acute thinker and a sensitive observer," of immense culture, but so refined that his appeal is limited. He is hardly American.

35 PEATTIE, ELIA W. "With Books and Authors . . . More of James's Youthful Memories." Chicago Tribune, April 18, p. 8.

(Review of Notes of a Son and Brother.) This book is whimsical, "touching and casual, sincere and sad" and beautiful. James's style is as tortuous and evasive as ever, but it makes "the pulsating fact" carry home.

36 QUINN, JOHN. "Some of the Best Books Found During Past Year." New York Sun, April 4, Part 2, p. 1.
(Note.) The best nonfictional books of the past year are James's "delightful" biographical studies A Small Boy and Others and Notes of a Son and Brother. James relives his youth "without sentiment or rhetoric," and is always "the great artist." The study of Minny Temple "would have delighted Meredith, and is almost as fine as anything of Meredith."

37 SKIDELSKY, BERENICE C. "New Books of the Month/Notes of a Son and Brother." Book News, 32 (May), 451.
(Review.) This is "one of the most stimulating books" in some time, and it contains much that is charming, interesting, and important. The verbose, maze-like style is typical of James, but so are the "wisdom, insight, [and] true penetration" into not-so-obvious aspects of life.

38 UNDERWOOD, JOHN CURTIS. "Henry James: Expatriate." Literature and Insurgency, Ten Studies in Racial Evolution. New York: Mitchell Kennerley, pp. 41-86.
At his best, James is a "brilliant critic" and incisive social observer, but he is also evasive, old-maidish, narrow and superficial, "superlatively patronizing," our most misrepresentative and un-American novelist of contemporary cosmopolitan life, and a "false prophet of sterile and reactionary culture." Women of a certain class have read and spoiled him. Insurgent American literary criticism justly finds him parochial, a microscopic observer of a contracted sphere, "a gradually clouding mirror" of a foggy, "characteristically feministic culture," a "highly unprofitable vivisector of vacuums." James is dull and misinterprets American life. Elisabeth Cary's book praising him is amateurish, "commercially interpretative hero-worship" typical of women. (See 1905.86, 1915.31.)

39 W., H. C. "Notes of a Son and Brother." America, 9 (June 20), 235.
(Review.) James is hard to read, but "a master of literary art" with "exquisite skill," "unerring judgment," and an almost dazzlingly brilliant "power of psychological analysis." The force and sometimes the ponderousness of his language and style overwhelm the reader, like a torrent of water or rocks. This book's main value is in showing the

influences on William James. The picture of earlier American society is "delightfully charming," and the account of La Farge's influence is "particularly happy and graceful."

40 WEST, REBECCA. "Mr. Shaw's Diverted Genius." New Republic, 1 (December 5), 14.
James has never "condescended to jostle with the ideas and affairs of his day," but maybe his abstinence is connected with "that indefinable but vital deficiency which makes his work not quite essential."

41 WILLIAMS, S. C. "Books and Authors/Henry James Reminisces." Boston Daily Advertiser, April 8, p. 10.
(Review of Notes of a Son and Brother.) The "remarkable" James brothers had a remarkable father. The most interesting passages in this book are the quoted ones, which are more direct than James's "finely woven cogitations." A patient reader may learn much about social conditions and important people.

42 YARROS, VICTOR S. "James on the Art of the New Novelists." Chicago Tribune, October 24, p. 14.
(Review of Notes on Novelists.) This book is "an intellectual treat," and although not always wholly just, is "delightful from beginning to end." The criticism is acute, profound, and comprehensive. James is by turns generous, enthusiastic, illuminative, conclusive, masterly, and authoritative.

1915

1 ANON. "General Literature." A.L.A. Booklist, 11 (January), 211.
(Review of Notes on Novelists.) These characteristic essays have "delicate delineation and fine insight." Their most interesting revelation, and the one to which the others add up, is of James himself.

2 ANON. "New Yorkers Join American Ambulance." New York Times, January 5, p. 2.
(News item from London mentions James as Chairman of the Ambulance Advisory Committee. Refers to his pamphlet "The Motor Ambulance in France.")

*3 ANON. Review of Notes on Novelists. Catholic World, 100 (February), 695.
(Cited in Foley and Ricks.)

4 ANON. "Literature and Art." Current Opinion, 58 (February), 115-116.
(Quotes James's "masterly" Notes on Novelists essay on the new school of British realists. Refers to James's comments on Compton Mackenzie.)

5 ANON. "Was Robert Louis Stevenson a Second-Rate Literary Artist?" Current Opinion, 58 (February), 119-120.
(Article ends with a quotation from Notes on Novelists on Stevenson's essays.)

6 ANON. "Mr. James on Punctuation and the War." New York Times, March 22, p. 8.
(Editorial. Response to 1915.40, a Times interview with James.) James has expressed as "subtly, powerfully," and eloquently as anyone the civilized world's feeling about the war. The interview is "a veritable masterwork," James is a master of the spoken as well as the written word, and one long sentence (quoted) is expressive, emotionally forceful, and "remarkable for both lucidity and cumulative effect." It has literary charm, though many passages in his books attend so much to shades of meaning that they bewilder all but the most attentive readers.

7 ANON. "The War and a Literary Style." Literary Digest, 50 (April 3), 752-753.
(References to and quotes from James's interview with Preston Lockwood of the New York Times, 1915.40.) In his humanitarian writings about the war, James's style is forceful and clear, much in contrast to the public's image of his famous literary style. A New York Times editorial agrees.

8 ANON. "Literary Notes." Harvard Graduates' Magazine, 23 (June), 723-724.
(Review of Notes on Novelists.) People who like criticism will read this volume with interest, wonder, and some regret at the increasing complexity of James's style. More and more he looks not at moral values, but at craftsmanship minutely and without proportion in interpreting sensations.

9 ANON. "Simple Home Remedies for Literary Troubles." Life, 65 (June 10), 1038.
(Brief humorous references.) Henry James indigestion may be relieved by taking one Shaw play, one Billy Sunday sermon, two Ade fables and six Mother Goose rhymes. James, Chaucer, Genesis, the Congressional Record, and Bulwer are sedatives to cure Jack London hysteria.

10 ANON. "Literary Notes." Life, 65 (July 1), 39.

(Humorous item.) James has made "excellent progress" on his new novel in the past month, having finished "the forty-third clause of the first sentence."

11 ANON. "James May Renounce American Citizenship/Novelist Said to Resent Failure to Protest More Strongly to Germany." New York Times, July 17, p. 1.
(Brief news item refers to James's dissatisfaction with the American government's failure to protest what he "regards as the gross violations of the rights of humanity by Germany.")

12 ANON. "Henry James Becomes Subject of Britain." Atlanta Constitution, July 28, p. 12.
(Notes James's change of citizenship, with quoted reasons.)

13 ANON. "Are We To Lose Henry James?" New York Times, July 28, Part 2, p. 14.
(Editorial.) James has become "wholly Anglicized in his tastes and his point of view, but there are no obvious causes for his proposed change of citizenship. He cannot like the state of things in England, and the memories of the traditions of his New England ancestry may keep him American.

14 ANON. "Henry James Now A British Subject/Took Oath of Allegiance on Monday--Sympathy for Allies His Impelling Motive." New York Times, July 28, p. 10.
(Brief news item contains long quotation from the London Times praising James's literary accomplishments and attributing his change in citizenship to his sympathy with the Allied cause and his ties to England.)

15 ANON. "Henry James Renounces His U.S. Allegiance." San Francisco Examiner, July 28, p. 1.
(News item on this "famous" author's change of citizenship, with portrait and quoted reasons.)

16 ANON. "Felicitate Henry James./Author Says if Teutons Won They Would Soon Attack Us." New York Times, July 29, p. 9.
(News item contains quotations from the London Daily Chronicle and the London Daily News on James's change of citizenship and its extraordinary significance.)

17 ANON. "Mr. James a British Citizen." New York Times, July 29, p. 8.
(Editorial.) James has always seemed foreign, he sees things with an introverted "delicacy of vision," he is "essentially critical and not creative," and Daisy Miller,

"once so famous, is still the dominant note of Jamesians." William James might have smiled at his brother's expressed idealistic reasons for becoming British, but a literary man must be granted his choice of scene.

18 ANON. "Editorial Notes." New Republic, 3 (July 31), 321.
Because so many of us are naturalized citizens, Americans should be able to understand James's becoming a British citizen. He is not lost to us, because possession of him is not a matter of nationality, and genius gives but does not take away.

19 ANON. "Giving the War a Credit Mark." New York Times, July 31, p. 6.
In commenting on James's change of citizenship, most of the American press has hidden "resentful wonder" under "suave and kindly phrases." The Portland (Maine) Argus, however, is forthright and not polite, and expresses American resentment of expatriates. (Quotation.)

20 ANON. "Rumored Expatriation of Mr. H. James." Life, 65 (August 12), 269.
(In discussion of James's rumored threat to renounce his American citizenship, writer makes a slap at James's style, but finds that "he is a good man, and his feelings about war are all right.")

21 ANON. "Thinks Henry James Dislikes Our Policy/Dr. White, American, Writes of Author's Feelings, But Hopes He Has Not Misrepresented Him." New York Times, August 14, p. 3.
(Long quotations from Dr. William White's letter to the London Spectator interpreting James's renunciation of his American citizenship.)

22 ANON. "All About Henry James." Life, 65 (August 19), 334.
(Humorous item.) If James tries to explain his intention to become a naturalized Englishman, no one will understand it.

23 ANON. "Missed His Calling." Life, 65 (August 19), 320.
(Brief humorous reference, following quoted complicated sentence from New York Sun financial column.) James should perhaps have been a financial writer.

24 ANON. "Our 'Great Renunciator.'" Literary Digest, 51 (August 28), 405-406.
(Discussion of James's application for British citizenship, with quoted comments from the Brooklyn Citizen, New York Times, Boston Herald, Boston Transcript, Portland

(Maine) Argus, St. Louis Republic, and London Evening Standard.) James's decision has provoked many newspapers' "sarcastic comment."

25 ANON. "A Tribute by Henry James." New York Times, September 12, Part 2, p. 4.
(Long quotation from James's written tribute to Allen D. Loney, who died on the Lusitania.)

26 ANON. "The Case of Mr. James." Outlook, 111 (September 22), 175.
James's change to British citizenship has provoked "cheap journalistic wit." Yet, although the Outlook regrets his decision, it admires his reasons and sees in them a moral lesson for other, less aware, Americans.

27 ANON. New York Times, October 17, Part 4, p. 1.
(Portrait by Sargent appears with James's article on the Belgian refugees in England, which "comes so to the core of national traits in their relation to the psychology of pity, that it ranks among the most important contributions to the pitiful literature of the war.")

28 ANON. "Henry James Very Ill." New York Times, December 9, p. 8.
(News account of the aftermath of James's stroke.)

29 ANON. "Mixed In His Jameses." Life, 65 (December 30), 1288.
(Humorous item. Reference to a writer's confusion of G. P. R. James with Henry James, Sr.) The elder Henry James was as interesting a man as either the younger Henry or William, but he was "not quite so extensively advertised."

30 BEERS, HENRY A. "Fifty Years of Hawthorne." Yale Review, 4 (January), 301-315.
James's biography of Hawthorne was at the time thought in America to be unsympathetic and patronizing, but now seems instead "cordially appreciative." James's reference to Hawthorne on the smell of peat smoke "is mentioned by nearly everyone who writes about Hawthorne." Like James in The Turn of the Screw, Hawthorne is ambiguous. (Quotes James on Hawthorne's allegorizing habit.)

31 COLBY, F. M. "Books and Things." New Republic, 1 (January 16), 26.
(Review of John Curtis Underwood's Literature and Insurgency.) Underwood's attack on James is ineffectual, since it is only an expression of disappointment that James's works are not more like the Ladies' Home Journal,

the Congressional Record, and other organs that promote "collective thinking." (See 1914.38.)

32 CROTHERS, SAMUEL M. Review of Notes of a Son and Brother. Yale Review, n.s. 4 (January), 414-415.

In this book everything "is seen in the act of becoming," and the verbal mist does not condense into "a shower of information." To one who likes James's style "the experience is rewarding," especially the glimpses of William.

33 GILMAN, LAWRENCE. "The Book of the Month." North American Review, 201 (May), 757-760.

(Review of Notes on Novelists.) These high-spirited, vivacious, playful, lucid, forthright studies are in contrast to James's forbidding, recondite reputation. In this remarkable book he is impetuous sometimes at the expense of precision, and so pathetically anxious to communicate that he is colloquial. He is "a great master of English prose" and of criticism. He has a long, firm and delicate line of thought, a charm and wit of expression, as well as "a literary conscience without parallel for sensitive and anxious probity." Although one of "the indubitable immortals," he would benefit from editing.

34 HACKETT, FRANCIS. "A Stylist on Tour." New Republic, 2 (May 1), 320-321.

Though the popular attitude among James's admirers is to prefer the early to the late style, this writer is happy that he enjoys "the later labyrinthine James." James's meticulousness about emotions may get impractical, but that quality is "intensely valuable" when applied to places and people in The American Scene. Few have succeeded as well as this "fine, inclusive, meditative spirit" at making "a justly sensitive analysis" of civilized intercourse.

35 HARRISON, HENRY SYDNOR. Review of Notes on Novelists. Yale Review, n.s. 4 (April), 608-611.

James criticizes from his base of "immense technical proficiency" as a distinguished novelist, and shows sympathy with other novelists. This book's main interest is as "a full correspondence course" for young writers, containing James's "brilliant dissertation on the theory and practice of the novel." This old master is "more celebrated than read," especially for profundity of insight, and his creed for storytellers is fundamentally sound.

36 HAY, JOHN. The Life and Letters of John Hay. Ed. William Roscoe Thayer. Boston and New York: Houghton Mifflin, 1:411, 416f. Rpt. 1916.

(John Hay's letters to Howells refer to James.)

1915

37 HUEFFER, FORD MADOX. Henry James: A Critical Study. New York: A. & C. Boni. 192 pp.

Of all the works currently being published, James's are the most worthy of critics' attention. He is the greatest of living writers. He has both a distinctive temperament and conscious craftsmanship, as well as "fineness of mind," nobility of character, high hope, a great quest, and genius. He tells a truth that both is and exceeds beauty. His greatness is as an historian. He is not didactic or a moralist, but rather a "philosophic anarchist." He is also the greatest living man because he, "more than anybody," has impartially observed and rendered "human society as it now is." His work is "intimately true to the life we lead." He should not be criticized for examining only the life of the comfortable classes, because assessing its worth assesses the worth of Western civilization. Though James is very American, one must understand Samuel Richardson to understand him. James's characters are real, "amazingly rendered," "skillfully and dispassionately dissected and laid bare." His only public mission has been to civilize America. The early 1890s stories of the literary life are wonderful, but James thought ordinary English people nasty and did not find his great good place in their country. He has carried the power of selection so far that he "can create an impression with nothing at all." His books deserve to be read by the great continental writers, and have a "vibrating reality," a movement between the apparent and the essential. The niceness of his sense of form is unrivalled. He refines all non-psychological action out of his work and writes purely in allegory. Through early 1897 his style was "almost unapproachable," lucid, picturesque, and forcible. If mankind can bestow immortality, James will receive it. (See 1914.9.)

38 KELLNER, LEO. American Literature. New York: Doubleday, Page, & Co., pp. 178-184.

(Translated from the German.) James protests the vulgar misuse, the crudeness and flatness, of the language of American newspapers. He keeps aloof from the common, the popular, the obvious, and the readily comprehensible. James's self-conscious art has finesse. The Portrait of a Lady has unforgettable characters, and Daisy Miller is James's most perfect work, a portrait unsurpassed in American literature.

39 LITTELL, PHILIP. "Books and Things." New Republic, 3 (July 3), 234.

(Quotation from and discussion of Littell's fifteen-year-old review of The Sacred Fount. Littell questions its conclusions and those of any review.)

40 LOCKWOOD, PRESTON. "Henry James's First Interview/Noted Critic and Novelist Breaks His Rule of Years to Tell of the Good Work of the American Ambulance Corps." New York Times, March 21, Part 5, p. 3.

(Portrait. Interview with James includes physical description and reference to his deliberate, hesitating speech. James discusses briefly his punctuation and his revision of his work, but focuses on the war and seeks American support of the Ambulance Corps.)

41 PACE, ROY BENNETT. American Literature. Boston: Allyn & Bacon.

(James is included on the "Supplementary List of Authors.") James "has small title to inclusion among American writers," his attitude toward his country is usually "patronizing or mildly contemptuous," and his most important works are novels, of which The Portrait of a Lady and The Princess Casamassima are representative.

42 PATTEE, FRED LEWIS. A History of American Literature Since 1870. New York: Century Co., pp. 186-197, 306, 380. Rpt. 1916.

James is one of a "school of deliberate workmen" who reacted against the Emersonian New England school and had "no message for their times, only technique and brilliancy." James is "cultured, cold, scientific," and influenced by Turgenev and the French. More than any other American author he stands for specialization. His art has finesse but is all "objective, external phenomena," of the intellect alone, inspiring no sympathy. Like George Eliot, he stripped himself of all illusions and considered outgrown "the ideal, the intuitive, the spiritual." His world is small, and he is "feminine rather than masculine," "exquisite rather than strong." His always brilliant characters analyze, philosophize, and all sound like him, yet James the critic lacks "perspective, philosophy, system." Self-study became a veritable obsession with him.

43 WELLS, H[ERBERT] G[EORGE]. "Of Art, of Literature, of Mr. Henry James." In Boon, The Mind of the Race, The Wild Asses of the Devil, and the Last Trump: Being A First Selection from the Literary Remains of George Boon, Appropriate to the Times. Prepared for Publication by Reginald Bliss, With an Ambiguous Introduction by H. G. Wells. New York: George H. Doran, pp. 86-130.

(This satirical work parodies James's method and includes him as a character whose speeches parody his style. Boon, the main character, says that in the field of criticism James is "a partially comprehensible essential," that he thinks novels are pictures and life a studio, and that he is too concerned with form, invents denatured, "eviscerated people," and makes very much of very little. Boon says that "the elaborate, copious emptiness" of what he does is redeemed only by his "elaborate, copious wit.")

44 WEST, REBECCA. "Reading Henry James in War Time." New Republic, 2 (February 27), 98-100.
(Review of Notes on Novelists.) The war's obscene perversion of every "warm passion" vindicates James's seemingly "inhuman incapacity for enthusiasm." His style has deteriorated into artificiality, he misjudges D. H. Lawrence's genius, and overrates Gilbert Cannan and Compton Mackenzie, but the presence of James's "marvelous brain" in his many volumes reinforces our faith in the intellect, and "nothing is innocent in man except the mind."

1916

1 ANON. "W. W. Astor is Made a Peer by King George." New York Times, January 1, p. 1.
(James is mentioned as receiving the Order of Merit from the King.)

2 ANON. "Henry James's Honor./Order of Merit Has Only Eleven Civilian Members." New York Times, January 2, Part 2, p. 3.
(Brief item mentions James's having received the honor given to very few civilians, and refers to his change of citizenship.)

3 ANON. "Henry James Very Ill." New York Times, January 22, p. 1.
(Brief news item on James's illness.)

4 ANON. "Henry James Unimproved./Mrs. William James Announces That His Condition is Serious." New York Times, January 23, Part 2, p. 5.
(News item on James's illness.)

5 ANON. "Mr. James's Order of Merit." Literary Digest, 52 (February 12), 377.
(Quotations from George W. Smalley's New York Tribune comments on James's being awarded the British Order of Merit.)

6 ANON. "Mr. James's Illness Grave/Even Temporary Improvement in Author's Condition Not Expected." New York Times, February 17, p. 11.
(Brief news item.)

7 ANON. "Novelist Henry James Summoned by Death." Atlanta Constitution, February 29, p. 8.
(Long standard obituary printed in a number of newspapers.) Even James's critics ranked him as "one of the most masterful writers of the past generation." James was independent of the public, had his own cult, and wrote in a complicated style stories with abrupt endings.

8 ANON. "Henry James Dies At London Home." Boston Daily Advertiser, February 29, p. 1.
(Obituary. James's death also mentioned under "Summary of Morning's News.")

9 ANON. "Loss to Letters, Judge Grant States." Boston Daily Advertiser, February 29, p. 1.
Judge Robert Grant says that James will be missed because he and Howells "'were two of the foremost exponents of the present time.'"

10 ANON. "Profound Critic of Human Nature." Boston Daily Advertiser, February 29, p. 1.
(Professor W. A. Neilson of Harvard is quoted as saying that James was "'a profound critic of human nature'" whose highly individual, "'strange and intricate'" style was "'extraordinarily adapted'" to his views.)

11 ANON. "Henry James Dead." Boston Evening Transcript, February 29, p. 4.
(Obituary, with biographical sketch.) From the early 1870s, James was accepted as "a new force in literature." His books in French and his essays "attracted much favorable criticism." He was never as popular in America as in England, but was ranked among "the masterly writers of the past generation."

12 ANON. "Henry James, Famed Author, Dies In London." Boston Journal, February 29, p. 1.
(This condensation of the standard obituary appearing in many newspapers emphasizes biography.)

13 ANON. "Henry James the Novelist is Dead." Boston Post, February 29, p. 3.
(Obituary, with large portrait.) James's work was more popular in England than in America. Even his critics considered him "one of the most masterful writers of the past generation," though his work has been controversial and hard to understand. His stories often ended abruptly and attempted "what other writers deemed as the impossible in literary art."

1916

14 ANON. "Henry James, Noted Writer, Dies in London." Chicago Tribune, February 29, p. 13.
(Long obituary, with portrait of the "Famous Novelist" and samples of his "difficult" writing also showing his "remoteness from American life.")

15 ANON. "Henry James Dies, Famed As Author." Cleveland Plain Dealer, February 29, p. 6.
(Standard obituary appearing in many newspapers.)

16 ANON. "Henry James, Famous Novelist, Is Dead." Colorado Springs Gazette, February 29, p. 1.
(Portrait and standard obituary noting James's alleged greater popularity in England than in America, the abruptness of his endings, the complexity and the mastery of his writing, and the controversy inspired by his prose.)

17 ANON. "American Novelist, Henry James, Dies a British Subject." Cincinnati Commercial Tribune, February 29, p. 4.
(Obituary refers to James's attachment to England and lists his books with little critical comment.)

18 ANON. "Henry James, Novelist, Dies." Louisville Courier-Journal, February 29, p. 5.
(Standard critical and biographical obituary appearing in many newspapers.)

19 ANON. "Henry James Dies A British Subject." Detroit Free Press, February 29, p. 3.
(Standard critical and biographical obituary, with portrait.)

20 ANON. "Henry James." New York Evening Post, February 29, p. 10.
(Editorial.) Average opinion identifies James with a European subject and a highly involuted style. His indifference to popularity and his desire to tell the untellable may account for that style. He did not achieve the highest art in character development, but because of the difficulty of his manner and because his subtle subjects, "the dimly conscious manifestations of the soul," are increasingly interesting to psychologists, he will be famous for some time.

21 ANON. "Henry James Dies in London at Age of 73." New York Evening Post, February 29, p. 6.
(Long obituary.) James was more popular in America than in England, and "his critics ranked him as one of the most masterful writers of the past generation." His short stories are less notable than his novels, which often ended

abruptly. He was indifferent to popularity, but had a cult of admirers. The complexity of his style and whether he could successfully tell untellable stories have been controversial.

22 ANON. "Famous Novelist, Henry James, Dies." Washington Evening Star, February 29, p. 5.
(Portrait, and standard obituary that appeared in a number of newspapers.)

23 ANON. "Henry James." New York Globe and Commercial Advertiser, February 29, p. 10.
(Editorial.) James offended more than American patriotism. Americans found tiresome the prolixity and nebulosity of a writer who pursued analysis for its own sake. Despite their air of significance, James's books often had little substance and their characters became meagre, queer, and monotonous, concerned with childish things. Yet, James showed literary genius in being himself and creating his own method, without regard to the public's desires. (Notes Frank Moore Colby's observation that James's works would be morally shocking if his characters were less cerebral and his style less obscure.)

24 ANON. "Henry James Dies In London." Hartford Courant, February 29, p. 19.
(Standard critical and biographical obituary.)

25 ANON. "Henry James, Novelist, Dies in His London Home." Indianapolis News, February 29, p. 5.
James created his own public and converted very able critics, but in recent years was heard from less and less. His style was brilliant and enigmatic, but people complained that he was "always analyzing and probing." (Obituary with large portrait.)

26 ANON. "Novelist James, Once American, Dies in London." Minneapolis Tribune, February 29, p. 1.
(Portrait. Parts of standard AP obituary referring to James's English popularity and his independence of the public.)

27 ANON. "Henry James Dead." Portland Morning Oregonian, February 29, p. 4.
(Portrait and standard obituary which refers to James's being more popular in England than in America, to his abrupt endings, and to his "intellectual mazes and verbal labyrinths.")

1916

28 ANON. "Henry James." New York Herald, February 29, p. 10.
(Editorial.) James was honored and leaves "an exquisitely fragrant literary memory." In his best novels he "wrote truthfully and with gentle, ironic humor." Daisy Miller is an unforgettable portrait, and The Bostonians rendered the patriotic service of helping counteract the foreign belief that the only good American society is the plutocracy. James's style "dimmed the brilliance" of his later works, but his earlier ones will long sustain an increasingly lustrous fame.

29 ANON. "Mr. Henry James, American by Birth, Dies a Briton." New York Herald, February 29, p. 7.
(Cable obituary, with portrait, is biographical rather than critical.)

30 ANON. "British Tribute to James./London Times Says His Relations with Home Were Constant." New York Times, February 29, p. 11.
(Quotes appreciations from the London Times, London Daily Telegraph, London Daily Mail, and London Morning Post.)

31 ANON. "Henry James Dead at His London Home." New York Times, February 29, p. 11.
(Obituary, with Sargent portrait, mentions James's renunciation of citizenship, his "very favorably criticized" fiction and essays, his being ranked "one of the most masterful writers of the past generation," his greater popularity in England than in America, his methods of composition, his manner of life, his dislike of publicity, and his feelings about the war.)

32 ANON. "Henry James Dies Subject of Britain; Famous Novelist." Detroit News, February 29, p. 8.
(Long, standard AP critical and biographical obituary, with portrait. Also quotes James on his ambivalence toward Theodore Roosevelt and on Rudyard Kipling.)

33 ANON. "Henry James Dead; American Novelist, But Became Briton." Philadelphia North American, February 29, p. 1.
(Standard long critical and biographical obituary, with portrait.)

34 ANON. "Henry James, Long Ill, Dies in London." St. Paul Pioneer Press, February 29, p. 1.
(Condensation and paraphrase of standard obituary.) James's works did not meet a "hearty response" from the American reading public, and they were endlessly controversial.

35 ANON. "Henry James Dead; 50 Years An Author." Philadelphia Press, February 29, p. 1.
(Augments information and critical remarks from the standard obituary with accounts of James's fainting at the premier of "The High Bid" and of his life at Rye. Portrait.)

36 ANON. "Henry James Dies, Noted as Novelist of Analytical Type." St. Louis (Mo.) Republic, February 29, p. 1.
(Standard obituary.)

37 ANON. "Henry James Dies In His London Home/Lives Less Than a Year After Renouncing Allegiance to U.S." Salt Lake Tribune, February 29, p. 1.
(Biographical obituary, with portrait, emphasizes James's change of citizenship.)

38 ANON. "Henry James, Novelist, Dies In London at the Age of 73." San Francisco Chronicle, February 29, p. 3.
(Standard obituary, with portrait.)

39 ANON. "Novelist James Dead in London/Famous American Writer Who Became British Subject Dies." San Francisco Examiner, February 29, p. 5.
(Brief obituary.)

40 ANON. "Death of Henry James." Springfield (Mass.) Republican, February 29, p. 1.
(Obituary, with portrait, summarizes the stages in James's career.) James was "one of the greatest writers of modern times," who created works of "amazing subtlety, completeness, and beauty."

41 ANON. "Henry James Dies in London, At 72." New York Sun, February 29, p. 1.
(Obituary, with portrait.) Daisy Miller was James's most popular work, and among "the best appreciated" of his later books are The Bostonians, The Princess Casamassima, and "London." His "intricateness of verbiage" often made his works difficult.

42 ANON. "Henry James Dies Suddenly in London After Brief Illness." New Orleans Times-Picayune, February 29, p. 1.
James's books are among the foremost in their technique by an American. He was early a "sensitive impressionist," able to portray the elusive and baffling. He requires much of his readers, and perhaps wrote for writers, yet is "unrivalled" as an interpreter of today's world.

43 ANON. "Henry James Dies In London After Long Suffering/His

1916

Novels, Covering a Wide Range of Life, Won Him Even More Fame Abroad Than in This Country." New York World, February 29, p. 4.
(Long, standard biographical and critical obituary, with portrait.)

44 ANON. "Henry James." Boston Daily Advertiser, March 1, p. 6.
(Editorial.) Despite his expatriation, James retained an American consciousness. His style, "though involved, was never ponderous," and his expression was always clear.

45 ANON. "Henry James." Boston Journal, March 1, p. 6.
(Editorial.) Because James made novel writing an art rather than a business, the public credited his artistry and neglected him for lighter entertainment. His works have been far more popular in England than here, but his change of citizenship has reminded Americans of his connection with them. A James novel is a history of emotions. Jocosely, but not grudgingly, the harsher critics of his style long ago gave him "an enduring place in American letters."

46 ANON. "Henry James." Cleveland Plain Dealer, March 1, p. 8.
(Editorial.) James and America disliked one another, but an English coterie pretended to enjoy and understand his "ponderous, dull wordy novels" and his "extravagantly involved style." Born rich, the highbrow James followed his own whims as a writer and "hated and shunned the common crowd." Like a foreigner, he showed America condescension and "patronizing contempt." His distinctive style was subject to parody, but rarely imitated. He "will stand for some time a unique figure in literature."

47 ANON. "Henry James." Detroit Free Press, March 1, p. 4.
(Editorial.) This noted literary figure wrote "penetrating and rather finical" criticism in "suave and studied diction." James was accused of creating unreal characters with unnatural talk, and of using his "vast command of language" to conceal thought. Yet, although in his novels of "minute observation and elaborate analyses" he "turned plot and action into a maze of mystification," his intricacies have "subtle shades of meaning not otherwise appreciable." His best work was in international contrasts, although Daisy Miller aroused "much feminine antagonism."

48 ANON. "Henry James' Body To Be Cremated." New York Herald, March 1, p. 12.
(Brief news item on funeral.)

49 ANON. "To Cremate James's Body." New York Times, March 1, p. 6.
(Brief news item.)

50 ANON. "Henry James." New York Times, March 1, p. 10.
(Editorial.) James was an old New Yorker, fortunate in his family and ancestry, misjudged by too many of his countrymen, and "a patriotic American." Americans know him best for Daisy Miller, but would find humor, sharp characterization, and power of creation if they read his mature works. He had great insight into human nature, and because he was so true to his art, artists honored and loved him. He "was never more loyal to American traditions and principles than when he became a British subject."

51 ANON. "Move to Honor James./Public Funeral in Westminster Abbey Proposed in London." New York Times, March 1, p. 11.
(Laudatory quotations about James from the London Morning Post and from Violet Hunt in the London Daily Mail.)

52 ANON. "Henry James." Philadelphia Press, March 1, p. 12.
(Editorial.) Changing citizenship because of the war did not make James an Englishman. He was a peerless and exceptionally clear-eyed pioneer in fictionally handling international relationships, in seeing and delineating social types. Like the impressionists, he used small strokes, minutiae, to mingle unforgettably "mood and manner" and reach a realism with "all the illusion of nature itself," as in The American Scene. In such masterpieces as The Ambassadors and The Golden Bowl, he realizes "the most vivid sense of actual personality." His humor is warm and kindly as well as "sharply ironical." At his best, James was a great figure, though not a great force, in American literature.

53 ANON. "Henry James' Body Will Be Cremated." Philadelphia Press, March 1, p. 14.
(Brief AP news item on funeral.)

54 ANON. "Henry James." New York Sun, March 1, p. 8.
(Editorial.) James's cosmopolitanism is British, but his works are forever part of American literature, and he is "truly great" because unclassifiable. His early books have a "fundamental humanity" and his later work is like nothing else, despite its somewhat justly maligned style.

55 ANON. "Henry James." New York World, March 1, p. 10.
(Editorial.) Despite his later, "incomparable wretched style," James held a very fair place in the literary world.

1916

He succeeded not because of his word-mazes, but "by sheer weight of thought."

56 ANON. "Born An American; Dies An Englishman." Hartford Courant, March 2, p. 8.
(Portrait, and note on funeral with reference to James's change of citizenship.)

57 ANON. "Henry James." Nation, 102 (March 2), 244-245.
(Obituary.) To most people, James is best known for his preoccupation with Europe and his "highly involuted style," which has been much parodied in the newspapers and has thus added to his fame. James's "real indifference to popularity" is reflected not only in this style, but in his rejection of obvious plots and emotions for more subtle, elusive material. The ultimate test of a great novelist is creation of character, and not since the "splendid" Portrait of a Lady has he produced "a vital, rounded figure." His recent characters lack immediacy, inevitableness, flesh and blood.

58 ANON. "Books and Reading." New York Evening Post, March 3, p. 8.
(Editorial.) James's conversation was "notoriously different from his writing." (Anecdote.)

59 ANON. "Henry James's Funeral./Our Ambassador Among Those Who Pay Last Honors." New York Times, March 4, p. 11.
(Brief news item.)

60 ANON. Editorial. New York Times, March 5, Sect. 7, p. 76.
(Describes the New York Edition, with its prefaces and revisions, as James's final literary legacy to posterity.)

61 ANON. "Gosse's Tribute to James./A Supreme Artist and a Hero of Whom England Shall Be Proud." New York Times, March 5, Part 1, p. 6.
(Quotes Sir Edmund Gosse's letter to the London Times praising James.)

62 ANON. "Henry James, Interpreter of American Types/Famous Writer, Who Died a Few Days Ago in England, Left Gallery of Literary Characters Derived from Lifelong Study." New York Times, Part 6, March 5, pp. 7-8.
(Two portraits.) In his autobiographies, James used "the slenderest" of vehicles to portray "a complicated social period." In fiction he was the only writer to commit "to definite form any impressive number of American types, any impressive mass of American characteristics." His abundance of thought separated him from the other novelists of his day,

and his reputation will live on "the high quality of his intellectual product," especially his fiction. He was artistically responsible, and rich and full in spirit. Time must pass before we can make an accurate critical and personal assessment of this kind, sympathetic, friendly man and his works.

63 ANON. "Nephew Hears of James's Death." New York Times, March 6, p. 20.
(Brief news item.)

64 ANON. "The Week/. . . Henry James." Outlook, 112 (March 8), 541-542.
(Obituary.) Since James's death, the British estimates of his work are even more laudatory than the American estimates. Many of his earlier works, written "directly and entertainingly rather than subjectively and involvedly," were "natural, sincere, and truly human stories," not over-elaborated. The Portrait of a Lady is among the best American novels. James's name was formerly linked with Howells's, but even then their work was very different. James's obscure later manner has reduced his audience almost to a narrow, overawed cult. Yet, despite all his faults as a writer, he had distinction, culture, and "penetrating thought."

*65 ANON. Country Life, (March 11), 332-333.
(Cited in Ricks.)

66 ANON. "Casual Comment." Dial, 60 (March 16), 268.
James has described his early literary likings entertainingly in A Small Boy and Others, and they have "an especial interest" just after his death. (Long quotation from Ch. 7.)

*67 ANON. Country Life, (March 18), 365.
(Cited in Ricks.)

68 ANON. "Letters and Art/The Baffling Henry James." Literary Digest, 52 (March 18), 714-715.
The American newspapers seem to show that James's death is "an event of first importance in the world of letters." He still baffles them, provokes the "old platitudes" about his literary style, and raises the issue of his "Americanism." (Quoted comments from the Brooklyn Citizen, Washington Star, New York Globe, Syracuse Herald, Rochester Herald, Indianapolis News, Milwaukee Evening Wisconsin, New York Sun, and Boston Transcript. Photograph by E. O. Hoppe.)

69 ANON. "Henry James." Life, 67 (March 30), 569.

1916

(Obituary.) James's character was not affected by the "degeneration which gradually engulfed his style." For a whole generation he was a literary institution, and although he had few readers in his later years, they were good ones.

70 ANON. "The Ineradicable Americanism in the Genius of the Most Misunderstood of Modern Novelists." Current Opinion, 60 (April), 280-281.

(Obituary.) The Springfield (Mass.) Republican's statement that at James's death England "'loses the greatest of American novelists'" summarizes the prevalent opinion of the American press. In general, this tribute due American genius lacks a certain warmth and enthusiasm, but whether editors express "admiration, respect, or cold appreciation" for James, they find him "ineradicably American." (Quotations from Springfield Republican, Boston Transcript, and New York Evening Post. Portrait by van der Weyde.)

71 ANON. "British Tributes to Henry James." Literary Digest, 52 (April 8), 970.

(Quotes tributes from the Spectator, London Daily Mail, London Nation, Saturday Review, New Statesman, and London Times.) No man of letters has "passed from the living world of England with finer expressions of grateful appreciation" from the British press than has James.

72 ANON. "Rebecca West Dethrones Some of our Literary Idols." Current Opinion, 61 (November), 343-344.

(Review of 1916.97.) This book will arouse interest not only for its "discriminating praise" of James, but also for its demolition of many of the other great nineteenth-century literary reputations, by which West tries to convince the reader of James's greatness. Yet, she is not overkind to him. (Quotations from a favorable review in the British Weekly and a mixed one by Arthur Waugh in the London Outlook.)

73 ANON. "Literary Criticism." New York Times Saturday Review of Books, 21 (November 12), 482.

(Editorials.) If James left any unfinished works, literary fragments, who would be able to imitate his complex style well enough to bring them "to a successfully mystifying conclusion"?

A biography of James or a volume of his letters would be "of unique literary interest."

74 CAIRNS, WILLIAM B. "Meditations of a Jacobite." Dial, 60 (March 30), 313-316.

The "paucity of striking events" in James's novels is "a necessary consequence" of his conception of fiction. His later novels contain "unforgettable pictures" even more admirable than those in his earlier works. His "moral tendencies" have been much discussed, and in his later novels "he has been much more free in his choice of subjects." The wickedness in his books is incidental, secondary to something else, and "this acceptance of evil as a natural and expected phenomenon of modern life" shocks many readers. Most readers prefer his earlier and middle style to his later manner, but his later prose contains many passages better than any in the early works. James "has always made much of the emotional significance of wind and weather, of light and shade," and successfully creates what has come to be called an atmosphere.

75 CANBY, HENRY S. "Henry James." Harper's Weekly, 62 (March 25), 291.

(Obituary.) James was not the greatest novelist of his century, but he was the greatest craftsman to come from America and "the greatest American critic since Poe." He is more American than the critics say, especially in his "keen, inventing greatness." Yet, his "great refusal of popularity" was atypical of Americans. His place is secure "as a great figure in the broad sweep of international English literature."

76 CONRAD, JOSEPH. "Henry James: An Appreciation." North American Review, 203 (April), 585-591.

(Reprint of 1905.88.)

77 D., G. "Henry James/Passing of One of the Greatest Men in American Letters." San Francisco Chronicle, March 5, p. 23.

James's death is the biggest recent event in the literary world, and will provoke more estimates, many derogatory, than would the death of any other American literary luminary. In life "no man was more severely assailed," but he was too sure of himself to be affected by criticism. His change of citizenship did not make him un-American, and one hopes he will now be more widely read.

78 DARGAN, E. PRESTON. "Henry James the Builder." New Republic, 7 (June 17), 171-174.

In the course of his fiction, James has been in effect the builder of two "exquisite" ideal cities: "the concentrated essence of a glorified Europe," and a place that houses and celebrates the artistic life. (Article reconstructs these two composite "James cities" from a number of his works.)

79 DE LA MARE, WALTER. "Henry James." Living Age, 289 (April 8),

122-125.
(Obituary. Reprinted from Westminster Gazette.)

80 FOLLETT, HELEN THOMAS, and FOLLETT, WILSON. "Henry James." Atlantic Monthly, 117 (June), 801-811.

Except for Meredith's, Henry James's genius is "the most lavish gift surely of our time." James has answered with silence "the tumult of jeers" that have over the years been the response of many reviewers and parodists, his "irresponsible tormentors" from the press. Now that his death has silenced their "profane laughter," those who appreciate him can try to address the important issues raised by his work. These include his intensely individual style, in which substance is diffused into elaboration with an "extraordinary felicity of phrase," the "nicest possible care" for the music of prose; his witty, "swift summarizing touch" in character portrayal; his subtlety and basic simplicity in presenting consistently the interpenetrating ideals of perfection of environment and perfection of the individual soul. For James and his characters the greatest thing in the world is "the social conscience, the inveterate human instinct of solidarity," expressed in a "reasoned" course of conduct arrived at through slow, patient gaining of self-knowledge and self-mastery. These characters "bring the issue out of their conflicts without the stress of a fiery or tragic denouement," yet are characterized by "passion and quickness of intuition, rather than profundity of thought." The body of James's work has a "studied formal exquisiteness," reflects his "will to know," and has as an important theme: renunciation.

81 HACKETT, FRANCIS. "The Rupert Brooke Legend." New Republic, 4 (February 5), 23.

(Review of Rupert Brooke's Letters from America. Some discussion of James's introduction to the volume.) James has spent much of his career "gently commiserating with the world" on its failure to fulfill his "delicate expectancies for it," but with Rupert Brooke "he was immensely, mutely charmed."

82 HALE, EDWARD E. "Henry James." Dial, 60 (March 16), 259-262.

James was "one of the most able and most representative leaders" of the great movement called realism, and stood for "the aims of dozens of younger writers, for the interests of thousands of readers." Later, James "was acknowledged a master," but writers of adventure stories and romances became more in fashion. When that romantic fashion waned, James was still a master, could still do "what everybody else was now trying to do." He has had "a fine and an extraordinary career." James followed the path of his genius "in spite of the ebbs and flows of popular sentiment," and "was at the end of his life a greater figure even than in those early days when he was felt to be so absolutely fine." Yet, his art did change, became deliberately obscure to portray something deeper and more elusive and all-pervading than mere words and actions. The Golden Bowl, which illustrates this method and purpose, seems "the veriest transcript" of life, and "the most consummate achievement."

83 HOWELLS, WILLIAM DEAN. "Mr. Henry James's Later Work." North American Review, 203 (April), 572-584.
(Reprint of 1903.112.)

84 LEACH, ANNA. "Henry James: An Appreciation." Forum, 55 (May), 551-564.
Despite his ability to make us approve his characters' questionable acts, James was essentially, even sternly, moral. Yet, he was sensitive to nuances and labelled nothing. What William James told by formula, Henry "worked out in terms of life." The "most wonderful" of his attributes was a youthful flexibility that he never lost. He remained interested in everything. Though critics say the heroine of the "brilliant study" Daisy Miller was an impossible type, now obsolete, she still is and will be with us. James is "an impressionist of the Velasquez school" and as much a realist as any great artist can be. He was wonderfully able to teach the commonplace "its own meanings," and had "the supreme charm" of the spontaneous. His expression is modern and supremely original, but also, like that of all great artists, impersonal. His people are symbols of the race. He almost magically turns a mere incident or "germ" into a work of art.

85 LITTELL, PHILIP. "Henry James's Quality." New Republic, 6 (March 11), 152-154.
Over the years James has come nearer and nearer mastery of his special world, and his insight into human relations has become more penetrating. His later landscapes are "more brilliant, more achieved, more done," and they match or illustrate something human. In three of his great late novels, the main characters seem too isolated.

86 _____. "Books and Things." New Republic, 6 (March 18), 191.
(For "your pleasure and for mine," quotations of landscape descriptions from a number of James's works.)

87 LUBBOCK, PERCY. "Henry James." Living Age, 290 (September 16),

1916

733-742.
(Reprint of July 1916 [London] Quarterly Review article.)

88 [LYEL, P. C.] "The World of Henry James." Living Age, 289 (April 22), 229-233.
(Reprint of article in London Times, March 23, 1916.)

89 MACDONNELL, ANNIE. "Henry James as Critic." Bookman, 43 (April), 219-222.
(Reprint of 1896.48.)

90 MORDELL, ALBERT. "The Early Lucid Henry James." Book News Monthly, 34 (April), 359-360.
(Portrait.) Although James's later style has made his name "synonymous with all that is obscure, dull and unintelligible" in literary form, his works before 1890 were lucid and readable. He has written "a few of the greatest novels and tales" ever produced in America. James was "a great critic." He helped make it fashionable again to write about "'high-brow' characters." He was a poet, whose characters are living, emotional, and sensitive. He understood women, and has created some "permanent types."

91 PHELPS, WILLIAM LYON. "Henry James." Yale Review, n.s. 5 (July), 783-797.
No American prose writer born since 1843 rivals James. He always did his best, appealed to a select few, did not worry about public opinion, and had perhaps a "higher artistic purpose" than anyone. He pursued "eternally elusive" shades of meaning, and admitted to the "common accusations" that he dealt with trivialities and that no one read him. He is "perhaps the best example of the psychological realist" in American literature. His best novels are from the 1870s, and his early manner is superior to his later. Few writers have felt "the terrible passion of love more deeply" than this specialist in "the finer shades of emotion." His mind was "powerfully reflective and speculative," but his reticence and apparent lack of sympathy with his characters keep his books from being popular. James's real life preference for cultivated over commonplace people did not narrow the range of his subjects. Few moderns have lived as keenly and abundantly as he, and his "brave explorations on the frontiers of human thought and passion" were as thrilling as the voyages of Drake and Columbus.

92 POWYS, JOHN COWPER. "Henry James." In Suspended Judgments, Essays on Books and Sensations. New York: G. Arnold Shaw, pp. 367-398.
James's fiction fills an essential place in our

interpretation of life. He is associated more than any other contemporary writer with "the actual stir and pressure" of the environment of educated people, but, although not snobbish, he says little to the lower classes. Free of a priori systems and philosophies, this "great urbane humanist" remains unrivaled "in his universal treatment of European society." He has a unique "cold, calm, detached intellectual curiosity," combined with "a deep and tender pity" for human frailty, a natural amiability. He relentlessly omits the spirit of class revolution from his work. In his distinctive style, the colloquialisms of superrefined people have a "grace and charm." James's works from 1895 to 1905 are his apogee. Although detached, he diffuses his personality more completely into his work than anyone else does. Despite the turbulence of the historical moment, James's humanistic emphasis on refinement, beauty, distinction, and toleration will return.

93 RANDELL, WILFRID O. "The Art of Mr. Henry James." Living Age, 290 (July 29), 281-290.
(Reprinted from April 1916 Fortnightly Review.)

94 SQUIRE, J. C. "Literary Affairs in London./Henry James, and His Unfinished Work." Dial, 60 (March 30), 316-317.
James was "one of those extraordinary men whose powers go on strengthening in old age." He did not reach a wide public, but younger writers were devoted to him. His works were "rich in beautiful detail," "full of revelations concerning the human mind and heart" and of "an implicit moral nobility." Despite his alleged obscurity, in his last years the British recognized his greatness, and his books "may safely be committed to Posterity."

95 No entry.

96 WALBROOK, H. M. "Henry James and the English Theatre." Living Age, 290 (August 19), 505-509.
(Reprint of article from Nineteenth Century and After, 80 [July], 141-145.) James loved the drama, but nearly hated the theater, whose commercialism, extravagant public deification of actors, and uncritical audiences sometimes "depressed this fastidious idealist." James tried hard to "adapt his subtle and exquisite art" to create the "bold and broad effects of the dramatist," but even The High Bid, more satisfactory than Guy Domville, appealed "chiefly to the fastidious" who could enjoy the delicacies of James's prose.

97 WEST, REBECCA. Henry James. New York: H. Holt, 128 pp.

(Chronological review and assessment of James's works.) Hawthorne was not altogether a happy influence on James's early stories. Roderick Hudson "is not a good book." James has "great genius" which will give "eternal comfort to the mind of man." The exquisite "Four Meetings" is his first of "many masterpieces," but with Daisy Miller James lost his American reaction to emotional stimuli. His early 1880s short stories are perfect in phrase but "incredibly naive" about people and situations. James continued to write about Americans in Europe after they had ceased to excite him. His work of the 1880s lacked purpose and unity as he searched for an intellectual basis to enable him to use his genius with noble or permanent results. Although French Poets and Novelists contains "the best reviews ever written," James the critic lacked the capacity for universal reference. The Aspern Papers begins his second phase of genius, in which he saw life as "a vale of tears." Sustained by the subjects of the literary life and the blessedness of the pure in heart, he attained near perfection for fifteen years, longer than any other writer. He produced masterpieces in the late 1890s and in The Wings of the Dove. He began to show his age in the works that followed it: the characters in The Golden Bowl say unspeakable sentences, do incredible things, and "are not even human." Yet, this not-very-good novel has beautiful metaphors, shows James's "genius for conversation." The prose of it and its successors has a "made" rather than a living beauty, and sometimes lapses into tiresomeness. (See 1916.72.)

98 WYATT, EDITH. "Henry James: An Impression." North American Review, 203 (April), 592-599.

One is often so dazzled by James's art that one forgets his "creative ideas." His "genius is supreme" in his creation and mastery of a mode of expression that "proceeds by chromatic shades and half-tones," the way we in fact experience and see revealed much of our existence. The similarity of the speech of James's characters eliminates distraction and shows "intimate motives." James has had a cosmopolitan purpose, but his criticisms of America are "far less contemptuous" than Thoreau's. James's characters acquiesce to the corruption they encounter not out of weakness of purpose, but with "high courage and vision." James could not have them behave inharmoniously or indecorously because they can exist only in a context of tradition and convention. He is able to rise above the "squalor of personal reference" that fills America, he has "a large inner life" that all must honor, and no one else's written words have better served civilization against the error of hatred among nations.

99 YOUNG, FILSON. "A Bunch of Violets." Living Age, 289 (May 27), 568-570.

(An appreciation of James, reprinted from the April 1916 English Review.)

Subject Index

Author Index

Newspaper and Periodical Index

Title Index

Index to Works by Henry James